JESUS
WEPT

JESUS WEPT

Seven Popes and the
Battle for the Soul of the
Catholic Church

PHILIP SHENON

ALFRED A. KNOPF
New York
2025

THIS IS A BORZOI BOOK
PUBLISHED BY ALFRED A. KNOPF

www.aaknopf.com

Knopf, Borzoi Books, and the colophon are registered trademarks of Penguin Random House LLC.

Library of Congress Cataloging-in-Publication Data
Names: Shenon, Philip, author.
Title: Jesus wept : seven popes and the battle for the soul
of the Catholic church / Philip Shenon.
Description: First edition. | New York : Knopf, [2025] |
Includes bibliographical references and index. |
Identifiers: LCCN 2024019372 (print) | LCCN 2024019373 (ebook) |
ISBN 9781101946411 (hardcover) | ISBN 9781101946428 (ebook)
Subjects: LCSH: Catholic Church—History—20th century. |
Papacy—History—20th century. | Catholic Church—Doctrines—
History—20th century. | Catholic Church—History—21st century. |
Papacy—History—21st century. | Catholic Church—
Doctrines—History—21st century.
Classification: LCC BX1389 .S518 2025 (print) | LCC BX1389 (ebook) |
DDC 282.09/04—dc23/eng/20240807
LC record available at https://lccn.loc.gov/2024019372
LC ebook record available at https://lccn.loc.gov/2024019373

Front-of-jacket image: *Christ Crowned with Thorns* (detail) by Dirk Bouts (workshop). National Gallery, London. Album / Alamy
Jacket design by Janet Hansen

Manufactured in the United States of America
First Edition

To the memory of the man born
Angelo Giuseppe Roncalli (1881–1963),
who might have been forgotten

They said unto him, Lord, come and see. Jesus wept.

—JOHN 11:34–35

The Catholic Church . . . desires to show herself to be the loving mother of all—benign, patient, full of mercy and goodness toward the brethren who are separated from her.

—POPE JOHN XXIII,
at the opening of the Second Vatican Council, 1962

Who am I to judge?

—POPE FRANCIS, 2013

Contents

PART VII

FRANCIS (2013–)

JESUS
WEPT

Introduction

THIS BOOK IS an investigative history of the modern Roman Catholic Church. Specifically, it is a without-fear-or-favor account of the battle for the soul of the church that began in earnest with the 1958 election of Pope John XXIII and his decision to call the world's bishops to Rome for what became known as the Second Vatican Council, or Vatican II. That battle continues to rage into the twenty-first century. It pits Catholics desperate for a more tolerant church—one that, in the words of Pope John, dispenses the "medicine of mercy instead of severity"—against those who see that vision as heresy.

To try to understand any part of the two-thousand-year history of the Catholic Church, even just a portion of the last two centuries, is daunting. It is easily the most important institution in the history of Western civilization, as well as one of the most complex and secretive. With more than 1.3 billion followers, it is the largest of thousands of nominally independent churches that venerate the Jewish prophet Jesus Christ as the son of God. The other branches of Christianity, broadly known as either Protestant or Orthodox, broke away from the Vatican centuries ago.

The impact of the Roman Catholic Church—for good and, with heart-breaking regularity, for ill—has always been disproportionate to its actual numbers. Wars and violent evangelical campaigns conducted in its name,

Left: Pope John XXIII carried on his portable throne to the opening session of the Second Vatican Council in St. Peter's Basilica, Rome, October 11, 1962

including the genocidal Crusades launched in the eleventh century, dominate the history of Europe, the Middle East, and much of Africa. From the
fifteenth century on, European kings and queens colonized much of the
Southern Hemisphere in the Vatican's name. Since the Middle Ages, Catholics have controlled an outsized share of the world's wealth and claimed
political and cultural influence to match. For most of the church's history,
popes exercised raw political power, especially in Europe; they governed
the Italian peninsula as dictators for more than a thousand years. Catholics
were at the forefront of the Industrial Revolution of the eighteenth century
that moved the world from subsistence farming to machine manufactur-
ing; it was an accomplishment tarnished in that same era by their role in
establishing a global slave trade. Many of the world's most esteemed universities were established by the church. In the United States, that includes
Georgetown University and the University of Notre Dame. In Britain, the
eleventh-century founders of the world's oldest English-language university at Oxford cannot be identified with certainty, but its great rival, the
University of Cambridge, opened its first college in 1284 under the patronage of the Catholic bishop of the nearby village of Ely.

What has always set the Catholic Church apart from other Christian
institutions, as well as from non-Christian religious faiths, is its insistence
that all decision-making be exercised from within the borders of a single
city—Rome, in which Jesus never set foot—and in the hands of its bishop,
who is known as the pope. He has traditionally exercised the powers of
an absolute monarch, albeit one democratically elected by his red-robed
peers in the College of Cardinals. There is nothing like that concentration
of power in Protestant or Orthodox churches. Muslims look to Mecca,
birthplace of the prophet Mohammed, as the spiritual heart of the faith.
For Jews, that city is Jerusalem (although Christians and Muslims claim
that sacred city as theirs too). Yet in those faiths there is no counterpart
to the power of Rome. The result today is that its bishop is the only living
religious leader whose face is instantly recognizable in every corner of the
globe. His pronouncements are taken seriously even in countries, notably
in Muslim nations, where he is viewed as a dangerous apostate.

In 1929, when the Vatican reached an accommodation with the Italian dictator Benito Mussolini, its authority became, geographically, even
more concentrated. Today the church controls a single neighborhood
inside Rome totaling 108.7 acres, less than a quarter the size of Central
Park in New York City. The Vatican City State, as it is formally known,

is the world's smallest independent nation as measured both by landmass and population. It is named for the area around one of Rome's fabled hills, Vatican Hill (Mons Vaticanus, in Latin), where St. Peter's Basilica was consecrated in 1626. The basilica's dome is said to have been built directly atop the tomb of the apostle Peter, claimed as the first bishop of Rome, who was buried there after his execution by the emperor Nero about AD 65. Visually, it is dominated by St. Peter's—452 feet tall and the biggest church in the world for most of its existence. (It lost that distinction in 1989 to the Basilica of Our Lady of Peace in Yamoussoukro, the administrative capital of the African nation of Ivory Coast.)

Although Vatican City depends on Rome's municipal government for supplies of water and electricity, it is otherwise proudly self-sufficient. It maintains its own telephone and banking systems—it mints its own euro coins—and its own post office, fire department, courts, and radio stations. The city-state has about six hundred citizens, including the pope, who are entitled to special passports; about half reside outside the Vatican. Several hundred other people, who remain citizens of their homelands, also live in Vatican City, including about 150 mostly young men who are the soldiers of the Swiss Guard, the smallest regular army in the world, since 1506 charged with defending the pope. By tradition, its recruits are unmarried Swiss Catholics between the ages of eighteen and thirty-five.

The universal worldwide government of the church is known formally as the Holy See (drawn from the Latin term for "Holy Chair"). Its chief administrator, a cardinal with the title of secretary of state, is appointed by the pope and has duties like those of a European prime minister. The secretary of state is also the Vatican's chief diplomat and oversees a string of embassies around the world. Many nations, including the United States, post two ambassadors to Rome—one for diplomatic contact with Italy's government, another for the Holy See.

Inside Vatican City, the pope is served by a bureaucracy of about four thousand workers—led by hundreds of cardinals and bishops, about a fifth of them Italian-born—known as the Roman Curia. Its central work is divided among administrative departments known until recently as congregations. (Under a 2022 restructuring, they were all renamed, along with a group of smaller agencies, as "dicasteries." There are a total of sixteen. Among the largest are the Dicastery for the Clergy, which administers the priesthood, and the Dicastery for Bishops.) Over the centuries, the most powerful and feared Curia agency was the one founded in 1542 as the

Supreme Sacred Congregation of the Roman and Universal Inquisition. It was later renamed the Holy Office and is known today as the Dicastery for the Doctrine of the Faith. Responsible for promoting church teachings and punishing heretics, its day-to-day methods once included secret trials, torture, and public executions. Popes have regularly been selected from the Curia. The most recent was Benedict XVI, the former Cardinal Joseph Ratzinger of Germany. Before his election in 2005, he had been in Rome for almost a quarter century as the Vatican's chief enforcer of doctrine. Although the Curia's ranks have included some of the church's greatest thinkers, it has also been the source of the worst scandals to plague the Vatican. Its history has often been one of venal, power-mad, even homicidal bishops struggling for influence.

The Vatican maintains a supposedly definitive roster of the 265 men who succeeded St. Peter as bishop of Rome, a list that currently ends with Pope Francis, the former Cardinal Jorge Mario Bergoglio of Argentina. But that list is incomplete, if not riddled with errors, since there was no reliable recordkeeping in the early history of the faith. More fundamentally, despite the Vatican's stubborn insistence to the contrary, many historians think it unlikely that Peter ever made the perilous twelve-hundred-mile journey to Rome from ancient Judea. If they are right, it means the concept of the Vatican as the indisputable center of Christianity has always been a myth. Beyond describing Peter in the Gospels as "the rock upon which I will build my church," Jesus says nothing explicitly to suggest he wanted an institutional church. The other eleven apostles would have been shocked at the idea, especially of a bloated hierarchy in faraway Rome, if only because Jesus preached the world would end soon after his death.

This book's timeline covers the reign of the last seven men elected bishop of Rome, beginning with the authoritarian Pius XII, supreme pontiff from 1939 until his death in 1958. Pius was celebrated in his lifetime for holding the church together during World War II. After his death, his legacy was badly tarnished by the discovery that, throughout the war, he received irrefutable intelligence about Nazi Germany's murder of millions of Jews and others in the Holocaust yet said almost nothing publicly in protest. Pius's final days are a logical place to begin this book, since his death was a turning point. His successor was an unlikely revolutionary: John XXIII, the former Cardinal Angelo Giuseppe Roncalli of Venice, a fat, jolly Italian who cherished his peasant roots and quickly became known to his countrymen as *il papa buono* ("the good pope"). Weeks after his election, John called the world's bishops to a so-called ecumenical council, later known as Vatican II, to end what he saw as the church's self-imposed isolation from the modern world. He mocked the concept of an infallible, all-powerful pope and promised that the council, which met for several weeks a year from 1962 to 1965, would chart the church's future without his interference. He defended some traditional teachings—he believed strongly in the need for an all-male, celibate priesthood—but was open to rethinking others. Although it was a secret until after his death, he established a commission that, in 1966, called for the church to lift its ban on birth control. He opened the Vatican, for the first time in centuries, to dialogue with people of other faiths, especially to Jews, and proposed a new, expanded role for women. In their early debates at Vatican II, the overwhelming majority of the world's bishops endorsed John's vision. As a result, the church was altered in ways that all Catholics could see and hear for themselves, including an end to the exclusive use of ancient Latin as the language of worship services.

In June 1963, just eight months after opening the council, John died of stomach cancer, and his opponents, led by a group of archconservative Curia bishops, set to work to block its reforms. The decades that followed can be framed as a struggle over whether John's vision of the church's "soul"—of a faith that, at its essence, put mercy ahead of punishing sin— would survive his death.

His successor, Paul VI, dithered. While resisting calls to shut down Vatican II, he refused to enact many of its reforms, especially its call for power sharing between Rome and the world's bishops. He is best remembered for the uproar he created in 1968 when he upheld the Vatican's ban on artificial contraception. In doing so, he rejected the findings of John XXIII's once-secret commission. The reign of Paul's successor, the genial Cardinal Albino Luciani of Venice, who took the papal name John Paul in honor of his two predecessors, is remembered mostly for its brevity. He passed away after just thirty-three days as pope. His sudden death, blamed on a heart attack at the age of sixty-five, inspired wild, unsupported conspiracy theories suggesting foul play.

The next two popes, John Paul II and Benedict XVI, were aggressive combatants for their vision of the church, in which traditional doctrine was strictly enforced. Although both men spoke of their pride at having attended Vatican II, they were regularly accused of ignoring the council's plea for a more tolerant, democratic church. The globetrotting John Paul II, the former Cardinal Karol Wojtyła of Poland, was the first non-Italian bishop of Rome since the sixteenth century. He reigned for nearly twenty-seven years, making him the second-longest-serving pope in recorded history. His greatest legacy may have been his role in promoting a peaceful end to the Cold War. His successor was his trusted deputy Ratzinger, who took the papal name Benedict and whose seven-year reign was plagued by scandal and humiliating, self-inflicted blunders. His poorly worded speeches and teaching documents managed to offend other religious leaders and led to violence in several Muslim nations. In 2013, he resigned, becoming the first pope to step down since the fifteenth century.

The legacies of John Paul II and Benedict have been permanently stained by what is regularly described as the worst scandal to confront the Vatican in centuries—the discovery that church leaders in Rome covered up the sexual abuse of thousands of children by priests. In the 1980s, the Vatican became, literally, a crime scene. The child-abuse crisis has shaken the faith of millions and darkened the reputation of the priesthood for generations to come. As this book will document, there is clear proof that John Paul and Benedict joined in a wide-ranging conspiracy to shield child molesters from justice. The bluntness of that statement may anger some readers, but anyone who doubts it should review just a small portion of the mountain of incriminating evidence the two popes chose to ignore—over decades— against high-profile churchmen widely known to be sexual predators.

Two events led me to write this book. One was the 2013 election of Francis, who seemed easily the most compelling public figure in the world at the time—a pope who, like John XXIII, had the potential to bring about a revolution. Francis made history as the first pope from South America, the continent that will soon be home to most of the world's Catholics. He was also the first bishop of Rome drawn from the influential, if often polarizing, religious order known as the Society of Jesus, or the Jesuits. Within days of his election, he abandoned much of the pompous formality of the papacy and frightened Vatican bureaucrats with pronouncements revealing his contempt for the Curia. He hinted at plans to reverse church teachings that he saw as intolerant, if not downright un-Christian, beginning with the Vatican's centuries-old condemnation of homosexuality. As he asked publicly weeks into his papacy, "If a person is gay and seeks God and has goodwill, who am I to judge?"

This project began as a joint biography of Francis and Benedict, who represented such sharply different visions of the church, but it expanded into a history of popes dating back to World War II as it became clear to me that the battles of Francis's papacy can all be traced back to those launched by "the good pope" at Vatican II. Like John XXIII, Francis has sought to dispense "the medicine of mercy." Similarly, the papacies of John Paul II and Benedict can be compared to that of Pius XII, who centralized power in Rome and silenced anyone who dared challenge his restrictive teachings on doctrine.

Catholics make up about one-fifth of the population of the United States. I am not among them. I was raised in a not particularly observant Protestant family in California and today describe myself as agnostic. Like so many other non-Catholics, however, I am fascinated by the Vatican, which has such outsized influence on American politics and culture. Much of this book was written at a time when the president of the United States, the Speaker of the House of Representatives, and six of the nine justices of the Supreme Court publicly embraced their Catholic faith. (A seventh justice, Neil Gorsuch, was raised Catholic but joined an Episcopal church.)

The other event that drew me to this subject took place in 2009, when the Catholic Archdiocese of Los Angeles revealed it was under federal investigation for covering up the crimes of pedophile priests. During more than two decades at *The New York Times*, I often reported on the American criminal justice system. For three years, I was the paper's Justice Department correspondent in Washington; then in 2010 I was asked to write about the Los Angeles investigation and had a chance to see for myself what the church there had been determined to hide. How was it possible that once-admired churchmen could be so corrupted that they allowed sexual predators to shatter the lives of children? That question helps explain this book's title. It is drawn from what is—at two words—the shortest verse in the King James Version of the Bible. It appears in the Gospel of John, in a passage in which the Savior cries when beckoned to see the corpse of his follower Lazarus: "They said unto him, Lord, come and see. Jesus wept." Surely, the Savior's tears would be justified today by the catastrophic failings of a church that claims to act in his name.

I was relieved in my research to discover how many heroes have existed in the church's modern history. That includes the now-sainted Archbishop Óscar Romero of El Salvador, assassinated in 1980 after challenging his nation's brutal military; Father Pedro Arrupe, leader of the Jesuits from 1965 to 1983, who turned the order's mission almost exclusively to the poor; and several of the brilliant churchmen selected by John XXIII to be architects of his revolution: Cardinals Leo Suenens of Belgium, Augustin Bea of Germany, and Franz König of Austria, and Archbishop Hélder Câmara of Brazil.

It is undeniable that women take a secondary role in this history, since they have always been denied formal, decision-making posts in the Vatican. Even so, there are fascinating Catholic women to salute, including Sister Pascalina Lehnert, the Bavarian-born housekeeper to Pius XII. Mocked as *la popessa* because of her influence with Pius, she has never been properly recognized for her role in saving the lives of thousands of Italian Jews after Hitler's troops marched into Rome in 1943. The truth about Mother Teresa of India, the most admired churchwoman of the last century, is far more perplexing and poignant than I ever imagined.

The rest of this book is told through the eyes of five men who played commanding roles in the modern battle for the church's soul. The first is John XXIII. To me, he is the model of what a pope—and a Christian—should be. I was disappointed in reporting trips to discover how few Catholics today know his name or can recognize his photo, proving just how successful his critics have been in erasing the memory of this great man. Two of this book's other central characters succeeded him as pope: Benedict XVI and Francis. Their career paths are mirror opposites of one another, pursued at roughly the same time and at opposite ends of the globe. Benedict went from trailblazing reformer in his youth to rigid conservative at the Vatican—"God's Rottweiler," as his enemies dubbed him. Late in life, he and Francis had something in common: a desire to rewrite their biographies. In Francis's case, that meant trying to ignore evidence tying him to right-wing militias responsible for terrible violence in the 1970s during Argentina's "Dirty War."

The other two central figures will be unfamiliar to some readers: the Swiss theologian Hans Küng, perhaps the most influential Catholic thinker of the last century, who died in 2021, and his former teaching assistant Cardinal Walter Kasper of Germany. Kasper abandoned his career as a university professor to establish himself in Rome as a bitter public opponent to then-Cardinal Ratzinger. The half-century-long rivalry between Ratzinger and Küng, once close friends, was even more poisonous, as they also came to represent the two sides in the battle for the church's soul.

My research, conducted across four continents, included hundreds of interviews, as well as an exhaustive search of church and government archives. Non-church records cited in this book come from sources as varied as the Central Intelligence Agency, the armed forces of Argentina, and the police departments of New York City and Sydney, Australia. Weeks of my research were spent paging through court files in criminal cases in which priests were accused of molesting children. I also spent weeks researching the history of the eleventh-century doctrine of priestly celibacy and came to understand how it has always been a matter of reversible church law, not eternal dogma. It is obvious to me that the demands of lifelong celibacy, which was not compulsory for priests in the first thousand years after the Crucifixion, help explain the child-abuse crisis.

Early chapters of this book are set largely in the Vatican and in Germany, home to Benedict, Kasper, and, as an adult, Küng. In later chapters, describing events in the 1960s, the battle for the church's soul shifts at times to Latin America, where millions of poor Catholics pleaded for—and were often denied—Rome's help in fighting to make a better life for themselves. It is then that the ambitious, often arrogant young Argentine Jesuit Jorge Bergoglio makes his appearance in this history, at the start of a climb to power that ends in 2013 with his election as bishop of Rome.

In the first decade of his papacy, Francis disappointed many admirers by failing to pursue the bold agenda he once seemed to promise. He proved unwilling to grapple with the magnitude of the child-abuse crisis, all the while refusing to acknowledge that he once shielded pedophile priests in Argentina. In Rome, he allowed rigidly conservative bishops to remain in power, including several who openly mocked and defied him. If Francis was timid to act, his defenders blamed it on the unexpectedly vicious opposition he faced from allies of his predecessor Benedict. The tension between the two popes in the years they lived uneasily as neighbors in Rome—an arrangement that ended in 2022, when Pope Emeritus Benedict died at the age of ninety-five—is explored closely in the pages that follow.

Many in the Vatican wondered if Benedict's death would embolden Francis to act decisively to secure his legacy. There was evidence it might. As this book was readied for publication, Francis shocked friends and enemies alike by appointing a fellow Argentine, Archbishop Victor Manuel Fernández, a reform-minded theologian whose provocative writings on sex have long been criticized in Rome, as the new prefect of the Dicastery for the Doctrine of the Faith, the agency that was Benedict's springboard to the papacy in 2005. Weeks later, Francis named Fernández a cardinal, instantly fueling speculation that the pope sees his countryman as a possible successor.

Whatever history's final judgment on Francis, his supporters are increasingly optimistic that his calls for a more merciful and open-minded church will outlast him. He may have guaranteed it, in fact. Since his election, he has remade the College of Cardinals by appointing more than three-quarters of the so-called cardinal electors who will choose the next bishop of Rome. Beyond the numbers, the cardinals selected by Francis are far more progressive and geographically and racially diverse than the men they replaced. They seem likely to elect a new pope who shares Francis's vision and may feel empowered to do much more to achieve it. They may yet win the battle.

PART I

PIUS XII
(1939—1958)

1

The Silent Pope

PIUS XII WAS the first pope to be a global celebrity in his lifetime. Thanks to newsreels and glossy photo magazines in the 1930s and 1940s, his face was recognizable to almost all Catholics on earth. His large, dark eyes, usually photographed behind rimless glasses, suggested an abiding devotion to God and absolute tranquility. He liked to pose for photos with his pampered pet goldfinch, Gretel, on his shoulder, or sometimes cradling a baby lamb trucked in from a nearby farm, as if to imply his presence could calm all God's creatures. He was celebrated nowhere more highly than in Rome. He was born there in 1876 as Eugenio Maria Giuseppe Giovanni Pacelli to a family of seminoble Vatican bureaucrats. After World War II, Romans hailed him for having singlehandedly saved the city from destruction; he repeatedly pleaded with Franklin Roosevelt and Winston Churchill to spare the Eternal City from Allied bombers.

Pius was especially beloved in Germany, where he was known as *der deutsche Papst*—the German pope—and the affection was mutual. He came to love the country after spending a dozen years there as a Vatican diplomat, beginning at the end of World War I. In its efficiency and orderliness, he came to prefer Germany to his homeland. Throughout his papacy, his household staff was made up almost entirely of German nuns led by a tough-minded Bavarian, Sister Pascalina Lehnert, who were ordered to address him only in German. The pope's personal confessor was a kindly German Jesuit, Father Augustin Bea, a renowned biblical scholar who would go on to become a powerful adviser to Pius's successors.

Pius was, at the time of his death, the most prolific *writing* pope of all time. He was author of forty-one of the supreme teaching documents known as encyclicals. They set down church policy on the most profound issues of the twentieth century—ranging from the rise of Marxism, which he saw as an existential threat, to artificial contraception; he joined with predecessors in describing birth control as a violation of God's natural laws. Other encyclicals offered surprisingly commonplace advice, including what movies Catholics should see (they must avoid films that "contain something contrary to Catholic belief") and what musical instruments their children should play (violins and other bowed instruments were best, because they "express the joyous and sad sentiments of the soul"). His stature seemed only to grow in the first years after World War II. As the Iron Curtain descended across Eastern Europe, he was saluted in Western capitals for his willingness to confront communism. Shortly after his death in 1958, however, his legacy was called into question. The controversy centered on his failure to speak out against the Holocaust. Church archives released after his death proved he received concrete evidence throughout the war of the genocide, yet chose to remain almost completely silent about it in public.

His legacy was also battered by testimony from former deputies, who told ugly, embarrassing stories about how erratic he had been. Through-out the 1950s, they reported, the long-ailing Pius had limited his circle of advisers to a handful of aides and family members. He was especially dependent on Pascalina. In written accounts, his former deputies gave a shocking appraisal of his failings. Cardinal Domenico Tardini, who man-aged foreign policy, described the pope as paralyzed by self-doubt. "He wasn't a fighter," Tardini wrote in his memoirs. "He was handicapped by caution." Church archives showed that other powerful bishops were appalled by the pope's conduct during the war. Cardinal Eugène Tisserant of France, a senior Curia bureaucrat later named dean of the College of Cardinals, wrote to a colleague in the early months of the war that Pius, by remaining silent about Nazi war crimes, pursued a policy "of selfish con-venience and not much else." The cardinal suggested future generations would—and should—judge Pius harshly.

No one would prove more indiscreet or better informed than Pascalina. "The mistakes of His Holiness brought tears to my eyes," she told an inter-viewer after his death. Although the public knew almost nothing about her during his papacy, she had been as influential as almost any cardinal. Her principal critic was Tisserant, who often warned the pope of a potential

Sister Pascalina Lehnert, housekeeper and adviser to Pius XII, was known inside the Vatican as *la popessa* because of her influence with the pope.

scandal over her influence. "It's a disgrace for a woman to be given such authority in the church," the cardinal told a colleague. She completed her memoirs in 1959, but the church declined to publish them for more than two decades, apparently fearing her account would create an uproar by revealing such an intimate, if nonsexual, relationship between a pope and a woman.

Pascalina controlled the pope's schedule, determining who could see him and when. She often canceled long-arranged meetings with Curia officials if a popular entertainer or politician visiting Rome requested a last-minute reception. She recalled how they were both thrilled to rearrange his schedule to grant an audience to the actor Clark Gable in the 1940s. She was by the pope's side at those meetings, holding a glass container of disinfectant that she used to wipe his hands after every encounter with a worshipper who kissed his ring. The two met in 1917, when then-Archbishop Pacelli stayed in a retreat house in Switzerland affiliated with the Sisters of the Holy Cross, an order of German-speaking nuns that Pascalina joined at the age of fifteen. Pascalina, by then a strikingly pretty twenty-two-year-old, had been assigned to tend to the forty-one-year-old Pacelli. She said she knew early on their relationship would inspire gossip, although no evidence ever emerged to show she was anything other than a treasured friend and adviser. "It wasn't that His Holiness had no needs of the heart," she said later, revealing that Pius, as a young man, had come close to abandoning his plans for the priesthood when he proposed to an Italian girl named Lucia. "If Lucia had said yes, he never would have become pope."

She claimed credit for significant acts of his papacy, including his decision in 1944 to serve as his own secretary of state. The move incensed many in the Curia who felt Pius already centralized too much power in his own hands. "He was the kind of pope who was accustomed to doing everything possible by himself," said Cardinal Richard Cushing of Boston, who was appointed that city's archbishop by Pius but never felt close to him. In later years, Pius insisted he did not need anyone's advice. "I want people to do what I say, not to help me think," he barked to Tardini. That helped explain why he blocked the promotion of a new generation of cardinals. After 1953, Pius failed to appoint a single one.*

The Germans on his staff were treated with respect by the pope, but he earned a reputation for humiliating everyone else, especially fellow Italians. Apart from Pascalina, Pius's closest aides were a pair of Italian priests who held the largely honorary title of monsignor: Tardini, named a cardinal after Pius's death, and Giovanni Montini, the future Pope Paul VI. Pascalina thought Pius was nasty to them both, especially the meek Montini. "I pitied him so," she said. "He was a thin little person and always had such a frightened look on his face." On some days, she recalled, Pius was "vocally cruel" to everyone. He was the first pope to use a telephone regularly, and he was notorious for angry calls to subordinates, who were expected to fall to their knees when they recognized his voice on the line.

Pascalina believed Pius's fondness for all things German was responsible for his worst decisions, and that he was dangerously naïve in his dealings with the Nazis in the 1920s and 1930s. His writings from the time suggest he believed Hitler could be a useful ally in containing communism, which he saw as a far greater threat than fascism. To a journalist, Pascalina recalled an astonishing scene in which Hitler paid a visit to then-Archbishop Pacelli

---

* The title "cardinal," which dates to the sixth century, is bestowed today on a relatively small number of bishops and archbishops honored by the pope with membership in the Sacred College of Cardinals, the body that gathers when a bishop of Rome dies to choose his successor. It had fifty-three members at the time of Pius's death in 1958. Beyond the more prestigious title and a wardrobe of scarlet-red robes instead of black, a bishop named a cardinal in modern times often sees no change in his day-to-day duties, although he will have more regular invitations to Rome and the opportunity for promotion to the Curia. By tradition, major Vatican agencies are led by cardinals, as are the archdioceses of major world capitals. After he was named to the College in 2001, Cardinal Bergoglio, the future Pope Francis, retained his title as archbishop of Buenos Aires.

in the nuncio's residence in Munich. During the meeting, Pacelli handed Hitler an envelope filled with cash to support political efforts to combat Marxism. "Go quell the devil's work," Pacelli told the rising demagogue, according to Pascalina's account. "Help spread the love of Almighty God." Hitler, who was born a Catholic but would turn on the church, replied: "Yes, for the love of Almighty God."

In 1929, Pacelli returned to Rome and was made a cardinal by Pius XI. The next year, the pope also named him secretary of state. In that post, Pacelli drafted the 1933 pact with Nazi Germany that guaranteed special privileges to the Vatican, including the right to appoint local bishops without the Nazis' interference, in exchange for the church's promise to remove itself from German politics. That meant withdrawing the church's support for the key opposition party, known as the Zentrum. The pact, modeled on one signed four years earlier with Mussolini, required German bishops to swear a loyalty oath to the Third Reich and compelled Catholic parishes to open up baptism and marriage records. That allowed the Nazis to identify Jewish converts to Catholicism.

Throughout the war, Pascalina said, she repeatedly urged the pope to condemn the Nazis, especially as the first horrifying intelligence reports arrived in 1940 about Hitler's plans for the Holocaust. She later remembered telling him: "If you, as Holy Father, were to reveal the extermination of Jews, people all over the world would believe you."* But Pius refused, saying he believed a protest would do nothing to stop the slaughter and might bring retaliation against Catholics. He knew how his silence might damage his reputation. "This Holy Father may go down in history as being anti-Semitic," he told Pascalina, according to her account. But that was better, he said, "than for the Holy See to wear its virtue on its sleeve so the Nazis can claim more victims." He did not deny that his love for the German people also explained his silence. When in 1943 the semiofficial

---

* The extent of Pascalina's influence with Pius XII remains a tantalizing mystery. She spoke to a veteran Boston newspaperman, Paul I. Murphy, who was also a contributor to *The New York Times,* for his 1983 book *La Popessa: The Controversial Biography of Sister Pascalina, the Most Powerful Woman in Vatican History.* Although many in the Vatican thought the book's depiction of Pius was scandalous, it was well reviewed in the United States and drew no public criticism from the church or Pascalina, and Vatican officials were convinced she enjoyed the attention it brought her before her death in November 1983, about a year after the book's release. Its New York–based publisher, Warner Books, would later be commissioned to publish the autobiography of Pope John Paul II. In her own memoirs, Pascalina offered a saintly portrayal of Pius and wrote that while the pope was publicly silent about the Holocaust, he had worked tirelessly behind the scenes to rescue Jews: "He saved many a life without anyone ever learning of it."

Vatican newspaper, *L'Osservatore Romano*, interviewed him and suggested he denounce Hitler, Pius replied, "You must not forget, dear friend, that there are millions of Catholics in the German army. Would you like to place them in the middle of a conflict of conscience?"

The war came to the pope's doorstep in 1943, when Mussolini was overthrown and the Nazis invaded Italy. Although Mussolini imposed so-called racial laws that placed draconian limits on the rights of Jews, they had not been targeted for outright extermination, as in Germany. So when Nazi troops marched onto the streets of Rome in September 1943, the threat was obvious and terrifying to the city's nearly twelve thousand Jews, most of them living in the riverside neighborhood known as the Ghetto di Roma. Pascalina panicked at the idea that Rome's Jews, whose community had existed there for more than two thousand years, would be rounded up within hours, and she pressed the pope again: "If you cannot bring yourself to denounce Hitler, then the least the papacy can do is to lend full support to the Jewish people" who lived in the city that the Catholic Church called its home. To her relief, the pope agreed. Ultimately, about ten thousand Jews were saved, many sheltered inside Vatican City. The effort came too late for more than thirteen hundred others, who were ordered into a tree-shaded square bordering Rome's largest synagogue, placed in sealed trucks, and shipped to death camps, most to Auschwitz in Poland.

Pius never expressed regret over his silence about the Holocaust. To the alarm of Truman administration officials directing the postwar occupation of Germany, the pope ordered Vatican diplomats to press for clemency for German Catholics accused of war crimes, including military officers who supervised the camps. In stark contrast to his neutrality in World War II, he became a fierce Cold Warrior. In 1946 the French ambassador to the Vatican reported the pope was "obsessive" in his hatred for communists, especially as Marxist politicians threatened to come to power in Italy. Three years later, Pius issued a decree excommunicating all Catholics who identified themselves as communists, a step he never took against German Catholics who were members of the Nazi Party. In speeches throughout the late 1940s, he expressed outrage about governments in Hungary, Poland, and other Soviet-bloc nations that jailed Catholic clerics. In 1949, he apparently saw no irony in a speech in which he denounced communist leaders in Eastern Europe over their persecution of Catholics and then turned to his audience to ask: "How can the pope be silent?"

2

"A Church of No, Not Yes"

HANS KÜNG'S FIVE SISTERS agreed that he looked like a movie star. He resembled one of those handsome Americans—Jimmy Stewart, maybe, or Van Johnson, who could have been his twin—whose films were as popular in the foothills of the Alps as they were in Hollywood. The tall, blue-eyed Küng, who styled his wavy blond hair in a pompadour above his high forehead, had a dazzling, gap-toothed smile. His family said he drew admiring stares from the opposite sex throughout his youth—first at home in Switzerland, where he was raised near the city of Lucerne, and then in Rome, where he went in 1948 to study at the Pontifical Gregorian University, the Catholic Church's most famous school of religious studies. Founded in 1551, it was called "the school of popes" for good reason. Its graduates included sixteen future pontiffs and more than fifty other men canonized as saints.

Küng radiated good health. He was a natural athlete and, whenever back in Switzerland, no matter what the time of year, went for a swim every day in the lake that bordered his family home. He taught himself to swim as a five-year-old by plunging into the icy waters one day and discovering that if he paddled his legs and kept his breathing steady, his head stayed above water: "It impressed me deeply that the water was supporting me," he wrote in his memoirs. It was an experience he later compared to his early, easy acceptance of Jesus as his Savior.

He was twenty years old when he began his studies in Rome, living ten blocks from the Gregorian in a German-language seminary that dressed its students in brilliant red cassocks. Italian neighbors gently mocked the seminarians as *gamberi cotti*—cooked prawns. As a priest-in-training, he was bound by the celibacy vows that would be formally imposed on him after ordination. Still, he *thought* about women during his studies in Rome, even as he tried not to obsess about the prospect of a life without them. As a teenager in Switzerland, he had girlfriends he cherished. "I was no stranger to falling in love," he wrote of his dream of a wife and children. At the Gregorian and for the rest of his life, he hoped the Vatican might someday find a way to allow priests to marry. In his university courses, he learned the detailed history of the doctrine of priestly celibacy—how it was a matter of church law, not dogma, which meant any pope could overturn it at will.

He was thrilled in 1951 when Pius XII agreed to make an exception to the doctrine by permitting married Protestant ministers who converted to Catholicism to be ordained as priests and remain with their wives and children. That was as far as Pius would go, however. In 1954, Küng was crushed when the pope declared in an encyclical that, apart from those few converts, "the celibacy of priests must be retained" and that "perpetual virginity is a very noble gift." The encyclical was written to address a twentieth-century problem—a collapse in the number of men entering the priesthood after World War II. Pius offered his solution in the document. He called on the church to redouble its efforts to convince parents to encourage young sons—at the time, boys commonly entered seminary before puberty—to see a life of priestly sacrifice, including celibacy, as noble: "We urge fathers

Father Hans Küng, the maverick Swiss theologian, whose 1960 book *The Council, Reform and Reunion* helped set the agenda for many bishops who attended Vatican II

and mothers to willingly offer to the service of God those of their children who are called to it."

Küng thought the Gregorian went to excessive, even comical lengths to ensure he was never tempted by lust. All women, including nuns, were forbidden inside buildings where students gathered. Use of the word "homosexual"—*homosexuales* in Latin, the Gregorian's language of instruction—was seen as scandalous and banned from conversation. Even so, students were warned repeatedly to avoid "particular friendships" with classmates; there was a prohibition on all physical contact among students, including handshakes.

Küng knew that some university administrators who enforced those rules were hypocrites. He and his classmates heard convincing reports about cardinals and bishops in Rome, including some of their professors, who had mistresses and even common-law wives and children. Other churchmen were rumored to have male lovers or to loiter in the backstreets around Rome's central railroad station, where male prostitutes offered their services. Over time, Küng came to see how compulsory celibacy led otherwise honorable churchmen to sin—sexually, with women or men—in order to keep their sanity. Many priests came to see all women as temptresses, Küng believed. Within the Curia, it was common for a bishop or priest to go years without a single significant conversation with a woman who was not a family member or housekeeper.

AT THE GREGORIAN, Küng pursued a degree in theology—the scholarly field broadly defined as the study of God and religious belief—and within a few years of his ordination in 1954, he achieved a degree of fame almost unheard of in the profession. By the late 1960s, there was only one young Catholic theologian who came close to his renown in the German-speaking world—Father Joseph Ratzinger. In the decades that followed, the two men found themselves tangled up in each other's lives, initially as allies in seeking reform of the church. As personalities, they were strikingly different. Küng was gregarious. He loved a heated debate and—once he tasted freedom after moving to Paris in 1955 to pursue a PhD at the Sorbonne—a raucous cocktail party. He boasted of his impressive capacity for alcohol. As a young priest, he had a special affection for the potent cocktail known as a Rusty Nail, made by mixing Drambuie and Scotch. Ratzinger, a year older than Küng, was shy and stayed close to home. He repeatedly passed up the chance to study outside Germany. He was charming in conversation, with a gently biting wit, and his students were devoted to him, but he liked solitude. That had been true since elementary school, when he discovered it was "torture to study with other boys."

If Küng glowed with youth, Ratzinger seemed older than his years. He had deep-set eyes, which gave him a raccoonlike, perpetually tired look. His hair grayed in his twenties. His posture had been poor since childhood, and he tended to hunch over while standing. The problem grew worse late in life when he was crippled by arthritis. He was sickly as a boy and came to loathe athletics after he entered a seminary in 1939, at the age of twelve. As a young man, he too saw priestly celibacy as a sacrifice, although he readily accepted it. Late in life, he hinted he had been romantically involved with a woman before his ordination in 1951, but his family and others who knew him well were certain he never experienced romance.

His greatest pleasure came from classical music—he was a fine pianist and revered Mozart, considered an honorary Bavarian by Ratzinger, since the great composer was born just across the border in Austria—and from the company of his close-knit, devoutly Catholic family. He lived with his parents on and off until his late twenties. Appropriately enough for a man who spent his life in the church, his mother and father had the names of Christ's earthly parents: Mary and Joseph (in German, Maria and Josef). Young Joseph (born Josef, he adopted the English spelling of the name in his writings) had one brother, Georg, who was three years older and also became a priest. Their sister, who shared her mother's name, would never marry. The Ratzingers were committed to their parish church, attending Mass daily and several times on Sunday. They made sure Joseph was baptized only hours after his birth on Holy Saturday, the day before Easter, in 1927. To delay baptism only a few hours was a risk, since the church taught that unbaptized infants who died shortly after birth—common at the time—were consigned to an interim celestial space known as "limbo" and not guaranteed a place in heaven.

There was "nothing mystical" about his decision to become a priest, Joseph said. "There was no lightning-strike moment." Given his parents' devotion to the faith, they instantly embraced his announcement as a ten-year-old that he would follow Georg into the priesthood. He said the idea had been in the back of his mind since he was five or six, when he became enchanted by prayer books he received as gifts. They included drawings of each step in the Mass, alongside a German translation of the liturgy—the words that would be spoken in church in Latin, a language Joseph found incomprehensible until well into his seminary training. The ceremonies of the Mass were difficult for a child to follow, but he loved the ornateness of the sacraments. When other boys grabbed their wooden toy guns to play cops and robbers, he play-acted the role of a priest leading Mass or performing a marriage or funeral.

Both Küng and Ratzinger described their childhoods as idyllic. They experienced World War II very differently. In neutral Switzerland, Küng, the son of shopkeepers, knew about the war only from what he read in newspapers or heard on the radio. Ratzinger was six when Hitler came to power in Germany. His father, a policeman, was known among neighbors for his opposition to the Nazis, but the family stayed out of politics. At the age of fourteen, Ratzinger, like his schoolmates, joined the Hitler Youth movement, as the government insisted. He said the only truly frightening moments of his youth came in the final two years of the war. In 1943, when he was sixteen, he was drafted into a Nazi antiaircraft unit responsible for protecting industrial plants. He saw combat only from a distance, he said. Before and during the war, his family was aware of the existence of Nazi

A 1951 family photo of Father Joseph Ratzinger, who established himself at Vatican II as one of the young reform-minded stars of Catholic theology. Left to right: sister Maria, brother Georg, Maria (mother), Joseph, and Josef Ratzinger Sr.

concentration camps where political dissidents were imprisoned and executed. One of the most notorious, in the Bavarian city of Dachau, was only
about seventy miles from his family's village, but Ratzinger insisted later his
family never suspected the Nazis had engaged in anything so nightmarish
as the Holocaust.

He thought he met Küng in 1957 at a theology conference in Austria.
By then, he already knew of, and admired, the young Swiss theologian.
Months earlier, Ratzinger reviewed Küng's first book, *Justification*, which
was controversial because it defied the Vatican by calling for Catholics and
Protestants to see beyond the differences that had divided them since the
sixteenth century, when that brave if fanatical German monk named Martin Luther launched the Protestant Reformation. In his review, Ratzinger
praised the book as a "gift" that "deserves the honest thanks of all who pray
and work toward the unity of divided Christianity." Küng remembered
the review with gratitude, although he was still convinced he did not meet
Ratzinger until the early 1960s, when they were both in Rome as theological advisers at the Second Vatican Council. Küng remembered thinking at
that first meeting that Ratzinger was hesitant to speak candidly: "Ratzinger
seemed very friendly, although perhaps not completely open, while to him
I possibly seemed too spontaneous and direct."

In their ambition and the quality of their scholarship, they had much in
common. During long careers, they would each write scores of books and
hundreds of scholarly articles. Both became fluent in several languages,
including Latin, Italian, French, and English. They had similar taste in
the arts, especially in their shared love of Mozart. Friends and colleagues
agreed that both men, throughout their lives, even in periods of turmoil
or despair that might have tested their faith, were unshakable in their
belief that Jesus Christ was their Lord and Savior. They *believed*. Pressed
to explain how he could put aside doubt and accept God's existence, Küng
often referred to the experience of closing his eyes and listening to Mozart
and being transported to "a divine place" that existed beyond human com-
prehension. "The music embraces me, permeates me, brings me happiness
from within, fulfills me completely," he wrote. "It points to the ultimate,
unspeakable mystery."

Küng and Ratzinger were raised to revere Pius XII. During World
War II, when Hitler portrayed the Vatican as his enemy, the pope never lost
the devotion of most German Catholics, who made up about a third of the
population. That loyalty was especially strong in Bavaria, where Catholics

outnumbered Protestants. In 1948, shortly after Küng arrived in Rome, he and his Gregorian classmates were invited to the sumptuous papal country residence in Castel Gandolfo, about fifteen miles south of the Vatican, to be received by the pope. Küng remembered Pius as "a tall, slim figure with a spiritual face and eloquent hands. With his perfect gestures, his knowledge of languages, and his rhetoric, Pius XII appeared generally to be the model pope." The visit had special meaning for Küng and his German-speaking classmates, since the pope addressed them flawlessly in their own tongue.

At the Gregorian, Küng could not escape the image of Pius, since photos of the pope were displayed at the front of every classroom and along every hallway. The pope was not, however, a universally beloved figure at the school, as Küng was surprised to discover. Students did not dare offer public criticism, but among themselves they regularly complained that the church had stagnated during Pius's long reign. Cormac Murphy-O'Connor, a young Englishman who was one of Küng's classmates, recalled his excitement at arriving in Rome for the first time in 1950. He was an untraveled eighteen-year-old thrilled to find himself studying in this "fabulously exciting city." That excitement was quickly tempered, however, by what he began to realize about the state of the church. Curia bishops lectured at the Gregorian, and the more Murphy-O'Connor listened to them, the more he realized the church was a "closed fortress." Instead of celebrating Christ's message of mercy, he wrote, the Vatican under Pius was fixated on "prohibitions—on dire warnings about sinful practices and false teachings." It was "a church of no, not yes."

Küng traced his doubts about Pius to 1949, his second year in Rome, when the Supreme Sacred Congregation of the Holy Office issued a declaration that appeared to undermine the church's budding campaign to promote dialogue with non-Catholic Christians. Küng had always considered the four-hundred-year-old rupture between Catholics and Protestants—and before that, the eleventh-century split between the Vatican and Orthodox churches, the so-called Great Schism—as "outrageous scandals" that kept Christians from celebrating a common belief in Christ. The Holy Office, however, suggested in the 1949 decree that the divisions were permanent and that non-Catholic Christians could save their souls only by converting to the Catholic faith. The document described non-Catholics as "dissidents" who had fallen away from "the one true Church of Christ." Among Catholic theologians, the Holy Office, the most powerful of what were then twelve Curia agencies known as congregations, had always inspired fear. Küng suspected most Catholics had no idea of the agency's dark and bloody history—and would be appalled if they did. Under its original name, the Supreme Sacred Congregation of the Roman and Universal Inquisition, the Holy Office launched the Roman Inquisition of the sixteenth and seventeenth centuries, in which people accused of heresy were regularly burned at the stake on the congregation's orders.

The Holy Office had been responsible for many of the Vatican's worst historical embarrassments, including the imprisonment of the great Italian scientist Galileo in the seventeenth century because he rejected the church's view that the sun rotated around the earth. The congregation played an important role for centuries in maintaining the Index of Prohibited Books, a list of works banned as blasphemous. The writers whose books appeared on the Index included Voltaire, Hugo, Descartes, Milton, and Copernicus. In the twentieth century, the French thinkers Jean-Paul Sartre and André Gide were added for works that won them the Nobel Prize. In 1906, in an obvious effort to distance itself from its past, the congregation removed the word "inquisition" from its name. Whatever it called itself, Küng wrote in his memoirs, it was clear to him as a student that the spirit of the Inquisition had never died: "They may no longer be able to burn dissidents at the stake, but they can burn them psychologically."

As a young theologian, Ratzinger shared the harsh criticism of the Holy Office. The Vatican under Pius XII, he wrote in the early 1960s, was a place of small-minded "baroque princes" who believed that they alone should decide how Catholics lived. He was reminded of the Curia's indifference to the faithful every time he went to church and watched parishioners struggle with the Latin liturgy. Since the fourth century, the Vatican had insisted that the Mass be offered throughout the world only in Latin, the formal language of the faith since the Roman Empire. In the twentieth century, many theologians urged the church to allow the Mass to be said in the vernacular—in local languages—so everyone could appreciate a ceremony meant to re-create the poignancy of the Last Supper. But Pius, while open to other liturgical reforms, would not abandon Latin. Ratzinger thought the Vatican's insistence on the ancient language had always exaggerated its importance, since Latin was not the language of Jesus and his apostles. The Savior addressed his disciples in Aramaic, a language related to Hebrew. After Aramaic fell into disuse, the principal language of the church for nearly three hundred years was Greek. In writings early in his career, Ratzinger blamed Latin—"a language in which the living choices of the human spirit no longer found a place"—for the "sterility to which Catholic theology and philosophy has in many ways been doomed."

He thought the Vatican's "crippling antimodern neurosis" on other issues dated back to another Pius—the autocratic Pius IX, the former Cardinal Giovanni Maria Mastai-Feretti, whose thirty-two-year papacy (1846–1878) was the longest in recorded history. Among his Italian countrymen, his papal name in their language—Pio Nono—had a double meaning, since it could mean both "Pius the Ninth" and "Pius No-No." To many Italians, Pope No-No was the appropriate title, since Pius IX rejected all change. His most famous papal decree, entitled the Syllabus of Errors (*Syllabus Errorum*) and published in 1864, condemned the concept of religious freedom, while questioning the whole idea of "progress, liberalism, and modern civilization." His successor, Pius X, stepped up the campaign of repression, ordering that all clergy swear an "oath against all modernity." He established a network of spy agencies across Italy, known as Committees of Vigilance, to root out heretics. Its tactics included blackmail and torture. "Kindness is for fools," the foul-tempered Pius X famously declared. The committees' targets included a young northern Italian priest, Angelo Roncalli, after he published an essay in 1909 in support of striking textile workers. True Christians, he wrote, had a "duty in charity toward the weak who are suffering for the triumph of justice." The local Committee of Vigilance branded Roncalli, the future Pope John XXIII, as a dangerous "modernist."

Throughout the 1940s and 1950s, there was widespread, if little publicized, criticism of Pius XII from Catholic theologians across Europe. Ratzinger's professors at the University of Munich were appalled by the pope's 1950 decree that proclaimed—as irrefutably true—an ancient theory that the Virgin Mary had not suffered a normal human death. She had, Pius declared, risen body and soul, apparently still alive, into heaven, although there was no reference to anything like it in scripture.

The situation for many Catholic theologians became treacherous that same year when Pius issued an encyclical entitled, in Latin, *Humani Generis* (Of the Human Race) that silenced the church's most progressive thinkers by branding them as dissidents. Its targets included the celebrated French theologian Yves Congar, a Dominican friar who championed unity between Catholics and other Christians. Congar told friends he fell into a nearly suicidal depression after he was ordered by the Holy Office to give up all teaching and banished from France. Some colleagues cut off contact, fearing to be associated with him. Congar described his despair as worse than what he had experienced in World War II, when his army unit was captured by the Nazis and he was held in prisoner-of-war camps for four years.

Humani Generis was a landmark in Küng's life. He thought it was so wrongheaded that it convinced him the pope, hailed by most Catholics as error-free in his every word and action, was in fact fallible. "For the first time, I was convinced that Pius XII was wrong," Küng remembered. Then in the middle of his graduate studies in Munich, Ratzinger had reached the same conclusion: This bishop of Rome, like all of his predecessors, was capable of making terrible mistakes. How else to explain so many bad, bloodthirsty popes—"men who would obviously not be picked by the Holy Spirit"—throughout history? It was a parlor game among his classmates: Who was the worst pope ever? Was it Sergius III, elected in 904 after assassinating two of his predecessors and whose favorite mistress gave birth to a son who succeeded him as pope? Or Innocent IV, the thirteenth-century architect of the Inquisition, who approved the use of the rack and other instruments of torture? Or maybe it was Alexander VI in the fifteenth century, reported to have had an incestuous relationship with an illegitimate daughter. He also had a fondness, it was said, for drunken orgies that ended with naked prepubescent boys jumping out of cakes. Popes from the eleventh through the thirteenth centuries mounted the Crusades, in which mercenary armies slaughtered more than a million Muslims and Jews.

Power-loving popes had always tried to create the perception that, because they were the successors to St. Peter, they were infallible. But Küng and Ratzinger—and anyone else familiar with the New Testament—knew that this was a misreading of Peter's biography. The Gospels portray Peter, a Jewish fisherman who abandoned his life on the Sea of Galilee to join the Savior's wandering band of disciples, as lovable but deeply flawed. Jesus mocked him for his weak character and, as the Savior predicted, a terrified Peter denied his loyalty three times in the hours around the Crucifixion. Besides, as Küng and Ratzinger also knew, the doctrine of papal infallibility held that the bishop of Rome was error-free only in limited circumstances, when issuing the most rare sort of proclamation, known as an ex cathedra decree. And far from being ancient teaching, the doctrine dated back only to 1870 and the First Vatican Council. At that council, many bishops rejected the doctrine but were overruled by the bullying Pius IX, who insisted he needed sweeping new authority because the Vatican was then under threat of invasion by the Italian army.* To his credit, after demanding the right to claim infallibility, Pius IX never once invoked it in his teaching documents. In the century that followed, it was invoked by only one pope and on only one occasion—by Pius XII in his widely ridiculed 1950 decree on the Virgin's assumption into heaven.

THE YOUNG WEST GERMAN PRIEST Walter Kasper was put straight to work after his ordination in 1957, at the age of twenty-four. "It was a crash course in my new life," he said of his first assignment in Stuttgart. The priest shortage in Germany meant he worked seven days a week. On feast days, he heard confessions all day long. He would sit there in his part of the dark wooden booth, listening quietly from behind a mesh screen as parishioners, one after another, asked forgiveness. "I learned in the confessional how wonderful it was to be permitted to tell people of God's abundant and inexhaustible mercy," he wrote later.

He was especially eager to comfort the many parishioners who confessed sins related to the collapse of a marriage. In the late 1950s, divorce was becoming common in West Germany. Typically, divorced Catholics were tormented by a feeling that in abandoning a marriage, they had abandoned their faith. In some parishes, divorced Catholics were treated as outcasts and asked to sit apart from the congregation. They were also barred from receiving the most important sacrament of the faith: the Eucharist, also known as Holy Communion, in which a priest re-creates the Last Supper and offers bread and wine transformed into Jesus's flesh and blood.† Divorced parishioners told Kasper of their anguish at being refused Communion. He felt their despair and how wrong it was to deprive them of the church's support at a moment when their lives were already in turmoil.

Kasper was a man of almost otherworldly calm, his parishioners agreed. He credited his unrelenting, even obsessive optimism—a bit perversely, he admitted—to the terrors of World War II. His childhood in southern Ger-

---

* Pius IX's power grab inspired Lord Acton, a devoutly Catholic nineteenth-century English historian who attended the council to lobby against the doctrine of papal infallibility, to compose his famous aphorism: "Power tends to corrupt, and absolute power corrupts absolutely."
† According to Catholic teachings dating to the twelfth century, the bread and wine are transformed into the Savior's actual flesh and blood—a process known as transubstantiation. After breaking from Rome, many Protestant churches rejected the theory, arguing that it diminished the significance of Christ's actual suffering on the cross and promoted a fantasy that priests had supernatural powers, and instead offered bread and wine as symbols of Jesus's sacrifice, not as his actual body.

many was framed by the rise and fall of the Nazi Party. He was born on an inauspicious day: March 5, 1933, when elections formally brought Hitler to power. Having survived the war, Kasper said, he woke up every morning grateful to be alive.

He initially wanted to be a parish priest. His bishop, however, urged him to become a theologian, in the hope such a bright, open-minded young priest might influence the church's future. In 1958, Kasper enrolled in a PhD program at the University of Tübingen, about thirty miles from Stuttgart, which had a theology school that was among the most renowned in Europe. The Catholic theologians on its faculty, which would soon include Professor Hans Küng, were known as independent-minded, often to the annoyance of their counterparts in Rome.

The 1933 pact between Germany and the Vatican remained in effect, which gave the church authority over Catholic religious education. At Tübingen, there were separate programs for Catholic and Protestant theology students. Germany's Catholic bishops, acting on instructions from Rome, insisted on it. As a younger man, Kasper never thought to question the reasoning behind that, but his arrival at the university was a jolt. He could see the goodwill that existed between Catholics and Protestants, students and professors alike, and wondered why Pius XII had allowed this "rigidity" to linger. When would the church "be able to enter the modern age?"

At the time, Pius's reign was nearly over. His health had been failing for years. Since the mid-1950s, he had limited public appearances because, to his obvious embarrassment, his health problems included chronic, round-the-clock hiccupping. Pascalina was appalled when he turned over his medical care to an obvious quack—Dr. Riccardo Galeazzi-Lisi. While he had graduated from medical school, Galeazzi-Lisi was better known in Rome as the owner of a small but centrally located eyeglasses shop. He met the pope in the 1930s, when then-Cardinal Pacelli noticed the shop's garish street sign, in the shape of a human eye, and wandered in to buy glasses.* Pascalina pressed the pope to find a more qualified doctor, but Pius refused. "This alleged doctor hasn't the ability to treat even your pet birds," she told

* Galeazzi-Lisi may have been incompetent in prescribing eyeglasses, too. The BBC's Rome correspondent at the time reported that Pius, who famously claimed to have seen apparitions of the Virgin Mary in the Vatican's gardens in 1950, had probably not seen her at all: "His alleged vision of the Virgin Mary was not due to the pontiff's devotion to the Mother of God but to an inefficient oculist, who prescribed the wrong spectacles" (Smith, *A Desk in Rome*, 112).

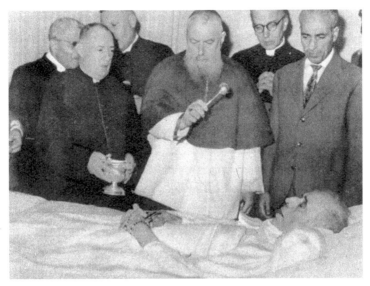

Cardinal Eugène Tisserant sprinkling holy water on the body of Pope Pius XII as he lies on his deathbed at Castel Gandolfo, the summer papal residence, October 9, 1958

him. His response wounded her: "You're jealous of everyone who is close to me." His other doctors, including a Swiss gerontologist who developed a so-called living-cell therapy that required the pope to receive daily injections of ground tissue from freshly slaughtered lambs, were not much more competent. Another doctor, trying to deal with the pope's chronic gastritis, treated him with a metallic liquid that discolored his skin and was blamed for his hiccups.

In the first week of October 1958, *L'Osservatore Romano* revealed that the pope's heart was failing. He died at Castel Gandolfo before dawn on October 9, at the age of eighty-two. With the announcement of his death, Rome came to a standstill. The pews in St. Peter's Basilica and in the city's nearly six hundred parish churches filled with Romans praying for his soul.

It would not be reflected in the reports of the world's major news organizations, which were always so deferential to the Vatican, but the pope's funeral was—up close—a catastrophe. The man responsible for the ghastly spectacle was Galeazzi-Lisi, who insisted on overseeing preparation of the corpse for burial. He called a news conference a few days after the pope's death to discuss his embalming methods, claiming he used "the same technique that had been used at the time of the Savior," with Pius's body covered with oils that would preserve it indefinitely. Galeazzi-Lisi was no better a mortician than he was a doctor, however, and the corpse began to decompose even before it was placed in an open coffin in St. Peter's. The skin turned a deep bluish-green and began to rupture. Within a day, the pope's nose fell off and had to be reattached with sculptors' putty. The smell was so offensive, even after the corpse was covered with thick sheets of cellophane, that one of the Swiss Guards watching over the coffin collapsed from the stench.*

It was evidence of Pius's failings as an administrator that he made so few preparations for his death. There was no secretary of state, since he gave himself the job, and he never bothered to appoint a so-called camerlengo, the title traditionally given to a senior Curia bishop to administer the Vatican in the period between a pope's death and the election of his successor. Those duties fell to Cardinal Tisserant, who was startled to discover how much needed to be done. He was required, first, to seal the pope's apartment and gather up his paperwork. Tisserant began a frantic search for Pius's will. Over the centuries, most popes left behind a will to divide up their earthly belongings. But if Pius had one, he had—characteristically—kept it to himself. Tisserant eventually found it hidden away at the bottom of a locked drawer in the pope's desk in the Apostolic Palace. If the cardinal had a reaction to the will, it was not recorded, but others in the Curia were shocked.

At first glance, the will, handwritten in Latin, was out of character, since it was so short, just eight sentences on a single page. Unlike the wills of his predecessors, Pius's made no mention of the accomplishments of his papacy. There was no word of thanks to Pascalina or others. It seemed to have been written instead as a desperate plea for God's forgiveness. The opening words were drawn from the Book of Psalms: "Have mercy upon me, O God." He expressed his fear that throughout his life he had damaged people: "I humbly ask pardon from all those whom I have hurt, harmed or scandalized." He suggested his sins were so grave that his name should be forgotten: "I ask those whose affair it is not to bother with any monuments to my memory. It is sufficient that my poor remains are buried in a sacred

* It was later discovered that as the pope lay dying, Galeazzi-Lisi kept handwritten notes at the bedside that he sold—secretly, within hours of Pius's death—to newspapers around the world. Curia officials later insisted they had been unaware that, for years, he had been on the payroll of *The New York Times* and several European tabloids as a confidential Vatican source. And it was not just his deathbed diary that was up for auction. He had also taken photos of the pope in his final hours—and of the corpse—that he also sold to the highest bidder.

place—the more hidden the better." The will was made public two days later, released in an Italian translation. Curia censors apparently hoped no one would notice that several words had been edited out from the original Latin; the words "sin" and "scandalized" were removed entirely.

The reasons for his despairing last words became a subject of fierce debate among his former deputies, an argument that had to be conducted behind closed doors because it threatened to undermine what became an aggressive, decades-long public campaign to have Pius declared a saint. Some Curia bishops thought Pius pleaded for mercy because he knew that once the record of his actions in World War II became known, his legacy would be forever tarnished. That furor began in earnest in 1963, with a play that was produced both in London and later on Broadway: *The Deputy: A Christian Tragedy*, by the German playwright Rolf Hochhuth. It depicted Pius as a moral pygmy who had abdicated his responsibility to protest the Holocaust. The play would eventually be performed in more than twenty languages. In a pivotal scene, as Roman Jews are rounded up under the pope's windows for deportation to Auschwitz, a priest watching from a distance expresses his disgust: "Doing nothing is as bad as taking part. God can forgive a hangman for such work. But not a priest. And not the pope."

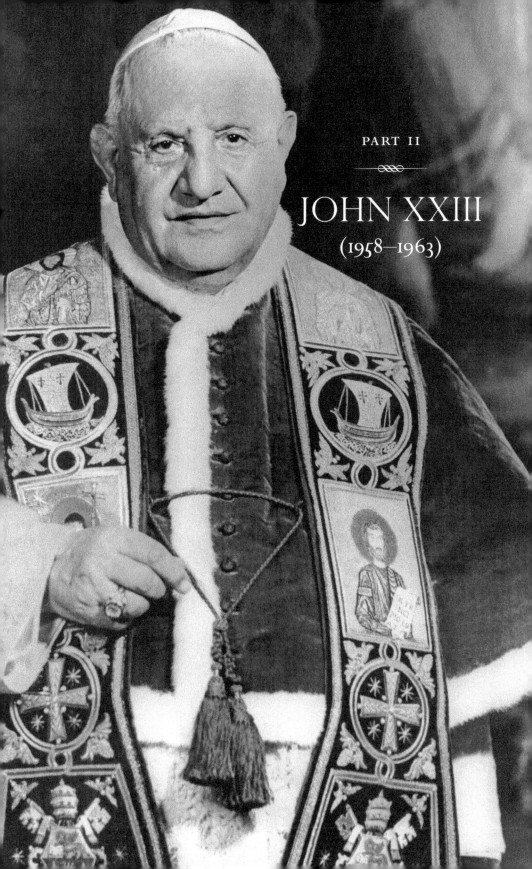

PART II

JOHN XXIII

(1958–1963)

3

A Pope for All the World

A T FIRST, it was hard to make out the color of the tiny wisp of smoke from the metal chimney. Was it black? Gray? Then, a few seconds later, the smoke above the Sistine Chapel was a pure, clean white, signaling to the world that the fifty-one members of the College of Cardinals, in their fourth day of deliberations, had elected a successor to Pius XII. It was 5:07 p.m. on Tuesday, October 28, 1958. The use of smoke signals—black after an inconclusive vote, white to signal a pope's election—was a bit of stagecraft first used in 1914 with the election of Benedict XV. Under the rules of that conclave, the paper ballots needed to be incinerated to preserve secrecy, and a few theatrically minded cardinals came up with the idea of burning them with damp straw in a stove to produce dense black smoke after an inconclusive vote. When a pope was elected, the ballots were burned with dry twigs, producing white smoke.

The new pope, John XXIII, the former Cardinal Roncalli of Venice, was surprisingly calm in the first minutes after his election. He recalled in his diary how he was immediately escorted from the Sistine Chapel to a side room to be fitted for the flowing white robes that would be his uniform for the rest of his life. By tradition, his identity remained a mystery to the public until the moment the billowing curtains parted on the balcony of St. Peter's and he stepped forward to receive the cheers of the crowd. When he did, he wrote later, it was the noise that overwhelmed him. The sound of cascading water from the pair of magnificent four-tier fountains in the square, designed by Bernini and his rival Maderno in the seventeenth century, was drowned out by the frenzied cries of "Viva Papa!" The new pope's next physical sensation was one of being blinded by the floodlights set up around the square. "I blessed Rome and the world as though I were a blind man," he wrote. "I could see nothing but an amorphous, swaying mass."

Hundreds of students from the Gregorian had rushed to St. Peter's to learn the identity of the new pope. Many admitted later they were unimpressed by the fat, bald little man who stepped forward. "He was this roly-poly old Italian," said Father Charles Curran of Rochester, New York, then a twenty-four-year-old theology student at the university. "There was none of the gravitas of Pius XII." Hans Küng, then at home in Switzerland, heard the news over the radio, and he was no more enthusiastic, although he tried to find reason for optimism. After years of Pius's repression, Küng said, at least this new pope was not known in advance to be "some kind of fanatical reactionary."

To the crowd in St. Peter's, the first, most obvious difference between the new pontiff and his predecessor was one of physical appearance. John was five foot six—almost half a foot shorter than Pius—and so overweight at more than 250 pounds that an embarrassed Vatican tailor, hastily trying to dress him in his first white cassock, needed safety pins to hold the fabric together. While Pius was born a Roman aristocrat, John celebrated the fact that he was an "absolute peasant," the fourth of fourteen children in a family of northern Italian sharecroppers.

Without saying so directly, he made clear in the first hours after his election that the grim sobriety of Pius's reign was over. John would rarely be seen in public without a smile on his face. In his early papal audiences, he joked with crowds in a way that traditionalists in the Vatican found undignified. He was aware of their disdain and told friends he often felt insulted by Curia bishops. They treated him like a simpleton, he complained in his diary. Still, he would never respond in kind to their rudeness. "I'm not aware of having offended anyone in my life," he wrote.

As pope, he quickly created a profitable niche industry for Italian publishing houses; they regularly issued book-length collections of his best wisecracks and latest, most quotable, off-the-cuff remarks. Most famously, at an early news conference after his election, the journalists' questions turned to the size of the Vatican's bureaucracy. One reporter asked the pope if he knew how many people actually worked in the Curia.

John thought for a moment.

"About half," he said with a sly grin. The journalists of the Vatican press corps, not used to a pope who cracked jokes, roared with laughter.

His wit was usually at his own expense, often about his weight. He joked, too, about the idea that he should ever be considered infallible. "Anybody can be pope," he said. "The proof of this is that I've become one." That humor was lost on Curia bureaucrats determined to keep alive the idea of an all-powerful pope whose decisions were error-free.

He often said that of the nine formal titles bestowed on him at the time of his election, beginning with bishop of Rome and vicar of Christ, the one that most appealed to him came last on the official list: "Servant of the Servants of God."* It reflected what he saw as his responsibility to the world's 800 million Catholics. He was their servant, not the other way around.

He decided as a young boy to dedicate his life to the church. In 1892, eleven-year-old Angelo left his family farm—he would never again live with his parents for more than a few weeks at a time—and entered a seminary. He told his mother his only goal in life was to be a simple parish priest. But he proved to be a fine student and, after earning a doctorate in theology at the age of twenty-three, attracted the attention of the Curia, which assigned him to the diplomatic corps. In 1925, he was appointed the Vatican's representative to Bulgaria. The thought of a posting in an obscure Eastern European nation was "terrifying" at first, but he came to love Bulgaria's "magnificent, soulful" people and developed a lasting respect for its Eastern Orthodox Church, which had broken away from Rome seven centuries earlier. Even so, during almost a decade in Bulgaria, he often felt "hidden from the world" and "forgotten" by the Vatican.

In 1934, he was dispatched to Turkey as Rome's diplomat in Istanbul. He was enchanted by the city and made sure, every night, to stop for a few minutes to gaze out the window and watch the "boats on the Bosporus come round from the Golden Horn in their hundreds—a spectacle of color and light." Turkey was a Muslim nation, but throughout the 1930s and 1940s, the country became a transit point for Jewish refugees and others

---

* "Pope" is not among those official titles even if it is the most common way in English to refer to the bishop of Rome. The word is a colloquial term taken from the Italian word *papa*, or father. The stuffier word "pontiff," drawn from the Latin word *pontifex*, meaning "bridge builder," is part of one of his official titles: "Supreme Pontiff of the Universal Church."

fleeing the Nazis. Roncalli found it exciting to be "lost in this weltering mass of Muslims, Jews and Orthodox."

In 1944, he was astonished when Pius XII named him papal nuncio—the church's term for ambassador—to newly liberated France. He remained in Paris, traditionally the most desirable assignment in the Vatican's diplomatic corps, for nine years, among the happiest of his life. He charmed the French, including the country's notoriously gruff president, Charles de Gaulle. Roncalli delighted in the cuisine and felt no guilt about it, even as he grew fatter by the day. His chef in the nuncio's residence would later help open the famed La Grenouille restaurant in New York City. At diplomatic receptions, Roncalli could often be found in a corner, a glass of champagne in one hand, a cigarette in the other, in excited conversation with a famous novelist or film star. His Parisian friends told funny, if slightly off-color, stories about parties at his residence, including one in which he was approached by a ravishing Frenchwoman who wore a massive gold crucifix between her ample breasts, leading him to exclaim in French, "Quelle Golgotha!" (What a Calvary!)

In 1953, he returned to Italy as patriarch of Venice—it was a sign of that fabled city's prominence that its archbishop has that additional, lofty title—and named a cardinal. Roncalli earned the affection of his new flock with his total lack of pretension. In an address in St. Mark's Basilica on the day he arrived in Venice, he announced he was "someone who simply wants to be your brother—kind, approachable and understanding." He was beloved for small gestures, including learning the names of the gondoliers who shuttled him across the canals, as well as the names of their children. He was grateful that, at long last, he fulfilled his dream of being a real pastor, albeit in service to an entire city. "I am excited to be ministering to souls even if I am beginning my direct ministry at an age—seventy-two—when others end theirs." He decided to keep St. Mark's open at all hours, since "someone may want to go to confession with me." He was regularly roused from bed at night to meet with a parishioner who had no appointment but needed comfort.

John took pride in not having engaged in any of the flattery or horse trading common for centuries among candidates for the papacy. He boasted that when he left for the conclave in 1958 he had a return train ticket to Venice in his pocket and expected to use it. Still, he had been identified in advance as a likely contender. Other cardinals were looking for a transitional pope who would serve only a few years and who, after the distant, ill-tempered Pius, had a reputation for calm and good humor. And so Roncalli was an obvious choice even if, on matters of doctrine, he was a blank slate. He said later his election was not certain until the last minute, with votes shifting "like chickpeas in a pot of boiling water." His choice of the papal name John was a surprise. It had been out of favor since the fifteenth century, when internal chaos at the Vatican allowed a wayward bishop from Naples with a criminal past—a former pirate on the high seas, it was said—to claim the papacy as John XXIII. After five tumultuous years, that John was deposed and denounced as an antipope. In reviving the name and number five hundred years later, Roncalli said he was honoring two men close to Jesus—John the Baptist and the apostle John. It had also been the name of Roncalli's father.

In public, the new pope offered only praise for his predecessor.* He kept many of Pius's deputies in place and promoted Cardinal Alfredo Ottaviani, a protégé of the late pope, as head of the Holy Office. He raised Pius's closest aide in the Curia, Monsignor Tardini, to the post of secretary of state and made him a cardinal—a surprise, since Tardini had been openly contemptuous of then-Cardinal Roncalli, mocking his intelligence to his face. When news of the promotions reached Hans Küng, he was horrified that these "dry reactionaries" held on to power. The new pope, he thought, was making "one wrong decision after another."

As Christmas approached, however, there was real change, as the stiff formality of the papacy began to disappear. John was appalled by the practice of earlier popes of having people fall to their knees in his presence, so he stopped it. He barred another custom in which some visitors tried to kiss his feet. He ordered *L'Osservatore Romano* to stop referring to him with flowery descriptions—in the past, the paper described all papal decrees as "Illumination from the August Lips of the Most Supreme Pontiff"—and to stop using the royal "we." He insisted to deputies that, when writing documents in his name, plain language be used. The model, he said, was Jesus, who spoke with "the most appealing simplicity."

His management style could not have been more different from Pius's. John held regular meetings with Curia bishops who had been denied face-to-face contact with his predecessor. Foreign diplomats marveled at

* Privately, John XXIII may have felt differently about Pius. After a newly promoted French bishop told John in confidence that he worried he would not succeed in his diocese, John reportedly replied: "Don't worry. Just do what I do: the opposite of my predecessor" (Hebblethwaite, *John XXIII: Pope of the Century*, 172).

what was happening. "Under Pius XII, the Vatican was chaotic," the British ambassador to the Vatican wrote. "John XXIII makes the organization work." After so many years in which Pius refused to appoint new cardinals, John named twenty-three in his first month, including his old friend Giovanni Montini, the archbishop of Milan. Over the next three years, he appointed a total of fifty-two cardinals, including the first Black African and the first from Mexico, the Philippines, and Japan.

The people of Rome agreed there was something special—and also intensely familiar—about the new pope. Beneath the white robes, he was one of them. In a different life, he might have been a neighborhood fruit peddler, or their slightly buffoonish uncle. Reporters in the Vatican press corps were delighted they had a pope eager to talk to them; he was the first bishop of Rome to hold regular news conferences. When First Lady Jacqueline Kennedy visited Rome to meet him, he was advised by the Curia's ever-finicky protocol experts that he should refer to her as either "Mrs. Kennedy" or "Madame Kennedy." When he caught sight of her walking toward him, however, he opened his arms wide and yelled out "Jacqueline!"

He ended the physical isolation of the papacy, becoming the first pope regularly to leave the confines of Vatican City and Castel Gandolfo since 1870, when Pius IX declared himself "the prisoner of the Vatican" in protest over the Italian government's seizure of church lands. Pius and his first six successors remained almost entirely inside the walls of Vatican City until their deaths. Yet on Christmas Day 1958, two months after his election, the "prisoner" went free. John XXIII declared that morning that he wanted to visit Rome's Bambino Gesù children's hospital to offer holiday wishes. As he moved from sickbed to sickbed, many of the children took him to be the Italian version of Santa Claus. The next morning, he panicked deputies with his announcement that he would pay an impromptu visit to the city's Regina Coeli Prison and meet with any prisoner who wished to see him. "Open up the doors," he told a warden who urged him to stay behind the iron gates in the cellblock where the most dangerous inmates were held. "Do not bar them from me. They are all children of the Lord." Many shocked prisoners fell to their knees at the sight of the pope, who smiled impishly as he announced that "since you couldn't come to see me, I came to see you." Newsreels captured prisoners in tears. A man convicted of murder pleaded, "Can there be forgiveness for me?" The pope took him into his arms and assured him of God's mercy.

He acknowledged in an impromptu speech to the inmates that he, like so many of them, came from grinding poverty. He revealed that one of his uncles, a sharecropper like the pope's father, had been imprisoned for poaching. "There are only three ways of losing money in Italy: farming, gambling, and women," he joked. "My uncle chose the least interesting way." Curia censors deleted the remarks in the official account of the visit; they thought it shameful for a pope to acknowledge a petty criminal as a relative. There were other, more significant early acts of defiance by the Curia. In a routine move for a new pope, John sent a letter to bishops who led large Vatican agencies, asking them to submit letters of resignation. That would allow him to put his own men in the jobs. To his shock, several refused.

"They refuse the pope?" he asked incredulously. When asked later why he didn't insist on having his way, John sighed. "I'm only the pope around here."

He prided himself on never showing anger, never raising his voice, never making a critical comment to a subordinate. "The secret of my success may lie there—in being content to be meek and humble," he wrote in his

Pope John XXIII meets with inmates at Rome's central prison on the day after Christmas 1958, two months after his election.

diary. "I am grateful to the Lord for the temperament he has given me, which preserves me from anxiety and tiresome complexity. This disposition in all things, large and small, gives me, unworthy as I am, a strength of daring simplicity." Other churchmen misread him, thinking his tranquility reflected a lack of intelligence. In fact, as his diaries revealed, he was clever and thought strategically. He could be downright cagey. He often said he lived by a set of rules known to all nineteenth-century northern Italian peasants: "See everything, overlook a great deal, correct only a little."

John, seventy-six on the day of his election, knew he was seen as a caretaker pope, but he had no intention of being one. In fact, from the moment he pulled on those white robes, he delighted in upending the common wisdom that his would be a dull, uneventful papacy. Instead, he wrote, "I have an immense program of work in front of me to be carried out before the eyes of the whole world, which is waiting and wanting."

His most momentous decision came three months after his election. On January 25, 1959, he announced in a speech that he would summon all the world's bishops to a meeting in Rome—a so-called ecumenical council—to plot the church's future. It would be the first such gathering since the First Vatican Council adjourned in 1870. The idea occurred to him, he said, after he noticed that his desk was "piling up with problems, questions, requests, hopes"—all tied to issues that the world's bishops should be empowered to resolve for themselves. In his speech to a group of cardinals, he offered no date for the Second Vatican Council, or Vatican II, as it came to be known, although he hoped it could be organized within two or three years. He said he wanted the church to approach the gathering with a spirit of *aggiornamento*—an Italian word meaning "bringing up to date." He dreamed the council could bring about reconciliation between Catholics and other Christians. In that hope, he said, the Vatican would issue a "friendly invitation" to representatives of the "separated churches"— Protestants, Eastern Orthodox, as well as the fast-growing evangelical communities of the United States and South America—to send observers. When his speech was finished, he expected to hear applause, maybe even cheers, from the cardinals. "But they did nothing of the kind," he wrote in his diary, remembering his disappointment. "There was only silence." *L'Osservatore Romano*, which the Curia controlled, buried news of the speech deep inside the paper. It censored the pope's remarks about his "friendly invitation" to non-Catholic Christians—"friendly" was removed, and the reference to "separated churches" was replaced with "separated communities," reflecting the Curia's view that there was only one true church. Cardinal Giacomo Lercaro of Bologna was incensed by John's announcement: "How dare he summon a council only three months after his election." The new pope, he said, was proving to be "rash and impulsive, lacking in experience and culture." As John's friend Cardinal Montini put it: "This holy old boy doesn't seem to realize what a hornet's nest he's stirring up."

In the history of the church, ecumenical councils had been momentous events—and often the setting for revolutionary change. There had been only twenty in the nearly two thousand years since the Crucifixion. According to early Christian teachings, a council had more authority than any individual pope, which explained why most bishops of Rome refused to call them. After the First Vatican Council ended by endorsing the doctrine of papal infallibility, many churchmen assumed there would never be another council, since an error-free pope could resolve all issues. John XXIII thought otherwise. He announced that the world's bishops would set the agenda at the Second Vatican Council and directed the Curia to mail a questionnaire to all 2,710 Catholic dioceses around the globe, asking local bishops what they wanted to discuss in Rome. More than two thousand replied, many with long, detailed lists of topics.

In Germany, the announcement of a council thrilled Joseph Ratzinger, then thirty-one. Among his new colleagues on the faculty at the University of Bonn it created excitement "to the point of euphoria," he wrote. It seemed "everything was open to revision; the council appeared to be like a great church parliament that could change everything." He would not say any of that too loudly, however. He understood the danger he faced as a young Catholic theologian if he became known as a champion of "everything that was new and progressive," since it could invite punishment by the Holy Office.

Especially then, Ratzinger was eager to enjoy some calm in his life. He still struggled to forget his humiliation two years earlier when his doctoral dissertation was rejected by an adviser at the University of Munich. The dispute between the two was complicated to explain, even among theologians, but came down to the adviser's belief that Ratzinger had a dangerously provocative view of how God revealed his existence to man. When his thesis was rejected, Ratzinger wondered what he would do for money; his family depended on him financially after his father's retirement. A year later, the thesis was approved, but only after Ratzinger edited out its most innovative passages; what had been a 700-page dissertation was now just

180 pages. Even after receiving his degree, "I could hardly feel any joy, so heavily did the nightmare of what happened weigh down on me." The incident scarred him. He would live for years with the fear that events could shift at any moment and destroy him.

He was still settling into his teaching duties in Bonn when he was approached by Cardinal Josef Frings of nearby Cologne. The cardinal, introduced to Ratzinger by a mutual friend, wanted his help in preparing for the council—and then to join him in Rome for the meetings themselves. Ratzinger was elated, even if he was essentially taking on a second full-time job. The seventy-two-year-old cardinal was nearly blind, so Ratzinger would be responsible for sifting through a flood of advance paperwork from the Vatican. Frings was a legend to many Germans because of his bravery during World War II, when he repeatedly described the persecution of Jews as a *himmelschreiendes Unrecht*—a crime that cries out to heaven. After nighttime air raids on Cologne, he pulled on a steel helmet and went onto the streets to help dig out survivors from the rubble.

HANS KÜNG KNEW only success in his early career. In 1960, at the age of thirty-two, he joined the theology faculty of the University of Tübingen, where he was introduced to Walter Kasper, then a year into his graduate studies.* The two became close, and Kasper worked for a time as Küng's research assistant. They shared an admiration for the new pope and were excited by his plans for a council. On the day John XXIII announced Vatican II, Kasper was in Tübingen, listening to the radio with friends when they heard the news. "We could not believe our ears. It was like lightning from a blue sky."

Küng insisted later he had never planned to attend Vatican II. He thought he was too young to be invited as a theological expert. Besides, he told himself, the meetings might go on for years, and he had no desire to live again in Rome. Despite happy memories of the Gregorian, he still equated the Eternal City with the oppression of Pius XII—the "black

---

* In an interview near the end of his life, Ratzinger insisted that he, not Küng, had been the University of Tübingen's first choice for the faculty post. Ratzinger said he turned down the Tübingen offer because he preferred to teach at the University of Bonn, "which was my dream destination." Some of Ratzinger's critics were skeptical of the story, since Tübingen's theology school was so much more prestigious—"the Olympus of German theology," as Ratzinger's authorized biographer noted (Seewald, *Benedict XVI: A Life, Volume I*, 503).

Rome" that he wanted no part of. Even so, he had great hopes for the council and wanted to express them in print. His first book had been a critical success, so he decided he would write another, addressed to the world's bishops, in which he would propose an agenda for Vatican II. The book's central message: the bishops—recognized by ancient church teachings as successors to the twelve apostles, with the pope identified specifically as successor to the apostle Peter—should reclaim the power stripped away over centuries by the Vatican. The book offered a checklist of reforms they should demand. Most important, he thought, the council should begin a formal process of ending centuries of hostility toward other Christians. As a symbolic first act, he wrote, the bishops should lift the ancient decrees of excommunication issued against "heretics," especially Luther. The council should also end the exclusive use of the Latin Mass, allowing worship services in local languages; abolish the Index of Prohibited Books; and overhaul the church's strict marriage laws.

After a lecture in Tübingen in which he outlined the book's themes, another theologian whispered in his ear: "People used to be burned at the stake for saying things like this." To shield himself from the wrath of heresy hunters in Rome, Küng sought to have the manuscript endorsed in advance by a prominent German-speaking cardinal. He sent it to Cardinal Franz König of Vienna, the most powerful churchman in Austria. The cardinal, who had also attended the Gregorian, was impressed and agreed to write a brief introduction: "I hope that this book, and the challenge which it presents, will be received with understanding and spread far and wide." When it was published in Germany in 1960, the book, *The Council, Reform and Reunion,* was a sensation, wildly praised by reviewers in and out of the church and released within a year in several other languages. Küng decided not to seek an Italian publisher, at least not immediately, since it might make the book too easily available to detractors in the Holy Office. The book's English-language edition climbed bestseller lists in the United States and Britain. Archbishop of Canterbury Geoffrey Fisher, leader of the Church of England, told his colleagues: "You should all read it. I have never read such a book in my life!" For Küng, the most thrilling evidence of his newfound celebrity came when *Time* magazine, then at the peak of its influence, published an article about the book under the headline "A Second Reformation for Both Catholics and Protestants." It was accompanied by images of three men: Martin Luther, John XXIII, and the boyish, now thirty-four-year-old Küng.

Küng was audacious enough to hope the pope might endorse the book, too. He packaged up a copy of the French edition and had it delivered to the Apostolic Palace in Rome, attaching a letter to the pope in Italian. Küng wrote in formal Curial style, beginning with the salutation: "Beatissimo Padre"—Most Blessed Father. The book, he explained, was a "modest work" intended to assist in planning for the council. Several weeks later, he received a letter back from the Vatican, with thanks. It reported that, even before the book arrived, John had obtained a copy for himself. A few weeks later, there was a second letter, this one from the papal nuncio in Bonn, who reported that the pope had finished the book and wanted its author to know that "it has met with his high approval." A delighted Küng read and reread the letter, wondering if this amounted to a formal papal endorsement.

He changed his mind about attending Vatican II. His invitation came in June 1962, when Bishop Carl Leiprecht of Rottenburg, near Tübingen, asked Küng to join him in Rome as his theological adviser at the council. Küng hesitated, but his faculty colleagues convinced him he *had* to go. This was the first ecumenical council in more than ninety years, and it had been called by a pope eager for reform. How could he think of saying no? "My friends tell me it's the event of the century," Küng wrote of his change of heart. "And they're right." He and Ratzinger were on their way.

4

To Summon a Council

THE SOCIETY OF JESUS, the fabled Catholic religious order also known as the Jesuits, has been home for almost five hundred years to many of the church's most courageous evangelists and finest scholars. The order was established in 1540 by St. Ignatius of Loyola, a Spanish nobleman-soldier who found God on the battlefield. Jesuits vowed total loyalty to the papacy, even when a sitting bishop of Rome was notoriously corrupt or otherwise wicked, and were known for their eagerness to risk their lives to spread the Gospel to exotic lands. They were often compared to soldiers—"the pope's shock troops"—and had an especially proud reputation in South America, where they were among the first Europeans to settle the continent. They administered many of the church's most famous universities, including the Gregorian. Under the order's written rules of conduct, Jesuits were banned from accepting appointment as bishops or to any other posts in the church hierarchy without receiving formal permission from the Society, and that was rarely granted without an explicit order from the pope. Until the twenty-first century, there had never been a Jesuit pope, and many Jesuits assumed there never would be one. For many Jesuits, the idea of such outsized ambition and power was unthinkable.

In Rome in the 1950s, few Jesuits were more revered than Father Augustin Bea, a German-born biblical scholar who wielded influence in the Vatican because of his relationship with Pius XII. Bea had been rector of the Jesuit-run Pontifical Biblical Institute, the church's most renowned center for Bible research, from 1930 to 1949, and his scholarship so impressed Pius that he named Bea as his personal confessor. Bea held that most delicate of assignments from 1945 until Pius's death. In the days after the pope's funeral, the birdlike, stoop-shouldered Bea, then seventy-seven, told friends he looked forward to a quiet retirement in Rome. But he put that thought aside in January 1959, when he was summoned to an audience with John XXIII, then three months into his papacy.

At that first meeting, both men were overcome by a sense of brotherhood. Born six months apart in 1881, they shared a reputation for extraordinary humility. In Bea's diary, he described a morning ritual in which he coached himself in his shaving mirror on the need to suppress his ego and demonstrate modesty at all times, with all people. Days after the meeting, Bea returned to the papal apartment with a daring suggestion. He urged the pope to begin the process of building bridges to Protestants and Orthodox Christians by establishing—ahead of the council—a Vatican agency with that explicit responsibility. A delighted John agreed on the spot. Weeks later, the pope announced the creation of the Secretariat for the Promotion of Christian Unity, with Bea as president. It would answer directly to the pope, bypassing the Holy Office, a status that infuriated Ottaviani, who for decades had rejected even modest efforts to reach out to other Christians.

The pope joked to Bea that, in accepting the assignment, he needed to make a sacrifice: He would have to be promoted—to become a cardinal. Bea noted that as a Jesuit, he was required to resist the honor, but John was insistent. He told Bea he needed the title in order to have his voice heard in the Curia. Bea grudgingly accepted, although he insisted he never felt comfortable in his red robes.

The two men settled on a vocabulary for their project. They agreed the words "heretic" and "dissident" were to be banished in referring to non-Catholic Christians. Instead, Protestants and Orthodox Christians would be described as "separated brethren." The Vatican would stop talking about other Christians "returning" to the Catholic Church, as if they were wandering sheep. The new word was "reunion." Bea oversaw secret arrangements for the head of the Church of England, Archbishop of Canterbury Fisher, seen as the world's most important Protestant churchman by virtue of his title, to travel to Rome to meet the pope that December. It would be the first-ever meeting between the leaders of the two churches. (The Church of England was established in 1534, after Henry VIII broke from Rome when he was denied an annulment from the first of his six wives.) The idea of a papal encounter with the Protestant archbishop scandalized Curia bureaucrats, who insisted photographers be barred from witnessing the scene, an order John chose not to overrule. The Vatican's only public confirmation came in a single, cryptic sentence in *L'Osservatore Romano* the next day: "Dr. Geoffrey Fisher had an audience with His Holiness." Fisher was delighted at what had taken place: "This is a complete revolution."

Conservatives who opposed John's initiative should not have been surprised by it. In his decades outside Rome, he formed close friendships with people of other faiths. He said he had no other choice in Bulgaria, where there were almost no Catholics, "unless I had wanted to live like a hermit." In a 1944 sermon in Istanbul, then-Archbishop Roncalli asked why Catholics had cut themselves off "from our Orthodox brothers, Protestants, Jews, Muslims. I have to tell you that in light of the Gospel and Catholic principle, this division makes no sense." (Church historians assume the text of that bold homily did not reach Rome at the time, since the Holy Office would likely have seen his outreach to non-Catholics as career-ending heresy.)

John XXIII next moved directly to end the most ancient rupture of all—between the church and the Jews. He held unpublicized meetings in the papal palace with Jewish leaders from the United States and Europe and with officials from Israel, even though the Vatican had no diplomatic relations with the Jewish state. (Pius XII refused to recognize Israel, citing ancient Christian claims to land that fell within its borders after its creation in 1948.) In those meetings, John repeatedly noted that Jesus, who considered himself a proud, obedient Jew, would be horrified by the rupture. "We are all sons of the same Heavenly Father," the pope told a delighted group of American Jews. In simply uttering those words, he rewrote two thousand years of history. As a child, he often heard neighbors describe Jews as "Christ killers" and, while the term was obviously a slur, it was not far from the formal teachings of the church. Ancient Catholic doctrine held that all Jews, including those not yet born, were responsible for the actions of a small tribe of their ancestors who, according to the Gospels, betrayed Jesus to their Roman occupiers. The Vatican stood by that wholesale condemnation into the twentieth century—Pius XII suggested Jews were members of a "cult"—and ignored Catholic theologians who had argued for years that the indictment resulted from the misreading of a single, ambiguous passage of scripture found in the Gospel of Matthew. The passage quotes Jews confronted by Roman governor Pontius Pilate as confessing that the blood of Jesus is "on us—*and on our children*" (my italics). In undoing the ancient libel, John XXIII thought he had a perspective shared by few in the Vatican.

Unlike many careerists who never left Rome, he had always befriended Jews—first in the Balkans in the 1920s—and had seen, firsthand, how anti-Semitism metastasized into the Holocaust.

The first public sign of his plan to reach out to Jews—and ultimately to seek their forgiveness—came five months into his papacy, when he prepared for services on Good Friday, the day of the Crucifixion. For centuries, that day's liturgy included a call for mercy for Jews but also described them with an insulting Latin word—*perfidis*, meaning "faithless" or "perfidious." John ordered the word removed, a decision that outraged some decidedly anti-Semitic Curia bishops.

At about the same time, reporters in the Vatican press corps, piecing together the life story of the new pope, stumbled onto intriguing records about his years as a diplomat in Istanbul. At a time when Pius XII was silent about the Holocaust, they discovered, then-Archbishop Roncalli acted to save Jews, often to the exasperation of superiors in Rome. By the count of independent historians, he helped rescue at least twenty-five thousand Jewish refugees across Europe, often by organizing transit papers that allowed them to reach safety in Palestine. In 1943, he called on old friends in the Bulgarian royal family to provide emigration permits to thousands of Slovakian Jews trapped in Bulgaria, who also reached Palestine. The next year, the grand rabbi of Jerusalem wrote to Roncalli to praise him for his "profound humanitarianism" in saving so many Jews "at this, the saddest moment of our history."

In June 1960, John granted an audience to the French Jewish historian Jules Isaac. After losing much of his family at Auschwitz, Isaac dedicated his life to promoting understanding between Christians and Jews. He recalled his excitement as he was ushered into the papal apartment. He was surprised by the pope's informality; Isaac had expected the bishop of Rome to sit on some sort of throne, but instead they sat next to one another in armchairs and chatted in French. Isaac told the pope that Jews were inspired by his election, then outlined what he had learned in his years of research: how so much of the anti-Semitism supposedly justified by the New Testament was the result of a historic misunderstanding of scripture. The pope agreed.

Days later, Bea was summoned back to the papal palace and given an additional assignment. His new agency, already responsible for promoting harmony with other Christians, would seek it with Jews as well. The pope asked him to draft a formal declaration in which the Vatican would apologize for its centuries of flagrant anti-Semitism—a document that the world's bishops could approve at Vatican II. Both Bea and the pope understood the significance of having it written by a German.

The cardinal returned to his office that afternoon to announce to his staff of theologians they were now responsible for "the Jewish project," as he called it. One of his brightest young deputies, a thirty-nine-year-old American, Father Thomas Stransky of Milwaukee, was thrilled by the news, although he was taken aback when Bea warned that this new assignment needed to remain "completely confidential." The cardinal said the pope insisted on secrecy, apparently fearing "the Jewish project" would otherwise be derailed by anti-Semites in the Curia. By then, Stransky, who had interrupted his theology studies at the Gregorian to go to work for Bea's new agency, had been in Rome long enough to know that keeping such a tantalizing secret would be a struggle. "I learned that the Curia is as leaky as Swiss cheese," he said. Among Vatican bureaucrats, "a secret was either not worth knowing—or it's too good to keep."

IN NOVEMBER 1961, Cardinal Frings of Cologne feared he was about to be dismissed. And if that was true, his young theological adviser, Ratzinger, shared the blame. Frings had been hastily summoned to the papal palace in Rome to meet with John XXIII. The summons came days after the cardinal delivered a bold speech written by Ratzinger to promote Vatican II, still a year away. The speech, delivered word for word from Ratzinger's draft, asserted that after centuries of "stagnation" inside the church, it was finally ready to embrace "humanity's future." Given its inherent criticism of the isolation of earlier popes, the speech attracted news coverage in Rome, which appeared to explain why Frings had been summoned, and he worried what it meant. Had he offended John XXIII?

On the day of the audience, as Frings pulled on his red garments, he told his secretary nervously, "Perhaps I am now wearing these robes for the last time." Minutes later, though, he found himself standing before a beaming Pope John, his arms outstretched in welcome. He had read Frings's speech closely. "Thank you, Your Eminence," the pope said. "You have said the very things I wanted to say myself." Frings explained he should not take credit for the address, which had been written by a talented young theologian named Ratzinger. The pope joked that he often got credit for speeches written by others.

Frings returned home to Germany to tell Ratzinger the exciting news—
that the pope shared their commitment to real reform. Ratzinger was
elated, especially at the thought that a speech he had written had been
praised personally by the bishop of Rome. Even so, he and Frings remained
in agreement about the battles to come at the council. By then, for more
than a year, Ratzinger had been paging through the paperwork dispatched
from the Curia in advance of Vatican II. They were draft documents known
as schemas, a term derived from ancient Greek, that the Curia intended to
force the world's bishops to rubber-stamp at the council. Ratzinger thought
many were dismal, written to enforce the idea that bishops should march
in lockstep on existing doctrine with a supposedly infallible pope. The language in the documents reflected the "cramped thinking" that had plagued
the Vatican for centuries. He could only assume John XXIII had little
involvement in writing the schemas, since most seemed designed to undermine the spirit of openness—aggiornamento—that the new pope made his
goal. Unless the drafts were rewritten top to bottom, they could "weigh
down" the church "like a heavy millstone," Ratzinger thought.*

The worst, he knew, had been drafted in the Holy Office at the direction
of Ottaviani. By then, it was clear throughout the church that the Italian
cardinal, then seventy-one, intended to use his power at Vatican II to block
any real reform, no matter what the pope desired. Ottaviani, eleventh of
twelve children born in a family of Roman bread bakers in the working-
class neighborhood of Trastevere, lived proudly by the Latin motto *semper
idem*—always the same. He embedded those words in his official coat of
arms and had them sewn into his robes. He was a tall, imposing man with
ballooning jowls and a hawklike stare. Simply a whisper of his name struck
terror in the Vatican, given his ability to destroy the career of any churchman seen as theologically suspect. His conservatism extended to politics.
Like his patron Pius XII, Ottaviani was a dedicated anticommunist and
insisted the church would banish any Italian who dared voice support for
Marxism. As he once told an Italian journalist, "You can say what you like
about the divinity of Christ but if, in the remotest village in Italy, you vote
Communist, your excommunication order will arrive the next day."

---

* Ratzinger claimed decades later, after he rose to great power in Rome, that he had not
been so critical of the draft documents: "I found no grounds for a radical rejection of what
was being proposed." But evidence made public after Vatican II suggests that this was not
true and that he and Frings had in fact been harshly critical of what they were reading. In a
1961 note to the pope, Frings dismissed the drafts as "completely unsuitable" (Allen, *Pope
Benedict XVI*, 53).

Cardinal Alfredo Ottaviani
of the Holy Office, feared
archconservative doctrinal
enforcer of the Vatican

Since John XXIII spent most of his career far from Rome and managed to avoid close scrutiny by the Holy Office, he insisted he never had reason to fear Ottaviani. In fact, he treated "my dear friend Alfredo" like a beloved, if cranky, uncle. The cardinal, he knew, was capable of great kindness; much of Ottaviani's free time was spent raising money to support a local school for needy children. The pope also appreciated the fact that not all of the cardinal's views could be labeled as conservative, especially on questions of war and peace. Ottaviani was among the first senior churchmen in Rome to conclude after World War II that nuclear weapons were immoral and should be banned. Many in the Curia thought the pope, aware he could always overrule or even oust Ottaviani, kept the cardinal in place as a way of reassuring conservative churchmen who might otherwise try to sabotage Vatican II.

John met regularly with bishops from outside Italy who, he sensed, would be his allies in promoting aggiornamento at the council. An early invitation went to Leo Joseph Suenens of Belgium, who had impressed him for years. Suenens earned his theology doctorate at the Gregorian in the 1920s and was considered an intellectual giant. In his many books he called for broad reform of the church, notably in its attitude toward women—and particularly toward nuns, often treated as little more than household servants by their parish priests. Suenens, a tall, lean man with graying temples, whose full but still angular face would not have been out of place in a painting by Rubens or one of the other Flemish masters, had a heroic story. As a university administrator during World War II, he defied the Nazi occupiers, earning him a place on a Gestapo list of Belgians to be executed at war's end. He survived because of the unexpectedly sudden retreat of German forces after the Allied invasion of Belgium in 1944.

In 1961, John named Suenens an archbishop and invited him to the Vatican. They formed an instant bond. Suenens, then fifty-seven, remembered the pope telling him, with a smile, that "I still do not understand why I have become pope. And I believe God is having some trouble explaining it to himself." Face-to-face, the pope was struck by Suenens's intelligence—he spoke with lawyerly precision in French, Italian, and Latin—and by his conviction that the Vatican too often put its interests above those of the faithful, especially impoverished Catholics in the developing world.

John immediately thought of Suenens as a confidant, maybe even a pope-in-waiting. When they met again a few weeks later, the pope announced, to the Belgian's astonishment, that he was being promoted a second time, to cardinal, to give him more stature at Vatican II. Over time, Suenens would be seen as the council's principal architect.

John explained to Suenens that he was serious about allowing the world's bishops to set their own agenda at Vatican II. He needed a structure for the meetings, though, so he asked Suenens to write out a detailed proposal for organizing the bishops' debates. Days later, he received a confidential letter from Suenens that harshly criticized the council's early draft documents, which had been written by so-called preparatory commissions that were under the Curia's thumb. Suenens said 80 percent of the schemas should be discarded, even if that gravely offended Ottaviani. He also urged the pope to set up a "brain trust" of senior clerics to guide the council, which would limit any attempt by the Holy Office to seize control. The pope agreed and when the brain trust was created, Suenens would lead it.

Given how much confidence John had placed in him so quickly, Suenens decided to press the pope on the most controversial issue facing the Vatican in the 1960s: its ban on birth control. The situation had troubled Suenens since he was a parish priest. In taking confession, he often heard a woman's anguished voice pleading for the right to control the size of her family. For centuries, the church opposed all contraceptive methods short of abstinence, since the Vatican saw birth control as a violation of God's law and associated it with promiscuity. The question became pressing in the 1920s, when an effective contraceptive method—latex condoms—went into mass production. In 1930, the Church of England declared birth control was not a sin; other Protestant churches soon agreed. Pius XI was appalled. Several months after the Church of England's decree, he issued an encyclical, *Casti Connubii* (Of Chaste Wedlock), banning artificial contraception. The document reflected the church's obsession with the idea that human sexuality existed only for procreation and that any effort to tamper with the natural journey of a woman's egg or a man's sperm was tantamount to murder. The church would eventually approve only one form of birth control—the so-called rhythm method, in which a woman abstained from sex around the days of ovulation, as determined by the calendar and her body temperature. It was notoriously unreliable.

Suenens was a progressive voice on questions of sexuality. He was careful not to say explicitly that the Vatican should allow birth control, but he left no doubt that sex had a value beyond childbirth. While the Book of Genesis encouraged Christians to see sex as an opportunity to "be fruitful and multiply," he knew the Bible also recognized the necessity of physical pleasure between husband and wife—how their bodies came together so "the two will become one flesh," as decreed in the Gospel of Mark. In a 1958 speech, he encouraged the medical profession to speed up research on birth-control methods that did not violate Catholic doctrine. He was excited about promising research for a pill that, by manipulating a woman's hormones, made pregnancy impossible. Catholic scientists hoped such a pill would win the church's approval, since it would not destroy eggs or sperm. They argued it would also reduce the number of women seeking abortions, an act the church equated with murder. It was no secret inside the Vatican that abortion was common across Catholic Europe. That included Italy, where it was a serious crime but still readily available in large cities, including Rome. In staunchly Catholic Poland in 1956, the Communist government legalized abortion. In France, where the population was overwhelmingly Catholic, opinion polls in the early 1960s showed 70 percent of women used contraception; one in three acknowledged having had an abortion. Suenens also questioned the Vatican's ban in light of growing threats of overpopulation and famine. It was a special concern, he said, in the devoutly Catholic nations of Latin America, where populations exploded after World War II, especially among the poor.

To Suenens's delight, the pope agreed, without much hesitation, that it was time to consider lifting the ban, although he felt the deliberations should be carried out in secret, since the subject was so controversial. In

Cardinal Leo Joseph Suenens of Belgium (left) and Cardinal
Augustin Bea of Germany, key progressive advisers to Pope
John XXIII and architects of Vatican II

late 1962, with no public announcement, the Pontifical Commission for
the Study of Population, Family and Births was created. Suenens chose its
six members, all Catholic men. Three were doctors, including the English
neurologist who devised the rhythm method. The panel's first meeting was
scheduled for early 1963.

The church faced another important debate about sexuality. Many
priests around the world dared not say it out loud, but their greatest hope
for Vatican II was that the world's bishops would rewrite church law to
allow them to marry. The Vatican had always portrayed the so-called doctrine of priestly celibacy as eternal and irreversible, but it was neither. It is
not demanded in the Gospels, nor was it a way of life followed by the twelve
apostles. There is a traditional understanding among Christian theologians
that Jesus was celibate and unmarried, but the New Testament does not state
that explicitly. There is, by comparison, compelling evidence in scripture
to show that most of the apostles, as well as most of Jesus's larger band of
disciples, were married. The apostle Peter had a wife whose ailing mother
was healed by the Savior, as recorded in three of the four Gospels. For a
thousand years after the Crucifixion, priests almost always took wives and

experienced both the comfort and the chaos of a family. Like Peter, other early popes were married. That changed in the eleventh century with the election of a strong-willed pope, Gregory VII, who rewrote church law to demand lifetime celibacy for all priests and bishops, including those already married. Historians believe the decision was motivated in part by Gregory's disgust over the scandals of a group of shockingly promiscuous Roman bishops. Other accounts suggest he was equally motivated by money—by the struggle to balance the Vatican's budget. By demanding celibacy, he guaranteed the estates of dead priests—their homes and anything else of value—were turned over to the church. Since churchmen were often drawn from families of great wealth, including royalty, his decision promised a vast new source of income.

Nine centuries later, the doctrine was blamed for a worldwide shortage of priests, which had become a crisis for the church by the 1950s, when thousands of men left the priesthood each year, most to marry. In many countries, there were not nearly enough new priests to replace them, in part because so many millions of young men died in battle in World War II, which emptied out seminaries. The situation was especially dire in South America, a continent where virtually every man and woman was born Catholic. The centuries-old migration of European-born priests to serve parishes in Latin America largely dried up. In some urban areas of Brazil, the world's most populous Catholic nation, there was a ratio of one priest to every twelve thousand people. Brazilians born deep in the Amazon rain forest might see a priest only a few times in their lives. It was well-known inside the Vatican, but never acknowledged publicly, that South American bishops turned a blind eye to the fact that many priests in rural areas had common-law wives and children.

John intended to maintain a celibate priesthood. "Celibacy is a sacrifice which the church has imposed on herself—freely, generously and heroically," he declared. Still, he acknowledged in private that as a matter of church law, it could be reversed with little more than a snap of his fingers. "Celibacy is not a dogma," he conceded to a French friend. "How simple it would be: We take up a pen, sign an act and priests who so desire can marry tomorrow." His own conscience would not allow it, however. He knew priests suffered from the demands of celibacy—how, for many churchmen, it was "a martyrdom." He had suffered himself. In his diary, he wrote of his struggles with the "evil impulses" of lust and how he welcomed old age, since it brought "silence and tranquility of the flesh."

Questions about priestly sexuality were a daily concern for others in the Vatican. Ottaviani was forced to address them, since the Holy Office was responsible for investigating churchmen accused of violating their celibacy vows. In 1922, the Vatican issued secret instructions to the world's bishops to refer all allegations of sexual crimes by priests, including rape and child abuse, to the Holy Office. In 1962, Ottaviani met with a visiting American priest, Gerald Fitzgerald, the director of a religious order in New Mexico, the Servants of the Paraclete, that was established in the 1940s to treat priests struggling with alcoholism. Over time, it also began to treat those suffering from sexual disorders. Fitzgerald went to Rome to warn Ottaviani of a brewing crisis in the American church—of widespread child molestation by priests.* He said his experience in New Mexico suggested that pedophiles were common in the priesthood, and that the problem was being covered up by bishops who moved child molesters from parish to parish. He felt so strongly about the danger posed by pedophile priests that he had begun raising money to purchase a small Caribbean island where they could be exiled. He eventually gave up on the idea, concluding that "an island is too good for these vipers."

Months after meeting Fitzgerald, Ottaviani dispatched a new set of instructions to the world's bishops, reminding them to be alert to the possibility of sexual crimes by priests, including child molestation. The document, *Crimen Sollicitationis* (The Crime of Solicitation), outlined detailed procedures for investigating accused priests. The instructions, which required all cases of serious sexual misconduct to continue to be reported to the Holy Office, also demanded secrecy. Ottaviani attached a typed note to each copy of the instructions, demanding the contents remain secret under penalty of excommunication. Although the document did not explicitly order bishops to withhold evidence of sexual crimes from the police, many dioceses read it that way, since that had always been their practice.

Another Vatican agency, the Congregation for Religious, was responsible

---

* Vatican archives from World War II made public in 2020 revealed that priestly sexual abuse had also been of concern to Pius XII, especially after the Nazi government prosecuted hundreds of German priests for sex crimes, including child molestation. The Vatican insisted at the time that in most of those cases, the allegations were false and intended to blacken the church's image. A transcript of a 1939 conversation with Pius XII quoted him as saying that when priests were credibly accused of sexual abuse, "we intervene immediately and severely." One newly released document showed that in 1938 the Vatican, concerned about a police investigation in Austria of priestly sexual abuse, decided to "burn all archival material concerning cases of immorality by priests and monks" in that country (Kertzer, *The Pope at War*, 63).

for investigating cases of sexual misconduct by priests and monks in religious orders, such as the Jesuits, the Dominicans, and the Franciscans.* By the late 1950s, it had been flooded for years with detailed, salacious allegations against Father Marcial Maciel Degollado, the Mexican-born founder of a wealthy religious order known as the Legion of Christ. Maciel, who established the group in Mexico in 1941, initially attracted attention in the Vatican for his fundraising skills. His first large donors were the wives of wealthy Mexican industrialists; the women were flattered by the attention the dark-eyed, seemingly mystical Maciel lavished on them. Their money was used to build seminaries and underwrite Maciel's frequent travels abroad. It was often noted that the order's seminarians, with their closely cropped hair, tended to be unusually attractive and fit, as if the boys had been recruited for their looks. They were required to swear an oath never to criticize Maciel, who was known to all as *nuestro padre* (our father), and to report on anyone who did. In the early 1950s, he moved his headquarters to Rome.

He had been dogged by rumors of misconduct since he was a teenager. He was ordained only after an uncle who was a bishop insisted on it. Maciel later complained that throughout his life, he was subjected to "waves of scandal" in which he was falsely accused of being "a liar, a drunkard and a thief." In 1956, his career seemed to end in disgrace when he was hospitalized in Rome for an opioid addiction. At about the same time, a seminarian in Mexico wrote to Rome to warn that he had seen Maciel inject himself with narcotics. Other allegations followed. The Vatican received reports about Maciel's obsessive affection for teenage seminarians, with the clear suggestion he was molesting them. After reviewing the evidence, an appalled Cardinal Valerio Valeri, prefect of the Congregation for Religious, ousted Maciel and placed the Legion under control of a different religious order. Maciel would not be stopped, however. In the two weeks between the death of Pius XII and the election of John XXIII, he convinced Cardinal Clemente Micara, a Curia bureaucrat who oversaw parish churches in Rome, to sign an order that returned him to full authority. The cardinal had reason to be grateful to Maciel, since in 1946 the Mexican priest had given him a secret cash gift of ten thousand dollars, an extraordinary amount of money

* In the Vatican, the word "religious" is used to refer to members of religious orders, so a "religious priest," as opposed to a regular parish priest, is a member of a priestly order like the Jesuits. Nuns are often described collectively as "women religious."

in postwar Italy, to rebuild churches damaged by Allied bombing.* Weeks after Maciel's reinstatement, Micara was present to bless the cornerstone of the Legion's handsome new church, the Basilica of Our Lady of Guadalupe, in the center of Rome. The cardinal died in 1965 without knowing the terrible mistake he had made. By returning Maciel to power, he enabled a serial child molester to continue his crimes for another fifty years.

* Maciel's gift would be equivalent to about $170,000 in 2024.

5

Planning the Great Debates

J OHN XXIII WAS DETERMINED to end the Vatican's reputation, so firmly established by Pius XII, as a ferocious anticommunist partisan in the Cold War. He had an early taste of what was possible when, at the 1960 Olympic Games in Rome, he met with a visiting army general from Communist Bulgaria. During their friendly chat, the pope reminisced about his years in the Balkans in the 1920s. Within weeks, a Catholic bishop and dozens of priests imprisoned in Bulgarian jails were allowed to go free.

In November 1961, when John turned eighty, he was astonished to receive birthday greetings from Soviet leader Nikita Khrushchev. It was the first formal diplomatic communication between the Vatican and Moscow since Russia's 1917 revolution. In the letter, Khrushchev hailed John as a man committed to "peace on earth." Sensing the opportunity, the pope replied with a handwritten note offering best wishes for "the entire Russian people." Months later, Khrushchev's daughter Rada arrived in Rome on holiday, and the pope agreed to an audience. During the meeting, she drew comparisons between the pope and her father. Both were reformers, she said, who came from peasant roots. She pointed to the pope's beefy, calloused hands: "You have hands that have been hardened by toil, like my father." The pope told her that, whatever his disagreements with Communist leaders in Russia, he had only good will toward its citizens.

Many in the Curia were furious that the pope agreed to the meeting, which they saw as a dangerous sign of appeasement, and barred reporters from witnessing the encounter. Even so, the pope wanted an official record—to signal his sincerity to Khrushchev—and had aides draft an article about the meeting for *L'Osservatore Romano*. To his shock, the Curia bishops who edited the newspaper refused to publish it. John chose not to protest, fearing a scandal if the editors' disobedience became public. Instead, he vented in his diary about the editors, describing the "unspeakable maneuvers" of "people I deplore and pity."

Among those horrified by the pope's contact with the Kremlin was Monsignor Joseph Fenton, the most prominent American churchman working under Ottaviani in the Holy Office. The ornery Massachusetts-born theologian, then fifty-six, wrote in his diary that John was the latest in a series of "weak and liberal popes, who have flooded the hierarchy with unworthy and stupid men" who coddled Marxists. "People believe what I have thought for several months—namely that John XXIII is definitely a lefty." He worried that, once the council began, the Vatican's "embrace" of communism would grow stronger. "If I did not believe in God," he added, "I would be convinced that the Catholic Church was about to end."

AT EASTER TIME in 1962, six months before the opening of the council, Joseph Ratzinger and his brother went to Rome on a short holiday. A springtime visit to the Eternal City might be the stuff of dreams for most travelers, but not for the Ratzingers. There was "no particular urge to go," Joseph remembered. He and Georg were excited to see St. Peter's Basilica, as well as the catacombs beneath the city where, beginning in the second century AD, persecuted Christians buried their dead after land became scarce above ground. Overall, though, they found much to dislike. Unlike a well-scrubbed German city, "life in Rome plays itself out on the street and everything is rather noisy," Joseph complained.

Still, the visit had real value to Ratzinger, since it allowed him to become familiar with the labyrinth that was the city map of Rome. At the council, he would not only serve as Cardinal Frings's theological adviser, he would also need to walk him to his appointments. The cardinal was, by then, almost completely blind and had to be assisted everywhere. After writing Frings's speeches that year, Ratzinger dictated them into a tape recorder so the cardinal could memorize them by listening to the tapes. They planned to use the same method at the council.

On the day he toured St. Peter's Square that spring, Ratzinger found himself stopping constantly to look up at the windows of the pope's apartment, where he imagined John XXIII and his deputies must be deep in solemn preparation for the council. In fact, the mood inside the Apostolic Palace in those weeks was one of happy frenzy, as the delighted pope put finishing touches on plans for what would be the largest gathering of senior Catholic churchmen in history. More than twenty-five hundred cardinals and bishops from around the world were expected to descend on the Vatican for meetings that would keep them in Rome, sporadically, for years.

John wanted to be involved in every detail. That included the seating charts in St. Peter's and the music played at the opening ceremony, scheduled for October 11. He decided to include the ninth-century hymn "Veni Creator Spiritus" (Come, Creator Spirit), because he knew it was commonly heard in Protestant services. He thought the planning was going well and waved away last-minute pleas from Curia bishops who urged a postponement—by several months, if not a year—since so much work remained. He teased them by threatening to move the council *up* a few weeks. He carefully planned his own role at the opening ceremony. He would write every word of the speech he would deliver to welcome the bishops to Rome and wanted it kept secret until the day of delivery. Although he would speak in Latin, he planned to release translations simultaneously in modern languages, so the public would know precisely what he said.

That summer, he understood the speech would be important for another reason: it would be one of his last public pronouncements as pope. In August, he learned he was dying.

It was his stomach, which had been bothering him for months, rumbling uncontrollably, sometimes causing him sharp pain in the middle of the night. "I notice in my body the beginning of some trouble that must be natural for an old man," he wrote in his diary. "I bear it with resignation, even if it is sometimes rather tiresome and makes me afraid it will get worse." On August 8, his doctors told him he had inoperable abdominal cancer and would live only several months. One of his sisters had died an agonizing death from the same disease a few years earlier. He asked his doctors to keep the illness a secret, fearing it might dampen excitement about the council, then only two months away. Perhaps, he wrote in his diary, he should be delighted by this news: "I await the arrival of Sister Death and will welcome her simply and joyfully."

SUENENS HAD BEEN a frequent visitor to the Vatican throughout the year, and Curia bishops admired his ability to do so much without a large staff. That would not be true for hundreds of other cardinals and bishops heading to the council. They each planned to bring a huge personal entourage to Rome, including secretaries, translators, cooks, chauffeurs, and valets. Many would also bring along their own theologians, to guide them through the complicated debates to come. The awkward truth for many bishops was that they had no special knowledge of theology or Bible scholarship beyond what they had learned in a seminary decades earlier. In the past, that ignorance was not necessarily an obstacle to a career in the church hierarchy. Under Pius XII, a bishop's duty was to slavishly follow the doctrinal teachings of the pope and the Holy Office. Under John, however, bishops were suddenly being encouraged to think for themselves. The pope wanted his own elite team of theologians at the council, so in 1960 he began to draw up lists of *periti*—Latin for "experts"—to help plan the bishops' meetings. The rosters shocked many in the Vatican, since they seemed an obvious slap at Ottaviani; they included the names of scholars who had been silenced or otherwise disciplined by the Holy Office. Most famous among them: Yves Congar of France and Karl Rahner of Germany.

As John must have known, Ottaviani *was* offended. The pope's move instantly ended Congar's decade-long banishment from the Vatican. Much worse for Ottaviani was the selection of Rahner, a Jesuit who had long been under investigation by the Holy Office. Over the years, Rahner, seen by many German Catholics as their country's greatest living theologian, had offended the Curia with essays that suggested atheists could enter heaven so long as they lived a life in accordance with the message of the Gospels. In the early 1960s, he was under orders to submit his writings to the Holy Office for "precensorship" before publication.

IN JULY 1960, as preparations for Vatican II began in earnest, Congar received an apparently hand-signed letter from John XXIII inviting him to serve as an official papal theologian at the council. Congar was dumbfounded—and suspicious. He thought at first the invitation was a forgery, a cruel joke by his enemies in the Holy Office. After a few discreet inquiries, however, he realized the letter was authentic. John, he was told, had long admired Congar's books about Christian unity—the writings the Holy Office had once branded as heresy. Copies of his books, filled with underlined passages and notations by John, would later be found in the pope's library.

Congar was honored by the invitation, although he feared he did not have the energy for this. His years of banishment had cost him both peace of mind and his physical health. In 1960, at the age of fifty-six, when he should have been in his prime, he felt decades older. "I feel fed up and crushed by everything," he wrote in his journals. "I feel betrayed by life." For many Catholic thinkers, Congar had long been the most poignant example of how small-minded Vatican bureaucrats could crush the spirit of a visionary scholar.

He traveled to Rome in November to join planning meetings for the council, which meant that he was suddenly face-to-face with his Holy Office tormentors. As expected, he wrote, he was appalled by "these idiots." He realized again that the Curia "understands nothing." He saw Ottaviani as "a man who personifies reactionary thought" and who had encouraged "the bottomless paternalism and stupidity" of Pius XII. Congar was even harsher in his appraisal of Cardinal Giuseppe Pizzardo, Ottaviani's predecessor at the Holy Office. In his diary, Congar described Pizzardo variously as a "cretin," an "imbecile," a "sub-human wretched freak," and a "sub-mediocrity with no culture, no horizon, no humanity." And then there was that "odious" American on Ottaviani's staff, Monsignor Fenton, who was "so hateful, so obstinately negative, so aggressive, so utterly insensitive."

Rome was itself an assault. It was so much less sophisticated—and so much dirtier—than Congar's beloved Paris. As he maneuvered down narrow, crowded streets between appointments near Vatican City, he found himself thinking of the people he walked past—average, working-class Romans—and how little the church had to do with their lives. To most Catholics, the Vatican functioned "neither as a true spiritual guide nor a source of comfort." He thought Jesus would be outraged to see the bureaucracy that claimed to act in his name. He noticed his fists clench whenever he passed the imposing sixteenth-century yellow-brick palace where Ottaviani had his offices. One night after dinner, walking with other theologians, he stopped near the palace and asked the others to wait; he then marched over and made a show of urinating on the wall. An American magazine correspondent who confirmed the story said that Congar "returned to the group with a satisfied smile on his face."

THE WORLD'S BISHOPS, representing 133 nations, began to arrive in Rome in large numbers in September 1962. At times, the city's international airport resembled a church procession, with long lines of robed men at the immigration counters. (They were all men, since no women had been invited to the council, even as observers.) Of the world's nearly twenty-eight hundred cardinals and bishops, all but about three hundred were in Rome in time for the opening ceremony. Most who failed to attend cited illness or old age. Seven Eastern European bishops were refused government exit permits. A Ukrainian archbishop had been imprisoned by the Communists there since 1946.

Some bishops came bearing bulky gifts for the pope, which made for delicate negotiations at the airport. Bishop Joseph Busimba of the Congo needed to explain to skeptical customs agents that his gift—three elephant tusks—would finish up on display at the Vatican and not in the hands of the ivory smugglers who lurked along Rome's seaport. Several Asian and African nations with tiny Catholic populations sent only a single bishop each. The largest delegation was from Italy, a total of 379 cardinals and bishops. The second-largest was from the United States—252 churchmen, led by five cardinals. The wealth of the US church was on display; several American bishops moved into plush suites in the Excelsior and other hotels along Rome's most fashionable boulevard, the Via Veneto, made famous two years earlier in the Fellini film *La dolce vita*.

The far less ostentatious German delegation also began to arrive in September, and most of its seventy-two cardinals and bishops settled into makeshift apartments in the church known as the Santa Maria dell'Anima (Our Lady of the Soul), which had been the German national church in Rome since the fifteenth century. Cardinal Frings moved in there, while Ratzinger was given a room in a small inn nearby.

Only one visiting churchman would join John XXIII in living in the papal compound in Vatican City during the council—Cardinal Montini, who was provided with an apartment there whenever he was in Rome. It was seen as more proof that Montini, a close friend of the pope's since the 1930s, was John's chosen successor.

6

The Medicine of Mercy

FROM THE DAYS of the apostles, gossip had been an occupational hazard among men of the church—and was considered a grave sin. St. Paul described gossips as "God-haters." According to scripture, Jesus was so alarmed that people were whispering behind his back that he quizzed his disciples: "Who do men say that I am?" Over the centuries, otherwise godly bishops and priests admitted they found it impossible to resist the temptation to pass along gossip in their isolated, often obsessive world. By definition, they focused their lives on their calling. Free time that would otherwise have been spent with a wife and children was often spent alone, pondering—and sometimes, cursing—the actions of other churchmen.

Once the world's bishops arrived in Rome for the council in the fall of 1962, several became early targets of gossip. Stories flew around the city that they were misbehaving in scandalous ways. A number were accused of drunkenness at restaurants near the Vatican, although the police hushed up the incidents at the Curia's request. Congar heard accounts of bishops sneaking out to visit brothels. In one case, he wrote in his diary, a South American bishop was discovered with prostitutes, but because he was "protected" in the Curia, there were no repercussions. Another, a Mexican, kept approaching policemen on street corners to "give them gifts and proposition them" for sex. Other, more common rumors centered on long-simmering jealousies among churchmen, suddenly forced to live together in a city that at times could resemble a small village.

Among German churchmen, rumors of a rivalry between Küng and

Ratzinger began swirling in the early days of the council. In many ways, it was only natural, even flattering, that people wanted to pit them against one another. They were two of the brightest young stars of Catholic theology anywhere in the world. At the start of the council, Küng was thirty-four, Ratzinger a year older. The gossip grew stronger in November, when John added new names to his roster of elite papal theologians. The most prominent was Küng, whose book had so impressed him. It was an extraordinary honor, especially since Küng was by far the youngest of the so-called *periti*. Ratzinger, whose name did not appear on the papal list, insisted later he had been pleased for his Swiss colleague; he said he was not jealous of Küng then or ever. Since Küng's book had already rocketed him to fame, the pope's recognition was only to be expected, Ratzinger thought.* Beyond that, Ratzinger had to admit at the time that he, unlike Küng, lacked a skill required of all world-class Catholic theologians—true fluency in Latin. When he arrived in Rome, he worried his imperfect grasp of the language meant he could not participate fully in the council's debates. Küng owed his fluency to his years at the Gregorian. Among German theologians, the school's alumni were considered an elite and known by a special term— *Germaniker*. Even late in life, Ratzinger admitted his regret that "I never spoke Latin like a *Germaniker*."

In the days before the opening ceremony, his enthusiasm about the council had evaporated, replaced by dread. Almost as soon as he and Frings arrived from Germany, they were presented with a stack of draft paperwork from the Curia—new documents to be debated at the council. There was now a total of seventy schemas, on every sort of issue, that Cardinal Ottaviani and other archconservatives apparently expected the world's bishops to approve without discussion. Ratzinger could see the new documents were no better—and often much worse—than what he had read back in Germany. Taken together, the final package of schemas to be presented to the council totaled more than two thousand pages. Only two schemas—one about limiting the use of Latin in the liturgy, another promoting dialogue with Orthodox Christians—pleased Ratzinger, since they suggested an openness to reform. The rest were full of condemnations—of Protestant and Orthodox churches, of atheists, of Marxists, of anyone who questioned

---

* While some of Ratzinger's biographers suggest he, too, was named one of the elite papal *periti* in 1962, the most authoritative roster of the nearly five hundred *periti* at Vatican II, prepared by American researcher Sharon Kabel, shows that he was not honored with the title for another year.

the power of the papacy. Hundreds of pages focused solely on sins of the flesh. "That man has a healthy sexual power does not give him the right to exercise it!" one draft raged. That document, entitled "Chastity, Marriage, the Family and Virginity," condemned the "cult of nudity" in the twentieth century and warned against adultery, pornography, homosexuality ("the shameful love for persons of the same sex"), and sex-change surgery. Given the bulk of the paperwork, Ratzinger knew many bishops would be overwhelmed. Just to read the drafts, which were written entirely in Latin, would be daunting. He was nagged by a "feeling that the whole enterprise might come to nothing—it would be a mere rubber-stamping of decisions already made."

On October 10, the day before the opening ceremony, he and Küng joined a final meeting of the German bishops. Many bishops were glum, convinced Ottaviani and his Curia allies intended to block any real debate, regardless of the pope's wishes. Even the weather was threatening. With so much else to worry about, the forecast was for pouring rain the next morning. The Germans feared their best formal robes and headwear would get doused in the planned street procession to St. Peter's.

The forecast was blessedly wrong. As dawn broke, crisp sunshine emerged from behind the clouds. At about seven thirty, a total of 2,540 cardinals and bishops began to assemble on the Via di Porta Angelica, near the Vatican museums. Half an hour later, they started walking slowly toward St. Peter's Square on streets that sparkled in the morning sun since they had been washed clean by the rain the night before. Ratzinger, witnessing his first grand Vatican ceremony, felt his pessimism lift, as an inner voice told him that "great things were about to happen." Once he got inside the basilica, the smell of sawdust was as strong as that of incense, since for weeks St. Peter's had been a construction site. It was now a magnificent meeting hall, with rising tiers of upholstered armchairs—red for cardinals, green for bishops—set along the six-hundred-foot-long nave. Italy's national television network placed thirty cameras inside and around St. Peter's, and the images were being broadcast live as far away as the United States via the new Telstar communications satellite. In the streets outside, hundreds of thousands of Romans lined up to witness the procession. The highlight, they knew, would come at the end of the march, with the arrival of John XXIII.

By tradition, the pope did not join the bishops in walking to St. Peter's. Instead, he was carried aboard a portable wooden throne, known in Italian as the *sedia gestatoria* (carrying chair). Its base was upholstered in red silk and attached to two long poles borne on the shoulders of eight men in crimson uniforms. Walking behind the throne were two other uniformed men; each held a fan made of ostrich feathers that on a warmer day would cool the pope.

As Küng watched from a sidewalk, he was appalled by the ostentation, beginning with the whole idea of a gilded portable throne. He put his cynicism aside, though, when he caught a glimpse of the approaching *sedia*—and the pope's face. John appeared indifferent to the pomp around him and was crying tears of joy. "If there is a good omen for Vatican II at all, it is that it is taking place under this pope," Küng remembered thinking to himself. Near the massive bronze doors to St. Peter's, the *sedia* was lowered, and the pope walked the rest of the way into the basilica, pausing every few seconds to accept the audience's applause.

The opening ceremony lasted seven hours. Ratzinger could see that many bishops, annoyed by the length, were squirming in their chairs by the end of it. He thought the event was much too formal, with the bishops remaining passive observers throughout. Also in the audience were about eighty non-Catholic observers, representing most of the world's Protestant and Orthodox churches. Observers from non-Christian faiths, including representatives of the World Jewish Congress and a handful of Muslim leaders, were in Rome, but most did not attend the ceremony, given its distinctly religious nature. The pope's campaign to foster goodwill with Khrushchev paid an important dividend, since two bishops from the Russian Orthodox Church were given last-minute exit visas to attend. The arrival of the heavily bearded Russian churchmen, in sweeping black robes and towering black-cloth headwear, created a sensation. One of the Protestant observers, Bishop John Moorman, representing the Church of England, had gone to St. Peter's assuming he and other non-Catholic Christians would be hidden away in a part of the basilica where "we wouldn't be able to observe anything at all." Instead, to their amazement, they were escorted to chairs directly in front of the papal throne. Moorman was told later that John had insisted they be given the best seats in the basilica. He said Cardinal Bea, who served as their host, stayed nearby throughout the ceremony. "Bea came to be the symbol of the new spirit of Rome," Moorman wrote. In Bea, "there is no trace of that triumphalism . . . that the Protestant mind had so hated." The cardinal provided the observers with Latin-speaking interpreters for simultaneous translation of the debates. They also had access to all important documents as they were issued to the Catholic bishops.

Moorman was put off by the opening ceremony's punishing length—"an endurance test." But he thought several moments were genuinely thrilling, especially when it came time for John XXIII to speak. In years to come, the pope's address that day would be hailed as revolutionary, as groundbreaking as any delivered by a bishop of Rome stretching back centuries. It was a speech that, at heart, demanded the church reject its past and end its self-imposed isolation from the modern world.

The pope began the address with a flowery, seemingly innocuous passage that Ottaviani and others in the Curia would welcome—about the need to honor the teachings of earlier popes and their advisers: "These are solemn and venerable voices." But he then took on a different, critical tone. His central message: sour, power-hungry Curia bureaucrats had become so wrapped up in demanding obedience to ancient teachings—and to punishing sin—that they ignored their larger responsibility to promote God's mercy. The pope was careful, many in the audience thought, to avoid making eye contact with Ottaviani, who would be seen as the target of the speech.

"In the daily exercise of our pastoral office, we sometimes have to listen, much to our regret, to voices of people who, though burning with zeal, are not endowed with too much sense of discretion or measure," the pope said, using the royal "we."* "They can see nothing but prevarication and ruin," he continued. "They behave as though they had learned nothing from history. We feel we must disagree with these prophets of doom, who are always forecasting disaster."

From that moment on, he declared, the church's days of heresy hunting and pessimism were over. It was time "to dispense the medicine of mercy instead of severity." The church must "show herself to be the loving mother of all—benign, patient, full of mercy and goodness toward the brethren who are separated from her." Those "brethren," it was clear, were the world's other Christian churches.

The pope might have expected most of the audience to be stirred by his words, but the speech was met largely with silence. There was an embar-

---

* While John XXIII tried to restrict the use of the royal "we," he bowed to that self-important tradition for formal addresses.

rassing reason for that. As the Vatican was reminded that day, Latin had fallen into such disuse that many of the world's bishops could barely speak it. Since they had not been given an advance text of the pope's speech, they did not understand what he was telling them. Those who did know Latin kept silent too. Ottaviani and his deputies were staring at the floor, motionless. They would not want to draw more attention to themselves as the focus of the pope's humiliating attack.

Unlike so many bishops, Küng understood every word of the speech and was thrilled. He wondered if he could believe his own ears: *Medicine of mercy? Prophets of doom?* He turned his head toward Ottaviani and thought that if he listened closely enough he might hear the gnashing of the cardinal's teeth. With his imperfect Latin, Ratzinger struggled to make out the pope's words, but he understood enough to be delighted.

The speech was followed by a burst of joyous choral music, which signaled the end of the ceremony, and the pope beamed as he walked back to the *sedia*, which returned him to the Apostolic Palace. He disappeared from St. Peter's in the days that followed, since he intended to honor his commitment not to meddle in the council. He planned to watch the debates on a closed-circuit television in his apartment. When the Italian translation of his speech was made public that afternoon, Romans could read for themselves what the pope had said, and the enthusiasm for his "medicine of mercy" became infectious. Hundreds of thousands of people poured into St. Peter's Square that night, hoping to coax the pope to address them. He appeared at his apartment window at about eight p.m., looking out on the largest crowd there since his election. It took several minutes for the cheering to quiet. "Dear children, dear children, I hear your voice," he said in his melodious Italian. "My voice is an isolated one, but it echoes the voice of the whole world." He thanked them for their support and urged them to look up at the dramatic full moon that night, which he saw as a sign of good fortune.

THE REAL WORK of the council began two days later, when the bishops gathered again. There was uneasiness, because they were still uncertain how they would organize the historic debates to come. Ignoring much of the structure that Cardinal Suenens had devised, Ottaviani and his allies wanted to impose *their* order. They announced there would be an immediate election of members of ten commissions that would divide up the council's work by subject, then prepare final documents for the bishops to approve. Ottaviani had come that day with a roster of candidates, including several Italian bishops from the Curia, and assumed the council would approve his list. Küng could hear bishops grumbling about this "Curial spoon-feeding." By controlling the committees' membership, Ottaviani and other conservatives would try to control the agenda. Ratzinger was dismayed, too. He thought the idea of an immediate vote was absurd, since most bishops were strangers to one another.

Cardinal Achille Liénart of the French city of Lille bravely stood up to insist the election be delayed, so the candidates could be properly introduced. Under the council's rules, bishops were forbidden from clapping or making any other sound of approval or disapproval for a speaker. As Liénart sat down, however, wild applause filled the basilica, which horrified Curia bishops. "Scandalo! Scandalo!" a few yelled out. Then, to Ratzinger's delight, his patron Cardinal Frings rose from his chair to join the protest, demanding the vote be postponed. There was more applause. The normally shy Frings was incensed over the Curia's effort to "torpedo" the council's independence, Ratzinger said later.

Caught off guard by this sudden challenge, Ottaviani and his loyalists backed down, agreeing to delay a vote for three days. And with that, the first business session of the council was over, barely twenty minutes after it began.

To most people, the events of that morning might have seemed a small procedural matter. To the world's bishops, however, this was historic, the first time they stood up to Vatican bureaucrats and acted on the independence that John had promised them. To Ratzinger, it was proof the council was not going to be a "mere sounding board" for the Curia's propaganda. Küng was ecstatic. He watched the bishops file out of St. Peter's, giddy over what had happened. Eager to celebrate, they gathered at two temporary coffee bars opened in side chapels. The bars were the pope's idea; he knew many bishops were heavy smokers and needed someplace to light up. ("If we don't let them smoke somewhere, they'll be hiding their cigarettes under their miters," he told Suenens.)

Reform-minded bishops had reason to hope other, much bigger victories would come quickly. The first substantive debate on the council's agenda centered on liturgy—specifically, on draft documents calling for an end to the exclusive use of Latin in worship. Küng was eager for the debate, especially since liturgy reform was a centerpiece of his best-selling book—a book that, as he had hoped, had shaped the thinking of many of the church-men arriving at Vatican II. Küng, already treated as a celebrity by much of the Vatican press corps, was flattered to see cardinals and bishops carrying dog-eared copies of *The Council* into St. Peter's.

A central proposal before the council would restrict use of the Triden-tine Mass, the tightly structured all-Latin Mass imposed on the church in the sixteenth century. Küng knew most German bishops felt as he did about the Mass, named for the Council of Trent, where it was created. The bish-ops saw the Mass as a vestige of that dark time when Rome overreacted—disastrously—to their countryman Martin Luther. Luther outraged the Vatican not only by daring to translate the Bible into German, but also by offering worship services in his native tongue. After Trent, the church responded by making the Latin Mass even more structured and, for most laymen, even more incomprehensible. Its unbendable rules required both priest and altar to face away from the congregation—and therefore, the Vatican insisted, toward God. As he argued in his book, Küng believed the Mass alienated the faithful in the pews by creating distance, literally and figuratively, between them and their priest. He hoped the council, beyond ending the exclusive use of Latin, would approve other changes to the Mass, including altering Communion, the high point of the ceremony. Since the twelfth century, only priests were routinely offered full Communion—both wine and bread. Most laymen received only the bread. That reflected a view in the Dark Ages that it was unsanitary for parishioners to sip from the same cup. Five centuries later, Küng and many bishops thought the situation was absurd—and a betrayal of the meaning of the Last Supper. By denying full Communion to the faithful, Küng thought, the Vatican ignored the plain words of Jesus, who instructed his followers to participate fully in the sacrament and "do this in memory of me." Most Protestant churches offered full Communion—bread and wine—to all parishioners.

The debate had laughable moments. It turned out that many of the car-dinals and bishops who most fiercely defended the use of Latin could barely speak it. They addressed the council in such "labored pidgin Latin" that much of the audience in St. Peter's was left snickering, Ratzinger remem-bered. Bishops on the other side of the debate were among those who spoke Latin most fluently. Ratzinger was impressed by Frings's elegant, classic use of the language. For many bishops, liturgy reforms were part of a larger mission—to stop the church from placing roadblocks of language and ceremony ahead of saving souls. Asian and African bishops were passionate on the subject; they said it was nonsensical to insist on the Latin Mass, especially in remote, impoverished parishes where most priests, like everyone in the pews, did not understand a word of it. "These beautiful rites are completely lost on our people," said Archbishop Eugene D'Souza of India.

Ratzinger thought the argument was made most memorably—and defiantly—by the Syrian-born patriarch of the Melkite Catholic Church, eighty-four-year-old Maximos IV Sayegh, who refused to address the council in Latin; he would speak only in French. The Melkite Church was one of a small number of Orthodox Christian communities that had remained loyal to Rome over the centuries in exchange for autonomy. The Melkites, whose followers were found throughout the Middle East, worshipped in Arabic and allowed priests to marry. To Ratzinger, Patriarch Maximos, in his elaborate black headdress, stroking his snowy-white beard, was a living reminder that Christianity was a faith born in the Middle East, not in Rome. "Latin is dead!" Maximos roared to the council in his heavily accented French. "We in the East never imagined that the faithful could be forced to pray in a language they do not understand."

The council's early debates proved most bishops were eager for change in the liturgy, beginning with an end to the Tridentine Mass, but traditionalists refused to give up. In impassioned, sometimes tearful speeches, conservatives sought to preserve every element of the old liturgy. They said they worried worship services would be badly translated from Latin and therefore misstate the word of God. The most powerful Catholic churchman in Britain, Cardinal William Godfrey, the archbishop of Westminster, warned of scandal if women, allowed to sip from the chalice of wine at Communion, "left behind traces of lipstick."

After three weeks of debate, the council moved to a vote. Among the last to speak was Ottaviani, who demanded the council preserve the Tridentine Mass. His jowls quavering in fury, he admitted he was incensed. "Are the bishops planning a revolution?" he asked. The church would be "scandalized" by so much change. He pressed on for several more minutes, confident he did not need to comply with a rule that limited speeches to ten minutes. After fifteen minutes, Cardinal Bernardus Alfrink of Holland, overseeing the debate that day, gently reminded him: "Excuse me, Eminence, but you have already spoken five minutes beyond the limit." Ottaviani just kept talking.

Alfrink, who said later he felt he had no other choice, ordered the microphone switched off. Ottaviani's amplified voice disappeared, replaced seconds later by applause, as hundreds of bishops clapped in support of Alfrink for silencing the man seen as the Vatican's ultimate reactionary. Ottaviani stormed back to his seat. "I'm finished now," he blurted out in a voice loud enough to be heard without amplification. As he sat down, he closed his eyes, his left foot trembling.

His fears were justified. When the bishops' punch-card ballots were counted, there were 2,162 votes to approve a preliminary document to restructure the liturgy, including an end to the exclusive use of Latin, with only 46 opposed. "The forces of renewal were stronger than anyone would have dared hope," Ratzinger marveled after the tally was announced. The debate was not over; the council still needed to approve a final document on liturgical reforms, and it would not be completed for another year. Still, Ottaviani was despondent over the vote. "I pray to God that I can die before the end of this council," he told an aide. "In that way, at least I can die a Catholic."

KÜNG AND RATZINGER SAID they got along well at Vatican II, whatever the rumors of a rivalry. Their roles at the council were different. Ratzinger, who needed to remain close to Frings at all times, helped draft several of the council's key documents on the cardinal's behalf. Küng saw his role mostly as that of commentator and behind-the-scenes strategist. He was always a favorite of reporters, who were grateful for his pithy, sometimes indiscreet on-the-record analysis of council debates. Although Küng and Ratzinger usually worked in different parts of Rome, they managed to meet regularly. They sometimes talked over a cup of coffee near St. Peter's Square or, when the weather was nice, which was most of the time in Rome, in one of the open-air cafés along the Tiber River.

They found they had a similar judgment on churchmen they met, and it was often unflattering. Many bishops, they knew, were desperate for radical reform of the church, although they could never find the nerve to speak up and demand it. That was especially true of bishops from outside Europe. They might be honored celebrities at home, as famous as any politician or entertainer, but they had no special status in the Vatican. Others stayed silent because they did not understand Latin, so they could not participate in the debates. Küng and Ratzinger were both struck by the inability of most American bishops to speak anything except English. Cardinal Cushing of Boston admitted he could not carry on even a simple conversation in Latin. At the council, "I can't understand a word these guys say," he conceded. "I just have to look intelligent and get someone afterwards to tell me what it's all about." Cushing, among the church's best fundraisers, offered to pay for the last-minute installation of a simultaneous translation service, like the one arranged for non-Catholic observers. But he was rebuffed by the Curia, only too happy, it was cynically suggested, to keep him and others ignorant of what was being said.

The situation allowed a handful of non-Italian bishops with language skills and theological training to make names for themselves. Western European churchmen dominated the council. Everyone recognized that Suenens spoke for the pope, as did Bea. The German delegation was so influential that non-German bishops came up with an expression to describe it: "The Rhine flows into the Tiber."

In the opening weeks of the council, Yves Congar was heartened to meet so many open-minded bishops and theologians from around the world. Many reacted with wide-eyed awe to be in his presence—an astonishing turnaround in the status of a churchman who just a few years earlier was shunned as a heretic. "I am overcome by this crazy respect that there is for me everywhere," he wrote. He was especially impressed by Suenens ("a positive man, well organized, realistic and precise"). He had long admired many German bishops and was impressed from the start by a pair of talented young theologians they brought to Rome: Küng, who was "full of intelligence, health, youth and insistent demands" and acted "like a revolutionary," and Ratzinger, who had none of Küng's star power but was "reasonable, modest, disinterested and helpful."

Congar had several encounters with the bishops' delegation from Poland, the largest from Eastern Europe. He had always admired the bravery of the Polish people, who spent so much of their history under siege or occupation. Patriotism and Catholicism were intertwined for Poles, and their faith had only grown during the Nazi occupation, then during the brutal domination by the Soviets. Still, to Congar, the country seemed stubbornly backward: "The Poles are always a people apart, with whom it is difficult to get on." Early in the council, he accepted an invitation to lecture to Polish bishops and take their questions. He came away struck that they "remained rather remote from current ideas." A few days later, he returned to his boardinghouse "in a state of complete exhaustion" and found a Polish bishop at his door. The visitor, forty-three-year-old Karol Wojtyła of

Krakow, Poland's second-largest city, was physically imposing. A former actor, Wojtyła (pronounced voy-TEE-vuh) was tall and muscular, with handsome Slavic features and a piercing stare. He carried a sheaf of papers, some of his recent theological writings, and pushed them into Congar's hands. Would he read them? Congar agreed, which became awkward when he returned the material: "Wojtyła gave me some texts which he had prepared and which are fairly confused, full of imprecisions." Later, Congar's appraisal of Wojtyła, the future Pope John Paul II, would be very different.

FEW CHURCHMEN AT the council, from any continent, were more admired than Archbishop Hélder Câmara—"the lovable Brazilian," in Küng's words. Câmara's diocese on Brazil's northeast Atlantic coast boasted dense tropical beauty—palm-fringed beaches, turquoise waters, and thick jungle—but it was also a place of crushing poverty. Câmara was a tiny man—five foot three inches tall—with sad eyes and an infectious smile. Then in his early fifties, he was more influential than other Brazilian bishops at Vatican II in part because of his ease in foreign languages. Beyond his native Portuguese, he spoke French fluently and was comfortable in Latin, Italian, and English. In any gathering, it was easy to make him out because he was invariably the shortest person there—and because his body was always in motion. "I speak 'Câmara,'" as he put it, "which means that I speak with my arms, my hands, my body and with all my heart." In his first visits to Rome in the 1950s, he befriended fast-rising members of the Curia, including then-Monsignor Montini, the future Paul VI. Montini described Câmara as a man with a "pastor's soul—there are few in the church whose voice deserves a hearing as much as his."

At the council, Câmara never once addressed the bishops in St. Peter's—it could be hard for bishops to get speaking time, since cardinals took precedence—but no one was more active behind the scenes. He was a natural, back-slapping politician. In Brazil, he was known as a champion of the poor, especially those living in the lawless shanty towns known as favelas that overwhelmed the country's big cities. He was often described as the "bishop of the slums," a title he wore proudly, even if it led to allegations that he flirted with Marxism. "When I give food to the poor, they call me a saint," Câmara joked. "When I ask why the poor have no food, they call me a Communist." He was never made a cardinal, in part because he offended so many other Brazilian bishops with his complaint that they ignored Jesus's command to serve the poor.

In the 1960s, few South American governments kept reliable poverty statistics, but, as Câmara put it, "any man with eyes in his head" could see that tens of millions of people across the continent were not properly fed, housed, or educated. He had trouble finding the right adjectives to describe the misery. In his writings, he called it "shameful," "revolting," "degrading," and "obscene." Many of his parishioners were penniless Black sharecroppers, the descendants of five million African slaves brought to Brazil before 1888, when the country became the last in the Western Hemisphere to outlaw slavery. In discussing poverty with outsiders, he stayed away from dry conversations about land distribution and calorie counts. Instead, he offered anecdotes about how his parishioners struggled to survive. He described the shacks in which the sharecroppers lived, built from scrap metal held together with twine. Since there was no running water, open-air pits functioned as toilets. When someone died, there was no money for a coffin, so corpses were wrapped in a blanket and laid directly in shallow graves, contaminating the groundwater. Since a baby's crib was an unimaginable luxury, it was normal for parents to "make a cradle out of an old packing case or an old gasoline can and lay the baby down among the pigs." But that came with a terrible risk, Câmara explained. "It sometimes happens that, when mothers have to go out to work, they come home and they find the pigs have eaten the baby." He would wait for the look of horror to cross the face of the person in front of him.

"Pigs eating the babies?" he would add with a shrug, suggesting just how common it was. "Isn't it terrible?"

He believed the Vatican bore ultimate responsibility for this misery, since South America was "*the* Catholic continent." European settlers claimed virtually all of it in the name of the church and, over hundreds of years, "every part of society has grown and developed under the influence of the faith." So why, he asked, did the church continue to allow millions of its faithful to live in squalor? He was appalled at how many Brazilian churchmen lived like royalty in church-owned estates dating from the days of Portuguese colonialism. Câmara was no hypocrite in his own life. He refused to move into the bishop's grand palace in Recife or don the traditional hand-embroidered black robes of a bishop, preferring a simple brown cassock. Around his neck he wore a cross made of wood.

Câmara traveled to Rome in 1962 with a revolutionary proposal to present to the council. It was so bold that, at first, he shared details with only a few trusted friends. He told them he believed that, with time, he could convince the world's bishops to embrace—completely—Jesus's commitment to the poor. Under his plan, the bishops would vote to compel the Vatican to divest itself of all material wealth. That would mean selling off every cathedral, church, chapel, office building, and plot of land, every university campus and seminary, every masterwork of art and piece of precious jewelry. The proceeds—the equivalent of billions of dollars, he assumed—would be used to benefit the poor, Christians and non-Christians alike. "If we have to auction off St. Peter's, so be it," he said. "Do you doubt the Savior would demand that of us?"

7

Death Be Not Proud

THE POPE'S CANCER was spreading, the pain constant. Until the end, though, John tried not to limit his schedule. He continued granting audiences to the famed artist Giacomo Manzù, a fellow native of the province of Bergamo, who had been commissioned to do an official sculpture of the pope. Manzù, whose friendship with John scandalized many in the Curia because he was an outspoken Marxist and atheist, worked quickly over several sittings. He wanted to capture the pope's image before the cancer affected his appearance. When they met for the last time in the spring of 1963, John was so thin that his face had become a "crumbled castle," Manzù remembered. Loose flesh bunched around his eyes and jaws, leaving him unrecognizable except for "that big nose of his and those immense ears." At about the same time, the Italian filmmaker Pier Paolo Pasolini, a defiant gay leftist who loathed the Vatican as a young man, set to work on a film about the life of Jesus, *The Gospel According to St. Matthew*. When it debuted shortly after the pope's death, the film opened with a dedication to Pasolini's hero: "To the dear, merry, familiar memory of John XXIII."

As the pope entered the final months of his life, he completed his last will and testament. Church historians often noted the contrast between his last wishes and those of his predecessor. While Pius's will was that bleak plea for forgiveness, John wrote he was grateful to the many friends who "made my life serene." He welcomed death, he wrote. "At the moment for saying farewell—or better still, *arrivederci*—I once more remind everyone of what counts most in life: Blessed Jesus Christ."

There was another consequential document he hurried to finish: an encyclical that would be his deathbed appeal to save the human race from Armageddon. Entitled *Pacem in Terris* (Peace on Earth), it was the first by any pope to be addressed to all humanity and was, by Vatican standards, written in clear, unambiguous language. It was completed just weeks after the October 1962 Cuban Missile Crisis, when the United States and the Soviet Union came close to nuclear war. The pope had played a role in resolving the showdown. Shortly after President Kennedy revealed that Soviet missile launchers had been detected in Cuba, the pope issued a public plea for the Americans and the Russians to listen to "the cry of humanity" and avoid war; he offered to serve as a go-between. A grateful Khrushchev had the statement published on the front page of the state-run newspaper *Pravda*. He said later that "the pope's message was the only gleam of hope" at the darkest moment of the crisis.

The encyclical called for a total ban on nuclear weapons and for urgent international negotiations to reduce stockpiles of all other arms, with a goal of "abolishing them entirely." The old theory of "just war," once promoted by the Vatican to justify the right of Christians to use violence, was no longer viable, given the "appalling slaughter and destruction that nuclear war would bring in its wake." The encyclical endorsed women's rights and saluted women who chose to shed a "purely passive role" in society to enter politics. The document included an assertion that would have been rejected as heresy by almost all of John's predecessors—that everyone, including non-Christians, was entitled to religious freedom. World leaders rushed to praise the encyclical. "As a Catholic, I am proud of it," Kennedy said. "And as an American, I have learned from it."

The pope's imminent death threatened to bring an end to Vatican II. From the first days of the council, it was obvious to most bishops that they would not complete their work in one session; but if John died, would his successor allow the meetings to resume? Some progressives, pleased by early victories, wondered if it might be best to declare the meetings over and go home before Ottaviani and other conservatives won battles of their own.

In fact, reform-minded bishops had reason to fear what was still on the agenda that year—a debate about the seemingly abstract concept of revelation. Putting aside the jargon that theologians applied to it, the central question was not so hard to understand: Were there two sources of God's message or just one? All Christians agreed truth was revealed in the

Bible, but did God also reveal himself through teachings of the Vatican—specifically, of the popes? And if there were two sources, were traditions established by papal teachings equal in value to scripture? In the twentieth century, theologians regularly used a shorthand term for the debate: "scripture versus tradition." Not surprisingly, popes throughout history had been champions of the two-source theory, but Protestants and Orthodox Christians rejected the idea outright. It was, in fact, an essential part of why they broke from Rome. Luther launched the Reformation by declaring the Old and New Testaments the only source of God's message. It became his rallying cry: "The Bible alone!"

Few men would influence Christianity—and the Western world, for that matter—more than Luther. Certainly, the Vatican took him seriously from the moment news of his "heresy" reached Rome in 1520. He and his followers were excommunicated, and the Curia set to work to undermine the threat these "Lutherans" posed. The result, the Council of Trent, was a turning point because it cemented divisions between Catholics and Protestants. The council declared the pope's words, like those in the Bible, were God's truth. It was scripture *and* tradition—separate and equal.

Now, at another council four centuries later, Ottaviani was ready to present the world's bishops with a document that reaffirmed Trent and proclaimed papal teachings, like the Gospels, as "free from all error." Protestant and Orthodox observers at the council were furious. To them, Ottaviani's document, by demanding non-Catholics bow down to the bishop of Rome, would crush their budding hopes for Christian unity. Bishop Moorman, the Church of England observer, was appalled: "Are we to believe that the Roman Church has access to a separate supply of divine truth which is not accessible to other Christians?" That anger was shared by many Catholic bishops. The document, especially its claim that every word in the Bible was true, was an affront to many of the Vatican's most prominent Bible scholars. Researchers at the Pontifical Biblical Institute, led by Cardinal Bea for almost two decades, had argued for much of the twentieth century that the church had always been wrong to claim the Gospels were error-free. They thought they were stating the obvious: The four Gospels, written in the first decades after the Crucifixion, contain glaring mistakes and contradictions about Jesus's life and teachings.* They do not agree on the

---

* Although the four Gospels are attributed to the evangelists Matthew, Mark, Luke, and John, church historians are convinced the books were almost certainly written by others whose names were lost to history.

most basic details about his birth and death, in fact. (Matthew and Luke state that Jesus was born in Bethlehem, while John suggests he was born elsewhere. As for the Crucifixion, the four books contradict one another even about Jesus's emotional state on the cross. In John, the Savior is perfectly composed as he is executed. In Mark, he is terrified.)

Ottaviani finally returned to St. Peter's on November 14—it had been two weeks since he stormed out after his microphone was cut off—to introduce his document on revelation. He described it as "safe doctrine" and said it should be adopted quickly since, he claimed, it had been personally approved by John XXIII. The decision to present the document to the council "belongs solely to the Holy Father." It was a statement that many bishops were convinced was untrue.

Once again, Cardinal Liénart of France stood to protest. He said Ottaviani's document was "cold and formulaic" and would needlessly offend other Christians at a moment when unity seemed within reach. Ratzinger looked on proudly as Frings again joined the protest. The paper's dense, technical language was out of place, Frings declared. "Truth is like music. This schema belongs to the wrong class of music. It's too rigid." Then Bea, seen by everyone as speaking for John XXIII, gave an address in which he effectively accused Ottaviani of lying when he claimed the pope's endorsement.

The debate threatened to go on for weeks, with most bishops lining up to criticize the document and, by extension, the Holy Office. In the face of the attacks, Ottaviani and his deputies came up with a plan that would later be described as a shameful dirty trick.

It was never entirely clear who controlled the council's agenda. "No one knows exactly who determines the schedule," complained Father Gregory Baum, a Canadian theologian on Bea's staff. "Everyone speaks about 'they'—'they' have announced, or 'they' have decided and nobody knows who 'they' are." Those decisions were supposed to be in the hands of a Curia bureaucrat, Archbishop Pericle Felici of Italy, who had the title of general secretary of the council, but few thought he acted independently of the Holy Office.

On November 20, he announced there would be an instant vote on Ottaviani's document. At first, Küng, Ratzinger, and several German bishops were pleased by the idea the council might quickly reject the document and move on to other issues. They realized minutes later, however, that the vote had been rigged. Ottaviani's plan was to word the ballot in such a baffling way—in Latin—that bishops would cast the wrong vote. Instead of asking them to vote "yes" to approve or "no" to reject, the question was presented in reverse: "yes" to reject the document or "no" to keep it alive and continue the debate.

Most bishops saw through the ploy and voted correctly, but the confusion was obvious on the face of others who voted "no" by mistake. The tally was more than a hundred votes short of the two-thirds needed to end debate and kill Ottaviani's document. To the cardinal's delight, the vote meant his draft remained open to discussion indefinitely; he now had more time to twist arms and lobby for its passage. Ratzinger could see many bishops were furious over how they had been tricked. The feeling inside the basilica was one of "deep dismay and anger," he later wrote.

As it turned out, Ottaviani and his loyalists overplayed their hand, because they had alarmed the pope, too. Until then, John had, as promised, stayed out of the council's debates, but his neutrality came to an end hours after the vote. With a sheepish look, Felici stood before the bishops the next morning to announce that Ottaviani's document was being withdrawn. The pope had decided overnight it would be rewritten by a committee led by Ottaviani and Bea.

Most bishops appeared relieved and grateful to the pope. "The fury dissolved," Ratzinger remembered. He looked back on those two days as "the real turning point" of Vatican II, when the pope sided with the world's bishops over the Curia.

The council was scheduled to end that year in early December, with the bishops expected to reconvene sometime in 1963, assuming John survived. The Vatican continued to hide the truth about his health, insisting he suffered only from a minor stomach ailment. *L'Osservatore Romano* took the dishonesty to new heights when it reported that the pope was "on his way to a complete recovery." John joined in what he apparently saw as a white lie, appearing at the window of his apartment on December 5 to bless the crowd. He appeared in good spirits, although pale and drawn, and claimed he was getting better, even though he knew it was untrue: "Slowly, slowly, we move from illness to convalescence." Two days later he delighted the bishops by appearing in St. Peter's for the last business session of the council. In a brief speech, he thanked them for their work: "You have heard the voice of the whole Catholic world." He failed to attend the next day's closing ceremony, announcing he would instead give a final blessing from his apartment window that afternoon. Küng, who believed the rumors that the pope was dying, made sure to be in St. Peter's Square to witness this. He looked up to the window, heartbroken to realize that "I am seeing the face of this pope, who has been the source of such hope and encouragement, for a last time."

Küng had a final appointment in Rome that year. It was a sign of his ever-growing fame that the American bishops' conference asked him to give a speech summing up what had just happened at the council. "A new freedom has broken through," he told them. "The church no longer gives the impression of being absolutist or totalitarian." At the age of thirty-five, he was easily the most talked about theologian in the world. That fall, he managed to dash off another book—*The Council in Action*—to be released simultaneously around the globe the following spring.

His publishers arranged an eight-week tour of the United States, to begin in March. He was excited, if only because he had never been across the Atlantic. He was curious to see if stereotypes about American Catholics were true. Among European theologians, the US, then home to about forty-five million Catholics, had always been treated as an afterthought. There was outright contempt for the country inside the Curia, Küng knew. Many Vatican bishops saw the US as a vulgar and backward place, where money was all that mattered and where popular culture, centered on Hollywood and the publishing industry in New York, was sinful. Küng's first lecture was in Boston, where an airport news conference drew a crush of more than thirty reporters and photographers. Wherever he went in the US, he was welcomed by crowds of devout, well-educated Catholics thirsty for talk of reform. He gave standing-room-only speeches "in my clumsy English" in New York, Chicago, and dozens of other cities. In California, sixty-five hundred people jammed into an auditorium at the Jesuit-run University of San Francisco to hear him. He was not welcome everywhere, however. The bishop of Trenton, New Jersey, issued a statement describing his writings as "nonsense." The Catholic University of America, the conservative, Vatican-accredited school in Washington, DC, barred him from speaking on campus—no surprise, since its theology dean was Monsignor Fenton, Ottaviani's American deputy. Küng lectured instead across town at Jesuit-run Georgetown University. The Washington newspaper columnist Mary McGrory, a devout Catholic, was in the audience and wrote: "Never before has a theologian received such a welcome. Three-thousand people went out to hear him and sat in rapt silence." In Minnesota, he was the guest of Senator Eugene McCarthy, also a proud Catholic. The senator chuckled years later in recalling how Küng asked to test-drive the lawmaker's new

Chevrolet sedan. A few minutes after climbing into the driver's seat, Küng gunned the car to a hundred miles an hour on an empty stretch of Minnesota highway. "I drive as I do theology," Küng told him. "Fast but safe."

The trip's most memorable moment came in April, when Küng was invited to meet President Kennedy. Ushered into the Oval Office, Küng found himself standing before "the most powerful man in the world—in a beige suit, slim, smart and tanned." He felt a special bond to the Catholic president, whose "New Frontier" mirrored what Küng wanted to achieve in the church. Kennedy introduced Küng to others in the office as "the New Frontiersman of the Catholic Church."

A week later, Küng flew back to Germany, where an alarming message awaited him at home in Tübingen. He was summoned urgently to the nearby city of Rottenburg by Bishop Leiprecht, his original patron at the council. They met in the bishop's office the next morning. As they sat down, Leiprecht nervously reported that he had received three separate letters from the Curia, one from the Holy Office, to protest Küng's lectures in the US. The bishop, frightened to be dragged into a controversy over Küng, would not show him the letters or describe them in any detail, so Küng could not be sure what had so offended Rome. Still, he now knew, formally, what he had long assumed. From that moment on, he could be certain the Vatican was monitoring his every word—and would try, someday, to silence him.

BY MAY 1963, John XXIII never left his bed. He was so weak his head rarely rose from the pillow. The thought of death was never far away, he said. "My time on earth is coming to a close," he told friends who gathered at his bedside. "In this last hour, I feel calm and sure that my Lord, in his mercy, will not reject me." He issued a last written order to his deputies banning photos of his deathbed. There was to be an absolute minimum number of people allowed into the crypt at the time of burial. He did not want the nightmare of Pius's death and funeral repeated, with images of his corpse leaked to tabloid newspapers.

On May 31, his doctors told him there was nothing more they could do. At the news, Monsignor Loris Capovilla, his devoted secretary, began to sob. John asked him: "Help me to die as a bishop should." The next day, members of his household staff, including the Bergamo nuns who had been his housekeepers, were brought in as he received the last rites—extreme unction, or final anointing, in which sacramental oil was applied to several points on his body.* He received Communion a final time, a rite known as viaticum, from a Latin word that refers to food for the journey that is starting.

His dying took two more days. In his final, agonizing hours, he told weeping family members he welcomed death, since it meant he would soon be in the eternal embrace of Jesus. Despite the pain, he tried—characteristically—to joke with his doctors: "Don't worry too much about me. My bags are packed and I'm ready to go."

He floated in and out of consciousness. At times, he seemed to think he was back in Paris and babbled happily in French. At other moments, he was in Bergamo, a child again, thinking his mother was close by. Once, when he was fully alert, he looked around and smiled weakly. "I'm still here," he said. At three a.m. on June 3, he woke up suddenly and exclaimed, "Lord, you know that I love you." They were his last distinct words. At seven forty-five that morning, his body shuddered and his breathing stopped. Moments later, Cardinal Benedetto Aloisi-Masella entered the bedchamber. A Curia veteran, Aloisi-Masella held the title of camerlengo, or chamberlain, which meant that he would run the Vatican until the election of John's successor. (It was a job that Pius XII left vacant, adding to the turmoil around his funeral.) He was now required to perform a series of rituals dating back to the twelfth century that are required before proclamation of a pope's death. He began by leaning over the corpse, looking for signs of life. Convinced he saw no evidence of a heartbeat, he tried to rouse the pope by addressing him, as the ritual dictated, by his birth name: "Angelo, Angelo, wake up." There was no response.

"The pope is truly dead," the cardinal declared as he removed the gold fisherman's ring from the pope's finger. It would later be shattered into pieces with a hammer and buried with John's body.

IN 1963, with the birth of satellite television only the year before and new methods of stretching telephone and telegraph cables beneath the sea, news could finally travel from one point on the globe to any other in seconds. So the bulletin announcing the pope's death reached most of the world's 800

---

* During the rite, oil is usually applied to the eyes, ears, nose, lips, hands, and feet, representing the senses of sight, hearing, smell, taste, and touch.

million Catholics at almost exactly the same moment, producing a torrent of grief unlike any the church had ever known.

For the first time in its history, the Church of England lowered flags outside all its places of worship in honor of a pope. Jewish and Muslim leaders joined in the tributes. In Israel, the Religious Affairs Ministry hailed John as "one of the truly righteous men of the world, whose loving spirit extended to the Jewish people."

Years later, many American Catholics could recall exactly where they were when they heard news of the pope's death—what room they were in or, if they were outside, what the weather was like that day. It was the sort of shock many would experience again five months later at the news that President Kennedy had been assassinated. Among Catholics in Latin America, the mourning was mixed with gratitude. The Vatican reported that in his final hours, the pope spoke of his "special hope and love" for the church in the nations of Latin America, which would soon be home to most of the world's Catholics. During his papacy, John, in meetings with the region's bishops, often talked excitedly of how he would visit them in their homelands one day. He told them how, during his diplomatic career, he had dreamed of being posted as papal nuncio to Argentina. He had seen photos of the capital city of Buenos Aires and was struck by its beauty. He loved the idea that because Argentina was home to millions of Italian immigrants, he would never be without good pasta or the sound of opera, even seven thousand miles from Rome.

His smiling face was as familiar to Argentines as it was to Europeans. And when news of his death reached Buenos Aires, residents were convulsed by the sort of mourning not seen there since the death a decade earlier of Eva Perón, the country's iconic former first lady. Store windows along the capital's wide, Parisian-style boulevards were covered in black bunting in honor of the pope. In some shops, it remained up through the Christmas holidays six months later. Within hours of his death, crowds of wailing mourners gathered outside the capital's grand Metropolitan Cathedral. Many women, their heads draped in black scarves, clutched rosary beads in one hand; in the other they held a framed photograph of *el buen papa* that had been taken down that morning from its place of honor on a wall of the family home.

Among the mourners elsewhere in the city that day was a twenty-six-year-old Catholic seminarian, Jorge Mario Bergoglio, then in training for the Jesuits. A native of Buenos Aires, he was in his second year of philosophy studies at a Jesuit college on the outskirts of the capital, and he made several trips to the school chapel that day to pray for the pope's soul. Bergoglio wanted to honor John not just as the bishop of Rome but also as a *paesano*, the word used by his Italian-born grandmother to refer to a kindly neighbor. Like so many of his reform-minded Jesuit teachers, he saw John as his role model, especially given the late pope's repeated pledge of his absolute commitment to the poor. As he neared death, the pope wrote in his diary, he had no possessions apart from family photos, a few sticks of furniture, and a small library of books: "I was born poor and I will die poor." It was the model Bergoglio intended to follow in his own career in the church.

In Germany, Küng and Ratzinger were shaken by the pope's death, even if they expected it. Küng remembered he fell to his knees in his university office in tears when the news crackled over the radio. Catholics had lost a bishop of Rome who "radiated Christian love and changed the church more than any other pope in five hundred years," he wrote. Ratzinger later insisted to friends that, unlike Küng, he did not shed tears over the pope's death ("We Ratzingers are not emotional" like that) but that he, too, was shattered. John, he thought, would be remembered as a pope "great both in humanity and humbleness." He remembered wondering with dread what would become of John's greatest achievement: Vatican II. "Would the council even continue?"

After Küng collected himself, it occurred to him there was an obvious way to honor John XXIII in death. He decided that if the council resumed, he would organize a campaign by the world's bishops to declare John a saint immediately—by acclamation. He knew the move, bypassing the Vatican's byzantine process of canonization, would delight most churchmen. Normally, church law required a candidate for sainthood be linked to two physical miracles, but Küng thought John had already done something miraculous—offering Catholics "a papacy with a human, Christian face." Others had the same idea. Cardinal Cushing of Boston believed that apart from the Savior himself, John XXIII had been "the greatest builder of spiritual bridges in the history of Christianity." Weeks after the pope's death, he published a book to make the case for John's instant canonization.

The adulation was far from universal, however. In fact, John's legacy was under siege within hours of his death. In Rome, the "prophets of doom" were determined to have their revenge. Even as funeral services were being organized at the Vatican, a few conservative bishops made shocking public denunciations of the late pope. Cardinal Giuseppe Siri of Genoa, the pope's most public critic in the Italian hierarchy, sneered that it would take "fifty years for the church to recover from the disasters of this man's pontificate." Siri and like-minded conservatives set out to end what they called *il culto* (the cult) of John XXIII, which meant undermining any attempt to honor his memory. First, they would derail the effort to have John declared a saint by acclamation. Then, they would move to undermine his larger legacy at Vatican II.

PART III

PAUL VI
(1963–1978)

8

The Hamlet Pope

FOR JOSEPH RATZINGER, 1963 was already an eventful year. In May, he left the University of Bonn to join the theology faculty at the more prestigious University of Münster, about a hundred miles north. He moved there with his sister, Maria, who would remain his housekeeper for the rest of her life. Students in Münster, eager to hear about his history-making work at Vatican II, rushed to join his classes. His inaugural lecture filled a six-hundred-seat classroom, requiring a loudspeaker to be installed in the next room so hundreds of others in the overflow crowd would not miss the chance to hear him.

His reception in Münster bolstered Ratzinger's self-confidence. The shame he felt in his twenties over the rejection of his thesis had mostly disappeared. At the council, he earned the respect of bishops from around the world. His writings became bolder that year. He published articles denouncing "the servility of the sycophants" in the Curia. What the Vatican needed, he wrote, were churchmen with "passion for the truth" willing to endanger their careers—"who love the church more than the ease and unruffled course of their personal destiny." If the Vatican was offended by his criticism, so be it. He would prepare himself for "misunderstanding, suspicion, even condemnation."

Almost as soon as he arrived in Münster, Ratzinger tried to recruit Hans Küng to the faculty. In a letter, Ratzinger urged his new friend to accept, saying they could teach together. Küng wrote back, noting how excited he was to discover at the council that they had a shared vision for the church, and said he would seriously consider the invitation. His students in Tübingen convinced him to stay, however. He was especially touched when they gathered one night for a candlelight procession to urge him not to go. As they walked, they joined in a happy chorus of the rhyme "Im Minschter isch's finschter!" (In Münster, it's dark!) In declining the job, Küng convinced Ratzinger that the University of Münster should hire his talented young Tübingen colleague Walter Kasper for the faculty post. Kasper's arrival in Münster that year marked the start of his long, and at times poisonous, relationship with Ratzinger.

The conclave to choose John XXIII's successor was scheduled to open on June 19, and all eyes were on Montini. For progressives, he was the obvious choice. He had already signaled that if elected, the council would continue. In a speech days before John's death, he praised what Vatican II had already accomplished: "The Holy Father has shown us paths it would be wise to follow."

Montini had none of John's magnetism, but he had warmth, intelligence, and a reputation in Milan as an agreeable, nonconfrontational manager. For many cardinals, he was, at sixty-five, young enough to serve many years as pope, but old enough not to remain in power so long he grew arrogant; the unhappy memory of Pius's nearly twenty-year reign was still fresh. Other Europeans were seen as *papabile*, the Italian term to describe a likely papal candidate, including Cardinal Suenens of Belgium, but it had been four centuries since a non-Italian was pope, and Italian cardinals had the votes to insist on one of their own. That preference went beyond national pride, they admitted privately. Many feared what would happen if a non-Italian pope decided to do business at the Vatican in his native tongue—or, heaven forbid, in Latin.

The membership of the College of Cardinals worked in Montini's favor, since by then more than half of its members had been given their red hats by John. (At the time, cardinals wore a broad-brimmed red hat known as a *gelaro*; they were phased out in the late 1960s.) The late pope, who so clearly wanted Montini as his successor, had increased the college's membership from fifty-three to eighty-two, and its newest members were far younger and more geographically diverse than the cardinals they replaced. The only fierce opposition to Montini came from older European cardinals who opposed John and were, by and large, allies of Cardinal Ottaviani. Ottaviani, then seventy-two, was also considered *papabile*, although his many enemies were certain to do whatever was necessary to block his election.

Montini's chief rival was Cardinal Siri, the archconservative from Genoa. Named a cardinal by Pius XII, Siri had the support of Spanish cardinals associated with an increasingly powerful Catholic sect called Opus Dei (Latin for "the Work of God"). The group, in which laymen outnumbered clerics, was founded in 1928 in Spain by a hyperambitious priest, Josemaria Escriva.

The biggest obstacle to Montini's election appeared to be the cardinal himself. He had always been tormented by self-doubt. John XXIII joked about his friend's chronic indecisiveness by comparing him to Shakespeare's vacillating prince: *il nostro Amleto di Milano*—our Hamlet of Milan. Friends said Montini was terrified at the prospect of becoming pope. Cardinal König of Vienna saw it up close in the first minutes of the conclave. At the moment the cardinals were sealed inside the Sistine Chapel, the massive brass doors bolted shut and then coated along their frames in scented wax, the look on Montini's face was one of "abject horror" at the prospect of his election, König remembered.

The two men had been given makeshift sleeping chambers next to each other off the chapel. König left his room that evening, took a step into the hallway, and knocked on Montini's door. He was invited in. "When I told him that I, too, shared the general view that he would be elected and that I was overjoyed, he kept trying to convince me I was wrong," König recalled. Montini was nearly in tears as he pleaded that any campaign to promote his candidacy be stopped: "I am enveloped by complete darkness and can only hope that the dear Lord will lead me out of this."

Others could only speculate about what he really feared. Some thought it was Montini's realization that, as pope, he would be stripped of any real privacy. He had always enjoyed a surprisingly full life independent of the church and treasured his free time. Given a pope's crushing workload, would he be denied the greatest pleasure of his day: plucking a book from the shelves of his library to savor for hours after dinner? When he left Rome for Milan in 1954, more than one hundred bulky crates, filled with thousands of books, went with him. It would later be disclosed that his library included many works that the Holy Office had declared blasphemous and placed on the Index of Prohibited Books.

Montini counted writers, artists, and actors among his closest companions, including self-proclaimed atheists and Communists, and he feared those friendships would be exposed to damaging scrutiny. In Milan, his best friends outside the church—all men, including a well-known Italian film actor—found themselves the subject of feverish gossip about how close they were to Montini. There would never be concrete evidence the friendships were romantic or sexual, but there had always been whispers about Milan's archbishop. He had reason to believe that speculation about his sexuality might detonate into a public scandal one day.

Although many of his personal papers were destroyed after his death, letters he wrote as a teenager survived, including what appeared to be love letters to a boy named Andrea. He referred to Andrea as *carissimo*—"dearest"—a surprisingly intimate way for Italian boys of the era to address each other. In one, he pleaded: "I beg you, continue this friendship, which has opened up for me, so withdrawn and alone, a living ray of goodness." There is no suggestion he ever knew romance with a woman before or after entering the priesthood. Nor would there ever be an equivalent to Pascalina or any other powerful woman on his papal staff.

The June 1963 conclave lasted only forty-three hours, one of the shortest in centuries. König worried that Montini, who won on the sixth ballot, would refuse election. But Montini hesitantly said yes, announcing he would assume the papacy even though it left him feeling "crucified with Christ." Moments later, he revealed that he had chosen the papal name Paul in honor of the apostle who, more than any other, spread the Gospel's message to foreign lands.

His election was proclaimed on the balcony of St. Peter's by Ottaviani. The crowd, clearly hoping for this news, exploded. The new pope, whose slight frame was draped in his new white robes, a red stole embroidered in gold silk thread around his neck, emerged to accept the cheers. He neither smiled nor frowned. He issued the Latin blessing *Urbi et Orbi*—"To the city [of Rome] and to the world"—and offered, also in Latin, the traditional prayer for the occasion: "May the blessing of Almighty God, the Father, the Son, and the Holy Ghost, descend on you." Despite his nerves, he spoke in a clear, somber voice.

The next day, he announced, as expected, that Vatican II would continue. In fact, he declared, he wanted the council to be remembered as "the preeminent part" of his legacy. He set September 29 as the opening date for the new session, only three months away. On his second full day as bishop of Rome, he made an appearance at his apartment window to introduce the crowd below to the visiting Suenens, now widely seen by the world's bishops as their most important champion of reform. That summer, Paul named Suenens and two other progressive cardinals to a panel of "moderators" to oversee all aspects of the bishops' meetings.

Küng and Ratzinger began to plan their return to Rome. Both were optimistic about the new pope, given his closeness to John XXIII. Küng knew the new pope slightly and had been impressed for years by his intelligence and open-mindedness. He first set eyes on him in Rome in the late 1940s, when Küng was at the Gregorian and then-Monsignor Montini was an aide to Pius XII. Küng had a clear memory from the time of watching Montini leave St. Peter's after an event in the basilica, and how odd it was that he made no effort to interact with anyone around him: "He just marched ahead with tightly folded hands, sunk in prayer, his head bowed in devotion."

The new pope's roots were solidly middle-class. He was raised in the northern province of Brescia, where his father was an antifascist newspaperman before winning election to parliament. As a boy, Montini was sickly, which prevented him from attending a regular seminary. After ordination as a priest at the age of twenty-three, he entered the Gregorian, with plans to join the Curia, and then spent most of his career as a Vatican bureaucrat. A Church of England theologian who was a frequent visitor to Rome in the 1930s and 1940s sent home a glowing description of the young Montini: "So good and lovable, a man of deep kindness, high intelligence and real wisdom. Slight, not very tall, dark, alert and capable of laughter, eyes both penetrating and bird-like. I liked him to no end."

In 1931, when Montini turned thirty-four, he was plucked out of the Curia to join the inner circle of then-Cardinal Pacelli. After Pacelli's election as Pius XII eight years later, Montini was given remarkable authority for a man of his youth, but it came at a cost, given Pius's bullying, autocratic ways. There was mystery over the pope's decision in 1954 to transfer Montini to Milan, especially since Montini was only made an archbishop, not a cardinal. Without membership in the College of Cardinals, he could not be part of the next conclave and therefore was out of the running to succeed Pius.

Montini did not welcome the move to Milan, writing of his "intense suffering" at leaving his beloved Rome. Even so, his loyalty to Pius never wavered. Just a week before his own election as pope in 1963, Montini wrote a long, passionate letter to the British Catholic weekly newspaper *The Tablet*. It was prompted by the London opening of *The Deputy*, the play that villainized Pius for his silence about the Holocaust. In the letter, which many in the Vatican thought ill-advised because it raised questions about Montini's own wartime record, he declared the play an appalling distortion. He insisted Pius was a man of "exquisite sensibility and the most delicate human sympathies" who had done all he could, behind the scenes, to save Europe's Jews. If Pius had raised his voice publicly, Montini wrote, it would have invited more slaughter of "innumerable innocent victims."

Many Vatican bureaucrats were alarmed about Montini's election, even if they expected it. He had worked at the heart of the Curia for most of his adult life and so he knew its failings. In a speech in September, he announced sweeping reforms of the Curia, declaring it needed to be "simplified and decentralized." He offered few details, although he suggested the restructuring would result in a shift in authority away from Rome. The next morning, *The New York Times* hailed it as "a speech of truly historic magnitude" that proved the new pope was ready "to share his powers in the church's government with the world's bishops."

Küng and Ratzinger, along with most of the German bishops' delegation, were delighted by the announcement, which came only a week before the new session of Vatican II. Ratzinger saw the pope's plans to remake the Curia as a "daring step into the future." However, as the church was about to discover, Paul's promises of reform usually proved hollow. Küng's first major disappointment came that same week, when the pope announced he was keeping Ottaviani in place at the Holy Office. In the battle for the church's soul, Küng thought, it was Ottaviani who personified the repression that Vatican II was meant to end. Küng pondered whether there was something he should do, and he settled on a daring plan. Once the council resumed, he decided, he would round up bishops to bring pressure on Paul VI. It was almost certainly the riskiest decision of Küng's young career, but "I will ask for the dismissal of Cardinal Ottaviani."

THE COUNCIL MEETINGS that fall were expected to last at least two months, ending sometime in early December, allowing bishops to return home in time for Christmas services. Almost as soon as he landed back in Rome, Küng had new evidence that he was in trouble with the Holy Office. An Italian-language edition of his 1960 book on the council had just been published and sold quickly, as Italians had a chance to read what had been exciting Catholics elsewhere for nearly three years. Then, suddenly, it disappeared from stores. Italian booksellers reported they received visits from Archbishop Pietro Parente, Ottaviani's deputy, warning them to stop selling a book that was "contrary to sound doctrine."

Parente gave an angry speech that fall in which he raged against the "iconoclastic" writings of young theologians at the council. "Many shameless things have been published during these months," he warned. He did not identify the wayward scholars by name, but there was no doubt that he was referring to Küng and Ratzinger. No two young theologians in Rome were more prominent.

Whatever the threat, Küng delighted in being the center of attention at the council. His hesitation about living in Rome had evaporated. He was reminded each day of the crumbling, sun-dappled beauty of the city. Even more, he loved the intellectual jousting with the church's finest minds. His days and nights at the council were filled with precisely the work he cherished: "I do theology every day with joy."

His risky behind-the-scenes campaign to oust Ottaviani began in earnest almost as soon as he arrived back in Rome. He wrote directly to the pope in September. "I composed, in French, a well-considered letter to His Holiness, which asks for Ottaviani's dismissal," he recalled. He also approached Cardinal Bea, given his influence with the pope, to ask for help in removing Ottaviani. Bea was understanding but suggested there was nothing they could do, at least not then. He urged Küng to be cautious, comparing the situation to a gun battle in which everyone would lose their lives.

The controversy that always surrounded Küng worried his admirers. Yves Congar feared Küng would so outrage the Holy Office that his career would be destroyed. "Küng charges at things," he wrote in his diary. "He goes straight ahead like an arrow." The older theologian's worry was mixed with envy: "I realize the fairly horrifying degree to which I myself have been too timid."

Congar returned to Rome that fall convinced that if Vatican II succeeded, it would be largely due to Suenens. The year before, the Belgian had demonstrated an ability to bat away challenges from Ottaviani and others in the Curia. Congar was impressed by everything about Suenens, beginning with his appearance. The cardinal dressed as modestly as possible. He wore no jewelry of any sort, representing his vision of a church dedicated totally to service, especially to the poor. "He usually dressed in a dark gray clerical suit without the least sign of office—no red collar, not even a ring," Congar recalled. It was startling to see Suenens—tall, thin, with perfect posture—standing alongside a group of aging, overfed Italian cardinals in their embroidered red silk robes. Suenens's influence was evident in the planning for the new session. The opening ceremony would be far less ostentatious than the year before, and only three hours instead of seven. For the event, the new pope simplified his own wardrobe, including his headwear. He would not be seen in one of the traditional jewel-encrusted crowns that popes had worn at such gatherings for centuries. Instead, he wore an embroidered cloth miter. He insisted, though, on arriving at St. Peter's on the *sedia*—the portable throne. The decision disappointed many bishops, since the *sedia* was the bit of Vatican pageantry they thought most ridiculous.

The ceremony on September 29 got underway the moment the portable throne was lowered near the doors to the basilica. Paul walked slowly toward Bernini's sculpted papal altar, a seventeenth-century bronze masterwork reportedly situated directly above the tomb of St. Peter. There was applause, which Paul acknowledged with a gentle wave. Despite the setting's magnificence, his speech that day was memorable for its modesty. He introduced himself in the humblest of terms—as the "servant of the servants of God," the title John XXIII had embraced—and described himself "the least" of the bishops in Rome that day. He welcomed the others as "the successors of the apostles," a choice of words that struck many bishops as significant. It was the new pope's most explicit statement to date suggesting he believed the bishops were entitled to real power in Rome.

The ceremony's most dramatic moment came when Paul turned to the corner of the basilica where the Protestant and Orthodox observers were seated. His voice trembled as he addressed them, expressing "the deep sadness we feel at our prolonged separation." Several observers were startled at what he said next: "If we are in any way to blame for that separation, we humbly beg God's forgiveness and ask pardon if our brethren feel themselves to have been injured." It had been nearly a thousand years since the split between Catholics and the Orthodox, and more than four centuries since the break with Protestants, and now, finally, a bishop of Rome acknowledged that the Vatican shared blame. "It was the first occasion in which Rome has offered anything in the nature of an apology," marveled Bishop Moorman, the Church of England observer. He described

Paul's concession as a landmark in the history of Christianity: "No wonder the pope's voice trembled, for he must have known that, while he greatly encouraged many of us in the audience, he was deeply offending many of his own friends."

The first business meeting was scheduled for the next day. With their votes the year before, the vast majority of the world's bishops proved they were ready for sweeping, democratic reform of the church; many returned to Rome convinced they were about to achieve it. Years later, their cause would be described as "liberal" or "progressive," but that description did not do them justice, since it suggested they faced a sizable number of "conservative" opponents. The truth was that, as measured by their votes, the conservatives represented only a small minority at the council. The central conflict, then, was whether this relatively tiny group of conservative bishops could bring enough pressure on an uncertain new pope to reject the majority's will.

There was relief on all sides that the council's workload was more manageable. Suenens and his fellow moderators cut the number of draft documents from seventy to sixteen. Some were merged, others discarded entirely. One moderator proved especially valuable to Suenens: Cardinal Julius Döpfner, the fifty-year-old archbishop of Munich. He was jokingly described in the German church hierarchy as their "child prodigy." In 1948, at the age of thirty-five, he became the youngest bishop in Europe. A decade later, John XXIII made him the world's youngest cardinal. He had a rich life outside the church; he was a mountaineer and reached the peak of the 14,700-foot Matterhorn at the age of fifty-two. Döpfner's contempt for the Vatican's bureaucracy was well-known to his parishioners in Munich; he often suggested from the pulpit they were right to see the Roman Curia as "an institution that enslaved freedom." He had been spared the wrath of the Holy Office over that sort of incendiary remark because he was given a bishop's robes—then a cardinal's—so early in his career. Like so many reformers, Döpfner was a graduate of the Gregorian, where he obtained a doctorate in 1941. He returned to Germany for the rest of World War II; church records confirm he had only routine interactions with the Nazi government.

The first item on the council's agenda that fall was a landmark document designed to establish a modern structure for the Catholic hierarchy. It was eventually given the formal title of Dogmatic Constitution on the

Church, or *Lumen Gentium*—Light of Nations.* An initial draft was circulated the year before by Ottaviani, but it was so flawed—so biased in the Curia's favor—that it was quickly withdrawn. Ratzinger could see the new version was the handiwork of Suenens. It was written to emphasize, above all, that the church should identify itself as "the People of God," a phrase repeated dozens of times. It offered a vision of a church in which the average worshipper in the pews was, in God's eyes, as important as any bishop. The Vatican's hierarchy *served* the church; it was not, by itself, the church. Ratzinger was excited by the document, especially its acknowledgment of "a sinful church continually in need of renovation." The big battle, he predicted, would come over passages of the constitution that encouraged power sharing between the pope and the world's bishops. If approved as written, it would end the monopoly on power that popes had claimed since the First Vatican Council. The document restored what was, in ancient times, a far more democratic arrangement between the bishop of Rome and bishops outside Rome.

There would also be a battle over another proposal in the document—to revive the regular appointment of deacons, low-ranking ministers who had some of a priest's authority to lead worship. Deacons were common in the first centuries of the church, when the title was granted to men and women. Among those early deacons, there was no celibacy rule, which meant that they—like priests at the time—had spouses and children. After AD 500, however, the routine appointment of deacons came to an end as the all-male priesthood grew more powerful. The title of deacon survived into the twentieth century, but it was given to a small number of seminarians in training for the priesthood.

After World War II, when the priest shortage grew into a worldwide crisis, many bishops urged the Vatican to revive the appointment of deacons and, as before, allow them to marry. The assumption was that many devout men who resisted the priesthood because they could not accept celibacy would become deacons instead. Ratzinger, Küng, and many German bishops thought the idea of married deacons made perfect sense; it was an obvious solution to a disgraceful situation in which tens of millions of Catholics had no clergy to serve them. The wording of the draft did not state explicitly that deacons would be allowed to marry, but it left open the

---

* By tradition, the title of Vatican documents is drawn from the opening words of the Latin text. The opening sentence of the constitution reads, in Latin: "Christ is the light of nations."

possibility. (The council's records show that the appointment of women deacons was never seriously considered.) Still, what so many churchmen saw as a sensible solution, archconservative bishops viewed as a threat; they worried a debate over married deacons would lead to a larger discussion of whether priests and bishops could marry too.

Many bishops, especially from Latin America, had returned to Rome determined to put the issue of priestly celibacy on the agenda. A few wrote speeches to deliver in St. Peter's in which they would plead to revise church law and allow priests to marry. But those speeches were never delivered—on orders of Paul VI, who sent word through the council's administrators that fall that he considered the doctrine of priestly celibacy to be a settled issue and therefore closed to debate.

In October, one of Mexico's most influential churchmen, Bishop Sergio Méndez Arceo of the city of Cuernavaca, was ready to defy the pope. The priest shortage was as dire in Mexico as anywhere else and Méndez Arceo, who held doctorates in history and philosophy from the Gregorian, planned to speak in St. Peter's to argue that, since mandatory celibacy was not dogma, it was time to end it. In adding his name to the speakers' list, he was required to identify his topic. He wrote a single word: "Celibacy." Hours later, he was confronted by Archbishop Felici, the council's general secretary, who told him angrily that the subject was taboo and that he would not be allowed to speak.

"Raising the subject of celibacy is not allowed," he told Méndez Arceo.

"Why?" the Mexican asked. "Who made this decision?"

"Higher authority," Felici shot back, clearly referring to the pope without using his name.

News of the confrontation spread quickly around St. Peter's, and many bishops were despondent over what it seemed to mean—an end to their hopes for truly open debate at Vatican II, with the newly elected pope ready to silence anyone who dared raise a topic that made him uncomfortable.

THE DEBATE OVER *Lumen Gentium* went on for weeks, and it was clear the draft attributed to Suenens had overwhelming support. Bishops talked excitedly of how, once it was approved, they would assert their renewed authority. Many proposed the creation of a bishops' "congress" or "parliament" based in Rome, its members elected by their regional colleagues. Patriarch Maximos, the Syrian-born leader of the Melkite Church, gave another defiant speech in October—again in French, since he continued to refuse to use Latin—to offer a blueprint for a bishops' parliament that would be nothing less than "the supreme executive and decision-making council of the church." Its elected members would live full-time in Rome and, working with the pope, control the Curia. "The church was given to St. Peter and the apostles, not to the Curia," he said. Maximos acknowledged explicitly what his plan would mean: it would end forever the idea of the pope as absolute monarch. "It is an error to say the pope is the head of the church," he continued. "The church has only one head: Jesus Christ."

The debate then turned to the question of deacons. South American bishops were passionate on the subject, saying the appointment of married deacons was the only way to deal with the grave shortage of priests. Tears poured down the face of Bishop Jorge Kémérer of the Argentine city of Posadas as he described how poor farmers in his diocese needed to travel by foot for hours simply to find a priest to hear a confession. "Do not take away our hope!" he pleaded. As expected, conservatives, especially those associated with the Holy Office, denounced the idea of married deacons as heresy. "With trepidation in my soul, I beg you, venerable council fathers, do not inflict a wound on the sacred law of celibacy," said Cardinal Ernesto Ruffini of Sicily, who was close to Ottaviani.

The larger debate on the constitution appalled conservatives. They opposed every part of the document, especially its call for power sharing between Rome and the world's bishops. Suenens, certain the critics represented only a small minority, decided to force the issue. On October 15, he announced a test vote the next day on central elements of the constitution. The vote, he was convinced, would prove the document could move quickly to final passage. He said ballots for the test vote would be distributed in the morning.

But bishops arrived in St. Peter's the next day to discover there were no ballots—and no explanation why. After morning Mass, Felici announced the vote had been postponed indefinitely. He eventually acknowledged that ballots had been printed but—on orders of the Curia, with the pope's approval—incinerated overnight. Many bishops were furious. Years later, the events of that day were seen as the first compelling evidence that Paul had fallen under the sway of Ottaviani and the Holy Office, and that John XXIII's spirit of aggiornamento was being extinguished.

Suenens pleaded with the pope to change his mind or risk losing the council's goodwill, and Paul backed down. The pope reluctantly agreed to

Cardinal Josef Frings of Cologne, Germany, patron of Father Joseph Ratzinger at Vatican II, delivered one of the council's most explosive speeches, denouncing the Holy Office as a "scandal to the world."

a series of votes on October 30 on the central provisions of the constitution, and all were approved by lopsided margins; each was supported by at least 80 percent of the vote. Suenens believed—prematurely—that the battle on the constitution was won that day, with the world's bishops about to reclaim a permanent voice in Rome.

Then, yet again, there was chaos, as Ottaviani worked behind the scenes to ensure the full constitution never got a final vote. His intention, it became clear, was to kill the document with endless delays. He all but confirmed that in a newspaper interview in which he said he did not consider any votes in the council—on the constitution or anything else—to be binding. He vowed there would never be any sort of permanent bishops' parliament since it would infringe on the "universal and supreme authority of the pope."

Cardinal Frings was enraged and asked Ratzinger to help him write a speech to allow him to vent his fury with Ottaviani.* On November 8,

* Ratzinger's role in drafting the speech became a topic of impassioned debate inside the Vatican decades later. Many German churchmen at the council left Rome certain it had been written by Ratzinger—he wrote all of Frings's other speeches, after all—and that

Frings added his name to the speakers' list in St. Peter's. Since he was a cardinal, the request was granted the same day. He walked slowly to the podium and cleared his throat as he prepared to give a speech that would be the most important of his career, a blistering public attack on the Holy Office and the brutal tactics it had wielded since the days of the Inquisition.

He began by insisting the council honor the bishops' votes on the constitution. He was astonished, he said, by Ottaviani's suggestion that their votes were not binding. "The Curia has no function but to obey the wishes of the council—and this goes especially for the Holy Office." His voice growing almost to a shout in his German-accented Latin, Frings said it was time for the church to recognize the larger truth about Ottaviani's congregation. The methods of the Holy Office, Frings declared, were "out of harmony with modern times—and are a scandal to the world!" *Scandal to the world?* There were gasps. Frings compared the Holy Office to a spy agency in a Cold War police state, with dissidents placed under round-the-clock surveillance and denied the ability to defend themselves against trumped-up charges at trial: "No one should be judged and condemned without having been heard, without knowing what he is accused of." For many in the audience, this was the moment at the council they had longed for. Here was a respected senior churchman identifying and denouncing their common enemy: Ottaviani and the Holy Office.

Frings said it was time for the Holy Office and all other Curia agencies to be led and staffed by laymen, ending the centuries-old concept of a clergy-led bureaucracy in Rome: "It is not necessary to be a bishop in order to serve in the Roman Curia, nor even to be a priest."

When he stepped from the podium, dozens of bishops joined in cheers and sustained applause. Ottaviani was incensed, and later that day rose to respond, his voice shaking with rage: "I most profoundly protest against the accusations made against the Congregation of the Holy Office." He did not identify Frings by name, but the German cardinal was his obvious target. Frings, Ottaviani charged, talked nonsense: "Without any doubt, this criticism is due to ignorance." He said he was offended personally by Frings's speech—this "defamation." Worse, Ottaviani continued, the

---

he endorsed every word of it. They recalled that at the time, Ratzinger was proud of the speech. Years later, however, as he rose to great power in the Vatican, he was coy on the subject. He suggested that the most heated passages of the speech were written by Frings, not him, and that he had not necessarily shared the cardinal's fierce criticism of the Holy Office, an agency that Ratzinger would one day lead under a different name.

speech amounted to an assault on Paul VI: "In attacking the Holy Office, one attacks the pope himself." The cardinal returned to his seat to scattered applause, most of it from his own deputies.

Church historians later described Frings's remarks as historic, among the most significant acts of public dissent against the Holy Office in its four-hundred-year existence. Many agreed that apart from the pope's opening address, it was the single most important speech delivered at Vatican II. There were widespread news reports that day that Paul telephoned Frings to offer support for what the cardinal said—reports that prompted an indignant Ottaviani to go to the pope and offer to resign. It was refused.

9

The New Pope Struggles

Paul VI found the pressures of his new life agonizing. It was just as he had feared. His friends said he treated every decision as a burden, one that only he could bear. Worse, he saw most choices as traps in which, whatever he decided, he would humiliate himself. The pressures weighed him down—literally, it seemed. He was so anxious when leading a worship service in St. Peter's that his shoulders hunched over the moment he opened his mouth, as if pushed down from above. Suenens said Paul appeared to be in physical pain in situations in which he needed to settle quarrels on even routine issues.

He involved himself in trifling decisions about Vatican budgets and staffing, the sort of bureaucratic matters that John XXIII gladly left to others. So much paperwork piled onto Paul's desk that, on some days, he stayed there nonstop from seven a.m., when he completed the morning Mass, until one a.m., when he went to bed.

Paul's anguish, and the growing sense that he allowed Ottaviani and the Holy Office to make decisions for him, alarmed Suenens and his allies. Even so, Suenens felt that reform-minded bishops were making progress in the early weeks of the council's new session. There was surprisingly quick, decisive approval of the document to allow the Mass to be said in local languages, ending the exclusive use of Latin, and to phase out the rigid choreography of the Tridentine Mass. The final decree, known in English as the Constitution on the Sacred Liturgy, was endorsed by the council in December on another wildly lopsided vote:

2,147 to 4.* By then, translators had been at work for months on the Mass in local languages—as well as on the rites of baptism, confirmation, and the anointing of the sick. Shortly after the vote, American bishops announced they would begin offering the all-English Mass the following spring. Altars in many churches and cathedrals around the world were uprooted and turned around, allowing priests to face their parishioners during worship. In most dioceses, Holy Communion was revised to allow parishioners, previously only offered bread at the altar, to sip from the chalice of wine as well.

Paul agreed to weekly meetings with Suenens and his team of moderators while the council was in session. Despite growing tension between the two men, the pope approved another controversial proposal from Suenens that fall—that women be invited to attend the council as observers. The cardinal often complained, with exasperation, that women should have been invited from the start: "Unless I am mistaken, women make up one-half of the human race!" Other decisions by the pope disappointed reform-minded churchmen. He was determined to limit the influence of the progressive theologians appointed by John XXIII. In November, many *periti*, including Küng and Congar, were invited to a papal reception and came away insulted. According to Küng, Paul suggested he saw the theologians as little more than bishops' note takers.

Just a few weeks into the new session, it was obvious the council would need to reconvene the following year—and probably again a year after that. The debate on *Lumen Gentium*, the document intended to make the church hierarchy more open and democratic, was nowhere near complete, and the last weeks of the session that year had been set aside to debate a document likely to be just as controversial: the long-awaited declaration on "ecumenism" and interfaith dialogue prepared by Cardinal Bea.†

The document had five chapters. Three were relatively uncontroversial and would be approved after brief debates. They called for the church to encourage dialogue with non-Catholic Christians, the campaign that John XXIII had launched in the first days of his papacy. The real debate

* It was the first of sixteen key documents approved by the council. Four of them, including the liturgy decree, were labeled as "constitutions," which was meant to signal that they were considered especially important to the church's future.
† The word "ecumenism" has different meanings in the church. In this case, it referred to the search for unity among people of different faiths, especially between Catholics and other Christians.

would come over the last two chapters. Chapter 4 was Bea's declaration on the church's relationship with Judaism, intended to end two thousand years of hostility. It affirmed the links between Judaism and Christianity, how one emerged from the other, and rejected the ancient claim that Jews were responsible for the death of Christ. Jewish leaders rushed to praise the document. Some bishops at the council were equally quick to denounce it and put their anti-Semitism on display. Other criticism came from Arab governments and from Christian churches in the Middle East. They saw the document as a de facto endorsement of Israel's sovereignty and warned it would threaten the safety of Christians living in Muslim nations. Egypt's government radio denounced the declaration as part of a "world Zionist plot."

The other groundbreaking chapter declared a universal right to religious freedom—a statement that American bishops, in particular, had been pressing the Vatican to make for decades. They saw it as a way of combatting the bigotry that had targeted American Catholics since the country's founding. The discrimination, they felt, reached a crescendo during the 1960 presidential campaign, when John Kennedy was accused of putting his Catholic faith above his loyalty to his country. Like the chapter on the Jews, chapter 5 faced heated opposition, especially from Curia bishops who insisted Catholicism remained the one true faith and that it was a sin to suggest otherwise.

Bea's full document was introduced on Monday, November 18, but the debate had to be suspended on Friday because of the terrible news from Dallas, where Kennedy had been assassinated that afternoon. The shock was felt across Rome, but most profoundly in Vatican City, since so many bishops felt a connection with the first Catholic president of the United States. That evening, the pope announced he would lead a special Mass the next day to pray "for the peace of the president's soul." In Washington, the funeral services were overseen by Cardinal Cushing, who was close to Kennedy's family. The cardinal had attended the opening ceremony of the council that year, then quickly flew home to Boston. He said he had departed Rome since the Curia once again refused his offer to pay for a simultaneous-translation system; he thought it was pointless for him to remain.

The council resumed business the following week. As expected, the attacks on Bea's document continued to focus on the chapters about the Jews and religious liberty. Yves Congar was appalled by so much organized opposition, especially to the chapter on the Jews. The attacks, he thought, were proof of how anti-Semitism still poisoned the thinking of powerful bishops in Rome. He came to believe reports that shortly before he died, John XXIII had proposed diplomatic relations with Israel, but the idea was scuttled because of the anti-Semitism of Cardinal Tardini, then secretary of state. "How can we establish diplomatic relations with the people who killed Jesus?" Tardini was heard to ask. On the Curia's orders, the two most contentious chapters in Bea's draft would later be made into independent documents, in an effort to make it more difficult to get them approved, since it would require two long debates in the council, not one.

Since the bishops' meetings needed to end by early December, Bea suspended debate on all five chapters, to resume the following year. The session concluded on December 4 with a ceremony led by the pope in St. Peter's. Many bishops felt uneasy as they sat there, since so much work remained undone. The new pope, despite his vow to shake up the Curia and allow greater independence to bishops outside Rome, had done neither. The excitement and optimism of the year before, when John XXIII opened the council with his promise of a church that dispensed "the medicine of mercy," had vanished. In his closing speech, Paul admitted that the council's debates that fall had been "arduous and intricate." Still, he insisted the disagreements were proof of the freedom the council now enjoyed. His delivery was wooden, his eyes rarely rising from the text.

There was one moment of great drama in the speech, near the end, when he departed from the text and revealed what was, by Vatican standards, a well-kept secret. He announced—"on behalf of peace among men"—that he would make a pilgrimage to the Holy Land the next month. The three-day trip would be the first outside Italy by a pope in more than 150 years. It would also be the first time since the Middle Ages that any bishop of Rome had made a pilgrimage to the lands where Jesus was born and preached. There was stunned silence at the announcement, followed by a long burst of applause.

Two days later, the spiritual leader of the world's Orthodox Christian churches, the Greek-born Patriarch Athenagoras, announced he had accepted an invitation to meet with the pope during his visit to Jerusalem. The meeting, the first between a pope and an Orthodox leader since the fifteenth century, would be proof of the Vatican's newfound commitment to Christian unity.

––––––––

THE POPE'S PILGRIMAGE began on January 4, when he left the Vatican in a thirteen-car motorcade bound for the airport. The bells of Rome's hundreds of churches pealed in unison, and crowds along the motorcade route witnessed something no living Roman had ever seen: a pope departing for a foreign land. The Vatican chartered a jet from the Italian national airline, Alitalia, for the trip, its tail repainted in yellow and white, the colors of the Vatican City flag.

The symbolism of the days that followed could not have been more profound, as a pope gazed out on landmarks tied to the life and death of the Savior. The meeting with the Orthodox patriarch came the second evening, when the two men entered the Vatican's diplomatic compound in Jerusalem and kissed each other on the cheek. The seventy-seven-year-old Athenagoras, who was six-foot-four and wore a black brimless head covering that exaggerated his height, towered over the white-robed pope. Paul remembered that the patriarch "embraced me like a brother—he shook my hand and held on to it." The patriarch told him: "We should show the world that we are once more brothers."

The trip offered fresh evidence of Paul's awkwardness as a public figure. There was a baffling moment for his Israeli hosts when, during a farewell meeting with the country's president, he put aside his prepared remarks and launched into an impassioned defense of the wartime record of Pius XII. His outburst was prompted by the continuing furor over the play *The Deputy*, which had just opened in more cities across Europe. He said that, as he prepared to depart the Jewish state, a nation born in the aftermath of the Holocaust, "I am happy to have the opportunity to state on this day and in this place that there is nothing more unjust" than slighting Pius's memory.

The pope's return home was triumphant. So many cheering Romans lined the fifteen-mile route from the airport back to the Vatican that the pope's motorcade slowed to a crawl; the ride to St. Peter's Square took nearly three hours.

His mood was brightened for a time by the excitement the trip created, but it did not last long. Back in the palace, he was flooded with messages from bishops around the world, many of them close friends, alarmed by what they saw as the council's stagnation; they worried that John XXIII's call for aggiornamento at Vatican II had been abandoned. He wrote back, assuring the worried bishops he was doing precisely what John would have wanted. He insisted his predecessor was falsely portrayed as some sort of bold revolutionary. As he told a French friend, "Pope John was much more conservative—much more traditional"—than most Catholics believed.

The constant comparisons to "the good pope" nagged at him. In fact, some bishops suggested simple jealousy explained what they saw as Paul's shocking decision that spring to ignore his predecessor's wish for his final resting place. In his will, John specified that he wanted to be entombed outside Vatican City on the grounds of the Basilica of St. John Lateran. The sixteenth-century basilica, three miles east of St. Peter's, was traditionally seen as the personal church of the bishop of Rome. After the will was made public, there was excited speculation that, if John XXIII were buried there, it would create a pilgrimage site to rival the Vatican. Paul guaranteed that would never happen. He sent a letter to the Curia directing, without explanation, that his predecessor be buried in vaults beneath St. Peter's, the resting place of more than one hundred other popes.

Paul thought of himself as bolder than John XXIII, certainly more modern and sophisticated in his thinking. "I don't want to brag," he wrote to a friend, but "in the field of work, of culture, of human and diplomatic relations, my life is characterized more clearly than anything else by the love of our time and of our world." In Rome, he surrounded himself with deputies who, he felt, were willing to break with stodgy tradition. Among them was Paul C. Marcinkus, an American priest who had worked in the Curia since the 1950s. The Illinois-born Marcinkus joined the Vatican diplomatic corps after earning a doctorate at the Gregorian. He was that rare thing in the Curia, a real man's man who, at six feet four inches tall, had the build of a linebacker, which earned him the nickname among friends of "the Gorilla." He liked to golf—he was proud of a five-stroke handicap—and was fond of cigars. In 1964, then forty-one, he helped oversee security for the pope's trip to the Holy Land. During the pilgrimage, Paul became enamored of the tough-talking Marcinkus and put him in charge of all papal travel. In 1968, the pope added to Marcinkus's responsibilities, appointing him as a director of the so-called Vatican Bank, known formally in Italian as the Istituto per le Opere di Religione—the Institute for the Works of Religion. It was an appointment for which Marcinkus was totally unqualified, he admitted; he had no background in banking or finance. Three years later, he was named the bank's president.

The pope often sought advice from a circle of businessmen he knew from his years in Milan, including his close friend Michele Sindona, an ambitious Sicilian-born lawyer and banker who, by the time of Paul's election, was in control of a sprawling international financial empire. He befriended then-Archbishop Montini in the 1950s after raising $2 million to build a church-sponsored retirement home. Just days after his installation ceremony, Paul contacted Sindona, then forty-three, and asked for help in managing the church's investments. The pope admitted to Curia deputies he had long heard troubling rumors about Sindona—that he was somehow tied to the notoriously violent Sicilian Mafia, known in Italy as Cosa Nostra. But the pope convinced himself the stories were untrue, and that Sindona was the victim of the sort of prejudice that even the most godly Sicilian faced in Italian high society. Among business leaders in Milan, Sindona was admired as a man of unusual self-discipline and good taste—he neither smoked nor drank, collected fine art, and was a patron of Milan's fabled La Scala opera house—who moved easily in global financial circles.

In years to come, Paul stood by Sindona, much as he remained stubbornly loyal to Marcinkus, even as those two men brought scandal to his papacy.

HANS KÜNG, already at odds with the Holy Office, was startled to learn in 1964 that the pope was angry with him too. That July, several weeks before returning to Rome for the council, he received an ominous note from a prominent theologian from his native Switzerland. The theologian had just met with Paul VI, an old friend, and the conversation turned to Küng. The pope was upset by what Küng was writing about the council's failings, and he wanted it to stop. "The Holy Father asked me to tell you that he is not very happy with you," the theologian warned. "Indeed, he is troubled. He asks you to moderate yourself."

A year after his election, Paul was tormented by criticism of his papacy, especially from outside the church. Major news organizations, which treated his predecessors with such respect, could be brutal, especially about his dithering. The British newsmagazine *The Economist* mocked him as "the Pope of Buts," since Paul seemed incapable of speaking directly, qualifying everything he said with "but" or "however." *The New York Times* said Paul had proved a grave disappointment—"a possessor of an exceptionally brilliant mind, very learned, but he is not a man of action." The most closely read foreign correspondent at the council was an American theologian who wrote for *The New Yorker* under the pseudonym Xavier Rynne. Copies of the magazine were air-freighted each week to Rome, where they were snapped up within hours because Rynne was so well sourced—and reliably gossipy. He was harsh about Paul—an "enigmatic and contradictory man" who dampened the "spirit of joyous expectancy that pervaded the world when John XXIII announced the council." Rynne, later revealed to be Father Francis X. Murphy, a Bronx-born theologian whose pseudonym was a combination of his mother's maiden name and his own middle name, described Paul as a man of "icy aloofness." No modern pope "had been so widely criticized by Catholics themselves."

Paul's fixation on defending the increasingly tarnished papacy of Pius XII continued to grow. The new pope was rattled every time he read news about the controversy whipped up by *The Deputy*. In March, he organized a hastily arranged ceremony in St. Peter's to dedicate a seven-foot-tall, ten-ton bronze statue of Pius. Much as Paul ignored the terms of John's will about his burial place, he was now brazenly ignoring the final wishes of Pius, who had insisted there be no monuments to him. And far from honoring John, there was new evidence that Paul wanted to dampen memories of his most beloved modern predecessor. On June 3, the first anniversary of John's death, the Vatican received a petition from fifty thousand residents of Bergamo, the late pope's birthplace, urging that *il papa buono* be beatified, the first step to sainthood. There was no reply from Paul.

In August, the pope released his first encyclical, a matter of great significance in any papacy. The Vatican revealed in advance that Paul wrote every word himself, and copies of his handwritten drafts were made public to prove it. But the encyclical, entitled *Ecclesiam Suam* (His Own Church), disappointed reform-minded churchmen because it offered no clear agenda for Vatican II and seemed to contradict itself on the council's purpose. The densely written encyclical stressed the pope's hope for dialogue with other faiths—the word "dialogue" appeared eighty-one times in the text—but it also accused Protestants and Orthodox Christians of a history of undermining the institution of the papacy. "Without the pope," it said, "the Catholic Church would no longer be Catholic."

By then, Suenens worried that the pope's mind had closed to the idea of any real reform of the church, no matter what he claimed publicly about his goals for the council. Above all, Paul resisted ceding any power to the world's bishops. Suenens said that while the pope claimed to support power sharing in principle—"collegiality," in the Vatican's jargon—he balked whenever pressed for details. "He spoke to me of his fear that collegiality would be abused to 'democratize the church,'" as if that were a dangerous thing, Suenens recalled. The cardinal tried to remain optimistic. He had learned an important lesson in his negotiations with Paul—that the pope was a profoundly lonely man, and it was important to spend time with him. There was a "thawing phenomenon," Suenens explained. "Whenever the audience was brief, Pope Paul's manner was reserved, conventional. If I stayed about an hour, however, the atmosphere became more relaxed, and it was possible to speak freely." He could see that Paul would never be comfortable in public settings: "His reserve and his personal style made it impossible." Suenens was always struck when he watched Paul try to engage with crowds. The pope would begin to wave, but the gesture "always stopped halfway, remaining somewhat unfinished." Suenens often encouraged the pope to put aside written remarks and speak from the heart in public audiences, but Paul rejected the idea, "because he felt that a pope's words must always be carefully weighed in order to avoid any cause for criticism."

In Germany that summer, Küng and Ratzinger stayed in touch, exchanging a few brief, friendly letters. They agreed that, despite the new pope's indecisiveness, there was no turning back for the church after the council. "A new spirit has come alive," Küng wrote. In an essay written that summer, Ratzinger made a bold proposal. He thought the council should announce an end to the concept of the pope as an all-knowing "monarch." Instead, the bishop of Rome would be given the role of "coordination" of the church—not as an all-powerful ruler but as the "first among equals."

PAUL VI WANTED the council to end that year, he told deputies. The logistics of bringing more than two thousand bishops to Rome for weeks at a time drained the Vatican of tens of millions of dollars a year. Older churchmen were exhausted by the journey. Conservative bishops, fearful they were about to lose important battles at the council, were especially eager for it to be over. In a meeting with the pope in early October, Cardinal Siri of Genoa urged him to shut down Vatican II immediately: "The atmosphere of the council makes one feel ill."

Suenens simplified the agenda of the next session. He again reduced the number of schemas, this time from seventeen to six. Still to be debated was a draft of a document, entitled "The Church in the Modern World," that would become Suenens's favorite project. He wanted it to be a sweeping, optimistic statement about the church's relationship to the twentieth century and to address controversial issues, including nuclear disarmament, sexuality, and women's rights. He told colleagues privately he hoped it would be a vehicle for the council to debate birth control, which by then was a fact of life across the United States and much of Europe. By 1964, six million American women were taking "the Pill," making it the most popular form of contraception in the US. A major opinion poll showed 25 percent of those women were Catholics.

The pope tried to short-circuit that debate. In June 1964 he authorized an announcement that became front-page news around the world: he revealed the existence of the birth-control commission that John XXIII had secretly created two years earlier. Paul said he hoped the panel finished its work quickly. In the meantime, he wrote, using the royal "we," the ban on contraceptives imposed by Pius XI in 1930 remained in place, "at least until we feel obliged in conscience to change it." His message was clear: the council should not debate birth control until the commission finished its work, and it was uncertain when that would be.

The ceremony in September to open the council's third session was tense. For many dispirited bishops, the only evidence of progress in St. Peter's that morning was the announcement that they would soon be joined by at least a few women, invited by the pope at Suenens's urging. A month later fifteen female observers—eight nuns and seven Catholic laywomen—arrived in Rome. They were led by fifty-six-year-old Sister Mary Luke Tobin, the Colorado-born president of a large American order of nuns. While the women were barred from participating in the council's debates or voting, Sister Mary Luke insisted their presence would still be historic, "a completely new phase in the life of the church."

The pope's opening speech was, for many bishops, infuriating. He acknowledged that the question of power sharing was at the heart of debates to come, but he made no commitment of what he would accept. He warned against "the fantasies and dreams" of anyone who expected quick change.

Suenens won important battles in the first days of the session. The first item up for debate was the so-called Dogmatic Constitution on the Church, the document that Ottaviani had tried to sabotage the year before, which proclaimed the right of bishops outside Rome to greater authority. There were lopsided votes to approve key passages. A chapter that recognized the world's bishops as a "college" with authority like that of the original twelve apostles passed 2,012 to 191. More than 70 percent voted to allow the appointment of married men as deacons, which meant the council endorsed the idea that at least some clergymen could be exempted from celibacy.

The next debate centered on a pair of even more controversial documents—one declaring religious freedom as a human right, another seeking to promote understanding with the world's Jews—that were left over from the year before, when they were originally part of Cardinal Bea's larger decree on interfaith dialogue. The new, stand-alone, religious-liberty document maintained much of Bea's wording and had overwhelming support, although it still faced ferocious opposition from a handful of arch-conservatives who warned it was blasphemous to suggest other religions had legitimacy. Cardinal Norman Gilroy of Sydney, Australia, one of the few church leaders from the English-speaking world to oppose the document, said it would "draw the faithful away from Christ" and lead them to worship in the "poisoned fields" of other faiths.

There was a far uglier debate to come over the document on the Jews, especially after Bea made clear he was alarmed by the way Ottaviani and his allies had rewritten it since the year before, largely to water down what had been a full exoneration of the Jewish people for the Crucifixion—the exoneration requested by John XXIII. Bea's original version said it was "wrong and an injustice" to blame any Jews for the Savior's death. The new draft argued instead that some Jews—the ancient Jews who denounced Jesus to their Roman occupiers—*did* bear responsibility. The exoneration that remained, of modern-day Jews but not their ancestors, was presented in a confusing and halfhearted way. Ottaviani insisted the revisions had the pope's support.

Bea, clearly at odds with Paul as well as Ottaviani, rose to speak to the council in protest over the rewriting. Drawing on his decades of biblical scholarship, he explained why the council needed to reinstate his original draft and offer a full exoneration to Jews. He used the speech as a history lesson, describing what scholars had determined about the circumstances of the Crucifixion. Yes, he said, a small group of Jewish elders in Jerusalem, known collectively as the Sanhedrin, led a campaign against Jesus that ended in his execution, but the Sanhedrin represented only a fraction of the Jewish population of the land that their Roman occupiers called Judea.*

---

* The Romans renamed the territory "Syria-Palestine" about a century after Jesus's death, formally reviving the name "Palestine," which had first been applied to the area by a Greek historian in 430 BC. In modern times, the region of Jesus's birth is commonly described simply as Palestine.

And even the Sanhedrin had been forgiven by the dying Jesus with words that every Christian should know from the Gospel of Luke: "Father, forgive them for they know not what they do."

To the embarrassment of many in the audience, a few conservative bishops replied to Bea with speeches that smacked of crude anti-Semitism. Cardinal Ruffini of Sicily said the Vatican should not back away from its centuries-old conviction that the Jewish people as a whole betrayed Christ. Modern Jews needed to "remove the veil" from their eyes and convert to the "true faith" of Christianity, Ruffini declared. If hate lingered between the faiths, he said, it was the Jews who were responsible. "It is clear that Christians love Jews, for such is the law of Christians. But Jews should be exhorted to cease hating us and regarding us as contemptible animals."

Before either document could come to a vote, there was pandemonium, similar to the year before, as bishops realized the pope was trying to muzzle them. Things happened so quickly during what became known as the "October Crisis" that it became difficult for stunned bishops to keep track of the bad news. Although it was not announced publicly, Ottaviani convinced the pope in early October to suspend debate indefinitely on both the religious-liberty document and the one on the Jews so they could be rewritten again—to Ottaviani's liking—by a committee of theologians who were mostly allied to the Holy Office.

Bea was informed of the decision in a private note from the pope, and the otherwise mild-mannered cardinal was incensed. He had good reason to fear Ottaviani would rewrite the two documents, this time to render them totally meaningless. Within hours, word of what was happening rocketed around Rome and reached reform-minded cardinals and bishops, who were appalled. It also reached Hans Küng, who recognized that "speed was of the essence" and decided to organize a protest. He telephoned Ratzinger, asking that Cardinal Frings intervene. Frings, who had already demonstrated his bravery at the council, called a meeting the next day with a dozen like-minded bishops. They gathered at his apartment at the German national church and signed a protest letter to the pope. In its opening passage, which was drafted in Latin, the cardinals announced they were writing to Paul *magno cum dolore*—with great pain.

Küng made another bold decision, which he kept secret at the time. He decided to leak the details of the backroom maneuvering by the pope and Ottaviani to Vatican correspondents for major European newspapers, briefing them on "the scandalous machinations against the two declarations." To his delight, the leaks resulted hours later in an "incredible storm throughout the international press." Front-page headlines the next morning suggested that anti-Semitism and other intolerance contaminated the thinking of the Curia, and that Paul VI acquiesced in it.

Within a day, stunned by the ugly headlines, the pope backed down and announced the writing of the declarations would remain in Bea's control. The cardinal moved quickly to put finishing touches on both documents so they could be voted on immediately, before the Curia had another chance to sabotage them. The declaration on the Jews was reworked to restore most of his original wording, then approved in nearly final form in an overwhelming vote, 1,770 to 185. Küng was relieved to discover that, with enough pressure, Paul could be forced "to do the right thing."

There was more chaos to come, however. The council's next debate centered on the latest draft of "The Church in the Modern World," the document that Suenens promoted so enthusiastically. As expected, its most provocative chapters dealt with marriage and sexuality. The draft rejected, once and for all, the idea that sex existed only for the purpose of procreation. Sex, the document said, existed also for a married couple's pleasure— "the intimate drive of conjugal love." The draft referred specifically to the debate over birth control, noting the "sense of responsibility" felt by Catholic married couples to limit the size of their families. It asked Catholics "not to be discouraged" as the birth-control commission continued to deliberate.

In the debate, many bishops said they wanted the document to go further and call directly for an end to the birth-control ban. Patriarch Maximos of the Melkite Church was, as always, direct—outrageously so for many in the Curia. He urged the pope to realize that millions of Catholic women around the world already used artificial contraception in defiance of the church because they had no other choice if they wanted to feed the children they already had. He raised a question other bishops were too diplomatic to ask: Why should married couples allow their sex lives to be regulated by a group of aging celibate men in Rome? The ban, he said, had always reflected a "bachelor psychosis."

Suenens followed, and his speech created another uproar. He called for an end to secrecy in the deliberations of the birth-control commission. He left no doubt he believed artificial contraception was no sin. He warned that if the council failed to address the issue, it would invite the sort of scandal and mockery that the church had not known since the Holy Office condemned Galileo in the seventeenth century.

"I beg of you, my brothers," Suenens said, his voice rising. "Let us avoid another Galileo affair! One is enough for the church!"

There were cheers, even though his words were seen as insulting to the pope, who wanted no debate on birth control. Within hours, Suenens was summoned to the papal apartment, where Paul VI was as angry as the cardinal had ever seen him. The pope insisted that Suenens make a public statement retracting the speech. The cardinal agreed, although his retraction was carefully worded, apparently to signal that he and the pope had a fundamental disagreement about birth control. It came several days later, when Suenens rose in St. Peter's to "clarify" his remarks, saying that the Vatican's teachings about birth control remained firmly in the hands of the "supreme magisterium"—the pope.

Paul realized that his hope to end Vatican II that fall was unrealistic. He announced in October that, after the success of his trip to the Holy Land, he would make a second foreign pilgrimage—to India, in December. Since that was only weeks away, he ordered the council to recess as soon as possible, with bishops invited back in 1965 for a fourth session. Much remained undone, including a final debate on "The Church in the Modern World." The delay disappointed Suenens and other bishops, but their regret was quickly replaced by another emotion—absolute fury, directed at the pope.

What became known as "the black week" began on Monday, November 16, when Paul made a series of announcements that undermined the council's earlier votes and blocked new ones. While he did not say it explicitly, it was clear Paul had become so alarmed by what he saw as the defiance of the world's bishops that he was prepared to reverse every major decision they had already made. He delayed, indefinitely, a final vote on Bea's Declaration on Religious Freedom, even though it had such broad support. He ordered nineteen last-minute wording changes to another document—a wildly popular declaration on Christian unity. Seemingly out of nowhere, he also announced what many bishops considered a peculiar formal designation of the Virgin Mary as "the Mother of the Church." He must have known that this would be an affront to Protestant observers at the council; their churches had protested for years over what they considered the Vatican's campaign to turn worship of Mary into a near-cult.

American bishops, otherwise such a secondary presence at the council, decided to act. They were infuriated by the pope's decision to delay the vote on the religious-liberty document, which they endorsed above all others. Cardinal Albert Meyer of Chicago and Bishop Francis Reh of the Bronx sputtered with rage on the floor of St. Peter's. "Let's not stand here talking!" Reh announced. "Let's do something! Who has some paper?" That minute, the two Americans drafted a letter to the pope, in Latin, and had copies circulated around Rome. It began: "To the Most Holy Father: Reverently, but urgently, *most* urgently, we ask that the Declaration on Religious Freedom be called for a vote before the end of this session of the council—lest the confidence of the world, both Christian and non-Christian, be lost." Within hours, more than a thousand bishops and cardinals—nearly half the churchmen at the council—had signed it. The letter went that night to the pope, but he was defiant and announced again there would be no vote on the declaration that year.

The pope, now widely branded an enemy of reform, was grim when he arrived for that year's closing ceremony on November 21. Many bishops made a point of keeping their eyes down and refusing to clap when he appeared in St. Peter's. The council's greatest accomplishment that fall was the adoption of the Dogmatic Constitution on the Church, which many bishops continued to hope would lead to the establishment of their "parliament" in Rome; the full document had been approved days earlier on a vote of 2,151 to 5. But given the events of "the black week," Suenens and others feared the pope would simply ignore or revoke the constitution. Paul's closing speech gave them no reason for optimism. He announced that while he welcomed the constitution, it would not result in any dramatic restructuring of the Vatican, since the church remained "both monarchical and hierarchical." Many in the audience were shocked at the remark, since it proved the pope continued to see himself as a "monarch," overseeing a "hierarchy" in which the world's bishops answered to him.

10

A Pope "in Agony"

A T HOME IN Germany in early 1965, Joseph Ratzinger wondered what the pope must be thinking back in Rome. Did Paul realize how angry and disappointed so many of the world's bishops were— with him? Many German bishops feared that, when they returned for the final session of the council that fall, Vatican II "would slowly disintegrate" and be "more or less doomed to be remembered as an embarrassing failure," Ratzinger wrote. The debates the year before had left "a bitter aftertaste due to the impression that, in the final analysis, the pope could do whatever suited him."

Paul was inscrutable in his rare public audiences that winter. In the second year of his papacy, he could go days without any significant contact with the public, which forced the Vatican to respond to persistent news reports that he was ill or depressed. In meetings with bishops as they passed through Rome, Paul tried to convince them he was still committed to broad reform at the council. But it was important, he said, that he be seen as an honest broker between conservative and liberal bishops. Increasingly, he allowed others to see his anger, particularly over the way he was being portrayed in the world's press. The reporting was "not corresponding to the truth at all," he said. Felici, the council's secretary general, made the same criticism in shocking terms in an essay in *L'Osservatore Romano*. He accused journalists covering Vatican II of being "parasites and fungi."

There were modest gestures of reform from Paul early that year. He ordered church publishers to reissue a book, banned by the Holy Office for decades, on the life of Galileo, and announced that the Vatican had begun the process of lifting the formal banishment decree imposed on the great scientist in 1633. Paul also pleased reformers with his repeated suggestion that when Vatican II ended, the logical extension of its work would be an intensified campaign by the church to eradicate poverty and promote social justice. His friend Bishop Câmara of Brazil was the de facto leader of that movement. During the council, Câmara was defiant in condemning the Vatican's failure to serve the poor, even if he was careful not to criticize the pope directly. That winter, the Brazilian granted interviews to launch his public campaign to demand the church sell off its real estate and treasury of great artworks and dedicate the proceeds to the poor. This "hoarding of the wealth" was an affront to the Gospels, he said. In what appeared to be a response to Câmara's plea, the pope announced in November 1964 that he would donate to charity—"for the benefit of the world's poor"—the jewel-covered tiara he wore at his coronation. The three-tiered crown, made of beaten silver encrusted with diamonds, rubies, and sapphires, had been a gift from his former parishioners in Milan.*

The pope's pilgrimage to India in December 1964 was, by distance traveled, easily the longest journey ever undertaken by a bishop of Rome, four thousand miles each way. The religious and cultural distance was just as great. Of the five hundred million citizens of India at the time, more than 80 percent were Hindus, the vast majority of the rest Muslim. There were barely a million Catholics in the entire country. *L'Osservatore Romano* announced in advance that the pope intended to visit India as a "simple pilgrim." He flew there aboard a regularly scheduled flight on Air India, albeit in a special compartment in front of the jet's first-class cabin. He used personal funds to purchase the $985 ticket.

The trip allowed Paul to demonstrate a human touch he rarely exhibited in Rome. Archbishop Thomas Roberts, an English-born Jesuit who had once led Bombay's archdiocese, had originally advised Paul against the pilgrimage, arguing that displays of Vatican pomp would be vulgar in such an impoverished nation, but Roberts changed his mind. At the council, he had called for the lifting of the ban on birth control, and so he realized it would be useful for the pope to see the "nightmare" of overpopulation for

---

* It was later seen as an empty gesture, since the tiara was never sold off. The pope turned it over to Cardinal Spellman in New York, who donated it for display in the Basilica of the National Shrine of the Immaculate Conception in Washington, DC, next to Catholic University. Spellman argued—unconvincingly, his critics thought—that the display would benefit the poor since it would inspire wealthy donors who saw the crown to give more generously to Catholic charities.

himself. On arrival in Bombay, the pope found himself looking out onto a massive airport crowd, estimated at more than a million people. Overcome, he pressed his hands before his chest in the traditional, prayerlike Indian sign of respect. In the three days that followed, he was frequently moved to tears in gatherings where, it was obvious, the vast majority in the crowd were not Catholics, or even Christians, but rather Hindu and Muslim slum dwellers. In his motorcades, he wrote later, there were so many people to bless along the road that his arm grew weak as he tried to wave. He used a blur of adjectives in remembering the crowds—"poor and spiritual, avid, packed, naked."

His exhilaration after India lasted only a few days. That spring he was overwhelmed with the burden of preparing for the fourth—and, he insisted, final—session of the council. The reforms of the earlier sessions were finally becoming evident to Catholics far from Rome; they could see and hear the changes for themselves. In March, the pope made a visit to a parish church near the Vatican to lead its first Mass in modern Italian. He told parishioners they needed to sacrifice "the beautiful and noble idiom" of Latin in order for the church "to reach everyone in languages they could understand."

He planned to visit New York City in October to speak at the United Nations. He had visited the US as a bishop, but this would be the first trip there by a sitting pope. The US was increasingly in his thoughts, both because of its status as an economic powerhouse—charitable donations from American Catholics were the source of most of the Vatican's day-to-day income—and because the nuclear rivalry between the US and the Soviet Union continued to threaten the world with Armageddon.

In June, the Jesuits elected a new worldwide leader, Father Pedro Arrupe, a fifty-seven-year-old Spaniard. Arrupe, assuming the title of superior general of the Society of Jesus, quickly sought to establish himself as a champion of the reforms of Vatican II. At a news conference in Rome, he told reporters the overriding mission of the Jesuits from that moment on was to improve the lives of "the world's poorest and most despised." His election, three months before the council resumed, was cheered by progressive bishops. It came at a time when they were eager for good news from Rome, since so much else they were hearing suggested disaster.

There were news reports that summer that Ottaviani was tampering yet again with Cardinal Bea's declaration on the Jews. The reports were contradictory but taken together suggested that Paul wanted to revise the document to limit the church's apology to Jews; he worried the original, full-throated confession of the Vatican's past anti-Semitism would be read as criticism of his predecessors, especially Pius XII. The reports came at a time when Paul was already under attack for public remarks seen as appallingly anti-Semitic. In April, in his sermon to mark Palm Sunday, the day memorializing Jesus's arrival in Jerusalem ahead of the Crucifixion, the pope described "the clash between Jesus and the Jewish people" that ended with the Savior's death. Jews had been "predestined to receive the Messiah," yet they "fought him, slandered and injured him and, in the end, killed him." Jewish leaders were stunned, especially since the pope's words revived the idea of Jews as "Christ killers." The Vatican later conceded the sermon could have been more delicately worded.

Among American Catholics, the birth-control debate grew more heated that year, becoming part of a larger struggle over women's rights and sexual freedom. In June, the US Supreme Court overturned state laws that banned artificial contraception, including birth-control pills, and decreed that Americans enjoyed a "right to privacy" in family planning. For many Catholics, the ruling was logical and humane. Several bishops said the government should never have been in the business of regulating women's fertility. "Catholics do not need the support of civil law to be faithful to their religious convictions," said Cardinal Cushing in Boston. "And they do not seek to impose by law their moral views on other members of society."

At the time, American priests complained they were being bombarded with questions from parishioners about why taking oral contraceptives was a sin. The Pill did not kill a living being or interfere with the physical structure of sperm and eggs, so how was that sinful? Many priests were forced to relearn the scriptural justification—the Old Testament story about a minor biblical character named Onan, who refused to impregnate his sister-in-law after his brother's death. (Many twentieth-century theologians were convinced the story was meant to condemn Onan's supposed lack of family loyalty, not birth control. Many also found it strange the Vatican wanted to remind Catholics of an otherwise distasteful scriptural passage about a man pressured to have sex with his brother's widow.)

In an interview that summer, Paul confessed he was "in agony" on the subject. "The church has never in her history confronted such a problem," he said, acknowledging how bizarre it was for celibate churchmen to dwell on questions about the functioning of a woman's body. "This is a strange subject for men of the church to be discussing—even embarrassing." In

1964, at the recommendation of Suenens, he enlarged the birth-control commission from fifteen members to fifty-eight, adding scientists and doctors—as well as, for the first time, women. The new members included an American couple, Patty and Patrick Crowley of Chicago, both in their fifties, who were co-presidents of the Christian Family Movement, a worldwide organization of 150,000 mostly Catholic couples who sought to make the Gospel more relevant to their lives. The logistics and morality of birth control were a regular topic of discussion in the group. After the Crowleys married, they wanted to postpone having children and so used the rhythm method. It meant Patty constantly had to watch the calendar and monitor her temperature to know which days were safe for sex. Both complained it drained spontaneity from their romantic lives. In 1947, while giving birth to their fourth child, Patty hemorrhaged and was left sterile at the age of thirty-three. With pregnancy no longer possible, the Crowleys began to take in foster children; over time, they welcomed fourteen to their home.

The couple eagerly accepted the pope's invitation to join the commission. In advance of traveling to Rome, they sent letters to members of the Christian Family Movement, asking how they had been affected by the church's birth-control ban. The Crowleys were shocked by the responses—of how couples suffered to follow the Vatican's teachings. Because she was sterile, the Crowleys could enjoy a full sex life without worrying about birth control, but Patty could see most couples agonized: "We began to ask ourselves: Does God really demand this of people who are trying to live a good, generous Christian life?"

Some letters were especially moving. One came from a Massachusetts couple who had been married thirteen years and had six children. The husband wrote that the "rhythm method destroys the meaning of the sex act" and "turns what should be a spontaneous expression of spiritual and physical love into mere bodily sexual relief." His wife said she found herself "sullen and resentful of my husband when the time for sexual relations finally comes." Another couple, both in their thirties and married ten years with three children, wrote in a joint letter that "we do not believe that every time a man and wife feel the need to express their love to each other that it is a 'call from God' to raise more kids."

The Crowleys brought one hundred of the letters with them to Rome in March 1965 to share at the first meeting of the newly enlarged commission. They quickly got a taste of the mindset they were up against in the Vatican. On arrival, they were told they would sleep apart. The Curia made no provisions for married couples to live together. Pat was assigned to a men's dormitory, while Patty and the other four women commissioners were taken to a convent a mile away. Patty tried to make light of it: "I guess that's one way to solve this problem."

Another new commissioner, John Noonan, a theologian and law professor at the University of Notre Dame, had just published a book on birth control and offered the other commissioners a two-hour lecture on his research. The Vatican's ban had always represented a misreading of scripture, he was convinced. The four Gospels said "not a word" about birth control. He explained that the Vatican initially banned crude contraceptive methods in the twelfth century in a frenzied reaction to apocalyptic Christian sects that believed the world was evil and so, therefore, was procreation. Later, Noonan said, the church kept the ban in place as a way of guaranteeing childbirth during famine.

There were now several physicians on the panel, all of them devout Catholics. They were quizzed about the functioning of the birth-control pill and other contraceptive methods, including the so-called intrauterine device, or IUD. The doctors were asked if they believed the Pill or IUD interfered with bodily functions in a way that defied church doctrine. Their unanimous conclusion: most birth-control methods were no more a violation of a human body than dozens of intrusive medical procedures the Vatican had permitted for years, including open-heart surgery and organ transplants. The panel's doctors appeared ready to urge the pope to overturn the ban.

On the last day of the commission's meetings that year, its members were invited to an audience with Paul VI. He told them he had great confidence in their work and encouraged them to debate "in complete objectivity and liberty of spirit." The Crowleys were honored to be in his presence, although they were both struck that, in his prepared remarks, the pope referred to the commission members several times as his "dear brothers." The Crowleys wondered if the pope had failed to notice that five women were sitting there, too.

KÜNG'S CELEBRITY kept growing. The Holy Office's unofficial ban on his books remained in effect in Italy in 1965, but in much of the rest of the world his writings crowded bookstore shelves. An editor in his British publishing house referred to him as "the Catholic Elvis," given the excitement he created. His publishers were disappointed when he announced he was unavailable for promotion that spring and had stopped accepting speaking invitations so he could ready himself for the final session of Vatican II. The meetings that fall would be the last opportunity—in his lifetime, he believed—to achieve what many bishops identified as their central goal: the creation of a parliament to give them a permanent voice in Rome. Küng was not optimistic, fearing that progressives who had "won so many battles at the council will finally lose the war."

In July, a French bishop wrote to Küng to warn of rumors that Paul VI was maneuvering to kill the idea of a bishops' parliament—to prevent it from being debated at all. He urged Küng to publish something quickly to keep the proposal alive. Küng replied with a defiant essay in the German newspaper *Frankfurter Allgemeine Zeitung* that pleaded for greater democracy in the church and, specifically, for a bishops' parliament. Within days, the essay was republished across Europe and the US.

The pope was even more agitated with Küng after the essay. Yves Congar heard from a senior Curia official that, behind closed doors, the pope often praised Küng and Ratzinger as two of the brightest young theologians in the world, the sort of scholars who would normally be recruited to work in the Vatican. But Küng's writings about the council proved that he, unlike Ratzinger, was a man "without love" for the church, the pope reportedly said. "He loves the truth—but has he any mercy for human beings?"

The council's final session began on September 14. At the opening ceremony, several familiar faces were gone; seventy bishops had died since the year before, a jarring reminder of how old and frail so much of the hierarchy was. The pope arrived for the ceremony by foot, the portable throne finally abandoned. The bishops were muted as he passed into St. Peter's, reflecting the indifference and, in some cases, outright hostility so many felt toward him.

Paul had a surprise that morning. In his speech, he announced the "happy news" that he was creating a new institution, the Synod of Bishops, that would allow the world's churchmen to have their voices heard in the Vatican after the council was over. In his typically hazy language, he portrayed the "synod" as a sort of mini-council. Bishops from different regions would elect local delegates to go to Rome to represent them. Many in the audience turned to one another, trying to figure out what this meant. "Synod" was a word traditionally used to describe a one-time meeting of senior churchmen to debate a particular issue; yet the pope suggested this synod would meet regularly.

By the end of his speech, it was clear this was a move by the pope to pre-empt any debate about a true bishops' parliament. He said he alone would control the timing of synod meetings and the issues they addressed. They would be convened "according to the needs of the church, by the Roman pontiff." And whatever the synod was, he said, it would not displace the power of the Curia, to which "we owe so much gratitude."

Curia bishops in the audience were thrilled, since it appeared the Vatican's bureaucracy would survive the council intact. Although the synod was far from what they had dreamed of, many reform-minded bishops made an instant calculation this was the best they could hope for. Ratzinger tried to be optimistic. If the synod meetings proved ultimately to be a "permanent council in miniature," he said, this was welcome news. Seated nearby, Küng had no similar hope. He saw the pope's announcement as a ploy to block the bishops from ever claiming any power in Rome. Ultimately, he suspected, these "synods" would "not have the slightest capacity to make decisions," a prediction that proved to be largely correct.

The pope had promised the year before that the Declaration on Religious Freedom, ultimately entitled *Dignitatis Humanae* (On Human Dignity), would be the first item on the council's agenda, and it was. American bishops were thrilled that the latest draft retained passages—written largely by an American Jesuit theologian, John Courtney Murray—that brought the church into line with the US Constitution. "This right of the human person to religious freedom is to be recognized in constitutional law," it read. "It is to become a civil right." The pope endorsed the declaration and asked for a vote before he left for New York and his speech to the UN. He thought its adoption would be seen as proof of the church's newfound commitment to religious tolerance. In a preliminary vote on September 21, 1,997 bishops voted in favor, 224 opposed. (A final vote was scheduled for December, when only 70 bishops voted against the document.)

The pope's trip to New York, which began on October 4, lasted only thirty-six hours. He left the papal palace early that morning, with his speech at UN headquarters in Manhattan set for that afternoon. In order to avoid any suggestion he was meddling in American politics, he declined to be met by President Lyndon Johnson on arrival at the newly renamed John F. Kennedy International Airport. Instead, they met privately at the Waldorf Astoria Hotel. The UN speech, delivered in the pope's elegant French, was widely praised. Much of it focused on his call for global disarmament. "No more war!" he declared. "It is peace that must guide the destiny of the people of the world." The moment in the speech that disappointed many in the audience—and, doubtless, many married Catholic couples around the world—came when the pope acknowledged the threat of global overpopulation and insisted the answer was increased food production, not family planning. It would be "irrational" to support population control, he continued, since that would reduce "the number of those sharing in the banquet of life." The remark was widely taken as evidence he intended to keep the birth-control ban in place, no matter what his commission recommended.

His whirlwind trip included a motorcade across Manhattan, where tens of thousands of New Yorkers gathered on street corners to catch a glimpse of the first pope to set foot on American soil. The motorcade route began in Harlem and ended at St. Patrick's Cathedral on Fifth Avenue. Inside the cathedral, he was greeted with applause as he walked past pews crowded with famous American Catholics, including Jacqueline Kennedy. (It was later reported that the pope had insisted on the motorcade, despite security concerns. His limousine was covered by a plastic bubble top that was not bulletproof, which meant he was not much better protected than Mrs. Kennedy's husband had been in his motorcade in Dallas two years earlier.)

There was an open-air Mass that evening at Yankee Stadium in the Bronx, attended by ninety thousand people. Press coverage was glowing. Columnist Walter Lippmann of the *New York Herald Tribune* wrote that, after centuries of isolation, "the church has finally brought itself into the mainstream of human affairs." After an overnight flight back to Rome, the pope appeared at St. Peter's, where he received thunderous applause as he delivered a brief speech on the trip's significance.

The council was in session that day, deep in debate over "The Church in the Modern World," the document that was supposed to address the most pressing issues of the twentieth century. Its tone remained defiantly positive, as reflected in its Latin title, *Gaudium et Spes* (Joy and Hope). It was more easily discussed than other council documents because it was initially written in French, a necessity since Latin lacked so many words needed to address modern issues. (There was no Latin expression, for example, for "nuclear war.")

The debate lasted for weeks and drew bishops into discussions that would once have been scandalous. That included an argument on the value of psychiatry, which the Vatican had long likened to witchcraft. A group of European-educated bishops from Mexico wanted *Gaudium et Spes* to endorse Freudian psychoanalysis and honor Sigmund Freud by name. (That would not happen, although the document did praise advances in psychology.) Others wanted the document to question the church's strict marriage laws. An Egyptian archbishop of the Melkite Church spoke of the agony of women deserted by adulterous husbands, who, because of the Vatican's ban on divorce, could never remarry unless their estranged spouses died. (Ultimately, those concerns were not addressed in the final document, either.)

Several bishops made one last attempt to revive the debate over priestly celibacy. Bishop Alfred-Jean-Félix Ancel of France gave a daring speech in a meeting hall near the Vatican—he would have been forbidden from making it in St. Peter's—in which he warned of a future worldwide "scandal of unfaithful priests" who took mistresses or even committed sexual crimes. Mandatory celibacy created a "psychosis" among priests, he declared. A Brazilian bishop published an essay calling for the Vatican to allow priests to marry in parts of South America where the priest shortage was most dire: "It is urgent that the number of priests in Latin America be multiplied a hundredfold."

The pope tried to shut down that debate once and for all on October 11, when he declared in a written statement that the doctrine of priestly celibacy would be retained so long as he was pope: "We not only intend to maintain this ancient, holy and providential law to the extent of our ability, but also to reinforce its observance." Ratzinger said later that he had understood the pope's decision, since a celibacy debate in the final weeks of the council would create a "climate of sensationalism" at a time when there was so much else to do. Still, Ratzinger felt sure the church would need to confront the issue someday, given the global priest shortage: "Evading it is impossible." Küng was, predictably, "disgusted" that the pope had silenced the world's bishops on such a fundamental subject as celibacy: "It is as if one were at a totalitarian party congress."

Küng's own freedom of speech remained in jeopardy. In early October, he was handed a typewritten summons from the Holy Office demanding he appear before Ottaviani. The reason for the meeting was not stated, but Küng was sure the cardinal wanted to join with the pope in condemning what he had written about the council.

He arrived at the Palace of the Holy Office several minutes before his noon appointment on October 14 and was ushered into a reception area outside the cardinal's suite of offices, which were furnished as Küng had expected, with baroque, oversized, age-worn furniture. The walls were covered with paintings of Ottaviani's predecessors, including some of the bishops who had once held the informal title of grand inquisitor.

At exactly 12:00, as the bells in St. Peter's began to chime, Ottaviani announced his presence when double doors leading to his inner office were thrown open and there he stood, "in all his purple splendor," Küng recalled. There were no words of welcome. Instead, in what Küng was convinced was an effort to intimidate him, Ottaviani burst into loud prayer in Latin: "Angelus Domini nuntiavit Mariae" (An angel of the Lord announced to Mary). Küng recognized it as the opening to a traditional prayer and responded in equally fluent, if German-accented, Latin: "Et concepit de Spiritu Sancto" (And she conceived by the Holy Spirit).

The two men stood there, continuing to pray for several more seconds. Finally, the cardinal invited Küng to take a seat in a stiff-backed chair in the center of the room. Ottaviani had lost most of the sight in one eye, "so he stares all the more at me with the other," Küng recalled.

The cardinal began the discussion, in Italian, by ordering Küng not to speak to the press about their meeting. Küng was not surprised by the demand, since "there is nothing that the Inquisition fears more than publicity," and agreed. Ottaviani then launched into an attack on Küng's recent writings, especially those critical of the pope, and suggested Küng was putting his career in danger. Küng listened for several minutes as the cardinal listed "all the Roman precepts, dogmas and principles" that required theologians to pledge total obedience to the Vatican.

Küng thought the tirade was proof of why, so long as Ottaviani and men like him clung to power in the Curia, the world's Catholics would never achieve the more tolerant, democratic church that so many of them prayed for. Even so, Küng realized as he sat there that he felt genuine pity for the cardinal: "He has grown old in the service of the Curia, is almost blind, and hopelessly left behind by the development of theology and the church."

After several more minutes of Ottaviani's harangue, Küng tried to interject: "Eminence, may I now also say something?"

"Yes, yes, go ahead."

"Eminence, you know I'm still young." Küng repeated it for emphasis: "I'm still young." It was a gentle plea for an old churchman to be forgiving of a young one whose mistakes might be explained by inexperience.

"Yes, yes, you're still young," Ottaviani said. "And when I was still young, I did many things I didn't do later." He seemed to soften.

The conversation instantly took on a gentler tone, Küng remembered. "I had spoken to his heart, and he had opened it up a little to me."

He was relieved when Ottaviani abruptly ended the conversation and suggested there would be no recommendation for discipline of Küng, at least not then. In a sense, the cardinal got what he wanted from the encounter since Küng decided as he left the meeting that, for the time being, he would temper his public criticism of Paul VI; he *had* been too tough. The pope might be a "prisoner of the Roman system," but he was still a godly, well-intentioned man.

It occurred to Küng that he should make that point to Paul himself, face-to-face. In November, he wrote to request a papal audience. To his amazement, he recalled, he got an answer within days: "It is positive. Pope Paul VI is immediately ready to receive me." It would be "just the two of us, in a private audience."

MOST THEOLOGIANS at the council marveled at the commitment of Yves Congar. No other theologian could claim credit for having drafted and edited so many of the documents that became the written legacy of Vatican II. It came at a terrible cost to his health, however. By his own account, he worked every waking hour, seven days a week, when the council was in session. In his 1965 diary, he documented how his sixty-one-year-old body was falling apart. Since his four years in a Nazi POW camp, he had never known a day without physical pain, and in the final weeks of the council his

Yves Congar of France, a Dominican friar and reform-minded theologian, whose banishment by the Holy Office was ended when Pope John XXIII named him an official papal theological expert at Vatican II

body ached like never before: "I cannot lift my right leg more than three centimeters. I slide it along the ground." He compared himself to a "tree struck by lightning—no longer alive, except for a few centimeters of bark."

The emotional exhaustion was worse, he admitted in his diary. He was plagued by the loneliness common to churchmen after middle age. He had friendships with other clerics, but there was nothing intimate about them. What kept him alive that year were his contributions to Vatican II. "Basically, I love the work and the atmosphere," he wrote. He was heartened by his continuing encounters with so many bright young churchmen, beginning with Küng and Ratzinger. Ultimately, he was dazzled by the young Polish bishop Karol Wojtyła, who had once seemed so unimpressive. Others complained that Wojtyła was difficult to understand in discussions about doctrine—he seemed to speak in riddles—but Congar thought that was simply a reflection of the Pole's university training, which was mostly in philosophy, not theology. By the end of the council, "Wojtyła made a very great impression," Congar said. "His personality is imposing. A power radiates from it." He could see Paul VI had taken a special interest in Wojtyła, too. In the 1920s, the pope had served briefly as a Vatican diplomat in Poland, and so it was not surprising he paid special attention to Polish bishops at the council. And Wojtyła was easily the most impressive of them.

Congar's notoriety in Rome brought him under attack during the council, and it unnerved him. In 1965, he was the target of a "filthy Italian conservative rag"—the magazine *Lo Specchio* (The Mirror)—that described him as "an agent of introducing Marxism into the church." He comforted himself by remembering all the encounters in Rome in which prominent churchmen, including his friend Paul VI, showered him with praise for his contributions to the council. Congar took his greatest pride at Vatican II from his role in drafting *Gaudium et Spes*. He was especially pleased with its gracefully worded opening passage, which called for Catholics to recognize the "joys and hopes" and the "griefs and anxieties" of the modern world.

In the council's final weeks, the pope sent word he wanted passage of what was now called the Declaration on the Relation of the Church to Non-Christian Religions—the document meant to answer John XXIII's plea for an end to centuries of hostility toward Jews. It had been rewritten, again, since the last session, and its title had changed as well. While it continued to focus on Judaism, the words "Judaism" and "Jews" had been removed from the title; Ottaviani described that as an effort to appease

Arab Christians and Muslim governments. The new version further limited the Vatican's apology to Jews. While it deplored "all hatreds, persecutions and displays of anti-Semitism," the new draft revived the idea that at least some Jews were responsible for the Crucifixion. While it was wrong to blame "Jewish people indiscriminately" for Jesus's execution, it alleged that Jews in ancient Jerusalem had indeed "pressed for the death of Christ."

The final draft represented a compromise by Bea. With so little time left, he and other reform-minded bishops decided to accept the flawed version of the document rather than risk no document at all. In a final speech to the council, he admitted his disappointment but urged that the declaration, ultimately given the Latin title *Nostra Aetate* (In Our Time), be recognized as the breakthrough that it was. The church was finally apologizing to the Jewish people, even if the apology was less than complete.

Even this more limited document had opponents, including bishops who, to the mortification of their peers, continued to express flagrant anti-Semitism. There was a last-minute effort by a reactionary Italian bishop, Luigi Maria Carli, to scrap the declaration entirely because, he argued, the condemnation of Jews had always been justified. He said he believed all Jews—living, dead, and yet to be born—were a "cursed" people and should forever bear responsibility for Christ's death.

The final vote to approve *Nostra Aetate* was 1,763 to 243. Prominent Jewish groups welcomed the declaration as proof the church desired a new relationship with their faith. The American Jewish Committee hailed the vote as an "act of justice long overdue."

AS VATICAN II WOUND DOWN, the pope had other decisions to make, including how to respond to the campaign by many bishops for instant sainthood for John XXIII. Paul's answer disappointed them. It came in a speech to the council on November 18, when he announced he would open the beatification process for his predecessor, but "nothing will be done in haste," and it would not be for John alone. Paul revealed that Pius XII would be a candidate for sainthood at the same time. There was enthusiastic applause, although many progressive bishops were aghast that canonization of John XXIII was now paired with that of his divisive predecessor.

Paul maneuvered to win passage of *Gaudium et Spes*, but on his terms. At the last minute, he wanted to rewrite the passages about sex, demanding that the final draft include wording that explicitly reaffirmed the ban on artificial contraception. Many bishops were furious, both that the pope was again trying to limit their freedom of speech and that he was, effectively, ordering them to take a stand against birth control. Some wanted to reject his editing demands. Ultimately, there was a compromise—the insertion of a passage that noted the birth-control commission was still at work and therefore "the council has no intention of proposing concrete solutions at this moment."

In the final debate about the document, several bishops realized to their horror that it said almost nothing to promote the role of Catholic women. Archbishop Paul Hallinan of Atlanta, Georgia, submitted last-minute amendments that called for nuns to be recruited to important positions in the Curia, but his amendments were rejected without debate. He was told that Ottaviani and other conservatives feared his proposal might encourage a larger discussion about the status of women, including whether they could someday be ordained. "Women priests—*that* was their nightmare," a livid Hallinan told other bishops.

On December 7, in the final hours of the council, *Gaudium et Spes* was approved by a vote of 2,307 to 75.

It was later described by many bishops and theologians as the most important document adopted at Vatican II, since it placed the church on record in support of social justice campaigns that championed the rights of "all those who are poor or in any way afflicted." They were the sorts of campaigns—for civil rights, labor rights, and voting rights—that the Vatican had once rejected as dangerously political. Within months, American bishops regularly cited *Gaudium et Spes* in sermons urging parishioners to become active in the nation's civil rights movement. Latin American bishops often cited it as the inspiration for a wildly popular social-justice movement that took hold across the Southern Hemisphere and became known as liberation theology.

In the council's last days, the pope signaled he was finally serious about reforming the Curia. His actions seemed groundbreaking at first. On December 6, two days before the closing ceremony, he announced he was restructuring the Holy Office. It would have a new name—the Congregation for the Doctrine of the Faith—and, significantly, it would no longer be labeled "supreme" among Vatican agencies. Ottaviani remained in place, but the congregation's central, centuries-old mission of hunting down heretics would be sharply curtailed. Instead, it would be responsible, above all else, for finding new, better, more optimistic ways to preach the Gospel.

There would be no more secret investigations and closed trials for suspected dissidents, Paul declared. Churchmen facing punishment would be
given due process, including the right to defend themselves. The Index of
Prohibited Books was abolished. Ottaviani and his colleagues could "disap-
prove" of books, but no longer ban them. For the rest of his life, Ottaviani
described the announcement as a *giorno nero* (black day) in the history of
the church.

The pope also revealed a historic move toward Christian unity: after
secret negotiations, the Vatican and the world's Orthodox churches would
formally make peace—more than nine hundred years after they split in
the Great Schism. Their differences were "consigned to oblivion," Paul
declared. The pope and the Orthodox leader, Patriarch Athenagoras,
announced jointly they would lift the excommunication orders that their
predecessors had imposed on one another in 1054. The ceremony to do so
took place on December 7, the final business day of the council, when the
pope appeared in St. Peter's alongside a black-robed Orthodox patriarch.
The two men embraced.

The closing ceremony of the Second Vatican Council was held the next
day in St. Peter's Square. The pope thanked the bishops: "Go forth and
meet mankind, taking with you the Good News of Christ's Gospel and
the renewal of the church." He urged them to promote the council's "pro-
digious accomplishments," especially its call for Catholics to rededicate
themselves to the poor.

Congar thought the ceremony was magnificent, but he was disturbed
that it centered on the pope, not the bishops. "The pope got all the attention," he wrote. "He appeared not so much to be *in* the church as *above*
it." While Congar wanted to believe the pope's words about an expanded
commitment to the poor, he had been unnerved the day before when he
learned that every one of the more than twenty-five hundred bishops at the
council had been given an expensive parting gift from the pope: a gold ring
engraved with an image of Jesus standing alongside St. Peter and St. Paul.
He was shown one of the heavy rings, which he bounced in the palm of
his hand, and wondered why no one recognized the hypocrisy of making
thousands of gold rings when so many millions of the faithful could not
feed themselves. "How can one still talk about the church of the poor?" he
asked himself with disgust.

11

"You Must Trust Me"

I N THE FINAL WEEKS of the council, the pope held farewell meetings in the Apostolic Palace with the bishops' delegations from several large countries. In most of those meetings, he heard expressions of wild enthusiasm for the results of Vatican II, especially the council's decision to end the exclusive use of Latin. Among the European delegations, one was notably unenthusiastic, however—the bishops of Poland, who sought to remind the pope how differently they viewed their faith. Their papal audience on November 13 was attended by thirty-eight bishops, led by the country's only cardinal, Stefan Wyszyński of Warsaw. The sixty-four-year-old cardinal, easily the most popular man in Poland, was widely credited with the church's survival in the face of communist persecution after World War II. In the meeting, he pleaded with the pope to excuse the Polish church hierarchy from being forced to enact the council's major reforms. He warned that the changes, especially an end to the Latin Mass, would be too disruptive in his deeply devout but tradition-bound country: "Our request may appear very presumptuous, but it is difficult to judge our situation from afar." Paul was startled and rejected the request on the spot, telling Wyszyński the council's decisions would be enforced "energetically and willingly" in Poland, as everywhere else.

The pope was relieved when he granted a separate one-on-one audience that week to Bishop Wojtyła of Krakow, considered far more open-minded than Wyszyński and seen as the only true intellectual among Poland's church leaders. It was the first time the pope had a significant conversation with Wojtyła, and it gave Paul VI a chance to experience the magnetism of the youthful Polish bishop for himself. It was the beginning of a friendship that, two years later, would lead to the pope's decision to raise Wojtyła to the College of Cardinals at the age of forty-seven.

A FEW DAYS AFTER his conversation with Wojtyła, the pope had a far less cordial meeting with Hans Küng—the one that Küng requested after his showdown with Ottaviani. Küng's papal audience was scheduled for December 2, at 12:15 p.m., and he arrived a few minutes early. Because he still had a badge identifying him as an official papal theologian, he could move easily around the Vatican and bypass security posts, so he walked straight into the palace and took the elevator to the pope's apartment on the third floor. He nodded to the Swiss Guards. "They recognized me as one of their countrymen and saluted in a friendly way."

At the door, he was met by one of the pope's secretaries, and together they walked through several large rooms that had been tastefully modernized by Paul VI on the recommendation of famed architects he befriended in Milan. The walls, once red and gold, had been repainted in muted colors, mostly gray and beige. It was a stark contrast to the fusty Old World furnishings that Küng had seen in Ottaviani's office a few weeks earlier. Küng heard a mysterious tinkling of bells, apparently to signal his arrival, as he entered a reception area to a larger room: the pope's personal library, with bookshelves stacked floor to ceiling.

Paul was seated at his desk, near the door, examining papers. He raised his head and looked toward his guest, offering a tentative smile. Küng was immediately struck, as he had been with Ottaviani, at how human the man in front of him seemed, less stiff and intimidating than he appeared in public.

The meeting had been carefully staged. "Evidently, the Holy Father had thought hard about how to conduct the conversation," Küng recalled. The pope, speaking in Italian, first commended Küng for his many *doni*—gifts—as a theologian. He said he was impressed by Küng's ability "to present the Christian truth in public beyond the *mura della Chiesa* [the walls of the church]." Küng was delighted by the praise, which he had not expected.

Then the pope's smile disappeared. "But when I look over everything you have written, I would really prefer that you had written nothing," he said. Küng, he suggested, had damaged the faith with his "irresponsible" campaign to promote democracy in the church.

Küng tried to stay calm. He remembered the pope then offered him a "slightly ironic smile." Küng thought it was probably similar to the way "the Caesars smiled at poor poets" who faced execution because their work displeased the emperor.

The pope urged Küng to consider giving up his teaching career in Germany and come to the Vatican: "How much good you could do if you were to put your great gifts at the service of the church."

"But I'm already at the service of the church," Küng said.

The pope: "You must trust me."

"I trust *you*," Küng replied, "but I do not trust those around you."

The pope seemed astonished by such directness. He insisted Küng should not be wary of working in Rome. At the start, he would encounter "many unknown, closed dark faces, but these would light up when they get to know you." Paul made no direct threat to Küng's career, but his message was obvious: whatever path Küng followed, he needed to tone down his criticism of the Vatican.

The meeting, scheduled to last fifteen minutes, went on for nearly an hour. When it did end, Küng said, the pope bid him "farewell with great friendliness" and gave him a rosary of white pearls for his mother.

MOST BISHOPS RETURNED home in glory after the council, seen by their parishioners as having helped the Vatican end centuries of isolation. Ratzinger resumed his teaching duties at Münster, welcomed back on campus as a hero. Almost as soon as he settled in, he was the target of a flattering job offer from Küng. Much as Ratzinger had tried to recruit Küng to Münster, the roles were now reversed; Küng wanted Ratzinger to come to Tübingen so they could teach together.

Ratzinger eagerly accepted, if only because Tübingen was hundreds of miles closer to his beloved Bavaria. He and his sister, who remained his housekeeper, arrived in Tübingen in the spring of 1966 and "the magic of this small town soon worked its spell."

Students were struck by the differences between the two professors—the bashful Ratzinger, the boisterous Küng—and it was a topic of joking on campus. Ratzinger brought his bicycle from Münster and rode it to class. Küng got around in his Alfa Romeo Giulia sports car, a purchase made possible by his best-selling books. (He was defensive about the car, insisting he chose it not for its flashy looks but because of its "advanced technology and safety," a claim that caused friends to roll their eyes.) Küng offered Ratzinger a ride when the weather was bad. They regularly dined in each other's home.

Küng's fame brought a troubling new development to his life—death threats and blackmail attempts, usually by letter. The messages were "quite repulsive," he remembered. Typical were anonymous, typewritten notes warning him that in times past, his provocative writings would have led to his church-approved execution. One letter was so threatening that the police consulted with a psychologist. In another case, detectives quizzed his faculty colleagues about what brands of typewriter they used. Some letters insinuated there was something sinful about Küng's friendships with local women. He assured his colleagues at the time that he never betrayed his celibacy vows: "There are no skeletons in my cupboard." He said he came under suspicion simply because, unlike so many misogynists in the priesthood, he actually enjoyed the company of the opposite sex.

AFTER VATICAN II, there was excitement among progressive Catholics that other reforms might come quickly. In 1966, the Vatican announced an easing of the rules for marriage between Catholics and non-Catholics, while lifting the excommunication of thousands of Catholics once banished from the church because of their mixed marriages. The Vatican also announced that year that bishops could decide for themselves if their parishioners should continue to honor the ancient ban on eating meat on Fridays as a sign of penitence. The doctrine dated from the church's early history.*

Among Europeans, the five million Catholics of the Netherlands, who made up about 40 percent of the nation's population, were especially eager for reform. Dutch bishops intended to exercise the authority they thought they had been given at the council and demand change. "It's in the nature of the Dutch to speak frankly," said Cardinal Alfrink, the country's most powerful churchman, who was best remembered from Vatican II for daring to cut off Ottaviani's microphone. In 1965, as the council was ending, Dutch bishops put theologians to work on a document—a so-called catechism—to bring the Gospels' message up to date. The idea, the authors said, was to explain the Bible in easy-to-understand language and "make

---

* The end of meatless Fridays damaged the American fishing industry, which had come to depend on the once-a-week Catholic market. Three years earlier, the McDonald's chain of fast-food restaurants introduced the Filet-O-Fish sandwich in part to satisfy Catholics.

the message of Jesus Christ sound as new as it is." The document, more than six hundred pages long, strayed far from traditional Vatican teachings. It stated flatly, for example, that the Bible was never meant to be taken literally: the New Testament was misunderstood as "some sort of scientific manual" when it was in fact largely a set of fables "written to throw God's light on the existing world." The catechism questioned the existence of angels and whether the Virgin Mary had really remained a virgin. It called for tolerance of homosexuality and Marxism and said that, while the papal commission continued to deliberate, Catholics should be permitted to use birth control. *De Nieuwe Katechismus* sold four hundred thousand copies in the Netherlands before it was translated into thirty-two other languages. The seventy-five-thousand-copy first printing of an American edition in English sold out in three weeks.

The excitement created by Vatican II helped explain something remarkable among Dutch Catholics: they mostly stopped going to confession. With bishops telling them that birth control and other once-forbidden acts were not sins, the reasons for confessing had disappeared. Dutch priests largely abandoned wearing white collars. Alfrink simplified his wardrobe, too, and began dressing in a plain black suit. Of the country's 5,000 priests, 1,750 joined in a public statement calling for an end to mandatory celibacy. Dutch bishops said they hoped that issue would be debated when Paul VI called bishops together at the first of the synods he had promised, scheduled for September 1967.

The Dutch hierarchy quickly came under siege by the Vatican. Within months of publication of the catechism, its principal author, Father Edward Schillebeeckx (pronounced skil-e-bayks), a Dominican theologian, was placed under investigation by the newly renamed Congregation for the Doctrine of the Faith. The congregation insisted it was honoring the new, less punitive mandate it had been given by the pope after Vatican II, but that the catechism was just too provocative to ignore.

The global priest shortage grew worse after the council. As of 1970, the Vatican had more than ten thousand pending applications from priests around the world who wanted to be relieved of their vows, the process known as laicization. Most wanted to marry. The call by Dutch priests for an end to mandatory celibacy was heard elsewhere, including in the United States. In New York City in 1966, thirty-one priests made a joint announcement that they no longer felt bound by their vows and believed they were free to marry.

The celibacy debate continued to gnaw at Küng, especially after what he discovered at Vatican II about the rampant hypocrisy of so many bishops. He was not some sort of "gossipmonger," as he put it, but he told friends he had been astonished to discover how many powerful churchmen ignored their celibacy vows, some of them shamelessly. That was true even in his own profession. At the council, Karl Rahner—who remained, apart from Küng himself, the most celebrated Catholic theologian teaching in Germany—argued in his writings that priests needed to dedicate themselves fully to God through chastity. Yet for more than twenty years, beginning in 1962, he carried on a passionate romance with a German writer named Luise Rinser, and it was no secret to other theologians at Vatican II. The couple often met in Rome. After his death, she published a book of some of her more than four thousand love letters to Rahner. (The Jesuit order in Germany refused to allow his equally voluminous correspondence—he wrote to her as often as four times a day—to be made public.) Her letters suggested his feelings of intimacy overwhelmed him. In a 1962 letter, she wrote: "I cannot express how shaken I was as you knelt before me. We are both touched in the innermost part of our being by something that is much

Cardinal Francis Spellman of New York with presidential candidates John Kennedy and Richard Nixon at the Alfred E. Smith Memorial Dinner, New York, 1960

stronger than we anticipated." Her letters offered no proof of a physical relationship, and Rinser was coy on that question.

In the United States, several of the nation's best-known churchmen were widely known to violate their celibacy oaths, although major news organizations would almost never pursue the story, if only out of fear of offending Catholic readers and advertisers. It was common knowledge among his parishioners in Chicago that Cardinal John Cody had been in a decades-long relationship with a woman, sometimes referred to as a distant relative. The relationship became the target of a federal grand-jury investigation. Criminal prosecutors working for the Justice Department demonstrated that Cody funneled as much as $1 million to the woman from church funds, allowing her to purchase a luxury vacation home in Florida, where they spent holidays together. Millions of dollars in no-bid church contracts were awarded to her son's businesses. The criminal investigation ended only because of Cody's death in 1982.

Cardinal Spellman of New York, the city's archbishop from 1939 until 1967, was for years the target of credible allegations that he violated his celibacy vows with men. Clarence Tripp, a respected psychologist associated with Indiana University's Institute for Sex Research, the pioneering research center founded by Alfred Kinsey, tracked down a Broadway dancer who was the subject of the most persistent rumors. Tripp was convinced that the male dancer, who was regularly chauffeured around Manhattan in the cardinal's limousine, had been in a long-term sexual relationship with Spellman. The American journalist Lucian Truscott IV reported that, when he was an army cadet at West Point in the 1960s, he was groped when he and two other cadets interviewed the cardinal for a student magazine. "Spellman put his hand on my thigh and started moving it toward my crotch," Truscott wrote. "He was just about to reach my private parts when a monsignor, who was standing behind him, reached over his shoulder, grabbed his wrist and put his hand back in his lap, as if this was a common occurrence." Allegations about Spellman's sexuality were due to be published in 1984 in a biography by a former reporter for *The Wall Street Journal*. The New York archdiocese pressured the publisher to remove the material. The pressure campaign was led by Spellman's longtime secretary, Monsignor Eugene Clark. There was no little irony when Clark, who went on to become rector of St. Patrick's Cathedral in Manhattan, was forced to resign from that post after New York tabloids revealed his affair with a female secretary.

Spellman began his career in 1916 as a protégé to Boston's most powerful churchman—then-Archbishop William O'Connell, later a cardinal. Years after O'Connell's death, a scholarly biography published by the University of Notre Dame reported that he was well known in Boston to be a sexually active homosexual. According to the book, he also tolerated sexual activity by favored heterosexual priests, including two on his staff who were secretly married.

When he arrived at the Vatican in 1967, Rembert Weakland, a Pennsylvania-born Benedictine monk, was happily ignorant of all this sexual hypocrisy. In fact, Weakland, who had just turned forty, tried to put the whole subject of sex out of his mind. That year, especially, he was overwhelmed with exciting new work. He moved to Rome after his election as worldwide leader of the fourteen-hundred-year-old Benedictine order. At first, most of his free time in the Vatican was spent performing or listening to classical music; he played several instruments and held a master's degree from the Juilliard School of Music in New York. He said that at the time, he had never touched another human being with passion, so "my only emotional outlet was my music."

He entered a seminary in 1940, at the age of thirteen, with plans to become a priest; he eventually chose to become a monk because he preferred the quieter, more cloistered life of a monastery. As a teenager, he feared he was gay. He was sexually attracted to men, although he hoped it was just a phase. "No one then used the phrase 'sexual orientation' back then," he remembered of his early seminary years. "If there was homosexual activity among my fellow students, I knew nothing about it." Still, there was a traumatic period in his junior year when one of his priest-teachers began molesting students. The priest was ousted from the school, but his victims were forced out, too. Some boys left voluntarily, others were expelled. The school offered them no counseling or other help. Weakland remembered that "the prevailing view about them was, 'They will forget all about it as they grow older.'"

Before arriving at the Vatican, Weakland did not find it difficult to suppress his sexuality, even as so many other churchmen found it impossible. He watched as friends left the church to marry. Their departure, he said, left behind two types of priests and monks: those who grew old gracefully and "lived full and positive celibate lives," and those who could not. "I observed many aging monks and nuns who seemed like dried-up old prunes. Their celibacy may have been perfectly intact, but their lives seemed a caricature of what God intended."

When he left for Rome in 1967, he was convinced he chose the right path, but the Eternal City proved to be a delightful jolt to his senses and he began to think differently about himself: "I was becoming acutely aware that I, too, was a sexual being. It became evident to me that the celibate commitment was not one of avoiding evil, but of giving up what was enriching and good."

His sexual awakening was poorly timed. That same year, Paul VI decided to make a definitive statement about the need to preserve priestly celibacy. In June, he released an encyclical that reaffirmed the doctrine as a "brilliant jewel" that "retains its value undiminished." Ironically, much of the document was a catalog of compelling arguments *against* mandatory celibacy. It noted the Gospels made no demand for it. Stranger still, Paul acknowledged that lifelong celibacy could do serious emotional damage to some priests, leaving them "in a situation that is physically and psychologically detrimental to the development of a mature and well-balanced human person." He insisted the church needed to enforce celibacy to preserve its own credibility, since reversing doctrine would be a dangerous admission that earlier popes who championed the doctrine were capable of error. "The church of the West cannot weaken her faithful observance of Her own tradition," he wrote. In the encyclical, he admitted he was condemning many priests to lives of despair. He urged them to remember that "Christ, too, in the most tragic hours of his life, was alone."

At the time, the world's Catholics were still awaiting a decision on birth control. In 1966, the pope's commission entered its fourth year of deliberations. He added sixteen cardinals and bishops to the panel in March and appointed one as its new chairman: Ottaviani, the Vatican's most outspoken opponent of artificial contraception. Anticipating a furor over naming Ottaviani, the pope also added noted liberals to the panel, including Cardinals Suenens and Döpfner. The fast-rising Archbishop Wojtyła of Poland was named a member as well. There was no suggestion at the time he had uncompromising views on birth control. In fact, he seemed surprisingly enlightened about sexuality. In 1960, he published a book in his homeland entitled *Love and Responsibility*, in which he argued that sex in a loving marriage had a value well beyond procreation.

The commission's final meetings were scheduled to begin in April 1966 and last three months, when a report would be sent to the pope. The Crowleys, the American couple, returned to the Vatican convinced that birth control did not violate church teachings and that Catholics deserved the right to control the size of their families. Back in Rome they were relieved that, this time, they did not need to sleep apart. The Curia found them an apartment with a double bed. In the meetings, they were honored and intimidated to be in the presence of the many famous churchmen who had joined the commission. The one new member who did not attend was Wojtyła. He refused to go to Rome out of solidarity with Cardinal Wyszyński, who had been banned from foreign travel. Ultimately, Wojtyła did not vote on the commission's report, although it was later revealed he had pressed the pope to keep the birth-control ban in place.

There would never be a formal, detailed account of the panel's deliberations, but several members reported later that, almost as soon as they gathered for the final debates, there was overwhelming support to lift the ban. An especially persuasive figure was Döpfner, who argued that Vatican II proved the church could reverse centuries of doctrine—and be strengthened by it.

Patty Crowley spoke up on behalf of a community that, she said, was always ignored by the church in the birth-control debate: Catholic women, "the real bearers of these burdens." She said the rhythm method was a disaster for women, forced to live at the mercy of "thermometers and calendars." She posed a larger question: Why was the Vatican obsessed with restricting sexuality in a loving marriage? "Is not the sex drive instilled by God a normal one?" she asked. Another American member, Thomas K. Burch, a Georgetown University professor of population studies, said he was angry the church had taken so long to realize that family planning was no sin. The Vatican had "caused millions of people untold agony" for no reason, he said.

The commission never revealed its final vote tally, but major news organizations reported an overwhelming majority of the panel—fifty-four of its sixty-six members, according to several accounts—voted to lift the ban. A group of theologians was then assigned to write a final report to be presented to the pope. The Crowleys returned home gratified to have been part of this historic debate. "I don't think there was a doubt in any of our minds that the pope would approve the commission's report," Patty said.

In June, fifteen of the commission's sixteen cardinals and bishops—all but Wojtyła—gathered for a final debate before turning the report over to the pope. When they took their own vote, nine, including Suenens and Döpfner, agreed artificial contraception was no violation of the church's teachings. Three, including Ottaviani, voted to keep the ban in place. Three abstained. That tally was leaked to *The New York Times*, which ran the news under a banner front-page headline. On June 28, Döpfner presented the pope with the report, as well as a five-foot stack of scientific and theological research supporting its conclusions. As the cardinal left Rome, however, he telephoned other commission members to report an alarming rumor that their work was somehow being undone by Ottaviani.

Paul VI was, characteristically, tormented by the decision he faced. That summer, he summoned a friend, the French philosopher Jean Guitton, for an interview in which he suggested he would reject the commission's findings. Lifting the birth-control ban "would have the effect of calling morality into question and showing the fallibility of the church," he argued. The Vatican would be seen as "a servant to science," willing to reverse itself "with each new scientific discovery." He worried medical research might show that artificial contraception did genetic damage and "produced monsters."

News reports that fall suggested the pope, buckling under the pressure, planned to resign. He hinted at it in September when he paid an impromptu visit to a shrine, inside a castle about forty miles outside Rome, where his thirteenth-century predecessor Celestine V, the last bishop of Rome to resign voluntarily, had died in 1294. In a brief homily at the site, Paul suggested cryptically that he understood why Celestine chose to abdicate, since his ancient predecessor apparently felt "deceived by those who surrounded him" in Rome.

The pope's dithering on birth control outraged progressives. It was the last straw for Father Charles Davis, the best-known Catholic theologian of his generation in Britain. He called a news conference in London in December 1966 to announce he was leaving the priesthood and would no longer worship as a Catholic. He said Paul VI's obvious intention to reject the findings of his birth-control commission proved the Vatican was beyond reform: "It is a vast, impersonal, unfree and inhuman system." The pope's claim that there might be sound theological reasons to maintain the ban on contraceptives was an "evasion of truth—one who claims to be the moral leader of mankind should not tell lies." He said his differences with the Vatican over birth control were the immediate cause of his departure from the church, but he acknowledged he had also decided he could no longer abide the "cruelty" of priestly celibacy. After entering a seminary as a teenager, he said, he was still a virgin at the age of forty-three—and had begun to fear terrible loneliness in old age. He revealed to the reporters that he had fallen in love with an American Catholic woman and that they planned to wed. When the couple did marry two months later, the ceremony was held in an Anglican church near Cambridge University, where he had accepted a teaching fellowship. He said he was saddened that his devoutly Catholic family refused to attend.

12

"A Thorn in My Flesh"

A FEW DAYS AFTER the closing ceremonies at Vatican II in 1965, Archbishop Hélder Câmara left for the long flight home to Brazil. At Rome's airport, he encountered Brazilian journalists who noticed his ticket was in the back of the plane—in economy class. Câmara laughed and told the reporters he would "rather be dead" than in the company of passengers sipping champagne in first class. Left unsaid was the fact that most of Brazil's other big-city bishops would fly home in luxury in the front of the plane. They would insist on it.

Câmara maintained his record of never speaking publicly in St. Peter's during the council. He thought that mattered little since his opinions were well-known—"my voice was being heard"—and that was true. He left more of a celebrity than any other bishop in Latin America and was, without doubt, the principal advocate at Vatican II for the world's poor. The French newspaper *Le Monde* described him as the "one bishop at the council who merits the title of prophet."

By the end of the council, he had given up on his plan to convince the world's bishops to sell off the Vatican's real estate and other wealth to benefit the poor. The council had gotten too bogged down in angry theological debates to allow it to take up such an audacious proposal. Still, he left Rome convinced he had achieved the next-best thing: the absolute commitment of the bishop of Rome, in writing, to end global poverty. In November 1965, in the final days of the council, Câmara helped the pope craft a statement in which Paul VI declared that Latin America would collapse into "violent revolution" if the church failed to do more to combat poverty and oppression. The statement was released in Rome at a news conference in which Câmara joined with fifty other bishops to vow they would live their own lives without material goods: "We renounce forever both the appearance and the reality of wealth, particularly in regard to clothing and housing. We will have no property, furniture or bank accounts in our own name."

Câmara invited European and North American church leaders to see the poverty of Brazil for themselves. In 1967, he led Cardinal Suenens on tours of the slums—the favelas—of Recife. "The images have never left me," Suenens said later. "They are like a thorn in my flesh. How can people be reduced to such an inhuman situation—a situation that cries out to heaven for vengeance?" He was both touched and heartbroken when he saw parishioners arrive for Mass in a slum church: "I watched the procession of poor people dressed in rags," carrying the only thing they could offer for the donation plate. "One carried a single banana." He joined Câmara at church gatherings in which slum dwellers organized to demand their rights from local landowners. He remembered, in particular, "a secret meeting of poor people who were trying to set up a sort of workers union in an attempt to resist expropriation of the tiny plots of land they owned."

The clash between new and old visions of Catholicism after Vatican II was starker elsewhere in South America. Colombia had long been one of the continent's most socially conservative countries, with a repressive Catholic hierarchy to match. Most Colombian bishops remained silent about their country's outrageous economic inequality, even as an estimated twenty-five thousand children died there each year of malnutrition. But inspired by Vatican II, many Colombian priests, over the objection of their bishops, announced their determination to work with the poor in the cause of social justice. In the late 1960s, hundreds of priests and nuns moved to slums in the capital of Bogotá and other cities and established what became known as *comunidades de base* (base communities). Beyond worship services, they helped slum dwellers establish schools, sanitation projects, and labor unions. Colombia's order of Marymount nuns, long famous for educating daughters of the elite, opened an experimental school in a Bogotá slum in partnership with Marxist educators. The nuns stopped wearing religious habits, a decision that local bishops saw as scandalous.

A leader of the slum-priest movement, Father Camilo Torres Restrepo, turned himself into a legend. The fact that Torres was handsome and charismatic and the scion of one of Colombia's most aristocratic families enhanced his fame. Local newspapers often noted his "machismo" made women swoon.

He felt he had no choice but to join the priesthood, he said. As a young man, "I realized that life as I understood it otherwise lacked meaning." After ordination, he earned a sociology degree at a Catholic university in Belgium. In 1960, at the age of thirty-one, he returned home to join the faculty of Colombia's national university. Inspired by Castro's rise to power in Cuba the year before, Torres never hid his radical politics. "The duty of every Catholic is to be a revolutionary," he wrote. Still, he insisted he was not a Marxist, even as he noted that Jesus, like Marx, demanded that wealth be shared.

His politics infuriated Colombia's church hierarchy. By 1965, the conflict was so deep he left the priesthood. "I have taken off my cassock to become a truer priest," he declared. There was shock several months later when he joined a Marxist guerrilla group. That December, the military announced it had killed Torres in combat and buried his bullet-riddled corpse at a secret location—an effort to prevent the site from becoming a shrine. Hours later, walls across Bogotá were covered with posters that read: "Camilo! We shall not weep for you! We shall avenge you!"

The early base communities in Colombia, Brazil, and elsewhere became the centerpiece of a movement known as liberation theology. As it swept across Latin America, it put priests and nuns on a path to violent confrontation with brutal, right-wing governments. In 1964, the Brazilian military, with the quiet encouragement of the United States, overthrew a left-leaning democratically elected government; the military would remain in power for twenty-one years. In 1966, the Argentine military launched a largely bloodless coup d'état—its fifth coup since 1930—to overthrow an elected, centrist president.

FOR CENTURIES, the Jesuits were at the heart of Latin American Catholicism—and the region's rigid social order. In much of Central and South America, it was taken for granted that government and business leaders received at least part of their education in a Jesuit school. After Vatican II, however, the Jesuits' mission changed. Their new leader, Father Arrupe, wrote to Jesuit educators in 1966 to demand they begin to recruit students from among the poor. He said he worried the order's schools in

Latin America were failing to instill students with a sense of social justice. The mission of Jesuit teachers should "now be completely pervaded by the spirit of Vatican II," which meant an end to the perception the Jesuits were aligned with the rich and powerful.

That September, the Jesuits held a so-called general congregation—a meeting in Rome of their leaders from around the world—to discuss how the society's thirty-six thousand priests would incorporate the reforms of Vatican II into their daily work. For many, that meeting was their first face-to-face encounter with Arrupe, and they were awed. In years to come, he was regularly compared to John XXIII—a figure of serene goodness, loved even by churchmen who otherwise agreed with him on nothing. Father Michael Campbell-Johnston, a British Jesuit who was one of his closest deputies, said Arrupe "bubbled with high spirits, laughed a lot and loved jokes against himself." Rembert Weakland, Arrupe's counterpart in the Benedictine order, said the Jesuit leader "was the most saintly person I have ever encountered."

Arrupe had been a legend among Jesuits for years, long before his election as their leader, because of the courage he displayed as a missionary in Japan after the American atomic bomb was dropped on Hiroshima in August 1945. Even before the mushroom cloud cleared, Arrupe, who had studied medicine before joining the church, turned his Jesuit fieldhouse on the city's outskirts into a makeshift hospital—the first in the world to treat victims of radiation poisoning. A few hours after the blast, he led a rescue party into the city center, even though he was certain he was going to his death from the "mysterious gas" left by the bomb. He would always remember a tiny, terrified thirteen-year-old Japanese girl who came up to him that day, weeping, pleading for help as she pointed to her head and "showed me how her hair was falling out in her hands in bunches." She died two days later.

Among Jesuits, there was another oft-told anecdote about Arrupe from earlier in the war—about his arrest by the Japanese on December 8, 1941, the day after the attack on Pearl Harbor, on charges of espionage. At the time, Arrupe said, the Japanese believed all Westerners were spies, and he assumed he would be beheaded, the fate of anyone accused of such a grave crime in wartime Japan. On Christmas Eve, he heard people gathering near his cell and feared it was his executioners. Instead, the rustling was the sound of a group of his Japanese novices who wanted to comfort him by singing Christmas carols. He remembered bursting into tears of gratitude.

Even the Japanese military came to see Arrupe's goodness—or at least his innocence. After a few weeks, he was released.

The one church leader in Rome who never warmed to Arrupe was Paul VI, who seemed threatened by the Jesuits—and by Arrupe personally. At the order's 1966 conference, the pope gave a mystifying speech in which he said he was hearing "strange and sinister" reports about the Society of Jesus. He did not explain exactly what he meant but suggested Jesuits were moving away from their traditional loyalty to the papacy. The remarks left many in the audience dumbfounded, including Arrupe. He held a news conference a few days later to say—delicately—that he did not understand what the pope was talking about. "I do not want to defend any mistakes Jesuits might have made," he said. But until the pope clarified his concerns, the Jesuits would press on with their new agenda of total commitment to the poor: "The greatest mistake would be that, out of fear of making an error, we would simply stop acting."

Under Arrupe, Jesuits sponsored thousands of base communities across Latin America. Many Jesuits thought it was an obvious answer to the region's calamitous shortage of priests; the communities organized informal worship services when priests were absent. In Brazil, the national bishops' conference, working with the Jesuits, set up a radio network to broadcast grassroots education programs to distant base communities. Over time, the

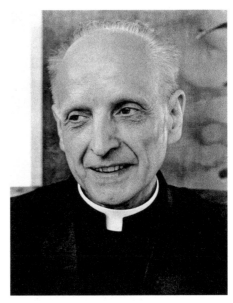

Jesuit leader Pedro Arrupe, a much-loved churchman often at odds with Paul VI

broadcasts began to include a Sunday-morning Mass, allowing millions of Brazilians who had no local priest to at least hear the sacraments.

At first, liberation theology appeared to have the pope's full endorsement. In 1967, he released an encyclical in which he declared that "the world is sick" and that only massive income redistribution would save it. "The continued greed of the rich nations should only provoke the judgment of God," he wrote in the eighteen-thousand-word document, *Populorum Progressio* (On the Development of Peoples). He cited Vatican II in condemning "atheistic materialism." There was no "absolute and unquestioned right" for people to own property, he decreed. For a pope normally so cautious, his language was radical; *The Wall Street Journal* described the encyclical's tone as "warmed-over Marxism." In its most explosive passage, the encyclical suggested there were times when injustice was so great—when a government engaged in "manifest, longstanding tyranny"—that violent revolution could be justified.

The effect was electric across South America, including in Argentina, where the church hierarchy was otherwise among the continent's most conservative. Two months after the encyclical, about one hundred Argentine clergymen organized a group that called itself Priests for the Third World. Over time, they committed themselves to moving into slums—known in Argentina as *villas miseria* (misery villages)—in Buenos Aires and other cities. The group eventually numbered four hundred priests in Argentina and expanded to neighboring countries. It suffered a setback in 1967 when one of its early patrons, Bishop Jerónimo Podestá of the city of Avellaneda, was abruptly ousted by the Vatican. The reform-minded Podestá insisted he was forced out under pressure from the Argentine junta, although the truth was more complicated. Podestá, it was later revealed, had fallen in love with his secretary, a mother of six separated from her husband. The Vatican was aware of the romance and sought to end his career before the relationship became a scandal.

IN APRIL 1967, Paul VI was appalled when the *National Catholic Reporter*, an independent progressive newspaper based in Kansas City, Missouri, published copies of both the majority and minority reports of his birth-control commission. The leaker turned out to be a Dutch priest based in Rome, who obtained the documents from a commission member. The pope complained to a friend that birth-control advocates were "trying to force my hand by publishing this, but I won't give way."

Increasingly, he was in no mood to compromise about anything. That summer, he announced another overhaul of the Curia, one clearly intended to bolster his authority. New power was concentrated in the job of secretary of state. The ailing eighty-four-year-old Italian cardinal then in the post, Amleto Cicognani, was given a new deputy: Archbishop Giovanni Benelli, a forty-six-year-old Vatican diplomat who had once been the pope's private secretary. There was little doubt that Paul was grooming the doggedly loyal Benelli for the job of secretary of state, if not for the papacy itself. Benelli was, literally, a man on the move—he was often seen roaring around the streets of Rome in his sleek Alfa Romeo sports car.

His role quickly grew, especially as Paul's health deteriorated. In September, when he marked his seventieth birthday, the pope was plagued by a urinary infection that forced him to wear a rubber catheter his visitors could see, which he found mortifying. It was left to Benelli and the always-influential Cardinal Ottaviani to oversee the final planning for the synod that month—the first of the "minicouncils" that the world's bishops had hoped would give them a permanent voice in the church after Vatican II. The synod, attended by 197 clergymen from around the world, dashed those hopes. In advance of the meeting, reform-minded bishops were blocked by the Curia, on the pope's orders, from putting birth control and other controversial subjects on the agenda. Although in pain from his infection, Paul appeared at the opening ceremony to make a speech that contained a dire warning to the bishops. He insisted there were "immense dangers" from the "modern mentality" inspired by Vatican II, and suggested the council's reforms had gone too far.

The month-long synod was widely seen by liberal bishops as a failure. Their only apparent victory was a majority vote calling on the pope to create a board of independent theologians to serve as a counterweight to Ottaviani and his deputies at the Congregation for the Doctrine of the Faith. Two years later, Paul established the so-called International Theological Commission, which, as its critics predicted, proved toothless.

Many bishops at the 1967 synod were despondent as they returned home. Weeks later, Canada's best-known churchman, Cardinal Paul-Émile Léger of Montreal, announced he was stepping down to devote the rest of his life to working with lepers in Africa. The sixty-three-year-old cardinal told colleagues the synod proved "nothing will change" in the Vatican, which explained his decision.

In November, Paul underwent surgery to remove his prostate, an operation carried out inside the papal palace after an operating theater was built next to his apartment, complete with oxygen tents, transfusion equipment, and an electric-shock stimulator to revive his heart if necessary. It was the most serious surgical procedure faced by any pope in decades. His painful convalescence continued into Christmas week. Even so, he agreed to a hastily arranged meeting on December 23 with President Lyndon Johnson, then on a whirlwind round-the-world tour. Johnson wanted to propose a role for Paul in peace talks to end the Vietnam War. The meeting was awkward, because the pope had condemned recent American bombing of North Vietnam. *Time* magazine reported the pope "slammed his hand on to his desk and shouted at Johnson," a claim the Vatican denied. The pope's deputies recalled a moment of comic relief during the tense encounter, when they were left snickering as Johnson presented Paul with a gift from the American people—a garish, foot-high plastic bust of the president himself.

That Christmas week was a memorable one for Hans Küng, since he was warned again that he was under scrutiny in Rome. His new book, *The Church*, had just been published in Germany and was scheduled for release in the rest of the world months later. On December 19, Küng's local bishop was notified by the Congregation for the Doctrine of the Faith that the book, which expanded on Küng's calls for reform of the Curia, should not be distributed further or translated. Küng responded with his usual impudence: "I telephoned my publishers in London, Paris and New York and told them to speed up."

Küng and other reform-minded churchmen had reason to celebrate weeks later. In January, Ottaviani, seventy-seven years old, announced he was retiring from the congregation. Although his departure was framed as voluntary, many in the Curia were convinced the pope, annoyed over the perception he was manipulated by Ottaviani, wanted new leadership. The cardinal's replacement was the sixty-two-year-old archbishop of Zagreb, Yugoslavia, Franjo Šeper. A Gregorian-trained theologian, Šeper was seen, initially, as more moderate than Ottaviani.

Other archconservatives were passing from the scene. A month earlier, Cardinal Spellman of New York died at the age of seventy-eight after a stroke. Hundreds of the city's priests, enraged for years by Spellman's enthusiastic support for the Vietnam War, risked their careers by signing a public petition to Paul VI, demanding a role in the selection of the next archbishop. The request was ignored, and in March the pope named Spellman's loyal forty-seven-year-old former secretary, Bishop Terence Cooke, to replace him.

The year 1968 was a traumatic one for Paul—and for much of the world. The pope's public calls for global disarmament were ignored, as were his repeated pleas for an end to the war in Vietnam. In January, Vietnamese Communists launched a surprise attack on American troops in South Vietnam in what became known as the Tet Offensive. In the US, the military debacle undermined public support for the war and led President Johnson to announce in March he would not seek reelection. There were political uprisings across Europe throughout the year, including in Czechoslovakia, where a popular revolt against the Communist government, known as the "Prague Spring," was crushed by a Soviet military invasion. In France, workers and students rebelled against the government of President Charles de Gaulle. There were violent antiwar protests at universities across the United States. In April, civil rights leader Martin Luther King Jr. was assassinated. In June, Senator Robert Kennedy of New York, seeking the Democratic presidential nomination to replace Johnson, met the same fate.

The turmoil reached Germany. In April, shops in Frankfurt were firebombed in a protest against the Vietnam War and Western capitalism. There was unrest days later in the normally placid university town of Tübingen. In May, three hundred students invaded the town hall and announced they would boycott classes; more protests followed by students who declared themselves to be Marxists or anarchists.

The campus unrest came at a time when Küng and Ratzinger, who had been teaching together for nearly two years, thought theirs was a solid friendship. They differed on some doctrinal issues, but Ratzinger said it was easy to overlook their disagreements given Küng's "winning openness and straightforwardness." Küng occasionally attended music performances with Ratzinger and his sister. That summer, the two men had plans to holiday together in Switzerland, although the protests made that impossible.

They were both alarmed by the campus demonstrations. Küng could be conservative when it came to politics. "I regard myself as a representative of the rational center," he said. "I am no left-winger." He felt students had no right to disrupt classes in their "megalomaniacal program" to overthrow Western society. One of his lectures was interrupted by about fifty demonstrators, and he was furious. "My whole Swiss character instinctively rebels against being intimidated." He was angry when students not involved in the protests just sat and gawked at the bad behavior of others. They were "like the old Romans in the arena, watching the outcome of the battle among the gladiators." He was so upset that, with two weeks left in the semester, he announced he was canceling classes and going on vacation. He said he would not return until order was restored.

The situation was more difficult for Ratzinger. He was also a dean of the theology school, which meant he had to deal directly with the protest organizers, and it was jarring. He was a man who had cocooned himself all his life—first with family, then with his studies. In his daily routine, he demanded little beyond the guarantee of several hours of solitude and quiet. So he was shocked when suddenly, without warning, he was confronted by angry students eager to insult him to his face. More than once, students interrupted his lectures with catcalls and whistles.

Faculty colleagues could see he was terrified, frightened even for his personal safety. More than one described what Ratzinger experienced as a nervous breakdown. Küng came to believe those months were a turning point in Ratzinger's life—that the "apocalyptic anxiety" produced by the protests caused Ratzinger to "snap," turning his back on all that he had stood for as a younger man, beginning with reform of the Catholic Church.

Ratzinger later compared the 1968 student protests to what Germany had experienced with the rise of Hitler in the 1930s—a time of "psychological terror" in which "every moral consideration could be thrown overboard." Student leaders of the "Marxist revolution" in Tübingen had shaken the university "to its very foundation," he claimed. Years later, he remembered with special horror how, one day that spring, he saw protesters handing out a pamphlet that depicted the cross and equated it with an implement of masochistic sexual practices. (Many professors and students at Tübingen recalled no such pamphlet.)

Others at the university thought Ratzinger badly overreacted to what was happening, but he insisted his fear was justified—that this was "not just another academic quarrel." His worst moment came at a chaotic meeting with student agitators in June, when they presented him with a long list of written demands for a voice in the running of the theology department. In justifying their protest, they presented him with a list of citations from Küng's new book, *The Church*, which called for an expanded role for Catholic laymen and laywomen in church affairs. Ratzinger sputtered with rage, telling the students they were misinterpreting his colleague's book. "Your intentions deviate from what Herr Küng has written," he said before packing up his briefcase and storming out of the room.

Years later, Küng thought it ironic that in many ways he agreed with Ratzinger—the students *had* misinterpreted the book. Still, he came to suspect that, as a result of that one confrontation with students, a bewildered, terrified Ratzinger decided to break off their friendship, in the mistaken assumption that Küng was "secretly behind" the protesters. Whatever his reasons, Ratzinger abruptly decided to leave Tübingen—and mostly cut off communication with Küng for the rest of their lives. "I had no inclination to live in a battle zone," Ratzinger wrote of his departure. Within weeks, he was invited to join the faculty of the newly opened public university in Regensburg, on the Danube River in his beloved Bavaria. The pretty medieval city was an especially good fit, he thought, because his brother, Georg, was director of its world-famous Catholic boys' choir.

Küng was shocked by the decision, if only because Ratzinger was moving from a theology school that was among the most respected in Europe to one that had no reputation at all. To an American audience, Küng later compared it to a move "from Harvard to Idaho State." He phoned Ratzinger with a final plea: "I told him how important it is to me that he should stay in Tübingen." Ratzinger had made up his mind, however.

Küng was distracted at the time by other troubles. In May, he received a letter from the Congregation for the Doctrine of the Faith, now led by Cardinal Šeper, summoning him to Rome to offer a defense of *The Church*. It gave a specific time and date for his appointment later that month. Küng thought the summons was preposterous since, at that point, he still had classes to teach. Besides, he was offended by the letter's threatening tone: "I do not want to be called to account as though I were in an authoritarian regime." He replied to Šeper with a four-word telegram: "UNFORTU-NATELY PREVENTED. LETTER FOLLOWS." He sent that letter a few days later, announcing he would go to Rome only if he could see the full disciplinary file kept on him at the congregation: "In all civilized states of the West, even criminals are guaranteed complete access to the dossiers that pertain to them." There was no immediate response from Rome.

Ratzinger arrived in Regensburg to find a vast building site. The theology department had been given temporary offices in a former monastery. He was disappointed to discover that there were student protests in his new home, too, and soon he confronted "a wave of Marxist revolt," especially among a group of Regensburg professors who were "determined leftists." Still, it was much less tumultuous than Tübingen.

He was excited that fall by the realization he was financially comfortable, and might be for the rest of his life, because of the success of his book *An Introduction to Christianity*, which was published that year and sold briskly. The book, which gathered material from his most popular lectures, was originally published in German but would eventually be translated into twenty other languages. Densely written, with long passages no layman could possibly understand, it was still acclaimed by theologians for its refreshing acknowledgment that faith in God was difficult and that many Christians were understandably confronted with the "oppressive power of unbelief."

In the book's preface, Ratzinger wrote that the state of modern Catholic theology reminded him of an old German folktale about a boy called Clever Hans, who foolishly exchanged a lump of gold for a series of increasingly less valuable items—a horse, a cow, a pig, a goose, and finally a stone. "Has our theology in the last few years not taken a similar path?" he asked, suggesting Catholics sought too-easy answers to difficult moral questions. He later denied that Clever Hans was a reference to Küng, but many theologians were convinced that it was, in fact, meant as an insult, especially since Ratzinger moved quickly to distance himself from Küng in other ways. That included his decision to resign as an editor of a theology journal, *Concilium*, that he and Küng established in 1965. Küng said that, initially, he didn't think Clever Hans was a reference to him, but later suspected otherwise, and was hurt. "Perhaps I should have taken more seriously the fact that a colleague for whom I felt nothing but friendship" was capable of "defamation," he wrote.

Ratzinger enjoyed his newfound celebrity as a result of the book, which gave him his first taste of fame outside Germany. It also brought him flattering attention at the Vatican. Almost as soon as he arrived in Regensburg, he was invited to join the new International Theological Commission. He accepted, which meant he began to travel to Rome regularly and meet with influential Curia bishops as well as with the pope.

Years later, he wrote in detail about what he believed had gone wrong in 1968—and in the church after Vatican II: the church, seized with dreams of reform at the council, had moved too quickly. The result was a "rebellion" of young, leftist Catholics who "viewed the entire course of history since the triumph of Christianity as a mistake." They believed they could create a "better world in the mainstream of Marxist thought." Marxists were not his only target. In Regensburg, he increasingly fixated on what he saw as the dangers of sexual sin and on the need for Catholics to reject the so-called sexual revolution of the 1960s, which he tied to left-wing politics of those years. He expressed his disgust to colleagues over the sudden availability of pornography in Germany and of sexually explicit advertising. He remembered his shock one day a few months after arriving in Regensburg when he noticed "crowds of people lining up in front of a large cinema to buy tickets for a pornographic movie."

Students in Regensburg who were otherwise devoted to Ratzinger said they were baffled by his obsessive warnings about sins of the flesh. In lectures, he insisted there was a clear-cut link between promiscuity and violence, an association many students doubted. When pressed, they said, Ratzinger offered clearly exaggerated, even fictional, anecdotes to try to support his argument. He regularly claimed he had read newspaper reports about dangerous incidents in which pornographic films were shown on long-distance international airline flights, which led to fistfights among the passengers. His students wondered what he could possibly be talking about. Sex films on planes? Fistfights among passengers? He insisted he was right and could never be convinced to double-check his claims. He often told friends at the time, and later wrote in detail, of his conviction that Germany had become such a decadent nation after World War II that child molestation was rampant and treated as socially acceptable. That assertion struck many of Ratzinger's colleagues and students as, at the very least, a wild misunderstanding. (He seemed to be referring to theories promoted by a small, discredited fringe of German sex researchers in the 1960s who claimed children could benefit from sexual contact with adults.) Years later, in light of those warnings in the 1960s and 1970s, Ratzinger was pressed repeatedly to reveal if he had any suspicion at the time that pedophilia was a problem inside the Catholic priesthood in Germany—in Regensburg, in particular. He denied it.

13

"Standing Before the World Alone"

I N JUNE 1968, Paul VI made an astonishing announcement: he declared that bones unearthed beneath St. Peter's Basilica decades earlier were those of St. Peter himself. According to tradition, the apostle Peter was crucified and buried there on the order of Emperor Nero about AD 65. Now, more than nineteen hundred years later, a new scientific analysis of the bones proved it, Paul declared.

Most prominent archaeologists knew his decree was nonsense. There was no way to be certain the bones, which were first dug up in 1939 and made up about 60 percent of a man's skeleton, were the apostle's remains. Beyond the limits of any scientific analysis, some church scholars had always questioned whether Peter ever reached Rome, let alone been its bishop; the New Testament says nothing about him traveling to the city. The theory that the bones were those of St. Peter had been promoted for years by the Vatican—and fiercely contested.

Paul's critics saw his announcement as a cynical attempt to bolster his authority as he prepared to reveal his long-awaited decree on birth control. The encyclical was nearly ready to be published and, the critics thought, he wanted the public to be convinced that when he spoke, it was with the authority granted him as the successor to St. Peter. By then, it was widely understood he would reject the majority report of his birth-control com- mission. Ottaviani, still a powerful adviser to Paul after stepping down from the Congregation for the Doctrine of the Faith, had been at work for nearly two years on an encyclical that would justify keeping the ban on artificial contraception in place.

Many senior churchmen around the world felt the pope was about to damage the church and permanently undermine his legacy. In Belgium, Cardinal Suenens, who had convinced John XXIII to establish the commission in the first place, was distraught. In March, he sent a blunt, confrontational letter to the pope, warning that the church's "credibility gap" would become a "credibility chasm" if the birth-control ban stayed in place. His letter, made public years later, was direct to the point of rudeness. He charged that the pope was isolating himself and making decisions unilaterally, consulting only with Ottaviani and a handful of other archconservative Curia deputies. The church, Suenens said, would be "endangered" if the "Holy Father were seen to take upon himself the role of sole defender and guardian of the faith." The pope would be left "standing before the world alone, cut off from the college of bishops, from the clergy and from the faithful."

His letter reflected a widely shared view of the pope, even among admirers. The more he felt himself under attack, the more he dug in. "He was simultaneously—and paradoxically—indecisive and authoritarian," said the French writer Jean Guitton, the pope's friend. "When he had taken a decision, it was quite impossible to get him to modify it in any way whatsoever." Suenens's letter arrived too late to make a difference. By then, the pope had already approved the final draft of the encyclical and planned to release it in July, when he would be on holiday in Castel Gandolfo. He hoped that at the height of summer, with Rome baking in the heat and mostly empty, the document would create less of an uproar.

Days ahead of the release, the pope's official spokesmen repeatedly lied to the press, insisting no decision was imminent. Then a copy was leaked a day early to *Time* magazine, which reported that the encyclical was "a massive blow to liberals in the Roman Catholic Church." The leak gave critics a chance to organize protests for publication day, July 29.

The seventy-five-hundred-word encyclical, *Humanae Vitae* (Of Human Life), was a rejection of all the key findings of the papal commission. The pope's central conclusion—that artificial birth control interrupted the workings of nature and was therefore a sin—was expressed in his typically convoluted way. Even by the standards of Vatican documents, the language was impenetrable.

The pope declared that birth control was a violation of God's command that every act of sexual intercourse "retain its intrinsic relationship to the procreation of human life." As a result, any action "intended to prevent procreation" is "absolutely excluded." According to the pope, Catholic couples could limit the size of their families only through abstinence or the rhythm method, even though he suggested the latter was morally questionable, too. Artificial birth control, he declared, could lead to infidelity and loss of respect for women.

For family-planning advocates, the only glimmer of hope in the document was that the pope had not labeled it as infallible, meaning his successors could overturn it. "This teaching will perhaps not be easily received by all," the encyclical declared in an absurd understatement. "Too numerous are those voices, amplified by modern means of propaganda, which are contrary to the voice of the church."

Conservative bishops rushed to defend and, in many cases, celebrate the decision. The church's new leader in New York, Archbishop Cooke, welcomed the encyclical as "authoritative teaching." Cardinal Cody in Chicago said it was a "message of faith regarding the dignity of life, love and the human person." Cardinal Wyszyński in Warsaw was delighted, since he knew the encyclical would outrage his enemies in Poland's Communist government, which advocated family planning and was about to open a factory to manufacture birth-control pills.

Other, equally prominent Catholic leaders challenged the decision and came close to denouncing the pope by name. Thomas Roberts, the retired archbishop of Bombay, told the BBC that the encyclical "flies in the face of reality." Eighty-seven Catholic theologians in the US, many of them professors at church-run universities, released a statement urging married couples to ignore the document, since it was so clearly wrong. In some European countries, bishops joined together to say the encyclical should be read as a suggestion, not a command. In the Netherlands, Cardinal Alfrink gave a defiant interview in which he said he would tell his parishioners to continue to use birth control if they wished. Since the pope had not declared his decision infallible, Alfrink explained, family planning remained a matter of individual conscience. The US bishops' conference declared that while birth control remained an "objective evil," American Catholics who continued to use it should not feel abandoned by their church: "We urge those who have resorted to artificial contraception never to lose heart."

Outside the church, the criticism was withering. In London, *The Economist* said that the encyclical was "not the fruit of papal infallibility but of papal isolation." Several American members of the pope's commission flew to Washington for a news conference to denounce the document. John Marshall, an English doctor who had been a member of the panel from the start in 1962, was angered at the pope's claim that contraception promoted infidelity: "The assertion casts a gratuitous slur, which I greatly regret, on the countless responsible married people who practice contraception and whose family life is an example to us all."

Küng was on vacation in Switzerland when he heard the news about *Humanae Vitae*. "It burst like a bomb on the world," he remembered. He called an editor at Swiss national television and said he was available for an interview, an offer the network instantly accepted. He was careful in the broadcast not to lash out at Paul VI: "We should take the conscientious decision of the pope seriously and respect it." But he urged Swiss Catholics to realize that bishops of Rome were capable of error. Couples who practiced family planning "should not accuse themselves of sin when they have acted in accordance with their best knowledge and conscience." It was a demonstration of Küng's global celebrity that Ottaviani learned about the interview within hours and shot back, insisting that criticism of the encyclical was coming only from "Catholics of Hans Küng's stamp."

Küng said later he had actually restrained himself in his initial criticism of the encyclical. The truth, he said, was that *Humanae Vitae* had "destroyed"

Archbishop Hélder Câmara of Brazil, "bishop of the slums" and progressive voice for the poor at Vatican II, champion of liberation theology

the Vatican's authority for a generation of Catholics. The pope, he said, would be remembered as a "tragic figure" who had arrogantly brushed aside the commonsense judgment of the church's most respected theologians. Ratzinger was in his final, tumultuous months at Tübingen when the encyclical was published, and he made no public comment about *Humanae Vitae* at the time. Still, he told friends he was appalled at how badly the document was written. Like many theologians who otherwise supported *Humanae Vitae*, Ratzinger was stunned by Paul's failure in the encyclical to explain himself clearly to the millions of Catholics who would be horrified by his decision.

Meeting with reporters in Castel Gandolfo days later, the pope said he "trembled before God" in rejecting the findings of the birth-control commission. He insisted Catholics should see his decision as a positive one—a recommitment to the sanctity of life. "This, our encyclical, is not a negative thing," he said, speaking in Italian before shifting—bizarrely—into German, which most of the perplexed journalists did not speak. His use of German that day was never explained by the Vatican, but many in the Curia were convinced he was trying to identify himself at a moment of unbearable stress with his mentor Pius XII.

THE POPE WAS GRATEFUL he had an important distraction that summer—preparations for a trip to Colombia in August, which would be the first pilgrimage to South America by a sitting bishop of Rome. He comforted himself at the thought of the rapturous crowds that were likely to greet him on the world's one truly Catholic continent—a place where, unlike Europe and the United States, his teachings were rarely challenged. The birth-control debate was never so heated in Latin America in the 1960s, when birth-control pills and other contraceptives were available only to a sliver of the population.

His two-day trip to Colombia was timed to a meeting of the Conference of Latin American Bishops, better known by the Spanish acronym CELAM, which represented more than six hundred cardinals and bishops from twenty-one countries across the region. The agenda for the meeting, which opened with a speech by the pope in Bogotá before the bishops traveled two hundred miles north to the industrial city of Medellín to continue their debates, centered on the reforms of Vatican II and how they should be implemented. The gathering had been organized largely by

Archbishop Câmara of Brazil, whose international fame was at its height. He appeared regularly on the shortlist of contenders for the Nobel Peace Prize, although he probably sabotaged his candidacy with public comments that were deliberately provocative: although he decried violence, he often praised violent revolutionaries, including Fidel Castro and Che Guevara.

In advance of the meeting, Câmara rounded up a group of Latin America's most impressive young theologians to write documents for debate in Medellín. None would make a mark like Father Gustavo Gutiérrez of Peru. Gutiérrez, a short, stocky man who turned forty that year, was a bundle of nervous energy. He walked with a limp, the result of bone infections that confined him to a wheelchair as a teenager. The experience gave him special insight into human suffering, he believed. He originally entered medical school to become a psychiatrist but felt drawn to the priesthood and went on to receive theology degrees in Belgium and France. He returned home to work as a priest in the slums on the outskirts of the capital city of Lima. In his early writings, he questioned whether the church fundamentally misled poor Catholics by telling them to accept their misery, with Jesus's promise of paradise after death, when in fact all human beings were entitled to a taste of the "Kingdom of God" while still on earth.

Ahead of the conference, he was asked to speak to a group of Peruvian bishops about how the church should combat poverty in light of Vatican II. His original draft called for the church to embrace a "theology of development," but at the last minute he revised the wording. The church, he decided, had a responsibility not just to offer development aid to the poor—housing, food, and medicine—but also to encourage their political liberation. The phrase in the speech was rewritten to refer to a "theology of liberation"—the first time many churchmen had ever heard the expression. In 1971, he published his most famous book, entitled *Notes on a Theology of Liberation*.

The crowds greeting Paul in Colombia were, as expected, overwhelming—hundreds of thousands of people overjoyed to witness the moment when a bishop of Rome first set foot on their continent. On arrival in Bogotá, the pope dropped to his knees, in his white vestments and skullcap, and kissed the airport tarmac. The brief trip seemed to revive him, and he thrilled crowds with his repeated call for the church to rise up to help the poor. At an open-air Mass the day after his arrival, speaking in Spanish before two hundred thousand mostly poor farmers and laborers gathered in a dusty cow pasture, he pledged that, after Vatican II, the church had ended its centuries-old alliance with the wealthy and powerful of Latin America. He addressed the cheering crowd as *campesinos*, a Spanish word to describe rural peasants. "We know that many of you live in miserable conditions," he told them. "Know that we are listening to the cry that rises from your suffering."

The Medellín conference was a landmark in the nearly five-hundred-year history of the church in Latin America. The bishops approved documents that expressed outrage over poverty and political inequality in their countries that was so brutal that it amounted to "institutionalized violence." They adopted Gutiérrez's wording and said that the church must encourage "liberation" for the poor, with a goal of a "profound transformation" of society. After the conference, the expressions "liberation theology" and "the spirit of Medellín" took hold across Latin America in describing the church's involvement in antipoverty and social-justice projects—especially in the base communities, where the poor gathered to pray and organize. In Brazil alone the church helped establish seventy thousand base communities. In the wake of Brazil's 1964 coup, the church and its base communities would be seen for years as the only organized opposition to the military.

Whatever pleasure he felt about the reception in Colombia, the pope fell into a deep depression on his return to Rome. Many aides said they had never seen him in such despair. He told friends he was convinced he would be under siege for the rest of his life, openly mocked and defied as a result of *Humanae Vitae*, and he was right. Across Western Europe and the United States, the encyclical was denounced as his ultimate betrayal of Vatican II and of the council's call for "the People of God" to have a voice in their church.

In his Christmas address that year, Paul delivered a bleak appraisal of the state of the faith, and of the world. It was easily the most pessimistic speech of his papacy, so darkly worded that aides urged him to revise it, a suggestion he rejected. While the holiday should inspire joy, "there comes forth anguish instead of hope," he declared. He warned of the threat of imminent nuclear war and how mankind might soon be destroyed "in dark clouds of terror and madness." Inside the church, "there are no longer any stable values of faith." At the end of the most momentous year of his papacy, a religion writer for *The New York Times* summed up the "tragedy" of Paul VI, noting that the beleaguered pope was often compared to Hamlet—"unable to make up his mind on birth control and other issues." The paper suggested a better comparison was to another figure from Shakespeare: "King

Lear—a man who was unable to recognize loyalty in his children when he saw it."

AFTER VATICAN II, Küng often visited Cardinal Suenens in Belgium. They had a friendship, Küng thought, built on their shared reputation at the council as troublemakers. Yet while Küng basked in his reputation as a rebel, the cardinal told Küng he found it painful to have so many adversaries in Rome. In 1968, when eighty-six-year-old Cardinal Cicognani was about to retire as Vatican secretary of state, many churchmen promoted Suenens as his obvious successor, given the extraordinary leadership he displayed at Vatican II. But the pope replaced Cicognani with an obedient, moderately progressive French cardinal, Jean Villot, the former archbishop of Lyon. Küng, who had promoted Suenens's candidacy, realized afterward that Paul would never have permitted a courageous, independent-minded churchman like Suenens to serve alongside him in Rome.

During their meetings in Belgium, Suenens and Küng often talked about the pope's failings and how they led to the catastrophe of *Humanae Vitae*. In March 1969, eight months after the encyclical, Suenens visited Rome to see the pope. They had a difficult conversation. The pope, Suenens remembered, was wracked with self-pity, at one point pleading: "Yes, pray for me; because of my weaknesses, the church is badly governed."

Suenens left Rome feeling his past public criticism of the pope had been too subtle. In May, he agreed to an interview with a popular French-language church magazine, and his blistering comments about the pope shattered their relationship forever. Paul VI, he declared, had fallen hopelessly under the influence of closed-minded Curia conservatives who convinced him to rule like a dictator: "The pope today does not give the impression of being St. Peter's successor, but rather the successor of emperors." In an interview with *Time* days later, he noted the worldwide priest shortage—"the hemorrhage"—and argued for allowing priests to marry; his remarks amounted to a public denunciation of Paul's 1967 encyclical on priestly celibacy. Predictably, the interviews created a firestorm in Rome. At first Paul did not respond directly. Days later, though, a trio of cardinals in the Vatican wrote to Suenens to protest, and their letters were leaked to journalists in Rome. The letter from Cardinal Tisserant, the eighty-five-year-old dean of the College of Cardinals, accused Suenens of "slander" and demanded he apologize to the pope. Suenens refused.

The pope found an important defender that year in Father Jean Daniélou, a prolific French theologian eager to make a name for himself as
Paul's most determined public champion. Daniélou had many detractors,
especially among fellow French Jesuits, who thought him outrageously
ambitious—always a grievous sin for members of the Society of Jesus. His
critics were not surprised when, in 1969, a grateful Paul raised him to the
College of Cardinals, a promotion that delighted Daniélou. At a ceremony
in Notre Dame Cathedral in Paris to mark his installation, leaflets fluttered
down from the balcony, attacking both Daniélou and the pope: "Paul VI,
you only choose your friends as bishops!"

The newly named cardinal jumped into battle with Suenens, describing
the Belgian's attacks on Paul as "excessive" and "unjust." In essays published across Europe, Daniélou wrote he was especially disturbed by Suenens's call for an end to the doctrine of priestly celibacy. By questioning
celibacy, Suenens was attempting "to strike at the authority of the pope."
Paul's reliance on Daniélou as a defender on that subject would embarrass the Vatican four years later when the cardinal was found dead in the
Paris apartment of a twenty-four-year-old nightclub stripper. His friends
insisted Daniélou was offering pastoral counsel to the young woman, but
that did not explain why his corpse was found in civilian clothes, with a
large amount of cash stuffed in his pockets. The mysteries of his death were
revived in news reports a few months later, when another bishop, visiting
Paris from his diocese in southwest France, died of a heart attack in a dingy
boardinghouse frequented by prostitutes.

The pope scheduled another worldwide bishops synod, the second since
Vatican II, for October 1969, but any hope it would rekindle the council's
spirit of reform was abandoned long before the bishops gathered in Rome.
In advance of the meeting, the pope gave speeches in which he called for
the synod to recognize his authority as supreme. Papal powers, he declared,
"derive from Christ himself." Suenens, who attended the synod, was not
cowed. In his speeches in Rome, he repeated much of what he said in his
now-notorious interviews. The pope's defense was offered most passionately at the synod by Daniélou, who demanded the church recommit itself
to the "firm and unique authority" of the papacy. He suggested Vatican II
encouraged "fantasies" about reform. The synod ended in a stalemate on
substantive issues.

Some frustrated bishops left Rome after the meetings determined to
press for broad reform of the church, even if that meant endangering

their careers. Apart from Suenens, no one was more resolute than Cardinal Alfrink of the Netherlands, already seen by many in the Curia as a renegade.

Alfrink announced after the synod he would sponsor a conference of Dutch churchmen and lay Catholics to decide whether his nation's priests should be allowed to marry. He acknowledged that might be seen in the Vatican as an outrageous act of defiance, but Alfrink argued that after the council, Dutch Catholics were convinced there were questions they should be permitted to answer for themselves. The Dutch church was forced to act, he insisted, because of a desperate shortage of clergymen. In the previous decade, ordinations of Dutch priests had fallen by 60 percent. Between 1967 and 1969, a fifth of the country's two thousand priests departed the ministry, and those who remained were eager for change. A 1968 survey showed four out of five priests felt they should be allowed to marry, and their parishioners were overwhelmingly supportive. Opinion polls showed that, by a huge margin, Dutch Catholics accepted the idea of married priests. A majority supported an even more revolutionary change—the ordination of women.

Ahead of the conference, which was scheduled for January 1970, Alfrink granted interviews to international news organizations in which he acknowledged something that he knew would appall the Vatican: with the quiet approval of their bishops, many Dutch priests had recently married in civil ceremonies and lived openly with their wives and children. The cardinal, who admitted he looked the other way when priests married, said his views on celibacy changed in the 1960s when he counseled churchmen tormented by the psychological demands of life without a family. He was also aware of something he did not share publicly at the time—how many priests violated their celibacy vows flagrantly. It would later be shown he was also aware of several cases in which Dutch priests had molested children.

As Alfrink might have expected, the pope was incensed. On Christmas Eve, he wrote to Alfrink and other Dutch church leaders, ordering them to cancel the meeting, then only two weeks away, but the bishops would not back down. The cardinal said he had no power to call off the gathering, since it had been organized under the auspices of the Dutch church's 108-member governing body. That group—half clergymen, including eight bishops, and half laymen and laywomen—had been established after Vatican II in response to the council's call for greater openness.

The January 1970 meeting became a global news event, with journalists from around the world crowding into the small Dutch town near the North Sea where it was held. A few conservative Dutch priests protested the gathering by chartering a small plane to fly above the school where the conference met. It trailed a banner that read "Einheet met Rome" (Unity with Rome).

The results were as Paul had feared. The Dutch governing board voted 86 to 3 to allow priests to marry. There were sixteen abstentions, which included the eight bishops, who agreed in advance not to vote. By a similarly lopsided vote of 72 to 8, the board urged that women be admitted to the priesthood. As the meeting ended, Alfrink announced he would immediately open negotiations with the Vatican about the ordination of married Dutch priests.

In Germany, Hans Küng followed the Dutch debate closely and was eager to be part of it. He still dared to hope it might affect him personally, since at forty-one there was still time for him to fall in love and begin a family. In February, he drafted a petition for German-language theologians to express solidarity with the Dutch. It was signed by eighty-four Catholic scholars and delivered to their local bishops.

Two of Germany's best-known Catholic theologians, Karl Rahner and Joseph Ratzinger, refused to sign. They said it would be inappropriate since they were both members of the pope's newly created International Theological Commission. Still, in private, they felt the German hierarchy had to weigh in on this debate as a matter of principle. The pope was trying to silence the Dutch church hierarchy—and by extension, all the world's bishops—on a vital question of church law, which amounted to a betrayal of the spirit of Vatican II. Together the two men drafted a letter to German bishops and labeled it "confidential." There was good reason for secrecy, since their message was harsh about Paul VI. It said German bishops, like their Dutch counterparts, needed to conduct an "urgent examination" of whether priests should be allowed to marry. It criticized Paul's 1967 encyclical as "supremely ineffective" in ending the celibacy debate and suggested German bishops should always have been offended by the document, since the pope had not consulted them before issuing it. The letter—eventually signed by seven other theologians, including Walter Kasper, Küng's former assistant and Ratzinger's former colleague—would remain secret for the next forty years. (When it was finally made public, Kasper stood by it. Ratzinger, who by then had great power in Rome, did not.)

The debate in the Netherlands effectively came to an end in July 1970, when Alfrink was summoned to Rome by the pope and ordered to shut down the celibacy debate forever. The cardinal reluctantly agreed, saying he had no choice but to show obedience to the pope: "This for him is a conviction of conscience."

The pope might have hoped that, given his decisive move against the Dutch, other threats to his authority would quiet. Suddenly, however, there came a new attack, and from a familiar source: Küng, whose latest book, *Infallible? An Inquiry*, savaged Paul VI by name. The book, published that summer, accused the pope of inflicting "damage on the unity and credibility of the Catholic Church" by aligning himself with the "power-hungry" Curia. The pope's failures culminated in *Humanae Vitae*, which "makes the weakness and backwardness of Roman theology evident to the astonished general public throughout the world." The book was timed to the one hundredth anniversary of the First Vatican Council and its declaration of papal infallibility. Much of the book was, in fact, a scholarly history of Vatican I. Küng argued that the concept of an infallible pope had never been valid and was imposed in 1870 only because of the bullying of Pius IX. Küng cited convincing historical research showing that the concept of an "error-free" pope had been dreamed up in the thirteenth century by an eccentric Franciscan priest whose views were rejected at the time as heresy.

The book was another sensation, and the initial German press run of ten thousand copies sold out in days. An Italian-language publishing house sold its four thousand copies almost immediately but refused to print more, fearing retaliation from the Vatican. Reviewers around the world praised the book for its boldness and easy-to-understand language, so rare for works about the church. In a review, a Lutheran theologian in Germany, Walther von Loewenich, described Küng as a modern-day Luther who had "said things that others had long been thinking quietly."

Küng knew his book would outrage the Vatican—more than anything he had ever written, he suspected—and so he braced himself for his "most important battle yet." He was grateful when the German bishops' conference refused a demand from the Vatican to force the book's German publisher to withdraw it. Instead, the conference issued a short statement that criticized certain passages of the book but made no blanket condemnation. "That is not our task," the bishops wrote.

Küng was saddened, however, by the reaction to the book from a few of his best-known German peers. Rahner wrote a scathing review. He said that by attacking Paul VI so directly, Küng had fallen away from his Catholic faith and now resembled a "liberal Protestant." Ratzinger, in his review, did not denigrate Küng personally and mentioned their "years of untroubled collaboration." Still, he accused Küng of using political jargon—the "language of class struggle"—to describe the relationship between the Vatican and its opponents. He cited what he said were seven historical mistakes in the book. That incensed Küng, who saw the "errors" simply as differences of opinion. The break between the two men was now complete and would only grow more vicious.

That May, Paul marked the fiftieth anniversary of his ordination with what was supposed to be a celebratory Mass in a small parish church in Rome. The pope was strangely somber throughout the service and failed to acknowledge friends in the pews, as if he no longer recognized them. It was a rare public appearance for the seventy-two-year-old pope. By then, he had largely given up day-to-day management of the Vatican to Villot. His withdrawal from public life reflected his vision of himself as a man now constantly under assault—and not just by liberal reformers. He had begun to make enemies among traditional allies as well. He outraged aging Curia conservatives that November when he rewrote church law to bar cardinals over the age of eighty from participating in papal conclaves. In his decree, the pope insisted he was doing elderly clerics a favor by lifting this "burden" from them. But many in the Curia suspected the decree was motivated principally by Paul VI's desire to prove his independence from one aging cardinal in particular—Ottaviani, who turned eighty just weeks earlier. The pope continued to be embarrassed over the portrayal of the cardinal as his puppet master, especially after *Humanae Vitae*. Ottaviani was furious over the decree. The pope's decision was "absolutely unheard of, arbitrary, revolutionary and in contempt of tradition," Ottaviani protested to an Italian newspaper. "I am pushed aside."

Paul's isolation made it easier for him—operating from a distance, communicating on paper—to launch what became a brutal campaign to punish the Dutch church. He began to remake the hierarchy there by appointing new, aggressively conservative bishops in the knowledge they would soon outnumber the progressives. His first move came in December 1970, when he named Father Adrianus Simonis, an outspoken opponent of birth control and married priests, as the new bishop of Rotterdam. It led all fourteen of the city's priests to protest; they said they could not work with Simonis since his views were so clearly out of line with theirs. Simonis refused to step aside, describing himself as a champion of "right-thinking people" who understood "the dangers of reform." Months later, the pope appointed an even more conservative priest, Joannes Gijsen, a thirty-nine-year-old church historian, as bishop of Roermond. The choice of Gijsen, a fierce defender of traditional doctrine who once said he would deny an abortion "even to a thirteen-year-old girl who gets raped by a psychopath"— was so shocking that several bishops petitioned the Vatican to cancel the appointment. A few hinted that the emotionally volatile Gijsen, known to colleagues to have suffered at least two nervous breakdowns, should be disqualified because of persistent rumors that he was a child molester. The pope refused to reverse the decision, but the rumors were true. In 2014, a year after Gijsen's death, the Dutch church hierarchy conceded it had long been aware of credible allegations that he sexually abused boys, including a ten-year-old who was forced to engage in oral sex when Gijsen was a seminary chaplain in the 1960s. Among the bishops who knew about the allegations was Simonis, who had heard rumors for years that his colleague Gijsen was a pedophile. After Gijsen's crimes were revealed publicly, Simonis insisted to church investigators that for most of his career, reports that a fellow bishop molested children were rarely investigated. What was considered criminal sexual abuse "wasn't so clear in those days," he said in explaining why he and others in the Dutch hierarchy had failed to stop Gijsen. "I know a lot about that now."

14

The Church's Front Line

ATHER ARRUPE SEEMED incapable of recognizing the pope's anger—
and that meant it only kept building. His deputies said the Jesuit
leader was guileless when it came to Paul VI. To Arrupe, the pope
was half father figure, half living saint. "I felt I was with a father who only
wanted his son to do better," Arrupe once said. "I felt encouraged, even if
he tweaked my ear."

Although the pope never said it directly, he made clear he felt that
Arrupe had turned the Society of Jesus away from its obligation to serve the
papacy—to serve *him*—above all else. Some Jesuits suspected that simple
jealousy explained the pontiff's hostility. It was similar, they thought, to the
envy that overwhelmed Paul in discussions of John XXIII. In many ways,
Arrupe was developing a reputation as Paul's saintly rival, a champion of
the oppressed at a time when the pope was turning his back on Vatican II.
In 1973, *Time* placed an image of the balding, gently smiling Arrupe on
its cover over a headline that saluted him as the leader of "Catholicism's
Troubled Front Line."

Other Jesuits were not blind to the pope's exasperation. "Arrupe did
not always understand the delicacy with which Paul VI expressed disagreement," said Cecil McGarry, an Irish priest working in the Jesuit bureaucracy in Rome. Arrupe would return from a papal audience convinced it
went well when, in fact, his aides knew the meeting had been a disaster.
Out of a sense of fairness, Arrupe refused to act blindly on papal instructions, especially since Paul spoke so opaquely, McGarry said. Occasionally,
the pope demanded that certain Jesuits be demoted or disciplined, or that a

policy be reversed, but Arrupe would not act until he himself investigated. "The Vatican expected that Arrupe would decapitate people, but he didn't," McGarry said.

Under Arrupe, no other religious order matched the prominence of the Jesuits in the second half of the twentieth century, nor would one be so closely associated with Vatican II. In his writings, Arrupe coined a phrase that became a rallying cry for liberation theology. The Jesuits, he said, needed to proclaim the "option for the poor"—the interests of the poor should always be put first. In that, he was convinced he was acting with the pope's endorsement. There was written proof of it, he said, in the documents of Vatican II—especially *Gaudium et Spes*, which demanded the church's involvement in social justice—and in the pope's bold encyclical *Populorum Progressio*, which helped give birth to liberation theology.

But Paul, characteristically, began to equivocate. At a 1968 ceremony to mark the first anniversary of *Populorum Progressio*, he backed away from the most radical passages in his document. He claimed it was never meant to condemn Western capitalism and free markets (even though it did, explicitly). Nor, he said, had he suggested the poor could be justified in using violence to overthrow a tyrannical government (even though the encyclical was nearly as explicit about that).

It was revealed years later that Paul backed away under pressure from powerful Catholics outside Rome, including American and European business leaders who were major donors to the pope's personal charity fund, known as Peter's Pence. They traveled to Rome to convince the pope to disown parts of the encyclical they branded as Marxist. The Americans included executives of Ford Motor Company, Goldman Sachs, and the First National City Bank of New York, later renamed Citibank. He also faced pressure from foreign governments—especially right-wing regimes in Latin America traditionally close to the Vatican, as well as from the United States—to renounce the encyclical. As declassified US government records from the 1970s showed, the Central Intelligence Agency was wary of Catholic social-reform movements tied to Vatican II. The spy agency monitored liberation-theology activists in Latin America, many of them Jesuits, for signs they were agents of the Soviet Union or Castro's Cuba. It was a fear, the CIA's own analysts would admit decades later, that had always been wildly exaggerated.

Arrupe was also in trouble with Paul because Jesuits were suddenly in the public eye. Many, citing the freedoms of Vatican II, began to speak out on politics, even if that put them at odds with church teachings. In 1970, the Vatican was furious when a trio of Jesuit scholars called a news conference only blocks from St. Peter's to assail the church for meddling in Italy's parliament to try to block legislation to legalize divorce. In 1973, a Jesuit sociologist invited reporters to a speech in Rome in which he hailed the population-control policies of Communist China, including coerced abortion, as the most "efficient" in the world.

The winds of change within the Jesuits were visible at the order's most famous outpost in Rome—the Gregorian. In the 1960s, the university began admitting a sizable number of women, including nuns, and it was often not possible to tell the nuns apart from other women students, since the Gregorian stopped enforcing a dress code. Similarly, many priests studying there had given up wearing clerical collars and, when the weather turned cold, arrived for class in the turtleneck sweaters fashionable at the time.

In the United States, Jesuits were at the forefront of the civil rights movement and protests against the Vietnam War. The most prominent was Father Daniel Berrigan, a Minnesota-born Jesuit who organized antiwar marches and was jailed in 1968 after he used homemade napalm, the sticky flammable chemical deployed by the US as a defoliant in Vietnam, to incinerate hundreds of files at an army draft board office in Maryland. Other Jesuits entered politics directly. In 1970, Father Robert Drinan, former dean of the law school at Jesuit-run Boston College, was elected as a Democrat to the US House of Representatives. He had been given permission by his Jesuit superiors to make the run, and his campaign centered on his opposition to the Vietnam War. That same year, the order's hierarchy refused permission to another Jesuit, Father John McLaughlin, to seek election to the US Senate from the state of Rhode Island. McLaughlin, a Republican who supported the war, entered the race anyway, only to lose. He left the priesthood to become a speechwriter for President Richard Nixon. Later he worked in television and was the host of a syndicated political talk show that bore his name, *The McLaughlin Group*.

THE SIGNIFICANCE OF their encounter would not be recognized for decades. But in Argentina in 1965, the most celebrated Jesuit of the twentieth century, Father Arrupe, met a young Argentine who would be the most important Jesuit of the century to come: Jorge Mario Bergoglio. At the time, Bergoglio was twenty-eight and still in training for the priesthood.

The encounter occurred in the city of Santa Fe, at the Jesuit high school where Bergoglio was teaching. He remembered sitting mesmerized as Arrupe, who was on a speaking tour of South America, lectured about the sacrifices that Jesuits made to evangelize Japan, where Christianity was unknown until the Society of Jesus arrived in the sixteenth century. Arrupe described how Jesuit missionaries were persecuted by Japanese warlords, most notoriously in Nagasaki in 1597, when twenty-six Jesuits and other Catholic missionaries and their parishioners were crucified, their bodies raised on poles and sliced open with spears. Despite the danger, the Jesuits remained in Japan until all Christians were expelled from the country in the midseventeenth century. Bergoglio was so inspired that he went up to Arrupe and asked to be considered for a mission in Japan. Arrupe was encouraging but told Bergoglio he should finish his education first.

Bergoglio, then seven years into his training as a Jesuit, felt no pressure from his family to join the Society of Jesus—or to become a priest, for that matter. Growing up, he thought of the priesthood as just another profession, "in the way you think about being an engineer, a doctor or a musician." As a teenager, he was, by all accounts, a smart, level-headed *porteño*, the slang term used to describe someone from Buenos Aires, his hometown. (The word refers to its river port.) He liked what his friends did—soccer, music, and girls. His family lived modestly: "We didn't have a car or go on vacation, but we didn't have any serious needs." At the insistence of his father, a factory bookkeeper, Jorge began to work part-time at the age of twelve. He also worked for a time in a chemistry lab. Later, he got a job as a nightclub bouncer.

He knew for sure he would become a priest when, in 1953, a few weeks shy of his seventeenth birthday, he walked past his parish church and felt compelled to go inside and make a confession. "I felt like someone grabbed me from inside and took me to that confessional," he explained, struggling to find words to describe an otherworldly experience. "Right there, I knew I had to be a priest." Two years later, he entered a seminary. Because of his pale skin and distinctly European features, other seminarians gave him the nickname *el gringo*. He was remembered by classmates for his intelligence. They saw no evidence of the extraordinary, sometimes ruthless ambition that would seize him later.

Young Jesuit Jorge Mario Bergoglio of Argentina (back row, second from left) in an undated family portrait taken in Buenos Aires several years before his 1969 ordination

As he prepared for a life in the church, he admitted he was conflicted about the demands of lifelong celibacy. He had his first girlfriend at the age of twelve. Years later, as a seminarian, he became infatuated with a young woman he met at a family wedding, and it almost derailed his vocation: "I could not pray during the entire week that followed because, when I prepared to pray, the girl appeared in my mind." Throughout his career, he was convinced he had a healthier attitude toward sex than other churchmen. Too many priests "think only from the belt down" and become obsessive about the sexual sins of others, he said many years later. "They smell sex everywhere." He credited his tolerant views to his high school, where he was taught by priests of the Salesian order, who had a reputation for open-mindedness. He also credited his tolerance to a basic understanding of the New Testament, since Jesus was constantly in the company of adoring but sometimes sinful women.

He thought his strong ego and some of the darker elements of his personality were shaped by his homeland. Among South Americans, Argentines had a well-earned reputation for arrogance and for seeing themselves as different. Native-born Argentines tended to identify themselves with the nations of their European ancestors instead of the one in which they were born, as if they would get on a boat someday and return to the old country. Despite pockets of poverty, Argentina was the most prosperous nation in South America for most of the twentieth century. It was blessed with natural resources, including the fertile soil of the region known as the Pampas.

The nation's Catholic hierarchy was among the most conservative on the continent, its bishops intensely loyal to the Vatican. Their devotion to Rome was explained in part by the fact that half of all Argentines were of Italian ancestry. Jorge, whose father emigrated from Italy in the 1920s, was raised speaking Spanish but became fluent in Italian thanks to his Italian-born grandmother. The family sat him down every Saturday at two p.m. to listen to the weekly radio broadcasts of Italian opera.

The pope of his childhood, Pius XII, was revered, his written pronouncements seen as infallible. That affected day-to-day life in the Bergoglio household. Because the pope so fiercely condemned divorce, the family refused to invite anyone into their home who was known to be divorced or separated. Since Pius saw Protestants as heretics, the Bergoglios did too. They credited their devotion to Pius to the fact that after they prayed for the intervention of both Jesus and the pope, Jorge survived emergency surgery in 1957 to remove a diseased portion of his right lung. The operation impaired his breathing for the rest of his life.

Throughout his youth, Argentine politics centered on one man: Juan Domingo Perón, first elected president in 1946, when Bergoglio was nine. Even after Perón was ousted in a 1955 coup and sent into exile, his fanatical supporters remained. For decades to come, political debates centered around the populist movement—Peronism—founded by Perón and his equally charismatic first lady, Eva Duarte, better known by her nickname, Evita.

Years later, Bergoglio was coy about his views on Perón, although as a young man he had been an enthusiastic supporter. His adversaries in the Jesuits would later draw comparisons between the two men. They saw Perón's influence in Bergoglio's personality-driven, sometimes cold-blooded style of leadership. Bergoglio credited his early fascination with Argentine politics to the woman who, outside his family, was the most influential in his life: Esther Ballestrino, a feminist and self-declared Marxist who ran the chemistry lab where he worked as a teenager. She did not force her leftist views on him but instead "taught me to think about politics," he remembered.

In 1957, at the age of twenty-one, he decided to seek admission to the Jesuits. That choice, he said, reflected his desire for a life of military-style discipline and intellectual rigor—"to be on the front lines of the church, to put it in military terms." He began his Jesuit training in Córdoba, Argentina's second-largest city. As a novice, Bergoglio lived a completely regimented life. His day was scheduled, down to the minute, between the clang of a wake-up bell at six a.m. and another at ten thirty p.m. that signaled lights out. A novice's life had changed little since the sixteenth century, when St. Ignatius, worried that idle time led to sin, set down strict rules for Jesuits-in-training. The Córdoba residence had a separate list of forty-two "instructions for living." Bergoglio was required to kneel while eating and to kiss the feet of his superiors as a greeting. He was compelled to spend much of the day in silence. When novices did speak to instructors, it was in Latin; Spanish was allowed only outside the classroom.

In 1960, Bergoglio took formal vows of poverty, chastity, and obedience, which meant he was considered a full Jesuit, although still not a priest. He then left for a year of study across the Andes Mountains in Chile. At the time, Chile was economically backward, especially compared with Argentina, and its Catholic hierarchy was far more progressive. Archbishop Raúl Silva Henríquez of the capital city of Santiago, named a cardinal in 1962, was a champion of the poor. He once revealed that had he been born in the poverty common among his parishioners, "I would be a Communist."

Chile's poverty shocked Bergoglio. He visited Jesuit schools where students were visibly malnourished. Some trudged to school without shoes, even in the frigid winter cold of the Andes foothills. In Chile, Bergoglio learned for the first time how it was possible for people in a devoutly Catholic country to live in the sort of misery he associated only with desperately impoverished corners of Africa or Asia. In 1960, he wrote his eleven-year-old sister to remind her how comfortable life was in Argentina: "As you sit at the dinner table, remember there are children who have only a small piece of bread to eat."

When he returned to Argentina, he began studies at the Colegio Máximo de San José, in San Miguel, about twenty-five miles from downtown Buenos Aires. The Jesuit-run college, where he studied philosophy, would be his home for most of the next quarter century. In Rome at the time, John XXIII might be promoting a new spirit of freedom at Vatican II, but there was none of that at the Colegio. Bergoglio found his studies there stifling. The school's textbooks, all in Latin, reflected "decadent or largely bankrupt" Catholic scholarship, he complained later.

In 1964, still several years shy of ordination, he was given an assignment typical for Jesuits of that era—teaching at the order's prestigious boys' schools around Argentina. He was assigned for a time to a Buenos Aires high school famous for educating sons of the capital's most influential families. Students there remembered him as stern but enthusiastic. While teaching in the city of Santa Fe in 1965, he convinced the country's most renowned living writer, Jorge Luis Borges, to make a six-hour bus trip from Buenos Aires to meet his teenaged literature students.

Among Argentine church leaders in the 1960s, a handful could be labeled as liberals, including the leader of the nation's Jesuits, Father Ricardo O'Farrell, who aligned himself with liberation theology and urged Jesuits to preach in the slums. In 1970, he approved the establishment of a Jesuit base community in a shantytown near downtown Buenos Aires. The project was the brainchild of Father Orlando Yorio, a left-leaning Jesuit theologian who had once taught Bergoglio at the Colegio Máximo.

Argentina's most famous slum priest, Carlos Mugica, was not a Jesuit, although he was close to Jesuits who shared his dedication to liberation theology. His parish was a slum in the heart of the capital, across the street from the main train station. Known as Villa 31, it was a community of scrap-metal shacks. Mugica organized residents to demand better living conditions, beginning with the installation of water lines and toilets. Their protests infuriated the junta, which saw slum priests as subversives, but the attacks only brought more flattering publicity to Mugica. He came from a family of wealthy landowners and was often described as Argentina's counterpart to Colombia's Camilo Torres. Unlike Torres, however, Mugica renounced violence and pledged his devotion to the church.

Bergoglio was ordained a priest on December 13, 1969, a few days before his thirty-third birthday. Ahead of the ceremony, during a week-long retreat to pray and meditate, he wrote a prayer for himself in which he seemed to acknowledge his faith was not absolute. Rather than stating directly that he believed in God, he wrote that he *wanted* to believe. He listed his failings, including the "egotism in which I take refuge" and "the stinginess of my soul, which seeks to take without giving."

He had still not completed his full training as a Jesuit, the process known as the "Jesuit formation." There was a final stage, known as the "tertianship," that he completed while continuing his studies in Spain. He returned to Argentina in 1971 for his full induction into the Jesuits, a ceremony in which he renewed his three earlier vows and then promised to honor the order's all-important "fourth vow," requiring submission to the papacy. He took a series of other sworn oaths, using the precise language written down by Ignatius in the sixteenth century. That included a pledge he would never "strive with ambition," nor accept any promotion without the approval of his Jesuit superiors. Years later, it was those vows that Bergoglio would be accused of violating.

His rise within the Jesuits began instantly. He was named to oversee the training of novices in Buenos Aires, a prestigious job normally held by a much older priest. At the time, those duties were not much of a burden since there were few Jesuits in training. The priest shortage was serious in Argentina, too. In 1972, only three novices joined the order in the entire country.

The government was then under the control of the Argentine military, which came to power in a 1966 coup. Despite their bumbling and brutality, military commanders remained in control for almost seven years with the help of the United States, which saw Argentina's armed forces as a bulwark against communism at the height of the Cold War, and the Vatican. The military pledged absolute loyalty to the church and, within months of the coup, delighted Paul VI by ratifying an agreement to grant the Vatican full control over its affairs in Argentina, including the appointment of bishops. Rome had previously been required to choose bishops from lists of government-approved candidates. Initially, the junta enjoyed civilian support, especially among Catholics who approved of its harsh morality laws. There was strict censorship; foreign films containing even a hint of nudity or drug use were banned. Crowds in the streets of Buenos Aires looked as if they were from a different era, since the military enforced a strict dress code. Men with long hair were marched by the police to a barber, while women were forbidden from wearing the miniskirts popular elsewhere.

By the late 1960s, the military struggled with an explosion of politically inspired bloodshed. Increasingly, Peronists split into two camps and both turned to violence. On one side were right-wing nationalists aligned with the military; on the other, leftist radicals, including a shadowy group known as the Montoneros, which was named for a band of nineteenth-century rebels who helped win Argentina's independence from Spain. Political kidnappings became a daily event. In 1970, in their most brazen act, the Montoneros abducted and executed General Pedro Aramburu, the retired strongman who ousted Perón in 1955.

Increasingly, Argentines gave up on their homeland, even though it remained easily the richest nation in South America. By 1970, they emigrated at a rate of almost a thousand people a week. The political and economic chaos of those years baffled Argentine political scientists; they described it as a case study in how a nation with every advantage could throw it away.

Desperate to restore order, the military agreed in 1973 to allow Perón, then seventy-seven and living in exile in Spain, to return home for the first time in seventeen years. What was supposed to be his triumphant homecoming on June 20 ended in chaos when an estimated two million people turned out at the airport in Buenos Aires for a rally to greet him. As it got underway, camouflaged assassins, later determined to be far-right Peronists, opened fire, shooting into areas where left-wing Peronists had gathered. Thirteen people died, and any hope for peace among warring Peronist factions collapsed.

In presidential elections that year, Perón returned to power in a landslide. His ill-chosen running mate was his third wife, Isabel, a former nightclub dancer three decades his junior. His return brought no stability. Within months, he publicly embraced the right wing of Peronism and denounced the left. His advisers secretly founded a far-right militia that called itself the Argentine Anticommunist Alliance, or Triple A, which began murdering its opponents. Later government investigations determined the group killed at least fifteen hundred people in the 1970s. Among its victims was the slum priest Carlos Mugica, gunned down in 1974 outside a church where he had just finished celebrating Mass.

Other Peronist militias were known for violence, although nothing on the scale of the Triple A. An organization known as the Iron Guard (Guardia de Hierro) portrayed itself as the most moderate of the right-wing groups. Its founders included alumni of the Jesuit-run Universidad del Salvador in Buenos Aires. They portrayed their mission, like that of their Jesuit teachers, as intellectually inspired and devoutly Catholic. Even so, some of the Iron Guard's four thousand members admitted years later that the group sometimes resorted to violence—mostly vigilante attacks on left-wing Peronists who were left bloodied and beaten. Human-rights investigators said later that there were credible reports of the group's involvement in assassinations and kidnappings.

In the midst of that turmoil, Jorge Bergoglio found himself thrust into the leadership of the entire Jesuit order in Argentina. In 1972, conservative Jesuits rose up to oust O'Farrell and wrote to Arrupe in Rome to ask for new leadership. O'Farrell's critics complained about his embrace of liberation theology and other social-justice movements that, they felt, involved the Jesuits in leftist politics. More fundamentally, they described O'Farrell as a poor day-to-day manager whose failure to recruit new men into the order threatened its very existence. Arrupe, who dispatched a deputy to Buenos Aires to investigate, determined weeks later the complaints about mismanagement were valid and demoted O'Farrell. There was no obvious successor, so Arrupe took a risk and appointed the unproven but promising Bergoglio, then thirty-six. His promotion brought protests from older Jesuits, including Father Ignacio Pérez, one of his former theology instructors. Pérez warned friends in the Jesuit hierarchy in Rome that, while Bergoglio had "imagination and energy," he was far too young and inexperienced for the post. Arrupe stood by his appointment, however, and it was announced in Argentina on July 31, 1973, two months before the national election that returned Juan Perón to power.

IN HIS FIRST WEEKS as Jesuit leader, Bergoglio impressed colleagues, including men who would later become bitter enemies, with his calm and decisiveness. "He had a cool head for what was to come," said Father Fernando Albistur. "Bergoglio was our *piloto de tormentas* [storm pilot]." Early reports about his competence were a relief to Arrupe. It helped explain why the Jesuit hierarchy in Rome appeared willing to look the other way as Bergoglio began to distance Argentina's Jesuits from the social mission that the order pursued in the rest of the world.

He moved to undo O'Farrell's legacy, especially when it came to promoting movements like liberation theology. Bergoglio was determined to end any perception that Jesuits were aligned with the left—with *zurdos*, an Argentine slang term that translates as "commies." Years later, he bluntly acknowledged that this had been his plan: "At that time, it was assumed that priests who worked with the poor were *zurdos*." He vowed no one would make that assumption again.

His critics acknowledged Bergoglio always showed an admirable dedication to the poor. Still, he shut down antipoverty projects that he saw as political. That meant pulling Jesuits out of the urban slums. The only significant Jesuit-run base community allowed to remain open was the one led by Father Yorio, who threatened a public protest if his project was closed.

Bergoglio upset other Jesuits when he announced plans to move the order's central offices from downtown Buenos Aires, where they had been since the sixteenth century, to the Colegio Máximo. The move out of the city center was designed, in part, to keep Jesuits safe from political violence, but it also meant moving the order's leaders away from the poor of the inner city. At the Colegio, too, Bergoglio seemed determined to eliminate any trace of O'Farrell's influence. He was offended by the way his predecessor had modernized the school's chapel by whitewashing its walls and removing religious artwork. Bergoglio rearranged the interior and installed a traditional tabernacle and a statue of the Virgin Mary.

His conservatism was evident in other ways. He insisted on a return to a strict dress code for priests, including the wearing of white collars. Novices were told to resume the practice of saying novenas, an old-fashioned type of prayer repeated nine days in a row, although many Catholics thought them an anachronism after Vatican II. Books promoting liberation theology disappeared from the Colegio's library.

Bergoglio's self-confidence turned into arrogance. Years later, many Jesuits said their sleep was still plagued by nightmares about their encounters with Bergoglio, who was known for his withering stare and icy, dismissive tone. He mocked young priests who were overweight. A few Jesuits recalled that he often sneered at a student at the Colegio who was notably effeminate, suggesting, in front of his classmates, that the young man was probably homosexual.

Bergoglio acknowledged years later that power went to his head as Jesuit leader and that he behaved atrociously. Arrupe, he said, made a mistake; he *had* been too young and inexperienced to run the national order. "I was only thirty-six years old!" Bergoglio said later. "That was crazy."

In his early days as Jesuit leader, he decided to involve himself in national politics by quietly volunteering to become spiritual leader to the Iron Guard. His ties to the Guard, given its reputation for bloodshed, appalled many Jesuits when they learned of it years later. There was never an allegation he approved of the group's violence, but former Iron Guard members say he must have realized what was happening. "Of course there was violence," said Julio Bárbaro, a former Iron Guard leader who remained friends with Bergoglio decades later. Bárbaro denied his group had ever carried out a murder, but he acknowledged lesser acts of bloodshed: "All the Peronist groups were involved in violence—against one another."

Bergoglio would have seen how the Iron Guard openly engaged in menacing rituals—full of fascist symbols and idol worship. In greeting one another, members performed a Nazi-style salute. They wore paramilitary brown shirts similar to those worn by Hitler's supporters in Germany.

Jesuits far from Buenos Aires tried to resist Bergoglio's conservative direction. In the early 1970s, Jesuit priests in the northwestern province of La Rioja mounted a campaign to organize local sharecroppers and factory workers into labor unions. Over time, those Jesuits, inspired by liberation theology, came to depend on the support of the local bishop, Enrique Angelelli. They had good reason to fear Bergoglio would close down their projects if he knew the details.

The sweet-natured Angelelli was beloved by most parishioners. After studying in Rome, where he earned a law degree at the Gregorian, he was named a bishop in 1960 by John XXIII and attended Vatican II. He rejected a bishop's trappings of power, including a car and driver, and made regular road trips around La Rioja in his pickup truck, driving himself, stopping every few miles to share a glass of mate, the traditional herbal tea of Argentina, with local priests. The motto of his career, Angelelli said, was to keep "one ear to the Gospels, the other to the common folk." He was known across Argentina as an advocate for the nation's coal miners, who regularly died in cave-ins, and farm workers. Those campaigns brought the wrath of coal executives and plantation owners, who organized paid mobs to threaten him with violence. In June 1973, during his visit to a rural church, a mob forced its way in as he offered Mass. Angelelli, hoping to spare the parishioners from bloodshed, walked out of the church alone, the mob right behind him. They pelted him with stones and screamed: "Zurdo! Zurdo!" The incident became national news and reached the Vatican. Days later, Paul VI directed Arrupe, then preparing for a visit to Argentina, to make a trip to La Rioja to offer support to the embattled Angelelli. Arrupe sent word to Buenos Aires that he wanted Bergoglio to join him.

They flew together to La Rioja and, moments after landing, got a taste of the danger Angelelli faced. The pilot stopped the plane on the runway while the police broke up a mob at the terminal—the same one that attacked the bishop weeks before. The thugs went to the airport because they knew Angelelli would be there to greet his Jesuit visitors.

Arrupe and Bergoglio spent hours with the bishop that day. He vowed to them that he would continue to campaign on behalf of the poor, whatever the risk to his safety, since he saw that as the mission demanded of him by Vatican II. Arrupe assured Angelelli he had the pope's full support. Bergoglio was impressed by the bishop's bravery and by the interactions he saw between Angelelli and his parishioners—"this dialogue of love." Even so, the encounter was not so moving that Bergoglio rethought his plans for the Jesuits. When he returned to Buenos Aires, he continued to move the order away from precisely the sort of social-justice projects that Angelelli promoted.

Perón's health collapsed after his election. He had suffered for years from heart disease, and months after his inauguration he began to show signs of dementia. In early 1974, prominent Argentines known to be loyal Peronists were approached to help write a document to be released by the president's office at the time of his death—a final tribute to Perón. Bergoglio was honored to be chosen for the secret project. The document, which took weeks to complete, was entitled *Nación Modelo* (Model Nation). On June 28, Perón suffered a series of heart attacks and died three days later, at the age of seventy-eight. Isabel, forty-three, was sworn in as the new president.

On behalf of the Jesuits, Bergoglio issued a written tribute. He used a religious term to describe the nation's reverence for Perón—the late president had been "anointed" by the Argentine people. A stone-faced Isabel appeared determined to show strength, not mourning, at the funeral, which explained one of her first decisions as president: She blocked publication of *Nación Modelo*, the document written to glorify her husband's legacy. Isabel was more interested in establishing her own.

At the time, Bergoglio was grappling with a financial crisis in the Jesuit order. The situation was so dire that he began to sell off buildings and plots of land that the Jesuits owned around Argentina, including the dormitory in Córdoba where he had lived as a novice. He also decided to give up control of the Universidad del Salvador, which the order established in 1958. Bergoglio drew up a list of charity groups and other religious orders that might take over the school. In August 1974, however, he shocked many Jesuits when he rejected the obvious candidates and announced he would transfer the university to the Iron Guard. He said he felt certain that, under the Guard, the school would promote "the Jesuit spirit," since so many of the group's founders were graduates. The decision created a furor within the Jesuits and among others who knew of the Iron Guard's reputation for violence. Decades later, many Jesuits were still angry. Father Guillermo Marco, a trusted aide and counselor to Bergoglio, acknowledged that "handing over the university to the Iron Guard was something for which many Jesuits have never forgiven him."

15

"Walking in Mud"

HIS PAPACY WAS in such turmoil that Paul VI decided there could be only one explanation: the devil. In a public audience in Rome in June 1972, he startled the crowd by announcing that Satan was a "real being" who was tormenting the church. "Through some crack in the temple of God, the smoke of Satan has entered," he declared. The remark became headline news around the world and appalled many mainstream Catholic theologians, who had long sought to portray the devil as a mythical personification of evil, not an actual being.[*]

A year later, Paul took part in ceremonies in Rome to mark the tenth anniversary of his election. His haggard appearance amid the pageantry revived speculation that he would abdicate. He denied it and told aides that, while he might like to step down, it would be pointlessly theatrical since his life would end soon anyway. Now seventy-six, he constantly felt ill, in part because of the aftereffects of his prostate surgery. He also became convinced, with reason, that his life might soon end in violence. He had been unnerved about the possibility since September 1970, when a man emerged from a crowd at Castel Gandolfo and threw two large, jagged rocks at his head, which missed by inches. The attacker was mentally ill and said "voices" had told him to kill the pope. Two months later, during a pilgrimage to Southeast Asia, Paul was the target of a more determined assassin in the Philippines. As the pope stepped from his plane in Manila, a

---

[*] Some of Paul's successors have also suggested that the devil is a real being, including Pope Francis, who revealed in interviews published in 2023 that he sent several of his former parishioners in Argentina to see exorcists.

man dressed in priestly robes lunged at him with a knife. The weapon was slapped out of his hand before the blade hit its target. The pope was rattled but unharmed. The attacker was a Bolivian painter who had lived in the Philippines for years and was known locally as "the mad artist." He said he wanted to kill the pope "to save the people from hypocrisy."

In 1970, a far-left terrorist group called the Red Brigades launched attacks across Italy. Over time, it would be responsible for dozens of assassinations and kidnappings. Its targets included politicians, business leaders, and anyone else associated with the Italian establishment, including the church. Beginning in 1973, fearing the Red Brigades would try to kill the pope, police snipers were placed on the roof of St. Peter's during his weekly public blessing.

Vatican buildings and the church's most cherished artwork were suddenly under threat. In February 1971, a bomb detonated in the middle of the night near St. Peter's Square, about a thousand feet from the pope's bedroom; the bomber's identity was never determined. A year later, Paul was devastated when Michelangelo's *Pietà* was damaged by a crazed thirty-three-year-old Hungarian man who shouted "I am Jesus Christ, risen from the dead" as he climbed over a marble balustrade in St. Peter's and attacked the beloved fifteenth-century statue with a hammer. The blows chipped the nose and left eye of the Virgin Mary and shattered her left arm. The pope, near tears, inspected the damage hours later and knelt to pray before the statue. The *Pietà* underwent extensive restoration before it was returned to public display behind thick layers of bulletproof glass.

Many of his deputies worried about the pope's emotional state. His personal confessor, Paolo Dezza, a Jesuit who had been rector of the Gregorian during World War II, revealed years later that the pope's "inner pain" was so deep that Dezza compared it to Christ's suffering on the cross.

By then, the pope's authority was being challenged on every sort of issue, by progressives and conservatives alike. The uprising against his authority in the Netherlands had not ended, as groups of Dutch priests continued to demand the right to marry. In France, a group of archconservative priests led by Archbishop Marcel Lefebvre established an unauthorized seminary and announced plans to name its own bishops. In 1976, Paul suspended Lefebvre from all priestly duties.

There was a brewing scandal in church investments, one that Paul set in motion with his disastrous appointment of his friend Michele Sindona to manage Vatican finances. In 1974, an American bank controlled by Sindona was declared insolvent, which led to the collapse of his entire financial empire. In 1975, the Vatican falsely claimed that it suffered only minor losses from investments tied to Sindona. In fact, it lost millions. Sindona died in an Italian jail cell in 1986 from cyanide poisoning; it was never established if his death was suicide or murder. He had been convicted four days earlier of ordering the assassination of the lawyer overseeing the empire's liquidation.

The calling of synods, which Paul had once portrayed as guaranteeing the world's bishops a voice in Rome, was seen more than ever as a sham by reform-minded churchmen. The pope called a synod in 1974, the fourth since Vatican II, and refused again to allow birth control and priestly celibacy on the agenda. That gathering was memorable because it raised the profile of a cardinal seen by Paul VI as a future leader of the church, maybe even his successor—Karol Wojtyła of Poland. The fifty-four-year-old Pole, who regularly spoke out in defense of *Humanae Vitae*, had proved himself fiercely loyal to the pope. Paul honored Wojtyła at the synod by naming him to the post of "relator," which put him in charge of writing the documents debated at the meeting. Many bishops found his drafts unredable. They were learning what Polish theologians had complained about for years—how Wojtyła's circular thinking made it impossible for him to communicate clearly on matters of doctrine. A friend of Wojtyła's in Krakow once joked that the cardinal's writing was so incomprehensible to his parishioners that it would be useful to have it "translated from Polish into Polish."

Nonetheless, bishops at the synod agreed it was extraordinary to be in Wojtyła's presence. There was something otherworldly about him. He glowed with religious passion. His compelling personal story—left without any close family by the age of twenty-one, educated secretly as a seminarian during the Nazi occupation, a defender of the church against the postwar Communist government—made his appeal all the stronger. The pope honored him again in 1976, when Wojtyła was the lecturer at the Curia's annual spring retreat. His speeches were dour, full of references to the modern world's sinfulness, but even those skeptical of his message came away impressed because he spoke with such conviction. His lectures were published as a book by the Vatican, another signal of the pope's support.

Paul's teachings on birth control and family life continued to be mocked and ignored, even in Italy. In 1970, over his protests, Italy's parliament legalized divorce. In 1975, France legalized abortion. By then, legal abor-

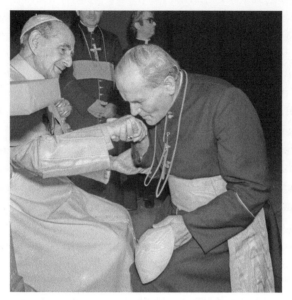

Cardinal Karol Wojtyła of Krakow, Poland, and his
patron Paul VI, 1977

tion had been available to Americans for two years under the Supreme
Court's *Roe v. Wade* ruling. Opinion polls showed American Catholics and
their clergymen overwhelmingly rejected *Humanae Vitae*. In 1971, the
American bishops' conference released a survey of five thousand priests
and found that two-thirds believed Paul had abused his authority with the
1968 encyclical.

The defiance caused the pope to dig in, especially to defend his view
of the evils of sexual freedom. His rhetoric became extreme. In a 1972
speech, he said mankind was falling victim to "animal, barbarous and sub-
human degradations" in the "disgusting and unbridled" hunt for sexual
pleasure. "We are walking in mud." He announced the church's enemies
included Sigmund Freud, since the father of modern psychoanalysis wrote
so openly about sex. The pope worried that even small, seemingly innocent
acts could lead to debauchery, including the way people cut their hair. In
a much-ridiculed 1971 speech, he told a convention of Italian hairdressers
to "work with sobriety." He became less understanding of priests who left
the church because they could not accept celibacy. Where once he had felt
sorrow over their decision, now he felt contempt. He compared departing
priests to Judas and suggested they were leaving the church "for vile earthly
reasons."

He felt similar disdain for nuns who left the church. It was a reflection of the status of women in the Vatican that, at the time, there was no reliable count of the worldwide population of nuns. In the early 1970s, there were thought to be about a million—and that as many as ten thousand renounced their vows each year. There were instances in the United States in which whole convents of nuns departed the church together. In Los Angeles in 1970, 315 nuns of the Order of the Immaculate Heart left the church but stayed together in what they called a "lay community." They abandoned the church in protest over what they saw as the backwardness of the city's cardinal, who had ordered them to give up jobs outside the church—many taught in public schools—and return to wearing head-to-toe black-cloth habits. He also directed them to return to calling themselves by the religious names given them by their convents. Anita Caspary, the convent's former mother superior, told reporters that, had she remained a nun, she would have been required to return to calling herself by her "literally humiliating" religious name: Sister Humiliata.

Under Paul VI, only one woman—a devout Australian laywoman and sociologist who had been one of the few women observers at Vatican II—held any significant position in the Curia; she was undersecretary of a committee that studied issues affecting Catholic laymen and laywomen. She was ousted in 1977, however, after the panel was given the more exalted title of "pontifical commission," a designation that required all members to be priests.

Paul promoted the work of one living Catholic woman above all others, an Albanian nun who opened hospices in the slums of the Indian city of Calcutta: Mother Mary Teresa Bojaxhiu, known there simply as Mother Teresa. In 1969, her work came to worldwide attention in a British television documentary. Two years later, the pope invited her to Rome to receive the inaugural Pope John XXIII Peace Prize, which he established as the Vatican's answer to the Nobel. In decades to come, the Vatican would cite Mother Teresa as proof of what women could accomplish even if they had no power in Rome.

The pope was wary of the women's rights movement in the United States and Europe, warning that feminist groups were "depersonalizing" women and making them "virile." He was adamant that women would never be priests, even as Protestants began to make way for women clergy. In 1976, the 2.9-million-member Episcopal Church of the United States began ordaining women. It came a year after Episcopal theologians agreed there was nothing in the New Testament to bar women priests. Nor was there any reason to prohibit gay priests of either sex, they concluded. In 1977, a lesbian priest was ordained in the diocese that included New York City.

The moves by the Protestants enraged the pope. In 1975, he declared that the ordination of Protestant women threatened to destroy the campaign for Christian unity begun at Vatican II. He issued a written protest to the Anglican Communion, the worldwide association of Protestant churches that included Episcopalians in the US and the Church of England. He restated the Vatican's centuries-old justification for its refusal to ordain women—because Jesus had chosen only men as his apostles—and warned that the Protestants were engaged in heresy.[*]

By 1975, the pope was so angry about defiance of his teachings on sexuality that he directed the Congregation for the Doctrine of the Faith to prepare a document to state—authoritatively, for all time—the church's views on sexual morality. That December, the congregation released its six-thousand-word Declaration on Certain Questions Concerning Sexual Ethics, with the Latin title *Persona Humana* (The Human Person). Progressive theologians and other church scholars were appalled by the document. "This is a giant step backwards for the church," said Eugene Kennedy, a priest in Chicago who was also a psychologist at the church-affiliated Loyola University.

Beyond the traditional condemnation of extramarital sex and masturbation, much of the report was a rejection of homosexuality: "Homosexual acts are intrinsically disordered and can never be approved of." While homosexuals should "be treated with understanding," it said, sexual contact between people of the same sex was properly described in scripture as a "serious depravity."

Paul did not foresee the disastrous chain of events that began with the document's release. He was about to be plunged into the gravest, most humiliating crisis of his life: a public discussion of long-standing rumors that he himself was homosexual. The allegations had long circulated in the Vatican press corps, in part because a popular Italian actor was a constant presence in the pope's apartment. The actor, Paolo Carlini, then in his

---

[*] That justification has long infuriated many prominent theologians, Catholics and non-Catholics alike. They note that while women were barred from formal positions of power in ancient Judea, a few were as important in the life of Jesus as the apostles. Two women in particular—Mary Magdalene, who witnessed the Crucifixion and its aftermath, and the Virgin Mary—were apostles in all but title.

mid-fifties, best known outside Italy for a minor role in the 1953 Hollywood film *Roman Holiday* with Audrey Hepburn, was trailed by news photographers whenever he was seen in Vatican City, although Italian news organizations that published the photos never dared suggest his visits were anything but innocent.

The allegations became public in April when the popular Italian newsmagazine *Tempo* published a three-thousand-word article by a prominent, openly gay French author, Roger Peyrefitte, who declared that Paul's homosexuality was well known among the pope's friends in Milan and that he had been in a long-term romantic relationship with a "movie star" he met while the city's archbishop. Peyrefitte claimed to know the man, "whose name I am not going to mention but whom I recall very well. He was an unknown actor when our friend Paul was Cardinal Montini." Peyrefitte, a former diplomat who had long shocked French readers by writing about his own sexual adventures, said he decided to reveal the pope's homosexuality as a protest over *Persona Humana* and what he saw as the pope's hypocrisy. *Tempo*'s editors suggested they had evidence, withheld from the article because it was so salacious, that proved the allegations were true. The police in Rome seized copies of the magazine from newsstands—they alleged the article amounted to criminal defamation—but it was too late to stop word of what was in the story from spreading across Italy. The pope was in a panic about the allegations, his deputies later revealed. He was reported to be nearly catatonic with fear about being publicly disgraced. At times, aides said, he was tearful and could not stop shaking.

There was no proof, certainly none that became public, that Paul VI violated his celibacy vows, but he had reason to believe *Tempo* was only the start of it. Others were peddling scandalous information about him, including a former journalist for *L'Osservatore Romano* who went on to publish a book in which he reported that the pope was the target of blackmail attempts over his sexuality.[*]

The initial response from the Vatican came in a statement issued by Italy's national bishops' conference. It denounced *Tempo* and appealed to Italians to join in prayer in a "day of consolation" for Paul VI. The bishops' conference provided parish priests across the country with the text of a ser-

---

[*] A well-reviewed 2000 book on the history of the British intelligence agency MI6 alleged that then-Monsignor Montini had an affair in the 1930s with a male MI6 agent based in Rome. The author, British historian Stephen Dorril, suggested the relationship opened Montini to extortion by foreign intelligence agencies.

mon to be delivered the following Sunday defending the pope. Paul's deputies urged him to say nothing about the article. They thought he should
take comfort from the fact that major news organizations outside Italy
ignored the story. Speaking out would only encourage more reporting, and
more questions, they warned. They reminded him how popes had always
been the target of scurrilous rumors, including his mentor, Pius XII, over
his relationship with Pascalina. Nevertheless, in his address in St. Peter's
Square the following Sunday, the pope denounced the "horrible and slan-
derous insinuations" made against him. He did not specify how he had
been slandered—many non-Italians in the crowd seemed uncertain what
he was talking about—but "we know that our cardinals and the Italian bishops' conference have urged you to pray for me." Vatican officials knew the
pope had made a terrible mistake in speaking out when, that evening, the
Associated Press, the world's largest news organization by many measurements, released an article under the headline "POPE PAUL VI DENIES
HE IS HOMOSEXUAL."

Years later, the question was often asked by church historians and government investigators: Did Paul VI and others in the hierarchy of the
church in the twentieth century, terrified their own sexual history might be
questioned, choose to ignore evidence that other churchmen were violating their oaths of celibacy, including in ways that were criminal?

Early in his papacy, Paul granted an audience to Father Gerald Fitzgerald, the American who ran the treatment center in New Mexico for emotionally disturbed clergymen, and who had warned for years that a growing
number of American priests were molesting children. When Fitzgerald
died in 1969, no one replaced him as a forceful internal advocate of the
need for the Vatican to confront the problem.

American bishops failed for decades to address serious allegations of
rampant child sexual abuse by priests. Even so, beginning in the 1970s, the
US hierarchy admitted publicly it was alarmed about the emotional stability of men entering the priesthood, especially on sexual matters, and the
threat it might pose. In 1972, the national bishops' conference published
the troubling results of a five-year study by Father Kennedy, the Loyola
psychologist. He found that two-thirds of the 271 priests he studied were
emotionally undeveloped and incapable of forming healthy, trusting nonsexual relationships with men or women. The study determined that most
priests had the emotional maturity of a teenager, especially when it came to
sexuality. Kennedy found that a sizable percentage were not just emotion-

ally underdeveloped, they were *"mal-developed."* Priests put so much energy into repressing their sexuality that it damaged their mental health, Kennedy concluded. "They became obsessed with suppressing it."

IN FEBRUARY 1975, Hans Küng was disappointed but not surprised at news he was being formally denounced by the Congregation for the Doctrine of the Faith. He had known for years that he had a "target on my back" in Rome. The congregation's written decree condemned Küng's book *Infallible?*, published four years earlier, in which he questioned the doctrine of papal infallibility. The book erred in "opposing Catholic Church doctrine which must be professed by all the faith," the congregation declared. "Professor Hans Küng must not continue to teach such views." It was the Vatican's harshest public condemnation of a theologian since well before Vatican II.

Even so, many in the Curia thought it represented a partial victory for Küng, since the Vatican did not announce any other disciplinary action. German churchmen credited Cardinal Döpfner of Munich with behind-the-scenes negotiations that saved Küng's career. Many German bishops were harsh critics of Küng, but he had a protector in Döpfner, who had been chairman of the national bishops' conference since Vatican II. While the cardinal was often infuriated by Küng, he was also convinced that the Vatican badly overreacted to the Swiss theologian, which only brought Küng more publicity and sold more of his books. "Don't be a fool," Döpfner told a colleague who suggested the Vatican had been right to denounce Küng: "His books are already bestsellers without the church's assistance."

On the day of the congregation's announcement, Küng released his own statement, declaring he would continue to defy the Vatican: "I will not tolerate being prevented from pursuing my theological service to my fellow man." He honored that promise with new books that were almost as controversial—and sold even better. In 1974, he published *On Being a Christian*, which offered a basic history of the life of Jesus. In the book, Küng wanted to undermine the idea that Jesus was a meek pacifist who had to be provoked into action, a description regularly promoted by the Vatican in arguing for complete obedience to the church's teachings. In fact, Küng wrote, "Jesus of Nazareth was a very clear-sighted, resolute and—if need be—militant and fearless young man" who was "more revolutionary than the revolutionaries."

On Being a Christian was also an effort by Küng to debunk what he considered myths about Jesus's supernatural powers and explain why Christians could still see him as their Savior. Küng argued, as did other modern theologians, that Jesus's resurrection as portrayed in the Gospels might be fiction meant to inspire with its symbolism. He thought the account of Mary's virginity might also be legend.

Küng admitted years later his book was largely a response to the success of Ratzinger's *Introduction to Christianity*, the book that seemed to contain a gratuitous insult to "Clever Hans." Küng insisted he had always been unimpressed by much of Ratzinger's scholarship—a judgment, he said, unrelated to his personal contempt for his once-close friend—and believed that Ratzinger's account of Jesus's life in *Introduction* reflected only the most traditional recitation of doctrine and sidestepped questions about the Bible's accuracy.

On Being a Christian was a massive worldwide bestseller by the standards of religious books, surpassing Ratzinger's sales within months. It was the best-selling religious book published in Germany in a quarter century, with 160,000 copies sold there in a year. In the US, it was nearly as successful. A reviewer for *The New York Times*, Father Andrew Greeley, a noted Catholic sociologist and novelist, declared it "the best defense of Catholic Christianity to appear in this century."

It was a sign of Küng's fame that some of Europe's most important theologians rushed to contribute essays to a book *about* his book, *Discussion of Hans Küng's "On Being a Christian."* Most of the essays complimented Küng, but a handful were stinging. None was more venomous than one by Ratzinger. He wrote that Küng's "shallow" book presented an "empty formula" for Christianity.

In July 1976, Küng lost his most important protector when Döpfner died of a heart attack at sixty-two. His death "ushered in a situation which is disturbing for the church in Germany and was highly dangerous for me personally," Küng wrote later. The conservative Bavarian state government opposed the Vatican's initial choice of Döpfner's replacement, a reform-minded bishop, and urged Paul VI to find another. The search continued for months.

BY THE MID-1970S, Ratzinger had created a satisfying life for himself in Regensburg. The university was quiet and conservative. He enjoyed daily walks along the banks of the Danube and across the city's twelfth-century stone bridge, considered a masterwork of medieval construction. The university was near the city's thirteenth-century cathedral, a twin-spired Gothic landmark that was home to the Regensburger Domspatzen, the famous Catholic boys' choir led by his brother. (The word *domspatzen* means "cathedral sparrows.") The oldest boys' choir in the world, founded in the year 975, it was now a constant presence in Joseph Ratzinger's life.

He built a home for himself and his sister in Regensburg, paid for from the continuing strong sales of *Introduction to Christianity*. Since his brother lived only a few minutes away by foot, all three ate together several times a week. Joseph assumed Regensburg would be his home forever, so he had the remains of his late parents reburied there; he planned to be buried beside them.

He was saddened by Döpfner's death and shocked by rumors he might be the cardinal's successor. At first, he said, he did not take the rumors seriously, since he had none of the administrative experience a bishop normally required; he had never managed anything larger than a university theology department. He also had little experience as a pastor, ministering face-to-face to real people.

Weeks later, he received an unexpected visit from the Bosnian-born papal nuncio in Germany, Bishop Guido del Mestri. Ratzinger remembered that "we chatted about insignificant matters and then finally he pressed a letter into my hand, telling me to read it and think it over." It was a letter from the pope naming him archbishop of Munich. He said he decided on the spot to reject the appointment, if only because he valued his scholarly career too much. He went to his personal confessor, Father Johann Auer, a fellow theology professor, and asked for advice. "Auer had a very realistic knowledge of my limitations, both theological and human," Ratzinger said. "I surely expected him to advise me to decline." Auer, however, replied without hesitation: "You must accept."

Ratzinger went to see the nuncio, who was staying at a nearby hotel, who also urged him to accept, and Ratzinger reluctantly agreed. His installation as bishop was set for May. Ratzinger said the weeks ahead of the ceremony were almost unbearably stressful; he felt ill and found it difficult to sleep. On the day of his installation in Munich's grand fifteenth-century cathedral, however, he was revived. "The day itself was extraordinarily beautiful—a radiant day."

Weeks later he was named to the College of Cardinals. That promotion was less surprising than his initial appointment, since Munich was traditionally led by a cardinal. In June he went to Rome for the installation ceremony and met privately with the pope, who seemed strangely chilly and distracted. One of Paul's secretaries later apologized to Ratzinger, explaining that the pope was heartsick over the imminent departure from Rome of his closest aide, Archbishop Benelli, who was also being installed as a cardinal that week and dispatched to Florence. Years later, Benelli recalled the day he was summoned to the papal apartment to be told of his promotion. He found the pope weeping at his desk, despondent at the thought of Benelli's departure. "The tears were so abundant that they marked his blotter." Many in the Curia were convinced Paul promoted Benelli to the College of Cardinals to position him for election as his successor.

In Munich, the newly installed Cardinal Ratzinger faced a crush of pastoral and administrative work. Beyond leading worship services in the cathedral, he now oversaw the staffing of parish churches and schools throughout Bavaria. Hundreds of priests and nuns and thousands of lay employees answered to him. He proved himself a cold, distant manager, which made for an ugly comparison to the agreeable Döpfner. Many priests bristled at Ratzinger's formality. He was reluctant to meet personally with individual clerics who wanted his time, citing his busy schedule. Several years after his appointment, a group of Munich priests joined in an extraordinary written statement of protest. Ratzinger, they wrote, "exalts himself in a triumphant manner above everything." Still, others admired his decisiveness. "I didn't dodge conflicts," he said later. In fact, he found it "repulsive" when bishops ducked important decisions. "In order to avoid conflicts, they let the poison spread." Many priests, when they did spend time in his presence, found him welcoming; they wondered if some people misread his shyness.

He was thankful that Regensburg was only an hour's drive away on the autobahn, and he returned there often to dine with former university colleagues and attend performances of the Regensburger Domspatzen. As cardinal for all Bavaria, he had nominal oversight over the choir, although he was convinced his brother was doing a brilliant job as choirmaster and needed no supervision—a disastrous conclusion, as it turned out.

16

The Dirty War

PERHAPS PAUL VI WAS simply too depressed and ill to understand the extent of the misery among millions of the faithful so far from Rome. Whatever the reason, it was undeniable that in the final years of his papacy, he was often silent about terrible human-rights abuses in Latin America. In Chile, General Augusto Pinochet came to power in a 1973 coup, overthrowing the democratically elected government of President Salvador Allende, a socialist. Pinochet's vicious dictatorship lasted for seventeen years. Immediately after the coup, Paul issued a statement decrying the military regime's "violent oppression," including the murder of scores of Pinochet's opponents. Behind the scenes in Rome, however, the pope's deputies were eager to excuse the Chilean general because of his dedication to the church. Allende, a self-described atheist, died during the coup, possibly by suicide, although his cause of death was never certain. According to long-secret cables from the US embassy in Italy, the pope's closest aide, then-Archbishop Benelli, was eager to downplay the extent of the violence. He insisted to Western diplomats there had been "exaggerated coverage" of Pinochet's abuses. The Vatican had been assured by the Chilean military that "stories alleging brutal reprisals are unfounded" and might simply reflect "the great success of Communist propaganda." Using language better suited to a steely-eyed Cold War diplomat than a man of God, Benelli explained that some violence was only to be expected: "As is unfortunately natural following a coup d'état, there has admittedly been bloodshed during mopping-up procedures."

Brazil's military government, in power since 1964, continued to imprison and murder opponents throughout the 1970s. Since civilian political parties were banned, Brazilian bishops emerged as the government's chief critics. At first, the most outspoken was Hélder Câmara in the city of Recife, but his voice was silenced—literally, for much of the country—in 1968, when the government declared him a Marxist and banned radio and television stations from broadcasting his voice or image. In the late 1960s, Cardinal Angelo Rossi of São Paulo, the country's biggest city, resisted confrontation with the military. He was called to Rome in 1970 to join the Curia and replaced by a deputy, Bishop Paulo Evaristo Arns, who was later named a cardinal. The appointment of Arns, then forty-nine, set a new path for the Brazilian church, since he immediately established himself as a human-rights champion and the junta's most determined foe. He insisted on living simply, adding to his moral authority. First, he sold off the opulent bishop's mansion, as well as the leafy park that surrounded it, after discovering to his astonishment that his predecessor Rossi had a staff of twenty-five household servants simply to tend to his daily needs. Arns used the proceeds to enlarge several base communities in the city's slums. He moved into a pair of simple rooms behind a local monastery, where he often greeted visitors not in a cardinal's finery but in casual clothes and slippers. Soon after his appointment, he bravely authorized a secret church-funded investigation to document the extent of the government's murder of political prisoners—information later used to prosecute army leaders.

Whatever the human-rights abuses in Brazil and Chile, the scale of government-sanctioned violence in neighboring Argentina in those years was always much worse. The term *los desaparecidos* (the disappeared) became part of everyday conversation in Buenos Aires, since almost everyone knew someone who had vanished without a trace—kidnapped by the military, it was usually assumed. International human-rights groups estimated that during the 1970s, thirty thousand Argentines were abducted and never seen again.

There was another important difference between what happened in Argentina and what went on across its borders: The hierarchy of the Argentine church remained almost entirely silent about the government's crimes. The most powerful figure in the Catholic hierarchy at the time was Cardinal Juan Carlos Aramburu of Buenos Aires, who was named the capital's archbishop in 1975, a year before a coup brought the military to power. He would later be described by human-rights investigators as a collaborator in the junta's worst atrocities.*

JORGE BERGOGLIO, entering his third year as Jesuit leader in 1976, was unlucky in choosing a moving day that year: Wednesday, March 24. He planned to spend all day packing up the Jesuits' office at 300 Bogotá Street in downtown Buenos Aires, then shutting its doors. Everything was being relocated to the Colegio Máximo. Just as the move was getting underway, there was the menacing sound of army helicopters overhead. Military jets whizzed by, so many that the skies darkened with exhaust. Tanks appeared at roadblocks and a police car suddenly pulled up in front of the Bogotá Street building, its sirens blaring. Officers asked suspiciously why the priests were moving. "This is a national emergency!" one policeman yelled. An emergency? Bergoglio and the other Jesuits had been so busy that morning that no one turned on the radio to hear the news: the military had ousted Isabel Perón and was now in power.

Bergoglio, then thirty-nine, said later that what he felt in those first hours after the coup, a mix of ignorance and dread, was typical of what he experienced throughout the seven-year nightmare that descended on Argentina that day.

For the rest of his life, he struggled to avoid conversations about the Dirty War—or *el Proceso* (the Process), the Orwellian name the junta dreamed up for its frenzied campaign to rid the country of a supposed Marxist threat. After the Dirty War, Bergoglio declined to meet with prosecutors and human-rights investigators, and his defensiveness was understandable, since he could not deny that he, like most church leaders, did nothing publicly to protest *el Proceso*. For many Argentines, the scandal over the church's silence in those years was their nation's equivalent to the Vatican's failure to protest the Holocaust during World War II.

The country's new leader was the army commander, General Jorge

---

* In 2023, a group of Argentine historians and theologians concluded that the country's Catholic hierarchy knew for certain by 1979 that the junta had a policy of "disappearing"— kidnapping and killing—its opponents. Despite that, Argentine bishops refused to protest publicly for "fear of weakening the military government and for fear of communism," the study concluded ("New research reveals Argentine bishops knew the military junta was 'disappearing' people," Gerard O'Connell, *America* magazine, June 23, 2023).

Rafael Videla, who named himself president. Many church leaders were enthusiastic about Videla, since he was a devout Catholic and made a show of it. He broke away from his duties several times a day to attend Mass. He shared power in the junta with the nation's navy commander, Admiral Emilio Massera, and their equivalent in the air force. Massera was the mastermind of many of the horrors to come, including the use of navy facilities to torture and execute thousands of alleged subversives. Years later, he would be described by deputies as a true psychopath, eager to kill indiscriminately. "I hate to use the word 'evil,' but you can't avoid it with Massera," said Robert Cox, the heroic, British-born editor of the *Buenos Aires Herald*, the city's English-language newspaper, which was one of the few in Argentina to try to expose the junta's abuses.

Many Argentines became alarmed by early pronouncements from Videla in which he boasted of the savagery to come. He pledged to rid the country of anyone who could be labeled a leftist, which meant killing them all: "As many people as necessary must die in Argentina so that the country will again be secure." He labeled all dissidents as terrorists: "A terrorist is not only someone who plants bombs but a person whose ideas are contrary to Western, Christian civilization."

After the Dirty War, Videla was convicted of mass murder and sentenced to life in prison. At trial, he admitted the truth of what had happened—how the military rounded up, often based on rumor, thousands of suspected leftists and secretly executed them without trial. "At one time, we thought of publishing lists of the executed, but then there was an objection," he explained. "If we say they have been killed, then the awkward questions will start: Who killed them? Where? How?"

Within days of the coup, masked soldiers flooded the streets of Buenos Aires and other cities in a fleet of unmarked Ford Falcon sedans—the vehicle of choice for the security services—to abduct anyone suspected of being a leftist. Most victims were taken into custody late at night and transported to one of more than three hundred detention centers across the country. Massera oversaw the abductions and personally devised many of the torture methods. He came up with whimsical names for his interrogation program, as if to mock the condemned. Torture centers were called "Rooms of Happiness." One routine interrogation technique was known as "the submarine," in which prisoners had their heads placed in buckets of toilet water, fouled with human waste, until they began to drown. In a classified report to the State Department in 1980, the US embassy in Buenos Aires offered a full list of the torture methods known to be used by the junta's interrogators: electric shocks, often inflicted with cattle prods; the burning of skin with boiling water, oil, and acid; prolonged immersion in water; the extraction of teeth and fingernails; rape and other sexual assault; and, in a handful of cases, castration.

When it came time for prisoners to be killed, the junta's execution methods included "the water solution," in which the condemned were sedated and then thrown—alive—from helicopters or small planes flying above the La Plata River. The corpses, unidentifiable after several days in the water, washed up on shore as a warning of the danger of defying the junta. Other prisoners were executed on land. In August 1976, the mutilated bodies of forty-six men were found in a pasture outside Buenos Aires, first killed by machine guns before their corpses were blown up with dynamite. A crudely lettered sign over the bodies read: "Montonero Cemetery—Executed for Being Traitors to the Homeland."

The rape of women just ahead of their execution was common. Pregnant women were not killed until after giving birth. About five hundred of those babies were turned over to childless military couples and others loyal to the junta. Through DNA testing years later, hundreds of the "children of the disappeared" learned the truth about the men and women who raised them.

Argentine President Jorge Rafael Videla (center) with Admiral Emilio Massera (left) and Cardinal Juan Carlos Aramburu of Buenos Aires, during the junta's independence day ceremonies in 1977, the second year of the Dirty War

Despite the junta's supposed devotion to the church, clergy suspected of being leftists were early targets for assassination. In July 1976, three Catholic priests were gunned down in a parish residence on the outskirts of Buenos Aires, all shot in the back of the head. Weeks later, two more priests were murdered in La Rioja province—Bishop Angelelli's diocese.

In July, Paul VI condemned the violence against Argentine clergymen and dispatched his chief diplomat in Buenos Aires, Bishop Pio Laghi, the Italian-born papal nuncio, to meet with junta leaders to demand the priest killers be brought to justice. Still, Laghi was seen by many Argentines to be an imperfect human-rights advocate, since he was Massera's regular tennis partner.

In August, Angelelli died in La Rioja in what was officially reported as a traffic accident. Many of his parishioners suspected his death was no accident; and years after the Dirty War, two senior military officers were found guilty of arranging his murder.

Cardinal Aramburu was eager to be seen as the junta's champion and brushed aside reports of state-sanctioned kidnappings and executions. He ignored pleas for help from the families of missing Argentines and refused to meet with leaders of the best-known of the family groups, the Mothers of Plaza de Mayo (Madres de Plaza de Mayo), which represented thousands of women whose children had disappeared.

Priests, nuns, and other church workers were collaborators in the torture and execution of political prisoners. Several priests volunteered to work in the most notorious of the detention centers, established on the campus of the navy's School of Mechanics in the heart of Buenos Aires. The school was known by the acronym ESMA (Escuela Superior de Mecánica de la Armada). Military records later showed that, of about 5,000 people held there during the Dirty War, only 150 survived. It was revealed years later that, in 1979, the archdiocese secretly transferred ownership of Aramburu's weekend beach house—on a tiny, bucolic island on a waterway about forty miles from downtown Buenos Aires—to ESMA's commanders, who then used it to hide political prisoners at times when international human rights investigators were in the country searching for them. The island was known to locals by the name El Silencio.

Bergoglio never joined Aramburu and other churchmen who defended the junta. Even so, at a time when his voice might have made a difference—as leader of the Jesuits, he had undeniable moral authority in Argentine society—Bergoglio said nothing about the military's human-rights abuses.

A protest in Buenos Aires by the Mothers of Plaza de Mayo, a group of Argentine mothers whose children had been kidnapped and killed by the junta during the Dirty War from 1976 to 1983

In defending himself years later, he said that in the first year after the coup, he did not know enough to justify a protest. He insisted he always had fewer sources of information about human-rights abuses than the country's bishops, since every bishop oversaw a diocese of thousands of parishioners who could act as his eyes and ears in gathering information. "There were bishops who realized immediately what was happening," Bergoglio said. He, by comparison, learned about the extent of the horrors "only little by little." After the junta's human-rights abuses were well documented, he said, he remained silent in the belief that a public protest would doom his behind-the-scenes efforts to save individuals abducted by the government: "I did what I could and, with the few contacts I had, pleaded for people who had been kidnapped." Witnesses came forward years later to report that Bergoglio had, in fact, put himself at risk to protect people targeted by the junta. He sheltered several accused dissidents at the Colegio Máximo and helped others reach safety outside Argentina. In one case, he gave his government identity card to a suspected leftist, who resembled Bergoglio, and dressed him in priestly clothes to help him escape across the border to Uruguay. "I was taking a big risk," Bergoglio said years later. "If he had been found out, the authorities would undoubtedly have killed him and then come looking for me."

Still, he regretted he had not done more and said he was haunted for the rest of his life by the memory of a meeting, shortly after the 1976 coup, with a terrified woman whose two sons, both accused of being Communists, had been kidnapped, which meant they would almost certainly be tortured and killed. She pleaded for Bergoglio's help to save them. "She was a widow, and her sons were all she had," he recalled. "How she cried! It was a scene I will never forget. I made some inquiries but got nowhere."

The pressures of those years were so great that Bergoglio feared his mental health was at risk. It led him to do something that would have been scandalous for a prominent Argentine churchman to admit in the 1970s. He secretly began to see a psychotherapist. He later joked darkly that, in seeking therapy, he was just being a good patriot, since psychiatry and psychology had been extraordinarily popular in Argentina since the early twentieth century.* He thought his therapist, a woman, was unusually gifted. "For six months, I went to her once a week to clear up certain things. She helped me a lot."

His actions during the Dirty War left him with bitter enemies inside the Jesuits. He confronted no more ferocious an adversary than Father Yorio, the slum priest, whose hatred for his Jesuit superior resulted in a voluminous written record that would eventually endanger Bergoglio's rise to power in the church. Yorio's allegations, if true, were shocking. Before he died in 2000, he insisted repeatedly, including in a formal petition he filed with the Jesuit hierarchy in Rome, that he and another slum priest, Franz Jalics, were betrayed by Bergoglio, which resulted in their kidnapping and torture in the early months of the Dirty War. Yorio believed he and Jalics became marked men because Bergoglio identified them to the junta as leftists. Bergoglio adamantly denied Yorio's "smears," insisting he tried repeatedly to shield the two priests from violence. Over the years, it became impossible to determine with certainty who was telling the truth, although witnesses came forward who cast doubt on Bergoglio's account.

———————

* By some estimates, Argentina has long had more psychiatrists, per capita, than any other nation on earth. One stylish Buenos Aires neighborhood is known informally as "Villa Freud" because so many psychiatrists and psychologists practice there.

BY 1977, complaints about Bergoglio's conduct during the Dirty War and his arrogant leadership style were widespread among Argentine Jesuits, and the hierarchy in Rome decided to act. In April, Arrupe dispatched one of his deputies, Father Michael Campbell-Johnston, to Buenos Aires to investigate. He found a sharp split among the country's Jesuits. Bergoglio was admired by older, conservative Jesuits who were grateful he kept the Argentine order out of politics and—with the exception of Yorio and Jalics—safe from violence. He had nearly as many critics, including priests who complained that the order was completely out of step with the social-justice mission of Jesuits in the rest of South America. Campbell-Johnston confronted Bergoglio, who said his silence about human-rights abuses in Argentina was justified because the situation there was more dangerous than elsewhere.

Arrupe decided to keep Bergoglio in place even if he was divisive. After hearing back from Campbell-Johnston, Arrupe worried it would be wrong to shake up the leadership of the Argentine order in the midst of so much political chaos. When he left Buenos Aires, Campbell-Johnston carried a letter, signed by leaders of the Mothers of Plaza de Mayo, that he had agreed to present to Paul VI. The letter pleaded for the pope to pressure the junta to release their sons and daughters. The women told Campbell-Johnston that—since Argentina's church leaders, including Bergoglio, refused to do anything to help—their only hope was that the pope himself would intervene.

IN HINDSIGHT, Bergoglio's failure to help the Mothers of Plaza de Mayo was confounding, since he had such a personal connection to the group. Its founders included Esther Ballestrino, the chemist who had been his beloved boss when he was a teenager. Two of her young male relatives disappeared early in the Dirty War. In 1977, her pregnant sixteen-year-old daughter was abducted by the military. The reasons for kidnapping a pregnant teenager were never clear, and she was released after four months. She provided chilling details of her imprisonment. Nazi swastikas and photos of Adolf Hitler were displayed everywhere in the detention center, she said. "They put on cassette tapes of Hitler's speeches to drown out the screams while they tortured us."

Earlier that year, Ballestrino had phoned Bergoglio and asked him to come to her home to say last rites for a dying relative. He was surprised by the request, since she was a committed atheist. He went as requested, only to discover there was no dying relative. Instead, Ballestrino asked him to help her get rid of her library of books on politics, including several volumes on Marxism; simply possessing them might be reason enough for the junta to arrest her. Bergoglio agreed and moved the books to the Colegio.

That December, the junta decided to infiltrate the Mothers of Plaza de Mayo. A junta spy, navy commander Alfredo Astiz, who was based at the ESMA torture center, began to attend the group's meetings, pretending a family member was among the disappeared. Astiz, later dubbed by the Argentine press as the "Blond Angel" because of his golden hair and movie-star looks, provided his superiors with a roster of the group's leaders, including Ballestrino and two French nuns. The three women were then kidnapped, never to be seen alive again. Bergoglio said that, while he raised no public protest about the women's disappearance, he worked behind the scenes with his government contacts to try to save them, to no avail. "Perhaps I didn't do enough for them," he admitted. He was horrified years later to learn that the three women were tortured at ESMA before they were executed by the "water solution." Their bodies, which could not be identified by forensic scientists for years, washed up on a riverbank near Buenos Aires after a heavy storm.

JESUITS WERE DYING elsewhere in Latin America in the 1970s—martyrs to the cause of liberation theology. There was an especially stark contrast between Argentina's Jesuits and those of the much smaller, much poorer nation of El Salvador. Unlike in Argentina, the Jesuits of El Salvador embraced liberation theology and other social-justice campaigns, which made them targets for assassination. Theirs was a land of especially shocking inequality. A few landowners, allied with the military, controlled 90 percent of the nation's wealth. Military-backed governments had ruled the country mostly uninterrupted since the 1930s. Government and business leaders immediately saw liberation theology as a threat, especially as the base communities sponsored by Jesuits inspired peasant workers to organize for better pay and housing.

In 1977, right-wing death squads allied with the military drew up lists of Jesuits and other priests targeted for assassination. The first to die was a forty-eight-year-old Jesuit, Father Rutilio Grande, who was assassinated in March along with two parishioners, one of them a sixteen-year-old boy. Gunmen surrounded their car on a road outside San Salvador, the capital, and opened fire. Human-rights groups later determined that Grande's name was at the top of the death list because he was so well-known for his work in establishing base communities. An autopsy found twelve bullets in his body. Human-rights investigators believed the number was no coincidence; it was meant, perversely, to represent the twelve apostles.

Grande had been a protégé of the country's most important churchman, Archbishop Óscar Romero of San Salvador, and Romero was radicalized by his friend's death. Almost overnight, the archbishop became the government's most outspoken critic and aligned himself with the Jesuits, even as the Jesuits became targets of more violence. In July 1977, a right-wing militia known as the White Warriors, made up of retired army officers, released a statement vowing to execute fifty more Jesuits because of their "Communist subversion." The response from the leader of El Salvador's Jesuits, Father César Jerez, was defiant: "We'll all stay until we are either killed or expelled."

AT THE END of his life, the Italian word for pain, *dolore*, appeared often in Paul VI's public statements. He spoke of the pain of the church, and of his own emotional and physical pain. He turned eighty in September 1977 and refused any public celebration on his birthday: "Let me spend that day alone, in solitude and prayer."

His closest confidante was John Magee, a kindly Irish priest who had been one of his private secretaries since 1969. Magee said years later that the pope was intensely lonely as he approached death, desperate for any sort of conversation. He recalled a rainy Sunday afternoon when Paul grabbed his hand and led him on a tour of the papal library. At one point, the pope pulled open a cabinet stuffed with letters and photos that dated from his childhood. He told Magee that his friends and family in the pictures were dead: "They're all gone, leaving me alone." Magee tried to comfort him, reminding him he would be reunited in heaven with his loved ones. Paul said somberly that he did not accept the premise: "It is not certain that I will go to Paradise."

He often told Magee he was convinced the world beyond Rome was in chaos, engulfed by "barbarism," and blamed it in part on the failures of his papacy. Magee worried Paul would try to die a martyr. That October, the pope's secretaries panicked when, overcome by news that a German passenger jet had been hijacked by Palestinian terrorists to the African nation of Somalia, Paul issued a public statement offering to fly there and be taken hostage in place of the ninety-one passengers and crew. Before the hijackers had a chance to act on the pope's offer, they were dead, killed when the plane was stormed by a West German commando unit.

Five months later, the pope agonized at news of another terrorist act: the Red Brigades' kidnapping of his friend Aldo Moro, Italy's former prime minister and the leader of the governing Christian Democratic Party. Moro was abducted from his car in Rome on March 16 in an ambush in which five bodyguards were killed. Within days, the Maoist-inspired Red Brigades announced that the sixty-one-year-old politician would be placed on trial by a "People's Court." The pope, who had been close to Moro since the 1930s, was so distraught that he canceled his public appearances for Easter and the preceding Holy Week.

In letters made public by his captors, Moro pleaded with the pope to save him by pressuring the Italian government to organize a prisoner swap. The Red Brigades suggested they would release Moro in exchange for a group of imprisoned radicals. The government refused to negotiate, so Paul decided to act. On April 21, on the eve of a deadline set for Moro's execution, the pope sat at his desk from nine thirty p.m. until almost midnight, composing a letter released publicly the next morning. "I write to you, men of the Red Brigades," it began. "Aldo Moro is a good and upright man, to whom no one can impute any crime. I beg you, on my knees, to free him."

In another letter to his family in late April, Moro charged that the Vatican, which had failed to convince the government to negotiate, was "condemning me." On May 9, his bullet-riddled corpse was found in the trunk of a car in the center of Rome.

The pope was so overcome with grief that he remained in his private chapel, on his knees, for the rest of the day. Four days later, he led Moro's memorial service at St. John Lateran, the central cathedral of the archdiocese of Rome. Many members of Moro's family refused to attend in protest of the church's failure to do more to save him.

In July, the pope left Rome to begin his summer retreat at Castel Gandolfo. He came down with a high fever, and on August 3, the last day he was fully coherent, he asked Magee to join him for dinner. He ate nothing but seemed eager simply for the presence of another human being. They watched the evening television news together, then an American cowboy movie. Magee recalled that the pope "did not understand anything about the plot, and he asked me every so often, 'Who is the good guy? Who is the bad guy?'" Paul became enthusiastic "only when there were scenes of horses." After saying the Rosary together, Magee said good night and went to bed.

At about three a.m., the pope's household staff heard three bells—a sign he needed help. Magee rushed to his bedroom and found him sitting up, gasping for breath. Paul was helped to an armchair. Magee asked him: "Your Holiness, should we pray together now?" "Yes," came the reply, "but not for me. Pray for the church." He returned to bed and stayed there until Sunday evening, August 6, when he suffered a massive heart attack. It was so violent his body convulsed, nearly throwing him from the bed. He survived another three hours. His last words were an effort to say the Lord's Prayer. At 9:41 p.m., his doctors pronounced him dead. At almost that same moment, Magee said, the pope's alarm clock went off at his bedside. Paul bought the clock in Poland in the 1920s, during his brief diplomatic assignment in Warsaw. Magee came to believe that the ringing of the Polish clock was a sign of momentous change to come.

WITH NEWS OF HIS DEATH, there were the expected tributes to Paul VI from world leaders, especially for his role in steering the Second Vatican Council to its conclusion. He was hailed as the first bishop of Rome to cross oceans in his travels. Still, his death resulted in nothing like the outpouring of grief the church experienced after the death of John XXIII. Many Catholics remained furious with him over *Humanae Vitae.* In Germany, Hans Küng was flooded by phone calls from major news organizations, eager to hear a final assessment of Paul's legacy from one of his best-known critics. Küng issued a conciliatory statement: "I personally am grateful to Pope Paul for holding his hand over me protectively all these years." Whatever their differences, the pope had never moved to silence Küng or seriously punish him.

Paul's body was moved by road from Castel Gandolfo to Rome. More than five thousand armed soldiers lined the route. The Italian military said the deployment was necessary because of the continuing threat from the Red Brigades. The funeral services in St. Peter's were understated, as Paul had requested in his will: "Let it be as simple as possible." Most of the 130 members of the College of Cardinals attended. The College, which had never been so large or diverse, included cardinals from fifty-one nations. The largest contingent, twenty-nine, was from Italy, but for the first time in the church's history non-Europeans would have a majority of votes in a conclave.

There was excited speculation a non-Italian would be elected pope—the first in 456 years. The last had been Hadrian VI, a Dutchman from the city of Utrecht, who reigned for twenty-one months in the sixteenth century. In 1978, the most talked-about non-Italian candidate was also a Dutchman from Utrecht, Johannes Willebrands, a well-liked Curia veteran. Another possible non-Italian contender was Franz König of Austria, seen as one of the progressive heroes of Vatican II. Ahead of the conclave, König said he supported the idea of a non-Italian, but ruled himself out as too old at seventy-two. Years earlier, Cardinal Suenens would have been an obvious candidate, but he was now seventy-four and had alienated too many conservatives in the Curia.

The name of Karol Wojtyła, the fifty-eight-year-old Polish cardinal, appeared on several lists of *papabile* candidates, and other cardinals were eager to promote his candidacy—König, in particular. Given Austria's self-declared neutrality in the Cold War, König had often been dispatched on sensitive Vatican missions to Poland, and he and Wojtyła became close. At the time of the 1978 conclave, he thought that Wojtyła was just the right age and had the magnetism that Catholics had missed since John XXIII. He knew there would also be powerful symbolism in electing a pope from Communist Eastern Europe.

Wojtyła had befriended many of the world's cardinals during his far-flung travels throughout the 1970s. He demonstrated a talent for attracting flattering publicity abroad, especially when cameras were around. He sensed what news photographers wanted, so often had his picture taken wearing native hats and costumes. In 1973, during a trip to Australia, his photo was splashed across several newspapers there after he made a point of visiting a wildlife preserve to feed a kangaroo. In 1976, he made an eleven-city tour of the United States, centered on cities with sizable ethnic Polish communities.

It was evidence of his charm that he never aroused the jealousy directed at other cardinals seen to be campaigning for the papacy. He had a strong patron in Paul VI, who had always been ambitious for Wojtyła. When Paul asked him to speak at the pope's Lenten retreat in 1976, he encouraged

Wojtyła to deliver the lectures in Italian instead of Latin, so Italian cardinals who might be kingmakers at a conclave could hear for themselves how well he spoke their language.

In any Vatican gathering, Wojtyła always stood out because of his physical presence. Even well into middle age, the Polish cardinal—five foot ten inches tall, with a full head of hair—remained ruggedly handsome and fit; he loved to ski and kayak.

His youth had been marked by loss. His mother died when he was eight, so he was raised mostly by his father, a retired soldier. In 1932, when Karol was twelve, his only brother died during a scarlet fever epidemic. Karol originally planned an acting career, but those plans were foiled by the Nazi invasion of Poland in 1939. Two years later, his father died of a heart attack, leaving twenty-year-old Karol so devastated that he felt compelled to rethink his life, which led to his decision to become a priest. The Nazis shut down Catholic seminaries, so in 1942 Wojtyła joined an illegal underground seminary, while continuing to work in a stone quarry and chemical factory.

Among cardinals outside Poland who knew him, there was a general understanding about his views on church doctrine; he was conservative and had been especially vocal in support of *Humanae Vitae*. But he spoke and wrote so vaguely, and could be so downright confusing at times, that no one could be certain exactly what he believed. Some progressive cardinals, including König, were reassured by Wojtyła's constant public praise for Vatican II, which suggested he would press forward with the council's reforms. Churchmen who wanted to understand his thinking often turned to translations of a book he had written in Polish in 1972, in which he offered a detailed analysis of the central documents of the council, but many bishops found it impenetrable.

Some friends thought he had trouble expressing himself because in his graduate studies, he had specialized in an obscure branch of philosophy known as phenomenology, in which clear-cut, easy-to-understand arguments were actually discouraged.* By the 1970s, the field, once promoted by the French philosopher Jean-Paul Sartre, was treated as little more than a curiosity by most major university philosophy departments.

---

* There is no simple definition of phenomenology. The *Encyclopaedia Britannica* defines it as a "philosophical movement" that pursues the "investigation and description of phenomena as consciously experienced, without theories about their causal explanation and as free as possible from unexamined preconceptions."

Years later, Joseph Ratzinger struggled to remember when he first met Wojtyła. They both attended Vatican II, but he thought they had not talked at the time. He knew his Polish counterpart slightly from the 1977 synod, but Ratzinger thought his first real conversation with Wojtyła did not occur until Paul VI's funeral in 1978. The two got along instantly, the German cardinal remembered: "You sensed that here was a man of God. Here was a person who had nothing artificial about him."

Ratzinger went to Rome for the 1978 conclave awed by the idea he would soon be locked inside the Sistine Chapel to elect the next vicar of Christ. He did not expect to be an active participant since, at fifty-one, "I was one of the youngest cardinals, and I didn't want to presume that I would somehow play a role."

The chapel was uncomfortably crowded when the conclave got under-way on August 25. Given the record number of cardinals, the central area was too small to accommodate all of them, so some had to be seated behind an ornate grille that divided the sanctuary in two. Rome was in the mid-dle of a traditional summer heat wave, and the cardinals were confined to makeshift sleeping quarters that were barely air-conditioned. "My room was an oven," Suenens complained. Their discomfort helped explain why the cardinals were eager to end the conclave quickly. The deliberations lasted only eight hours over two days, the shortest since the election of Pius XII in 1939. The 1978 deliberations were also short because the Ital-ian delegation settled on one of its own as a candidate—Albino Luciani, the popular primate of Venice, who was elected pope on the fourth ballot.

PART IV

JOHN PAUL I
(August–September 1978)

17

The Smiling Pope

MANY CARDINALS LIKED the idea that the shy, genial Luciani, the son of a northern Italian bricklayer, was mostly an outsider in Rome. He had never worked in the Curia, which meant he might bring a fresh eye to the church's creaking bureaucracy. At sixty-five, he was also seen as the right age—young enough to serve several years, but not several decades, as pope. He had a theology degree from the Gregorian but was far better known as an approachable pastor. His best-known writing was a 1976 book of charming letters he addressed to important figures in history, including Jesus, and fictional characters from literature. The letters, originally published in his archdiocese newsletter in Venice, offered a message of charity.

His choice of the papal name John Paul in honor of his two immediate predecessors was welcomed by reform-minded churchmen—as an early sign of his willingness to break tradition, since it was the first papal double name in two thousand years. He established himself from the start as unpretentious. He was the first pope in centuries to refuse to wear a jeweled tiara at his coronation: "I am only a poor man, accustomed to little things." He immediately won over crowds at the Vatican with his ever-present smile, which was so different from the grim Paul VI. He quickly became known to Romans as *il papa del sorriso*—the smiling pope.

On doctrine he appeared to be staunchly conservative. In Venice, he had spoken out to oppose abortion, divorce, and the ordination of women. He seemed wary of liberation theology: "It is a mistake to state that political, economic and social liberation coincides with salvation in Jesus." At the same time, he was open to developments in modern science that the Vatican opposed. That included in-vitro fertilization, which Curia theologians saw as sinful since it replaced the normal process of reproduction. When the world's first so-called test-tube baby was born in England earlier that summer, then-Cardinal Luciani wrote to parishioners that he extended "the warmest wishes to the little English girl. As for the parents, I have no right to condemn them."

The cardinals left Rome confident they had chosen a pope who would hold to tradition and whose personal warmth would be welcomed. The selection was praised by other prominent churchmen, including some who might have worried he would prove too conservative. "I am truly happy," Hans Küng wrote in a diary. He had corresponded with Luciani over the years and been impressed by his "modesty, judgment and serenity."

And then, on September 28, thirty-three days after his election, the smiling pope was dead. According to the Vatican's official account, he was found in bed that morning, his heart stopped, after he failed to appear for sunrise Mass; the body was discovered by Father Magee, who had remained on the papal staff. Magee said he entered the bedroom at five thirty a.m. after there was no response to his knock and found the pope in bed, his head propped up on pillows in a half-sitting position. The reading light was on. The semiofficial Vatican Radio reported he had been reading *The Imitation of Christ*, a fifteenth-century handbook on Christian devotion. The Vatican said a papal physician determined that the pope, who had been sickly as a young man, died of a heart attack at about eleven the night before. Many in the Curia encouraged journalists to assume the pope's death was the result of the extraordinary stress of his new responsibilities.

It would be years before the Vatican acknowledged that much of the initial account was a lie, beginning with a crude cover-up of the body's discovery. The pope was found in bed not by Magee but by a thirty-seven-year-old Italian nun who worked on his household staff. She went into the bedroom after another, older nun noticed the pope had not collected a tray with his morning coffee. The younger nun gave testimony in which she recalled how she entered the room and "touched his hands—they were cold." She yelled out for others to come quickly. She thought his death was especially shocking because he had not seemed at all overwhelmed by his duties. In the days before his death, she testified, he had been "calm, serene, full of trust, confident."

The motive for the cover-up seemed obvious. The pope's aides feared a scandal at the disclosure that a woman, albeit a nun, entered his bedchambers and touched his flesh, even if it was simply her attempt to determine if he was alive. The official story began to unravel when news organizations disputed Vatican Radio and reported that the pope was not reading a book when he died. He had actually been reviewing routine Curia paperwork, it appeared. Medical experts said it was impossible to imagine the corpse in the condition described by the Vatican—the pope's glasses propped up on his nose, a serene expression on his face—when in fact a heart-attack victim would thrash about in reaction to the pain. Items from the pope's bedroom disappeared immediately after his death, including a bottle of blood-thinning pills.

American reporters in the Vatican press corps began to compare mysteries about the pope's death to what they encountered after the 1963 assassination of President Kennedy. The facts of the pope's death, like Kennedy's, had become so muddled—intentionally, it seemed—that conspiracy theories ran wild. Years later, polls showed a vast majority of Italians were convinced John Paul had been murdered. Several best-selling books insisted the pope had been assassinated; the suspects included senior figures in the Curia as well as the CIA and the KGB. The most persistent theories centered on the possibility the pope was murdered because he was about to expose corruption within the Curia, especially inside the Vatican Bank.

The swirl of conspiracy theories so worried Vatican officials that they agreed to cooperate with a respected British journalist, John Cornwell, as he conducted his own investigation. In his book *A Thief in the Night*, published in 1989, Cornwell concluded the pope had in fact died of natural causes—possibly from a blood clot that reached his lungs, not a heart attack—and that he might have survived had he received proper medical care. He had complained of chest pains the day before, Cornwell reported. He believed Magee had discovered the pope dead the night before, on the bedroom floor, "his hands bunched in agony." According to the book, a panicked Magee summoned another papal secretary to meet him in the bedroom. The pair were terrified they would be blamed for having failed to call a doctor after the pope complained of chest pains, so they rearranged the scene to suggest he died hours after he actually did. They picked up the corpse and put it back in bed, propping it up with pillows and placing the pope's glasses on his nose. They left the body to be discovered the next morning. Magee and the other secretary adamantly denied the allegations, and they were never formally charged with wrongdoing.

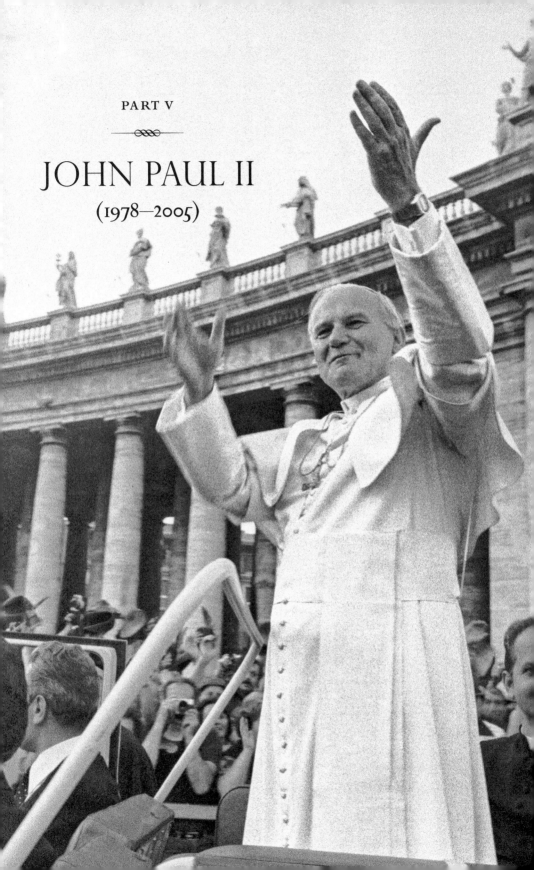

PART V

JOHN PAUL II

(1978—2005)

18

The Superstar Pope

THE WORLD'S CARDINALS, shocked by John Paul's death, planned their return to Rome. The year's second conclave was scheduled to begin October 14, ten days after the pope's funeral. Cardinal König announced publicly he was now ready to vote for a non-Italian pope; privately, he had settled on Wojtyła. He approached fellow German-speaking cardinals to urge them to consider the Pole. Ratzinger didn't need convincing, given what he had seen of Wojtyła that summer. König said there was enthusiasm everywhere he turned, with one notable exception: Cardinal Wyszyński of Warsaw, often seen by his countrymen as a jealous rival to the younger Wojtyła. "He could never be pope," Wyszyński scoffed to König. "He's too young. He's unknown."

The cardinals began their deliberations on the opening day of the conclave by swearing an oath of secrecy, but there were the usual leaks. Major news organizations eventually reported Italian cardinals split their votes between two countrymen: Giuseppe Siri, the rigidly conservative archbishop of Genoa, and Giovanni Benelli of Florence, Paul VI's protégé. After several rounds of balloting, however, neither could achieve the necessary margin for victory: two-thirds of those voting.

König then announced his compromise candidate—Wojtyła. The idea was greeted enthusiastically. Cardinal John Krol of Philadelphia, the Ohio-born son of Polish immigrants, urged the US delegation to back the Pole. Cardinal Vicente Enrique y Tarancón of Madrid, one of Spain's most progressive churchmen, knew little about Wojtyła's detailed views on doctrine but had always assumed the delightful Polish cardinal was a centrist in the mold of John XXIII. "We wanted more of a pastor than an intellectual," he said. "We were not looking for a conservative or a progressive, but someone in line with Vatican II."

Wojtyła was elected on the eighth ballot. According to several news accounts, he received the votes of 99 of the 111 cardinals. That included most of the Italians, who had come to accept the idea of a non-Italian pope—a decision made easier because Wojtyła spoke their language so well. The conclave erupted in applause. Wojtyła announced he would take the name John Paul II, in memory of his predecessor. There was relief among the cardinals at the thought that, after two papal deaths in a matter of weeks, there would not be another conclave for decades. At fifty-eight, John Paul II was the youngest pope since 1846.

As white smoke rose from the vent above the chapel, an estimated two hundred thousand people rushed to the square to learn the identity of the new bishop of Rome. It was revealed by Cardinal Felici of Italy, who struggled with the Polish name: "Ka-ro-olum Woj-ty-la." There was confusion, since many in the crowd mistook it for the name of an aging Italian cardinal. ("He's too old!" someone shouted.) Then others recognized the name and yelled, in Italian, "È il polacco!" (It's the Pole!) The appearance on the balcony of the tall, muscular Pole, so different physically from all of his modern predecessors, was met with cheers. Arms outstretched, he broke precedent by delivering a brief speech and prayer in Italian before offering the traditional Latin papal blessing of *Urbi et Orbi* ("To the city and to the world"). Even though his Italian was nearly fluent, he joked: "I am not sure I can express myself in your—in *our*—Italian tongue. You will correct me if I make a mistake." There was more applause as he continued: "The eminent cardinals have elected a new bishop of Rome. They have called him from a far country. I was afraid to receive this nomination, but I did it in the spirit of obedience to our Lord Jesus Christ."

In Germany, Hans Küng "honestly welcomed Wojtyła's election." He remembered thinking at the time that with the Cold War raging, "it was a good idea to elect a man from the East." Polish friends assured him that Wojtyła was open to reform. They predicted John Paul II would prove to be a moderate during what was likely to be a long papacy.

HIS CORONATION WAS a week later. From the moment he stepped out of St. Peter's and into the morning chill to begin the ceremony, John Paul II proved his mastery of Vatican stagecraft. There was nothing inauthentic about him—no one doubted his faith was deep and genuine—yet more than any of his modern predecessors, he understood how to convince an audience that through him, they were in the presence of God. He sensed how a well-timed gesture or facial expression—a slight, mischievous smile, perhaps, or by squeezing his eyes closed tight in prayer at an unexpected moment—communicated his feelings in a way words never could. He acknowledged to friends they were talents developed during his acting career in Poland.

The ceremony began when the pope seated himself in a beige, high-backed chair set just outside the doors of the basilica. Aides draped his shoulders with the decorative white scarf known as a pallium. Then, as banks of television cameras captured the scene, the College of Cardinals left their seats and filed toward him. Most doffed their red skull caps and knelt to kiss the gold ring on his right hand. The ceremony's most moving—and surprising—moment came when Wyszyński bent down to kiss the ring. Instead, John Paul II jumped up and lifted his fellow Pole to his feet and embraced him. He then kissed the cardinal's own ring.

The pope demonstrated that day why he would be a nightmare for the Vatican's security agencies. (Two police forces protected him: the Swiss Guard, easily identifiable to tourists because of their brightly colored Renaissance-era uniforms, and the more somberly dressed, mostly Italian-manned agency known as the Gendarmerie.) Once the ceremony finished, John Paul pushed past his alarmed bodyguards and marched into the crowd. When a young boy ran toward him clutching a bouquet of flowers, guards tried to hold the child back. The grinning pope called out to the boy to come forward for a hug.

His election signaled the arrival on the world stage of a religious and cultural phenomenon. The Broadway musical *Jesus Christ Superstar* had opened a few years earlier, and *Time* magazine could not resist the obvious, if slightly sacrilegious, cover headline: "John Paul II, Superstar." American journalists tried to capture the excitement by drawing comparisons to John Kennedy and Frank Sinatra. The Rome tourism board calculated that in the first six months of his papacy, he drew an extra five million visitors to the Eternal City.

The election of a Polish pope suggested a new role for the Vatican in the Cold War. The Soviet Union reacted cautiously to John Paul's election, issuing a boilerplate statement about its hopes for "friendship and peace."

The Polish government, by comparison, offered hearty congratulations, noting its "great satisfaction" about the election of a countryman. That enthusiasm surprised some Vatican diplomats, given the conventional wisdom that all Polish church leaders were militantly anticommunist. (In fact, internal documents from Poland's spy agencies later showed many Communists saw Wojtyła as less of a troublemaker than other bishops. He was certainly easier to deal with than the ornery Wyszyński.)

Before heading home, the College of Cardinals returned to the Sistine Chapel for a final meeting with the new pope, who gave a speech setting out his agenda. He portrayed himself as an open-minded centrist and pledged to carry out the reforms of Vatican II, especially its call for closer ties to the world's other religions. He insisted he was committed to sharing authority with bishops outside Rome—"collegiality"—and described it as an issue "on which we can never focus enough attention." He vowed he would not involve the Vatican in geopolitics: "We have no intention of political interference."

Years later, it was fair to ask if the pope really meant what he said that day—or if words like "collegiality" and "political interference" had a different meaning for him. His actions in the first weeks of his papacy proved that, far from being the moderate many hoped for, he was an iron-willed conservative who would further centralize power in the Vatican. He quickly proved his intention to intervene—selectively, but often—in the political affairs of other nations, especially Poland. On October 23, the day after his inauguration, he released a statement to "my beloved countrymen" that many Poles read as a call to arms: "I ask you to oppose everything that violates human dignity and diminishes the habits of a healthy society, often threatening its very existence."

Almost immediately, he tried to shut down the lingering doctrinal debates that plagued Paul VI. In an audience in St. Peter's a month after his election, John Paul reaffirmed *Humanae Vitae* and denounced all forms of birth control. He proved himself a traditionalist in almost every way. In November, he declared that nuns should immediately return to wearing head-to-toe cloth habits: "It is the means to remind yourselves constantly of your commitment to God."

Days after his election, he issued a secret order to Curia agencies to suspend laicization—the process by which men were given permission to leave the priesthood and be relieved of their celibacy vows. Under Paul VI, those requests were granted routinely. Of thirty-two thousand submitted during his papacy, all but about one thousand were accepted. John Paul, whose order would remain secret for almost a year, approved almost none. That meant priests choosing to leave the church, to marry or for any other reason, were subject to excommunication. They either remained true to their vows or they could no longer call themselves Catholics. For many, it was an unbearably cruel choice.

Hans Küng first sensed something wrong when, a week after John Paul's election, he picked up a copy of *L'Osservatore Romano* and saw a display of photos of the new pope taken throughout his career. Küng's eyes widened when he saw a picture of then-Cardinal Wojtyła speaking to a group in Rome years earlier. The caption described it as one of a series of lectures he delivered to priests who were part of a mysterious conservative sect.

"Opus Dei?" Küng recalled saying to himself. "What? This is ominous news."

For decades, Opus Dei had been easily the most controversial religious order in the Catholic Church. Some of Küng's colleagues in Tübingen had a similar reaction to the photos. They were alarmed by the discovery that the new pope had a long-established relationship with what they considered a sinister right-wing cult. One colleague worried that John Paul was a "Manchurian Candidate," a reference to the 1962 film about an American presidential contender who turns out to be a brainwashed Communist spy.

News reports days later revealed that, in the week before the conclave that elected him pope, Wojtyła made an unannounced visit to Opus Dei's headquarters in Rome to pray at the tomb of the group's eccentric Spanish founder, Father Escriva. It was seen by many in the Vatican as a bizarre show of reverence by a Polish churchman toward the leader of a controversial sect that, at the time, had no formal presence in Poland.*

Inside the Curia, suspicions about Opus Dei dated back to the 1930s, shortly after the order was founded in Spain. Many in the Vatican had always been unnerved by Opus Dei's fixation on secrecy—members were forbidden to admit publicly they were part of the group—and by Escriva's close affiliation with the dictatorship of General Francisco Franco. Others in Rome were uneasy about the group's zeal for corporal mortifica-

---

* Decades later, Opus Dei's reputation outside the church would be damaged by block-buster mystery novels and films, which made outrageous allegations about the order. The most famous of the books, the 2003 mystery *The Da Vinci Code* by Dan Brown, depicted Opus Dei as a murderous, sadomasochistic cult determined to preserve secrets about Jesus, including the possibility he was married. It sold eighty million copies worldwide.

tion; many members constantly wore a spiked metal belt, known as a cilice, on their upper thighs beneath their clothing, the inward-pointing spikes meant to be a constant reminder of Christ's suffering. Escriva's deputies said he regularly bloodied the floor after self-mortification sessions.

Escriva lobbied in Rome for decades to have his organization recognized as an alternative to the Jesuits—like them, an elite, military-style religious order pledging absolute loyalty to the pope—and the Jesuits felt the rivalry. In 1941, the Jesuits' worldwide leader, the Austrian-born Wlodimir Ledóchowski, warned Pius XII that Opus Dei was "very dangerous for the church" and might have a "covert inclination to dominate the world." English-speaking Jesuits nervously mocked it as "Octopus Dei."

Escriva's lobbying worked, however. In 1946, he moved his headquarters to Rome in what he said was a sign of his devotion to Pius XII. The pope was so flattered that he granted official papal accreditation to the group. By the 1970s, Opus Dei was reported to have seventy thousand members around the world—10 percent of them priests, the rest laymen and laywomen. About 25 percent of its lay members were known as "numeraries" or "associates"—men and women who took celibacy vows and lived together in sex-segregated dormitories and practiced self-mortification.

Beginning in the 1940s, Opus Dei established orders throughout Latin America and cultivated ties to the region's most repressive governments. It was known as fiercely anticommunist and seen as a powerful enemy of liberation theology. Its most relentless critics included the parents of members, especially in Spain and Italy, who accused the organization of brainwashing their children after recruiting them as teenagers.

The full truth about the relationship between John Paul and Opus Dei would never be known, but Vatican officials acknowledged years later that Opus Dei had been an important financial patron of the pope before his election and helped underwrite his foreign travels as a cardinal. Those trips allowed Wojtyła to befriend far-flung members of the College of Cardinals—the men who elected him pope. In 1974, Opus Dei published hundreds of copies of a handsome book of his lectures, which Wojtyła handed out to fellow churchmen as a gift during his travels.

He entered the papacy determined to grant Opus Dei the full independence that Escriva sought. In a confidential letter a month after his election, John Paul II notified the order's hierarchy that there would be "no further delay" in granting its designation as a special arm of the papacy, with the title of "personal prelature," similar to that of the Jesuits. Once it took effect, Opus Dei priests would no longer answer to local bishops, only to the order's superiors in Rome.

John Paul also agreed—secretly—to begin work on fulfilling another of Opus Dei's dreams: sainthood for Escriva, who died in 1975. The idea struck many Curia bishops as absurd, given Escriva's reputation for egomania and a cruel, volcanic temper, to say nothing of his ties to Franco. He was also widely reported to be anti-Semitic. A former top deputy, a British priest who left Opus Dei in the 1980s, said Escriva did not hide his "pro-Nazi sympathies" and believed Hitler had been treated unfairly in history. The priest said he was startled one day to hear Escriva say, with conviction, "Hitler couldn't have been such a bad person. He couldn't have killed six million Jews. It couldn't have been more than two or three million."

In the first weeks of his papacy, John Paul met almost daily with Opus Dei's leaders, much more often than with the leaders of other religious orders. In January 1979, he led a ceremony in St. Peter's for the installation of his successor in Krakow. Fearing it would be awkward if there were empty pews, he asked Opus Dei to fill the vast basilica. The order responded by organizing thousands of its followers, many from outside Italy, to attend the ceremony.

John Paul's election turned the Apostolic Palace into an outpost of Polish culture, with Polish its de facto language. That alarmed many of the Italian bishops who still dominated the Curia, since they found themselves cut out of conversations; some began to refer dismissively to the papal apartment as the *ambasciata polacca*—the Polish embassy. The pope appointed a fellow Pole as his chief secretary, Father Stanisław Dziwisz. The thirty-nine-year-old Dziwisz held the same job under the pope in Krakow, and the relationship was often described as that of father and son. Five black-robed Polish nuns, members of the Sacred Heart of Jesus Convent in Krakow, moved into the palace as the pope's cooks and housekeepers. They said he was an easy-to-please boss. While he had a hearty appetite, he cared little about what was actually on the menu, and even less about the upkeep of his apartment or the condition of his wardrobe. In Krakow, he was notorious for wearing clerical robes that were frayed or torn; there were usually holes in his shoes and socks.

Dziwisz and the Polish nuns were witnesses to the pope's faith in a way others were not. They knew, for example, that he was a devoted practitioner of self-mortification, a fact made public after his death, and denied himself basic physical comforts. Both in Krakow and in Rome, he often slept on the cold, bare floor rather than in bed, for example. His household staff would sometimes hear him whipping himself behind a closed door. They knew he used a particular belt for the purpose, and that he always returned it to the same hook in his closet when he was finished.

Many Curia bishops later said that Poland figured in every significant conversation they had with John Paul, since it was the easiest way to hold his attention. His passion for his homeland and its tragic thousand-year history was something that non-Poles could not fathom, he believed. He said that, during his many trips to the United States, he was struck that Americans, for all their boasts of patriotism, did not have a similar, fierce love for their country.

His patriotism colored several early decisions as pope. Just weeks after his election, he ordered Vatican auditors to shut down their investigation of a multimillion-dollar fraud orchestrated by the Pauline Fathers, an order of thirty monks, based in Pennsylvania, that was affiliated with the Polish Catholic Church. Documents unearthed by a newspaper in Pennsylvania revealed that the monks squandered almost $20 million in charitable donations and loans and used it to underwrite a luxurious lifestyle. The monks were bailed out at a cost to the local archdiocese of $5 million.

The papal apartment became a gathering place for Polish clerics working in the Curia. They were honored with invitations for meals with John Paul, who relished nothing more than a conversation, in Polish, about news from back home. Other topics were forbidden. He had a special disgust for scandalmongering about other churchmen. That was explained in part by his experience in Poland throughout the Cold War. Government opponents, including churchmen, were the targets of vile disinformation by Polish spy agencies, often involving false allegations of womanizing or alcoholism. In Rome, as in Krakow, he assumed the best about other churchmen unless there was absolute proof of wrongdoing, and even then he was slow to act. That explained why he never pursued widespread, credible reports about a Polish priest, Father Juliusz Paetz, who was a frequent guest at the papal dinner table. A Curia bureaucrat since the 1960s, Paetz was dogged throughout his career by allegations that he preyed sexually on boys and young men. He was known for an obsessive desire to be in the presence of teenage seminarians and to spend time in their dormitories. If any of that reached the pope, it did not stop Paetz's advancement under John Paul, who sent him back to Poland as a bishop in 1982. It would be several more years before his career collapsed in scandal after he was accused of molesting Polish seminarians.

Like Opus Dei, other religious orders sought favor from the new pope. He granted an early audience to Father Marcial Maciel Degollado, the Mexican-born founder of the Legion of Christ, known by then as one of the church's best fundraisers. With twenty thousand members, the Legion was smaller than Opus Dei, but similarly promoted itself as a conservative alternative to the Jesuits. Maciel made himself central to the success of the pope's first international trip, in January 1979, to Mexico. It would be the first visit by any pope to Mexico, a nation where 90 percent of the population was Catholic but where the Vatican had a checkered history. In the three centuries before Mexico's independence in 1821, the Catholic hierarchy there had been allied with Spain's colonial government. After independence, Mexican leaders forced the church underground, and that hostility continued into the twentieth century. As of the 1970s, the Vatican had no diplomatic relations with Mexico, which meant John Paul could receive no formal invitation to travel there. Maciel swung into action. The mother and two sisters of Mexican president José López Portillo were generous donors to the Legion. Maciel convinced the three women to pressure the president to override the Interior Ministry and grant a formal invitation to John Paul II, which they did.

On January 25, the day the chartered jumbo jet carrying the pope headed to Mexico, there was a special guest on board: Maciel. Their friendship would last the rest of their lives—and bring scandal to John Paul's legacy. Decades later, the Vatican insisted the pope had no idea there was anything controversial about Maciel's past and never thought to investigate. If he had, he would have turned up the voluminous disciplinary files in the Vatican, dating back to the 1940s, about Maciel's rampant sexual misconduct with children. In November 1978, just a month after John Paul's election, the Vatican's diplomatic mission in Washington, DC, received a detailed account of Maciel's pedophilia. The report accused him of molesting at least twenty boys, all identified by name in the document. The evidence had been compiled by Bishop John McGann of Long Island, New York, who began to investigate after taking the confession of a local Mexican-born priest who described the "moral torture" of the sexual abuse he had suffered at Maciel's hands. The priest, Father Juan Vaca, the Legion of Christ's former US director, told McGann he had been molested by Maciel—repeatedly, over more than a decade—beginning in 1949, when Vaca was twelve. McGann's report was passed on to Rome in early 1979, where it was filed away and forgotten.

19

Gossip and Sin

JOHN PAUL II HAD special reason to disdain gossip, since he had so
often been the target of it. There is no evidence he ever violated his
celibacy vows, but throughout his life he loved being in the company
of women. Early in his papacy, news organizations kept stumbling onto
stories about his intense relationships with women before and after he was
ordained a priest, at the age of twenty-six. At times, he had the sort of
friendships with women that clerics were urged to avoid, since they invited
rumors and undermined the idea of a celibate priest dedicating his heart
solely to God.

A week after his election, *Time* magazine reported "persistent rumors"
in Poland that "he had been engaged or married." The Vatican angrily
denied that, although it could not deny that he had a rich romantic life in
his youth. As archbishop in Krakow and later in Rome, he alarmed deputies because of what they saw as his passionate relationship with a married
Polish American philosophy professor, Anna-Teresa Tymieniecka. Born to
an aristocratic family in Poland, she left her homeland in 1946 and settled
in the US, where she was married to a Harvard University economist. Her
training, like the pope's, was in phenomenology. In 1973, he accepted her
offer to prepare an English-language edition of what he considered his
definitive book on the subject. Tymieniecka, then fifty, began commuting
to Poland, remaining there for weeks at a time. *The Acting Person: A Con-
tribution to Phenomenological Anthropology* was published in English in 1979,
a year after John Paul's election. Tymieniecka, who needed several years

Then-Cardinal Wojtyła of Krakow on holiday with Anna-Teresa
Tymieniecka, a Polish American academic whose close friendship
with the future John Paul II worried his deputies in Poland and Rome

to finish the translation because the pope's writing was so dense, acknowledged that general readers would find the book incomprehensible.

She adamantly denied to friends she had a physical relationship with
the pope, but letters and photos made public years later offered evidence
of an unusual intimacy.* In 1976, two years before his election, he wrote
to her: "God gave you to me and made you my vocation." He seemed
to acknowledge the risk of scandal, even as he honored his "conviction,"
which seemed a reference to his celibacy vows: "If I didn't have this conviction, some moral certainty of grace, and of acting in obedience to it, I
would not dare act like this." That same year, he sent her an item of religious clothing given him by his father—a scapular, made up of two cloth
rectangles joined together and worn next to the skin over the chest and
back. He told her he hoped she would treasure it. It allowed him to imagine
he could "feel you everywhere in all kinds of situations, whether you are
close or far away." Photos showed the then-cardinal and Tymieniecka on
holiday together, including one at a lakeside tent, with Wojtyła in T-shirt

* In 2008, the National Library of Poland purchased the archive of letters and photos
from Tymieniecka for a reported $1 million. The library blocked public access to the mate-
rial until 2016, two years after John Paul was declared a saint.

and shorts; another showed them on a skiing vacation. A friend of hers, Professor George Huntston Williams of the Harvard Divinity School, later wrote that the relationship was one of "erotic energy," although he had no reason to believe it had ever been consummated.

In the mid-1970s, Hans Küng found his own joy with a woman, Marianne Saur-Kemmer, a widowed neighbor in Tübingen. In a discreet reference to her in his memoirs, he described her as "an attractive, intelligent, warm-hearted and self-confident widow of about my own age." They had been neighbors for years, long before their friendship blossomed. When he first met Marianne, her husband, a local dentist, was in need of constant medical care "and she impressed me because she devotedly cared for her incurably ill husband." Küng's colleagues never thought to press for details of the exact nature of their relationship. In 1978, he turned fifty and told friends he wanted to share more of his life with Marianne. That year, he decided to build himself a new home, and moved into Marianne's house for a time. When construction was over, they moved in together.

Küng's friends at the university welcomed Marianne to their close-knit social circle and were pleased he would avoid the loneliness that came to so many priests in middle age. "Marianne is a stroke of luck for Hans Küng and all of us here in Tübingen," said Jürgen Moltmann, the school's best-known Protestant theologian. There were occasional quiet jokes about the fact that the two most prominent Catholic theologians in Germany, Küng and Karl Rahner, had put aside their scholarly differences to agree on the value of the love of a good woman. The romance between Rahner and the German novelist Luise Rinser would continue until his death in 1984.

A frequent guest to Küng's home was Father Walter Kasper, his former research assistant and a fast-rising faculty member at Tübingen. Küng had recruited him back to Tübingen from the University of Münster in 1970 to take Ratzinger's place. Kasper could be controversial, and he occasionally drew scrutiny in the Vatican. In 1974, he published a book that questioned whether Jesus actually performed the miracles in the Gospels, including walking on water and converting two fishes and five loaves of bread into enough food to feed five thousand people. Kasper, however, had something Küng lacked—modesty, and a preference for diplomacy over intellectual combat—and it was widely assumed he could still have a career in the church hierarchy someday.

In a liberal university town like Tübingen, it was no longer a surprise to learn that a Catholic priest had struck up a romance with a woman. By then, opinion polls showed German Catholics, like those across Western Europe and the United States, were ready to accept married priests. In 1971, the Gallup organization, the US polling company, reported that for the first time in its research, a majority of American Catholics supported an end to the doctrine of priestly celibacy. The once-taboo subject was suddenly embraced in popular culture around the world, especially after the 1977 publication of the best-selling novel *The Thorn Birds*, which depicted the passionate affair between a Catholic priest and a beautiful young woman on a remote sheep station in the Australian outback; the book sold thirty-three million copies. There was only a muted scandal in the US a few years later after publication of the diaries of the renowned Catholic writer Thomas Merton, an American Trappist monk who wrote several best-selling books about spirituality and social justice. In the journals, Merton described his affair in 1966 with a nineteen-year-old nurse he met when hospitalized in Kentucky. He was fifty-three at the time. "There is no question I love her deeply," he wrote after calling off the affair. "I keep remembering her body, her nakedness."

By the late 1970s, the fact that so many prominent Catholic churchmen had active sex lives came as no surprise to the American psychotherapist Richard Sipe, who taught at the renowned medical school at Johns Hopkins University in Baltimore. He was then more than a decade into what would be the most authoritative research in the world on the sexuality of Catholic priests. When his findings were published in 1990, he outraged many in the Vatican, even as his findings became widely accepted in medical and legal circles—and in much of the church.

Sipe, a devout Catholic, was a former Benedictine priest and monk. He had been raised in an observant home in Minnesota and attended a Benedictine high school. After ordination in 1959, he pursued a graduate degree in psychotherapy. By 1965, he was working at the Seton Psychiatric Institute in Baltimore, a church-administered hospital for priests suffering from behavioral problems. His patients included clergy who had been forced to seek counseling for child molestation. He felt pity for some pedophile priests, since so many had themselves been abused as children, but was also convinced most should be defrocked and prosecuted. At the time, church leaders almost always refused to consider that option, insisting instead that child-molesting priests undergo psychological treatment and, when "cured," return to church work.

As a priest, Sipe appreciated the self-discipline that came with his celibacy vows. "I learned a great deal from the practice," he said. But in 1970, he left the clergy and married a former nun, who was a fellow psychotherapist. That did not end his professional relationship with the church, since he continued to provide counseling to troubled priests.

Years before he published the results of his research, Sipe had already reached his central conclusions. He believed that the church's centuries-old demand for celibacy had created a mental-health crisis, as well as a shockingly perverse system in which criminal sexual abuse by priests was ignored. He was convinced the situation would someday explode into a scandal so grave it would threaten the church's survival. After treating thousands of clergymen, he was certain that the vast majority of American priests violated their celibacy vows. The result was a culture in which bishops and cardinals, often sexually active themselves, readily covered up for other churchmen.

He saw no correlation between sexual orientation and pedophilia. American crime statistics showed that, in the general population, the vast majority of child molesters were men who preyed on girls, suggesting most pedophiles would identify themselves as heterosexual. Still, he thought the church should acknowledge that a disproportionate number of priests were gay, which explained why most victims of child-molesting priests were boys. He was convinced the percentage of gay men in the priesthood grew dramatically in the 1960s, when so many heterosexual clerics left the church to marry. From his own years in the church, he knew many gay men became priests as a way of dealing with a sexual orientation they considered sinful. By the late 1970s, he estimated that of all priests who were sexually active, more than half were having sex with other men.

20

On the Road

J OHN PAUL II WAS grateful to Father Maciel for helping arrange his extraordinary welcome in Mexico in January 1979. The reception, first in Mexico City, was rapturous. After stepping from his plane, the pope fell to his knees and kissed the tarmac, an act repeated in each of the 129 countries he visited over the next twenty-seven years. He celebrated Mass that afternoon in the Mexican capital's central cathedral, then spoke to an open-air gathering of more than three hundred thousand people in the Plaza de la Constitución.

Two days later, his entourage made the eighty-mile journey to the city of Puebla, where John Paul addressed a meeting of CELAM, the Conference of Latin American Bishops. It was the group's first full meeting since its landmark 1968 gathering in Medellín, when the region's bishops embraced liberation theology for the first time. In the years since, the movement had continued to sweep across Latin America. By the late 1970s, tens of thousands of "slum priests" worked in more than 150,000 Catholic base communities across the region.

Even so, the fate of liberation theology was in doubt when John Paul arrived in Mexico. In the decade after Medellín, the movement's opponents seized control of CELAM. In 1972, a rigidly conservative Colombian, Archbishop Alfonso López Trujillo of Bogotá, was elected its general secretary. He was known to parishioners for two types of sermons: those condemning the dangers of sex—he preached constantly about the sinfulness of homosexuality and birth control—and those denouncing liberation theology. (Churchmen who worked with López Trujillo would later expose his hypocrisy—how he was sexually active with men throughout his career in Colombia and Rome.) López Trujillo packed CELAM's leadership with other conservatives, who drafted documents ahead of the Puebla meeting that if approved at the conference would be a death blow to liberation theology.

Ahead of his Mexico trip, John Paul had not made a clear-cut statement about his views on liberation theology. Even so, many Latin American bishops were hopeful he would endorse the movement. They saw its goals as virtually identical to those that John Paul had pursued as archbishop of Krakow, where then-Cardinal Wojtyła regularly organized parishioners to demand their political and economic rights from Poland's Communist leaders.

On the plane to Mexico, the pope held a news conference with Vatican reporters and offered his first assessment of the movement, and it was perplexing. "Liberation theology is true theology," he declared, "but perhaps it is also a false theology. Because if one starts to politicize theology, this is no longer theology." A "true" theology? A "false" one? The confusion remained until the day he spoke to the 184 cardinals and bishops in Puebla. To most, his speech came as a bitter disappointment. He did not use the term "liberation theology" but suggested that Catholic social-reform movements like it were wrong because they involved the church in politics. He rejected the idea of Christ "as a political figure, as a revolutionary, as the subversive man from Nazareth." The church's mission is "not social nor political." The address received warm applause from López Trujillo and other conservatives, convinced that the demise of liberation theology was at hand.

The pope made another speech in Puebla that day, in the city's soccer stadium, which was packed with eighty thousand Mexicans who appeared jubilant, at first, to be in his presence. Then came passages of his speech in which he repeated his message to the bishops—about the need to keep the church out of politics. Many in the stadium took that as a repudiation of liberation theology. Suddenly there was an astonishing sound from the crowd—hissing, which grew louder. The pope's eyes widened at the sound of the protests.

In the hours that followed, Mexican newspaper and radio commentators suggested the new pope was a hypocrite. In Poland, they noted, he encouraged the church to be active in social justice, but he was telling Catholics in Latin America to abandon the same fight. One Mexican writer said the pope's remarks would be "used by governments and paramilitary goons across Latin America in beating up clerics demonstrating for their people's rights." There was evidence he had done just that. In Chile, the country's dictator, General Pinochet, said the pope's speeches in Puebla proved that the Vatican rejected liberation theology and "wanted nothing to do with politics."

John Paul was so alarmed by what had happened in the stadium—his first taste of any real protest as pope—that he left Puebla ahead of schedule and returned to Mexico City. He wanted time to rewrite a speech scheduled for the next day to fifteen thousand indigenous Mexicans in the impoverished province of Oaxaca. In it, he would back away from much of what he said in Puebla. "The poor have a right to demand fair wages and humane living conditions," he declared, sounding suddenly like a social justice warrior. Inequality in places like Oaxaca "is not just, it is not human, it is not Christian." The church needed to battle against "the powerful classes" on behalf of the poor. Both supporters and opponents of liberation theology were now bewildered about where the pope stood, and that confusion would continue for years.

After his departure from Mexico, Latin American bishops began the formal debate over the draft documents prepared by López Trujillo and rejected them. The conference released a final statement that, while not referring to liberation theology by name, once again embraced the movement: "We ask all Christians to collaborate in the changing of unjust social structures."

Despite the confusion he created, the pope returned to Rome in triumph. Outside of Mexico, news coverage of the trip was uniformly glowing and stressed the massive crowds he had drawn. He announced that he intended to make foreign travel a centerpiece of his papacy. There was delight in Poland days later when the church released the itinerary of his trip to his homeland that June, followed by a tour of the United States in October.

In March, he released his first encyclical, *Redemptor Hominis* (Redeemer of Man). At twenty-four thousand words, it was one of the longest encyclicals in the history of the papacy. (*Humanae Vitae*, the most consequential encyclical of modern times, was one-third the length.) Many passages were so vaguely worded that, once again, it was uncertain what the pope was trying to say. He was clear enough, however, in condemning the worst abuses of both Western capitalism ("a consumer attitude uncontrolled by ethics") and Marxism. He reaffirmed the doctrine of priestly celibacy and demanded an end to any lingering debate on the subject. He warned theologians and other church scholars that freedoms they won at Vatican II had limits.

He backed that up with action a few weeks later, launching a crackdown on the work of progressive theologians, the sort of assault not seen since the days of Pius XII. His first target was a French academic, Jacques Pohier, a Dominican priest, who had just published a book that questioned papal infallibility. In April 1979, the pope denounced the book and blocked its distribution inside the church, the first such action since 1967, when the Vatican shut down the Index of Prohibited Books. Pohier was later stripped of his teaching credentials as well as his right as a priest to say Mass. He left the priesthood in 1984.

The Congregation for the Doctrine of the Faith, still led by Cardinal Šeper, became central to the pope's campaign to enforce his conservative views. That fall, Šeper ordered Edward Schillebeeckx, the most famous theologian in the Netherlands and the lead author of the best-selling Dutch catechism, to travel to Rome for formal hearings to defend his most controversial writings, especially about sex. Outraged Dutch Catholics saw it as a new front in the Vatican's assault on their national church. More than sixty thousand of them signed a petition urging Schillebeeckx to refuse to take part in what amounted to a modern-day heresy trial. He went anyway. The investigation targeting him would continue for years.

In December, the congregation publicly denounced five American theologians who, on behalf of the mainstream Catholic Theological Society of America, had published a book-length study on sexual morality two years earlier. The study, *Human Sexuality: New Directions in American Catholic Thought*, gently questioned church teachings on birth control, homosexuality, and masturbation. It was the Vatican's first censure of American theologians since before Vatican II.

FOR ARCHBISHOP ROMERO of El Salvador, a trip to the Vatican was always a homecoming. He had been such a promising seminarian in the 1930s that the church hierarchy in El Salvador sponsored his studies at the Gregorian, where he received a theology degree. Still, his trip to Rome in April 1979 was nerve-wracking as he prepared to introduce himself to John Paul II. He had been promised a papal audience weeks earlier, so he was insulted when he arrived in Rome and was told to wait, day after day, for an exact date for the meeting. He found the papal secretaries unfriendly, even rude.

Romero, sixty-one, was without doubt the best-known Catholic bishop in Central America. His fame—and to church conservatives, his infamy— came because he repeatedly risked his life to defend the poor against his country's murderous right-wing government. He did not describe himself as a supporter of liberation theology, but he was a hero to the movement. Lawmakers in the United States and Europe repeatedly nominated him for the Nobel Peace Prize. Romero, named an archbishop in 1977 by Paul VI, had always been grateful for the warmth the late pope showed him. He hoped for the same support from John Paul II, but the signs were not promising.

In his diaries at the time, he wrote about his assumption he would soon be dead—assassinated by one of the military-backed death squads roaming El Salvador. Four Salvadoran priests had been murdered in the previous two years. Weeks before Romero's visit to Rome, Father Octavio Ortiz, thirty-four years old and the first priest he had ever ordained, was gunned down at a Catholic retreat center in San Salvador, the capital. The military insisted, falsely, that it was a guerrilla hideout. Ortiz's corpse was then run over by an army tank. Hours later, Romero went to the morgue and, tears streaming down his face, asked to see the remains. A morgue worker recalled he hesitantly removed a sheet that covered the mangled corpse. "You couldn't tell it was Ortiz," the attendant remembered. "His body was completely flattened, his face destroyed to the point where it looked as if he didn't even have one." At the funeral, Romero eulogized Ortiz as one more victim of the government's injustice. "The conflict is not between the church and the government; it is between the government and the people," he declared. "The church is with the people."

He had almost no support from fellow Salvadoran bishops, who aligned themselves with the military and the country's wealthy elite. A few bishops poisoned Romero's reputation in Rome, arguing he was too close to leftists, especially to the Jesuits who championed liberation theology. Bishop Pedro Arnoldo Aparicio, president of the national bishops' conference, alleged Romero was "manipulated" by Jesuits and popular only among "students and those who are part of the guerrillas."

Romero was finally granted an audience with John Paul in early May, and it did not go well. John Paul listened as Romero outlined the crisis in El Salvador. The bishop brought reports from international human-rights

Archbishop Óscar Romero of
El Salvador with parishioners in
San Salvador, El Salvador, in 1979,
a year before his assassination

groups that documented the government's brutality, which he handed to
the pope. He also brought photos taken at the scene of the murder of
Father Ortiz, including one that showed how the corpse had been mutilated by the army tank.

"Holy Father, know that I have preached the Gospel and I am ready to
keep on preaching that Gospel in defense of the beloved people entrusted
to me by the Lord," Romero explained. He was distressed by the pope's
response. John Paul seemed less interested in the extent of the violence in
El Salvador than in the need for the church there to find compromise with
the country's brutal leaders. He urged Romero to tone down his antigovernment protests. Citing the strength that came from unity among Polish
bishops, he advised Romero to put aside his differences with other bishops
in El Salvador, the same men who had long denounced him.

At the end of the conversation, the pope had humiliating news. In what
Romero remembered to friends as a cold, matter-of-fact tone, John Paul
revealed that, given the "extremely delicate" situation in El Salvador, he
was considering the appointment of an outside bishop, a so-called apostolic administrator, to run Romero's archdiocese, leaving him archbishop
in name only.

Romero, despondent as he left the meeting, knew he was returning home to chaos. Two days after his papal audience, police opened fire on antigovernment demonstrators outside San Salvador's cathedral, killing twenty-five. The next month, a priest was shot dead near the capital, the fifth Salvadoran cleric assassinated since 1977. A sixth was killed in August, gunned down as he approached the altar in his parish church.

ROMERO WAS NOT the only bishop to receive a chilly reception in Rome that year. Reform-minded churchmen said they often felt unwelcome at the Vatican during the papacy of John Paul II. The pope, so buoyant and joyful in public, could be distant and gruff behind closed doors. That was the experience of Archbishop Rembert Weakland of Milwaukee, the former leader of the Benedictine order, who had been dispatched to the Wisconsin archdiocese by Paul VI in 1977. In June 1979, Weakland was in Rome for his first formal audience with John Paul. Ahead of the meeting, Curia officials warned him that he was the subject of damaging, perhaps career-ending "rumors" and that "the pope was displeased with me." Weakland had established himself in Milwaukee as a champion of social justice and women's rights—he once made headlines by suggesting women could be priests someday—so he knew he and the new pope had sharp differences on doctrine. Still, he was taken aback that John Paul could have soured on him so dramatically, so quickly. "What rumors?" he asked Cardinal Sebastiano Baggio, who led the Congregation for Bishops, in a meeting before the papal audience. Baggio explained to Weakland that he had become the target of a Polish "pipeline" between the sizable Polish American community of Milwaukee and the pope's Polish deputies in the Curia. As Weakland learned that day, his ethnic Polish critics back home were forwarding regular written reports to Rome about what they saw as his heresy.

His meeting with the pontiff lasted only a few minutes. "He never looked me in the eye and never betrayed his feelings," Weakland recalled. John Paul asked only two questions. "How long have you been a bishop?" (two years) and "How long were you primate of the Benedictines?" (ten years). After that, Weakland said, "we had the usual photo opportunity" before he was hurriedly ushered out of the papal palace.

He wanted to believe the pope had not been intentionally rude—that perhaps he had been distracted, since John Paul was then only days away from the start of his historic first trip home to Poland.

DURING THE NINE-DAY PILGRIMAGE to his homeland, John Paul was given a welcome befitting the man already recognized there as the most famous Pole since the sixteenth-century astronomer Copernicus (or perhaps the nineteenth-century composer Chopin). The enthusiasm of the crowds was impossible to restrain in a nation where the church had always been its most potent symbol of unity. The pope's grueling schedule—thirty-six public events in barely a week—had elements both of a spiritual crusade and of a political campaign. On arrival the first day in Warsaw, a beaming pope stepped from his plane and knelt to kiss his native soil. Later that day, he led an open-air Mass before an estimated five hundred thousand people in Victory Square.

Fearful the visit would stir up political protests, the Communist government placed severe restrictions on the pope's public appearances. Events were limited to local audiences. In Warsaw, liquor sales were banned to prevent drunken antigovernment riots. The fears of Communist leaders may have been justified, since the pope offered pronouncements during the trip that the government complained were overtly political. He called on the Polish church to confront the authorities and speak up for the political and economic rights of parishioners. In a speech in southwestern Poland, he urged Catholics to defend the faith even if that meant physical danger: "Do not give up that noble effort that enables you to become a witness for Christ. A witness, in biblical language, means 'martyr.'" As news reports about the pope's trip home reached Latin America, many bishops there were baffled, since the pope had said precisely the opposite to them in Mexico.

Exhausted but clearly exhilarated, John Paul returned to Rome to complete arrangements for his trip to the United States. The planning was interrupted briefly for the funeral of Cardinal Ottaviani, who died in August at the age of eighty-eight. John Paul hailed Ottaviani, so widely seen as the Curia's most important opponent of the reforms of Vatican II, as a man who dedicated his life to "safeguarding of the sacred patrimony of faith and of Catholic morality."

The pope's six-city US visit in October 1979, which began in Boston and included stops in New York and Washington, was perhaps the most anticipated event in the history of the American Catholic Church, and the excitement was shared by non-Catholics. The evangelical preacher Billy Graham described John Paul as "the most respected religious leader in the world." President Jimmy Carter, a devout Southern Baptist, welcomed him to the White House: "God blessed America by sending you to us."

For many of the nation's fifty million Catholics, there was disappointment, however. In advance of the pope's trip, the Associated Press conducted a poll of the nation's Catholics and found 66 percent wanted the Vatican to lift the ban on birth control, 53 percent believed priests should be allowed to marry, and 50 percent believed women should be granted abortion on demand. In the pope's speeches in the US, he made clear he would compromise on none of those issues. He often adopted a scolding tone, suggesting Americans were out of step with the church's moral teachings, especially about sex.

Catholic women had special reason to feel slighted during the trip. Since Vatican II, nuns had been allowed in many US dioceses to join priests at the altar and handle communion wine and wafers. It was seen by bishops as a way of dealing with a shortage of priests. In advance of the pope's trip, however, the Vatican announced that women would be barred from any role in worship services that he attended. When he gave a speech in Philadelphia to twelve thousand clergy from around the country, priests were invited to sit in the audience on the main floor of the auditorium, while nuns were

Sister Theresa Kane, the Bronx-born president of the largest nuns' organization in the United States, led a silent protest against John Paul II before his speech in Washington, DC, October 7, 1979.

moved to the balcony. In that address, the pope made his most explicit statement to date of his conviction that women could never be priests: the all-male priesthood was "a tradition that cannot be altered."

He faced his most direct public protest in Washington. After he took the stage there before an audience of seven thousand nuns, about fifty of them stood up in silent protest. They were led by Sister Theresa Kane, president of the Leadership Conference of Women Religious, the nation's largest organization of nuns. She read out a statement to the pope in which she spoke of the "intense suffering and pain that is the life of many women" inside the church. The forty-two-year-old, Bronx-born Kane drew applause when she said that "the church must regard the possibility of women being included in all ministries," including the priesthood.

The pope sat impassively as she spoke and, in his remarks a few minutes later, did not directly address the protest. Instead, he spoke, as he often did, of how women should see their role model in the Virgin Mary, "the handmaiden of the Lord." Women, he said, should embrace their role as mothers—mothers, in particular, to boys who grew up to be priests and bishops: "Women make all our hierarchy possible." The pope suggested he was disappointed to see so many nuns in the audience in street clothes—Kane wore a tailored tweed suit and blouse—instead of traditional nuns' habits. He called again for nuns to return to "simple and suitable religious garb."

Reporters swarmed around Kane after the speech. She insisted she had not meant to offend the pope, but the protest seemed to be the only way of making him aware of how strongly American nuns felt about the "evil" of having no voice in their church. The nuns organized the protest after the Vatican failed to respond to their request for a meeting with the pope during his US tour, she said. On several visits to Rome in the years that followed, Kane asked repeatedly for an audience with John Paul—and was told he did not have time.

21

Punishing a Theologian

JOHN PAUL HAD his eye on Cardinal Ratzinger for a job in Rome. That appeared to explain why, to the surprise of some of his jealous future rivals in the Curia, Ratzinger had been honored with an invitation to join the pope's pilgrimage to Poland in 1979.

In the first months of John Paul's papacy, Ratzinger made a concerted effort to track down and read all of the pope's books and other writings, at least those that had been translated from Polish into other European languages, to try to better understand him. And the cardinal's aides in Munich could see that he was unimpressed by most of what he was reading. John Paul's writing style, especially on issues of Catholic doctrine, was so convoluted that even a celebrated church scholar like Ratzinger found it difficult to make out what he was trying to say. From what the cardinal had witnessed in Poland, John Paul demonstrated his "true genius" in face-to-face meetings with the faithful—"he is a person who needs conviviality, life and movement"—and decidedly *not* in what he put on paper.

By then, Ratzinger had established himself as one of the German church's most outspoken conservatives. He distanced himself as much as possible from his early reputation as a reformer; he quietly asked German publishers to stop reprinting some of his early, reform-minded books. In sermons in Munich, he described himself as a Catholic "betrayed" by the modern era. He reversed progressive policies of his predecessor, Cardinal Döpfner. Many young parents were upset when Ratzinger reimposed an ancient rule that children preparing for their First Communion, typically in the first years of grade school, needed to make a confession to a priest.

Döpfner stopped enforcing the rule, since he worried that children were needlessly frightened when forced into a dark confessional to repent for sins they didn't understand in the first place. Ratzinger disagreed: "The child *has* to confess." He was eager to be seen as an anticommunist partisan in the Cold War and denounced liberation theology because of what he saw as its link to Marxism, which he described as "the disgrace of our age."

The year 1979 proved to be a turning point for Ratzinger and several old friends in the field of theology, because it was the year those friendships ended. Some theologians spoke openly of their belief that Ratzinger was aligning himself, in the most public way possible, with the new pope's rigidly conservative agenda, in hopes of winning himself a powerful assignment in the Vatican.

He exercised his authority as Bavaria's archbishop that year to reject the appointment of a renowned Catholic theologian, Father Johann Metz, to the faculty of the University of Munich. Ratzinger was vague at the time when questioned about why he had blocked the appointment, saying only that it was motivated by "appropriate pedagogical considerations." But Metz was known to be a fine teacher, and Ratzinger's decision was seen as especially baffling since they had once been friends and taught together in Münster. To deny Metz the post, Ratzinger overruled the unanimous recommendation of Munich's faculty senate.

Metz was the father of a movement he called "political theology," which demanded the church's involvement in social-justice campaigns like liberation theology. He said his views were born from the horrors of World War II and specifically from the most searing moment of his life: in 1945, as a sixteen-year-old soldier drafted into the Nazi army in the final months of the war, he returned from a mission to discover his entire unit—most of them teenagers, too—wiped out from an Allied ground assault. Because of that, he said, his work as a Catholic theologian was dominated by a single question: How could the church have stood by as the evils of Nazism overtook Germany? In discussing his faith, he said, he would never allow himself to "forget the perspective of Auschwitz."

After blocking the appointment, Ratzinger was the target of furious attacks from other theologians. It destroyed forever his once close relationship with Karl Rahner, who made his wrath clear in letters published in German newspapers. He accused Ratzinger of bowing to conservative winds blowing from the Vatican. "You had no reason for rejecting Metz," he wrote. "This violation of a century-old tradition in the manner of appointing professors makes a farce out of your responsibility to protect academic freedom." He said Metz had obviously been rejected because he supported the church's involvement in social justice. "Cardinal Ratzinger, could your real reason be that Metz has influenced the development of Latin America's liberation theology, which you criticize?" Rahner asked. "One must protest this injustice."*

THAT FALL, Hans Küng returned to the firing line with his enemies in Rome. In October, on the first anniversary of John Paul's election, he published an essay in many of the world's most influential newspapers, including *The New York Times* and *Le Monde*, that was a stocktaking of the pope's first year. Küng made no definitive judgments about John Paul—the essay was written in the form of questions—but his tone was blistering. The article was meant to jolt Catholics into realizing that, despite the global outpouring of enthusiasm for their new pope, John Paul II was proving himself a reactionary. Küng suggested the pope had allowed himself to be turned into a "living cult figure" for many Catholics—even "a new messiah for our time"—in a campaign to extinguish what remained of the reforms of Vatican II. Several German bishops reacted angrily to the essay, including Ratzinger, who suggested in a newspaper interview that the Vatican should revoke Küng's credentials to teach as a church-accredited theologian: "Quite simply he no longer represents the faith of the Catholic Church."

Küng was appalled by Ratzinger's comments and frightened that any senior German cleric would suggest so publicly that he be stripped of his church teaching license, since Küng felt it gave him standing as a serious Catholic scholar. Losing the credentials might endanger his post in Tübingen, given the church's power over faculty appointments, and might even be the first step toward his excommunication: "I would become a non-person."

Küng released a statement that accused Ratzinger of misrepresenting him. "A cardinal should stick to the truth," he wrote. "I have never claimed to speak for the official Catholic Church. That is not my task. But I have claimed and still claim to speak as a Catholic theologian." In a private let-

---

* After Metz's death in 2019, Ratzinger conceded to a biographer that he had rejected the appointment largely because he considered Metz to be "so madly political" in trying to tie the Gospels' message to social activism (Seewald, *Benedict XVI: A Life, Volume II*, 125).

ter to his tormentor, Küng accused Ratzinger of a "frontal attack on my Catholicity and intellectual and moral integrity."

Ratzinger seemed eager to calm things down, at least for the moment. "Dear Herr Küng," he replied in a letter. "I completely agree with you that controversies over issues must not become too personal." He said he wanted to "express the wish for a friendly conversation in a spirit of collegiality."

After a faculty meeting in Tübingen on December 15, Küng drove several hours to a ski resort in Austria to spend the Christmas holidays with Marianne Saur. Three days later, at ten thirty in the morning, while high on the slopes, he showed his pass to a ski-lift operator, whose face went grim: "Professor Küng? You're being called at all the stations. You must return to the valley immediately." Küng sped down the mountain as quickly as he could. When he reached the ski lodge, he was told his university office was searching for him urgently.

He called his teaching assistant in Tübingen, who announced the bad news from Rome: the Congregation for the Doctrine of the Faith, with the pope's endorsement, had revoked his teaching credentials. The timing was no coincidence, Küng was convinced. His enemies in the Vatican had cynically waited until Christmas to launch "an insidious surprise attack" to end his career, since they knew he would be away from the university and unable to defend himself at a time when most Germans ignored the headlines.*

There were instant protests at the university, even in the middle of Christmas vacation. Students rushed back to campus to defend Küng. About a thousand supporters joined in a torchlight parade, several carrying banners that read: "The Pope Is Fallible, Küng Must Stay." The next day, two thousand students attended a special lecture that Küng arranged, and he was greeted with bouquets of flowers as well as a standing ovation.

John Paul's decision to discipline arguably the world's most famous living Catholic theologian was a major international news story. In Germany, newspaper editorials defended Küng, even if some suggested he had

---

* It was later established that the plan to lift Kung's teaching credentials had been under discussion in the Vatican for weeks, with the knowledge of Ratzinger and other German bishops. The date on the document announcing his punishment was December 15, when Kung was still in Tübingen, but it was not made public until after Kung left town for the holidays.

brought this on himself by being needlessly provocative. Father Walter Burghardt, a theologian at Georgetown University, wrote in *The New York Times* that the Vatican had made a terrible mistake. While Küng suffered from "intemperate pride," he was "a theologian whose learning, sincerity and warmth have brought fresh Christian life to many a tottering believer."

On the day of the Vatican's announcement, journalists flooded into Tübingen. Radio reporters camped out on the first floor of Küng's home, while a television crew set up on the second. At the university, the theology faculty met in an emergency session that afternoon. Hours later, eleven deans and professors issued a statement defending Küng: "We see serious dangers for the credibility of the church in today's society and for the freedom of theology."

Küng released his own statement. "I am deeply ashamed of my church," he wrote. "People are scandalized by a church that appeals to Jesus Christ but defames and discredits its own theologians." He attacked German bishops who had "collaborated with the Roman inquisition in order to destroy the credibility of one of their own."

The move against Küng posed a dilemma for the university. Under the 1933 concordant, the Vatican believed its authority was needed for a professor to teach Catholic theology, and that Küng should be fired if he did not resign. At the same time, he was a civil servant at a public school. The university president announced Küng would remain on the faculty, although his teaching duties would be limited; he would lose authority to direct the work of Catholic graduate students, for example.

German church leaders began to panic over the news coverage, which was wildly supportive of Küng. Bishop Georg Moser, whose diocese included Tübingen, refused to take Küng's phone calls on the day of the Vatican's announcement. The next morning, however, he rushed to Küng's home for a three-hour conversation, with the bishop offering to mediate personally with the pope. The next day, Küng drafted a polite letter to John Paul, stating he had not meant to "unsettle Catholic men and women in their faith."

The pope understood the threat created by the furor. He interrupted his Christmas-week holiday to confer with a delegation of five German bishops at Castel Gandolfo, to debate whether to reconsider his action. Ratzinger was among them. The five-hour meeting ended with no announcement, nor was there news the next day.

Küng was in agony as he waited. "I will never forget what were perhaps the most oppressive hours of my life," he wrote. On December 30, he got a call from the papal nuncio's office in Bonn with news that the pope would not reverse his decision. Hours later, Küng issued a new statement: "The pope is condemning a man whom he has not heard. An uncomfortable critic is to be silenced with all possible spiritual force. John XXIII and the Second Vatican Council are forgotten."

Ratzinger insisted years later he had nothing to do with the initial debate at the Vatican about punishing Küng. In fact, he said, he had always been wary of the idea of disciplining Küng, since it would allow him to portray himself as a martyr. "Küng had a big mouth and said impudent things," as Ratzinger put it. But he did not question Küng's faith, nor much of his scholarship. "In previous years I had occasionally been asked to give an opinion about Küng. I always said: 'Let him be.'" Years later, Ratzinger said he always regretted the perception that he had somehow betrayed Küng: "Why he identifies me as an enemy, I do not know."

Küng fought for weeks to convince the university to allow him to remain a member of the Catholic faculty, which would have required support from a majority of the university's twelve other Catholic theologians. That battle ended in February, when seven said they would abide by the pope's decision. "This is a betrayal that strikes me deeply," Küng wrote later. He was stung especially that his friend Walter Kasper, a frequent guest in his home, whose career he had guided, was among the seven. Küng had once thought of Kasper as the sort of independent, reform-minded theologian who would stand with him in promoting a more tolerant church. Instead, Kasper turned out to be another fair-weather friend and colleague, like Ratzinger, who had "an eye towards Rome" and put ambition ahead of principle. Years later, Küng sneered that when Kasper was eventually named a bishop, then a cardinal, "he must have attained his goal on earth."

JOHN PAUL II, even more than Paul VI, was determined to rein in the Jesuits and end their centuries of independence. John Paul's public assault began in September 1979, when he spoke in Rome to a gathering of Jesuit leaders, including Father Arrupe. The pope's speech was cryptic, but his disdain was obvious. The Jesuits, he said, had been plunged into "crisis" from "regrettable shortcomings" that were causing "discomfort for the Christian people." He said there were so many problems within the Society of Jesus that it was impossible to list them all, although he identified one: the Jesuits needed to "stay away from all secularizing tendencies." Many in the audience understood that as a reference to the order's support for social-justice movements like liberation theology. In the audience, Arrupe appeared baffled by the pope's attack, just as he had often been mystified by the anger of Paul VI. Arrupe remained committed to liberation theology.

John Paul followed up with concrete action. In December 1979, a prominent Jesuit activist in Washington, DC, Father William Callahan, who made headlines by campaigning for the ordination of women, was silenced by his local Jesuit order. He was told he had been disciplined at the pope's request. Four months later, Father Robert Drinan, the Jesuit who had been a member of the House of Representatives since 1971, announced he was leaving Congress on the explicit order of John Paul. Drinan had long rankled the Vatican by supporting public financing for health-care programs that provided birth control and abortion services.

RATZINGER WAS SUMMONED to Rome in the first weeks of 1980. There was a vacancy at the top of one of the Vatican's largest congregations, the agency that administered Catholic schools and universities around the world, and John Paul wanted Ratzinger: "We need you in Rome." But Ratzinger turned him down. "I've been in Munich such a short time," he told the pope. "I've made a vow. I can't just go now." The pope accepted the decision, although it was clear to both that Ratzinger would be in the Vatican before long.

Many in the Curia were convinced Ratzinger said no because he suspected a far more powerful job in Rome, as prefect of the Congregation for the Doctrine of the Faith, was about to become vacant, and he knew he was an obvious candidate. For a theologian, there could be no more important assignment. The congregation was where all judgments about Catholic doctrine were made and enforced.

Ratzinger accepted other important, temporary duties in 1980, when John Paul asked him to organize a worldwide bishops' synod that fall to discuss questions involving marriage and family life. The pope intended to use the synod to demand compliance with church teachings on birth control and divorce. Ratzinger also agreed to oversee arrangements for the pope's visit to Germany in November.

The cardinal accepted both assignments reluctantly, he said. At the time, he regularly complained that he felt overwhelmed with his duties in Munich, especially in managing a workforce of thousands of people across

Bavaria. The most distasteful part of his job, he said, came in disciplining priests and other church workers accused of misconduct, including violating their celibacy vows. Archdiocese records showed that, during his five years in Munich, several of his priests were accused of criminal sexual abuse, including child molestation. The paperwork suggests those cases were handled mostly by subordinates. Decades later, however, the question of how much he knew—and why any pedophile priests were allowed to remain in the church—would come back to haunt him. Many victims, their childhoods shattered by the abuse, would never forgive Ratzinger.

In 1980, no misconduct case before him was more troubling than that of Peter Hullermann, a thirty-three-year-old priest who had been transferred to Munich for psychiatric care after he admitted molesting an eleven-year-old boy in the northwest German city of Essen. Church authorities there eventually accused him of "indecent advances" toward several other boys. Ratzinger's staff accepted responsibility for supervising Hullermann during his treatment by a Munich psychiatrist. Archdiocese records confirm that on January 15, 1980, Ratzinger led the meeting in which Hullermann's transfer to Munich was approved. In accordance with church policy at the time, there was no consideration in either Essen or Munich of referring Hullermann to the police. Nor was there any thought of forcing him to leave the priesthood, even though Ratzinger's staff was explicitly warned that Hullermann was likely to continue molesting boys. One document described him as a "clear danger" to children.

Despite those warnings, church records made public decades later showed that just days after arriving in Munich, Hullermann was allowed to resume his full priestly duties, with no restriction on his access to children. He went on to molest at least a dozen more boys across Germany. Years later, Ratzinger would claim ignorance of the details of Hullermann's case, but his top deputies could not. The cardinal's records showed that his chief personnel officer, Father Friedrich Fahr, had been determined to find a way to preserve Hullermann's career despite his confession that he was a child molester. Fahr wrote in 1980 that while the young priest required urgent psychiatric care, he should be treated with "understanding," since he was a "very talented man."

AS THE 1970S DREW to a close, much of the world, Catholic and otherwise, remained in awe of John Paul II. He had created an excitement about the church not seen since the papacy of John XXIII and Vatican II. His constant globetrotting meant that people in scores of distant lands had a chance to see a bishop of Rome for themselves for the first time, and they found him mesmerizing.

Even so, mainstream Catholic theologians and other scholars began to step forward in the early 1980s to criticize the pope openly, even if, as Hans Küng had proved, that put their careers at risk. Their common complaint was that John Paul and his Curia deputies had turned their backs on Vatican II and abandoned the idea of any sort of power-sharing between Rome and the world's bishops. "In a certain sense, they're trying to repeal the council," wrote Father Francis X. Murphy, the theologian who famously chronicled Vatican II under a pseudonym for *The New Yorker*. At the end of his career and feeling he had less to lose for his candor, Murphy wrote a series of essays, under his own name, in which he described John Paul as a closed-minded authoritarian. He pointed out what he considered the pope's blatant double standard in demanding that Latin American priests who "risked their lives for justice" stay out of politics, while John Paul himself intervened constantly in the politics of his Polish homeland.

In January 1980, the pope summoned the bishops of the Netherlands to Rome for what amounted to a dressing down over what he saw as their outrageous disobedience over the years, especially their campaign to allow priests to marry. Their meetings with the pope, which were conducted in secret and lasted almost two weeks, ended with what many Dutch Catholics saw as a humiliating surrender by their bishops, who backed down on almost all of the initiatives they had promoted since Vatican II. They were each required to sign a twenty-two-page document in which they promised the debate over priestly celibacy was over. Many Dutch Catholics cited that document as the reason they decided to leave the church. Within several years, the share of the population worshipping as Catholics dropped by half, from about 40 percent to 20 percent.

Two months after his confrontation with the Dutch, the pope issued a letter to the world's bishops granting them authority to resume regular use of the Latin Mass, seen before Vatican II as the ultimate symbol of the church's isolation, if they wished. The letter suggested the council had created "scandal and disturbance" by encouraging the exclusive use of local languages for worship. Latin, he declared, deserved "full respect." In other ways, church services began to look and sound as they had before the council, on his orders. In April, the Congregation for Divine Worship issued a declaration demanding an end to "undue experimentation" in the sacraments. The document condemned the "reprehensible" conduct of priests who allowed lay people to help distribute communion wine and bread at the altar. It directed that Gospel passages be read aloud only by a priest or deacon, never by a layperson. It ordered an end to so-called guitar masses, in which folk music was played, that had become popular in the United States and Western Europe. It also imposed restrictions on the type of bread and wafers distributed from the altar; they must not be made with yeast or any other ingredient that caused dough to rise. (In Judea during Jesus's lifetime, yeast was sometimes associated with sin.)

The legacy of Vatican II was challenged in other ways. One of the council's great accomplishments, the establishment of dialogue between the Vatican and other Christian churches, was badly dented in the early years of John Paul's papacy. The divide between the Vatican and the worldwide Anglican Communion, which included the Church of England and the US Episcopal Church, became almost insurmountable, given John Paul's protests over the ordination of Anglican women priests.

The role of women inside the Vatican continued to stagnate. John Paul,

Father Hans Küng and his longtime companion, Marianne Saur, at a 2003 awards ceremony in Berlin. Küng's university colleagues said they never pressed him for details of the couple's thirty-year relationship.

like Paul VI, came to depend on the fame of Mother Teresa to argue that the church encouraged Catholic women. In 1979, the year after John Paul's election, she was awarded the Nobel Peace Prize, which increased her global celebrity. He used her as a roving ambassador for his most conservative causes, especially his opposition to birth control and abortion. Sadly, her association with John Paul appeared to bring her no personal spiritual comfort. In fact, although she would never say it publicly, she feared her work with the Vatican was all a charade. Her private correspondence, made public after her death in 1997, showed she was tormented by uncertainty about the existence of heaven—and even of God. She felt no presence of God whatsoever in her life. She admitted in her writings that her public smile was a "mask" or "cloak that covers everything" and that if people truly knew what was in her heart, they would say, "What hypocrisy!"

IN JANUARY 1980, Archbishop Romero was in Rome for a second audience with the pope, and it did not go much better. In a diary entry, Romero wrote he was grateful that John Paul "received me very warmly and told me he perfectly understood how difficult the political situation of my country is." Still, rather than give full backing to Romero's brave protest against the savagery of El Salvador's military, the pope once again urged caution. He said Romero should be worried about the possibility of "score-settling" violence by the government's "popular Left opponents, which could be bad for the church." Even more than the year before, Romero returned home convinced he would soon be assassinated. In February, the church radio station was bombed, as was the library of the Catholic university. He stopped sleeping in his own home, hoping to make it more difficult for the death squads to find him. He had taken to driving alone. "I prefer it this way," he wrote. "When what I'm expecting to happen, happens, I want to be alone. So it's only me they get. I don't want somebody else to suffer."

More than nine hundred Salvadoran civilians were killed in political violence in the first three months of the year. In a sermon in March, Romero warned that the nation was "in a prerevolutionary stage," with worse to come. He wrote in his diary that he could not understand why the pope, who regularly condemned Mafia violence in Italy, did not say more about political violence in Central America. He was puzzled that John Paul would "speak out about the cruel killings in Italy" but remain mostly silent about the "many killings in El Salvador every day."

In his final speeches, Romero said he was comforted that, in defending the poor and oppressed, he had done the work demanded by the Savior. In his last radio address, he said: "I know that many are scandalized at what I say and charge that it forsakes the preaching of the Gospel to meddle in politics. I do not accept that accusation." His diaries show he was unaware at the time that the pope had formally decided to strip him of his authority. In March, senior Curia officials met to plan his ouster from his archdiocese. "He was acting without responsibility," said Cardinal Silvio Oddi, who then led the Congregation for the Clergy. According to Oddi, Romero had to go because the government in El Salvador "interpreted Romero's doctrine to be in favor of communism."

Before he could be ousted, however, Romero was dead. On March 24, he was assassinated as he said Mass in a small hospital chapel in San Salvador. The assassin, later identified as a member of a government-backed death squad, fired a single bullet into Romero's chest, just as the archbishop was raising a chalice to begin Communion. A photographer captured the moment, as Romero gasped for breath, blood pouring from his mouth. A week later, his funeral descended into chaos; twenty-six people were killed and hundreds injured when gunfire broke out on the steps of the Metropolitan Cathedral.

Romero's murder was denounced by government and religious leaders throughout the world. In their tributes, many Catholic bishops, especially in Latin America, agreed that Romero was bound for sainthood—as a martyr to the cause of liberation theology. In London, the Catholic magazine *The Tablet* compared him to the great twelfth-century British churchman Thomas Becket, sainted by both the Catholic and Anglican churches, who was also murdered at an altar.

There was no similar mourning at the Vatican. In fact, there was a remarkably callous reaction to Romero's death, including from the pope himself. In a telegram to El Salvador's bishops, the pope called the murder a "sacrilegious assassination," but he pointedly offered no words of admiration for Romero, apart from describing him as "zealous," which may not have been meant as a compliment. A week later, after the massacre outside Romero's funeral service, the pope—grudgingly, it seemed—issued a statement of praise. He said Romero had "united his life with the service to the poorest and most underprivileged."

The Vatican's failure to do more to honor Romero appalled churchmen across Latin America, especially in Brazil, where liberation theology had been so widely embraced and where Romero was instantly hailed as a saint. Brazilian bishops remained bewildered by the pope's continued waffling on liberation theology, and they planned to press him on it during his pilgrimage to their country in June. It would be the first trip by any pope to Brazil, home to more than one hundred million Catholics. In preparing for John Paul's arrival, Cardinal Arns of São Paulo traveled to Rome four times for long conversations with the pope. The cardinal said later he tried to convince John Paul that in Brazil, he should publicly champion liberation theology once and for all, especially after Romero's assassination. "Archbishop Romero did not die because he was some sort of Marxist," Arns told the pope. "He died trying to defend the rights of the people in the slums."

Before visiting Brazil, John Paul made a six-nation pilgrimage to Africa in May. He reveled there in the colorful displays of tribal dance and music that he encountered. He repeatedly hailed the continent, home to fifty million Catholics, as "ripe for harvest" in the search for converts. At the time, the number of African Catholics was growing rapidly, by more than 5 percent a year, due largely to his star power. Still, throughout the trip, he made pronouncements that seemed strangely insensitive, if not tone deaf. He rejected pleas that he say the Mass, or listen as others did, in tribal languages, as had become common in African churches after Vatican II. In Kinshasa, the capital of Zaire, a nation of almost twelve million Catholics, he insisted on conducting an open-air Mass in Latin and French, even though a local bishop warned him that "absolutely no one" there would understand him. Dissident groups were angered by his public embrace of Zaire's Catholic-born dictator, "President-for-Life" Mobutu Sese Seko, despite Mobutu's dismal human rights record and outrageous, well-documented corruption. Mobutu was widely quoted that year as boasting he was the world's third-richest man, with an estimated $3 billion in assets, from the plunder of the nation's diamond mines and other mineral resources. After leaving Zaire, John Paul appeared to concede he held his tongue about Mobutu's sins, since the former Belgian colony had been independent only since 1960. "Sometimes there are sinful governments," he said. "But at least these people are their own masters."

In Brazil the following month, he was welcomed by what were reported to be the largest crowds ever encountered anywhere by a bishop of Rome. Police estimated that more than one million people lined his motorcade route in Rio de Janeiro. At the start of the visit, Cardinal Arns told deputies he was hopeful he had finally won John Paul over to the cause of liberation theology. The pope continued to avoid using the term, but he delivered speeches that embraced the goals of the movement. He repeatedly criticized human-rights abuses by Brazil's military and called for the church to align itself with laborers. In Recife, he made a point of embracing Archbishop Câmara in front of news cameras. It was the first time in years that the Brazilian government allowed Câmara—the "Red bishop," as the junta dubbed him—to be seen on television. In the city of Salvador, the pope sounded as if he had always been a champion of liberation theology. In his speech there, he warned dictators across Latin America that they faced a stark choice: social justice would come through "profound and courageous reform" or through "the forces of violence."

Then, just as quickly, that message evaporated. At the end of the trip, John Paul held a contentious, hours-long meeting with Brazil's 345 bishops that left many of them angry and dispirited. The pope had returned to his stubborn insistence that liberation theology promoted Marxism and involved the church in partisan politics, and he would forbid it. "We are not experts in politics or economics," he told them. "We are ministers of the Gospel."

THERE WAS ALWAYS one glaring exception to the pope's demand that the church stay out of politics: Poland. In August, weeks after the pope returned from Brazil, Poland was seized by labor unrest tied to the Communist government's decision to raise food prices. Workers went on strike in the shipyard in Gdansk. The strike committee was led by a thirty-seven-year-old electrician, Lech Wałęsa, who went on to lead a national opposition movement. The city's archbishop announced his support for the workers, whose rallies were often held at a shrine they created at the front of the shipyard gates, covered with images of the Virgin Mary and photos of John Paul. The strike was immediately recognized within Poland as not simply a challenge to the shipyard managers but, as it grew, a threat to the survival of the Communist government in Warsaw.

The pope would not wait long to take a side. On August 20, during an address in St. Peter's Square, he noticed a group of several hundred Poles. Many were waving Polish flags, while others carried banners expressing support for the shipyard workers. Unexpectedly, the pope burst into song in Polish—an emotional hymn often heard at the Gdansk protests. Many Poles in the crowd wept openly and began to sing along. After the last verse, the pope called for those in the square to join him in a "prayer for my homeland."

Days later, he dispatched telegrams to Poland's bishops to offer his backing for the Gdansk protests and organized a special Mass in St. Peter's in support. The situation in Poland continued to deteriorate, with Wałęsa's trade union growing increasingly militant. The pope's deputies said he monitored the news minute by minute. There were some days, they said, when he would talk about nothing else.

The interior of St. Peter's Basilica during the opening ceremony of the Second Vatican
Council, October 11, 1962.

Above: Pope Pius XII (1939–1958) often preferred to be photographed with his pet birds. Right: Pope John XXIII (1958–1963) welcomes First Lady Jacqueline Kennedy to the Vatican, March 11, 1962. Standing behind them is Father Paul Marcinkus, an ambitious, American-born Curia bureaucrat who brought scandal to two future popes.

Pope Paul VI (1963–1978) with the newly appointed archbishop of San Salvador, El Salvador, Óscar Romero, 1978.

Pope John Paul I, whose papacy lasted only thirty-three days in 1978, offers blessings to Cardinal Karol Wojtyła of Poland.

Above: German theologian Joseph
Ratzinger, the future Pope Benedict XVI
(2005–2013), and his sister, Maria, in
the garden of the home they shared in
Regensburg, Germany, in the 1970s.
Right: Pope Benedict and his brother,
Father Georg Ratzinger, director of the
famed Catholic boys' choir of Regensburg,
after a concert in the Sistine Chapel, 2005.

Left: Pope John Paul II (1978–2005) and Cardinal
Joseph Ratzinger of Germany ride in a motorcade
in Munich, November 1980. Right: John Paul II
and Mother Teresa of India embrace, 1988.

Sexual predators: (left to right) Cardinal Hans Hermann Groër of Austria; Father Gilbert Gauthe of Lafayette, Louisiana; Father Stephen Kiesle of Union City, California.

Father Marcial Maciel, Mexican-born founder of the Legion of Christ and a child molester for decades, leads male students in prayer at a Legion school in Ireland, 1962.

Left: Father Theodore McCarrick, future cardinal of Washington, DC, and a sexual predator throughout his career, with a victim in a 1974 poolside photo that the victim released to news organizations. Right: Cardinal McCarrick of Washington appears between President George W. Bush and Chief Justice John G. Roberts Jr. at the capital's annual Red Mass in October 2005.

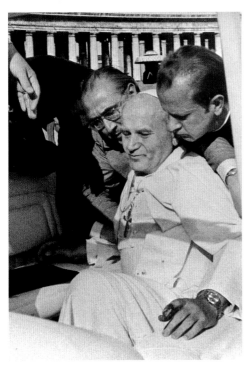

Left: John Paul II moments after he was shot in an assassination attempt in St. Peter's Square, May 13, 1981. Above: Mourners at the funeral of the assassinated Archbishop Óscar Romero of El Salvador, March 30, 1980.

Rebels: (left to right) Friar Leonardo Boff, Brazilian champion of liberation theology, in 1986; Orlando Yorio and Franz Jalics, kidnapped Argentine slum priests.

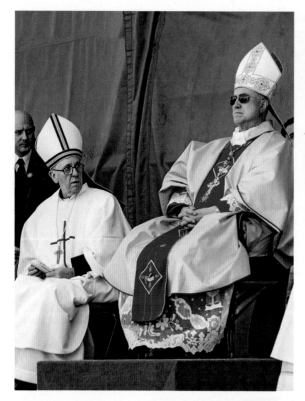

Left: Cardinal Jorge Bergoglio of Buenos Aires looks up at Cardinal Tarcisio Bertone, the Vatican's secretary of state, at a ceremony in Argentina, November 2007. Above: Cardinal Raymond Burke of the United States, future archconservative opponent of Pope Francis, at a prize ceremony in Rome, 2011.

Pope Benedict XVI seated between Cardinal Walter Kasper of Germany, left, and Cardinal Bertone during his first visit as pope to Rome's synagogue, January 17, 2010.

Left: Pope Francis prays alongside Pope Emeritus Benedict XVI at the papal country residence at Castel Gandolfo during their first meeting after Francis's election, March 2013. Above: In the 2019 film *The Two Popes*, Hollywood fictionalized the relationship between Benedict, left, portrayed by Anthony Hopkins, and Francis, right, portrayed by Jonathan Pryce.

Pope Francis washes the feet of refugees during the annual Holy Week foot-washing ceremony, March 2016.

Francis encounters President Joseph Biden, a devout Catholic, at the G7 summit of world leaders in Apulia, Italy, June 2024.

Vatican City today: (1) St. Peter's Basilica; (2) Sistine Chapel; (3) St. Peter's Square; (4) Apostolic Palace, the traditional papal home; (5) Palace of the Holy Office; (6) Casa Santa Marta guesthouse, home to Pope Francis; (7) Mater Ecclesiae Monastery, home to the late Pope Emeritus Benedict XVI.

22

Cardinal Ratzinger Rises

IN OCTOBER 1980, Ratzinger had his opportunity to shine in Rome. It was a final audition, it seemed, for a much larger role. The venue was the bishops' synod on the Catholic family, the event the pope had asked him to organize. The gathering of more than two hundred bishops from ninety countries produced the outcome the pope desired—a full commitment to conservative doctrine on marriage, child-rearing, and sexuality.

Ratzinger maneuvered to keep the subject of birth control—for millions of Catholics, still the most pressing issue confronting the church—off the agenda. He made clear the pope considered it a settled matter. There was a moment of drama, however, when the president of the US bishops' conference, Archbishop John Quinn of San Francisco, gave a speech calling for a new, "completely honest" debate on the subject. He warned of a crisis among American Catholics, since so many rejected *Humanae Vitae*; he cited opinion polls showing that three-quarters of married Catholic women in the United States used birth-control pills or other methods of artificial contraception. His request went nowhere. If other bishops supported Quinn, they were not brave enough to speak up to endorse his words, and the synod hurriedly moved on to other subjects. It was widely recognized that after the speech, the pope lost faith in Quinn permanently, and the archbishop, once seen as a rising star, would never be promoted to cardinal.

During the synod, the pope created controversy by promoting his most conservative views on sex. In his weekly audience, he revealed his belief that a married man who lusted for his wife was guilty of "adultery in his heart," as if the physical passion felt by a loving married couple could be sinful. The comment was seized on by reporters in the Vatican press corps to suggest the church was reverting to its pre–Vatican II view that sex was meant purely for procreation. The next week, at a Mass to celebrate the synod, John Paul praised married couples who abstained from sex entirely as a demonstration of "serene and generous self-control." In his closing speech, he stressed his commitment to teachings that barred Catholics who left their marriages—through separation or divorce—from receiving Communion unless they committed to giving up all sexual activity for the rest of their lives. The synod ended with a document, written largely by Ratzinger, that was a complete reaffirmation of the church's opposition to divorce and birth control.

The next month, John Paul's pilgrimage to Germany, which Ratzinger had also organized, did not go so smoothly, and many in the Curia thought the cardinal was to blame. When Ratzinger's mistakes were pointed out to him, he proved defensive and unpleasant. The trouble began when the country's Protestant leaders protested that Ratzinger had set aside almost no time for them to meet the pope. Lutherans and other Protestants made up about half the German population, yet the pope originally planned to meet with their leaders in a single brief gathering. After the protests, individual meetings were hastily arranged.

Worse, Ratzinger paid little attention to written material issued to promote the trip. Germany's Catholic bishops published a booklet on the history of Catholicism that outraged Protestants by describing Martin Luther as a man of "vehement anger" who "brought no reform, but only a schism of the church." The Vatican was forced to issue a statement in which it regretted the booklet's "errors." The trip's most awkward moment was also a result of sloppiness by Ratzinger and his deputies. When the pope visited Munich, a local twenty-nine-year-old Catholic social worker named Barbara Engl was asked to give a brief speech to welcome him. She submitted the text in advance, and it was approved. To their horror, however, Ratzinger's staff looked at the speech again—and realized it contained several lines that would offend the pope, including a protest over the Vatican's "many prohibitions" on sexuality and women's rights. The cardinal's aides demanded Engl remove the passages, but it was too late, since the text had already been distributed. Engl delivered the speech as written, with the pope seated six feet away from her, his head bowed. Ratzinger would claim that she had "tricked us" and delivered remarks that were neither "tactful nor appropriate." Engl said that was blatantly untrue.

The year ended with the pope focused on the crisis in Poland, which left him little time to concentrate on news elsewhere. The bloodshed across Central America worsened in the final months of 1980, yet there was little public response from the Vatican. John Paul put out only a brief statement to condemn the murder that December of three American nuns working in El Salvador, who had been gunned down by a right-wing death squad. Political violence flared across the border in Guatemala as well, forcing an entire Catholic diocese to shut down. Its bishop and priests were relocated, leaving the faithful without anyone to conduct services—or offer any protection from the bloodshed.

John Paul now promoted himself as a mediator in the Polish crisis. He issued repeated statements defending the Gdansk shipyard workers, who had unified under the Polish name Solidarność (Solidarity). He championed the movement by citing documents of Vatican II that called for the protection of labor rights. In September, the Communist Party leader was ousted and replaced by a former domestic spy chief who promised a return to "Leninist norms." In October, the Polish bishops' conference issued its first definitive statement supporting the workers' demands. On December 7, President Jimmy Carter's Polish-born national security adviser, Zbigniew Brzezinski, telephoned the pope to warn him—in their native language—that Soviet troops were moving toward Poland's eastern border. Days later, the pope wrote a letter to Soviet leader Leonid Brezhnev, urging him to "do everything you can in order to dispel the tension." He said that Soviet invaders would confront "the forces of the entire society of Poland" acting "in solidarity." The choice of the word "solidarity" appeared intentional. There was no invasion.

In the United States, Ronald Reagan was sworn in as Carter's successor on January 20, 1981. On the campaign trail, Reagan had made clear he shared the pope's hopes for an end to Soviet domination of Poland and the rest of Eastern Europe. John Paul sensed an opportunity and, a month before Reagan's inauguration, dispatched a savvy Vatican diplomat to serve as the church's ambassador to Washington—Archbishop Pio Laghi, who had just completed six years as nuncio in Argentina. News reports about the appointment, attributed to Vatican sources, suggested Laghi had heroically confronted the Argentine junta during the Dirty War. Laghi admitted to his new aides in Washington that was a gross exaggeration of any bravery he had shown. He was directed by the pope to open early, confidential lines of communication with the Reagan administration—in particular, with the

Central Intelligence Agency. Reagan had appointed his close friend William Casey, a devout Catholic, as director of central intelligence. Days after the inauguration, Casey and Deputy Secretary of State William Clarke called on Laghi at the Vatican's mission in Washington. It was the first of what would become regular meetings between Casey and Laghi. From the start, the Reagan White House, through Laghi, urged the Vatican to rein in a campaign by American bishops to end US military intervention in Central America. The White House also asked the Vatican to keep a close watch on activist priests across Latin America tied to liberation theology, still seen by the CIA as a Marxist threat. Clarke later described the logistics of how he would call Laghi to arrange the secret meetings: "We had kind of a code word, 'Could we stop in for cappuccino?' That would mean that we had to see him right away."

The White House dispatched Vernon Walters, a former CIA official who was a roving ambassador for Reagan, to meet regularly with the pope in Rome. Walters, yet another devout Catholic, pressed John Paul for help in trying to stem leftist church movements in Latin America. In return, Walters offered detailed intelligence about the crisis in Poland. Over time, the pope was shown American spy-satellite photos of the movement of Soviet troops near Poland's borders. Declassified CIA records released decades later suggested, but did not prove, that the pope encouraged the CIA's efforts to funnel millions of dollars into Poland in support of Solidarity.

ON MARCH 30, 1981, a mentally ill twenty-five-year-old man named John Hinckley attempted to assassinate the new president. Six weeks later, on May 13, the pope was also targeted for death by a gun-wielding assassin— a twenty-three-year-old Turkish nationalist, Mehmet Ali Ağca, who fired four bullets at John Paul as he was being driven in his "popemobile" through a crowd of ten thousand worshippers in St. Peter's Square. The pope, hit in his stomach and left hand, fell backward into the arms of his private secretary, Monsignor Dziwisz, and stared at his blood-stained hands as more blood began to pool in front of his snow-white papal cassock. Minutes later, Dziwisz, assuming the pope was close to death, administered last rites.

Ağca, an ultranationalist Turkish militant tied to the 1979 murder of a journalist in his homeland, tried to flee but was tackled by a policeman and others in the crowd. Several handwritten notes in Turkish were found in his pockets, including one that read: "I am killing the pope as a protest against the imperialism of the Soviet Union and the United States and against the genocide that is being carried out in El Salvador and Afghanistan." The CIA and other foreign intelligence agencies pursued reports—never confirmed—that Ağca was acting on behalf of the governments of the Soviet Union or Poland.*

The pope underwent five hours of surgery, as doctors removed several inches of his intestines. After three weeks in the hospital, John Paul, painfully thin and weak, was allowed to return to the papal apartment to continue his convalescence. In August, over the opposition of doctors who said it was too soon, he insisted on a new round of surgery to restore the normal functioning of his intestines: "I don't want to continue half dead and half alive." On his return to the Vatican, he went to pray in the grottoes beneath St. Peter's Basilica, at the tomb of St. Peter. "I wanted first to thank St. Peter for wishing to keep alive his latest successor," the pope later joked.

His recovery was made more difficult by a deluge of bad news. On May 19, just six days after the assassination attempt, Italian voters, by a two-to-one margin, rejected a plea from the Vatican and upheld the country's liberal abortion laws. A week later, Cardinal Wyszyński died in Warsaw at the age of seventy-nine. It was a serious blow to the labor uprising in Gdansk, which he and the pope had so eagerly championed. In June, the pope settled on Wyszyński's successor, Bishop Józef Glemp, whose training was as a church lawyer. It would be the first of a string of disastrous personnel decisions by the pope. Glemp proved he had none of his predecessor's courage or decisiveness and, over time, embarrassed the Vatican with public remarks that were flagrantly anti-Semitic. Then came another catastrophic staffing choice. In September, the pope promoted Archbishop Marcinkus, the head of the Vatican Bank and the best-known American in the Curia, to the additional role of chief administrator of Vatican City, effectively making him its mayor. The move astonished many in the Curia, since the fifty-nine-year-old Marcinkus had been tied for years to so much incompetence, if not outright criminality. He had run the bank in the mid-1970s when it lost tens of millions of dollars in the collapse of the business empire of the sinister Michele Sindona. Marcinkus had proved a cunning survivor,

---

* In December 1983, the pope visited Ağca in prison and said he forgave his would-be assassin, in a demonstration of the Gospels' call for forgiveness. At the pope's request, Ağca was pardoned by the Italian government in 2000 and deported to Turkey. In 2007, he revealed he had converted to Roman Catholicism.

however. He charmed John Paul with his brash, cigar-chomping style and reminded the pope constantly of their shared ethnic roots. Marcinkus's father was a Lithuanian immigrant to the US. In the sixteenth through eighteenth centuries, Poland and Lithuania were one country—the pope's mother was of Lithuanian descent—and their cultural ties remained strong after they separated. That made Marcinkus an "honorary Pole," John Paul often said.

The pope demanded another momentous personnel change that summer—in the Society of Jesus. In August, Father Arrupe, seventy-three, suffered a stroke that left him partially paralyzed. His deputies agreed he would never recover sufficiently to return as leader, so they organized a meeting in Rome to elect a successor. Under the Jesuits' four-hundred-year-old constitution, the choice of a new superior general rested solely within the order itself. In the interim, Arrupe named his American-born deputy, sixty-two-year-old Vincent O'Keefe, the former president of Fordham University in New York, to serve as temporary leader.

On the pope's orders, those plans were abandoned weeks later. In a letter to Arrupe, still confined to his hospital bed, John Paul announced he had assumed day-to-day control of the Jesuits and was suspending its constitution. He pushed O'Keefe aside and declared that Father Paolo Dezza, the conservative Jesuit academic who had been Paul VI's personal confessor, would succeed Arrupe. The moves outraged Jesuits around the world, convinced that John Paul intended to end forever the order's special role in the church; they saw the pope's treatment of the saintly Arrupe as unconscionably brutal. In Germany, eighteen prominent Jesuits, including Karl Rahner, issued a letter of protest. They said that it was "hard to recognize the hand of God" in the pope's actions.

In November, the pope was faced with the most consequential personnel decision of his papacy when Cardinal Šeper retired from the Congregation for the Doctrine of the Faith, citing ill health. John Paul did not struggle in choosing his successor: Cardinal Ratzinger of Munich, then fifty-four. Many of Ratzinger's friends were convinced he was thrilled by the appointment even though, in public, he insisted he resisted a transfer to the Vatican, describing his new job as a "bed of nettles." He relented this time, he said, only because he felt that, after turning down a Curia post the year before, he could not disappoint the pope a second time.

The choice made for banner newspaper headlines in Germany, but there was a shudder among the country's progressive Catholics, who believed

Ratzinger had turned his back on everything he stood for as a reform-minded young theologian. German newspapers dug up copies of the essays he had written in the 1960s in which he condemned the closed-minded "sycophants" of the Curia. They also found copies of the historic 1963 speech that his mentor Cardinal Frings had delivered at Vatican II—the speech that Ratzinger had almost certainly written—in which the Holy Office was denounced as a "scandal to the world." It was the same agency, now called the Congregation for the Doctrine of the Faith, that Ratzinger had been chosen to lead.

He moved to Rome several months later with his sister. They were provided with a grand, church-owned apartment—three thousand square feet, complete with its own chapel, on the fourth floor of a palazzo overlooking the barracks of the Swiss Guard. It was so large that Ratzinger had trouble filling it. He arrived with not much more than his library of books, his beloved antique wooden desk, and his piano. He quickly became known to his Italian neighbors, who found him quiet but charming, as *il tedesco*—the German.

His new workplace was the Palace of the Holy Office, the off-yellow, five-story stone structure built in the sixteenth century for Cardinal Lorenzo Pucci, best remembered as a patron of Michelangelo's. It was located just outside the borders of Vatican City, close to St. Peter's Basilica. Ratzinger received a warm reception from the congregation's staff, which included about forty theologians and canon lawyers.

In Rome, as in Munich, he proved himself a man of absolute routine. He rose at six a.m. for prayer and was at his desk precisely at nine. He had a chauffeured car at his disposal—the congregation's handsome 1960s-era Mercedes sedan had been a gift to Cardinal Ottaviani from the German carmarker—but he liked to walk to work, clutching his scuffed leather briefcase. Much of his morning was spent reading documents. At eleven a.m., if there were no staff appointments, he met with outsiders, usually bishops visiting Rome. At precisely one fifteen, he returned home for lunch and a nap. The rest of the day was spent studying documents and editing the work of his deputies. He mostly dined in the apartment with his sister. If he went out for a meal, it was usually to his favorite Roman restaurant, Cantina Tirolese, which served home-style German food. He insisted on being in bed by ten p.m.

His relationship with the pope, he said, was easy from the start. They had one extended meeting every Friday in the papal apartment. They spoke in German. In describing the conversations, Ratzinger was careful to note the two addressed each other in the formal version of the language. (They used the formal *Sie*, for the word "you," and not the informal *du*.) Ratzinger said he arrived first for the meetings, took a seat, and waited a few minutes. "Then the pope comes in. We shake hands, sit down together at the table and have a little personal chat" before launching into a discussion of issues before the congregation. In their early years working together, Ratzinger insisted he took direction from John Paul. "I had a say in the pope's official teachings and contributed something," he said. "But the pope very much set his own course." Inside the Vatican, however, those remarks were seen as false modesty. Over time, the pope so respected the cardinal that he would regularly bow to Ratzinger's views. The cardinal arrived at the Vatican with a reputation as a famed scholar and intellectual heavyweight, much more so than the pope. And the cardinal was undoubtedly the better, clearer thinker.

Ratzinger's new job brought him international celebrity. He was regularly described as the second-most-powerful man in the Vatican, and by many measurements that was true. At first, he seemed to enjoy the recognition. Quickly, though, he began to experience a type of notoriety he found unpleasant, even alarming. Journalists in the Vatican press corps were different from what he had known back in Germany. The journalists in Rome were far more intrusive and eager to track down embarrassing stories about his past. Family members in Bavaria were suddenly badgered for anecdotes about his youth, and his talkative brother posed a special problem. Georg embarrassed him by sharing tales with nosy reporters about their childhood. He revealed, for example, that Joseph, who always insisted publicly he never had ambition to work in the church hierarchy, had in fact boasted about it since grade school. Georg recalled how, as a young child, Joseph startled the family one day when he announced, "I'm going to be a cardinal!" Ratzinger, his deputies said, was also bothered by stories told by his family about how frail he had been as a child, as if questioning his manliness. "He was very slight and delicate," Georg said of his brother. "He would have preferred to stay home with Mother." Joseph, he revealed, had never had a girlfriend or known any other sort of romance in his youth, despite his brother's occasional public suggestion to the contrary.

What distressed Ratzinger most of all were the stories told about his family life during World War II. Hitler came to power in 1933, when Joseph was only six. The fact that the Ratzinger brothers had been members of the

Hitler Youth movement was no surprise, since membership was considered compulsory. Nor did the brothers ever deny they had been soldiers in the Nazi army. Joseph was insistent, however, that he and his family had no suspicion about the extent of the Nazis' barbarism—certainly no idea that they were slaughtering millions of Jews and others in the Holocaust.

Some journalists in the Vatican press corps questioned that account. Many noticed Ratzinger's childhood home was only seventy miles from the Dachau concentration camp, where tens of thousands of Jews and other prisoners were executed, beginning in 1933. And so they again tracked down Georg, who acknowledged that the family had actually been well aware of atrocities: "Of course, we knew already during the Nazi period that there were concentration camps in which people were murdered." He revealed that the Ratzingers had experienced, directly, the terror of Nazi euthanasia campaigns to rid the country of "undesirables," including people who suffered from birth defects. He recalled how one of his cousins—"a very sweet, happy boy" who was "mentally handicapped" and had trouble speaking—was abducted and murdered by Nazi police. He also remembered how his family befriended an "old, childless married couple who were always so happy when we came to visit. One day the husband died of pneumonia, and the wife had a gradual onset of dementia." She was taken away and, as the Ratzingers understood it, killed.

The fact that the brothers offered such starkly different accounts of their upbringing did not attract much attention at the time outside Italy, but Joseph sensed it could be a damaging controversy later. And so, in his early years in Rome, despite the crush of his new duties at the congregation, he set to work on the first volume of his memoirs. It was a book that would rewrite, and misrepresent, much of his early life story.

23

Banishing a Jesuit

THE DIRTY WAR WAS still raging in Argentina in the early 1980s, although there was reason to believe the worst of the violence was over. According to human-rights groups, there had been a sharp drop in reports of government-ordered kidnappings and secret executions, explained in part by growing international scrutiny—and condemnation— of the junta. In 1980, the country's best-known human-rights activist, Adolfo Pérez Esquivel, was awarded the Nobel Peace Prize. A classified study by the US State Department completed the year before suggested another, more chilling reason for the drop-off in violence: the military had simply run out of opponents to kill. There were relatively few people still alive who could be branded as "terrorists or subversives," the study found.

In Rome, the Jesuits continued to be alarmed about the failure of the order in Argentina—and Father Bergoglio, the former national leader, in particular—to make any public protest against the junta's savagery. Bergoglio's legacy was one of "troubling ambiguities and silence," said Father Francisco Ivern, a Spaniard in the Jesuit hierarchy in the Vatican.

If Bergoglio was aware of the criticism in faraway Rome, it did not seem to concern him. He was cheered by the first years of John Paul's papacy. The pope's decision to suspend the Jesuits' constitution and oust Father Arrupe's chosen successor suggested it was Argentina's tradition-minded Jesuit leaders, not their left-leaning superiors in Rome, who were in line with the thinking of the new pope.

In 1979, Bergoglio completed his full six-year term and took up a new post as rector of the Colegio Máximo, a job just as prestigious. He established himself at the school as a forceful leader and moved quickly to balance its books. With the help of European donors, he oversaw the construction of a new library and lecture hall. Those accomplishments came at the cost of unity, however. Many priests said Bergoglio encouraged an almost cultlike following at the college. Those refusing to pledge loyalty to him became pariahs. His name became an adjective—there were "Bergoglio Jesuits" and everyone else. Several clerics left the order to protest his leadership.

He imposed new disciplinary rules on students and faculty, requiring both to wear clerical cassocks at all times. There was an insistence on displays of patriotism. Students were ordered to sing the Argentine national anthem at school gatherings. In classes, there was a stress on conservative doctrine. Teaching about liberation theology was still strongly discouraged. Bergoglio promoted a home-grown alternative called "theology of the people," which rejected left-wing economic theories and encouraged the poor to find strength by embracing traditional Argentine culture.

Bergoglio continued to make a priority of serving the poor, which his critics grudgingly admired. He donated land around the campus for the construction of food kitchens to serve deprived neighborhoods nearby. Other land was converted into a farm, complete with livestock. Some students, who felt they should be allowed to focus exclusively on their studies, protested when Bergoglio ordered them to do farm work. "I joined the Society to study, not to look after pigs," said Ernesto Giobando, a seminarian.

Desperately poor local families often arrived at Bergoglio's office door, asking for shelter or food. Father Ángel Rossi recalled that he was once summoned to the rector's office and found a distraught woman standing in the hallway. He was given an order by Bergoglio: "Don't come back until you have found a home for this lady here. She has four children and no roof over her head." Bergoglio's community projects created new divisions, however. Many Jesuits thought he was trying to turn what had been an elite educational institution into a sprawling antipoverty organization— one that brought glory, principally, to him. Father Rafael Velasco, who studied at the Colegio, said the welfare projects were "all identified with one man—Bergoglio."

The end of the Dirty War, and the junta's collapse, began in earnest on April 2, 1982, when the military launched an ill-fated invasion of the Falkland Islands, a tiny archipelago in the South Atlantic about three hundred miles off Argentina's eastern coast. A British territory since the early nineteenth century, it had a population of about eighteen hundred English-speaking residents. Argentina had always claimed sovereignty and knew the islands by a different name, the Malvinas. The invasion by ten thousand Argentine troops was a poorly disguised effort to divert attention from the country's disastrous economy and civil unrest. It quickly turned into humiliation. The British launched a naval armada to retake the islands and seized them again in June, at a cost of 907 lives—649 of them Argentine soldiers and sailors.

The invasion initially had popular support among Argentines, including church leaders. Bergoglio praised soldiers who died in "the Malvinas war"—he would never call them the Falklands—as heroes: "They went out to defend the fatherland, to claim as theirs what had been usurped." The invasion led to an abrupt decision by John Paul II to visit Argentina in June; it was the first pilgrimage to the country by any sitting pope. The awkward two-day trip, which came in the final days of fighting, was an attempt by the Vatican to appear even-handed. Aides said the pope went largely because he did not want to cancel a long-planned visit that same month to Britain. On arrival in Buenos Aires, he called for negotiations to end the war, a plea that came too late, since Britain was only days from victory. Still, the junta was eager to exploit the visit to suggest a papal endorsement, and military leaders were delighted when the pope said virtually nothing during his time there about human rights.

The military's disgrace in the Falklands led to massive street demonstrations against the junta, which quickly announced a return to civilian rule. The protest leaders included Raúl Alfonsín, a human-rights lawyer and democracy activist elected president the following year. Many Jesuits recognized instantly that Alfonsín's presidency meant trouble for Bergoglio. The new president's advisers included a Jesuit priest, Fernando Storni, once seen as a liberal rival to Bergoglio, whom he despised. In his first week as president, Alfonsín, with Storni's encouragement, announced the creation of a national commission to investigate human-rights abuses during the Dirty War, an inquiry that would last for years and lead to the trial and imprisonment of several junta leaders for mass murder. It also brought a spotlight to the actions of other prominent Argentines accused of collaborating with the military, including members of the Catholic hierarchy. In years to come, the investigations would regularly target one churchman in particular—Bergoglio.

THE POPE'S SUSPENSION of the Jesuits' constitution lasted from 1981 until 1983. During that time, John Paul left no doubt that, whatever the order's future, the centuries-old concept of the Jesuits as the elite "shock troops" of the papacy was over. As Jesuits had long feared, the pope intended to transfer much of that role to Opus Dei. In 1982, the pope announced that, after years of secret planning, Opus Dei would report to him directly as his "personal prelature," allowing its priests around the world to operate independently of local bishops. There were quiet protests over the move, notably from Cardinal Basil Hume, the archbishop of Westminster and the most powerful church leader in Britain. Only the year before, he had grown so alarmed about what he saw as Opus Dei's sinister behavior that he imposed strict limits on its recruiting in Britain; he barred anyone under the age of eighteen from joining the order.

In 1983, the pope allowed the Jesuits to pick a new permanent leader, and in September they elected Father Peter Hans Kolvenbach, a respected Dutch linguist, as Arrupe's successor. From the start, Kolvenbach was eager to show loyalty to John Paul. He spoke often, almost obsessively, of his love for the pope, even as he quietly revived much of Arrupe's agenda. Kolvenbach shared his predecessor's commitment to social justice, and especially to liberation theology.

Early on, Kolvenbach was forced to deal with a stream of complaints from Buenos Aires about Bergoglio, by then the head of the Colegio Máximo. Kolvenbach was shown letters from Argentine Jesuits who had written to Rome to protest what they saw as Bergoglio's divisive, egomaniacal leadership. Kolvenbach decided to act, ordering an investigation of Bergoglio.

When word of the investigation reached Argentina, Bergoglio began to look for an exit—a way to lie low, perhaps for years. He stunned colleagues in 1985 when he abruptly announced he would step down from the Colegio and move to Germany to complete his long-delayed theology dissertation.* He had another good reason to flee Argentina that year, since human-rights investigators for the new civilian government were at work, reviewing allegations that Bergoglio and other churchmen collaborated with the military during the Dirty War. For Bergoglio, there was an even

---

* The subject of his never-finished dissertation was the Italian-born twentieth-century German theologian Romano Guardini (1885–1968), whose students at the University of Munich included Joseph Ratzinger.

more immediate threat: the imminent publication of *Iglesia y Dictadura* (Church and Dictatorship), a book that would revive the ugly allegations about his actions before and after the 1976 kidnapping of Yorio and Jalics, the two slum priests. The book's author, Emilio Mignone, a renowned legal scholar and diplomat, became one of Argentina's most outspoken human-rights campaigners after the 1976 disappearance of his twenty-four-year-old daughter Monica, who was abducted by the military in the early days of the Dirty War and never seen again. He had long suspected that Bergo-glio bore some responsibility for her kidnapping since she had worked in the slum project run by Yorio and Jalics, who disappeared the same week. Mignone's book identified church leaders who, he believed, were complicit in the junta's crimes, most notoriously Cardinal Aramburu, but also made a target of Bergoglio. Mignone suggested that Bergoglio never told the truth about Yorio and Jalics—that he had in fact betrayed the two priests, which resulted in their abduction as well as his daughter's. He questioned whether Bergoglio was one of those "shepherds who abandoned his sheep to the enemy." The book did not come close to offering conclusive evi-dence of wrongdoing by Bergoglio, but Mignone urged the new govern-ment to investigate.

Just months after arriving in Germany, Bergoglio startled his colleagues again when he turned around and went home, abandoning his PhD research there before it had really begun. He insisted his abrupt return to Buenos Aires was motivated by homesickness, but his Jesuit enemies scoffed at that explanation. They saw his early homecoming as a cynical move to try to reestablish a power base among Argentine Jesuits, since he knew there would soon be a vacancy in the national Jesuit order for the elected post of "procurator." (The job, which exists in Jesuit orders around the world, is held by a priest who serves as the local eyes and ears of the Jesuit hier-archy in Rome.) Back home in Buenos Aires, he accepted an invitation to live at the Universidad del Salvador—the school that, to the consternation of so many Jesuits, he had turned over to the Iron Guard militia a decade earlier—and won election as procurator in March 1987, proof of his still-considerable support among colleagues. He also began teaching part-time at the Colegio Máximo and sought to reestablish himself as a powerful fig-ure on campus. Other faculty members were unnerved by what they saw as his bizarre displays of arrogance and self-importance. Father Andrés Swin-nen, his successor as national Jesuit leader, remembered hearing disturb-ing reports from the Colegio about Bergoglio's "out of control" behavior after his return from Germany—how he presented himself on campus as the school's "parallel" leader and barked out orders to administrators and students. "There was something very unhealthy about this thirst for leadership that he has," Swinnen said.

In May 1990, Bergoglio's bad behavior finally caught up to him, leaving his career inside the Jesuits at a dead end at the age of fifty-three. The Colegio and the national Jesuit hierarchy received permission from Kolvenbach to force Bergoglio into internal exile. With no warning, he was ordered to move immediately to Córdoba, four hundred miles away, to begin an indefinite period of "reflection," cut off from his Jesuit allies in the capital. He was fired from his teaching post at the Colegio, which left his stunned students without a professor for their theology classes. What Bergoglio later described as the darkest period in his life, his time of "great interior crisis," had begun.

24

The Distracted Pope

I N THE FIRST MONTHS after he was stripped of his Catholic teaching credentials in 1979, Hans Küng sank into a deep depression—as deep as he had ever known. He remained a professor in Tübingen's theology department, but the word "Catholic" was removed from his title and he was barred from meetings of Catholic faculty members. On March 19, 1980, his fifty-second birthday, "I realized I hadn't laughed for a long time," he wrote later. "It was a dark period." He wondered how the church "could leave a man feeling so crushed." He felt his mood begin to lift late that year, which he credited to his students' devotion. Now freed of responsibility for teaching "boring" standard theology classes, he offered a lecture series on the ties between religion and world literature, which regularly attracted more than a thousand people to his classroom.

It was not long, in fact, before he began "an extremely hopeful period of my life," with Marianne Saur by his side. He made plans to spend several months a year in the United States, where he saw so much fresh thinking. There was even a momentary, surprisingly cordial reunion with Ratzinger. In 1983, at the encouragement of mutual friends, a meeting was arranged while the cardinal was on vacation in Bavaria. It was the first time the two men had seen each other in years.

Küng was an hour and a half late—his sleek BMW had "shamelessly let me down" when the engine stalled on the autobahn—and recalled that Ratzinger was gracious about the delay, greeting him at the bottom of the steps of the monastery where he was vacationing.

"You're doing well, Herr Küng?" the cardinal asked.

"Yes, I'm doing well, Herr Ratzinger, even if that's not what the Congregation for the Doctrine of the Faith intended," Küng replied with a sly smile.

The conversation was polite, Küng said. Ratzinger—"evasive in a friendly way"—addressed what happened in 1979, insisting again he had not participated in the initial decision to revoke Küng's credentials.

The meeting proved to Küng that he and Ratzinger "live in two different worlds, in two different paradigms." They discussed Küng's recent trip to Canada and how the church in the province of Quebec, a Catholic stronghold, was plagued by an exodus of nuns. Küng said the nuns might have remained in the church had they "been given more freedom in dress and lifestyle." Ratzinger responded by gently chiding Küng for having "contributed to the loosening of discipline with your talk of the church and freedom." They discussed John Paul, and Küng was struck that Ratzinger could not offer "even the slightest criticism" of the pope. They parted with a friendly handshake.

BY THEN, two years after his arrival at the Vatican, Ratzinger felt completely at home in Rome. The city that once seemed so foreign—so noisy, so dirty—now felt like a place where he could happily spend the rest of his life. He missed Bavaria, he said, but there was real pleasure in *la dolce vita*. The Italians had a "humanness that always leaves room for play," he told friends. Compared to Bavarians, Italians were less focused on details and deadlines, and perhaps that was a good thing. "Postponing things can be positive, make a situation less tense." He said he had set aside his old skepticism about the competence of Vatican bureaucrats: "In Rome, I came to realize that the Curia was far superior to its reputation."

There was a jarring disconnect between the contentment he found in his new life in Rome and the world he imagined beyond the borders of Vatican City. He often said he was horrified by modern society. He saw "filth" and "decadence" and "disobedience" everywhere he looked, he wrote at the time. That had much to do with the paperwork that landed on his desk at the congregation—the flood of correspondence from conservative church officials and theologians around the world protesting at what they saw as some local act of disobedience or blasphemy.

Although Ratzinger would adamantly deny it, the Congregation for the Doctrine of the Faith under his leadership largely abandoned the mission given to the agency in 1965, in the wake of Vatican II. That year, when the agency's name was changed from the Holy Office, Paul VI had decreed it would put aside its centuries-old fixation with identifying and punishing dissidents. Even before Paul's death, however, and especially after the election of John Paul II, the congregation returned to its old ways—to heresy hunting, conducted mostly out of public view. Theologians were again subjected to secret investigations and career-ending punishment. John Paul's decision to strip Küng of his teaching license in 1979 was only the best-known example of it.

With his arrival in the Vatican in 1982, Ratzinger accelerated the process—usually, but not always, with John Paul's encouragement. By the time Ratzinger left the congregation almost a quarter century later, dozens of the world's most prominent Catholic theologians and other scholars had been subjected to his discipline, including many who would have their careers ended.

At first, Ratzinger had one target above all others—liberation theology. Within the congregation, he was not shy about his intention to crush the movement, since he saw it as Marxism masquerading as social justice. His campaign became public in 1983, when he wrote to Peru's bishops, urging them to investigate the country's most famous theologian, Gustavo Gutiérrez, the father of liberation theology. Because Gutiérrez's writings often cited the theories of Karl Marx, "there are grounds for being deeply worried," Ratzinger's letter warned. At the same time, he expanded an investigation of another champion of liberation theology, the Brazilian Leonardo Boff, a Franciscan cleric who had been under scrutiny by the congregation since 1975.

When he learned about Ratzinger's letter, Gutiérrez was heartsick. He told friends he wondered if Ratzinger understood the terror that a decree from the Congregation for the Doctrine of the Faith struck among churchmen in a small, impoverished country half a world away from the Vatican. He decided to be proactive and wrote to Ratzinger, requesting a meeting. The cardinal agreed, and Gutiérrez flew to Rome weeks later, only to return home despondent. Ratzinger seemed ready to destroy Gutiérrez's career.

Years later, Gutiérrez remained perplexed by Ratzinger's refusal to see a distinction between a social movement that made use of Marxist theories and Marxism itself. In his writings, the Peruvian acknowledged that liberation theology owed something to Marx's concept of a "class struggle" in which the poor organized themselves against oppression. It was not so different, Gutiérrez often noted, from what Jesus declared in the Gospel of Matthew: "Blessed are those who hunger and thirst for justice." Gutiérrez and Boff often stated explicitly that they were not Communists. "I declare I am not a Marxist," Boff wrote. "What I am is a Christian and Franciscan who is in favor of liberties, of rights, and of the noble struggle for justice."

Prominent theologians in Europe and the United States stepped forward to defend Gutiérrez and Boff—and denounce Ratzinger. Among them was Karl Rahner, who issued a public statement in March 1984, just days before his death, to praise Gutiérrez and the movement he had created: "The theology of liberation that he represents is entirely orthodox."

Ratzinger faced one important, possibly insurmountable obstacle in his campaign against liberation theology: the pope he served. During the cardinal's first year in Rome, John Paul kept waffling on the subject, offering comments one day in support of the movement, only to back away the next. In March 1983, however, Ratzinger had reason to hope that the pope's indecision was finally over. John Paul had just returned from a grueling seven-nation tour of Central America, which included a stop in El Salvador, where he made amends for his initial, callous response to Archbishop Romero's murder. He prayed over Romero's tomb and offered seemingly heartfelt praise for "a pastor who always tended to his flock." His public events drew a joyous outpouring from hundreds of thousands of Salvadorans. That was in stark contrast to the hostile reception he had received two days earlier in neighboring Nicaragua. The leaders of that country's newly installed socialist government, former leftist guerrillas who called themselves Sandinistas, came to power in 1979 after overthrowing the corrupt dictator Anastasio Somoza, whose family had ruled over Nicaragua for four decades. Somoza's ouster had been widely celebrated by the public, and the senior ranks of the Sandinista government included four priests who were champions of liberation theology. One of them, Father Ernesto Cardenal, the culture minister, was a proud, self-declared Communist. "Christ led me to Marx," he said. The decision by priests to accept government appointments infuriated Nicaragua's conservative church hierarchy. It also alarmed the United States, which protested to the Vatican that Nicaragua was an example of liberation theology run amok. The Reagan administration was then arming right-wing anti-Sandinista insurgents known as contras.

There was a sour expression on the pope's face throughout his twelve-hour stay in Nicaragua. He did not hide his agitation during a welcoming ceremony in which Sandinista leader Daniel Ortega announced that "Christian patriots" were central to "the popular Sandinista revolution." At a Mass for hundreds of thousands in the capital city of Managua, the pope was heckled by Sandinista supporters chanting "Power to the people!" and "Liberation!" Infuriated, he yelled back, "Silence!" At a reception line with cabinet ministers, Cardenal dropped to one knee to kiss the pope's ring. John Paul pulled his hand back and wagged his finger at the priest, telling him to "straighten out your position with the church," a public scolding caught on camera.

The experience there so unsettled the pope that, back in Rome, he asked Ratzinger to draft a formal decree, to be issued by the congregation, that would restrict churchmen from being involved in the sort of left-leaning, overtly political displays he had witnessed in Nicaragua. Others in the Curia were uncertain what exactly the pope intended the document to do, but Ratzinger took it as a papal command to ban liberation theology, and he eagerly began to write. Months before his decree was made public, Ratzinger previewed what it would say, publishing an essay under his own name in the conservative Italian magazine *30 Giorni* (30 Days) in which he denounced liberation theology as "heresy." The essay shocked Curia officials who thought it scandalous for the Vatican's chief enforcer of doctrine to make such an important statement on his own, especially in a publication not controlled by the church. An American theologian compared it to the chief justice of the Supreme Court announcing a landmark ruling in the pages of *Reader's Digest*.

The article created an uproar, especially among bishops in Latin America, and was seen as Ratzinger's first great public stumble. He appeared to realize his mistake and called a news conference in Rome in which he awkwardly backed away from much of the essay, claiming it was a draft that had been published without his approval. In front of reporters, he now offered qualified praise for liberation theology, since it promoted "the necessary responsibility of Christians toward the poor." That comment struck some of his colleagues at the congregation as deceptive, since they knew Ratzinger was still secretly hard at work on a document intended to dismantle the movement once and for all.

He faced other criticism from reform-minded churchmen that year when it became clear that his congregation would return to the regular practice, supposedly abandoned after Vatican II, of banning books. His first targets were a pair of books published in the United States. One, entitled *Sexual Morality*, had been written by a Baltimore priest, Father Philip Keane, who questioned the church's views on sexual matters, including its definition of homosexuality as a sin. The book had been endorsed as "theologically sound" by Archbishop Raymond Hunthausen of Seattle, whose stamp of approval appeared in its opening pages. The second was the bestselling *Christ Among Us*, which had sold 1.6 million copies in the US after its publication in 1967 and was found in the libraries of most Catholic high schools. Written by a former priest, it was a commonsense guide to the church's teachings on contemporary issues, including marriage and birth control. The book, endorsed by Archbishop Peter Gerety of Newark, New Jersey, had long been the target of right-wing Catholic groups. On Ratzinger's order, Gerety revoked his endorsement. *Time* magazine noted that "while book burning by censors of the Roman Catholic Church sputtered out long ago," it appeared that, under Ratzinger, "a new purifying heat is coming out of Rome."

That fall, Ratzinger returned in earnest to his campaign to dismantle liberation theology. In September, he released the congregation's report on the movement, the one the pope had supposedly requested the year before, and it was the sort of blistering, unqualified condemnation that progressive churchmen had feared. Ratzinger described liberation theology as a "perversion of the Christian message as God entrusted it to His Church." The movement threatened to "create new miseries and new types of slavery" among the world's poor by exposing them to Marxism.

The incendiary language outraged even some conservative critics of liberation theology, who thought Ratzinger's overheated rhetoric undermined his argument—a criticism of the cardinal that became common in years to come. The report was "breathlessly alarmist in tone and ill-conceived," wrote Thomas Sheehan, a philosophy professor at Jesuit-run Loyola University in Chicago. He compared what Ratzinger had done to "Red baiting" in the US in the 1950s, with the cardinal in the role of Senator Joseph McCarthy. In the Netherlands, the famed theologian Edward Schillebeeckx warned: "The dictators of Latin America will receive this document with joy."

Curia bishops, who by tradition would never dare publicly criticize another senior churchman in Rome, made an exception this time. Cardinal Agostino Casaroli, the secretary of state, issued a withering statement to denounce the "negative" tone of Ratzinger's document. Casaroli, named to his post by John Paul in 1979, complained to colleagues that he had been blindsided by Ratzinger, who broke tradition by failing to provide the secretary of state's office with a draft before publication. Kolvenbach, the new head of the Jesuits, also joined the protest. He described liberation theology as "positive and necessary" and said the movement had improved the lives of millions of poor Catholics. In Brazil, hundreds of the nation's bishops gathered in an emergency meeting to denounce Ratzinger's document— and recommit themselves to liberation theology.

It quickly became clear that Ratzinger had made a terrible miscalculation—because the pope signaled that he was critical of the document, too. The president of the Brazilian bishops' conference flew to Rome days after the document's release to urge the pope to renounce it. The Brazilian, Bishop Ivo Lorscheiter, said churchmen across Latin America were appalled that Ratzinger had released "this screed," condemning a social-justice movement they championed, without consulting anyone outside his congregation. Lorscheiter left Rome convinced the pope agreed with him.

A month later, in what was widely depicted as a public humiliation for Ratzinger, John Paul ordered up a second declaration on liberation theology—to "stand alongside" what the cardinal had written—and asked that it have an entirely different tone. The pope told deputies he wanted the new decree to express optimism about liberation theology and recognize the support the movement enjoyed in the developing world—in other words, to repudiate most of what Ratzinger had written. The pope assigned the writing of the new document to Cardinal Roger Etchegaray of France, a veteran Curia bureaucrat seen as far more moderate than Ratzinger. Visitors to his office noted that the crucifix on Etchegaray's wall was surrounded by framed photographs of two men he considered personal heroes: One was the American civil rights leader Martin Luther King Jr. The other was John XXIII.

RATZINGER SEEMED CALM, even indifferent, to the furor he created. He later told aides he was convinced the controversy over the liberation theology decree ultimately strengthened his relationship with John Paul. As Ratzinger learned, public controversy tended to reinforce the bond between this pope and his embattled advisers. In Rome, as in Poland, John Paul prided himself on rushing to the defense of colleagues who found themselves under attack.

In his years at John Paul's side, Ratzinger regularly boasted of his closeness to the pope, and of how little attention either of them paid to detractors. The cardinal jokingly compared himself to the great Russian cellist Mstislav Rostropovich: "I'm like him—I never read my critics." Since he had the pope's total support, he said, he had no reason to fear anyone, with a single exception: "I'm only afraid at the dentist."

From John Paul's early days in Rome, he demonstrated no interest in day-to-day administration of the Vatican, which he happily left to others. The pope's closest deputies, including Ratzinger, shared two traits: a commitment to his conservative views on doctrine and total personal loyalty. He had a special need to trust the Curia, since he was so often away from the Vatican on globetrotting pilgrimages. In 1985, a typical year, he visited sixteen countries on four continents—journeys that required months of advance planning, including tutoring so he could speak at least a few words of the local languages. He spent another two weeks that year traveling inside Italy. Throughout the 1980s, his time in Rome was focused—on some days, almost entirely—on the latest news from Poland.

The result was that, so long as a deputy demonstrated loyalty, the pope was willing to overlook mistakes. That explained why so many Curia bishops held on to their jobs for a decade or more, much longer than under other popes, even when they clearly should have been replaced. That had been true in Poland as well. "He would leave incompetents at their posts rather than face the bother of removing them," said Jerzy Turowicz, editor of a church-supported magazine in Krakow, who had known the pope since the 1940s. Senior Curia posts were given to members of the pope's preferred religious orders, especially Opus Dei.

John Paul showed similar loyalty to others far from Rome. He was reluctant to investigate, much less discipline or remove, a bishop, no matter what questions were raised about his competence or honesty. That first became obvious in the United States in the early 1980s, when the Justice Department revealed that Cardinal Cody in Chicago was the target of a criminal investigation over his transfer of about $1 million in church funds to the woman assumed to be his mistress. The pope remained steadfast in his support.

Within a few years of arriving in Rome, Ratzinger's authority extended far beyond his congregation. With John Paul's encouragement, he became directly involved in the selection of bishops and cardinals, and it was widely understood he could make or break the careers of other churchmen. His growing self-confidence explained his eagerness to court publicity—and, at times, outrage. His most famous modern predecessor, Ottaviani, never sought, or attained, anything like Ratzinger's fame or power.

In 1984, Ratzinger demonstrated how confident he was when he granted hours of interviews to a little-known Italian journalist, Vittorio Messori, for what would be a book-length profile of the cardinal. Messori, who hadn't met Ratzinger before, wrote later he had been startled by the cardinal's candor in answering "even the most delicate questions." When the book was published in 1985, in separate editions in Italian, German, and English, many assumed Ratzinger had been grossly misquoted, since the comments attributed to him were so outrageous. In fact, he read the manuscript in advance—and approved it. The book, published in English as *The Ratzinger Report*, was, simply put, a declaration of war on virtually all progressive Catholic thinking.

Ratzinger told Messori the church was in the midst of an "authentic crisis that must be treated and cured." After Vatican II, he said, the church had moved from "self-criticism to self-destruction." He blamed that on Catholics who intentionally misread the documents of the council to promote a dangerous "cultural revolution in the West." It was time, he said, for the church to recommit itself to identifying and disciplining theologians and other Catholic scholars who questioned traditional doctrine.

He said the liturgical reforms approved at Vatican II had gone "too far, too fast" and that the Latin Mass needed to be widely revived. He suggested the campaign begun by John XXIII to seek unity among Christian churches was over, given the refusal of non-Catholic Christians to accept the pope's authority. He dismissed the worship practices of Orthodox Christians as "static" and "petrified." Within the Catholic Church, he said, it was time to abandon the idea of power sharing and accept the bishop of Rome as an absolute monarch. "The Church of Christ is not a political party," he said. "Authority is not based on the majority of votes."

He offered a checklist of everything wrong in Western society, beginning with the women's rights movement—"radical feminism," as he described it. Women, he said, were being forced to separate themselves from their traditional roles as wife and mother, especially as they entered professions like medicine and law. They had adopted a "trade-union mentality." He had contempt, he said, for modern mental-health care, including the work of psychiatrists and psychologists ("experts of the soul" who were in fact "profane confessors"). He warned about modern medical procedures, especially in vitro fertilization, which he described as an effort to "uncouple man from nature." He offered criticism of popular culture and denounced "rock music and all its related forms." He condemned the growing popularity of yoga, which reflected a worrying "fascination for what is Eastern."

He warned, in detail, of the grave dangers of sexual freedom. "Pleasure—the libido of the individual—has become the only possible point of reference in sex," he said. The church needed to reassert its traditional opposition to all sex outside of a monogamous marriage. He was outraged, he said, that "masturbation is now presented as a normal phenomenon of adolescence." He denounced homosexuality and said sex-reassignment surgery—"the right to be male or female at one's will or pleasure"—was an affront to God.

Many conservative Catholic thinkers were thrilled by the book. "There are zingers and then there are *Ratz*-zingers," wrote a delighted Ralph McInerny, founder of the American Catholic magazine *Crisis*. He praised Ratzinger's frank language in describing the "systematic perversion of Vatican II." Other commentators were appalled that the Vatican's senior official on doctrine would say such extreme things. Fergus Kerr, a Scottish priest who taught theology at Oxford University, said the book was "alarmist and lurid" and reflected the Vatican's "tradition of hyped-up, panic-mongering hyperbole." George Lindbeck, a Lutheran theologian at the Yale Divinity School, said that non-Catholic Christians, including Protestants who considered themselves "friends of Rome," should be "appalled" by *The Ratzinger Report*, since it essentially dismissed them as heretics. Monika Hellwig, a German-born Catholic theologian at Georgetown University, wrote that she found it hard to believe that Ratzinger would agree to have his name associated with "some of the really foolish statements in this so-called report."

Vatican officials acknowledged that John Paul was uncomfortable with the book, since Ratzinger clearly contradicted some of the pope's own views, especially about the need for Christian unity. When asked by reporters about the book, the pope said only that Ratzinger was "free to express his opinion."

Among those distressed by the book was the new theology dean at the Gregorian, Father Gerald O'Collins, a gregarious, Cambridge-educated Australian Jesuit who had taught in Rome since the 1970s. If only by virtue of his university post, he was one of the most influential Catholic theologians in the world. While holding his tongue publicly about *The Ratzinger*

Report, he agreed to write a scathing anonymous review for *The Tablet*, in which he dismissed "Ratzinger's sad book" as a "one-sided and negative assessment of Catholic life after Vatican II."

O'Collins had once considered the cardinal a friend. During a brief research project in Tübingen in the 1960s, the Australian lived next door to Ratzinger and his sister. After attending several of his university lectures, O'Collins was struck that there were two Ratzingers—the shy, timid man he encountered on the street and the self-confident scholar behind the classroom lectern: "At the podium, he was transformed." He understood why Ratzinger became so valuable to John Paul, since the cardinal was so much better able to express the pope's thoughts. Ratzinger had no personal magnetism, but he could explain himself in ways that were "clear, brief and intelligent," especially on paper. The pope, by comparison, had magnetism to spare, but his speeches and writings were full of "abstract terminology" and "tired old clichés" that meant nothing to most lay Catholics. O'Collins's sister, visiting from Australia, went to a speech in St. Peter's in which the pope spoke about the Book of Genesis and the story of Adam and Eve. "It was very abstract, like a boring university lecture," she complained. "I couldn't get the point of much of what he wanted to say, apart from the fact that he does not seem to be in favor of human sexuality."

Like many churchmen in Rome, O'Collins saw Ratzinger's hand in the choice of conservative bishops around the world who were "sycophants or worse." The appointment of uninspiring, often incompetent bishops would be remembered as one of the great failings of John Paul's papacy, O'Collins believed. It was a view shared even by some archconservatives in the Curia, who complained that John Paul regularly appointed small-minded bishops, with miserable personalities, because he and Ratzinger were convinced they would fight to uphold traditional doctrine. Father Richard O'Brien, a renowned American theology professor at the University of Notre Dame, concluded in 2005 that John Paul was responsible for—"and I'm not exaggerating"—the "worst group of bishops in modern church history." O'Collins knew of bishops who were selected solely because they had some family tie to Poland. Others were appointed, he thought, mostly because the pope believed they somehow looked or sounded the part, much like an actor might get a role because of a strong jawline or resonant voice: "He would select someone simply because he liked the look of them."

Ratzinger was instrumental in the selection of several bishops who were loathed in their homelands. In 1983, he helped secure the promotion of

Archbishop Lopez Trujillo of Colombia, that country's most powerful critic of liberation theology, to the College of Cardinals. Lopez Trujillo, then forty-seven, had long presented himself as Ratzinger's protégé; he gave copies of Ratzinger's books as gifts to newly ordained Colombian priests. In the mid-1980s Ratzinger offered a strong, public endorsement to the pope's choice of conservative, politically savvy bishops to lead the two archdioceses traditionally seen as the most important in the United States—Bernard Law in Boston and John O'Connor in New York. The pair, both quickly named cardinals, were dubbed "Law and Order."

Many European churchmen agreed that, in the 1980s, the most shocking senior leadership change in the church came in Austria, where Catholics made up about 80 percent of the population. In 1985, the beloved eighty-year-old Cardinal König of Vienna wanted to retire and asked to be replaced by a deputy, Bishop Helmut Kratzl, who shared König's progressive views, but the pope rejected the idea. Although John Paul knew he likely owed his election to König, the Austrian had fallen out of favor in Rome, seen as too liberal. So, in a decision that left König shocked and embarrassed, John Paul rejected Kratzl in favor of Hans Hermann Groër, a Benedictine priest best known for publicizing his claim he once saw an apparition of the Virgin Mary in an Austrian country shrine.

The appointment appalled Austrian clerics who had long heard the same ugly stories about the sixty-seven-year-old Groër—that throughout his career as a teacher in all-male Catholic schools beginning in the 1960s, he molested students, including prepubescent boys. Church records released decades later established that, although Groër's superiors were aware of the abuse, they refused to report him to the police or investigate him themselves. Two years after his appointment as Vienna's archbishop, Groër was named a cardinal.

THE UPROAR OVER *The Ratzinger Report* was at its height when the pope announced early in 1985 that he would hold a bishops' synod that November to mark the twentieth anniversary of Vatican II and to reexamine the council's legacy "in light of new needs." Liberal churchmen around the world panicked at the announcement, given what they now knew about Ratzinger. They worried *The Ratzinger Report* had set the agenda for the synod, which would become a vehicle for dismantling the council's reforms. Catholic bishops in Britain released a defiant joint statement complaining that, with the announcement of a synod, the Vatican could be on the verge of a "new fundamentalism."

Ratzinger welcomed the controversy. In advance of the synod, he cooperated with *The New York Times* in a six-thousand-word profile that identified him as "the second most powerful man in the Vatican." Ratzinger offered long written answers to the paper's questions and was just as combative and undiplomatic as he had been in *The Ratzinger Report*. The church, he said, needed to uphold conservative doctrine, no matter how unpopular. In 1968, the year he fled Tübingen during the "terror" of student protests, "I learned where discussion must stop—because it is turning into a lie—and resistance must begin." The *Times* duly declared that the upcoming bishops' meeting would be remembered as "Ratzinger's Synod."

IN THE FIVE YEARS since Hans Küng was stripped of his church credentials, he had gotten on with his life. He continued to teach at Tübingen, to publish best-selling books, and to travel the world on lecture tours. He had resisted most opportunities to speak out to criticize the pope, even as he grew more alarmed about the Vatican's growing repression under John Paul.

That changed in 1985. After *The Ratzinger Report* and the announcement of the synod, Küng felt he could no longer keep silent. He had come to see Ratzinger, seemingly unrestrained by the pope, as "power-mad." That fall, Küng published an essay in many of the world's most important newspapers and magazines to sound the alarm. His account, which first appeared in *La Repubblica* in Italy, the newspaper that was most avidly read in the Vatican, was targeted principally at Ratzinger. The cardinal, Küng charged, had become "exactly the definition of the prophet of doom" that John XXIII denounced at Vatican II: "Just like Dostoyevsky's Grand Inquisitor, he fears nothing more than freedom." Under Ratzinger, "the Inquisition is once again in full swing." Küng was almost as tough on the "authoritarian" John Paul: "Far from healing the wounds of the church, this pope rubs salt in them, promoting more strife than harmony."

Ratzinger did not respond to the essay, but several of the cardinal's allies defended him from what they saw as Küng's vicious attack. The conservative Swiss theologian Hans Urs von Balthasar said Küng was "no longer even a Christian."

25

"So Much Filth"

I N THE FINAL YEARS of John Paul II's papacy, the question plagued the Vatican and would drive millions of Catholics from the church: Why did the pope and Cardinal Ratzinger do so little in response to reports that thousands of children had been sexually abused by priests?

John Paul's defenders, including those who secured his sainthood after his death, insisted he was never fully aware of the extent of priestly child molestation, and that he would have acted more forcefully if he had been. Some compared it to his mishandling of the scandals that overwhelmed the Vatican Bank. In the case of the bank, they argued, the pope was distracted by vast responsibilities elsewhere and placed too much trust in others.

Ratzinger offered a similar defense. He said that for years after his arrival in Rome, he did not suspect that clerical sex abuse was a significant problem anywhere. When it erupted into a global scandal in 2002, Ratzinger insisted that it came as "an unprecedented shock."

He claimed the events of 2002, when news organizations led by *The Boston Globe* exposed the cover-up of thousands of child-molestation cases around the world, stunned him because he had never suspected that "so much filth, darkening and soiling everything," existed within the priesthood.

As a blizzard of once-secret Vatican records would later prove, however, his claim of "shock" never made any sense. Evidence from his own files showed that within weeks of arriving in Rome in January 1982, he received detailed briefings about priestly sex-abuse cases in several countries, many involving the molestation of children. From public news reports alone, he should have been aware of hundreds of cases in the early 1980s, especially in the United States.

Later, he tried to fall back on another defense—that there had been confusion in the Curia over which agencies had responsibility for investigating clerics accused of child molestation. Over the years, some cases had been referred to the Congregation for the Clergy or, if they involved priests or monks in special religious orders, the Congregation for Religious. But if there was confusion after 1982, that was Ratzinger's fault. He eventually acknowledged his congregation had explicit responsibility for the investigation of all priests accused of sex crimes. And since his congregation had responsibility for defrocking priests, every serious case should have ended up before him anyway.

Vatican documents made public in court records proved Ratzinger had always been involved personally in the handling of especially notorious child-abuse cases and that he regularly acted to delay the punishment of pedophile priests, even though that put more children at risk. The first case was brought to his attention almost as soon as he arrived in Rome, and it would later be described by child-victims' advocates as a brazen early example of his failure to grapple with the crisis.

In that case, the bishop of Oakland, California, John Cummins, wrote to the Vatican in June 1981 to ask for quick action to defrock a thirty-four-year-old priest, Stephen Kiesle, of nearby Union City, who had already admitted he was a child molester. As part of a plea bargain that spared him a prison sentence, Kiesle confessed to tying up and molesting two preteen boys in his church rectory. He would later be charged with abusing more than a dozen other children, including a seven-year-old girl who remembered how "Father Steve" had tried to portray the molestation—the fondling of her genitals and chest—as an exorcism: "He told me the devil was inside me."

Cummins's letter, addressed to John Paul, was passed on to Ratzinger. Although Kiesle had already been barred from priestly duties, Cummins assumed the Vatican would want to act immediately to defrock him—to cut off any tie between the church and a confessed pedophile. Instead, to the bishop's astonishment, Ratzinger did no such thing. On February 1, 1982, Cummins wrote directly to Ratzinger, who had taken up his duties at the congregation the month before, to plead for action. The bishop warned of the potential for a "scandal in the community" if it became known that Kiesle could still legitimately call himself a priest and might seek contact with children. There was no reply. Cummins sent another letter to the cardinal in September, asking for any sort of update. One of Ratzinger's deputies responded to Cummins weeks later with a curt letter stating that the case would be "examined at an opportune time." It would take the cardinal another three years to reply personally. In a letter to Cummins in November 1985, Ratzinger, acting on orders from John Paul to make it difficult for priests to leave the church through laicization, said there were no immediate plans to defrock Kiesle given his "young age"—by then, he was thirty-eight—and that the investigation would continue. The letter, which raised no concern about the well-being of Kiesle's many victims, directed Cummins to continue to offer "as much paternal care as possible" to Kiesle, who had sought work outside the church while he continued psychiatric treatment. Cummins said he could barely believe what he was reading. After the congregation finally agreed to defrock Kiesle in 1987, he went on to abuse several more children. In 2004, he was sentenced to six years in prison after pleading no contest to molesting a teenage girl in his Northern California vacation home.*

A CRUSADING AMERICAN CHURCHMAN, Father Thomas Doyle of Sheboygan, Wisconsin, played a central role in exposing the global clerical sex-abuse crisis and, as a result, became a pariah in the Vatican. Ordained in 1970, he worked early in his career in parishes around Chicago. He developed a specialty in counseling divorcing couples as they navigated the labyrinth of the church's marriage laws in seeking annulments. In response to Vatican II, the Chicago archdiocese made it easier for couples to obtain an annulment, a decree that effectively declared a marriage had never existed in the eyes of God, allowing them to remarry with the church's support.

The archdiocese was so impressed by Doyle that it urged him to earn a degree in church law. He studied at the law school at Catholic University in Washington, DC, where he received a doctorate. In 1981, he accepted a flattering job offer across town from Archbishop Laghi, the Vatican's newly arrived chief diplomat in Washington, who hired Doyle to conduct background checks on priests being considered for promotion to bishop. Laghi

---

* In December 2023, Kiesle returned to prison for an additional six years after pleading no contest to charges that he was driving drunk when he ran over and killed a neighbor in Walnut Creek, California. Kiesle, seventy-six, remained a defendant in several civil lawsuits brought by people who alleged they had been molested by him as children.

told Doyle that John Paul believed too many American bishops were liberals, and that all future candidates must share the pope's views on doctrine.

In the summer of 1984, Laghi asked Doyle to review a letter he had just
received from the diocese of Lafayette, Louisiana. The diocese, in a region
of small farms and bayous, was home to much of Louisiana's devoutly
Catholic Cajun community. Doyle was shocked by the letter, which had
been written to notify Laghi—and through him, the Vatican—that lawyers
for the diocese had reached settlements totaling $4.2 million with families
of nine boys who had been molested by a thirty-nine-year-old priest named
Gilbert Gauthe. The families agreed to keep the settlements secret. Laghi
did not want Doyle to intervene, only to write a formal acknowledgment
for Laghi's files.

Several days later, there was a second letter from Louisiana, which Laghi
also shared with Doyle. The diocese wrote to report that one family had
withdrawn from the settlement and was preparing to sue, which meant the
abuse would become public. The family had also begun cooperating with
the police, meaning a criminal case was probably imminent as well.

Doyle contacted the diocese and learned the stomach-churning details
of Gauthe's crimes. The priest's own lawyer admitted that the sexual abuse
of the boys—the youngest was seven—involved "every sexual act you can
imagine," including rape. After molesting a boy, Gauthe often threatened
to harm the child's family if he dared report what had happened. One victim said that Gauthe, who displayed a large gun collection in his home,
said he was ready to kill the boy's father and use his powers as a priest
to "make sure your daddy goes to hell." Doyle discovered that the local
bishop, Gerard Frey, had failed to investigate child-molestation allegations
made against at least six other priests.

In September, a state grand jury indicted Gauthe on thirty-four counts
of sexual abuse. He pleaded not guilty by reason of insanity and, in doing
so, admitted he had molested at least thirty-seven children—there were so
many he did not know the precise number—and maybe as many as a hundred. Frey admitted he had known since 1974 that Gauthe was a pedophile.
The bishop said that, every time a victim came forward, Gauthe was sent
for psychological treatment and eventually returned to his duties in a new
parish, where he preyed on new victims. It was a routine that would prove
to be common in dioceses around the country.

Doyle had an early meeting with Gauthe's lawyer, Ray Mouton, a devout
Catholic who was horrified by his client's crimes. He told Doyle he had

become convinced there was a "cult of pedophilia" in the priesthood and offered to help expose others. By then, both men had been introduced to Father Michael Peterson, a psychiatrist who was the founder of the Saint Luke Institute, a psychiatric hospital near Washington, DC, that treated troubled priests and other church workers. Peterson told Doyle that his hospital was, at that moment, treating ten priests who were child molesters.

By February, Doyle decided he was ready to act, first by demanding Bishop Frey be ousted. He wanted to send an outside investigator, Bishop James Quinn of Cleveland, a noted canon lawyer, to Louisiana to build the case against Frey. Laghi agreed and ordered Doyle to write up a report on the case that could be forwarded directly to the pope, with a request for a papal endorsement of Quinn's appointment. The obvious messenger, Laghi thought, was Cardinal Krol of Philadelphia, the pope's close friend, who was heading to the Vatican that week. Krol agreed to help and, days later, hand-delivered Doyle's report to John Paul. Within a week, Laghi received a telex from the Vatican, confirming that the pope had been briefed and agreed to dispatch Quinn. That telex would later be cited as concrete evidence that the pope knew personally—at least by early 1985— of a dire child-abuse scandal in the United States.

Doyle alerted other members of the American hierarchy to a looming crisis. His first call was to an old friend, then-Archbishop Bernard Law of Boston, a leader of the national bishops' conference who was about to be promoted to cardinal. Law was alarmed and agreed to set up a special committee to study clerical child abuse and recruited Bishop William Levada of Los Angeles to help. Levada, a Gregorian-educated theologian, was close to many in power in the Vatican, especially Ratzinger.

The Gauthe case became national news in 1985 because of groundbreaking reporting by journalist Jason Berry in the *National Catholic Reporter*, and the scandal spread. Berry identified clerical child-abuse cases in seven other states. Over the next two years, the papal nuncio's office learned of abuse cases involving more than forty priests.

By July 1985, Doyle, Mouton, and Peterson had completed a final draft of a ninety-two-page manual for the nation's bishops, entitled "The Problem of Sexual Molestation by Roman Catholic Clergy," to warn them about the extent of the crisis. It included a checklist of actions for bishops to take when a local priest was accused of child abuse. It called for the priest to be suspended immediately from regular duties and sent for a psychological examination, while his supervising bishop personally oversaw an aggressive investigation of the charges. The manual noted that in many states, bishops aware of credible child-molestation allegations had a legal obligation to report them to the police.

The nuncio's office received a visit that spring from Cardinal Silvio Oddi, the seventy-four-year-old Italian-born prelate of the Congregation for the Clergy. Doyle was struck by how Oddi looked the part of an old-fashioned Curia cardinal. "He reminded me of the cartoon character The Little King." On one finger, "he wore a cardinal's ring with a stone as big as a golf ball." Doyle was asked to brief Oddi on the Louisiana crisis. At one point, the cardinal, shocked by what he was hearing, made a clipping motion with his fingers, suggesting pedophile priests be castrated.

"Your Eminence, it's against the law in America to castrate men," Doyle replied.

"They're our priests!" Oddi shot back. "We can do what we want."

He promised Doyle he would immediately report back to the pope about this "terrible crisis."

Doyle thought the meeting had been useful, even if Oddi misunderstood part of what he was told. At the end of their conversation, the cardinal asked a series of bizarrely specific questions—not about pedophilia, but about homosexuality. When two men had sexual intercourse, he asked, does "the one in the passive position receive the same satisfaction as the one in the active position?"

"Your Eminence, I truly have no idea," Doyle said.

He realized afterward he should have corrected Oddi over the cardinal's assumption of a correlation between homosexuality and child molestation— something that, serious researchers were convinced, did not exist. Doyle would come to understand later how widespread that misunderstanding was throughout the Vatican.

As he prepared to publish his manual, Doyle could see the bishops who initially encouraged him were getting nervous. He could not get calls returned from Cardinal Law. Despite Oddi's promise of action, Doyle heard nothing back from Rome. So he took matters into his own hands. Without Laghi's approval, he made photocopies of the manual and mailed one to every one of the 260 cardinals and bishops in the United States, as well as to the *National Catholic Reporter*. After that, American bishops could no longer argue they were ignorant of a national crisis of priestly child abuse.

Doyle quickly found himself an outcast, branded by the church as a reckless whistleblower. Laghi sidelined him from his duties and suggested he look for work elsewhere. Catholic University's law school ended his part-time teaching appointment, on Laghi's orders. Doyle realized his career inside the church was over and, in 1986, at the age of forty-two, enlisted in the air force. He would serve as a military chaplain while continuing his advocacy for the victims of child-molesting priests.

When clerical sex abuse later exploded into a global crisis for the Vatican, Law, Levada, and Quinn would all claim—under oath—they could not recall basic details about the scandals in the 1980s in Louisiana or elsewhere. Nor, they claimed, could they remember most of their interactions with Doyle.

AS RATZINGER'S POWER GREW, so did his arrogance. Not everyone saw it. His closest deputies insisted he was always civil and open to debate. For churchmen who worked outside the congregation, however, the cardinal was increasingly high-handed. For years, he had used harsh rhetoric in defending church doctrine, and now it was matched by insensitivity and plain nastiness with people, especially in his written communications. (He almost always wrote to the congregation's targets instead of dealing with them face-to-face, even those who worked a few blocks away in Rome.) A respected American journalist, John Allen of the *National Catholic Reporter*, the author of three authoritative biographies of Ratzinger, attested to the cardinal's increasingly obvious "mean streak." He proved himself "capable of being petty when his full emotional energies were engaged in a fight."

Ratzinger's critics thought there was an early display of that in 1983, when he abruptly rescinded a policy—approved a decade earlier by Paul VI, at the urging of American bishops—that allowed priests who were recovering alcoholics to use unfermented grape juice instead of wine during Holy Communion. Ratzinger was adamant that Paul's policy could not stand, since the Gospels state explicitly that the apostles drank wine at the Last Supper. American bishops protested, warning it might condemn many priests to return to their addiction. After more than a year, Ratzinger revised his order, but only in part. He agreed to allow alcoholic priests to use grape juice but required them to apply to the congregation for permission. It was a bureaucratic process that many priests resisted since it meant creating a detailed paper record in Rome of their alcoholism.

By then, Ratzinger's crusade against liberation theology—and virtually every other type of progressive Catholic thinking—was well underway. It was a crackdown unlike anything since the 1950s, when Pius XII silenced scores of theologians who would later be hailed as among the church's greatest thinkers. It was impossible to say precisely how many scholars were disciplined by Ratzinger, since much of his congregation's work was done in secret, in clear violation of the spirit of transparency promised after Vatican II. In some cases, investigations were resolved without a public record, with theologians privately ordered to revise their writings or accept a period in which they would not lecture or publish.

Ratzinger had a consistent strategy in pursuing his agenda. As his congregation launched a campaign against a particular branch of theology, he singled out one or two scholars for punishment as a warning to all others. In his campaign against liberation theology, for example, he targeted one theologian in particular, Leonardo Boff, perhaps the most important Catholic thinker in Latin America. From the start, Brazilian bishops predicted Ratzinger would regret tangling with their charismatic countryman. Boff, a Franciscan friar, was often described as his country's answer to Hans Küng.* Telegenic, charming, with a penetrating stare and a mop of thick, curly hair, the multilingual Boff was the author of more than twenty-five books and editor of Brazil's most influential theological journal. He put his dedication to liberation theology into action by helping establish base communities near his home in Petropolis, Brazil's former royal capital.

Boff and Ratzinger had known each other for years. Boff received his PhD in 1970 from the University of Munich, where he attended lectures by then-Professor Joseph Ratzinger, who had so admired Boff as a student that he helped him find a publisher for his thesis. Years later, their bitter struggle over liberation theology would end any semblance of a friendship.

By 1984, Boff was convinced he knew why Ratzinger had singled him out for punishment—because he was the best-known theologian in the world's largest Catholic country, where liberation theology had taken hold like nowhere else: "When they hit me, they're hitting the church in Brazil." His face-to-face showdown with Ratzinger came that September, when he was summoned to Rome for what amounted to a trial. Boff, then forty-six, was told the interrogation would center on books and essays in which he

---

* The title of "friar" is given to members of several Catholic religious orders, including the Franciscans, the order founded by St. Francis of Assisi in the thirteenth century, who work alongside monks but do not live a monk's cloistered life. A friar's robes are similar to those of a monk.

had both championed liberation theology and attacked the Curia—in particular, the Congregation for the Doctrine of the Faith. In a 1981 book, he accused the congregation of turning its back on Vatican II and returning to the tactics of the Roman Inquisition, "a Kafkaesque process wherein the accuser, the defender, the lawyer and the judge are one and the same." The book did not target Ratzinger personally; it was published just before the cardinal arrived in Rome. Nonetheless, Ratzinger was furious about the book and accused Boff of a "pitiless, radical assault" on the congregation.

In an extraordinary demonstration of the Brazilian church's support for Boff, three of the country's bishops, led by Cardinal Arns of São Paulo, flew to Rome to sit in on his interrogation. Ratzinger initially refused to allow them to attend, but the Brazilians appealed to Secretary of State Casaroli, who negotiated an agreement to allow them to observe the second half of the session.

The confrontation with Boff threatened a public-relations debacle for Ratzinger. It was a story, seized on by the Vatican press corps, that almost wrote itself: the theological equivalent of David and Goliath. "Boff was cast as the boy with the slingshot," said Harvey Cox, a Harvard Divinity School professor who later wrote a book about the event. When Boff arrived in Rome, he waved away a mob of reporters gathered at the airport. "I am in Rome not as a pilgrim, not as a tourist," he told them. "I have been summoned by the prefect of the Sacred Congregation for the Doctrine of the Faith. I intend to respond to questions he asks me, not those of journalists."

The press corps could tell that Ratzinger was rattled about the unflattering headlines, because his congregation began leaking outrageously false stories about the Boff meeting. *L'Osservatore Romano* quoted the cardinal as saying that Boff's presence in Rome was his—not Ratzinger's—idea, and that this would be no interrogation; Boff would merely "confer" with the congregation in a friendly chat about his recent writings. The newspaper articles were laughably untrue. No one in the Curia doubted that Boff faced serious punishment, including the loss of his teaching credentials—and possibly even excommunication.

On September 7, the day of the interrogation, Boff celebrated morning Mass with Cardinal Arns, a fellow Franciscan, in their order's Rome headquarters. Two of Ratzinger's deputies appeared with a car at 9:40 a.m. Boff asked if they could make room for another passenger—a Franciscan priest who wanted to ride along to keep up Boff's spirits—but Ratzinger's deputies said they were under strict orders to bring Boff alone. As the car raced through the streets of Rome, Boff, by himself in the back seat, thought he must look to passersby like a criminal headed to prison. He tried to ease the tension with a joke as the car neared the palace. "Aha, is this the torture chamber?" he asked. Ratzinger's deputies chuckled, he remembered.

He was met at the entryway by Ratzinger, who greeted Boff in German. Boff's German was a bit rusty, but it was the language they used for their encounter, even if that put the Brazilian at a disadvantage. The two men traded pleasantries as they walked to the room where the interrogation would be held. Ratzinger complimented Boff for wearing his friar's robes that day instead of the civilian clothes he preferred at home.

Ratzinger gestured for Boff to take a seat at a table in the center of the room and invited him to speak first. Boff began by asking about the false newspaper reports. Ratzinger acknowledged the stories were riddled with errors but did not apologize or explain how they had occurred. Boff then offered a brief presentation on the struggles of the church in Brazil and how liberation theology offered hope to hundreds of millions of poor Catholics across Latin America. He cited several of the documents of Vatican II in arguing that liberation theology was simply an outgrowth of the council, which had urged the church to promote social justice. He was confounded, he said, why Ratzinger kept equating liberation theology with Marxism, as if priests involved in the movement were "bearded guerrillas in a jungle." In fact, he stressed, they were devout, mostly apolitical Christians helping the poor seek a better life. He said the movement's architect was not Karl Marx, it was the "historical Jesus who was poor, weak, powerless and critical of the social and religious status quo of his time."

His one-on-one meeting with Ratzinger had been surprisingly "tranquil and cordial," Boff remembered. It was in the second two-hour session, attended by the three Brazilian bishops, that the conversation became heated. Arns was furious about what he saw as the "persecution" of Boff and at Ratzinger's continuing assault on liberation theology.

Boff remained in Rome for a few days to grant interviews to dozens of the world's major news organizations. He told reporters his encounter with Ratzinger had been valuable—"a blessing in disguise"—because it had focused the Vatican's attention on the value of liberation theology. His optimism was misplaced, however. The following May, Ratzinger announced that Boff's writings defied doctrine and ordered him to submit to a year-long period of silence. Boff would not be allowed to publish anything or make public appearances. It was a punishment imposed by the church on only one other theologian since Vatican II, the French scholar Jacques Pohier, who went on to leave the priesthood. Boff said he was saddened by the order but accepted it: "I prefer to walk with the church rather than walk alone."

Ratzinger's campaign against liberation theology quieted in 1986, if only because the pope—to the cardinal's exasperation—spoke out again in support of the movement. At a meeting with visiting Brazilian bishops in March, he announced that in seeking justice for the poor, liberation theology "is not only orthodox, but necessary." The next month, the Vatican released its new, more positive report about the movement—the document ordered up by the pope to counteract the bad publicity over Ratzinger's stark denunciation two years earlier. The new decree saluted the poor's "aspiration to liberation" and praised liberation-theology base communities as a "source of great hope for the church." In Peru, Gutiérrez, the movement's founder, hailed the new document as a "relaunching" of liberation theology. A delighted Boff wrote to Ratzinger from Brazil. "Dear Brother Ratzinger," his letter began. "Now there can no longer be any doubt: Rome is at the side of the oppressed."

The Brazilian was wrong again. Within months, Ratzinger returned in earnest to his crusade against liberation theology and sought to end Boff's career forever. In 1987, the congregation blocked publication of a new book by Boff, then in 1991 ordered him to step down as editor of his theology journal. The next year, Ratzinger banned Boff from teaching and required him to present his writings for approval before publication. This time, Boff refused to submit. The Vatican's power "is cruel and remorseless," he said in announcing he would leave the clergy. "It forgets nothing. It forgives nothing. It demands everything."

Ratzinger targeted other prominent liberal churchmen in Brazil. In 1989, Curia officials confirmed he was a key architect of the Vatican's plan to dilute the authority of Cardinal Arns. The central archdiocese of São Paulo was reduced to a handful of relatively prosperous neighborhoods. The rest of the city, including the slums where Arns had always spent much of his time, was divided into four dioceses to be led by new, conservative bishops. There were similar moves across Latin America. Throughout the 1980s and 1990s, as older, reform-minded bishops across the region retired or died, they were succeeded by fierce critics of liberation theology. On Rome's orders, liberal seminaries were closed. Tens of thousands of base communities in Central and South America were disbanded, usually because they had been starved of the support of their local diocese.

WHEN RATZINGER BEGAN to sense victory in his campaign to dismantle liberation theology in Latin America, he turned to a new cause, this time in the Northern Hemisphere: combatting what he saw as the wanton sinfulness of Catholics in the United States and Western Europe. In this, he had the pope's full support. John Paul was always sharply critical of the US for what he saw as its moral decay. Ratzinger believed Americans were obsessed with money—"money and wealth are the measure of all things"—and accused the country's more than fifty million Catholics of allowing themselves to be swept up in the sexual revolution. Even as John Paul demanded bishops elsewhere remove themselves from politics, he made an exception for conservative churchmen in the United States. In the 1984 US presidential campaign, Cardinal O'Connor of New York attacked the Democratic vice-presidential nominee, Representative Geraldine Ferraro, a Catholic, for her support for abortion rights, while he described President Reagan, who opposed abortion and was seeking a second term, as a "friend of the unborn." Many saw that as an explicit call by the church for Reagan's reelection.

At the time, the best-known and most controversial Catholic theologian in the United States was Father Charles Curran, a professor at Catholic University in Washington, DC. Educated at the Gregorian, he was often described as the American counterpart to Küng and Boff in his willingness to battle the Vatican. Known to everyone on campus as Charlie, Curran had called for years for the church to relax its teachings on divorce and sexuality, and in 1968 had organized a campaign of theologians to reject *Humanae Vitae*. He had openly criticized John Paul, describing his papacy as "pervaded by authoritarianism."

In 1983, Curran received his first threatening letter from Ratzinger, who warned him that he was under investigation by the Congregation for the Doctrine of the Faith for his writings on a long list of subjects, most of them related to sex. The list included: "artificial contraception, the indissolubility of marriage, abortion, masturbation, homosexuality and premarital sex." As he read and reread that list, Curran thought that Ratzinger was engaged in a "gross oversimplification" of his views on those questions. He wrote back, insisting there was far more subtlety to his thinking than the congregation suggested. (He shared the Vatican's opposition to abortion, for example, although he thought the church was wrong to impose its views on the larger public by demanding lawmakers adopt anti-abortion laws.)

In a letter to Curran's bishop in September 1985, Ratzinger announced that Curran would be stripped of his Vatican-approved teaching credentials, which would force him out of Catholic University, unless he repudiated his most controversial writings. Ratzinger directed him specifically to declare that birth control was a sin; that abortion and euthanasia were "unspeakable crimes"; and that masturbation, premarital sex, and homosexuality were "intrinsically immoral." Curran could appeal, but only if he traveled to Rome to be interrogated by Ratzinger. Curran agreed to the meeting, scheduled for the following March.

Ratzinger allowed Curran to bring along an adviser to serve, effectively, as his defense lawyer in the meeting: Father Bernhard Häring, a prominent German theologian who had taught in Rome for years. Like Ratzinger, Häring made a name for himself as a reform-minded theological adviser at Vatican II. He went on to become one of the most prolific writers in the church's history, author of more than eighty books. Over the years, Häring, then seventy-three, had remained true to his progressive views, even as Ratzinger turned away from reform. They had remained publicly cordial.

That cordiality threatened to come to an end during the 1986 interrogation of Curran, however. Häring, it turned out, was appalled by what he saw as Ratzinger's closed-minded leadership of the congregation, especially his campaign to silence talented theologians like Curran. Häring had known the American since the 1960s, and while he thought Curran could be "undiplomatic" at times, he was also "scrupulously honest" and had "absolute loyalty to the church."

Ratzinger opened the meeting in a calm tone, but the conversation quickly became testy and threatening. Häring had come ready for a fight. He brought along a written statement, which Ratzinger asked one of his deputies in the room to read out loud. It was a brief history of disastrous decisions made by the congregation since its creation in 1542: the trial of Galileo; the church-sanctioned public execution of thousands of women across Europe accused of witchcraft in the sixteenth century; the silencing of many of the church's greatest intellectuals earlier in the twentieth. Häring wanted Ratzinger to acknowledge that throughout its history, his congregation made catastrophic errors—and that it might be making another by lashing out against a thoughtful scholar like Curran.

Curran had gone into the meeting determined not to raise his voice. "I need to avoid all expressions of anger and name-calling," he remembered telling himself. After Häring's presentation, though, he worried the meeting would collapse into a shouting match. It became difficult to remain calm as Ratzinger demonstrated he had no interest in hearing any challenge to his views.

Both Curran and Häring said later they were astonished when Ratzinger argued that, whatever the "fantasies" of some church scholars, the Vatican had the right to demand obedience from them on all controversial teachings, even those that had never been declared infallible. There could be no dissent on any significant doctrinal matter in which John Paul—and by extension, Ratzinger—had expressed an opinion. At heart, that meant the end of free speech for the world's Catholic theologians.[*]

Curran pressed Ratzinger to explain why he was being targeted for punishment when so many mainstream theologians shared his views, especially on sexual morality. Off the top of his head, he could name five well-known Catholic scholars in Germany who wrote just as boldly.

Ratzinger replied angrily: "We are only talking about you."

Curran persisted, which led Ratzinger to make an extraordinary demand: he ordered Curran to give him—that minute—the names of the five Germans so they could be investigated as well. Curran refused: "Surely I am not expected to report on my colleagues!" After two difficult hours, the meeting ended. Curran left Rome "drained and exhausted."

Back home in Washington, where his battles with Ratzinger were headline news, Curran called a press conference to reveal what had happened in Rome. The room was crowded with reporters and his devoted students. One journalist asked why Ratzinger was so fixated on "destroying" Curran when other theologians held similar views. Curran shrugged: "It is hard enough being a moral theologian in the church without being a psychiatrist."

He was gratified by the support he received from American theologians and other church scholars, including more than seven hundred who signed a petition in which they said they were "profoundly disturbed" by his case. It had no effect. In August, Ratzinger announced that his decision to revoke Curran's teaching credentials was final. Curran was left with the choice of resigning from the university or being fired. Ratzinger told him the order had been explicitly approved by the pope.

---

[*] Ratzinger did not publicly challenge details of the accounts of the meeting offered over the years by Curran and Häring.

26

Ratzinger's Crusade

IN EARLY 1986, Father Michael Peterson was gravely ill, for reasons he shared with few people outside the church. Although only forty-three, he suspected he would die within a year or two, and so, before his health got any worse, he decided to go to Rome to make one final plea for the Vatican to deal with the crisis of pedophile priests.

Many in the Curia had been impressed for years by Peterson's work with troubled priests at the Saint Luke Institute, his psychiatric clinic near Washington, and so he was able to set up meetings with influential bishops in Rome. He explained to each of them how the American hierarchy was covering up cases in which priests molested children. He wanted the Vatican to adopt a worldwide policy of identifying and punishing sexual predators in the clergy.

He returned home to Washington with dispiriting news for his friend Tom Doyle: Curia bishops were aware of the crisis and about to make it worse. They intentionally confused several issues, Peterson complained. They saw no need to deal directly with priestly pedophilia, which they saw as a problem only in the US. Instead, they sought to declare war on homosexuality, which they blamed for pedophilia. No matter how much Peterson argued that there was no link, they could not be talked out of it. What he heard was especially painful for reasons the bishops in Rome did not understand: Peterson was gay and had contracted HIV, facts he would keep secret from most colleagues until shortly before his death from AIDS in 1987.

By then, the arrest and prosecution of pedophile priests had become shockingly common in the United States. Cases became increasingly common outside the US, too. In 1988, the Australian bishops' conference established a commission to investigate a growing crisis of child sex abuse by clergymen there. A year before, Catholic dioceses across Ireland agreed to take out joint liability insurance to avoid bankruptcy because of lawsuits brought by the families of child victims.

The Vatican remained almost completely silent on the issue throughout the 1980s, treating it as a problem to be handled by local churches. Ratzinger said nothing on the subject, at least not publicly, and focused instead on what so many in the Curia claimed was the related but much larger threat—homosexuality. It became the subject of his congregation's next great campaign, in fact.

His preoccupation with homosexuality surprised some colleagues, if only because his congregation had already written extensively about the subject in 1975, when it issued its supposedly definitive decree that declared homosexuality to be "intrinsically disordered." It was the document that prompted the scandalous debate over Paul VI's sexuality. Ratzinger's campaign seemed odd for another reason: he was effectively condemning revered colleagues widely known to be gay. Over the years, gay priests had served on his staff, including a Polish theologian who went on to write a book about how he came to accept his sexual orientation. Ratzinger's campaign appeared to have the pope's full support, however. In his writings, John Paul II repeatedly described homosexuality as a violation of natural law, the same sort of argument he used against birth control.

To their credit, neither the pope nor Ratzinger gave voice to the ugliest prejudice of other Catholics as AIDS began to devastate the gay community, while killing millions of heterosexuals as well. In 1987, Cardinal Siri of Genoa described AIDS as "divine punishment" for homosexuality, a comment widely condemned by other churchmen. The pope and Ratzinger consistently spoke of their compassion for homosexuals, even as they rejected their sexual orientation. Catholic hospitals in the United States were at the forefront of treating gay men stricken with AIDS.

Ratzinger set to work in 1985 on a decree to condemn homosexuality, a document that would go much further than the one released a decade earlier. In the meantime, he took concrete action to make his views clear. In 1985, he ordered bishops throughout the world to cut off contact with organizations that advocated for gay Catholics. Months later, he decreed there would be no exceptions to the church's ban on the use of condoms, despite clear-cut scientific evidence that they blocked transmission of HIV, especially among gay men. He remained unmoved even though priests were dying of AIDS in unusually large numbers—hundreds a year in the US, four times the rate of men in the general population, according to one study. He repeatedly rejected pleas from bishops to approve condom use in limited situations—for example, when one partner in a heterosexual marriage was HIV positive. "A proposal for 'safe' or at least 'safer' sex . . . ignores the real cause of the problem—namely, permissiveness," he insisted.

His fixation on homosexuality figured in his decision in 1983 to open an investigation of Archbishop Raymond Hunthausen of Seattle. While beloved by most of his 350,000-member congregation, Hunthausen, then sixty-two, had outraged some parishioners by campaigning for nuclear disarmament and by refusing to abide by some church teachings. He allowed divorced couples to receive communion, for example, and for girls to serve alongside altar boys. He justified his rule breaking by declaring himself a "Vatican II bishop" who put mercy ahead of punishing sin.

The two-year investigation by the Congregation for the Doctrine of the Faith began after news reached Ratzinger in September 1983 that Hunthausen had sponsored a Mass in the city's cathedral that month for twelve hundred members of the Catholic gay-rights organization Dignity, which held its annual convention in Seattle. The archbishop made a videotaped welcome to the group. Ratzinger told deputies in Rome it was disgraceful that an "organization of sinners" had been invited to gather in such a sacred place. A year later, at the height of the investigation, Hunthausen flew to Rome to explain himself to Ratzinger. He had never met the cardinal before and found him ill-tempered and confrontational. The conversation turned poisonous as Ratzinger began to list what he saw as the bishop's failings, particularly his outreach to gay people. Hunthausen replied with a Gospel story from the Book of John, when an adulterous woman is brought before Jesus by the Pharisees, who want her stoned. Jesus refuses to judge her, telling the Pharisees, "Let he who is without sin cast the first stone."

Ratzinger angrily interrupted: "Are you presuming to lecture me?"

A startled Hunthausen tried again to answer. In allowing gay Catholics to meet in the cathedral, he said, "I tried to do what I thought Jesus would do. Jesus didn't wait until people changed before he talked to them. He began a dialogue and I think that's what the church ought to do with the gay community."

"Don't preach to me," Ratzinger warned before abruptly ending the meeting.

In September 1986, on the cardinal's orders, Hunthausen was stripped of day-to-day authority over his archdiocese, the most serious disciplinary action taken against an American bishop in a century. Friends said the inquiry had so demoralized Hunthausen that they blamed Ratzinger for a heart attack that nearly killed the Seattle bishop the year before.

A handful of American bishops risked their own careers by protesting to Rome over the case. Bishop Thomas Gumbleton of Detroit described the punishment of Hunthausen as "cruel" and an attempt by Ratzinger to intimidate all American Catholics. Archbishop Rembert Weakland of Milwaukee praised Hunthausen as a man "totally without guile, strongly principled and profoundly pastoral." In his diocese newsletter, Weakland wrote that Hunthausen's demotion suggested the Vatican had entered an era of "fanaticism and small-mindedness." The church, he said, needed to recommit itself to the "medicine of mercy" promised by John XXIII at Vatican II.

At the time, Weakland feared his own career could end in scandal at any minute. By the mid-1980s, he had told a few friends what had been, for most of his life, his greatest secret—that he was gay—even as he kept another to himself: in 1979, two years after arriving in Milwaukee, he had a brief affair with a local man. He could only hope the relationship would remain a secret. He knew that, in the era of John Paul II and Ratzinger, a bishop's public admission of an affair—and especially one with another man—meant the end of his career.

In October 1986, the Congregation for the Doctrine of the Faith issued a three-thousand-word document under Ratzinger's name that gathered up his darkest fears about homosexuality. Entitled "On the Pastoral Care of Homosexual Persons," it declared that homosexuals had a "strong tendency toward an intrinsic moral evil." It condemned the "pro-homosexual movement" and its "deceitful propaganda." As proof of the cardinal's intended audience, the proclamation was initially issued in English—not in Latin or Italian, as would be traditional.

The declaration had instant consequences in the United States. Dignity, the gay-rights group, was permanently barred from meeting in Catholic churches in the US. Father John McNeill, an openly gay Jesuit journalist who was also a practicing psychiatrist in New York, described the document as a reflection of a "mean and cruel spirit that is in conflict with both the spirit and the letter of the Gospels." Ratzinger struck back by demanding McNeill's Jesuit superiors expel him from the Society of Jesus, which they did, reluctantly.

In March 1987, Ratzinger launched a bold new campaign on another issue involving human sexuality when he released a forty-page document that condemned virtually all methods of artificial reproduction, including in vitro fertilization. It was an assault on a whole school of medical research, including that carried out in many Catholic universities. "What is technologically possible is not morally admissible," the document declared. The report distressed many of Ratzinger's usual defenders, who said it was cruel to crush the dreams of Catholic couples struggling with infertility. Dr. Patrick Steptoe, the British obstetrician who became famous in 1978 after delivering the world's first so-called test-tube baby, known to the public as Baby Louise, said the Vatican's decree was "rubbish." He pointed out that when Baby Louise was born through in vitro fertilization, her parents were publicly congratulated by then-Cardinal Luciano of Venice, who went on to be elected John Paul I that same year.

AS JOHN PAUL II APPROACHED the tenth anniversary of his papacy in 1988, senior Curia officials operated with near-total independence. On matters of doctrine, he relied almost completely on Ratzinger. By then, the cardinal hinted at how their relationship had changed and how he increasingly functioned as the teacher, with the pope his eager student. "I admired his willingness to learn," Ratzinger said.

In 1987, the pope toured both North and South America, as well as West Germany and Poland. When in Rome, he was preoccupied by the political turmoil in Poland, which he monitored by the hour, and by scandals at the Vatican Bank. In March, an Italian court issued an arrest warrant for Archbishop Marcinkus. He was under criminal investigation for fraud in the collapse, five years earlier, of Banco Ambrosiano, Italy's largest private bank, in which the Vatican Bank had been a major shareholder. The scandal was so byzantine and sordid that whole books were written about it, but even that could not do justice to how outrageous it was. Over time, the Vatican Bank's investments were tied to money laundering for drug cartels and prostitution rings. The events exploded into a global scandal in 1982 when Ambrosiano's president, Roberto Calvi, was found dead, hanging by the neck from a bridge in London with thirteen thousand dollars stuffed in his pockets. The circumstances of his death, and whether it was suicide or murder, were never established with certainty. In 1984, John Paul agreed to pay $244 million to make the scandal go away, with the money turned over to Ambrosiano's creditors. The pope defied the police and refused to allow Marcinkus to surrender to the warrant, which created an embarrassing standoff in which John Paul sheltered a criminal suspect inside Vatican City.*

By the late 1980s, the pope had begun to slow down, physically and intellectually, even as he continued his relentless globetrotting. He complained of constant pain, some of it related to the surgeries following the 1981 assassination attempt. His physical decline was matched by growing irritability. In public gatherings, he struggled to smile, and became shockingly callous in some of his decision making. In 1989, Jesuits were outraged when he failed to hold a public Mass in St. Peter's after six Jesuits, along with their housekeeper and her daughter, were slaughtered in El Salvador by a military death squad; the dead priests were targeted because they were known to be champions of liberation theology. They were honored instead with a Mass at the Church of the Gesù, the Jesuits' mother church in Rome. The pope did not attend.

A similar insensitivity resulted in what many in the Curia saw as the most damaging—and unnecessary—scandal of the first decade of his papacy: his decision in June 1987 to grant an audience to Austrian president Kurt Waldheim, the former secretary general of the United Nations, who had just been branded a war criminal by the United States Justice Department. The department determined that Waldheim, a Nazi intelligence officer in World War II, oversaw the 1944 deportation of thousands of Greek Jews to death camps. As a result, the US, several European countries, and Israel had cut off all contact with Waldheim, but the pope met him anyway. Israeli prime minister Yitzhak Shamir described the papal audience as "outrageous" and asked if the pope was trying to offer "justification for the crimes of which Waldheim is accused."[†]

The event was startling to Jewish leaders, who had come to see the pope as a champion of the dialogue between Jews and Catholics begun at Vatican II. During his papacy, John Paul regularly denounced anti-Semitism in

---

* An Italian court eventually dismissed the warrant, ruling that Marcinkus, as a Vatican employee, was immune from prosecution. He retired from the bank in 1989.
† The pope never expressed regret over the meeting, and in 1994, granted a papal knighthood to Waldheim, citing his "humanitarian achievements" at the United Nations, as well as his contributions to the church. Waldheim was a practicing Catholic.

his speeches. He made a special point during his first pilgrimage to Poland in 1979 to stop at the Auschwitz death camp to pay his respects to its Jewish victims. After the Waldheim meeting, however, that goodwill seemed to evaporate—and then Ratzinger made everything worse. In perhaps the most outrageous blunder of his early years in Rome, the cardinal granted an interview weeks later to an Italian newspaper to discuss his views on other faiths, including Judaism. When his comments were published, they were denounced by Jewish groups as blatantly anti-Semitic. Within the Curia, the furor was seen as more proof that Ratzinger spoke recklessly, assuming no one would dare correct him.

In the interview, Ratzinger called for Jews to convert to Christianity and accept "the reality of Jesus Christ." Insisting he spoke directly for the pope, Ratzinger said John Paul endorsed "a theological line" that Jews—like Christians and Muslims, descendants of the prophet Abraham—would find fulfillment in the "faith of Abraham" only if they accepted Jesus as their Savior. He cited the pope's recent, controversial decision to grant sainthood to Sister Edith Stein, a German-born Carmelite nun and Jewish convert who died in the gas chambers of Auschwitz in 1942. When she abandoned Judaism and "found faith in Christ, she entered into the full inheritance of Abraham," Ratzinger said.

Jewish leaders, already on edge over Waldheim, were incensed at the cardinal's suggestion that theirs was a lesser faith, whose followers would find salvation only by accepting Jesus as the Messiah. At Vatican II, John XXIII said repeatedly that Jews and Christians, one faith born from the other, were equal in God's eyes. Had Ratzinger decided otherwise? The American Jewish Committee said he had, effectively, shut down the lines of communication between Catholics and Jews opened at Vatican II: "Ratzinger simply provides no place for Judaism and hence no space for dialogue." The World Jewish Congress said Ratzinger had "besmirched the legacy of John XXIII."

He tried frantically to tamp down the controversy, claiming the translation of the interview, which was conducted in German, was imperfect and expressed his views too bluntly. The damage was done, however. Ratzinger faced protests weeks later when he traveled to New York to deliver a lecture. Local rabbis refused to meet with him. The cardinal, stung by the protests, held a news conference in New York in which he repeatedly—and awkwardly—expressed his admiration for Jews as "the owners of the Old Testament."

The pope said nothing in public about Ratzinger's blunder, and it appeared to do no lasting damage to their relationship. In fact, in the months that followed, the cardinal's authority seemed to grow again, especially when it came to the appointment of bishops around the world.

By then, John Paul had selected about a third of the world's nearly four thousand cardinals and bishops. His choices continued to fit the same mold—staunchly conservative and loyal to him personally. He appointed several bishops known to be, or at least strongly suspected of being, members of Opus Dei. (Even after their promotion, some refused to confirm their ties to Opus Dei, in line with the secrecy oaths they took in joining the order.) Most priests labeled as liberal or progressive were rejected for promotion to bishop, no matter how respected they were in their local communities, although there were exceptions. One of the most notable occurred in 1979, when John Paul named the biblical historian Carlo Maria Martini, a Jesuit who was the former rector of the Gregorian, as archbishop of Milan. Martini was notably liberal on many issues, but the pope seemed willing to overlook that given his reputation for extraordinary scholarship. Similarly, in 1989, the pope selected the fifty-six-year-old German theologian Walter Kasper, once seen as a protégé of Hans Küng's, as bishop of Rottenburg and Stuttgart. Kasper's ties to Küng were not a hindrance, since he had publicly broken with his onetime colleague. Unlike Küng, Kasper continued to have fine instincts about church politics. He was careful, for example, never to describe himself as "liberal," which might have sunk his hopes for appointment to the hierarchy; he instead called himself "open-minded."

His appointment delighted progressive Catholic theologians in Germany. Many hoped he might emerge one day as a rival to another renowned German theologian serving in the hierarchy: Ratzinger. After working together at the University of Münster in the 1960s, the two men considered themselves friends, if not especially close ones.

Kasper had always impressed other churchmen for something that Ratzinger lacked—a desire to be out among people, as a true pastor. Throughout his teaching career, he always found time to do priestly work. In Münster, he celebrated Mass every day for mentally impaired patients at a local hospital. The experience taught him the value of simplicity in discussions of faith. His sermons, he said, "had to convey the point in simple words."

The timing of his appointment was not a coincidence. It was seen as part of an effort by Rome to placate German Catholics who were furious over their treatment by John Paul. The year before, many were incensed when the pope selected a fiercely conservative, often foul-tempered archbishop for the city of Cologne, Cardinal Joachim Meisner, former bishop of Berlin. In fiery sermons condemning abortion, birth control, and homosexuality, Meisner was notorious in Berlin for his over-the-top rhetoric; he compared his opponents to Hitler and Stalin. In appointing Meisner, John Paul rejected three candidates proposed by diocese leaders in Cologne, a violation of a sixty-year-old treaty between the Vatican and the diocese, which previously had a veto over its bishop. For his part, Meisner showed little grace in accepting the assignment. This was a "shotgun marriage," he declared at a meeting with priests in Cologne. "We have something in common. You did not want me. And I did not want you."

It was widely reported in Rome that the appointment had been orchestrated by Ratzinger, a close friend of Meisner's, and that Ratzinger had assured the pope that the controversy in Cologne would blow over. By then, Ratzinger's profile in his homeland had never been higher, even if it was often unflattering. In German tabloid newspapers, he was commonly referred to as either *der Panzer-Kardinal* or *Gottes Rottweiler* (God's Rottweiler).

The furor over Meisner did not quiet, however. In fact, it set off what would be an historic uprising against the Vatican—and against the pope, personally—by hundreds of Catholic theologians and other church scholars. The protests began when 163 German-speaking theologians drafted a statement, timed to Meisner's arrival in Cologne, that denounced John Paul for his "authoritarianism." Within months, hundreds of other theologians added their names to what became known as the Cologne Declaration. In modern times, there had never been anything like it, a public denunciation of the bishop of Rome by hundreds of Catholic scholars who would otherwise feel bound to serve him. Under John Paul, the declaration said, the church had been "smothered by a new Roman centralism." The idea that bishops outside Rome had their own authority—the concept of "collegiality" promoted at Vatican II—had been demolished, it argued.

John Paul ignored the revolt, at least publicly. Ratzinger, however, was furious and decided to reply. In interviews with newspapers across Europe, he accused the theologians behind the Cologne Declaration of engaging in a "political power play" worthy of Machiavelli. There would be no negotiation over the issues they raised, he announced. In fact, he suggested, he was willing to end the careers of scholars who signed the document. In one interview, he hinted darkly that the church would soon cut the size of theology faculties at German universities to make sure they included only "qualified" scholars.

John Paul had special reason to be distracted at the time, given the astonishing news in 1989 from across Eastern Europe, where popular uprisings brought freedom to nations long trapped behind the Iron Curtain. In January, negotiations between Poland's Communist leaders and the Solidarity labor union cleared the way for free elections. In June, Solidarity, now certified as a political party, won control of the country's first democratically elected government in half a century. Communist regimes were toppled within months in Hungary, East Germany, Czechoslovakia, and Romania. The Berlin Wall fell in November. The collapse of the Soviet Union was imminent.

Publicly and privately, the pope remained involved in every part of the drama in Poland. He was constantly on the phone to Warsaw, or to intermediaries in Washington and Moscow, to negotiate political deals that would bring democracy to his homeland without bloodshed. Even his harshest critics found it hard to deny that the pope's statesmanship had helped end the Cold War.

That made the irony inside the Vatican all the greater: just as much of the world was congratulating John Paul for his role in securing freedom in Eastern Europe, his deputy Ratzinger was at work a few blocks away writing and editing documents that demanded an end to free speech inside the Catholic Church. The first document, released by Ratzinger in March 1989 and an obvious slap at the signers of the Cologne Declaration, demanded that professors at all church-run universities around the world swear a loyalty oath to the Vatican, at the cost of their jobs if they refused. The "oath of fidelity" required scholars to uphold the validity of all church teachings. A year later, he went further, releasing a second document that was breathtaking in its demand for submission to Rome. The seventy-five-hundred-word statement, entitled "On the Vocation of the Theologian," declared that the Vatican would no longer tolerate dissent of any sort from theologians—and it seemed, by extension, all Catholics—on issues of doctrine. The pronouncement was written in opaque language, but Ratzinger held a news conference to explain it in terms anyone could understand. It was time, he announced, to silence theologians who falsely portrayed themselves as the "real masters of the church."

With the pope fixated on Eastern Europe, and Ratzinger consumed by his crackdown on dissident scholars, the Vatican did virtually nothing in response to a flood of new cases of child sexual abuse by priests. Canada, where Catholics made up about 40 percent of the population, became an epicenter of the crisis. The diocese in the eastern province of Newfoundland was plagued by a wave of cases in 1990; twenty priests and former priests there were charged with child molestation. In Calgary in 1989, a sixty-three-year-old priest pleaded guilty to sexual abuse of eighteen boys; the youngest of his victims was eleven years old. In New York City in February 1990, Father Bruce Ritter, the seventy-three-year-old founder of Covenant House, a charity for homeless teenagers with an $80 million annual budget, resigned amid reports that he had regularly molested boys who sought the group's help. Although he was never criminally charged, an independent investigation identified at least fifteen cases in which Ritter had sex with homeless boys and young men. The church never sought to defrock Ritter, who remained a priest when he retired to a small town in upstate New York.

Those scandals coincided with the publication of the long-awaited findings of the research of the psychotherapist Richard Sipe. He was honored

The American psychotherapist Richard Sipe, a former Benedictine priest, conducted exhaustive research of priestly sexuality and warned in the 1980s and 1990s of a dire crisis over clerical sex abuse of children.

when he was invited to announce his findings, based on treatment of more than a thousand priests over a quarter century, at the 1990 annual conference of the American Psychological Association. His research had been reviewed in advance, and praised, by a Harvard Medical School psychiatry professor, as well as by a sociologist at Catholic University in Washington.

Sipe had concluded that the church's determined portrayal of the priesthood as a brotherhood of men who readily accepted celibacy had always been a myth. He estimated at least half of all American priests were sexually active during some or all of their careers. At any given time, he said, at least 20 percent of the nation's priests were engaged in a sexual relationship with a woman. He believed another 20 percent were gay or inclined to homosexuality, and that at least half of them were having sex with other men. Only 2 percent of the priests he studied achieved happy, celibate lifestyles. His most frightening finding was that 4 to 6 percent of the nation's priests were pedophiles and molested children, mostly boys. Because the church had never dealt honestly with the problem, the priesthood had been turned into a perverse "secret society" in which these men kept each other's secrets, even if that meant covering up for sexual predators.

He hoped his research, published as a book, *A Secret World: Sexuality and the Search for Celibacy*, would stir a new debate, and sent copies to friends in the Vatican. He timed the book's release to a synod called by John Paul that fall, at which two hundred bishops from around the world were being asked to debate the future of the priesthood.

The book instantly came under attack by the church. The United States Conference of Catholic Bishops dismissed Sipe's research and suggested a random survey of all priests, not just the troubled men who sought his help, would have produced less alarming findings: "What Dr. Sipe has done is the equivalent of walking into a cancer hospital and concluding that 30 percent of the world has cancer." Ahead of the synod, a group of Canadian bishops attempted to place questions about priestly sexuality—including child abuse—on the agenda, but they were rebuffed. Instead, the meeting in Rome ended with a ringing declaration to reaffirm the "precious gift" of celibacy.

The pope had invited several guests to attend the synod as observers, including Father Maciel, the founder of the Legion of Christ. That May, Maciel joined the pope on a week-long pilgrimage to Mexico and was often at his side in Rome. Years later, photos of the pope greeting him at the synod—and of the two men together in Mexico—would be painfully awkward for the Vatican. The photos proved that in 1990, a dozen years into his papacy, John Paul either was still ignorant of the voluminous, decades-old Vatican disciplinary files about Maciel, identifying scores of the boys he had molested, or had simply decided to ignore the allegations against his old friend.

27

Polishing an Image

IN NOVEMBER 1991, Cardinal Ratzinger's sister, Maria, died at the age of sixty-nine. She had been the only constant female presence in his adult life—for most of it, his housekeeper. There had always been affection between them, and they were both close to their brother, Georg. Still, it was clear to everyone who met Maria that she never engaged in conversations with her brothers that were the least bit intellectual. Gerald O'Collins, the theology dean at the Gregorian, was struck that she seemed to know nothing about Joseph's work and that he never tried to explain it to her, even in simple terms. O'Collins remembered meeting her in Germany in the 1960s and praising a theology book that her brother had just published. "Never even heard of it," she replied. Theologians who dined in the Ratzingers' home said Maria was not invited into discussions about church issues. Many of the dinner guests wondered if Maria had no interest in Catholic scholarship, or whether it reflected something about her brother's views on women.

In 1992, Ratzinger marked his tenth anniversary at the Congregation for the Doctrine of the Faith. O'Collins shared the view of many of his colleagues at the Gregorian that the cardinal had done terrible damage in Rome. As part of his university duties, O'Collins met regularly with Ratzinger's deputies, and found many were embittered, second-rate scholars who had been harmed psychologically by the work. "What happens to people whose daily task is to search for heresy?" O'Collins asked himself. Many had no doctoral training in theology or Bible studies, even though they were being asked to judge the work of the world's most distinguished religious scholars.

O'Collins thought the congregation's secretive methods would shock most Catholics if exposed. Under Ratzinger, it had abandoned a tradition dating from the nineteenth century known as "subsidiarity," which held that church problems should be handled on the lowest-possible level of authority, without any involvement by the Vatican. Ratzinger had turned the process on its head. Under Ratzinger, O'Collins said, the congregation encouraged ultraconservative "vigilantes" around the world to mail in reports identifying local priests, teachers, and writers who should be targeted by Rome. Hundreds of tips flooded in each week, typically in the form of a handwritten letter, accompanied by the text of a sermon or essay that the outraged tipster saw as promoting heresy. O'Collins said some of his most respected colleagues at the Gregorian found themselves under investigation by Ratzinger on the basis of "patently false allegations" leveled by "right-wing dissidents" or embittered students. The investigations were usually conducted in secret, which meant the targets could be under scrutiny for years without their knowledge. O'Collins would never confront Ratzinger about this, nor would anyone who valued their position in the church, given the cardinal's essentially unchecked power. O'Collins believed that, as a result of the partnership of the pope and Ratzinger, "the centralization of the power of the Catholic Church in Rome is now more pronounced than at any other point in its history."

Some of Ratzinger's friends guessed that 1992 was the year he began seriously to consider the idea he would succeed John Paul. In July, the pope, then seventy-two, underwent radical abdominal surgery. A large, benign tumor on his colon was removed, along with his gallbladder, and his surgeons predicted the recovery would be long and painful. That summer, the pope's health problems prompted major international news organizations, for the first time since the assassination attempt in 1981, to speculate in earnest about his successor.

Over the years, Ratzinger waved away speculation that he might be a candidate for the papacy, although friends knew he was offended when his name was left off the popular lists of those considered *papabile*. He recognized that some cardinals would strongly oppose his candidacy because of his conservative views, and others would want a younger candidate. He turned sixty-five in 1992 and had his own serious health problems. He suffered a stroke the year before and, as a result, could effectively see out of only one eye. Although he had never admitted it publicly, he had heart surgery years earlier to install a pacemaker. He said he cited his failing health when he asked the pope in 1991 for permission to retire: "I said I can't do this anymore. His response was 'no.'"

It was at about this time that Ratzinger took steps to soften his public image. His insistence that he ignored his critics had never really been true. He was stung by the insulting nicknames that newspapers continued to apply to him, especially in Germany. "The *Panzer-Kardinal* nickname really got to him," said Peter Seewald, a German journalist who became central to Ratzinger's campaign to polish his image. The cardinal was also alarmed by how often newspaper and magazine profiles noted his boyhood membership in the Hitler Youth and his service in the German army, as if the Nazis had given him any choice.

In 1996, he gave another of his book-length interviews, published in English under the title *Salt of the Earth*, in which he depicted himself above all else as a humble servant of the church—"I don't feel particularly powerful"—and described his immediate family, especially his mother, Maria, in loving detail. "My mother was very warm-hearted and had great inner strength." He expressed pride in his most famous relative, his great-uncle Georg Ratzinger, a nineteenth-century priest-politician who campaigned to end child labor in Bavaria: "He was really a champion of the rights of the peasants and the other simple people." (What Ratzinger failed to mention in the interview was that his great-uncle was also a notorious anti-Semite who compared wealthy Jews to "parasites.")

A year later, he published the first volume of his memoirs, *Milestones*, chronicling his life through his appointment as cardinal in Munich. The book would be seen by many critics as an attempt to whitewash parts of his early life story, especially his youth in wartime Germany. He presented his Bavarian childhood as idyllic, far removed from the terror experienced by other Germans during Hitler's rise and the outbreak of World War II. "It was the kind of happy life that boys should have," he wrote. Even when local newspapers carried grim reports about Nazi battle plans and troop movements, the war usually seemed "far from us." The book had no suggestion of what Ratzinger's brother and others had revealed over the years—how friends and even a family member were probably executed in Nazi euthanasia programs, and how the Ratzingers were aware of atrocities at Dachau. (The word "Dachau" appears only once in the book, in a reference to Ratzinger's seminary rector, who survived five years' imprisonment there.) Nor did it reveal how the Bavarian town of Traunstein, where he lived from the ages of ten to sixteen, beginning in 1937, was the scene of terrible violence, much of it directed against his Jewish neighbors. When a Nazi pogrom broke out across Germany on the evening of November 9, 1938, the event known as Kristallnacht, or the Night of Broken Glass, a squad of brown-shirts attacked the homes of the town's Jews. Traunstein's most prominent Jewish family fled the next day; most of the family would die in Dachau. The town, which had a population of about twelve thousand people at the time, was also home to a notorious prison for political dissidents. The writer Luise Rinser, who would later fall in love with Karl Rahner, was imprisoned there in 1943 and wrote afterward of the horrors of confinement in a cell overrun by rats and insects. In 1945, as the war was ending, the Nazis evacuated concentration camps and marched prisoners to their deaths. At least thirty-six died in the Traunstein area. On May 3, a column of sixty-six prisoners was marched past the neighborhood where the Ratzingers lived and into a nearby forest, where the SS opened fire on them. "The horrors of the Reich were right there in Traunstein, staring Ratzinger in the face," his biographer John Allen would later write in criticizing *Milestones*.

Elsewhere in the book, Ratzinger argued that German Catholics and the national church hierarchy had been mostly unified against the Nazis. Despite the "human failings" of a few Catholic leaders, "the church was the alternative to the destructive ideology of the brown rulers," he wrote. "In the inferno that had swallowed up other powerful institutions, she had stood firm." That was simply not true, however. When Hitler came to power in 1933, Germany's bishops issued a public statement to salute the "national awakening" that the Nazis represented. There had been a handful of brave German bishops who defied Hitler—his patron Cardinal Frings in Cologne, for example—but there had been no systematic Catholic opposition. The Vatican signed the 1933 concordat with Hitler that gave him international legitimacy, and a number of individual German bishops were proud Nazi collaborators.

Critics said *Milestones* offered stark evidence of what they saw as Ratzinger's exaggerated perception of the church as an institution so pure that it did not need to adjust itself to the horrors of the world around it. "A theme which seldom appeared in Ratzinger's writings was that of human evil and suffering," O'Collins noted in a review. "Ratzinger did not place his theology in a world torn by war, oppression, hunger." (The cardinal once acknowledged to a biographer that, having survived World War II, he felt no special obligation to write about its terrors and whether they had influenced his faith: "I did not see it as my job.")

Journalists did not challenge the accuracy of *Milestones* in earnest until years after it was published. In the meantime, the book humanized Ratzinger and explained away controversies that might have cost him the papacy. Several clergymen rushed forward with praise. "The book gives us finally Ratzinger the person," Cardinal O'Connor of New York wrote. "He is a joy to meet."

BY THE MID-1990S, many of the progressive churchmen who made names for themselves at Vatican II had retired or died, replaced by ambitious conservatives. In 1990, Ratzinger's friend López Trujillo of Colombia was brought to Rome to lead the pope's Council for the Family. He established himself as one of the Vatican's most ferocious defenders of traditional values, especially on sexual matters. He was outspoken on the AIDS crisis, denouncing the use of condoms to stop the spread of HIV as not only immoral but also ineffective. He repeatedly claimed that the virus was so tiny it could pass through the walls of a latex condom—a statement so outrageously false that he was denounced by name by the World Health Organization for promoting "dangerous" misinformation. Given the well-established accounts of his active sex life with other men, his hypocrisy remained astonishing.

The sexual and criminal hypocrisy of another church leader, Cardinal Groër in Vienna, was revealed publicly in 1995. A year before, when Groër turned seventy-five, he submitted his retirement letter, but John Paul refused it and asked Groër to stay on indefinitely. The following March, an Austrian newsmagazine published the first of several stories documenting how Groër had molested young boys when he taught at all-male Catholic schools and seminaries. A respected Austrian investigative reporter who wrote a book about the scandal said Groër had molested an estimated two thousand boys and young men, beginning in the 1950s. In interviews, the journalist repeated that number several times, to establish it was not a misprint.

It was easily the worst scandal in the history of the Austrian church, and the outrage of millions of Catholics there only grew as the national church hierarchy and the pope rallied to Groër's defense. Days after the first reports, he was re-elected president of the national bishops' conference. The pope at first appeared determined to defend Groër no matter how ugly and detailed the abuse charges. In September 1995, six months into the scandal, the Vatican announced the pope had accepted Groër's resignation from the Vienna archdiocese, although he remained a cardinal in good standing. Days later, the pope sent a letter to Austria's bishops in which he compared Groër to the crucified Jesus, who had also faced "unjust accusations." In the year that followed, tens of thousands of Austrian Catholics left the church in disgust.

Ratzinger seemed determined to remain uninvolved in the case, at least publicly. Vienna's next archbishop, Cardinal Christoph Schönborn, insisted years later Ratzinger had wanted to open an investigation of Groër in 1995, when the allegations became public, but the idea was vetoed by the pope and the Vatican's secretary of state, Cardinal Angelo Sodano. It was among the first of several well-documented cases in which Sodano intervened to shield a child-molesting bishop from scrutiny.

The church in neighboring Germany remained badly troubled in the 1990s. Opinion polls showed German Catholics, by huge margins, rejected Vatican teachings on birth control, abortion, homosexuality, and priestly celibacy. The shortage of clergymen was so severe that one in three German parishes had no priest. The uproar over the Meisner appointment in 1988 had not faded. For many German Catholics, Ratzinger was as much to blame as the pope for what had gone wrong in their church.

There were a handful of bishops in Germany at the time who still offered hope to progressive Catholics, none more than Walter Kasper. By then, his parishioners in Rottenburg had given him a nickname: *der Anti-Ratzinger.* He continued to present himself as a humble pastor who wanted to be out among the faithful. He visited a different church in his archdiocese every weekend, and he would take charge of the local Mass, which meant that, over time, every man, woman, and child in his archdiocese had the chance to meet him and hear him preach.

In years to come, the contrast between Kasper and Ratzinger was a regular topic of conversation in Rome. Observers were struck that two Germans from the same generation—Ratzinger was six years older—were so different. Kasper's writings showed that, unlike Ratzinger, he was tormented by memories of World War II, and that it had a profound influence on his faith. He believed the church needed to be flexible and show mercy as people struggled to live decent lives in "this dark and bloody century." In his early years as a bishop, Kasper acted on that belief, and it produced his first bitter clash with Ratzinger.

Bishop Walter Kasper of Germany, the rare progressive
churchman allowed to advance into the church hierarchy
under John Paul II, greets parishioners on the streets of
Rottenburg after his consecration ceremony, June 17, 1989.

The showdown centered on Kasper's wish to end the suffering of his
many divorced parishioners—men and women who, no matter how honor-
ably they lived their lives, were branded as sinners. As a bishop, he thought
he had the power to begin to relieve their misery by allowing them to
receive Communion, even if that was forbidden elsewhere in the church.

In 1993, Kasper and two other German bishops issued a public letter:
"In a show of the mercy at the heart of Jesus's message," they declared, they
had opened a debate over whether—in their dioceses, at least—divorced
Catholics should be welcomed to the altar for Communion bread and wine.
The three bishops said they were acting under the principle of "collegiality"
embraced at Vatican II—that they, as descendants of the apostles, should
make some decisions for themselves, independent of the bishop of Rome.

The letter was an important news story in Germany, since it suggested at
least a few churchmen were finally ready to stand up to John Paul. Within
hours, though, Kasper and the others received urgent, angry phone calls
from the Congregation for the Doctrine of the Faith, summoning them to
Rome. In the Vatican days later, Ratzinger told the trio they were promoting heresy. He ordered them to abide by the church's teachings and continue to refuse Communion to divorced parishioners. Kasper was insulted
by the cardinal's condescending tone. Another of the three, Karl Lehmann

of the city of Mainz, reminded Ratzinger of an awkward fact—that as a young, progressive theologian, Ratzinger had called for the church to show mercy to divorced Catholics by offering them Communion. Lehmann produced a copy of a 1970 speech in which Ratzinger called for a "clear turn" on the issue. Ratzinger angrily told Lehmann it was immaterial what he thought as a young man.

The following year, Ratzinger issued a declaration that undermined the three bishops completely. Divorced Catholics, he wrote, "find themselves in a situation that objectively contravenes God's law" and could not be allowed to receive Communion. The declaration came as Ratzinger prepared to rein in the power of all bishops outside Rome, individually and collectively. He was at work on a document, eventually issued under the pope's name, that muzzled the world's 108 national bishops' conferences and effectively barred them from ever speaking out on controversial issues.

Before then, the national conferences—the largest were in Italy and the United States—were permitted to issue public statements challenging Vatican teachings so long as the challenge had the support of a majority of their members. Those statements had often infuriated the Vatican, notably in 1968, when conferences across Europe questioned *Humanae Vitae*. In the 1980s, national conferences in Latin America provoked a similar, angry reaction in Rome by issuing statements endorsing liberation theology.

Ratzinger intended to make sure those sorts of challenges were never heard again. The 1998 decree, issued as a so-called apostolic letter, the most authoritative papal document after an encyclical, declared that national bishops' conferences could speak out on Vatican teachings only with unanimous support; a single dissenting bishop could block a protest. That effectively silenced the conferences on all controversial issues. (At the time, the US conference had a membership of about three hundred bishops, and there were few subjects on which every one of them could agree.)

Ratzinger also set out to dilute the authority of the larger, often more powerful continent-wide bishops' gatherings—such as CELAM, the Conference of Latin American Bishops, which had been instrumental in creating liberation theology. In 1993, the pope and Ratzinger demanded a restructuring of CELAM's counterpart in Europe—the Council of European Bishops' Conferences, which represented churchmen from more than thirty countries across the continent. The moves resulted in the departure of the group's longstanding, decidedly progressive president, Cardinal Martini of Milan.

In 1995, several European bishops, fed up by what they saw as never-ending power grabs by Rome, began to meet regularly—and secretly—to plot how to reclaim some of their lost authority. Over time, their meetings would take on the appearance of an insurrection against Ratzinger. The bishops came to call themselves the St. Gallen Group, named for the Swiss city where they met every January for years. Its membership included both Kasper and Lehmann, as well as Martini. Another member, Cardinal God-fried Danneels of Belgium, who revealed the group's existence years later, acknowledged how secret its deliberations had been: "We had one simple rule: Everything could be said, so long as no notes were taken." He came to describe the group—jokingly, he insisted—as a "mafia" of like-minded liberal bishops. Once asked by reporters if the "mafia" plotted to stop Ratzinger from becoming pope, Danneels grinned and said nothing, although he confirmed that the group did discuss possible successors to John Paul II. In some of their early meetings, he remembered, they talked about a promising contender from South America—the impressive new archbishop of Buenos Aires, Argentina, Jorge Mario Bergoglio, who was known there as the "bishop of the slums."

IN 1995, Ratzinger appointed his new chief deputy at the congregation—Archbishop Tarcisio Bertone, an arrogant sixty-one-year-old Italian who had spent most of his career in Rome as a professor of church law. It was instantly recognized inside the Vatican, by those who knew Bertone best, as a disastrous choice. Although he shared Ratzinger's conservative views on doctrine, he was the cardinal's opposite in many ways. He was notorious for his big mouth and obsessive love of Italian football, a subject in which Ratzinger had no interest. The cardinal brushed aside criticism of the appointment, telling friends that he saw in Bertone what the pope had seen in Father Dziwisz—a doggedly loyal deputy and confidant. A year later, Bertone was at the center of his first great controversy after publishing an essay in *L'Osservatore Romano* that called for all major papal pronouncements to be treated as infallible, and therefore closed to debate. That appeared to include *Humanae Vitae*. Colleagues assumed Bertone would never have floated the idea, seen by critics as an outrageous assertion of new papal authority, without Ratzinger's approval.

Worry about John Paul's health dominated conversations inside the Vatican in 1996. His doctors confirmed that fall that the seventy-six-year-old pope was suffering from Parkinson's disease, a progressively disabling neurological disorder. News organizations speculated over whether the pope, who already had trouble walking and whose left hand trembled constantly, could continue to lead the church.

John Paul II's health crisis came as Ratzinger was about to launch his next, sweeping theological crusade—to reassert Catholicism as the one true church. It was the campaign, above all others, in which he proved himself capable of outrageous misstatement, poor scholarship, and cruelty, and the one that John Paul might have curtailed had he been in better health.

Neither the pope nor Ratzinger acknowledged it publicly, but behind closed doors they disagreed sharply about the value of interfaith dialogue. Although the pope's critics said his stirring words on the subject were too rarely backed up by action, John Paul had been consistent in calling for closer ties between the Catholic Church and other religions, Christian and non-Christian alike. The outrage of Jewish groups over his meeting with Kurt Waldheim was a rare instance in which the pope stumbled in that cause. His passion on the subject was most famously on display in October 1986, when he invited leaders of all the world's major religions to join him for a day of prayer in the northern Italian hill town of Assisi, the birthplace of the beloved thirteenth-century friar St. Francis. The event drew representatives from virtually every non-Catholic Christian church, as well as leaders of a dozen different non-Christian faiths, including Muslims, Jews, Hindus, Shintoists (the Japanese nature-worshipping sect), and Native Americans. The pope's guests included the Dalai Lama, the exiled Tibetan Buddhist leader, who placed a statue of Buddha on the altar of Assisi's most famous church. Ratzinger did not make it known outside the Vatican—since he never wanted to be seen as at odds with the pope—but he had been violently opposed to the Assisi gathering. He viewed it as sacrilege since it allowed pagan worship in a sacred Christian setting.

Ratzinger had never hidden his doubts about the legitimacy of other faiths. There was an extensive record of it, in fact, beginning with his comments in *The Ratzinger Report* in 1984 about the "petrified" practices of Orthodox Christians, followed by his disastrous remarks three years later about the need for Jews to accept Christ as their Savior. He often warned about the "autoerotic spirituality" of Buddhism. As for the world's one billion Hindus, he said their faith promoted the "morally cruel" concept of reincarnation, which he depicted as a "continuous circle of hell."

His campaign to promote the Catholic Church as the only genuine faith was launched in earnest in 1996. In another book-length interview, he made sweeping and insulting characterizations of Islam. It was a religion, he said, that was so rigid in its teachings that it could not be "included in the free realm of pluralistic society." He suggested that Africans should be wary of Islam since, for centuries, Arab Muslims "were at the head of the slave trade and by no means displayed any great regard for the blacks." He added, "The idea that all religions are equal is disproved by the simple facts of history." In a speech that year, he declared that debates over "religious pluralism"—the idea that "one religion is as good as another," as he put it—had replaced liberation theology as "the central problem for the faith."

In the late 1990s, the congregation began drawing up lists of church scholars to be disciplined for dissenting from Ratzinger's views on the subject. And unlike his earlier theological campaigns, in which he singled out one or two high-profile targets as a warning to others, this time there would be several targets, disciplined almost all at once.

In 1997, he announced that the congregation had imposed its ultimate punishment—excommunication—on a Sri Lankan theologian, Father Tissa Balasuriya, who suggested God could communicate through religions other than Christianity. The penalty, seen by many theologians as absurdly punitive, was lifted the next year after Balasuriya signed a document acknowledging "perceptions of error" in his work. In 1998, a Munich theologian, Perry Schmidt-Leukel, was stripped of his Catholic teaching credentials after publishing a book, later considered a classic, that compared Christian and Buddhist views on salvation. That same year, Ratzinger issued a posthumous censure of an Indian Jesuit, Father Anthony de Mello, whose bestselling books blended Eastern and Western spirituality. The congregation accused de Mello, who had died a decade earlier, of promoting the idea that there might be more than one god.

In 1998, Ratzinger launched an investigation that, more than any other in his years at the congregation, would outrage the world's theologians with its heartlessness. It targeted a revered professor at the Gregorian, Father Jacques Dupuis, a seventy-four-year-old Belgian Jesuit who had spent much of his career working with refugees in India. He had just published a book, *Toward a Christian Theology of Religious Pluralism*, in which he argued that since God existed before Jesus, there would be evidence of God in other, even more ancient religions. He urged Catholic missionaries in the developing world to focus less on converting souls and more on dialogue.

He cited Vatican II documents championing the idea that other religions had wisdom to offer Christians.

In a review, O'Collins, Dupuis's colleague at the Gregorian, described the book as a "genuinely magisterial work" that reflected the "profound shift in the Christian understanding of other religions." Cardinal König of Vienna, who had taken on several Vatican assignments in retirement to promote interfaith dialogue, declared the book a "masterwork" that reflected views he often heard from John Paul. The Catholic Press Association of the US named it Book of the Year.

Ratzinger, however, condemned the book—and was prepared to destroy Dupuis's career. The congregation opened its investigation of Dupuis in the spring of 1998. He knew nothing about it until October, when Father Kolvenbach, as head of the Jesuits, received a nine-page letter from Ratzinger that cited "errors and doctrinal ambiguities" so serious that the book "cannot be safely taught." The letter contained a list of purported examples of heresy throughout the book, along with a demand that its author respond in writing.

Dupuis, chronically ill throughout his life, was so physically sickened by

Father Jacques Dupuis, a Belgian Jesuit theologian targeted for punishment by Cardinal Joseph Ratzinger over a book encouraging interfaith dialogue. Dupuis's friends blamed the investigation for his emotional and physical collapse.

news of the letter that he immediately checked himself into a hospital. He looked back on it as the day his life ended. "The joy of living has gone," he said. "I feel like a broken man who can never fully recover from the suspicion that the church—a church which I love and have served during my whole life—has thrust upon me."

He asked O'Collins to defend him in the investigation. O'Collins, then visiting the United States, immediately faxed back: "You have not only my affection and sympathy but my total support." The Australian was flabbergasted when he saw Ratzinger's letter and the detailed list of supposed errors in the book. O'Collins said later he would never have imagined the congregation's work could be so shoddy. "One would have expected basic competence from the CDF in at least correctly reading and interpreting what Dupuis had written."

It was clear to O'Collins that Ratzinger and his deputies had not read the book with even a minimum of care. The congregation accused Dupuis of writing things that were not in the text and failed to understand the meaning of simple words and phrases. Dupuis used the word "distinction" in a reference to the Trinity of Father, Son, and Holy Ghost, which the congregation seemed to think was interchangeable with the word "separation," which might be heresy in reference to "separating" the Trinity. Dupuis was charged with sacrilege in noting that God had characteristics of both a loving father and mother and might be referred to as "Father-Mother" instead of the usual "Father." O'Collins found a transcript of a 1978 speech in which John Paul II had noted that God was "Father and Mother" and had "all the characteristics of fatherhood and motherhood."

O'Collins was shocked most of all that Ratzinger had pursued the investigation for months without any notice to Dupuis. Ratzinger and Dupuis lived only a few miles away from each other in Rome. "The misgivings of the Congregation for the Doctrine of the Faith might have been resolved by a phone call or by a personal invitation to join Cardinal Ratzinger over afternoon tea for a serious face-to-face discussion," O'Collins said.

Over the next two years, as the investigation continued, Dupuis's health collapsed. He was hospitalized again in July 1999. O'Collins was disgusted by the congregation's indifference: "It never occurred to anyone at the congregation that a get-well card, a phone call or even a visit to Dupuis in hospital might be something that Jesus would expect of them." Dupuis heard from Kolvenbach about an encounter with Ratzinger in which the Jesuit leader expressed his worry about Dupuis's health. Ratzinger replied in an annoyed tone that Dupuis's problems were probably all "psychosomatic."

Dupuis's admirers were appalled at the way he was treated. König was so outraged that he decided to speak out. The resulting public dogfight between König and Ratzinger became so heated that it was dubbed "the Battle of the Cardinals" in newspaper headlines across Europe. König's initial protest came in an essay in *The Tablet* in January 1999. He wrote he was distraught for Dupuis: "My heart bleeds when I see such an obvious harm being done." The essay was a direct attack on Ratzinger, accused by König of trying to ruin Dupuis over a book that should be celebrated as a "pioneering achievement." The Austrian cardinal made a broader attack on Ratzinger's congregation as small-minded in its views of non-Western religions, an attitude that was "reminiscent of colonialism and smacks of arrogance."

Ratzinger, who had never been attacked like this by a fellow cardinal, replied in an angry letter in the same magazine. His letter, which expressed "astonishment" about König's criticism, contained several blatant exaggerations, if not outright falsehoods. He suggested König overstated the seriousness of the investigation of Dupuis. "Our action consisted simply in sending some confidential questions to Father Dupuis and nothing more," Ratzinger wrote, ignoring the fact that his office had prepared long, formal lists of supposed heresies in Dupuis's book. Ratzinger denied he had accused Dupuis "of directly or indirectly violating the church's teachings" when in fact the congregation had done precisely that, in almost precisely those words.

König wrote a second, even angrier article for *The Tablet*, in which he accused Ratzinger and his deputies of casually destroying Dupuis's life: "The congregation has hurt Father Dupuis deeply and the shock he received has led to ill-health and depression."

Two years into the investigation, Dupuis was ordered to appear for a face-to-face interrogation by Ratzinger. It was scheduled for Monday, September 4, 2000, and the timing was not coincidental. Ratzinger planned to release a document that same week that would be the Vatican's definitive rejection of the sort of religious dialogue that Dupuis's book endorsed.

O'Collins went with Dupuis to the congregation's palace. The meeting room was so hot and stuffy that both wondered if it was intentional—to make them feel under siege physically, too. The session lasted more than two hours, without the coffee break that would be a normal courtesy at the Vatican.

Dupuis left his defense to O'Collins, who presented Ratzinger with a long written list of the mistakes in the congregation's paperwork on the case. O'Collins noted the many instances in which Dupuis was accused of advancing a theory that appeared nowhere in the book. "He can hardly retract views that he never endorsed!" O'Collins said in exasperation. He then took a larger shot at the work of Ratzinger and his deputies—"We all know that the Congregation for the Doctrine of the Faith has a negative public image"—and proposed a face-saving compromise. He suggested Ratzinger and Dupuis agree on a "positive" joint statement about the value of interfaith dialogue and make no mention of the book: "That would end the affair happily, surprise the media and do some real good."

Ratzinger was insulted and threatened that O'Collins might now come under investigation, too, "since you share the views of Father Dupuis."

In adjourning the meeting, Ratzinger had a strange request. He asked Dupuis if he could help draft the congregation's final report on the investigation. Dupuis was puzzled. Was Ratzinger suggesting he help "improve on a text about my own condemnation?" he asked. Besides, he noted, he had provided Ratzinger with 260 typewritten pages of answers to the congregation's questions over two years; surely Ratzinger could find the appropriate wording in those pages.

The reply stunned O'Collins and horrified Dupuis. Ratzinger said he and his staff had never taken the time to read most of what Dupuis had written in his defense.

"Father Dupuis," Ratzinger said. "You can't expect us to read and study all that material." Two hundred and sixty pages was "just too much."*

The next day, the congregation released a document entitled *Dominus Iesus* (The Lord Jesus), which it billed as its definitive statement on the Vatican's relationship with other faiths. It unleashed what Ratzinger later acknowledged was a "firestorm" of criticism, mainly from the leaders of the world's other great religions. They questioned whether Ratzinger intended to abandon completely the teachings of the Second Vatican Council, when the church announced its hope for closer ties to other faiths, and return the Catholic Church to its old fortress mentality.

---

* Ratzinger did not publicly challenge details of the account of the meeting offered over the years by O'Collins and Dupuis.

Most of the thirty-six-page document was written in the traditionally dense language of the congregation, but its central passages were clear enough. There was only one true religion—Roman Catholicism—and it alone offered the path "to spiritual salvation for all mankind." Worship of Jesus Christ can "exist only in the Catholic Church." Protestants and all other non-Catholic Christian communities "are not churches in the proper sense" and "suffer from defects," while Judaism, Islam, Hinduism, Buddhism, and other non-Christian faiths were "gravely deficient." The "principle of tolerance and respect" promoted by Vatican II had been "manipulated" by dissident theologians to suggest that all religions had equal worth, when they clearly did not. In a broad sense, Ratzinger argued, there was nothing new in this. At Vatican II, the world's bishops had declared Catholicism to be the "one true religion," a phrase that appeared in the council's documents.

The attacks on *Dominus Iesus* began within hours of its release. The Lutheran World Federation, representing fifty-nine million Protestants, expressed "dismay and disappointment" over the decree and said it marked the end of the dialogue begun at Vatican II. The World Council of Churches warned of "tragedy," since the document threatened to drive a permanent wedge between the Vatican and other faiths. The criticism was almost as stinging within the Curia. Cardinal Edward Cassidy of Australia, president of the Council for Promoting Christian Unity, the agency created by John XXIII before Vatican II, said he was alarmed by the document's "insensitive tone." In Milan, Cardinal Martini found it so poorly written it was almost guaranteed to be misunderstood: "It is theologically rather dense, peppered with quotations, and not easy to grasp." Hans Küng described it as "a mixture of medieval backwardness and Vatican megalomania."

Many in the Curia found it impossible to believe the pope endorsed the document, since it so clearly undermined his own views. News reports suggested he was so ill that he approved it without understanding it. He eventually issued a statement confirming he had read and agreed with the decree, although he insisted that "the commitment of the Catholic Church to ecumenical dialogue is irrevocable."

Dupuis was appalled by *Dominus Iesus,* but he did not dare to speak out and make more trouble for himself. His health would not permit it, he said. Ultimately, the congregation's investigation of Dupuis ended when Ratzinger released a document in 2001 that criticized Dupuis's book for "notable ambiguities and difficulties" but did not call for the author to be disciplined. O'Collins said Dupuis, who died in 2004 at the age of eighty-one, never recovered from the emotional torment of the investigation. At his funeral in a chapel in the Gregorian, a fellow Jesuit noted in his eulogy that as a result of Ratzinger's investigation, Dupuis's life became one of "endless sadness."

28

Bergoglio in Exile

THE FIERCE BATTLES over doctrine and papal authority being waged in Rome mostly did not reach Argentina in the 1990s. John Paul II was revered there, his power unquestioned. The Argentine church hierarchy remained decidedly conservative. In 1990, Cardinal Aramburu of Buenos Aires retired at the age of seventy-eight, unrepentant about his friendship with military leaders accused of mass murder. He was succeeded by Archbishop Antonio Quarracino from the nearby city of La Plata, who was nearly as conservative. Quarracino was named a cardinal the following year.

In 1990, Jorge Bergoglio was trying to adjust to a life in exile. He knew his banishment to Córdoba could last for years. He was assigned "cell 5"—a room about twelve feet square, with bare white walls—on the ground floor of the city's Jesuit residence. There was barely enough space for his bed. He shared a communal bathroom, and the inadequate plumbing often meant a cold shower in the morning. His "cell" looked out on a bus stop. He could hear passengers chatter away as they waited for buses that screeched to a halt at all hours.

The purpose of his exile, he knew, was to crush his ego and, through isolation, break what had been his hold on the nation's Jesuit order. Father Victor Zorzín, the order's national leader at the time, urged Bergoglio to see his humiliation as an opportunity for redemption: "Pain can ripen into something else."

He was given few duties, which he found degrading. His mail and phone calls were censored to prevent him from reestablishing contacts in Buenos Aires. His visitors recalled that Bergoglio did not hide his depression. He complained to a friend that he was being treated like "an old piece of furniture." Word spread among Jesuits around the country that he had suffered a nervous breakdown.

Bergoglio's mood lifted slightly after he established a daily routine. He woke up between four thirty and four forty-five a.m. By five, he was washed and dressed. He was often found before dawn in the bathroom, polishing his shoes. The Jesuits in Córdoba admired his extreme frugality. He had, for example, only two pairs of socks. "Why would I need more?" he asked, each day wearing one pair while the other was washed and dried.

He spent much of the day wandering the residence, volunteering his labor. He was often seen collecting dirty laundry and stuffing it into washing machines. At midday, he would arrive in the kitchen to help prepare lunch. He said he found his greatest satisfaction in caring for aging or bedridden priests. Ricardo Spinassi, a lay worker, admired how Bergoglio "had no problem rolling up his sleeves" and washing the bodies of ill, elderly priests when they urinated or soiled themselves. When one monk, a man Bergoglio had known from his days as a novice, was close to death, he placed a mattress next to his bed to pray alongside him through the night.

His desire to serve the poor remained strong. He came to the rescue of a penniless Córdoba woman whose husband had been unfairly imprisoned, finding the money to pay a lawyer who won her husband's freedom. He also helped Spinassi, the lay worker, and his extended, impoverished family. After learning that Spinassi's niece was getting married but that her family had no money for a reception, Bergoglio bought the makings of a small wedding feast and spent much of a day preparing the food himself.

Years later, Bergoglio described his banishment to Córdoba as among the most valuable experiences of his life. Friends agreed he became a far gentler, more tolerant man than they had known before, although that did not mean his ambition had gone away. His Jesuit critics insisted that, in exile, he simply learned new ways of masking what he really wanted. With so much free time in Córdoba, he read constantly, and other Jesuits thought his reading list suggested a man who still saw an important and perhaps historic role for himself. He devoted months, for example, to reading a forty-volume collection of biographies of the popes, written by the

German Ludwig Pastor.* He also read and reread collections of the writings of John Paul II and Ratzinger. In his own writings, Bergoglio began to regularly cite passages from the pope and the cardinal's books, which his critics saw as a calculated effort to flatter the two most powerful men in Rome.

In 1992, Bergoglio was allowed to end his exile. Cardinal Quarracino in Buenos Aires had settled on Bergoglio as his new deputy and convinced John Paul to approve the appointment of Bergoglio as an auxiliary bishop in Flores, the neighborhood of the capital where he was born and raised. Quarracino knew about Bergoglio's reputation for divisiveness in the Jesuits but thought his intelligence and dedication to the poor more than compensated. The cardinal gave his new deputy a nickname: *el Santito*, the Little Saint.

As a Jesuit, Bergoglio should have struggled with a promotion to the church hierarchy but, desperate to end his exile, he readily agreed to become a bishop. The decision was made easier, he said, since he would return to Buenos Aires—and to Flores, no less.

For years to come, his relationship with the Society of Jesus proved impossible to repair. He continued to call himself a Jesuit and write "S.J." after his signature, but the divisions that he had created would linger. His appointment as a bishop "was a relief" to most Argentine Jesuits, said Father Rafael Velasco, a Jesuit critic of Bergoglio's who had once been his colleague. Velasco thought pure ambition explained Bergoglio's decision to step away from the Jesuits and become a bishop and that even then he had designs on much higher office, including even the papacy: "When he could no longer get power inside the Jesuits, he looked outside." It was widely reported that Kolvenbach prepared a written report at the time of Bergoglio's appointment that was a scathing appraisal of his character. If it existed, however, it was never made public.

On June 27, 1992, Bergoglio was formally installed as a bishop at a ceremony in Buenos Aires. He initially chose to live in a Society of Jesus residence in the capital, but many Jesuit priests found his presence disruptive, given the hostility he still faced within the order.

Father Ignacio García-Mata, the new national Jesuit leader, told Bergoglio he would need to live elsewhere.

* Decades later, he denied he made the commitment to read the dense papal biographies with any thought that he might be pope one day. Still, he admitted that "the way things turned out in my life, I must say it served me well" (Pope Francis, *Life*, 129).

"But I'm very comfortable here," Bergoglio replied.

"Jorge," García-Mata said with annoyance, "it's not right for a bishop of Buenos Aires to be living in a Jesuit community."

In a flash of his old arrogance, Bergoglio said he would not leave without a direct order in writing, and so García-Mata obtained a suitable letter from Kolvenbach in Rome. Bergoglio's break with the Jesuits was evident in his occasional trips to the Vatican. Jesuit bishops usually retained close ties to the Society and stayed in the order's dormitories near St. Peter's. Bergoglio stayed elsewhere.

He was one of several auxiliary bishops in Buenos Aires, all of them answering to Quarracino. As a bishop, Bergoglio was entitled to a car and driver, as well as a household staff, but he rejected them and insisted on riding public buses or walking to appointments. He established a reputation for being available to attend to parishioners at all hours and was regularly found in the middle of the night at accident scenes, maternity wards, or funeral homes.

He also earned a reputation for glumness—"the bishop who never smiles"—although parishioners were quick to overlook the sour expression on his face because they so admired his sense of duty and the simplicity of his lifestyle. He cooked his own meals, made his own bed, answered his own phone. He never went on vacation.

By tradition, bishops in Buenos Aires were prominent members of high society, found at banquet tables and glittering charity balls, but Bergoglio rejected that, too. As a bishop, he was a loner, more than at any other time in his life. "He didn't have very many friends," said Father Guillermo Marco, one of his closest aides. "He has always been, I'd say, monkish in his lifestyle. His main relationship is with God." Bergoglio rarely saw his own family, a remarkable thing in Argentina, where family bonds are usually so close. "He didn't even see them at Christmas," Marco remembered.

Bergoglio insisted to colleagues that he remained true to conservative church teachings promoted by John Paul II and Ratzinger and praised both men in his homilies. Even so, as a bishop, he resisted being drawn into detailed debates about doctrine, especially about sexual morality. His relationship with Quarracino was close, which proved awkward, since the cardinal outraged some parishioners with his fiercely conservative views on sex. As the gay-rights movement took hold in Argentina in the 1990s, Quarracino was criticized for his ugly intolerance. In 1994, he said that gay

Cardinal Jorge Bergoglio, who refused a church car and driver, traveling by subway in Buenos Aires in 2008

Argentines should be "locked up in a ghetto" in order to "clean an ignoble stain from the face of society."

Bergoglio was required to overlook dark rumors about church finances—specifically, about Quarracino's spending habits. The cardinal was trailed throughout his career by allegations that he misspent church funds on himself. It related to his love of luxury, especially in his frequent travels to the Vatican. He flew only first-class and insisted on being chauffeured around Rome in a late-model Mercedes limousine. He stayed in plush suites in the finest hotels, as did the two priests who served as his private secretaries and always traveled with him. It would later be revealed that the cardinal's lifestyle was underwritten by a prominent Argentine banking family, the Trussos, whose patriarch had been the country's ambassador to the Vatican. Two of his sons were directors of an Argentine bank, Banco de Crédito Provincial. Over the years, Quarracino had ordered the archdiocese to open large accounts there.

In his first weeks as bishop, Bergoglio was presented with direct evidence of corruption inside the city's church hierarchy. He received a visit from two businessmen "who claimed to be very Catholic" and said they could arrange a $400,000 government grant for church projects. The men explained they had organized similar grants for Bergoglio's predecessors in

Flores. There was a catch, however. Bergoglio was asked to sign a receipt acknowledging the full sum, even though the two middlemen would keep half as a kickback. Bergoglio refused. He was startled to realize that other bishops "had been open to such a corrupt operation." He was about to learn that corruption in the Argentine church went much deeper than that.

AS BISHOP, Bergoglio set aside several days a week to travel around Buenos Aires and stop in parish churches. He frequently filled in to say Mass when a local priest was ill or needed to travel. Father Fernando Giannetti, a priest in the impoverished neighborhood of Mataderos, once home to the city's slaughterhouses, remembered it was startling to encounter "a bishop this humble."

Bergoglio did not call himself a supporter of liberation theology—the term was still too controversial in conservative Argentina—but he now embraced it. In 1996, he supported slum priests who went on a hunger strike in Buenos Aires to protest plans to destroy several blocks of a shanty-town to make way for a new highway. The priests went for almost two weeks without food. Bergoglio convinced Quarracino to join him at the protests, which eventually shamed the government into abandoning the project.

In 1993, Bergoglio was promoted to be Quarracino's vicar general, a post that made him the cardinal's right-hand man, with responsibility for administering parishes across the city. The new assignment threatened to draw him directly into the financial scandals that would engulf Quarracino. In 1996, the cardinal convinced a military pension fund to deposit the equivalent of millions of dollars into accounts at the Trussos' bank, then arranged for the fund's president to attend a papal Mass at the Vatican and meet John Paul. In a string of complicated transactions, the bank convinced the pension fund to underwrite $10 million in loans—money that was supposed to go to Quarracino for use in the archdiocese—but weeks later the bank collapsed, leaving twenty thousand outraged depositors. Many blamed the cardinal for the loss of their life savings. The pension fund asked for its $10 million back, but a panicked Quarracino insisted the archdiocese had never received the money. His chief secretary, a priest, was arrested for fraud. Bergoglio kept his name out of the headlines, which surprised some churchmen, given how close he was to the cardinal.

Quarracino's health collapsed during the scandal. In 1997 he arranged with John Paul II to bypass other candidates and have Bergoglio named "coadjutor" bishop of Buenos Aires, which meant he would replace Quarracino automatically when the cardinal retired or died, and that moment came quickly. Quarracino died of a heart attack in February 1998 at the age of seventy-four.

Bergoglio, sixty-one and suddenly the most powerful churchman in Argentina, said he did not allow himself to become emotional on the day of the cardinal's death. "I didn't have time to feel anything" because there was too much work to be done, especially since the archdiocese was still entangled in the banking scandal.

Many of Bergoglio's old Jesuit critics saw calculated self-promotion in his first decisions as Quarracino's successor, although they welcomed most of what he did. He dealt first with the banking crisis, calling in an international accounting firm to conduct a full audit of the archdiocese. The audit found that Quarracino had involved the church in shady transactions for years. Next, Bergoglio began a campaign to raise his profile by offering himself up to Argentines as their humble servant. He announced he would refuse to live in the palatial archbishop's residence and instead created a small apartment for himself in the administrative headquarters of the archdiocese. Since the heat was shut off on weekends, he used a small electric heater in his bedroom in winter. He continued to prepare his own meals, often boiling up a pot of water for a simple dish of pasta for dinner. He abandoned the elegant high-ceilinged office traditionally used by the archbishop and moved his desk to a smaller office on the same floor.

A new archbishop of Buenos Aires would, by tradition, purchase a new wardrobe of clerical clothing, but Bergoglio refused new robes and asked nuns working in the archdiocese offices to adjust Quarracino's clothes to fit him.

Bergoglio ended the alliance between the church and the nation's political and military leaders. He refused a request from President Carlos Menem, who had been close to Quarracino, to allow the cardinal's body to lay in state in the Casa Rosada, the presidential offices. By tradition, the government paid for Bergoglio to fly to Rome in June for his installation as archbishop, since he was going as a representative of Argentina, and Menem's office dispatched a first-class air ticket. Bergoglio walked to the Casa Rosada personally to insist that it be changed to economy class.

In May, on Argentina's national independence holiday, Menem attended Mass in the cathedral. He faced a chilly reception from the new archbishop.

Bergoglio's homily startled many in the pews, since he seemed to suggest that corrupt, self-interested politicians—including Menem—were failing the poor: "A few are sitting at the table and enriching themselves while the social fabric is being destroyed."

Bergoglio refused early interview requests, though he understood the value of a dramatic news photo. During his first Holy Week as archbishop, he invited photographers to join him at services to mark Holy Thursday, commemorating the Last Supper, when Jesus dined with his apostles a final time and ritually washed their feet. The photographers were summoned to a ward at Buenos Aires's central infectious-diseases hospital, where the ceremony would be held. Days earlier, Bergoglio asked the hospital to gather up twelve patients who were in especially grave condition and who would allow him to wash their feet. Bergoglio was greeted by the patients—men and women, eight of them suffering from AIDS, including a transvestite. He invited them to take a seat as he began the ritual of washing, drying, then kissing their feet, as photographers and television cameras captured the emotional scene. "Everyone was in tears," said Father Andrés Tello, who arranged the ceremony.

Bergoglio insisted he had no further ambitions in the church and that he would end his career in Buenos Aires. As an archbishop, and later as a cardinal, he knew he might someday be offered a post in the Curia, but Bergoglio scoffed at the idea of living in Rome, saying he would "rather die" than work in the Vatican bureaucracy. Compared to his predecessors in Buenos Aires, he never developed close ties to bishops in the Curia, especially to those at the top of it. He later maintained he always had a cordial relationship with Ratzinger and his deputies at the Congregation for the Doctrine of the Faith. But given Ratzinger's strict demands for obedience to traditional doctrine, Bergoglio had reason to avoid unnecessary contacts with the congregation, since he was proving himself a rebel back home.

That was especially true on questions of sexuality. From his early days as archbishop of Buenos Aires, Bergoglio encouraged the city's priests to look the other way when it came to sex and marriage. "The least serious sins are the sins of the flesh," he told them. He urged priests to comfort, not condemn, women who had undergone an abortion, which was a serious crime in Argentina but still common. "That does not mean trivializing abortion," he said. "It's a serious sin. The murder of an innocent. But if there is a sin, pardon must be facilitated."

He ordered priests, in taking confessions about sexual matters, to stop asking for details about a parishioner's sins in the bedroom. He found it appalling that so many priests wanted to hear a checklist of their parishioners' taboo sexual activities, as if God needed to forgive each act, one by one. "Some priests, when they receive confession of a sin of this kind, ask, 'How did you do it? And when did you do it? And for how long?'" he complained. "These questions must stop." He encouraged priests to recognize that parishioners were entitled to enjoy sexual pleasure—that "sex is a good and beautiful thing"—and urged them to see his favorite movie: *Babette's Feast*, a 1987 film about a puritanical nineteenth-century Danish village that comes alive after a mysterious, pleasure-seeking Parisian refugee prepares a lavish banquet. "What you see is the transformation of people who have been 'locked up' in their world."

In 1999, he sought a meeting that a few years earlier would have created a scandal. He asked to see Jerónimo Podestá, the former bishop who resigned in 1967 after falling in love with a married woman. Bergoglio wanted to offer spiritual comfort to Podestá, who had been shunned by the church for almost thirty years and was near death. Bergoglio visited him in the hospital and would telephone his widow weekly for the rest of her life.

Years later, friends suggested it was his tolerance on questions of sexual morality that helped explain the darkest stain on his legacy as archbishop in Buenos Aires: his failure to acknowledge the crimes of pedophile priests. In nearly fifteen years as archbishop, he almost never discussed the subject, even as clerical child-abuse scandals devastated the church elsewhere in the world. On the few occasions he broke his silence, it was to congratulate his archdiocese for protecting the city's children from sexual predators. In a 2010 interview, he appeared to make the astonishing claim that in the dozen years since his appointment, there had not been a single clerical child-abuse case in the city. "It never happened," he declared, insisting he had "zero tolerance" for pedophile priests. He said the central Catholic seminary in Buenos Aires prided itself on a rigorous selection process that filtered out candidates for the priesthood suspected of "perversion."

He recalled he once got a phone call from a bishop outside Buenos Aires who wanted advice about the discovery that a local priest was a pedophile. Bergoglio advised the bishop to deal harshly with the priest and move to defrock him. "Even one Catholic priest doing that is horrible," he said. "If a priest is an abuser, it means he is a sick person."

Years later, child-protection advocates accused Bergoglio of willful blindness, if not much worse, in his failure to recognize that priests under his supervision were abusing children. His claim "it never happened" was, on its face, untrue, since abuse cases occasionally became public, even if they did not result in criminal charges. The most notorious centered on a celebrity priest, Julio Grassi, who had been close to Bergoglio for years. Grassi, a fixture on Argentine television talk shows in promoting his Happy Children Foundation, a charity that provided shelter to homeless youth, was arrested in 2002 on charges that he molested as many as five boys in his care. After a prosecution that dragged on for more than a decade, Grassi was convicted of child abuse and sentenced to fifteen years in prison. A year before Grassi's arrest, a priest in Flores was publicly accused of molesting two girls—one twelve years old, the other thirteen. In 2003, a priest from a neighboring diocese fled to Buenos Aires after admitting to his local bishop that he had sexually abused a fifteen-year-old boy. Bergoglio's office refused to provide prosecutors with information on the whereabouts of the priest—who was in fact living in a vicarage in Flores before he died in 2005 of AIDS. The boy's mother said she went to Buenos Aires to plead to Bergoglio for help and that he refused to see her.

His deputies acknowledged years later that Bergoglio demonstrated an astonishing blind spot on the issue. They said he seemed incapable of acknowledging the truth—that the archdiocese regularly, and secretly, investigated cases in which priests were accused of child molestation.* Under an unwritten policy that predated Bergoglio, the cases were never reported to the police. Instead, priests determined to be pedophiles were sent for psychological treatment before being returned to ministry in a new parish. It was known in Buenos Aires as the *cura geográfica* (geographical cure). In extreme cases, priests were quietly defrocked and dismissed.

Bergoglio was aware of dozens of well-publicized criminal cases brought against child-molesting priests outside Buenos Aires. From news accounts and court filings, the US-based group BishopAccountability.org compiled a list of one hundred priests, monks, and nuns across Argentina who were accused of child sexual abuse during Bergoglio's years in the church hierarchy. He would eventually acknowledge he had been aware in 1994 of a then-secret Vatican investigation of a fellow Argentine bishop, Edgardo Storni, in Santa Fe. Storni was accused of a staggering number of sexual

---

* The exact number of cases was never revealed by the archdiocese, although church officials suggest there were at least several dozen during Bergoglio's tenure.

crimes, including the molestation of forty-seven seminarians. The seven-month investigation was closed without charges after Storni flew to Rome to make a personal appeal to John Paul II, insisting he was innocent. A later police investigation ended in Storni's conviction in 2009 for sexual assault of a teenage boy. He was sentenced to eight years in prison.

THE EXTENT OF Bergoglio's failure to grapple with cases of priestly sexual abuse would not be revealed until years after he departed Buenos Aires. In the meantime, he became celebrated—first across Argentina, then through-out the worldwide Catholic Church—as a bishop of exceptional humility, committed to the Gospels' message to serve the poor. He became famous for his regular visits to the sprawling, and often dangerous, shantytowns of Buenos Aires. He was regularly seen on subway trains and public buses on his way to the slums. Reporters and news photographers followed him on the trips, eager to witness interactions between Argentina's most powerful churchman and the country's most desperate citizens.

By then, the controversy over his legacy in the Dirty War was mostly a distant memory. Even so, as archbishop, he was eager to apologize on behalf of the church for what happened in those dark years. In 1999, he agreed to a request to move the body of Father Mugica, the slum priest murdered in 1974, to a newly built tomb in Villa 31, the shantytown where he had become famous for mobilizing the poor. On the day the remains were transferred, Bergoglio said Mass at the tomb. News coverage of the ceremony caught the eye of one of Argentina's best-known investigative journalists, Horacio Verbitsky, known to colleagues as *el Perro* (the Dog) for his doggedness in pursuing a scoop.[*] He was fascinated by the new arch-bishop, who seemed willing to make enemies as he set a new course for the Argentine church, and decided that Bergoglio's past would be the target of his next great reporting project. Initially, the archbishop told Verbitsky he would cooperate, since he had nothing to hide. It was a decision he would come to regret.

---

[*] Verbitsky, whose unlikely surname was explained by his Russian-Jewish immigrant grandparents, had a controversial past. As a youth, he was a leftist guerrilla in the Mon-toneros and was indicted after the Dirty War for involvement in a 1976 terrorist bombing in which twenty-three people died. The charges, which he denied, were dismissed in 2007 because they fell outside the statute of limitations.

IN FEBRUARY 2001, Bergoglio was called to Rome for his installation to the College of Cardinals, an honor that had been expected given the importance of his archdiocese. Traditionally, a newly named Argentine cardinal took a large group of family and wealthy benefactors to the Vatican for the ceremony in St. Peter's, but Bergoglio insisted he go by himself. He asked friends to give the money they would have spent on the trip to the poor.

He stayed in a simple guesthouse not far from Vatican City. On the day of the ceremony, he rose as usual at four thirty to pray. Most churchmen would have arranged a car and driver for such a momentous occasion, but Bergoglio walked to St. Peter's. Other bishops being installed as cardinals that day had spent the previous week being outfitted for sumptuous new scarlet robes at Gammarelli, the famed ecclesiastical tailors. Bergoglio wore robes that had belonged to Quarracino.

The installation of 44 new cardinals, a record for a single day, increased the voting membership of the College of Cardinals to 135, which John Paul II grudgingly acknowledged was a violation of the official limit of 120 set by church law. The ailing, eighty-year-old pope seemed to know this would be his last opportunity to shape the group that would choose his successor. The new cardinals were mostly identified as conservatives, although a handful were notably progressive, including Walter Kasper and Karl Lehmann of Germany.

Bergoglio knew many of the other men honored at the ceremony. Ten were fellow Latin Americans. He was pleased to see his old friend Cardinal Martini, a fellow Jesuit, who introduced Bergoglio to Kasper and Lehmann. Bergoglio was told in confidence that all three were members of a small group of reform-minded bishops who had begun meeting annually in Switzerland.

That fall, Bergoglio was given his first assignment by the Vatican—to help organize a synod, the tenth since Vatican II, which would focus on the role of bishops in the church. Cardinal Edward Egan of New York was named the synod's rapporteur, which meant he would set the agenda and determine who spoke. A stern defender of Catholic orthodoxy, he made clear he would not allow a freewheeling debate, certainly not one that might upset the pope. Bergoglio was named Egan's deputy.

The arrangement came undone with the terrorist attacks in New York and Washington, DC, on September 11, 2001. Egan attended the synod's opening session, then went home to deal with his shattered city. Bergoglio was left to run the synod and impressed fellow bishops with his humility and quiet, efficient management style. His leadership was all the more valued because John Paul II, who attended the meetings, seemed so ill and unfocused. The four-week synod ended without any substantial recommendation for change, which was just as the pope had seemed to want it. Nonetheless, many bishops left Rome so impressed by Bergoglio that they began to promote him as a possible successor to John Paul. Late that year the Italian magazine *L'Espresso* reported that "the thought of having Bergoglio return to Rome as the successor of St. Peter has begun to spread with growing intensity. The Latin American cardinals are increasingly focused on him."

Bergoglio needed to return home quickly. At the time of the synod, the Argentine economy was nearing one of its periodic collapses, which set off rioting in the streets of Buenos Aires, leaving more than twenty people dead. The country's centrist president, Fernando de la Rúa, would be forced out of office within weeks. Halfway through a four-year term, he came to office pledging to end the corruption that was rampant under Menem, his Peronist predecessor. Instead, there was more economic chaos, with the currency devalued by 40 percent in a matter of days. Unemployment was close to 50 percent. Looting emptied supermarkets, and there was alarm over the possibility of widespread food shortages.

The police and military responded with brutality, some of which Bergoglio could see from his third-floor window in the archdiocese building. In a series of public statements, he announced that demonstrators were right to protest the government's corruption and mismanagement: "We bishops are sick of systems that produce poor people for the church to look after." He accused business leaders of "rapacity" in their treatment of their poor countrymen.

The economic devastation left the church as the only large institution capable of helping an increasingly desperate public, and Bergoglio stepped in—in ways that would quickly burnish his reputation, especially among those who had rejected the church during the Dirty War. He mobilized the 186 parishes of Buenos Aires, instructing the city's priests to go to the streets to search for people short of food. The relief effort caused many to re-embrace their faith. Two years later, opinion polls showed that the share of Argentines identifying themselves as Catholics had jumped from 83 to 90 percent, representing hundreds of thousands of newly committed believers. Bergoglio deserved much of the credit.

29

The Crisis in Boston

I N APRIL 2000, Ratzinger agreed to a secret meeting at the Vatican. It had been requested by seventeen bishops from English-speaking countries. Both sides agreed on the need for confidentiality, given the subject. The four-day meeting was not held in the Holy Office palace, since it was outside the central Vatican security perimeter, which meant the bishops' comings and goings might be seen. Instead, it was held inside the perimeter in the guesthouse used by the pope for visiting dignitaries.

The bishops had gone to Rome to insist that Ratzinger deal with the explosion of cases around the world in which priests were accused of molesting children. They complained that the Vatican gave them no direction, apart from a general instruction that pedophile priests be disciplined within the church and not turned over to the police. Bishop Philip Wilson of Wollongong, Australia, who organized the meeting, spoke on behalf of the others when he said it was infuriating to be given so little instruction—and out of character for Ratzinger, who for nearly two decades had inundated the bishops with explicit directions on how they must deal with everything else.

Ratzinger listened patiently but mostly allowed other Curia cardinals in the meeting to reply on his behalf. The visiting bishops were dumbfounded as one of Ratzinger's closest allies, Cardinal Dario Castrillón Hoyos of Colombia, the head of the Congregation for the Clergy, suggested they were overreacting. A certain number of child molesters was only to be expected in an institution as large as the priesthood, he insisted. The problem was being exaggerated by irresponsible journalists, especially in the United States, he said. These were matters that should be "kept within the family."

Bishop Wilson, appalled by this attempt to play down the crisis, then spoke up to reveal something that came as a shock to the others. He said he understood there was a secret Vatican document that gave Ratzinger direct responsibility for investigating cases in which priests were accused of child molestation. Wilson was referring to the 1962 decree written by Cardinal Ottaviani that called for all allegations of priestly sex abuse to be reported to the agency now called the Congregation for the Doctrine of the Faith. The Australian said he understood the document was distributed to the world's bishops in the 1960s but was treated as so confidential that its existence had largely been forgotten outside Rome.

Ratzinger stiffened at mention of the document but grudgingly acknowledged that Wilson was right—dealing with priestly child abuse was the congregation's duty.* The meeting ended with Ratzinger's promise to act on the bishops' complaints. The following April, he issued a letter to the world's bishops to clarify once and for all that his congregation had ultimate authority in investigations of clerical sex abuse. He ordered that paperwork for all abuse cases be forwarded to Rome immediately, so that his staff could decide how they should be investigated. The letter ordered the cases to continue to be kept secret within the church, which many bishops took as an explicit order not to report offenders to the police.

In years to come, Ratzinger often dissembled, in ways that could be easily documented, about his failure to deal with the crisis. He would claim his 2001 letter was proof that "I immediately took matters in hand when they came to me" and that "this task had the highest priority for the church." With each passing year, however, there was new evidence—often in the form of confidential documents Ratzinger had signed—to show that one of two things was true: either he suffered from such a faulty memory that he did not remember the grisly details of sex crimes against literally thousands of children, or he was lying. That included several cases in which Ratzinger knew that bishops and even cardinals had been credibly accused of molesting children.

By 2001, for example, there had still been no church investigation of Cardinal Groër in Austria, despite clear-cut evidence he had abused scores,

---

* Ratzinger's defenders would later insist that the 1962 document did not give him sole, unquestioned responsibility for investigating priestly child molestation and was meant to focus instead on cases in which priests solicited sex, with an adult or a child, in a confessional. That defense was undercut by an explicit statement in the document, *Crimen Sollicitationis* (Crime of Solicitation) that the congregation was charged with investigations of sexual abuse of "youths of either sex," regardless of whether it took place in a confessional.

Father Marcial Maciel of Mexico, founder of the Legion of Christ, being blessed by Pope John Paul II in Rome in November 2004 despite extensive evidence dating back decades of Maciel's sexual abuse of children

if not hundreds, of boys and young men. Many Austrians were disgusted when after Groër's death in 2003, John Paul praised him as a churchman entitled to "the eternal reward that the Lord promised to his faithful servants."

In January 2001, the pope played host at a ceremony in Rome to honor Father Maciel on the sixtieth anniversary of the Legion of Christ. Maciel, who videotaped the ceremony to use in fundraising appeals, was seated near the pope throughout the event, which was attended by more than twenty thousand people. In his remarks, John Paul praised his "beloved" friend Maciel as a "courageous messenger of the Gospel." Ratzinger did nothing to try to stop the ceremony even though, at the time, he had been aware for years of credible reports that Maciel was a serial child molester. In the United States, the abuse allegations had been public knowledge since 1997, when the *Hartford Courant*, the largest newspaper in Connecticut, where the Legion had its US headquarters, published articles that documented allegations by nine men who said they had been sexually abused as boys by Maciel. The *Courant* articles brought no public response from the Vatican. The following year, three of Maciel's victims flew to Rome and retained a lawyer, an Austrian woman who specialized in church law, to press Ratzinger to act. She organized a meeting with one of the cardinal's deputies, who listened as the three men detailed the trauma of Maciel's abuse. Four months later, the lawyer reported welcome news: the congregation had decided to investigate. Another year of silence followed, however. A Mexican bishop who wanted to support the three victims, Carlos Talavera Ramírez of the city of Veracruz, traveled to Rome in 2000 to confront Ratzinger and ask why the investigation had stalled. Talavera returned home defeated. He suggested to the three victims that, if there had ever really been an investigation, it was over. The cardinal, he said, praised Maciel as "a man who has done so much good for the church" and whose friendship with the pope meant an investigation would not be "prudent." Ratzinger told the Mexican bishop he questioned whether one of Maciel's central accusers was really "trustworthy."

BY 2002, the 1.8 million members of the Catholic archdiocese of Boston had grown used to regular scandals involving pedophile priests. None was more horrifying than that of Father James Porter of Fall River, Massachusetts, who pleaded guilty in 1993 to molesting dozens of children and was sentenced to eighteen years in prison. Prosecutors revealed that local bishops had known since the 1960s that Porter was a pedophile yet, rather than defrock him, tried to hide his crimes by moving him from parish to parish. At the time of the guilty plea, Cardinal Law of Boston decried the "media circus" in the case and called for heavenly retribution against news organizations, especially *The Boston Globe*, the city's largest newspaper. "By all means, we call down God's power on the media, particularly the *Globe*."

A decade later, frustration over the church's failure to grapple with the crisis of clerical sexual abuse finally boiled over around the world, beginning in Boston. In January 2002, the *Globe* published the first of a series of articles, based on court documents, that revealed how Cardinal Law and his deputies covered up for dozens of child-molesting clerics in the Boston archdiocese, shielding them from law enforcement. The records showed that Law routinely tried to comfort pedophile priests and silence their victims. Several articles centered on the cardinal's effort to protect Father John Geoghan, who had a well-documented history, inside the church, of child rape.* The documents showed that shortly after Law arrived in Bos-

---

* *Globe* reporters acknowledged that much of their early reporting, especially about the Geoghan case, was built in part on work published the year before by Kristen Lombardi, a reporter for *The Boston Phoenix*, a weekly newspaper.

ton in 1984, he granted Geoghan's request to move to a new parish, even though the cardinal knew Geoghan was a sexual predator who had been removed from other parishes for child abuse. In one earlier assignment, Geoghan acknowledged molesting seven boys from a single family. Archdiocese records showed that Law often sent bizarrely affectionate notes to Geoghan and other priests who admitted their crimes. In 1996, the cardinal told Geoghan, who by then had already confessed to molesting scores of boys, that "yours has been an effective life of ministry," even if it had been "sadly impaired by illness." In 2003, Geoghan was murdered in prison after his conviction the year before for molesting a ten-year-old boy.

The *Globe* articles turned Law into the villainous face of what became a national, and then a global, scandal. Several articles targeted Ratzinger for blame, given evidence that his congregation had long been aware of some of the worst Boston cases. Within months, thousands of sexual-abuse lawsuits, demanding billions of dollars in damages, were filed against 180 Catholic dioceses in the United States. In 2002, current and former bishops in eighteen American cities—including Phoenix, Arizona; Palm Beach, Florida; and Lexington, Kentucky—were accused in court documents and news reports of being sexual predators. In most of those cases, the alleged victims were children at the time of their abuse.

In May, Archbishop Weakland of Milwaukee, long seen as a voice for progressive Catholics, stepped down after admitting he made a $450,000 payment with church funds to silence a man who accused him of sexual assault. The bishop denied the assault but acknowledged a consensual sexual relationship with the man two decades earlier. There was a similar explosion of cases outside the US. In the pope's homeland, his old friend Archbishop Paetz of Poznań resigned in March over charges he had been molesting seminarians for years. In South America, bishops in Argentina and Paraguay resigned after public allegations that they groped young men and boys. Late that year, Archbishop George Pell of Sydney, Australia, faced what would be the first of several public allegations of molesting boys.

In a letter to the world's priests in March 2002, the pope referred to the "dark shadow of suspicion" cast over the church because of the revelations in Boston, but he offered no solution beyond prayer. Ratzinger largely disappeared in those weeks. He turned away interview requests and avoided large church gatherings in Rome. He was not eager to acknowledge what others in the church had realized—that he, more than anyone apart from the pope, had been responsible for combatting priestly sex abuse, and he had mostly ignored it.

In April, recognizing the crisis that began in Boston was spinning out of control, the pope summoned all thirteen cardinals of the United States, including Law, to an emergency meeting in Rome. The two-day gathering was held behind closed doors and ended inconclusively. The Americans said the pope was wary of any dramatic policy change given his experience in Poland, where priests were smeared by the Communist government with false allegations of sex abuse. Still, Cardinal Theodore McCarrick of Washington, DC, who emerged as spokesman for the American delegation, was convinced the pope would eventually approve a tough response to the crisis. *The New York Times* reported that the choice of McCarrick as a spokesman made sense since he was "relatively untainted by the sexual abuse scandals," an assertion that would prove horribly wrong.

That spring, as Ratzinger maintained his silence, others in the Curia launched an aggressive campaign to deny the Vatican had any responsibility for the scandals in the US and to put the blame instead on the sexual decadence of Americans, especially homosexuals. Archbishop Julián Herranz of Spain, who ran the Vatican agency that investigated misconduct by Curia officials, delivered a widely publicized speech in which he blamed the scandals on the climate of "exaggeration, financial exploitation and nervousness in the United States." American news organizations, he said, had "sullied the image of the Catholic Church and the Catholic priesthood." Herranz said he had personally concluded that pedophilia was a "concrete form of homosexuality." Ratzinger's former deputy Bertone, named archbishop of Genoa in 2002, gave an interview in which he offered his "well-founded suspicion" that Americans were falsely claiming to be victims of priestly sex abuse so they could "make money through civil litigation."

In a meeting with reporters in November, Ratzinger finally stepped forward to defend his record and to argue that he too was a victim. He charged that he had been defamed in a campaign led by the *Globe* and other American news organizations: "One comes to the conclusion that it is intentional, manipulated—a desire to discredit the church." He claimed the extent of priestly child molestation was wildly exaggerated, and that priests were no more likely to abuse children than doctors, lawyers, or bankers. Citing no source, he stated—apparently as fact—that "less than 1 percent" of priests were child molesters. Richard Sipe, the psychotherapist whose landmark studies suggested that at least 4 percent of American priests sexually abused children, told reporters that Ratzinger was "making up his numbers."

After 2002, Ratzinger was regularly named as a defendant in lawsuits brought by child-abuse victims in the US and Europe. In a project begun for the British newspaper *The Guardian*, the former UN war-crimes judge Geoffrey Robertson sought to determine if the cardinal was criminally liable for covering up the crimes of child-molesting priests. The project resulted in a book, in which Robertson concluded that Ratzinger could be charged with crimes against humanity since his "shameful and scandalous" inaction over twenty years meant that thousands of children became victims of pedophiles who could have been stopped.

In December 2002, Cardinal Law resigned and moved to Rome, just ahead of a Massachusetts state grand-jury subpoena, which he ignored. The pope found a prestigious new assignment for Law, who was named to administer a beloved Roman church. On the day of Law's departure from Boston, Cardinal McCarrick released a statement: "Cardinal Law accomplished many good things that should not be forgotten in the sad turmoil of this terrible scandal." It was a moment for the church to "rededicate itself to the protection of children." It would be several more years before McCarrick's hypocrisy was revealed—how the churchman who liked to be known as "Uncle Ted" had shattered the lives of the many boys and young men he molested.

THE VATICAN ACKNOWLEDGED decades later that John Paul II received his first explicit warnings about McCarrick in 1999 and that he dismissed them. That September, Cardinal John O'Connor of New York, then seventy-nine, underwent surgery to remove a brain tumor. It proved to be malignant, and his surgeons warned him that he might have only weeks to live. He took the news stoically and told his staff he wanted to get his affairs in order quickly. He had one task, above all others, that he needed to complete: he wanted to warn the pope about the danger of a "grave scandal" if he promoted then-Archbishop McCarrick of Newark, New Jersey, to any higher post.

O'Connor's letter, which remained secret in the Vatican's archives for two decades, was dated October 28, when the cardinal was at home recuperating from his final surgery. At the top of the first page were the words, in bold type: "HIGHLY PERSONAL AND CONFIDENTIAL."

"This is an extremely difficult letter for me to write," he began. But he said he felt compelled to act after hearing from the pope, during a meeting in Rome that summer, that McCarrick was in line to be named a cardinal and promoted to lead a large archdiocese. "With deep regret, I would have to recommend very strongly against such a promotion."

He listed what he knew of the allegations against McCarrick, including accounts from seminarians in New Jersey who were invited to dinner parties at the bishop's residence, then persuaded to share his bed at night. McCarrick, he wrote, was also well-known as the host of weekend parties at his beach house on the Jersey Shore: "The arrangement was for seven seminarians, six of whom shared the guestrooms and one of whom shared the bed with the archbishop."

O'Connor could not prove McCarrick molested any of those young men, although he was aware of a priest who sought psychiatric care after alleging he had been "victimized" by McCarrick. The psychiatrist, O'Connor wrote, "seemed certain of the validity of these charges." O'Connor enclosed several anonymous letters he had received that made more explicit allegations against McCarrick. The cardinal's letter was sent first to the papal nuncio in Washington, Archbishop Gabriel Montalvo, who then dispatched it to Rome along with a note saying he agreed. A promotion for McCarrick threatened a "scandal of great proportions," the nuncio warned.

John Paul refused to accept what he was reading. He liked McCarrick and was grateful to the archbishop for establishing the Papal Foundation, a US-based charity created in 1988 that raised millions of dollars a year to be spent at the pope's discretion. John Paul knew there would soon be an opening for a new cardinal in Washington, DC, and he thought McCarrick would be a good fit. So rather than accepting O'Connor's allegations, the pope asked deputies to conduct a discreet survey of other American bishops who knew McCarrick. Most praised him without qualification, but two bishops in New Jersey acknowledged that they knew about the abuse allegations and that they were serious. One, Edward Hughes of the diocese of Metuchen, wrote that he knew a young priest who had been a victim of "sexual aggression" by McCarrick. "It would be unwise to consider the archbishop for any promotion," Hughes wrote.

On July 4, Archbishop Giovanni Battista Re, a Curia bureaucrat who

US Cardinal Theodore McCarrick of Washington, DC (right), receives
the blessing of Pope John Paul II at the Vatican, February 23, 2001. The
pope named McCarrick a cardinal despite repeated warnings from other
American bishops that he was a sexual predator.

was about to be promoted to lead the Congregation for Bishops, wrote
a memo to the pope warning against McCarrick's promotion, since "the
accusations against him, even if unfounded, could surface."

Through a friend in the Curia, McCarrick got wind of O'Connor's
letter—and panicked. He wrote a desperate letter to the pope in which he
said he was "bewildered" by O'Connor's allegations: "I have made mistakes
and may have sometimes lacked in prudence, but in the seventy years of
my life, I have never had sexual relations with any person, male or female,
young or old, cleric or lay. Nor have I ever abused another person."

The letter convinced the pope that McCarrick was an innocent man. In
October, John Paul signed documents confirming McCarrick as the archbishop of Washington, DC. He was named a cardinal the following year.
Before leaving Newark, McCarrick ordered his staff to gather up his personnel files, which he took to Washington, never to be seen again.

RATZINGER HAD HOPED his May 2001 letter to the world's bishops would
be seen as proof he took the clerical sex-abuse crisis seriously. That Decem-

ber, however, an investigation by the *National Catholic Reporter* revealed his role, over several years, in blocking any investigation of the pedophilia allegations against Father Maciel. Other news reports in 2001 questioned Ratzinger's failure to act on evidence of the rampant sexual abuse of nuns by priests in the developing world. The problem was dire in parts of Africa ravaged by AIDS; nuns became sexual targets because they were seen as free from the deadly disease.

The Boston scandal erupted the next year. In July 2002, with Ratzinger's approval, the US bishops' conference appointed an independent review board to study the crisis. Its first chairman, Frank Keating, was the former Republican governor of Oklahoma. When he took the assignment, Keating, a devout Catholic, predicted in interviews that several American bishops would be forced to resign because of their mishandling of child-abuse cases. A year later, it was Keating who stepped down. In resigning, he alleged that American bishops acted like "La Cosa Nostra" in hiding information from the investigation. A year after that, his successor, Illinois state judge Anne Burke, accused US bishops of "backsliding" in their commitment to protect children from pedophiles.

In 2004, a study prepared for the bishops' conference proved the child-abuse crisis was far more dire than the American church—or Ratzinger—had admitted. The study, by the John Jay College of Criminal Justice in New York City, revealed that at least 10,600 American children, 80 percent of them male, had reported sexual abuse by priests since the 1950s. The researchers estimated that about forty-four hundred priests, roughly 4 percent of the nation's priests in those same years, had molested minors. The report made clear that the Vatican had never approved the resources needed to deal with the problem. In 2001, Ratzinger assembled a preposterously small staff—about ten investigators—to deal with the thousands of sex-abuse cases that began to flood into the congregation each year. By comparison, there was a staff of almost a hundred investigators in the Vatican agency that vetted candidates for sainthood.

At the time, Ratzinger had other reasons to feel under siege. He faced a surprisingly public challenge in Rome from a new, charismatic German rival: Walter Kasper. After a decade as bishop of Rottenburg, Kasper was summoned to the Vatican by John Paul in 1999. In Germany, Kasper had continued to express liberal views on doctrine, the sort that would normally block a promotion under John Paul, but the pope was always willing to make an exception for Kasper, given his brilliance and his charm. He was asked to lead the Council for Promoting Christian Unity, the agency created by John XXIII to encourage dialogue between the Vatican and other faiths. In 2001, Kasper was made a cardinal.

He was still smarting from his confrontation with Ratzinger in the early 1990s, when German bishops had been refused permission to give Communion to divorced Catholics, and he came to the Vatican girding for a fight.

As he prepared to take up his new post in Rome, Kasper set a trap to draw Ratzinger into a showdown. He published an essay in an obscure German theology journal that effectively accused Ratzinger of upending Vatican II by trying to restore all power to Rome. Under Ratzinger's leadership of the Congregation for the Doctrine of the Faith, Kasper argued, the concept of "collegiality"—power sharing—embraced at the council had mostly been abandoned. The idea that bishops outside Rome had their own authority had been reduced by Ratzinger to a "naked fiction." Kasper's choice of the little-known journal appeared strategic. Had he published his essay in a large newspaper, he could have been accused of an unseemly public attack.* His friends said he calculated that, while the journal might be obscure, Ratzinger would still see it—and fire back. And he was right. Ratzinger read the article, became enraged, and replied in an essay in the *Frankfurter Allgemeine Zeitung*, one of Germany's most prestigious newspapers. He suggested Kasper was engaged in "theological fanaticism."

The debate was on, and Kasper responded in a similarly public forum, with an essay in the influential US-based Jesuit magazine *America*. The essay was, by standards of the Curia, ferocious in its criticism. He portrayed Ratzinger as dishonest—"he badly misrepresents and mischaracterizes my positions"—and painfully out of touch with the average Catholic. He accused Ratzinger of cold-bloodedness, of treating the church's problems from a "purely abstract and theological point of view." Ratzinger, even more incensed, accepted the magazine's offer of space to reply. His counterattack dripped with sarcasm. He described his shock that "so great a theologian as Walter Kasper" could make baseless, defamatory allegations against him, and said Kasper's central argument about the powers of local bishops "makes no sense."

---

* Kasper knew that Cardinal König of Austria had been criticized for attacking Ratzinger the year before in the pages of *The Tablet*, which was widely read in the Vatican.

Kasper denied any hidden motive in such a frontal attack on Ratzinger, then being so widely promoted as John Paul's obvious successor. The timing raised dark suspicions among Ratzinger's friends, however. Years later, they still wondered if, on the eve of Kasper's arrival in Rome, this had been a not-so-thinly-veiled declaration by the charming, charismatic German bishop of his own candidacy for the papacy—and, if not that, a de facto plea that the next bishop of Rome be someone other than his rigidly conservative countryman Joseph Ratzinger.

30

The Saint Factory

AT THE END of his papacy, John Paul II had few higher priorities than to speed up the work of the Congregation for the Causes of Saints, the Vatican agency mocked by cynical Italian bishops in the Curia as *la fabbrica dei santi*—the saint factory.*

John Paul saw the naming of saints as an important tool to inspire the faithful, so he canonized more saints, 482 of them, than all his predecessors combined dating back five centuries. At the time of his death, another eight hundred candidates were in the pipeline after he had "beatified" them, an initial step in the process. (The exact number of Catholic saints can never be known, since records were kept only after the sixteenth century, but scholars believe the church has probably canonized a total of between three thousand and four thousand over time.)

In 1983, John Paul eased the centuries-old rules for making saints. Previously, the Vatican needed to document two physical miracles that could be credited to a candidate. The new rules dropped the number of miracles required in some cases, especially for martyrs. The pope also streamlined

---

* The canonization of saints dates back to the early history of the church. For centuries, it was overseen by local bishops, without Vatican involvement, but came under papal control in the twelfth century. The procedure today has three central steps. First, a sitting pope identifies a candidate for sainthood and asks for a review by the Curia agency that in 2022 was renamed the Dicastery for the Causes of Saints. The candidate is given the title of "venerable." In most cases, if a candidate is found worthy and can be credited with a scientifically inexplicable miracle, he or she is declared "beatified," or "blessed." The dicastery then begins a final investigation that, if a second miracle is verified, leads to a recommendation to the pope that the candidate be "canonized" as a saint. The pope can accept or reject the recommendation.

the process by effectively shutting down the office of the so-called Devil's Advocate, which searched for derogatory information about candidates to determine if they truly deserved the honor.

Most of his nominations were noncontroversial—devout Catholics who had demonstrated "heroic virtue," as church law required—but some were preposterous, men and women who were neither heroic nor especially virtuous. They were chosen, it was clear, because they represented conservative Catholic teachings or organizations that John Paul wanted to promote. In 2002, he declared sainthood for Josemaria Escriva, the Opus Dei founder, only twenty-seven years after his death—lightning fast by the standards of the process. The pope insisted on Escriva's sainthood despite testimony about the Spaniard's abusive treatment of subordinates and his alleged anti-Semitism, as well as his ties to the dictator Franco. John Paul also declared sainthood that year for a mystical Italian friar known as Padre Pio, who developed a cultlike following before his death in 1968. He became famous in Italy after exhibiting stigmata—bleeding wounds on his hands and feet that mirrored Jesus's on the cross. John Paul insisted on his canonization despite Vatican reports suggesting Pio was a fraud whose wounds were self-inflicted. There was also evidence he violated his celibacy vows with women followers. In 2004, John Paul beatified the Austro-Hungarian emperor Charles I, even though some historians described the emperor as a war criminal who had authorized the use of poison gas in World War I.

It had been rare for dead popes to become saints—there had been only five in a millennium—but John Paul II changed that, too. He was fixated on granting sainthood to a pair of archconservative predecessors: Pius IX, the nineteenth-century pope responsible for the doctrine of papal infallibility, and Pius XII, whose public silence about the Holocaust had stirred up such a fierce debate after his death. The campaign for Pius XII stalled in 1999 after publication of *Hitler's Pope*, a best-selling biography that alleged he was motivated by anti-Semitism in appeasing the Nazis. Sainthood for Pius IX was just as complicated, given his indisputable, flagrant anti-Semitism—he confined Rome's Jews to the Ghetto and effectively kidnapped a Jewish boy he raised as his son—and his dictatorial, antimodern pontificate.

John Paul failed to promote other, more clearly worthy candidates for sainthood, apparently because they were seen as too progressive. He turned aside constant pleas on behalf of Archbishop Romero. He was also in no hurry to canonize John XXIII, his most beloved modern predecessor, or any other hero of Vatican II. For years, the Congregation for the Causes of

Saints refused to act on John's candidacy because it could find no evidence of miracles credited to him—a strange argument given how flimsy claims of saintly miracles often were. (Escriva was sainted on the basis of a Spanish doctor's claim he had been cured of a skin disorder by praying to the memory of the Opus Dei founder; some of the doctor's colleagues said his skin problems might simply have gone away with time.)

In 2000, there was newfound interest in canonizing John XXIII, since John Paul's deputies realized it might ease the way for a more controversial candidate—Pius IX. Sainthood for the pair became a package deal, and that September John Paul proclaimed his "great joy" at their simultaneous beatification. The idea of sainthood for Pio Nono immediately drew protests from the Israeli government, which expressed "deep sorrow" over canonization of a nineteenth-century pope who described Jews as "dogs."

At the time, there was an aggressive, if private, campaign for sainthood for another controversial churchman—Father Maciel of the Legion of Christ. In 2000, Maciel turned eighty and announced to deputies that he would be worthy of canonization after death. He wanted the Legion to press his case, just as Opus Dei had for Escriva. The swirling reports about Maciel's pedophilia suggested the idea was ludicrous, but the Legion was not deterred, especially since its founder continued to enjoy enthusiastic displays of support from the pope.

As part of the campaign, the Legion organized a roster of Catholic celebrities willing to make statements of support for Maciel, a list that included opera singer Plácido Domingo, Florida governor Jeb Bush, US senator Rick Santorum of Pennsylvania, and Professor Mary Ann Glendon of Harvard Law School. In 2002, Glendon, the US ambassador to the Vatican under President George W. Bush, described Maciel as a man of "radiant holiness" who had been defamed by "irresponsible journalists."* Father Richard Neuhaus, editor of the conservative religious-affairs magazine *First Things*, announced that he had conducted a "scrupulous examination of the claims and counterclaims" about Maciel's alleged child molestation and "I have arrived at a moral certainty that the charges are false and malicious."

Maciel also stepped up an effort to buy goodwill among bishops in Rome, a pattern established after his hospitalization for narcotics abuse in the 1950s. During his papacy, John Paul II did nothing to crack down

* Glendon was harshly critical of *The Boston Globe* for its Pulitzer Prize–winning coverage of the clerical child-abuse scandal in 2002. She said awarding the prize to the *Globe* was like "giving the Nobel Peace Prize to Osama bin Laden."

on a centuries-old practice that allowed Curia bishops to accept large cash gifts. Many came to depend on the money, since it allowed them comforts they could not otherwise afford on a Vatican salary. Maciel's gifts to Curia bishops also included lavish feasts and other celebrations. The Legion was famous in Rome for distributing Christmas hampers that contained bottles of vintage wine and enormous Spanish cured hams. In the 1970s, Maciel paid for the renovation of the Vatican apartment of Cardinal Eduardo Pironio, an Argentine who led the congregation that oversaw the Legion.

Maciel was especially generous with Bishop Dziwisz, John Paul II's private secretary, and Cardinal Sodano, the secretary of state.[*] Legion officials eventually confirmed that Dziwisz received an envelope stuffed with thousands of dollars in cash each time he arranged for Legion members to attend the pope's seven a.m. Mass. The extent of Maciel's generosity with Sodano, his most powerful defender in the Curia, would never be determined with certainty. Within the Legion, it was known that the cardinal was paid thousands of dollars each time he spoke before the order's members, which happened regularly, and was given an additional ten thousand dollars at Christmas. The Legion organized banquets in his honor, including one for two hundred family members when he was named a cardinal in 1991. Sodano's family capitalized on his name in doing business with the church. In the 1990s, his nephew Andrea, an engineer often criticized by Italian construction companies for shoddy work, was hired by Maciel as an architectural consultant for the Legion's new university in Rome. He also dropped his uncle's name in obtaining church contracts in the US. He was drawn into a scandal in New York City in which a thirty-year-old Italian con man named Raffaello Follieri—a favorite of the city's tabloids because of his glamorous girlfriend, the Hollywood actress Anne Hathaway—pursued real-estate deals with the American church. According to the Justice Department, which obtained Follieri's guilty plea on charges of swindling investors out of millions of dollars, Andrea Sodano received at least $365,000 from Follieri for "engineering studies" and other services during a single two-month period in 2005. The cardinal's nephew, who was not criminally charged in the case, insisted he had done legitimate consulting work for Follieri.

The pudgy, white-haired Cardinal Sodano, the son of a member of the

---

[*] The extent of Maciel's gift giving, especially to Dziwisz and Sodano, was documented in 2010 articles in the *National Catholic Reporter* by journalist Jason Berry.

Italian parliament, was described even by friends as Machiavellian—a man dedicated above all else to accumulating power. Among the pope's deputies, his most important rival for authority was Ratzinger. But the two cardinals, born within months of each other in 1927, usually managed to stay out of each other's way, given their different portfolios. Ratzinger oversaw doctrine, Sodano almost everything else. Unlike Ratzinger, Sodano did not court publicity, since he sensed danger in it. He frequently found his name on the lists of possible successors to John Paul, but many Italian cardinals discounted the idea of him as pope, given his sinister reputation.

While Ratzinger would more often be blamed for the Vatican's disastrous response to the sex-abuse crisis, Sodano played an important role in shielding pedophile churchmen. In a handful of interviews over the years, he said priests belonged to a "brotherhood" in which members understandably protected one another, even when they were accused of serious misconduct. "Only the angels and saints in heaven are flawless," he said. No member of the College of Cardinals would be more publicly critical of Sodano than Cardinal Schönborn of Austria. He blamed Sodano for having single-handedly derailed any investigation of Schönborn's predecessor, the notorious child molester Groër, after Groër's crimes were exposed in the 1990s. Schönborn said that despite the "moral certainty" among Austrian bishops that Groër was a pedophile, Sodano insisted he be kept in place.

Sodano was controversial throughout a career spent mostly in the Vatican diplomatic corps. He was papal nuncio to Chile from 1977 to 1988 and was close to General Pinochet, the country's dictator. In Chile, Sodano befriended two priests, both wildly successful fundraisers, who were later exposed as child molesters: Maciel and Father Fernando Karadima, a Chilean who billed himself as spiritual leader to his country's aristocracy. It was widely reported that Sodano took large cash gifts from Karadima, just as he had taken them from Maciel.

After returning to Rome, Sodano took cash gifts from a third prominent churchman, another successful fundraiser, who was also a pedophile: Cardinal McCarrick. In 2001, McCarrick established a personal charity fund that over the years distributed more than $6 million. The "Archbishop's Special Fund" was separate from the Papal Foundation, the much larger charity McCarrick founded in the 1980s. Years later, ledgers from his "Special Fund" were leaked to news organizations and identified McCarrick's donors. His largest contributor was a federal appeals court judge in

New Jersey, Maryanne Trump Barry, sister of future US president Donald Trump. The judge, a convert to Catholicism, donated at least $450,000 to the charity.

McCarrick knew he had a reputation as a man with easy access to cash: "I think some people thought I was a millionaire or something." Much of the money from his personal fund went to legitimate charities, but at least $600,000 went directly to individual churchmen in Rome. John Paul II received at least $91,000 over the years, the ledgers show, while Sodano received at least $19,000.

McCarrick spent hundreds of thousands of dollars from the fund to underwrite his foreign travel. He promoted himself as a global trouble-shooter and often visited countries wracked by civil war. "I'm just trying to get people to talk to each other," he insisted. He regularly sent handwritten notes to the pope to alert him to his good works abroad. Years later, church investigators suspected his overseas travel had a second purpose—to allow him to find young male sexual partners abroad when he realized he was under too much scrutiny in the US.

McCarrick maintained perplexing ties to a gurulike Argentine priest, Carlos Buela, who would also be accused of rampant sexual abuse of boys and young men. Over the years, McCarrick donated nearly $1 million to Buela's Institute of the Incarnate Word and regularly visited its churches in remote parts of Argentina. The ties between the two men confounded other churchmen, since McCarrick and Buela seemed to have little in common. On Catholic doctrine they were opposites: McCarrick was among the most progressive church leaders in the US, while Buela modeled his institute on Opus Dei.

Over the years, Argentina's national church hierarchy repeatedly protested to the Vatican over Buela's heavy-handed recruitment of seminarians and passed along reports that he was molesting them. Many of the country's bishops refused to ordain priests who studied in Buela's institute. In 2001, when Cardinal Bergoglio was named archbishop of Buenos Aires, he joined fellow Argentine bishops in a formal complaint to Rome about Buela. That resulted in a decision by John Paul to shut down three of Incarnate Word's seminaries.

Even so, McCarrick's baffling ties to Buela did not undermine a budding friendship with Bergoglio. In December 2004, as McCarrick prepared to visit Incarnate Word projects in Argentina, he wrote to Bergoglio to ask for a meeting in Buenos Aires, and the two cardinals established a lasting bond. Over time, McCarrick promoted Bergoglio as a promising candidate for the papacy. Bergoglio would later insist that in his years in the church hierarchy in Argentina, he saw nothing to suggest McCarrick was a sexual predator. He said he knew only that the American cardinal was an "indefatigable traveler, engaged in church work throughout the world."

31

The Cardinals' "Mafia"

WALTER KASPER, so rare to show anger, was fed up. He told German colleagues in Rome that he was tired of cleaning up *das Durcheinander*—the mess—that their countryman Ratzinger kept creating. In 2001, when Kasper was made president of the Council for Promoting Christian Unity, his overriding mission was to encourage understanding between the Vatican and other faiths. Instead, he spent much of his first year as a cardinal trying to undo the damage caused by *Dominus Iesus*, the 2000 document in which Ratzinger had branded other religions as "gravely deficient."

Kasper and Ratzinger, both now working in Rome after years of battling from a distance, became neighbors in a church-owned apartment block near St. Peter's Square. Kasper lived at no. 4, across the hallway from Ratzinger's larger, more desirable apartment, no. 8. Guests at Kasper's housewarming party remembered Ratzinger made only a brief visit and barely acknowledged his host. A few weeks after Kasper's arrival in Rome, at a time when he "hardly knew anyone" in the Vatican, he was invited to a lecture by Ratzinger that was attended by John Paul and senior Curia bishops. Kasper said the first two-thirds of the lecture were a "brilliant" exploration of various issues confronting the church, but the last third was a mocking critique of Kasper—by name—for his views on power sharing among the world's bishops. He felt blindsided by Ratzinger: "This was not the reception into the Roman Curia that I had wished for."

He was among several Curia officials who continued to express public alarm over *Dominus Iesus*. In an interview in 2001, he faulted the document's "doctrinaire" tone and its "clumsy and ambiguous" references to other faiths. In a speech in New York to American rabbis, he apologized for the "offense" that *Dominus Iesus* had caused.

The furor over the document was the major topic of discussion the following January at the annual gathering in St. Gallen of the "mafia" of reform-minded bishops, including Kasper. For most of them, *Dominus Iesus* was more evidence of why Ratzinger would be a disaster as pope. The topic of succession came up in almost all of their conversations that year, given John Paul's fading health.

Some St. Gallen members, whatever their differences with Ratzinger, were always careful to say they liked the man personally. Cardinal Murphy-O'Connor of Britain found Ratzinger "unfailingly courteous, intelligent and, above all, kind." While Cardinal Martini of Milan made headlines when he appeared to question Ratzinger's views on doctrine, especially when it came to birth control and homosexuality, he avoided any criticism that might be seen as a personal attack.

Martini, a serene, open-minded progressive, had once been seen as a leading candidate to succeed John Paul. It was often said that Martini, like John XXIII, had "critics but no enemies." Italian cardinals were thought likely to accept him as a compromise pope if only to return the papacy to a countryman. Murphy-O'Connor was convinced that had there been a conclave in the 1990s, Martini would have easily won. But hopes for his candidacy were dashed in 2002 when he turned seventy-five and revealed that he, like John Paul II, had been diagnosed with Parkinson's disease.

Other St. Gallen members were thought to be *papabile*, including Kasper, who turned sixty-nine that year. His magnetism and outspokenness had won him many admirers in the Curia and in the Vatican press corps. In a bow to the children's cartoon character in the US, American reporters dubbed him "Kasper the Friendly Cardinal."

BY 2005, there was evidence of a chill between John Paul and Ratzinger, which many linked to the pope's distress about *Dominus Iesus*. The two men were spending less time together, if only because conversation had become so difficult for John Paul. As death approached, his loss of muscle control was so severe that he had difficulty sitting up for meals; others had to cut up his food and lift it to his mouth. Increasingly he wanted to be surrounded by fellow Poles and to hold his conversations in Polish.

The chill became more obvious as John Paul took a final turn for the worse and Ratzinger disappeared from his side entirely. In February 2005, the eighty-four-year-old pope was admitted to a hospital with a throat inflammation and surgeons performed a tracheotomy, robbing him of his voice. He was discharged from the hospital two weeks later. The minivan transporting him back to the Vatican was trailed by a motorcade of news photographers who assumed this would be the pope's last journey through the streets of Rome. The Vatican acknowledged his death was imminent, and crowds of thousands gathered day and night in St. Peter's Square.

Notable by his absence was Ratzinger, who visited the pope only twice in the final month of his life. He made one trip to the hospital and one to the palace on Friday, April 5, when John Paul was hours from death. The pope was given last rites by Dziwisz that day. Ratzinger offered a surprisingly bloodless account of their final encounter, saying he asked the pope "for his blessing, which he gave me. Then we parted with a cordial handshake, conscious that this was our last meeting."

John Paul held on for another day. His death was recorded at 9:37 Saturday night. In the pope's final hours, Ratzinger was forty miles away in a Benedictine monastery in the city of Subiaco, where he was receiving an award.

In their tributes the next day, Western politicians praised John Paul, above all else, for his role in ending the Cold War. Former Soviet leader Mikhail Gorbachev wrote that without him, the Berlin Wall might never have fallen: "Everything that happened in Eastern Europe in these last few years would have been impossible without the presence of the pope." There was the expected chorus of praise from conservative Catholic leaders, who credited John Paul with holding firm on doctrine. In Germany, Hans Küng released a diplomatic statement in which he said that while John Paul had made "many bad decisions," he would still be remembered as "a pope of many great gifts."

Other critics noted that despite the globetrotting that won the pope a reputation as the church's greatest modern evangelist, Catholicism was in retreat in much of the world. That was especially true in Western Europe and the US, where church attendance continued to plummet. "Americans clearly loved this man's goodness, but we were very, very uncomfortable with his absolute claims to moral certitude," said the American Catholic writer James Carroll, a former priest. In several Latin American countries, the church's membership as a share of the population had dropped sharply, as hundreds of millions of former Catholics turned to less rigid evangelical churches.

Despite his early vow to share authority with the world's bishops, John Paul left a legacy that was precisely the opposite. He centralized power in Rome in a way unknown since Pius XII. Progressive Catholic scholars, beginning with Küng, had been silenced or forced out. Much of the rest of the legacy of Vatican II, especially its call for the church's commitment to social justice and interfaith dialogue, was in doubt.

In hindsight, it was remarkable how little was said at the time of John Paul's death about his culpability in the child-abuse crisis. Commentators seemed determined to assume that he had never grasped the extent of the catastrophe. In its fourteen-thousand-word obituary, *The New York Times* dedicated only a few hundred words to the abuse scandals in the US, beginning in earnest in the sixty-eighth paragraph, and made no reference to those in other countries.*

As planning began for the largest funeral in the history of the church, Ratzinger was everywhere to be seen in Rome. As dean of the College of Cardinals, he was responsible for administering the conclave to elect John Paul's successor. He dismissed speculation that he was a papal candidate. "Of course, my name had been mentioned a lot," he said later, "but I really wasn't able to take it seriously." Even so, many cardinals were convinced that Ratzinger longed to be pope. If not, they noted, it would have been easy enough for him to withdraw his candidacy. Martini, another oft-mentioned candidate, had already declared he would not accept election that year, given his health. Ratzinger would have had good reason to withdraw his name given his age and his own health problems. He turned seventy-eight two days before the conclave, and his two strokes were not a secret.

He did not rule himself out, however, nor did he shut down an aggressive lobbying campaign on his behalf. Cardinals Meisner of Cologne and Schönborn of Vienna led the effort. Another loyalist, Cardinal López Trujillo, rounded up votes among Latin American cardinals. The Brazilian newspaper *Globo* quoted a Brazilian cardinal who complained about how aggressively he was lobbied: "They made it clear that they had consulted Ratzinger and he had given a green light for the campaign."

---

* In 2023, a documentary shown on Polish television and a book by a Dutch investigative journalist documented several cases in which then-Cardinal Wojtyła appeared to have known about—and covered up—the crimes of pedophile priests in Krakow.

Ratzinger went into the conclave with a head start since so many cardinals knew they owed their red robes to him, given his influence with John Paul. All but two of the 117 cardinals participating in the conclave had been named by John Paul. (Ratzinger was one of the two.) Murphy-O'Connor assumed Ratzinger had a guarantee from the start of at least forty votes, which might make him unbeatable.

More than four million people poured into Rome for John Paul's funeral, the single largest gathering of heads of state in history. (The previous record was set at Winston Churchill's funeral in 1965.) Four kings, five queens, and seventy presidents and prime ministers were there. Prince Charles postponed his wedding to his companion, Camilla Parker-Bowles, so he could attend on behalf of Queen Elizabeth. The United States was represented by President George W. Bush. The leaders of fifteen non-Catholic Christian churches were there, including the archbishop of Canterbury, the first leader of the Church of England ever to attend a papal funeral.

Ratzinger's performance at the funeral and in the traditional nine-day period of mourning that followed, known as the *novemdiales*, was widely praised. His eulogy at the open-air funeral Mass, delivered on the steps of St. Peter's, was so touchingly personal that many in the crowd were moved to tears. Eager to overcome his reputation for aloofness, Ratzinger focused less on the accomplishments of John Paul's papacy—"this is not the time to speak of the specific content of this rich pontificate"—than on the dramatic and often poignant details of his life.

His well-received eulogy did nothing, however, to derail the campaign to stop Ratzinger from becoming pope. Members of the St. Gallen Group spent days lobbying discreetly for other candidates. Murphy-O'Connor organized secret strategy sessions of the group, including a private supper at the English College, the Roman seminary for English-language students.*

The preconclave politicking took an ugly turn when Italian newspapers reported that two German cardinals—Kasper and Lehmann—were actively campaigning to block Ratzinger's election. The two cardinals denied it, even as Kasper did something that all but proved the story true. Days before the conclave, he gave a speech in Rome that was read as a shockingly direct plea for Ratzinger to be denied the papacy. He did not

* Ratzinger told a biographer years later that he knew nothing at the time of the conclave about the existence of the St. Gallen Group and its secret campaign to block his election (Seewald, *Benedict XVI: A Life, Volume II*, 265).

use Ratzinger's name, but did not need to, since he offered a checklist of qualities the new pope should have, beginning with a "truly pastoral" style that would allow him to communicate easily with laypeople. It was a list that clearly disqualified Ratzinger.

ON THE DAY of John Paul's death, Cardinal Bergoglio led the memorial Mass in the Metropolitan Cathedral in Buenos Aires. Then, after the long flight across the Atlantic, he mostly disappeared from public view in Rome. He attended the pope's funeral and participated in the business meetings of the College of Cardinals. Other than that, he was little seen as he waited for the conclave to begin. His name appeared on many journalists' lists of cardinals considered *papabile*. Italian newspapermen were especially eager to promote his candidacy, given his reputation as Argentina's humble "bishop of the slums," which made for a welcome contrast to other contenders. "Shy, reserved, of few words, Bergoglio doesn't move a finger to campaign—and that is what is considered one of his great assets," the magazine *L'Espresso* wrote. "His austerity and frugality, along with his intense spiritual life, are the personal qualities that increasingly elevate him to be *papabile*."

Bergoglio insisted he was appalled by the attention and feared people would assume he was whipping up this speculation. "My reaction was shame, embarrassment," he said later. "I thought the journalists must have taken leave of their senses." Those comments drew some eye-rolling back in Argentina, however. His critics, especially his old Jesuit adversaries and his new enemies in the Argentine government, suspected he was secretly thrilled by the thought of being elected pope.

FOR A MAN OF GOD, Bergoglio had always had a remarkable number of enemies. None would prove more determined than the husband-and-wife team who dominated Argentine politics for a generation: Néstor and Cristina Kirchner, often described as the twenty-first-century equivalent to Juan and Eva Perón. They met in law school in the 1970s and were self-proclaimed Peronists. Néstor, who had been governor of the oil-rich, sparsely populated province of Santa Cruz, came to power in the presidential election in 2003. Cristina, who succeeded her husband four years later, liked the Evita comparison, saying she identified with Eva Perón's "hair in the bun and clenched fist before a microphone."

The Kirchners promoted themselves as devoted champions of the poor, which might have made them allies to Bergoglio, but the relationship became poisonous. The couple was always dogged by rumors of corruption. In 2004, after a year in power, Kirchner had little to show in improving the lives of most Argentines, even as his political cronies cashed in on government contracts. He spent much of that year trying to explain away news reports revealing that as governor in Santa Cruz, he had deposited an astonishing $500 million of the province's funds in Swiss bank accounts. Opposition parties saw it as a massive political slush fund.

Bergoglio made his disdain public that year. At the annual Mass in May to mark Independence Day, with Kirchner in the pews, he accused the government of "exhibitions and strident announcements" that did nothing to help the poor. "The people are not taken in by dishonest and mediocre strategies," he declared. Kirchner was insulted and stormed out of the cathedral. Asked the next day to confirm that the president was the target of the homily, Father Marco, Bergoglio's spokesman, answered: "If the shoe fits, wear it." Kirchner shot back, describing the cardinal as "the spiritual leader of the opposition."

The president had many ways to take revenge against Bergoglio, especially by reviving the unresolved allegations about Bergoglio's actions in the Dirty War. Kirchner's predecessor, Carlos Menem, had halted trials for the worst of the war criminals and pardoned others. Kirchner effectively reversed the pardons and promised new investigations. In years to come, the inquiries would often focus on Bergoglio.

Kirchner had an ally in that cause, the journalist Horacio Verbitsky. By the time of Kirchner's election, Verbitsky had been gathering derogatory information about Bergoglio for almost four years, with a focus on the most controversial chapter in the cardinal's past—his actions before and during the 1976 kidnapping of the two Jesuit slum priests.

At the start of the reporting project in 1999, Verbitsky interviewed then-Archbishop Bergoglio and initially came away convinced he was telling the truth when he insisted he had not betrayed the two priests—Orlando Yorio and Franz Jalics—and fought for their freedom. "He depicted himself as a hero," Verbitsky remembered. But then he interviewed Yorio and obtained a copy of the twenty-seven-page document that Yorio sent to the Jesuits' leadership in Rome years earlier, laying out the damning allegations against Bergoglio. With that, Verbitsky said, Bergoglio's story "began to unravel."

With Kirschner's help, Verbitsky was granted access to military archives that described secret contacts between the junta and the Catholic hierarchy in the 1970s, and he thought some of the documents referring to Bergoglio were devastating. By 2004, Verbitsky had enough material for a book, and his publisher announced the title in advance: *El Silencio. De Paulo VI a Bergoglio. Las relaciones secretas de la Iglesia con la ESMA* (The Silence. From Paul VI to Bergoglio. The Secret Relations of the Church with ESMA). It suggested just how much the cardinal had to fear, since Verbitsky apparently intended somehow to tie Bergoglio personally to the horrors of what had happened at ESMA, the junta's notorious torture center in the Dirty War.

El Silencio neared publication just as John Paul neared death. At any other time, the book, published only in Spanish, would have drawn few readers outside Argentina. But with the pope fading and Bergoglio openly promoted as a candidate to succeed him, the cardinal's many enemies wanted to see the book's damaging information circulated widely in Rome.

The book, published in February 2005, did not provide absolute proof of wrongdoing by Bergoglio, but it offered new evidence that he had indeed denounced the two priests as leftist radicals in the 1970s, which put their lives in danger. Verbitsky obtained a 1976 army intelligence memo in which Bergoglio was praised for his "goodwill" toward the junta even if the Jesuit order under his control "has yet to be fully purged." Verbitsky thought his most damaging evidence was a 1979 document from the foreign ministry that suggested Bergoglio cooperated with the junta and continued to defame the two priests even after they were freed. It referred to a request by Jalics, then living in exile abroad, for a new passport. According to the memo, the ministry interviewed Bergoglio, who disparaged Jalics as a leftist and accused him and Yorio of "working with guerrillas."

Bergoglio tried to ignore the book. His spokesmen suggested Verbitsky had misunderstood the archives' material, especially the foreign-ministry memo, but the damage was done.* The cardinal now had an influential new critic: Adolfo Pérez Esquivel, the Nobel Prize–winning human-rights activist, who went on television to say he believed Bergoglio had indeed slandered slum priests in the 1970s as "being communists, subversives and terrorists." He suggested the cardinal should never be pope: "I hope

* According to the cardinal's spokesmen, Bergoglio did not disparage the two priests to the foreign ministry and had in fact tried to help Jalics get his passport. It was Bergoglio's office that submitted the passport application on the priest's behalf.

the Holy Spirit is awake on the day of the election and does not make a mistake."

The Kirchners had good reason to fear Bergoglio as pope. As bishop of Rome, he could use his influence to undermine them, just as John Paul II had helped bring down the Communist regime in Poland. And so, a shadowy campaign was launched in Buenos Aires to make sure Bergoglio was denied the papacy. He detected it almost as soon as he landed in Rome. Spanish-speaking cardinals warned him they had received emails from an unidentified sender that included excerpts from Verbitsky's book. Other cardinals were slipped manila envelopes containing the same material. The source of the emails would later be identified as Argentina's ambassador to the Vatican, although he denied it. Then, three days before the conclave, an Argentine human-rights lawyer filed a criminal complaint against Bergoglio in a courthouse in Buenos Aires, charging him with crimes against humanity during the Dirty War. The complaint, citing Verbitsky's book, made for headlines first in Argentina, then in Rome. The Italian newspaper *Corriere della Sera* described the allegations as an "infamy fueled by Bergoglio's enemies," while the Associated Press published a more damaging story under the headline "Cardinal Accused in '76 Kidnapping of Two Priests." The AP suggested the allegations would derail Bergoglio as a papal candidate.

Marco, the cardinal's spokesman, issued a statement in Rome that dismissed the lawsuit as an "old slander." Verbitsky's book, he said, was "full of lies." In Buenos Aires, church officials alleged the Kirchners were behind both Verbitsky's book and the campaign in the Vatican to defame Bergoglio. The government denied it. Verbitsky insisted the timing of the book's release was coincidental. He pointed out that he had been investigating Bergoglio years before Néstor Kirchner was elected.

As he waited for the conclave to open, Bergoglio told friends he was mortified by the controversy and feared he was being branded in front of the entire world as a war criminal. Several cardinals sought him out to offer comfort and urge him to continue to see himself as a viable contender in the conclave. They told him he remained an appealing alternative to rigidly conservative candidates, especially to Ratzinger, who otherwise seemed likely to win.

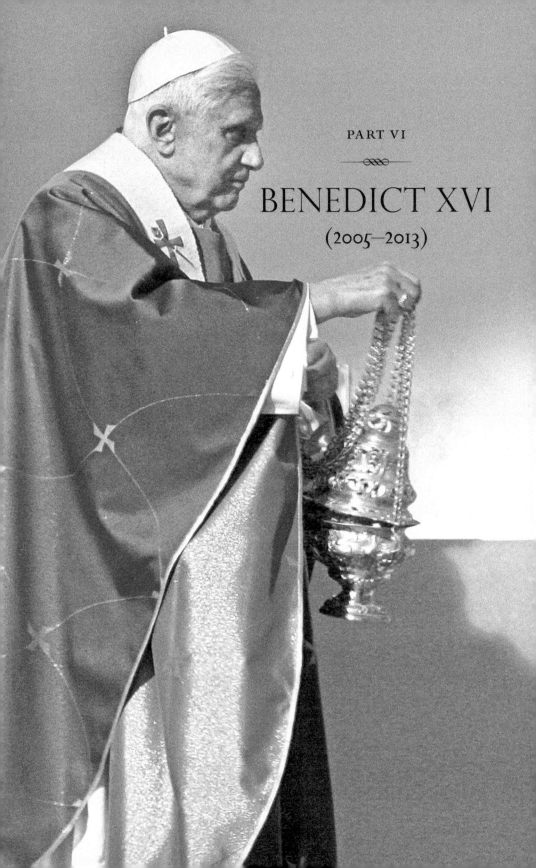

PART VI

BENEDICT XVI

(2005–2013)

32

The Unwelcome Challenger

A S MEMBERS OF the College of Cardinals entered the Sistine Chapel to choose a new pope, a few glowered up at the ceiling—at what had become of Michelangelo's beloved frescoes. The 2005 conclave was the first since the chapel underwent a $4.2-million restoration—paid for by a Japanese television network in exchange for filming rights—that had been roundly criticized by art historians. In removing centuries of grime from Michelangelo's sixteenth-century depiction of the creation of Adam and other scenes from Genesis, the restorers were accused of botching the job. The restored colors were so jarringly bright that they were compared by one critic to "Hollywood Technicolor."

Of the 117 cardinals eligible to join the conclave, all but two were there. The missing pair, one from Mexico, one from the Philippines, had been too ill to travel. In the two weeks since John Paul's death, carpenters had been busy installing a wooden floor over what had been different levels of hard pavement. Tables and padded seats had been set along two long rows. At one end, in front of the altar, was a separate table where three cardinals—the "scrutineers"—would tabulate the votes.

As dean of the College, Ratzinger led the proceedings. He was the first to stand up, place his hand on a copy of the Gospels, and take the oath never to reveal what went on during their deliberations. One by one, the other cardinals did the same. Under church law, the penalty for violating the oath was excommunication. Once all were sworn in, the TV cameras were shut down. Cardinal Murphy-O'Connor heard someone yell out—in

Latin—the traditional warning to outsiders, "Exeunt omnes!" (Everybody get out!), before the doors closed with a thud.

The day before, he and other cardinals had moved into the Vatican guesthouse, the Casa Santa Marta, where they would eat and sleep between sessions. The $20 million guesthouse, opened in 1996, had been built on orders of John Paul II, who had seen for himself how elderly cardinals suffered during the two conclaves in 1978, when they lived in makeshift accommodations around the chapel. Rooms in the Casa Santa Marta had been altered for the conclave to make sure no cardinals leaked information: the landline telephones had been removed and the shutters on the windows sealed shut. Electronic jamming equipment prevented the use of cell phones.

At least one participant at the conclave violated his oath of secrecy—by releasing a diary. Leaked to an Italian foreign-affairs magazine months later, it was the most complete timeline of a conclave ever made public. While decrying the leak, the Vatican did not dispute the diary's authenticity.

Murphy-O'Connor, who insisted he was not the diarist, later wrote about the nonsecret logistics of the conclave. This was his first papal election, and he was fascinated by the intricate, time-honored method of choosing a new bishop of Rome. The first vote took place on the opening evening, when each cardinal was presented with a list of every member of the College, along with several rectangular pieces of paper with the Latin words "Eligo in Summum Pontificem" (I Elect as Supreme Pontiff) printed across the top, with space beneath for the name of the preferred candidate. "We each wrote a name on the ballot paper, folded it in half, walked in turn to the front of the chapel, held up the ballot in the air, placed it in a saucer, then tipped it into a silver urn shaped like a flying saucer."

After all 115 ballots were cast, one of the scrutineers shook the urn and began pulling out ballots, one by one. After silently examining each ballot, he passed it to the second scrutineer, who also examined it, before the name was read out by the third. "Each ballot was then pierced with a needle and thread and strung together," Murphy-O'Connor remembered. Under church law, a winning candidate needed two-thirds of the votes, plus one, to win election. In a conclave of 115 cardinals, a victor needed seventy-seven votes.

The secret diary reported that in the first round, Ratzinger received forty-seven votes—40 percent of the total—followed by Bergoglio with ten votes and Martini with nine. Since Martini continued to insist he would refuse election, his votes were seen as a protest against Ratzinger, which meant they would likely go to Bergoglio in later rounds. In the first ballot, the remaining votes went to a mix of thirty other candidates, including four for Secretary of State Sodano. There was some surprise that Kasper received no votes, suggesting he had become too controversial.

After the tally was announced, the ballots were placed in the chapel's famous stove and burned with chemicals to create black smoke, signaling a vote had been taken but without a definitive result. The cardinals returned to the guesthouse to reflect. For the St. Gallen Group, the first tally was promising. If Martini's votes went to Bergoglio, this would likely be a two-man race with Ratzinger.

Bergoglio appeared astonished that he was a real contender. He would always adamantly deny he ever had designs on the papacy, at that conclave or afterward, or that he had campaigned in any way. After the first round, though, he knew he might win, which meant he had a decision to make—to stay in the race or, like Martini, bow out and throw his support to another candidate. He stayed in. In fact, he said later, he saw his prospects as so real that he settled on the papal name he would take if he won. He would be Pope John XXIV, in honor of John XXIII. It was a name, he knew, that would thrill Catholics who revered "the good pope."

The next morning, the cardinals took two more votes. In the first, Ratzinger edged up to sixty-five—twelve shy of victory—with thirty-five for Bergoglio. In the second ballot that day, Ratzinger's tally increased to seventy, while Bergoglio's went up to forty. That meant the Argentine had the support of more than a third of the cardinals and could deny Ratzinger the two-thirds needed for victory. The secret diary suggested that, by then, Bergoglio was overwhelmed by the pressure and had second thoughts about his candidacy. In the third round of voting, he displayed a "suffering face, as if he were begging, 'God, don't do this to me.' "

The idea of a stalemate was alarming to progressives because they knew it might open the way for another conservative, maybe even the feared Sodano, to offer himself as a compromise. It was left to Martini to ensure that did not happen. The account of what he did in those hours—of how he swung the election to Ratzinger in a secret deal between the two men—was offered years later, after Martini's death, by his personal confessor, Father Silvano Fausti. A renowned Jesuit theologian and biblical scholar in Milan, Fausti was also known to be Martini's closest friend.

Fausti's account was offered in a videotaped interview days before his own death in 2015. He said Martini swung the vote because he feared a plot had been hatched to deny election to both Ratzinger and Bergoglio—to "make them both fail." Martini suspected the plotters would then move to elect a "very slippery" cardinal, possibly Sodano. To avoid that, Martini believed the conclave needed to elect Ratzinger and hope for the best. Ratzinger, he said, was "honest and intelligent" and might be emboldened to end the Curia's worst abuses.

According to Fausti, Martini pulled Ratzinger aside and offered him a deal. He told Ratzinger he would round up the votes needed to win, so long as the new pope vowed to try to reform the Curia, and if that failed, resign. Ratzinger accepted the proposal, committing himself to become the first pope to abdicate voluntarily since the thirteenth century if he failed to complete the overhaul of the Vatican bureaucracy that he had just promised Martini.

Ratzinger always denied there had been any such agreement, although other churchmen close to Martini were convinced there was a deal; Fausti's colleagues said he would not make up such an extraordinary story.[*]

After a third inconclusive vote, the cardinals returned to the guesthouse for lunch. "We ate quietly," Murphy-O'Connor remembered. "There was a sense of serenity among us." That calm was a result of hushed conversations between other members of the St. Gallen Group and Martini, who did not give up details of the secret deal but suggested there were fewer reasons to fear a Ratzinger papacy.

When the cardinals returned to the chapel, a fourth vote was held. This time, according to the secret diary, Ratzinger had the necessary votes—plus seven more, for a total of eighty-four. When his name was called out for the seventy-seventh time, reflecting two-thirds of the votes, the cardinals burst into applause.

Sodano, as vice dean, approached Ratzinger and asked: "Your Eminence, do you accept to be the Supreme Pontiff of the Catholic Church?"

Ratzinger paused a moment before replying: "I accept it as the will of God."

Sodano then asked: "What name do you wish to be called?"

---

* In interviews shortly before his death, Benedict XVI, the former Cardinal Ratzinger, acknowledged for the first time that he did have private conversations with Martini during the conclave in which they discussed Ratzinger's candidacy. "To tell the truth, I did speak with Martini," he said, insisting that—far from making a deal to win election—he told Martini he did not want to be pope: "I don't want it, and if you tell your friends that, I will be grateful" (Seewald, *Benedict XVI: A Life, Volume II*, 278).

"Benedict."

He would be Benedict XVI. He chose the name in honor of Benedict XV, pope from 1914 to 1922, best remembered for campaigning passionately for peace talks to end World War I. The new pope said he had considered naming himself John Paul III as a tribute to his immediate predecessor but decided against it "because a standard had been set there which I couldn't match." He acknowledged that constant comparison with John Paul would harm him since "I had a different sort of charisma—or rather a non-charisma." He said he felt no particular emotion at the moment of his election, apart from fear. "The thought of the guillotine occurred to me," he joked later. From the chapel, he was escorted into the side room where a tailor waited, ready to fit him for his first set of white robes. Benedict reappeared about ten minutes later, entirely in white, and sat as the cardinals lined up, ready to pay their respects.

At 6:42 p.m., under clouds threatening rain, Cardinal Jorge Arturo Medina Estévez of Chile, one of the conclave administrators, stepped onto the balcony of St. Peter's to announce, "Habemus Papam" (We have a pope). He then uttered the name Joseph Ratzinger and introduced him as Benedict XVI. The initial reaction in the crowd was notably muted. For millions of reform-minded Catholics around the world, this was news they had dreaded. But after a moment, any grumbling in the square was drowned out by cheers in Italian of "Benedetto! Benedetto!" The bells of St. Peter's, and across Rome, pealed for hours.

Many of Benedict's friends had never seen him so happy or relieved. He beamed as he stood on the balcony and uttered his first public words, in Italian, as pope: "Dear brothers and sisters. After the great Pope John Paul II, the cardinals have elected me—a simple, humble worker in the vineyard of the Lord." He then did something totally out of character—he raised his hands above his head and clenched them together triumphantly, like a prizefighter.

World leaders welcomed his election. Many had been in Rome two weeks earlier to hear his moving eulogy for John Paul. Benedict was the first German pope in a thousand years, and his election was banner headlines in his homeland. The front page of the German tabloid *Bild* rejoiced: "WIR SIND PAPST!" (We Are Pope!).

The dismay among progressive Catholics was predictable. They worried that Benedict's election meant that the battle for the church's soul begun at Vatican II might really be over, with victory in the hands of the archconservatives who had opposed the council's reforms. Before the conclave, Father Thomas Reese, editor of the Jesuit magazine *America*, had hoped for the election of an open-minded pope who could lift the church "from its intellectual ghetto" and revive debates over sexual morality and social justice shut down under John Paul II. With Ratzinger, he said, it would be more of the same. The large American victims-rights group known as SNAP, or Survivors Network of those Abused by Priests, was alarmed by Benedict's election, given his failure over decades to deal with the clerical-abuse crisis: "He is a polarizing figure who seems to prefer combativeness to compassion." Hans Küng released a statement in which he said he was "enormously disappointed," describing the "pattern of persecution" that Ratzinger had pursued at the congregation. Still, Küng held out a small hope: "The papacy is such a challenge that perhaps it can change even Joseph Ratzinger."

At first, major news organizations offered inaccurate accounts of what happened in the conclave. Most failed to identify Bergoglio as Benedict's key challenger, and no reporter suggested there had been any sort of deal between Ratzinger and Martini. The record would be partly clarified only after the leak of the secret diary that fall.

After the conclave, Martini flew home to his beloved Jerusalem. As his health faded, he intended to spend his final days in the city where the Savior had preached and died and where Martini had spent the most rewarding years of his career as a Bible scholar. He would rarely visit the Vatican again. Nor would he ever say anything publicly to suggest he had been the central figure in securing the election of Benedict XVI.

IN THE DAYS BEFORE the 2005 conclave, Cardinal McCarrick was little seen in Rome. That was a surprise to the Vatican press corps, since he was the American cardinal usually most eager to be in the public eye, especially when television cameras were turned on. He had good reason to lie low, as it turned out, since he knew the Vatican had just been alerted to detailed new allegations of his sexual misconduct.

A few weeks earlier, in a letter stamped CONFIDENTIAL, Archbishop John J. Myers of Newark wrote to the papal nuncio in Washington to inform him—"with a heavy heart"—that the archdiocese had been approached by a lawyer representing a priest who alleged he had been molested by McCarrick in the 1980s. The lawyer was ready to open negotiations with

Myers, McCarrick's successor in Newark, over a settlement that would buy the victim's silence. Myers wrote that he had also become aware of a secret financial settlement reached with another man sexually abused by McCarrick. Myers told the papal nuncio he was panicked that local journalists might discover this. "Pray God this does not happen," he wrote.

Three months after the letter, the archdiocese agreed to pay $80,000 to the priest, who in turn agreed to drop plans for a lawsuit. McCarrick, back from the 2005 conclave in Rome, contributed $10,000 of the settlement money from his personal charity fund.

McCarrick told aides in Washington he had voted for Bergoglio at the conclave. Over the years, McCarrick and then-Cardinal Ratzinger had butted heads on doctrinal issues, and McCarrick thought the Argentine offered a "fresh start." There would have been a more craven reason for his support. As McCarrick later told his criminal defense lawyers, he believed Bergoglio, unlike Benedict, was ignorant of the sex-abuse allegations that had swirled around him for years.

Even so, McCarrick wanted to make an early show of loyalty to Benedict. The day after the conclave, he called a news conference in Rome to shower praise on the new pope: "He is a genius—and not just a genius. He is also a very spiritual man." In a comment that would prove strikingly ironic years later, he told reporters that Benedict would be especially sensitive to the victims of priestly sex abuse: "If they are looking for someone whose heart will break when he hears those stories, they are looking for someone like Pope Benedict."

He backed up those words a month later with a secret gift from his charity fund to celebrate Benedict's election—a check for $250,000, made payable directly to the pope. Many in the Vatican later questioned whether the gift amounted to a brazen effort by McCarrick to ensure he remained in place in Washington. The Vatican would deny there was any such arrangement. In July 2005, two months after sending the check, McCarrick reached his seventy-fifth birthday and submitted his mandatory letter of resignation. Benedict refused it and extended McCarrick's assignment for two years. In Rome, that decision was not seen as surprising. McCarrick had been valuable to the Vatican given his friendship with then-President George W. Bush.

At the time, Benedict was aware of allegations that McCarrick was a sexual predator, as the pope later admitted. Still, he insisted, he felt justified keeping McCarrick in place in Washington given the lack of "concrete" evidence of misconduct.

In Benedict's first months as pope, he was eager to calm fears his election would stir new divisions in the church, and between the Vatican and other religions. In his first speech as pope, he promised "open and sincere" dialogue with other faiths, precisely the dialogue he had regularly shut down at the congregation. His allies were dispatched to give interviews to major news organizations to dispel the image of him as aloof. Their remarks were heavily scripted; many cardinals offered identical anecdotes, especially about the pope's love of cats. Benedict stepped up the goodwill campaign by keeping many of his former Curia critics in place, including Kasper. Sodano remained as secretary of state. The new pope set to work that fall on his first encyclical, which was made public in January. It offered none of his usual rhetoric about traditional doctrine but instead was a surprisingly lyrical seventy-one-page meditation on love. Entitled *Deus Caritas Est* (God Is Love), it praised all forms of love, including the erotic.

In September, he granted an audience to the man long seen as his mortal enemy: Hans Küng. The meeting, only their second since Küng was stripped of his teaching credentials in 1979, was held at Castel Gandolfo and lasted four hours. They shared what was described as a leisurely dinner with good German stout. In a statement released by the Vatican and approved by Küng, the two said they had enjoyed a "friendly" conversation; they did not discuss "persistent doctrinal questions." Küng suggested afterward that he and the pope might restore some semblance of the friendship they had once known. "It's clear that we have different positions," he said. "But the things we have in common are more fundamental."

Benedict delighted in the trappings of the papacy, including extravagances his predecessor disdained. He cared passionately about his wardrobe, to a degree that startled colleagues who remembered Joseph Ratzinger as a bookish, unfashionable theology professor. He insisted that much of what he wore be handmade in the famed Gammarelli clerical tailoring shop, where a simple shirt could cost hundreds of dollars. He declared that every day's papal clothing include at least one item from the store: "Anything without Gammarelli is a no-no." His red papal shoes and slippers were hand-made at a small cobblers' shop near the Vatican called Arellano. (He denied persistent news reports his shoes came from the Italian fashion house Prada.) John Paul had worn a simple, unadorned gold cross, a gift from his former parishioners in Krakow. Benedict preferred a filigreed gold cross with a large emerald set at its center. He wore costly sunglasses by the manufacturer Serengeti; the Vatican justified the expense because the company's blue-tinted lenses were known for advanced eye protection.

He also cared deeply about the interior design of the papal apartment. He continued to live in the Santa Marta guesthouse for several days after his election while his new home on the third floor of the Apostolic Palace was renovated. He ordered the installation of new heating, plumbing, and electrical systems, as well as a new kitchen, complete with state-of-the-art German appliances. He had photos taken in his old apartment of his twenty-thousand-book library so it could be reassembled, book by book, in the palace. He was eager to promote himself as a figure in popular culture and enjoy a taste of John Paul's global celebrity. He opened negotiations with the American recording company Geffen Records to produce an album of him singing traditional hymns; it was released in 2009.

His efforts to demonstrate a newfound openness had limits, however. Two months after his election, he demanded the resignation of Father Reese, the editor of the magazine *America*, which had outraged then-Cardinal Ratzinger with articles challenging doctrine on birth control, homosexuality, and papal infallibility. The magazine had also published the cutting exchanges between him and Kasper. He also stepped up his old campaign against the "intrinsic evil" of homosexuality. That summer, the Vatican effectively banned all gay men from entering the priesthood. Under new regulations, seminarians with "deeply rooted homosexual tendencies" could not be ordained unless they "overcame" those tendencies three years before becoming priests. The Vatican also announced plans to send investigators to two hundred American seminaries to determine the extent of homosexuality among priests-in-training.

For most of his first year as pope, Benedict remained silent about the child-abuse crisis. Even so, victims' advocates were heartened by news reports, the day after his election, that the Vatican had quietly reopened its inquiry into Father Maciel, the investigation that then-Cardinal Ratzinger had closed down in 1999. Vatican spokesmen portrayed it as proof that Benedict intended to take early, decisive action to crack down on clerical sex abuse. Maciel's victims were told nothing about why the investigation had been reopened. "But it's better late than never," said José Barba-Martín, a former Legion priest who was one of Maciel's original accusers. "This is a good sign."

As it turned out, the decision to revive the investigation had nothing to do with seeking justice for Maciel's victims. It was prompted instead by the discovery in late 2004, in the final months of John Paul II's papacy, of a VHS videotape that showed Maciel in the company of one of his secret families. The tape, turned over by a disgruntled Legion official, showed Maciel with a young woman identified as his daughter, along with the girl's Mexican-born mother. The older woman would later allege that, as a girl, she had been molested by Maciel, became pregnant, and had been exiled along with their infant daughter to Spain. Their living expenses had been covered for years by the Legion. The videotape supported rumors that Maciel, beyond molesting scores of children, had violated his celibacy oath with women and fathered their illegitimate children. It was eventually determined that he had at least six children by three women. Two of his sons would allege they were raped and sodomized by their father. They would also report that Maciel brought them to the Vatican for private audiences with his friend John Paul II.

In Rome, the videotape was first seen by Cardinal Franc Rode of Slovenia, the prelate of the Vatican congregation that supposedly oversaw the Legion. Rather than confront Maciel himself, Rode shared the tape with the Vatican's chief sex-abuse investigator, Monsignor Charles Scicluna of Malta, who then secured Ratzinger's approval to launch a new investigation. Told of the inquiry and fearful of what lay in store, Maciel, eighty-four, hastily announced his retirement in November, citing ill health.

In the first months of 2005, Scicluna traveled to Mexico and the US to interview Maciel's victims. He was horrified by what he discovered and questioned how John Paul II, Sodano, and Ratzinger could have failed to stop such a terrifying sexual criminal. Still, despite the damning evidence, Scicluna's investigation was reportedly shut down, too. In May 2005, barely a month after Benedict's election, the Vatican announced the newly reopened inquiry of Maciel had been closed without charges. A Legion spokesman said Maciel was delighted by the news and thankful to Benedict for allowing the Legion's work to continue; the order then had an annual budget of $650 million.

BENEDICT'S MOST IMPORTANT early personnel decision was his appointment of Archbishop William Levada of San Francisco, a like-minded conservative, as his successor at the Congregation for the Doctrine of the Faith. The choice of the California-born Levada, the highest-ranking American ever to serve in the Curia, was denounced by Catholic gay-rights activists in famously progressive San Francisco, who often clashed with him. He had also regularly been accused of covering up the crimes of pedophile priests across northern California, which he denied.

Just weeks after arriving in Rome, Levada was shocked when he stumbled across paperwork from the congregation's secret disciplinary files on another American church leader—McCarrick. Levada asked to see the full file and was horrified to discover how the cardinal had regularly been accused of molesting boys and young men. He told colleagues he was haunted especially by the "gut-wrenching" written account offered by one of McCarrick's victims, a young priest in New Jersey. The priest reported that, in the mid-1980s, when he was a seminarian, he had been invited by McCarrick to a late dinner in New York City and then went to an apartment that the then-archbishop maintained on Manhattan's Upper East Side. McCarrick announced they would sleep there, since it was too late to head back to their own homes in New Jersey. The priest said he was startled to discover there was only one bed, which the archbishop insisted they share. In bed, McCarrick started to kiss his back and wrap his legs around him. Seconds later, he tried to force his hands "under my shorts, and then I felt his erect penis against me." The young man ran to the bathroom and began to sob, as McCarrick urged him to return to bed. The victim refused: "Instead, I went to the recliner and pretended to fall asleep."

Levada rushed to Benedict to tell him what was in the files, and the pope instantly realized it had been a terrible mistake to keep McCarrick in place in Washington. The cardinal, he declared, needed to retire immediately. McCarrick was summoned to Rome, where he offered what would become his standard defense to abuse charges. He admitted he occasionally invited young men into his bed, although he insisted there was never sexual contact. During a meeting with Cardinal Giovanni Battista Re of the Congregation for Bishops, McCarrick agreed to retire, but he pleaded for a delay of several months. He wanted to announce his departure on the same day his replacement was named, "so that my exit from Washington appears completely normal." Re agreed since at that point McCarrick's victims, while young, were all believed to be over the legal age of consent. "If there had been any involvement of minors, the approach would have been completely different," Re said in justifying the delay.

The retirement was portrayed as routine when it was announced the next spring. In June, President Bush and First Lady Laura Bush hosted a candlelit dinner for the cardinal in the family's private residence on the second floor of the White House. In a glowing farewell to McCarrick, an article in *The Washington Post* said his tenure as archbishop was marked by "prolific fundraising, a heightened profile overseas and a tone of civility." In retirement, McCarrick remained a full member of the College of Cardinals. He announced he would continue his charity work and worldwide travel.

IN JUNE 2006, Benedict announced a reshuffling of the Curia. He named Cardinal Bertone of Genoa as secretary of state, replacing Sodano, who was seventy-eight, three years past normal retirement age. The choice of the seventy-one-year-old Bertone as the Vatican's de facto prime minister was seen inside the Curia as proof that in Benedict's papacy, loyalty counted more than competence. By tradition, the secretary of state should be a multilingual career Vatican diplomat. But Bertone, who spoke little English and struggled in other major languages, had no experience in the diplomatic corps, and his personal style had never been described as diplomatic. He had been widely mocked the year before after announcing he would lead a global boycott of the best-selling 2003 novel *The Da Vinci Code*. By then, the book had already sold forty million copies. Vatican officials found the book outrageous, since it questioned Jesus's divinity and suggested the Savior was married to Mary Magdalene. Bertone's campaign backfired spectacularly, however. News coverage of his boycott caused sales of the book to soar again across Europe.

33

A Speech in Regensburg

MANY IN THE VATICAN could identify the exact day, even the exact hour, when the papacy of Benedict XVI began to unravel. It was Tuesday, September 12, 2006, a day intended to be a joyous homecoming for the pope in Regensburg, the Bavarian city where he had taught for so many years. The visit came during a six-day pilgrimage to Germany, his first extended trip to his homeland as pope. He planned to have lunch with his brother, who had retired several years earlier from the city's famed boys' choir; to lay flowers at the graves of his parents and sister; and to speak at the university at five p.m.

His speech was delivered in the school's central lecture hall, the audience packed with his former faculty colleagues and students. He had written the address himself, as he almost always did, since he never felt comfortable reading what others wrote for him. He spoke in part about the relationship between Christianity and other faiths, and most of the speech had a dry, scholarly tone. In discussing historic tensions between Christians and Islam, he quoted, with essentially no context, an insult that a fourteenth-century Byzantine emperor had directed against the prophet Mohammed. The emperor sneered when asked about the prophet's legacy: "Show me just what Mohammed brought that was new, and there you find things only evil and inhuman, such as his command to spread the faith by the sword."

While making clear he was quoting someone else, Benedict failed—inexplicably—to distance himself from the emperor's insult and pressed on with the speech. He then discussed the Islamic concept of jihad, which he defined as "holy war," and suggested it was a violation of God's will. A few in the audience turned to one another in bafflement, thinking the same question: Why had the pope revived an ancient slur against the prophet Mohammed without making clear he denounced it?

Cardinal Kasper, still in charge of the Vatican's efforts to build ties to other faiths, was in the audience and sensed disaster. He realized Benedict's remarks would be read as an insult against all Muslims. While the pope was still speaking, the Italian news agency ANSA sent out a bulletin on its wire service: "POPE: ISLAMIC HOLY WAR IS CONTRARY TO GOD." Minutes later, other news organizations began to report on what seemed to be the pope's stinging attack on Islam.

That night, street protests against the pope erupted in Muslim capitals throughout the world. He was burned in effigy in Egypt. Rioters in Indonesia, the world's most populous Muslim nation, took to the streets, crying out: "Crucify the pope!" The Pakistani national legislature voted unanimously to condemn Benedict. The deputy leader of the ruling party of Turkey said the pope had a "mentality that comes from the darkness of the Middle Ages." Benedict, he said, would be remembered alongside Hitler and Mussolini.

The violence went on for days. Several Christian churches were firebombed in the Palestinian city of Nablus. An Italian nun working in a charity hospital in Somalia was gunned down along with her bodyguard by Muslim militants who said the murders were in retaliation for the pope's insult. The Al Qaeda terrorist network warned that Benedict and his deputies were targets for assassination. Osama bin Laden said in an audiotape that the pope was leading a "new Crusade" against Islam.

Benedict frantically tried to calm the furor, issuing what was seen as an unprecedented papal apology: "I am deeply sorry for the reactions in some countries for a few passages in my address which were considered offensive." He insisted he did not share the views of the fourteenth-century emperor. The debacle became known among Italian clerics in the Curia as *l'incidente*, and it had elements of all that would go wrong during the rest of Benedict's papacy.

The Regensburg disaster could easily have been averted had Benedict followed the example of his predecessors and allowed deputies to read his speeches in advance. John Paul always had two or three aides edit his prepared remarks before delivery, but Benedict remained adamant about speaking without filters. A group of sharp-eyed Vatican reporters had saved Benedict from a similar calamity during a papal trip to Poland earlier that year. Handed an advance copy of a speech Benedict would deliver at the Auschwitz death camp, the reporters noted it failed to use the word "Holocaust" or refer directly to Hitler's Final Solution—omissions likely to appall Jewish leaders, all the worse coming from a pope who had been a soldier in Hitler's army. The reporters alerted the Vatican, which hastily inserted a suitable reference. Even with the revision, the address was criticized as strangely insensitive. Benedict failed to acknowledge any complicity of the German people in Nazi crimes and suggested that he and other Germans were "used and abused" by Hitler, as if they were innocent victims too.

The Regensburg debacle was an early reminder of an uncomfortable truth about the new pope. He had always been wary of other faiths—Islam, in particular. Journalists went back to find copies of then-Cardinal Ratzinger's remarks in 1996 in which he said Islam was so backward that its followers could not participate in the "free realm of pluralistic society."

BENEDICT FACED other setbacks that spring, including another wave of priestly sex-abuse cases. Several American dioceses announced they were nearing bankruptcy because of legal settlements with victims of pedophile priests. The Los Angeles archdiocese announced in December it would pay out $60 million to settle forty-five child-molestation lawsuits. Months later, it reached a $600 million agreement to settle five hundred more.

In 2006, Benedict attempted to put an end, once and for all, to the potential for a larger scandal over Father Maciel. Just a year after the Vatican had appeared to exonerate the Legion of Christ founder, the pope reversed course and announced that he had ordered the eighty-six-year-old Mexican priest to withdraw from public life because of "inappropriate conduct." Maciel remained a priest but would spend the rest of his life in "prayer and penitence." The announcement offered no details about Maciel's misconduct, nor was there any apology to his victims. The Legion released a statement in which Maciel accepted his punishment but compared his suffering to the Savior's. "Father Maciel has declared his innocence," it read. "But following the example of Jesus Christ, he has decided not to defend himself." The pope was praised by major news organizations for finally disciplining Maciel, even if so much about the investigation remained a mystery.

At first, the pope had reason to believe he had neutralized the threat of a massive public scandal over the sexual misconduct of another churchman, Cardinal McCarrick, whose departure from the Washington, DC, archdiocese in 2006 appeared to go off without incident. But on June 14, four days after the cardinal's triumphant farewell sermon in St. Matthew's Cathedral in Washington, church officials in New Jersey met with a lawyer representing yet another priest who had been molested as a seminarian by McCarrick. Months later, the priest was paid $100,000 in exchange for his promise never to identify McCarrick as his abuser. The settlement was reported to the Vatican.

That fall, Cardinal Bertone, newly settled in Rome as secretary of state, took charge of what became an increasingly desperate effort in the Vatican to prevent the McCarrick allegations from becoming public. In November, he received an alarming letter from the new papal nuncio in Washington, Archbishop Pietro Sambi, who wrote he was "on edge" after learning McCarrick might be the target of new abuse allegations, this time involving children. It was the first time Sambi had heard about the possibility that the cardinal, previously accused of groping young men, was a child molester, too. He pleaded for the Vatican's help to rein in McCarrick, who had stepped up his global travels and moved into an apartment in the Maryland suburbs of Washington—next to dormitories of a Catholic seminary. Sambi was appalled to discover that McCarrick had regular contact there with young seminarians, some still in their teens.

Made public years later, the correspondence between Bertone and Sambi, and hundreds of other long-secret Vatican documents about McCarrick, painted a damning portrait of decision making under Benedict. They showed that the pope, Bertone, and others refused to act against McCarrick even after an explicit warning in 2006 that he might be molesting children. The documents express little concern for victims and focus almost entirely on preventing a scandal that would embarrass the pope.

On December 6, 2006, Bertone's staff completed a memo summarizing all that was known about McCarrick's misconduct. The subject line: "CARDINAL THEODORE MCCARRICK: ALLEGATIONS OF HOMOSEXUALITY." The memo listed grave sex-abuse charges dating back more than twenty years. Its author, Archbishop Carlo Maria Viganò, a career Curia bureaucrat, said the allegations should be brought immediately to the attention of the pope, who could then defrock McCarrick "and restore a little dignity to a church so tired and humiliated for so many abominable behaviors on the part of some pastors."

On January 15, 2007, Bertone met with the pope and presented him with Viganò's report. According to Bertone, he and the pope discussed whether to launch a full investigation of McCarrick by the Congregation for the Doctrine of the Faith. Benedict rejected the idea, since he continued to hope the allegations might all be gossip. Even so, he told Bertone he "wished that McCarrick's activities be constrained in some manner." At the pope's direction, Bertone asked his staff to contact McCarrick and politely urge him—again—to withdraw to a "reserved life of prayer." It was guidance the cardinal ignored.

Then and for years to come, McCarrick thought he enjoyed Benedict's full support. Whatever his private misgivings, the pope allowed McCarrick to continue his far-flung travels and often asked him to represent the Vatican abroad. In 2007, he was the pope's personal envoy to a conference in Greenland on religion and science. The following January, McCarrick attended the global economic summit in Davos, Switzerland, before traveling to Rome, where he met briefly with Benedict during a papal audience in St. Peter's. In a letter to a senior Curia official after returning home, McCarrick wrote that, during the encounter in the basilica, the pope had greeted him with the remark, "You sure are traveling a lot!"

IN APRIL 2008, Benedict made his first pilgrimage to the United States as pope. There was intense speculation in the Vatican press corps about how he would address the child-abuse scandals. It was widely noted that he failed to include Boston, the epicenter of the crisis, on his itinerary. Instead, he went first to Washington, where he was greeted by President George W. Bush. On the flight from Rome, he told reporters he intended to apologize to American victims of pedophile priests: "We are deeply ashamed." In Washington, he met privately with several victims, including survivors flown in from Boston. In an open-air Mass in the capital's Nationals Stadium, the pope's homily included another apology to the survivors: "No words of mine could describe the pain and harm inflicted by such abuse."

In New York, he led a special Mass at St. Patrick's Cathedral. The pews were filled with the city's most powerful Catholic politicians, business leaders, and other celebrities. Benedict was surrounded at the altar by a group of American cardinals and bishops who had been honored with special invitations to participate in the papal Mass. To the horror of some in the audience, a beaming McCarrick was among them. The Vatican would later say it was unclear who had invited the cardinal, and his presence stunned Curia officials in the pope's entourage who knew something about the abuse allegations. That evening, McCarrick attended a banquet in the pope's honor.

News photos of the pope and McCarrick together in St. Patrick's circulated among some of the cardinal's victims hours later, and they were disgusted. They forwarded the photos to Richard Sipe, the psychotherapist who remained the nation's leading expert on priestly sexual abuse. Still a devout Catholic who considered himself loyal to the pope, he assumed Benedict would never have agreed to meet McCarrick in New York if the Vatican knew the extent of the cardinal's misconduct, which Sipe had heard about for years. So, on his personal website, Sipe posted an open letter to the pope to warn him about a brewing scandal. The statement, placed online the day after the pope returned to the Vatican, had a respectful tone.

Sipe wrote he had been moved by the pope's trip and his "heartfelt demonstration of concern for victims of priestly abuse," and so "I bring to your attention a dimension of the crisis not yet addressed." He wrote that, over the years, he had often heard about McCarrick's sexual misconduct, including his flagrant violation of his celibacy vows. In fact, he said, "I know the names of at least four priests who have had sexual encounters with Cardinal McCarrick. I have documents and letters that record their first-hand testimony and eyewitness accounts." He offered to send the material to Rome.

Sipe's post created a panic at the Congregation for the Doctrine of the Faith, which forwarded a copy to Bertone. Days later, Archbishop Viganò prepared a new memo for Bertone, noting that Sipe's allegations were more proof of the need to investigate and defrock McCarrick. Viganò's pleas were brushed aside again, however. Instead, in May, Bertone sent a letter to the Vatican's embassy in Washington asking that McCarrick be urged again to limit his public events. The letter also recommended the Washington archdiocese move him out of his apartment next to the seminary and find him a "worthy home" somewhere else—somewhere, it was hoped, away from boys and young men.

McCarrick refused to step out of the public eye. In correspondence with Benedict in 2008 and 2009, he promoted himself as a valuable go-between in Washington with newly elected President Barack Obama. He was especially close, he suggested, to Vice President Joseph Biden, a devout Catholic, and Secretary of State Hillary Clinton. His travels were never a

secret at the Vatican since he regularly sent the pope his detailed itinerar-
ies, which in 2009 included visits to more than twenty countries across five
continents. He was delighted that year when he was issued a new Vatican
diplomatic passport. The brownish-red passport, its cover stamped with
the papal seal, allowed him to travel almost anywhere, at will. Since the
passport guaranteed him full diplomatic immunity, he was comforted to
know he would never have to fear arrest or detention.

34

The Pope Stumbles

B ENEDICT'S HUMILIATING STUMBLES came every few weeks. He would announce a policy or deliver a speech that resulted in an uproar over his perceived insensitivity or carelessness. His small circle of doggedly loyal aides, frightened of giving him bad news, failed to protect him from his missteps. George Weigel, a conservative American Catholic writer who was close to John Paul II, condemned the "chaos, confusion, and incompetence" that became hallmarks of Vatican decision-making under Benedict.

In early 2007, the Vatican was still struggling to mend relations with Muslims after the Regensburg speech. Then, just as that furor died down, the pope outraged Jews too, as well as many reform-minded Catholics. In April, the Vatican revealed that Benedict was at work on a document to revive the widespread use of the traditional Latin service, the so-called Tridentine Mass, for the first time in forty years. The decision, which went well beyond John Paul II's move to allow occasional use of the Latin liturgy, was seen as the latest step in Benedict's years-long effort to undo Vatican II. He insisted that he simply wanted to increase options offered to the faithful. But bishops around the world reported almost no demand for Latin services, and many worried the decision would drive away Catholics who had come to treasure worshipping in their own languages, in the so-called New Mass. Father Keith Pecklers, a liturgical scholar at the Gregorian, thought the revival of the Latin Mass would alienate millions of worshippers: "This runs the risk of being misinterpreted as calling into question all of the Second Vatican Council."

Jewish leaders were dumbfounded. They had always considered the Tridentine Mass to be blatantly anti-Semitic, especially a prayer that called for their conversion. The prayer, dropped when the New Mass was adopted in the 1960s, called for Jews to end their "blindness" and "lift the veil from their hearts" by accepting Jesus as their Savior. The International Council for Christians and Jews said the pope's decision to revive the Tridentine Mass was "profoundly demeaning." The Anti-Defamation League of the US denounced the move as "nothing less than a body-blow to Catholic-Jewish relations."

Benedict, startled by the attacks, agreed to revise the Tridentine Mass, acknowledging that some of its wording was "really offensive," as if that had never occurred to him before. In early 2008, he announced the revisions, which Jewish leaders saw as only slightly less derogatory. Instead of referring to the "blindness" of Jews, the new version urged them to "enliven their hearts" by becoming Christians.

The pope next offended Protestants, especially the leaders of the eighty-five-million-member Anglican Communion, which included the Church of England and the Episcopal Church in the US. In 2008, he took advantage of a growing split among Anglicans over the appointment of women and openly gay priests by inviting disaffected Anglicans to leave their church entirely. His plan called for the creation of a church within the church, a so-called Catholic ordinariate, so Anglicans could worship as Catholics while honoring Protestant traditions. The Anglicans' global leader, Archbishop of Canterbury Rowan Williams, told deputies he was startled by what appeared to be a "dawn raid" by the Vatican, intended to split his church.

In May 2007, Benedict, on his first papal visit to South America, managed to outrage people across an entire continent with a speech in which he appeared shockingly ignorant of the history of European colonization. He told the audience in Brazil that the continent's native populations had been thrilled by the arrival of Christianity in the fifteenth century—that they had been "silently longing" for the faith to be brought to them by European settlers. "The proclamation of Jesus and of his Gospel did not at any point involve an alienation of native cultures, nor was it the imposition of a foreign culture," he said. For indigenous leaders, this was an absurd effort to whitewash the crimes of colonizers. Historians had long ago documented the deaths of millions of native Indians—through slaughter, disease, or enslavement—as a result of European settlement backed by the Vatican. President Hugo Chávez of Venezuela demanded an apology from Benedict. An Ecuadoran indigenous group condemned the pope, asking why he was defending Catholic missionaries who took part "in one of the most horrific genocides in all humanity." Benedict quickly realized his mistake and, in a public audience after he returned to Rome, acknowledged "unjustifiable crimes" committed by colonizers.

In January 2009, he lifted the excommunication of four self-declared bishops who were members of an ultraconservative Catholic order known as the Society of Saint Pius X. The cultlike group, which had about four hundred thousand followers, opposed the reforms of Vatican II and had never abandoned the Latin Mass. Its late founder, the conservative fire-brand Archbishop Marcel Lefebvre of France, had been banished from the church by John Paul in 1988, in part because Lefebvre ordained priests without the Vatican's approval. In announcing that the four bishops had been invited to worship again as Catholics, Benedict overruled Curia deputies who thought it was disgraceful for the Vatican to try to appease a dissident sect. His mistake became obvious just minutes after the announcement in Rome. Vatican reporters went to their computers and determined with a quick internet search that one of the bishops, Richard Williamson, was a fierce anti-Semite and Holocaust denier. In fact, just days earlier, Williamson created an uproar after a Swedish television interview in which he denied the existence of gas chambers at Auschwitz and other Nazi death camps. "It was all lies, lies, lies," the British-born Williamson declared. He thought perhaps three hundred thousand Jews had died in the camps, not millions, and most from natural causes. It turned out that all four of the now-rehabilitated bishops had said shockingly offensive things.*

Outrage over the pope's blunder was nearly universal, and the attacks were astonishingly personal. In Germany, Cardinal Lehmann, no friend to the pope, said the scandal threatened to undermine Benedict's legacy permanently: "There have to be consequences." Chancellor Angela Merkel phoned the pope to insist that as a German, he needed to make a "very clear" public rejection of Holocaust denial. Rabbi Marvin Hier of the

---

* Many of Benedict's critics said they found it hard to believe that the pope and his deputies knew nothing about Williamson's past as a Holocaust denier, since the bishop had stirred up controversy for years in his outrageous writings on that subject and others. Williamson believed women should not be allowed to attend university or wear pants, and equated feminism with witchcraft. He called for sweeping censorship, including global bans on many of the era's most popular books and films, since he considered them obscene. He denounced *The Sound of Music* as "pornographic soul-rotting slush," since it depicted a romance involving a Catholic nun-in-training: "Clean family entertainment? Nothing of the kind!"

Simon Wiesenthal Center, a Holocaust research center in Los Angeles, said that "this was absolutely a matter that was bungled at the highest levels of the Vatican. If they had just Googled the name Williamson, they would have found out he was a Holocaust denier!" Major newspapers in Germany openly questioned the pope's competence.

A wounded Benedict released a statement expressing his "full and unequivocal solidarity" with the Jewish people. He ordered Williamson to renounce his Holocaust denial. When Williamson refused, the pope moved to excommunicate him once again. In March, weeks into the controversy, Benedict issued a contrite letter to the world's bishops in which he accepted blame for the "avalanche of criticism" over Williamson. The letter suggested the pope was overwhelmed by feelings of self-pity; he wrote he was shocked at how many Catholics "attack me with open hostility."

Benedict saw the Williamson debacle as the turning point in his papacy. After that, "there was a huge propaganda campaign against me," he told a sympathetic German writer. "The people who were against me finally had the tangible evidence to say that I was unfit." He began to pray regularly for God "to get me out of this situation," as he weighed resignation. During a trip to central Italy in April to offer comfort to survivors of an earthquake days earlier, he arranged to travel to a basilica near the epicenter that held the remains of Pope Celestine V, the thirteenth-century monk who had been the last bishop of Rome to abdicate willingly.* While praying before a glass casket containing Celestine's mummified corpse, Benedict removed one of his most treasured papal garments—the V-shaped white woolen bands of cloth known as a pallium, which he had worn at his inauguration—and placed it on the casket to leave behind in tribute. His aides knew that this was freighted with symbolism, and that Paul VI had visited a separate shrine to Celestine in 1966 amid speculation that he was considering abdication.

By then, Bertone was also under heavy fire. In the modern history of the Curia, few senior Vatican bureaucrats were so widely loathed, viewed as both incompetent and power-hungry. Behind his back, Bertone was ridiculed by Italian colleagues as *il buffone* (the buffoon), although his authority was undeniable. As secretary of state, he had centralized all Curia decision-

---

* Celestine, who preferred the life of a hermit, stepped down voluntarily in 1296 after only five months as pope; he was later ridiculed by Dante, whose *Inferno* consigned the ex-pope to hell. In 1415, Pope Gregory XII resigned under intense pressure as part of an agreement to end the so-called Western Schism, in which rivals in Rome and Avignon, France, claimed to be the true pope.

making in his hands, and his loyalists were seeded throughout the Vatican. Foreign diplomats rolled their eyes at the mention of his name. In 2007, a classified cable leaked from the US embassy in Rome described Bertone as a classic "yes man" who served the pope poorly. Other Western diplomats noted that when things went wrong in Rome, Bertone was often nowhere to be found. He traveled abroad for weeks at a time, far more often than his predecessors, and delighted in first-class air travel and luxurious hotel suites. "Benedict XVI is left practically alone," *L'Espresso* commented. "And the Curia is abandoned to chaos."

Several German-speaking cardinals and bishops went to Rome in the spring of 2009 to plead with the pope to oust Bertone. The delegation, led by Cardinal Meisner of Cologne, one of the pope's best friends, noted that Bertone turned seventy-five that year and would need to submit his mandatory letter of resignation, which meant that his departure could appear routine.

"Listen to me carefully," the pope replied indignantly, according to Meisner's account. "Bertone will remain. Basta! Basta! Basta!" (Italian for "Enough! Enough! Enough!") Years later, Benedict still seemed blind to the damage Bertone had done. "He certainly was no diplomat—that is true," the pope told a biographer. "But who actually makes no mistakes?"

In 2009, Benedict made his first papal pilgrimage to the Holy Land, and his words and actions were roundly criticized by Jews, Muslims, and Christians alike as tone-deaf. He showed little interest in touring important biblical sites in Israel and Jordan, which baffled the dozens of journalists who accompanied him. Driven by golf cart to the shores of the Jordan River, scene of so many of the miracles depicted in scripture, he declined to step out of the vehicle and gaze out at the waters in which Jesus had been baptized. When he spoke at the Yad Vashem Holocaust memorial in Jerusalem, he made no reference to Nazi Germany or his own service in Hitler's army. The memorial's chairman, Rabbi Yisrael Meir Lau, said the pope's words were "almost sterile."

A month later, he issued his third encyclical, entitled *Caritas in Veritate* (Charity in Truth), that condemned economic inequality, a theme addressed in encyclicals by all his modern predecessors. What struck many church scholars was how badly it was written, as if Benedict no longer felt a responsibility to make himself understood. George Weigel, the American writer, derided the encyclical as "clotted and muddled." A religion writer for *The New York Times* said the "molasses-like text" left him baffled. "Not everyone will agree that *Caritas in Veritate* is hard-going," he wrote. "After all, some people enjoy visits to the dentist."

The sex-abuse scandals flared up constantly, especially in Ireland, one of the most devoutly Catholic nations in Europe. In November 2009, an Irish government investigation found that the country's bishops had conspired with police agencies to cover up hundreds of cases in which priests molested children. In the archdiocese of Dublin alone, bishops had shielded at least a hundred pedophile priests from arrest. One Dublin priest confessed to investigators that during twenty-five years in the priesthood he molested a different child every two weeks, as if meeting a quota.

By then, reporters in the Vatican press corps had become numb in writing about such horrors. How to explain to their editors, year after year, why the church refused to do more? Behind closed doors, Benedict was forced to deal with shocking new sex-abuse cases. In June 2009, he quietly accepted the resignation of a fifty-eight-year-old German-born bishop, Georg Müller, who stepped down after admitting he had molested a nine-year-old boy. The Vatican portrayed his resignation as routine. The ugly details only became public a year later because of the digging of journalists in Norway, where Müller was posted at the end of his career.

The Maciel case came back to haunt the pope. In 2009, a year after Maciel's death, the Legion of Christ was forced to make the first of what would be a long series of public admissions of its late founder's depravity.* Church investigators eventually identified thirty-three other Legion priests who sexually abused children—at least 175 boys and girls—since the order's founding in the 1940s. Curia officials urged Benedict to dissolve the Legion, but he refused. He declared that the order, still home to one of the church's most successful fundraising operations, remained a "sound" organization of "young men who enthusiastically want to serve the faith." In his only extensive comments about Maciel, Benedict said in a 2010 interview that the Mexican priest's crimes were "concealed very well." That was flatly untrue, however. The voluminous written record showed that then-Cardinal Ratzinger had been repeatedly alerted, over several years and in detail, to Maciel's sexual abuse of children, and he did virtually nothing.

---

* Maciel died in January 2008, at the age of eighty-seven, in his sprawling home in a gated community in Jacksonville, Florida. On the day of his death, the Legion issued a press release to announce that Maciel was so saintly that he was instantly received in heaven, where he had been reunited with his great friend John Paul II.

———

A NEW WAVE OF child-abuse scandals overwhelmed the Vatican in 2010, beginning with an explosion of reports about priestly sex abuse in Germany. Suddenly, the crisis that had taken hold in the US and elsewhere in Europe arrived in earnest among the twenty-five million Catholics of the pope's homeland. The first accounts came in January from a Jesuit school in Berlin that identified seven cases in which priests had sexually abused students. A total of 193 other ex-students came forward to report they had been molested there, as well.

The scandals became much more personal for the pope in March, when the Bavarian church hierarchy announced it had received reports of the rampant sexual abuse of choirboys in the Regensburger Domspatzen—led for thirty years by his brother, Georg. Then eighty-six and retired for a decade, Georg was accused of beating choirboys—he admitted he slapped and punched students when they misbehaved—but not of sexual abuse. He claimed he was shocked at the belated discovery that his staff had included several child molesters. Church investigators identified hundreds of choirboys who were physically abused by priests and other church workers between 1945 and the 1990s. At least sixty-seven were victims of sexual abuse, which ranged from "forced consumption of pornography to unwanted sexual touching to forced sex." Many boys described their years in the choir as a combination of "prison, hell and a concentration camp," the investigators reported. Attention turned to what the pope had known, since he lived in Regensburg for years and was so close to his brother. In 2010, a group representing German child victims demanded he reveal if he had been aware of the abuse: "How could the pope have had no sense at all of what was happening to these innocent boys who were in his brother's care?" The pope insisted he had never suspected any mistreatment.

That year, one news organization in particular tormented Benedict: *The New York Times*. The paper had not been in the forefront of covering priestly sex-abuse scandals, but in 2010 it turned its global reporting firepower to the crisis—and to questions of what the pope had known, and when. An early article detailed the crimes of Germany's most notorious pedophile priest, Peter Hullermann, believed to have molested scores of boys. The story explored then-Cardinal Ratzinger's involvement in the 1980 decision to allow Hullermann to resume his priestly duties even after admitting he molested an eleven-year-old boy. The *Times* tracked down the psychiatrist who treated Hullermann in Munich, who said he had repeatedly gone to Ratzinger's office with the same desperate plea: "For God's sake, he has to be kept away from working with children!"

Weeks later, the *Times* revealed how then-Cardinal Ratzinger had ignored urgent requests in the 1990s to defrock an American priest, Lawrence Murphy, who had molested an estimated two hundred boys at a Catholic-run school for the deaf in Wisconsin. In 1993, Murphy confessed his crimes to a social worker hired by the church; yet it would be another four years before the Congregation for the Doctrine of the Faith allowed Wisconsin bishops to organize a secret canonical trial to defrock him. And that trial was called off after Murphy wrote directly to Ratzinger, saying he was in poor health and wanted to finish his life "in the dignity of the priesthood." After he died in 1998, his victims were disgusted when Murphy, still a priest, was given a formal church funeral and buried in his priestly robes.

The *Times* revisited Ratzinger's role in the scandals of Cardinal Groër of Austria. The paper documented how even after Groër was exposed as a serial pedophile, Ratzinger held off any investigation. In May 2010, the paper published a sweeping investigation of the pope's involvement in the cover-up of Maciel's crimes.

In the year that followed, there was an unprecedented string of resignations by bishops caught up in abuse scandals. The longest-serving Catholic bishop in Belgium, seventy-three-year-old Roger Vangheluwe of the city of Bruges, stepped down in April 2010 after admitting he had regularly molested his own nephew for years. Although Vangheluwe insisted he was not a pedophile ("I never felt the slightest physical attraction to children"), he later admitted molesting a second nephew.

In September 2011, a team of prominent human-rights lawyers filed a complaint with the International Criminal Court in The Hague, accusing the pope personally of crimes against humanity. They charged that he was responsible for a "systematic and widespread" practice of concealing child rape. (The court declined the case, since most of the abuse cited in the complaint occurred before 2002, when the court was established.)

Benedict launched a ham-handed campaign to defend himself. He once more portrayed himself as a victim of irresponsible news organizations, the *Times* in particular. Reporters in the Vatican press corps were called in, one by one, to meet with Cardinal Levada and listen as he condemned the media's "persecution" of the pope.

The campaign only brought fresh attacks on Benedict. He managed to offend both child-victim advocates and Jewish leaders after he invited an Italian theologian on his staff to give the Good Friday sermon in St. Peter's Basilica in April 2010. As the pope listened a few feet away, the theologian compared the criticism directed at Benedict in the sex-abuse crisis to the "collective violence" that Jews had faced throughout history, culminating in the Holocaust. Germany's Central Council of Jews described the remark as "repulsive, obscene and offensive toward all abuse victims and to all victims of the Holocaust."

Two days later, at Easter services in St. Peter's Square, Cardinal Sodano created a similar uproar when he gave a homily defending the pope in the abuse scandals: "Holy Father, the people of God are with you and will not let themselves be influenced by the petty gossip of the moment." Benedict broke into a smile and rose from his chair to embrace Sodano.* The cardinal's remarks were condemned around the world. "When we speak up and tell how our childhood innocence was shattered by sexual assaults by priests, it is not 'petty gossip,'" said Barbara Blaine, president of SNAP, the victims' rights group.

Throughout the year, there were reports that the pope intended to resign, and for the first time he acknowledged it was a possibility. "If a pope clearly realizes that he is no longer physically, psychologically and spiritually capable of handling the duties of his office, then he has a right and, under some circumstances, also an obligation to resign," he told a German reporter.

The sex-abuse crisis so overwhelmed the Vatican that year that it crowded out other news about the pope, including what appeared to be his stepped-up campaign to defend conservative doctrine. He identified an important new target in 2012—Catholic nuns—and seized administrative control of the fifteen-hundred-member Leadership Conference of Women Religious, the largest nuns' group in the United States. The organization outraged American bishops two years earlier when it endorsed President Obama's national health insurance plan, known as Obamacare. The US national bishops' conference opposed Obama's plan because it might allow federal funding of abortion and birth control. The Vatican said the nuns' group also needed to be reined in because its members had challenged church

---

* While the pope denied asking Sodano to defend him in the homily, Benedict's private secretary, Archbishop Georg Gänswein, acknowledged years later that he—Gänswein—made the request to Sodano on behalf of Curia bishops who were alarmed by increasingly ugly personal attacks on the pope (Seewald, *Benedict XVI: A Life, Volume II*, 426).

teachings on homosexuality and the male-only priesthood, as well as promoting "radical feminist themes incompatible with the Catholic faith."

Under Benedict, as under all his modern predecessors, women had almost no influence in the Vatican. Mother Teresa, cited constantly by John Paul II as proof of what women could accomplish, died in 1997, and Benedict found no one to take her place. During his papacy, only one woman had any significant authority in the Vatican—Lesley-Anne Knight, a respected British laywoman who led Caritas, the umbrella group for the world's Catholic charities, with a combined annual budget of $5 billion. In 2011, however, she was forced out on orders of Bertone, who wanted the Curia to have more control over how the money was spent. She was replaced by a man.

FOR ALMOST FIVE YEARS, Hans Küng held his tongue in public about Benedict. After their unexpectedly friendly meeting at Castel Gandolfo in 2005, Küng had wanted to give his old rival the benefit of the doubt. In 2010, however, Küng decided he had lost all hope for Benedict: "He had become a disappointment to the world." Küng was shocked over the explosion of priestly sex-abuse cases across Germany that year, as well as the revelations about Benedict's personal involvement in cover-ups dating back decades. He thought Benedict was lying when he claimed he knew nothing about the molestation of boys in the Regensburg choir, given how close he was to his brother.

In March, Küng arranged for a group of leading newspapers and magazines in Europe and the United States to publish an open letter to the world's bishops, calling for them to demand a Third Vatican Council. He blamed Benedict directly for the abuse crisis—"a scandal crying out to heaven"—and suggested the pope's actions to shield pedophile priests amounted to a criminal conspiracy. Küng wrote that as a result of Benedict's disastrous papacy, the church had been plunged into "the worst credibility crisis since the Reformation." In response, the Vatican press office handed out copies of an essay by Weigel, who demanded Küng make an apology to the pope for these "vicious smears." While often a critic of Benedict, Weigel thought the pope had a "genuine commitment to combatting pedophilia in the priesthood." What Küng had written, Weigel charged, was a "piece of vitriol" unworthy of "a priest, an intellectual or a gentleman."

35

The Vatican vs. Buenos Aires

W HEN CARDINAL BERGOGLIO RETURNED home to Argentina after the 2005 conclave, he had reason to fear he would spend the final years of his career in tiresome battles with the Vatican. After Benedict's election, it became common wisdom in Buenos Aires that the new pope's craven deputies in the Curia intended to punish Bergoglio for having come so close to defeating him.

There was a telling sign of trouble in Rome in the days immediately after Benedict's election, when the new pope made a decision many Argentines saw as an unmistakable snub. It came at a press conference Benedict held to thank journalists for their coverage of the conclave. As had been routine for such events, he read out a statement of thanks in several languages, beginning with Italian, then English, French, and German. And then he stopped. He did not offer the greeting in the customary fifth language—Spanish, the tongue common to almost half the world's Catholics. It was a notable violation of tradition, all the stranger since he had addressed hundreds of audiences in Spanish over the years. Puzzled Spanish-speaking reporters turned to one another in exasperation.

Father Marco, Bergoglio's spokesman, called the office of Cardinal Sodano, still the secretary of state, and was told the pope had decided "the Spanish-speaking world would understand the Italian." Marco knew it was an absurd explanation.

Sodano had always been trouble for Bergoglio. During his years as nuncio in neighboring Chile in the 1970s and 1980s, Sodano had established a network of fiercely conservative protégés across Latin America who disdained what they saw as Bergoglio's willingness to ignore church teachings, especially on sexuality. It was well known in the church hierarchy in neighboring countries that Bergoglio's homilies rarely touched on what the Vatican saw as the evils of birth control, homosexuality, and promiscuity.

The ill will between Bergoglio and the Vatican came to a head in 2006 in the wake of the furor over the pope's speech in Regensburg. Leaders of Argentina's sizable Muslim community protested at what they saw as an attack on their faith. Bergoglio was appalled too. By then, he had established himself as Argentina's most important champion of religious tolerance. In 2002, he joined with Jewish and Muslim leaders to found a national institute on interfaith dialogue. The next year, as the US military prepared to invade Iraq, he set up a day-and-night open-air meeting place in Buenos Aires for Christians and Muslims to join in prayers for peace. The archdiocese television station sponsored thirty episodes of a program in which Bergoglio and one of the city's most prominent rabbis discussed the Bible. The cardinal was beloved among Argentine Protestants after word spread of his open invitation for aging priests from small Protestant denominations to spend their final days in a housing complex for retired Catholic clergy. When he learned an evangelical Protestant minister had become disabled from multiple sclerosis and could communicate only by blinking his eyes, he agreed to take him in and pay for his treatment. "If we have to sell chalices, we'll sell them," Bergoglio vowed.

After the Regensburg speech, Bergoglio felt he needed to speak up, even if that risked the Vatican's wrath. His office issued a press release: "Pope Benedict's statements don't reflect my own opinions. These statements will serve to destroy in twenty seconds the careful construction of a relationship with Islam that Pope John Paul II built over the last twenty years." A copy of the press release reached Rome hours later, and Sodano's office ordered Bergoglio to retract the statement. Within days, Marco, Bergoglio's spokesman, took the blame and announced his resignation, insisting the words should have been attributed to him.

Churchmen in Buenos Aires who had to deal with the Curia came to despise Bertone, Sodano's successor. As pope, Benedict never visited Argentina, but Bertone found reason to go there regularly and became notorious for insisting on the sort of pomp associated with the pope. His visit in November 2007 became infamous inside the Argentine church hierarchy because of an iconic photograph taken of Bertone seated next to Bergoglio at a beatification ceremony for an Argentine candidate for sainthood. Bertone, wearing aviator sunglasses, with an ornate gold-embroidered miter on his head, is seen staring out at the crowd, stone-faced, like an emperor. He is seated in a thronelike wooden armchair set on a platform putting him at least six inches higher than Bergoglio, who is wearing simple white robes and seated in a plastic chair. The photo shows Bergoglio unsmiling, his mouth open, looking up at the secretary of state, seemingly appalled by the gaudy spectacle.

IN HIS FINAL YEARS as archbishop of Buenos Aires, Bergoglio remained almost entirely silent on the issue of clerical sex abuse. When pressed, he continued to suggest his city had been spared the crisis that had so damaged the church elsewhere. His deputies rejected occasional local news reports suggesting the archdiocese hid evidence of the crimes of pedophile priests from the police, which explained why relatively few had been prosecuted. Bergoglio was regularly accused of an un-Christian callousness in dealing with the victims of clerical sex abuse elsewhere in Argentina. Since he was the country's most powerful Catholic leader, victims from outside Buenos Aires often asked to see him, and he turned them down. Ernesto Moreau, an Argentine lawyer who represented abuse victims, said he was startled by what he saw as Bergoglio's heartlessness in refusing to comfort his clients. "He's been totally silent," Moreau said.

In two notorious cases, Bergoglio was eager to jump to the defense of churchmen accused of sexual misconduct. The first was Father Grassi, the celebrity priest accused of molesting as many as twenty boys in the care of his Happy Children Foundation, which was based outside Buenos Aires. After his conviction in 2009 on charges of sexually abusing a thirteen-year-old boy, Grassi revealed that throughout his trial his greatest supporter had been Bergoglio, "who never let go of my hand" and "is always by my side." The victim's lawyers were astonished when they discovered that Bergoglio used church funds to pay for a four-volume, two-thousand-page forensic study of the case by a prominent criminal-defense lawyer, who argued that Grassi's many accusers were lying. Appeals courts rejected the claims and sent the priest to prison.

In the second case, Bergoglio was eager to offer public support in 2005 to Bishop Juan Carlos Maccarone, a sixty-four-year-old bishop in a northern province of Argentina, after news organizations obtained a grainy videotape of Maccarone having sex with a mostly naked twenty-three-year-old man, his chauffeur. The young man claimed he had been in a sexual relationship with Maccarone for years. The bishop's resignation was instantly accepted by Pope Benedict, even as Bergoglio issued statements defending Maccarone and suggesting he was a victim of a vendetta by a local political clan.

Bergoglio continued to demonstrate a serious blind spot on another issue—his actions in the Dirty War. The government of President Cristina Kirchner, who succeeded her husband, Néstor, in 2007, remained eager to stir up that controversy. After refusing for years to testify about allegations of his complicity with the junta, Bergoglio was finally forced in 2010 to submit to four and a half hours of questioning under oath in a criminal investigation of military officers assigned to ESMA, the Dirty War torture center. Even the cardinal's friends agreed his videotaped testimony before three judges was halting and evasive.

His constant battles with the Kirchners left Bergoglio sure that he was under surveillance by the national spy agency, the Secretariat of Intelligence, or SIDE. He insisted that sensitive church meetings be conducted with radios playing in the background, to make it difficult for conversations to be monitored by bugging equipment. He believed the Kirchners and their deputies were determined to destroy his reputation—"people in the government wanted to cut off my head"—by spreading lies about his conduct in the Dirty War.

His relationship with the government deteriorated further in 2010 in a national debate over legislation, sponsored by President Cristina Kirchner, to legalize gay marriage. Buenos Aires had long been seen as the gay capital of South America, and Bergoglio had often said publicly he welcomed gay Catholics to the pews, but he felt the gay-marriage bill boxed him in, given Pope Benedict's uncompromising rejection of homosexuality. The cardinal's opposition to the bill also pitted him against most of his countrymen, since opinion polls showed that 70 percent of Argentines supported same-sex marriage. He tried to negotiate a compromise, telling lawmakers that if they put aside the bill, he would support alternative legislation to recognize civil unions of gay couples. Kirchner rejected the compromise, however, and attacked Bergoglio; she said the church's thinking about sexuality had not changed since "the time of the Crusades." Bergoglio made a final plea for rejection of the bill, describing gay marriage as a "destructive attack on God's plan," but it was approved in July, making Argentina the first country in Latin America to allow gay couples to wed.

The Curia's hostility toward Bergoglio only grew. During his occasional trips to the Vatican to meet with Benedict's arrogant deputies, the cardinal was forced to "suffer in silence," said Father Victor Manuel Fernández, an Argentine theologian who was a graduate of the Gregorian and learned much about the cravenness of church politics during his studies in Rome. Within the Curia, Fernández knew, there was "a certain contempt toward those 'poor Latin Americans'—and especially toward Bergoglio." That was in stark contrast to the cardinal's popularity among his counterparts in Latin America. He was celebrated as a hero by many of the region's bishops after it became known that he had nearly defeated Benedict for the papacy in 2005. The region's few openly progressive bishops, who had managed to rise in the hierarchy despite the conservatism of John Paul II and Benedict, admired Bergoglio for his evolution on social justice. While still resisting any public affiliation with liberation theology, he had become, by his actions, one of its greatest champions.

He cemented that reputation in 2007, when the Conference of Latin American Bishops, or CELAM, decided to meet for the first time in fifteen years. The conference, then made up of 160 cardinals and bishops, had fallen out of favor under John Paul and Benedict, given its reputation as the organization that gave birth to liberation theology.

Bergoglio was the star of the gathering, held in the Brazilian city of Aparecida. He was easily elected to its most important job—writing the policy statements that the bishops would release at the end of the meeting. The documents were vintage Bergoglio, written in flowery, often difficult-to-understand language. Even so, the bishops' central message was unmistakable. The region's church leaders had not lost their enthusiasm for liberation theology: "We pledge to work harder, so our church may continue to accompany our poorest brothers on their journey, even to martyrdom." The reference to "martyrdom" was widely noted, since it meant the bishops knew the fight for justice could end in violence.

Bergoglio took his own theological expert to the conference, Father Fernández, and it was the start of a partnership in which they would both rise to extraordinary power in the church. Fernández, then forty-four, described Bergoglio as "a great father figure" always willing to overlook their differences on questions of doctrine. Fernández admitted he was far more liberal, even radical, on some issues, especially when it came to sexuality, and was best known for a controversial 1995 book entitled *Heal Me with Your Mouth: The Art of Kissing*, in which he urged Catholic couples to kiss passionately, since kisses were "the thermometer of love." The book, which even some of Fernández's friends saw as bizarrely explicit, included several of his erotic poems, including one that ended:

> *How was God*
> *so cruel*
> *as to give you that mouth?*
> *There is no one who resists me,*
> *bitch,*
> *hide it.*

BERGOGLIO SAW the bishops' conference in Brazil as the highlight of his career, which seemed to be nearing its end. In 2011, when he turned seventy-five, he would need to submit his resignation, and he assumed Benedict would accept it immediately. Bergoglio began planning for a quiet retirement. He picked out a comfortable room on the second floor of the Catholic priests' retirement home in Buenos Aires. He was offered a higher floor, with a nicer view, but he charmed the nuns who were the building's

Catholic theologian Victor Manuel Fernández of Argentina, a reform-minded protégé of Cardinal Jorge Bergoglio of Buenos Aires, was rudely rebuffed by the Vatican for years over a university appointment arranged by Bergoglio.

caretakers when he explained that he liked the symbolism of a lower floor since "I don't want to be above anyone else."

The closer he got to retirement, the more the Curia seemed determined to make his life uncomfortable. In 2009, he named Fernández as rector of the Pontifical Catholic University in Buenos Aires, among the most prestigious Catholic-run schools in South America. The appointment required approval from the Vatican, however, and the Curia delayed a decision for years. The approval was initially held up after an anonymous critic sent a package of Fernández's writings to the Curia, including passages from *The Art of Kissing*, and urged that he be rejected for the university post. The package ended up at the Congregation for Catholic Education, led by Archbishop Jean-Louis Bruguès of France, and at the Congregation for the Doctrine of the Faith, which then opened a secret disciplinary file on Fernández. When it became clear his appointment had stalled, Fernández decided to go to Rome to clear up any confusion over his credentials, but he was flabbergasted that he could not get an appointment, month after month, with Bruguès: "Can someone have his credentials questioned by anonymous people and have no chance to defend himself?" Bergoglio intervened and sent a stern letter to Bruguès, insisting Fernández be given an interview. Fernández soon received an email confirming the date of his appointment. He flew to Rome weeks later, but a day before the interview, it was canceled. Fernández was told, without explanation, that the congregation had no plans to reschedule it. He was despondent and telephoned Bergoglio in Buenos Aires. The cardinal sputtered with rage, Fernández remembered. It was clear to both of them that this was, above all else, a way of insulting Bergoglio. The runaround continued for three more years. In November 2012, Fernández asked again for a hearing in Rome. This time, he remembered despairingly, "the congregation did not even bother to reply."

36

What the Butler Saw

MARION WESTPFAHL WAS among the most respected criminal defense lawyers in Munich. A former judge and prosecutor, she was the logical choice in 2010 when the city's Catholic archdiocese needed a hard-nosed and discreet lawyer to lead an investigation that would be among the most sensitive in the history of the German church. Her assignment: to review all priestly child-abuse cases in the archdiocese dating back decades, with a special focus on how they were investigated during then-Cardinal Ratzinger's five years in Munich. The incumbent archbishop, Cardinal Reinhard Marx, did not want to be blindsided if there were more cases like that of the notorious pedophile priest Peter Hullermann—a case the future Pope Benedict had clearly mishandled—sitting in the files.

Westpfahl's investigation ended almost as soon as it began. The disciplinary files she needed had disappeared in what she suspected was a systematic cover-up. Documents that should have been stored in the Bishop's Palace, the eighteenth-century mansion that Ratzinger and his predecessors had used as both a home and an office, were nowhere to be found. "We are dealing with extensive destruction of paperwork," she declared. She did not allege Ratzinger had anything to do with the cover-up but noted that recordkeeping during his tenure had been "catastrophic."

What was in surviving files was still appalling. She could identify 250 priests and religious teachers who had been accused of abuse over the years and, given the missing documents, "we must assume the real number is much higher." The files reflected the archdiocese's "contempt" for victims, she said. Acts of child molestation, including rape, were described in "euphemistic, trivializing language." The Vatican had no comment on her report, apart from noting Pope Benedict's insistence that he had nothing to do with the missing documents.

The situation in Munich made for a dark contrast with the bulging files that continued to grow—in Rome and the United States—about the sex-abuse allegations made against Cardinal McCarrick in Washington. By then, other American bishops talked regularly among themselves about a looming scandal. "We *all* knew," said Bishop Steven Lopes, who had been a seminarian in New Jersey when McCarrick was bishop there. Lopes said later that when the scandal became public, he was disgusted to see "cardinals and bishops rushing to the television cameras, clutching their pectoral crosses, saying, 'I knew nothing.' Don't believe it."

The pope continued to greet McCarrick regularly in Rome and was host at a Vatican reception in April 2010 to honor the cardinal and other trustees of the Papal Foundation. The charity continued to raise tens of millions of dollars a year that Benedict, like John Paul before him, could direct to projects of his choice. McCarrick told colleagues in Washington that he had also quietly pledged to raise money that year for a pair of German-based charities. The first, the Ratzinger Foundation, was established in 2007 to promote theology "in the spirit of Joseph Ratzinger." The second was the Benedict XVI Institute, created to organize publication, in all major modern languages, of a sixteen-volume set of the pope's collected writings.*

The pope understood the risk of public displays of friendship with McCarrick. In June 2010, he turned down a request to send an otherwise routine letter of congratulations to McCarrick on his eightieth birthday. A confidential memo prepared by Bertone's office noted that the pope was advised against the letter because *The New York Times* was about to publish a "nasty" article about McCarrick's "moral life." (The *Times* did not publish such an article that year.)

A year later, Archbishop Carlo Maria Viganò, the Curia bureaucrat who wrote the blistering memos in 2006 and 2008 cataloging the molestation allegations against McCarrick, was named papal ambassador to Washing-

---

* In 2010, Benedict announced his foundation would begin handing out annual awards to honor distinguished theologians—the Ratzinger Prizes. They were intended to be the "Nobel Prize of theology," one of the foundation's trustees said. The first three prizes were handed out the next year, and each winner was given the equivalent of $87,000. There is no suggestion in public records that the foundation or the Benedict XVI Institute was aware of McCarrick's fundraising plans.

ton. He was sent there with explicit instructions to keep watch on McCarrick. Even so, in public, he treated the cardinal with deference. At a charity dinner in 2012, he gave an address in which he pointed to McCarrick in the audience, praising him as an invaluable "ambassador" for the church who was "very much loved by us all."

The remainder of Benedict's papacy was consumed by the sex-abuse crisis and by his inability or unwillingness to grapple with it. For many Catholics, especially in Germany, the disclosures tying him personally to the cover-up of abuse cases had shattered his credibility. He was reminded constantly of the Vatican's historic failure to protect children from pedophiles. In 2010, the Dutch hierarchy announced that a decade-long investigation had determined that as many as twenty thousand Dutch children had been abused by priests and other church workers since the 1940s. The following month, a Dutch newspaper revealed that ten boys were castrated in the 1950s on orders from Dutch bishops, either to "cure" their homosexuality or as punishment for accusing clergymen of molesting them. The castrations were carried out in church-affiliated psychiatric hospitals.

With no end to the crisis in sight, Benedict appeared increasingly frantic to find others to blame, including the devil. In a widely mocked speech in 2010 the pope said Satan was ultimately responsible for "the abuse of the little ones."

The final undoing of his papacy began in March 2012, when he made a three-day pilgrimage to Mexico. The trip was plagued by constant reminders of the scandals of Father Maciel. Days ahead of the pope's arrival, a Mexican magazine published excerpts of a new book by one of Maciel's victims, a former Legion priest who said he could document how Benedict had ignored evidence of Maciel's pedophilia. Benedict, who regularly met with victims of priestly sex abuse in his travels, refused to do so in Mexico.

Then came a devastating scandal that was quickly dubbed Vatileaks. It had its origins in a secret meeting in Rome the year before between Italian journalist Gianluigi Nuzzi and a mysterious source who promised damaging information about the Vatican. The source, a shy, forty-five-year-old Italian man, had contacted Nuzzi using a code name—Maria, after Jesus's mother. When they met, "Maria" revealed to Nuzzi that his real name was Paolo Gabriele, and that he was Benedict's personal butler. He insisted he loved the pope, which explained why he needed to expose internal church documents revealing how others in the Vatican were conspiring behind Benedict's back.

Paolo Gabriele, Pope Benedict's butler, was the source of leaked papal correspondence that exploded into the "Vatileaks" scandal in 2012.

Gabriele had worked in the Vatican since the 1980s, initially as a janitor, then from 2006 as Benedict's butler, which put him at the pope's side day and night. He was so trusted that he was also given sensitive secretarial work. Gabriele became so alarmed as he read some of the pope's correspondence, which documented systemic mismanagement and possible corruption by Bertone and others in the Curia, that he smuggled thousands of pages of the documents out of the Vatican.

Nuzzi began to release the papal correspondence in January 2012, initially on a television program. The most explosive letters had been written to the pope by Archbishop Viganò at a time when Viganò was still a senior Curia bureaucrat—the number-two official in Vatican City's municipal government—and facing transfer to Washington. In the letters, Viganò said he was being banished to the US because corrupt Curia officials wanted him out of the way after he exposed waste in the awarding of Vatican contracts. He suggested Bertone protected Italian businessmen who wildly overbilled the church for routine services. Viganò offered examples of how he had ended wasteful spending—for example, cutting the cost of the annual Nativity scene in St. Peter's Square from 550,000 euros in 2009 to 300,000 the next year. Viganò told the pope that rampant mismanagement was being hidden from him—"the Holy Father has certainly been kept in the dark"—and pleaded that he be allowed to remain in Rome. The pope did not cancel Viganò's transfer, however, and the despondent archbishop left for Washington.

Other Vatileaks documents revealed the details of what had long been rumored in the Vatican—that large cash gifts bought face-to-face access to the pope. In a single day, the files showed, Benedict could bring in $40,000 to $150,000 in exchange for private audiences. An Italian television anchorman sent a ten-thousand-euro check at Christmastime in 2010, attaching a note: "When can I have a meeting with the Holy Father?"

The Vatileaks scandal, which consumed the attention of the Vatican press corps for months, was seen as final proof both of Benedict's incompetence as a manager and of his willingness to turn a blind eye to corruption. He was humiliated by the criticism and, against the advice of Vatican lawyers, sued the German satire magazine *Titanic* for defamation at the height of the scandal after it published a cover photograph of Benedict under the headline "The Leak Has Been Found!" The photo had been altered to suggest a large urine stain on the front of his white cassock. The magazine was forced to pull the issue from newsstands.

In March, the pope asked three semiretired, archconservative cardinals to find the source of the leaks. The probe was led by his friend Cardinal Herranz of Spain, best known in Rome as the most prominent member of Opus Dei working in the Curia. The trio of cardinals—they became known in Italian tabloids as *i tre detective* (the three detectives)—had barely begun work when, in May, Gabriele was arrested. The police raided his apartment and found eighty boxes of the pope's correspondence. There were the predictable, embarrassing newspaper headlines, many with the punchline "The Butler Did It." At trial, Gabriele confessed under cross-examination and was sentenced to eighteen months in prison—confined in one of the small jail cells inside Vatican City. That Christmas, the pope pardoned him.

Gabriele's confession did not end the investigation by the three cardinals, who were urged by the pope to press on with the hunt for co-conspirators. The investigation became increasingly aggressive, and the pope authorized the use of wiretaps.

Few Italian church leaders were more disgusted by Vatileaks than Cardinal Martini, then eighty-five and living in retirement in Milan, where he received round-the-clock care for his Parkinson's disease.* He had confided to friends throughout Benedict's papacy that he was appalled by the pope's self-inflicted catastrophes, from the 2006 Regensburg fiasco to the endless disclosures about clerical child abuse. After Vatileaks, Martini was convinced that Benedict's papacy could never be salvaged. In June, when the pope was due in Milan for a church-sponsored conference, Martini asked to see him, and Benedict agreed. Exactly what was said that day would be known only to the pope and Martini. But according to the account from Father Fausti, Martini's confessor, the cardinal told the pope bluntly that he had to step down. He reminded Benedict of their 2005 pact—that the pope would abdicate if he failed to reform the Curia. According to Fausti, Martini looked Benedict in the eye and said somberly: "The Curia is not going to change. You have no choice but to leave." Fausti was unsure if the pope made a formal promise that day to resign, but Martini sensed that Benedict was already near that decision.

The pope received bad news that summer from "the three detectives" that added to the pressure to abdicate. While the cardinals could not identify co-conspirators in Vatileaks, they had turned up evidence of wrongdoing throughout the Curia, including blackmail plots by cardinals and bishops against one another, often involving threats of exposure of their sexual misconduct. That several Curia bishops were sexually active, and that many were homosexual, was not news to Benedict. What was shocking was the extent of it. Herranz reported the existence of what he called "gay lobbies" of homosexual bishops and priests who banded together to protect one another and damage others. Benedict was also warned to ready himself for a new wave of sexual-abuse scandals, including some that would target members of the College of Cardinals. Herranz told the pope that Cardinal Keith O'Brien of Scotland, then seventy-five, was about to be accused by a British newspaper of molesting seminarians and young priests throughout his career.

Within weeks, Benedict decided to abdicate, although he delayed the announcement for several months. He insisted his resignation had nothing to do with Vatileaks or the child-abuse scandals or that he was being coerced. "No one had tried to blackmail me," he told a biographer. "If that

* Martini's plans to spend his final days in Jerusalem had been foiled by the illness, which required him to return to Italy for constant medical care.

had been attempted I would not have gone. One cannot submit to extortion." He said the decision became unavoidable after he returned home from Mexico, a journey that left him, at eighty-four, close to physical collapse. He did not despair at the thought of resigning: "It did not tear me to pieces." In fact, he claimed, it turned out to be a simple calculation: "My hour had passed, and I had given all I could give." He told only four men in advance—Bertone; Sodano; his brother, Georg; and his private secretary, Archbishop Georg Gänswein of Germany—and all were sworn to secrecy.

On August 31, Martini died, which produced an outpouring of grief unlike any for an Italian churchman since John XXIII. The next day, Milan's leading newspaper, *Corriere della Sera*, published an interview that Martini had granted weeks earlier, to be published after his death. It was a stinging account of how the Vatican lost its way after the Second Vatican Council. The church "is 200 years out of date," Martini said. "It is tired. Our culture is aged. Our churches are big and empty. Our rituals and our cassocks are pompous. The church must admit its mistakes and begin a radical change." He suggested the closest the church had come to producing a modern saint was the slain archbishop of El Salvador, Óscar Romero, whose holiness had never been recognized by the Vatican: "Where are the heroes among us who can inspire us?" he asked. "Why don't we rouse ourselves? Are we afraid?"

AT THE TIME, Hans Küng suspected his life would end soon, too. In 2012, at the age of eighty-four, he was also diagnosed with Parkinson's, the ailment that killed both his ally Cardinal Martini and his foe John Paul II. Küng thought it was an especially cruel diagnosis since he had been so physically active all his life. He also suffered from macular degeneration, an eye ailment that would eventually rob him of his sight. "That will be the worst thing, no longer to be able to read." He told friends that when the time came, he would end his life by returning home to Switzerland, where assisted suicide was legal, unlike in Germany. "I can do it like Socrates," he joked, suggesting he would drink poison. While the church considered suicide a grave sin, Küng was convinced his Maker would understand: "The God of the Bible is a god of compassion and not a cruel despot who wants to see people spend time in a hell of their own pain."

He said he was not frightened about dying since "I am firmly convinced there is life after death." He was sad only at the thought of losing "my ideal companion in life," Marianne Saur. They had been together thirty years. Asked by an interviewer in 2012 if he honored priestly celibacy, he temporized: "I am not married, and I have neither a wife nor children. I have nothing else to say about it."

He felt that, with death approaching, he needed to write one last book—his sixty-first—as a final plea for the church to embrace the spirit of reform that he knew he had helped inspire at Vatican II. The book was well timed, since 2012 marked the fiftieth anniversary of the opening of the council. He chose a title in the form of a stark question: *Can We Save the Catholic Church?* Its hero was John XXIII, its villains John Paul II and Benedict. Küng accused Benedict and his Polish predecessor of conspiring to erase all that John had accomplished at Vatican II. He compared Benedict to the Russian strongman Vladimir Putin: "Putin also inherited a legacy of democratic reforms—and then did everything he could to reverse them."

The book was published as another great German-speaking theologian headed into retirement: Cardinal Kasper. In 2010, at the age of seventy-seven, he stepped down as president of the Council for Promoting Christian Unity. In retirement, Kasper wanted to revive the campaign he had pursued as a bishop—to convince the Vatican to extend mercy toward people condemned as sinners, especially by allowing divorced Catholics to receive Holy Communion. In 2012, he published a book in German entitled *Barmherzigkeit* (Mercy). Although it attracted little attention at the time outside his homeland, the book was the most important of his career—because it was about to set the agenda for a new pope. The book, like Küng's, noted the imminent fiftieth anniversary of Vatican II. Kasper recalled his thrill in 1962 when he first read Pope John's "revolutionary" speech opening the council, the one that promised "the medicine of mercy." It was a promise that many in the Vatican had since been determined to forget, Kasper's book declared: "Words like 'mercy' and 'pity' have largely gone out of fashion."

The book made no direct criticism of Benedict, but it was implicit in Kasper's warning that the Vatican had become "strict, harsh and pitiless," especially in its treatment of those "who lead a way of life that doesn't conform to church order." He offered a list of people who fell into that category, including divorced Catholics, gay people, AIDS sufferers, prostitutes, and drug addicts.

As Küng and Kasper were ending their careers, another prominent German-speaking theologian was arriving in Rome: Archbishop Gerhard Müller of Regensburg. In July 2012, Benedict announced that the sixty-four-year-old bishop, a close friend and protégé, would be the next prefect of the Congregation for the Doctrine of the Faith. Müller replaced Levada, who retired at the age of seventy-six at Benedict's request. By then, the pope had already decided to abdicate, but it was still a secret. With the last-minute installation of a new, younger loyalist as the Vatican's chief heresy-hunter, Benedict appeared to calculate that, even in retirement, he would still have great influence inside the congregation for years to come. News of Müller's promotion outraged child-rights advocates in Germany. They had long accused him of stalling clerical sex-abuse investigations in Regensburg, including those of the boys' choir. Müller mocked local journalists who reported on the abuse scandals by comparing them to "silly geese who hiss and spit."

The pope originally planned to abdicate in December but decided to postpone the announcement until February so he could have more time to make his retirement plans. In resigning, he confronted logistical questions not faced by any other pope since the Middle Ages, including where he should live. He briefly considered returning to Bavaria, but after three decades in the Italian sun he would find it hard—at the age of eighty-five—to deal with the frigid winters of his homeland. Aides convinced him it would be easy to justify remaining in Rome, since he would still need round-the-clock police protection. He decided to make his new home in the Mater Ecclesiae (meaning "Mother of the Church") Monastery, a former office complex on Vatican Hill that John Paul II had converted into a residence for cloistered nuns in the 1990s. On Benedict's orders, the nuns were quietly moved out of the four-story building in the summer of 2012 so secret renovations for its new tenant could begin. That summer, Benedict also chose a new title for himself, to be announced the day he revealed his abdication: "Pope Emeritus," although he still wanted to be addressed in conversation as "Holy Father." He decided he would continue to wear an all-white papal cassock but would no longer drape himself in a mozzetta, the traditional elbow-length cape worn over his robes. Instead of red shoes, he would wear brown. During his Mexico pilgrimage, he was given a pair of handcrafted coffee-colored loafers that he found "beautiful and comfortable," and the same Mexican shoemaker would provide for him in retirement. He decided he would stop wearing the solid-gold fisherman's ring, the piece of jewelry most closely identified with the papacy. It would be destroyed, as it would have been had he died in office.

He also delayed his departure because he did not want to step down until Vatileaks was out of the news. In mid-December, he received the final report of the "three detective" cardinals. The document, about three hundred pages long, each page stamped PONTIFICAL SECRET, was delivered in a stiff red file folder marked with the papal seal. Although never made public, Vatican officials said it confirmed that there was vicious infighting within the Curia. The report made clear that senior churchmen were violating their vows of celibacy, sometimes with women, often with men.*

Benedict had the report locked away in a safe in the papal apartment. It would remain there, waiting for his successor. He refused to discuss publicly what was in it, except to acknowledge after his resignation that it identified senior gay Curia bishops, "a group of individuals—a small one, perhaps four or five people—that we dismantled."

The final weeks of his papacy were difficult. He appeared exhausted in public and almost dozed off during midnight Mass on Christmas Eve. He announced his resignation on February 11, during a meeting in the papal palace with a group of cardinals. He had worked on the speech for about two weeks, much of that time spent making sure his Latin phrasing was correct. He originally considered speaking in Italian, but "when you do something so important, you do it in Latin."

The setting was the Hall of the Consistory, a reception area in the residential wing of the palace, its walls decorated with sixteenth-century tapestries by Raphael. British archbishop Leo Cushley, a member of Benedict's personal staff, walked the pope to the meeting and watched him ascend his throne, which was on a platform set above the red-robed cardinals, who were seated in a horseshoe shape in front of him. Cushley recalled that, without warning, the pope took out a piece of paper and began to read from it. The use of Latin caught the cardinals by surprise, Cushley said. "I felt my stomach turn over as I realized that here before us was something not seen for centuries: the voluntary resignation of the Roman Pontiff."

"Dear brothers," Benedict began, "I wish to communicate a decision of great importance for the life of the church. Having repeatedly examined my conscience before God, I have come to the certainty that my strengths,

* According to a semi-authorized biography of Benedict published in 2021, the Vatileaks report identified locations near the Vatican where the Curia's "homosexual lobby" met regularly, including a Roman villa and a suburban sauna. The biography's author, Peter Seewald, who was close to Benedict, said the central findings of the investigation took up only thirty pages of the report; the rest of it reproduced images of documents gathered in the inquiry (Seewald, *Benedict XVI: A Life, Volume II*, 484).

due to an advanced age, are no longer suited to an adequate exercise of the Petrine ministry."* The bishop of Rome must have "both strength of mind and body—strength which in the last few months had deteriorated in me to the extent that I have had to recognize my incapacity.

"For this reason, and well aware of the seriousness of this act, with full freedom I declare that I renounce the ministry of the bishop of Rome."

He said his resignation would take effect on February 28, at eight p.m., and that in retirement he would lead a "life dedicated to prayer" and "hidden from the world."

World leaders issued polite tributes to Benedict. German chancellor Merkel said she admired the pope as "one of the most important religious thinkers of our time" and commended him for recognizing it was time to go. In London, Cardinal Murphy-O'Connor said the resignation "was a very brave decision" by a "kind and gentle man." He felt pity.

The public was not so kind. A poll by *The New York Times* days later found that 70 percent of American Catholics believed Benedict had done a poor job, especially in dealing with the sexual-abuse crisis. A majority said the scandals of his papacy led them to question the Vatican's authority on all issues. In Germany, a few magazines and newspapers had brutal headlines. The left-leaning *Tageszeitung* left most of its front page blank, apart from the words "Gott Sei Dank!" (Thank God!).

Days later, Hans Küng published an essay in which he described Benedict's papacy as one of "breakdowns and bad decisions." Under Benedict, "there has been a fatal return to the church's old monarchical habits." He feared Benedict's decision to remain in Rome meant he could emerge as a "shadow pope" who would plot against his successor: "He is not exactly going to the mountaintop to pray."

The world's cardinals made preparations for travel to Rome, both to witness Benedict's departure and to choose his successor. Of the 207 members of the College of Cardinals at the time, 117 were under the age of eighty and could therefore join the conclave.

ON FEBRUARY 27, his last full day as bishop of Rome, Benedict addressed the crowd in St. Peter's Square for a final time as the sitting pope. He said he was departing with "profound serenity of spirit" even if at times "the

---

* The adjective "Petrine" is used in the church to refer to anything involving St. Peter.

Lord seemed to be sleeping" during his papacy, given its many scandals. At 5:07 p.m. the next day, he boarded a sleek white helicopter and lifted off to Castel Gandolfo.

The next five days were set aside for the College of Cardinals to settle into Rome. All cardinals, of all ages, were invited to the preconclave meetings. Among them was Murphy-O'Connor, who could not participate in the conclave because he had turned eighty the year before. He remembered the conversations that week as the most spirited and angry he had ever heard among senior churchmen. He said many cardinals expressed indignation over the Curia's duplicity and incompetence, especially in its failure to deal with the child-abuse crisis.

Bertone, seventy-eight, attended the meetings and appeared oblivious to how much of this criticism targeted him. In fact, he seemed to believe he was still a leading candidate to become the new pope. Benedict was widely reported to have a favored successor: Cardinal Angelo Scola of Italy, the conservative seventy-one-year-old archbishop of Milan.

If one cardinal could be credited with the outcome of the 2013 conclave, it was Murphy-O'Connor, who had been so eager to deny the papacy to Benedict eight years before. The English cardinal was convinced that Scola should not be pope, nor should any candidate unbendingly loyal to Benedict. There was an obvious candidate, he believed—the same man of "humility, sanity and holiness" who had come close to beating Benedict in 2005: Cardinal Bergoglio of Argentina.

At the last conclave, Murphy-O'Connor had watched how an intensive, political-style lobbying campaign won Benedict the papacy. Now, he decided, he would do the same for Bergoglio. The English cardinal might be too old to vote, but he could still be a "kingmaker," he knew.

In Washington, McCarrick rearranged his always jam-packed travel schedule so he could be in Rome. While the eighty-two-year-old could not participate in the conclave, he planned to join the weeklong meeting of cardinals. His trip to the Vatican drew no special news coverage, since the allegations of his sexual abuse were still largely a secret outside the church. Another American cardinal, seventy-seven-year-old Roger Mahoney of Los Angeles, was not so fortunate. He faced public protests across southern California over his decision to attend the conclave. Many parishioners thought it was outrageous for him to go to Rome since he was then the subject of a federal grand jury investigation of the cover-up of the crimes of child-molesting priests. While Mahoney was never criminally charged, files revealed in civil lawsuits exposed the elaborate methods he had used to shield pedophile priests from law enforcement.

Several European cardinals were similarly tainted. Two weeks before the conclave, Cardinal O'Brien in Scotland, best known to British Catholics as a fierce campaigner against gay marriage, which he described as a "grotesque subversion of God's will," abruptly retired after admitting "inappropriate behavior" with a group of priests, seminarians, and other young men who had accused him of sexual abuse dating back to the 1980s.

By 2013, the St. Gallen Group had disbanded, in part because its de facto leader, Cardinal Martini, had been so gravely ill for years before his death. It also stopped meeting because another member, Cardinal Danneels of Belgium, had become such a scandalous figure. In 2010, when he retired, Belgian newspapers obtained tapes of secretly recorded conversations in which he was overheard cynically plotting ways to derail a police investigation of serial child molestation by his colleague Bishop Vangheluwe. Days before the tapes were made, the bishop confessed to Danneels that he had sexually abused his own nephew over a thirteen-year period, beginning when the boy was five. In one tape, Danneels could be heard confronting the victim, by then an adult, to urge him to delay any police report for at least a year, allowing his seventy-three-year-old uncle to retire quietly and with some dignity. "Why drag his name through the mud?" the cardinal asked. "I don't think you'd do yourself or him a favor by shouting this from the rooftops." The victim is overheard replying incredulously that his uncle "dragged my whole life through the mud from the ages of five to eighteen. So why do you feel sorry for him and not for me?" The cardinal had no good answer.

PART VII

FRANCIS

(2013–)

37

"Carnival Time Is Over"

A T THE END OF 2011, Bergoglio signed his mandatory letter of resignation. It had an effective date of December 17—his seventy-fifth birthday, the occasion on which all churchmen had to be ready to go into retirement. He thought Pope Benedict would accept his resignation immediately, given the ill will of the Curia, but Benedict asked him to remain in his post for the time being, since there was no obvious successor. By early 2013, still waiting, Bergoglio had been archbishop of Buenos Aires for fifteen years and his reputation as the "bishop who never smiles" was truer than ever. He faced constant attacks from right-wing Argentine critics over what they saw as his refusal to abide by Vatican decrees on doctrine, especially about sex. His friend Father Fernández, the theologian, could see the fatigue in the cardinal's face: "There were many persecution campaigns orchestrated by some very conservative groups in the Church, and I believe that worried him greatly."

Others in Argentina wondered if Bergoglio was really so eager for retirement. They suspected that, having come close to the papacy in 2005, he kept that ambition alive. They thought it might explain his decision to take the risk of cooperating in a biography published in 2010, *El Jesuita* (The Jesuit). The book consisted of questions and answers between Bergoglio and two journalists and revealed his willingness to defy the Vatican on conservative teachings. He was open to the idea of overturning the doctrine of priestly celibacy and imagined the Vatican would someday follow the model of Orthodox churches and allow married priests. While he always denounced abortion as a grave sin ("a pregnant woman isn't carrying a toothbrush in her stomach"), he urged compassion. He favored universal sex education in public schools, even for young children, and was more open than ever in expressing support for liberation theology.

The pontiff he praised most in the book was John XXIII, who met his definition of what a pope should be—concerned with people, not doctrine. He recalled reading how John, when a cardinal in Venice, often strolled along the city's fabled lagoons, eager to talk to anyone: "He would be sitting in the shade of a tree or outside a bar, drinking a glass of white wine and spending a few minutes speaking with parishioners. For me, this is a true pastor."

El Jesuita, published at first only in Spanish, was distributed among church leaders in Latin America. His most determined critic, the journalist Horacio Verbitsky, saw the book's timing as anything but coincidental; he thought it was one last attempt by Bergoglio to promote himself for the next conclave.

Bergoglio said news of Benedict's resignation on February 11, 2013, came as a shock, although the logic of it was undeniable, given the pope's age and health problems. "Benedict had surely meditated and prayed for a long time before making his brave and historic decision," he wrote later. He flew to Rome at the end of the month, in time to witness Benedict's departure, and checked in at the modest church-run hostel, just outside Vatican City, where he had stayed for years, although he would move to the Santa Marta guesthouse when the conclave began. Once again, he appeared on newspaper lists of cardinals considered *papabile*, but at the age of seventy-six he was widely perceived as a man whose time had passed. The leading contenders appeared to be Cardinal Scola of Milan and two conservative non-European cardinals close to Benedict: Odilo Scherer of Brazil, sixty-three, and Marc Ouellet of Canada, sixty-eight, who then worked in the Curia. The two non-Italians seemed to have an edge, since so many cardinals were disgusted by the plotting of Italian clerics revealed by Vatileaks.

As soon as he landed in Rome, Cardinal Murphy-O'Connor swung into action on Bergoglio's behalf. His campaign was modeled on what he had witnessed in 2005, down to small details. The lobbying began in earnest when he invited Bergoglio to a risotto supper on March 3, the night before the College gathered for its preconclave meetings. Murphy-O'Connor insisted that during their meal, Bergoglio never suggested he considered himself a papal candidate, "nor did I raise the issue."

Many cardinals felt Bergoglio clinched election when, during the meetings, he gave a brief, impassioned speech in which he said the church had become "too wrapped up in itself." It needed "to come out from itself and go to people on the periphery of society where there is sin, pain, misery and injustice and to bring them the good news of the Gospel." Speaking in his accented but otherwise flawless Italian, he repeated the word "periphery"—*periferia*—several times. "There was stillness when he sat down," Murphy-O'Connor recalled. "I looked at the faces around me." Many cardinals were clearly moved and ready to vote for the Argentine.

Murphy-O'Connor kept up his lobbying throughout the week. He hosted a reception at the British embassy for a dozen cardinals from India and other former British colonies to ensure that Bergoglio was being "talked about." (Ouellet of Canada, a rival papal candidate, and the harshly conservative George Pell of Australia were left off the guest list.) On the conclave's opening day, cardinals of all ages were invited to Mass in St. Peter's, led by Cardinal Sodano in his role as dean. Normally a dealmaker in a conclave, Sodano, eighty-five and too old to vote, seemed resigned to leave the decision to others. Every one of the 117 cardinals under eighty was in Rome except the primate of Indonesia, who was ill, and the newly disgraced Cardinal O'Brien of Scotland. Of those who remained, seventy-seven votes would be needed to meet the threshold for a pope's election.

As a papal candidate, Bergoglio benefited from his lower profile; there was no organized effort in Argentina to block his election, as there had been in 2005. In Rome, the allegations about his possible duplicity in the Dirty War were seen as old news. He also benefited from the fact that many cardinals wanted to assume that the priestly sex-abuse crisis was less serious in faraway Argentina than elsewhere.

Unlike in 2005, there was no reliable account of the vote tallies at the conclave. It was widely reported, though, that on the first ballot Scola received the most votes, about thirty, while Bergoglio got twenty-five votes, the Canadian Ouellet ten. (Ouellet's candidacy had been damaged by news reports days earlier about his brother's conviction in 2009, when Ouellet was archbishop of Montreal, for sexually abusing two underage girls.)

The cardinals adjourned for the day. After supper in the Santa Marta, Bergoglio chose not to join in the animated conversations going on throughout the guesthouse. Instead, he returned to his room—no. 207—to try to sleep. Before bed, he had a friendly chat in the hallway with Cardinal Kasper, who had just received copies of the Spanish-language edition of his new book. He handed one as a gift to Bergoglio, who noticed the title—in Spanish, *La misericordia* (Mercy).

"Ah, mercy," Bergoglio said, thanking Kasper for the book. "That is the name of our God."

The next morning, there were two more inconclusive votes, although additional ballots shifted to Bergoglio. In both ballots, he received more votes than any other candidate—fifty in the count just before lunch. During the meal, Scola suggested he was ready to throw his support to Bergoglio. The rumors of the Argentine's imminent election spread wildly outside the Sistine Chapel, and the Rome correspondent of the Argentine newspaper *La Nación* confidently sent out a message on Twitter: "Bergoglio Could be the Surprise of the Conclave."

The first vote that afternoon was inconclusive, although Bergoglio's total went up again. The next vote, the fifth, was taken at six p.m. but had to be set aside after the scrutineers counted one more ballot than there were cardinals. It turned out that a blank card had become stuck to a filled-out one, which required the voting to start over. An Indian cardinal sitting near Bergoglio, Oswald Gracias of Mumbai, said the Argentine was remarkably serene that evening: "He knew, as we all did, that the Lord had chosen him." Bergoglio later acknowledged that he had felt surprisingly calm throughout the final hours of the conclave—a "deep and inexplicable peace and interior consolation," as if this were meant to be.

The sixth ballot was taken at six thirty p.m. When the seventy-seventh vote was called out for Bergoglio, the conclave burst into applause. (News reports the next day stated that Bergoglio had received a total of at least ninety votes.) The cardinal seated next to Bergoglio, his old friend Claudio Hummes of Brazil, hugged him and whispered in his ear: "Jorge, don't forget the poor."

As the senior official in the conclave, Cardinal Giovanni Battista Re of Italy had responsibility for confirming that Bergoglio would accept election. Re asked: "Acceptasne electionem de te canonice factam in Summun Pontificem?" (Do you accept your canonical election as Supreme Pontiff?)

Bergoglio replied, also in Latin. "I accept even though I am a great sinner."

"What name will you take?"

"I choose the name Francis. In honor of Saint Francis of Assisi."

There were delighted gasps. Bergoglio would be the first Pope Francis,

in tribute to the mystical, rag-wearing thirteenth-century Italian vener-
ated as patron of the world's poor. There was a reason no earlier bishop of
Rome had chosen the name, since it was a challenge to the idea of a rich,
all-powerful church. Francis said later that, while he had originally planned
to call himself John XXIV in honor of "the good pope," he changed his
mind the moment he heard Hummes's plea. "Those words came to me: the
poor, the poor. Then, right away, thinking of the poor, I thought of Francis
of Assisi."

His election made history in other ways. He was the first pope from
Latin America—or from anywhere in the Southern or Western Hemisphere for that matter. He was the first Jesuit pope in the 472-year history
of the Society of Jesus; the first from outside Europe since Gregory III, a
Syrian who reigned in the eighth century; and the first to speak Spanish as
his native language.

He insisted later he operated "by instinct" in the hours that followed,
but friends in Buenos Aires were convinced he had what was, effectively, a
script. It was the one he committed to memory years before and which had
served him so well in his first days as archbishop of Buenos Aires, when he
earned the goodwill of his parishioners by rejecting—often theatrically—
anything that suggested self-importance.

Moments after his election, he was fitted for his white robes. By tradition, this took place in a small space off the Sistine Chapel known as the
Stanza delle Lacrime (Room of Tears). After donning the white cassock,
he was offered a jewel-studded gold pectoral cross, along with a red papal
mozzetta—the hand-embroidered, ermine-trimmed cape that most popes
donned for their first appearance on the balcony of St. Peter's—and the traditional red papal shoes. He rejected all three and instead put back on the
pewter-colored cross and scuffed black orthopedic shoes he brought from
Argentina. He was still wearing the cheap plastic wristwatch he had carried
from home. The tailor urged him to at least wear the beautiful mozzetta.

"No, thank you," the pope was reported to have said in a joking tone.
"Carnival time is over."

Curia officials shared the "carnival time" remark with the press that evening, and while never officially confirmed as the pope's words, the comment
was seized on as evidence that Francis intended his papacy to be different.

He returned to the chapel in his white robes to greet the cardinals who
had just elected him. Violating protocol, he did not first go to the altar to
pray. Instead he went to the side of Cardinal Ivan Dias of India, who was

seriously ill and attended in a wheelchair. Dias teared up, clearly moved. The other cardinals lined up to present themselves. By tradition, Francis should have received them seated in a throne. Instead, he stood. When cardinals from China and Vietnam tried to kiss his hand, Francis rejected the gesture with a smile and kissed theirs. He was then escorted to the upper balcony of St. Peter's. There he would be introduced to the crowd in the square below, estimated at 150,000 people. It occurred to him that before giving his address, he should telephone Benedict and offer his respects. An aide placed the call to Castel Gandolfo. Benedict picked up the receiver and later recalled telling Francis: "I thank you, Holy Father, that you have thought immediately of me."

At eight twenty p.m., the long red curtains parted on the balcony, and a cheer went up as Cardinal Jean-Louis Tauran of France, a conclave administrator, announced in Latin: "Habemus papam!" ("We have a pope!") The cheers quieted as he revealed the name: "Eminentissimum ac Reverendissimum Dominum, Dominum Georgium Marium, Sanctae Romanae Ecclesiae Cardinalem Bergoglio qui sibi nomen imposuit Franciscum" ("The most eminent and most revered lord, Lord Jorge Mario Bergoglio, cardinal of the Holy Roman Church, who has taken the name Francis").

Murphy-O'Connor, who was in the crowd in St. Peter's, brushed away tears of happiness and relief, proud of his role in electing "this humble man whose papacy will be such a blessing for the world." On the balcony, Francis walked forward slowly, his right hand raised in a gentle wave. He smiled slightly, clearly overwhelmed by the huge audience below. Since he was not a familiar face in Rome, it took the crowd several seconds to realize who he was. A handful of Argentines in the square, including some who waved their country's blue-and-white flag, screamed out, "Bergoglio! Bergoglio!"

Then he began to speak, and the mostly Italian crowd was quickly won over by his simple message, offered in fluent Italian. He opened with a joke, which delighted the crowd even more. "You know that it was the duty of my brother cardinals to give Rome a bishop," he said. "It seems that they have gone to the ends of the earth to find one."

His address was brief, barely four minutes long. He asked for prayers for "our bishop emeritus Benedict XVI," then prayers for all mankind. "I need to ask you a favor," he ended. "I ask you to pray to the Lord that he will bless me: the prayer of the people asking the blessing for their bishop." Many in the crowd were touched by the idea of a pope so modest that he knew he needed God's help as much as they did.

His formal installation was scheduled for six days later. In the meantime, the Vatican press corps tracked his every move in hopes he would make news, and he gave the reporters and photographers what they wanted. A *New York Times* correspondent described his public-relations effort that week as one of "radical humility," which the pope's aides acknowledged was precisely his strategy.

On his first full day as bishop of Rome, Francis woke up at five forty-five a.m. and went to the chapel in the Santa Marta guesthouse. He was wearing a sweater, trousers, and shoes, all black—his usual morning wardrobe in Buenos Aires. The staff was startled, since these were not the clothes—even the informal clothes—of a pope. After prayers and then breakfast with a few cardinals at a common table in the dining room, he asked to be driven to one of the oldest and most beloved churches in Rome, the Basilica of Santa Maria Maggiore, which dated from the fifth century. He insisted he be driven in a modest, unmarked Vatican sedan, not in the famous papal Mercedes with the license plate SCV1 (an abbreviation of the Italian and Latin names for Vatican City, along with the number 1). At the church, he prayed in a side chapel where St. Ignatius had marked his first Christmas as leader of the Jesuits in 1538. When security officers tried to close the church to the public during his visit, Francis gently protested: "Leave them alone. I am a pilgrim too."

As the car headed back to the Vatican, trailed by a motorcade of reporters, he asked to stop at the hostel where he stayed before the conclave. He had left luggage there and wanted to pay the bill. It would become the most iconic photograph of that first week, the new pope standing in front of the hostel's mahogany reception desk, holding his own suitcase and trying to settle his account. The receptionist told him that paying the bill was unnecessary. "On the contrary," the pope replied loudly enough to be overheard by all. "That is precisely why I must set a good example."

That evening, he was given a tour of his apartment in the Apostolic Palace, home to popes since the seventeenth century. He inspected room after room, most with inlaid marble floors and decorated with masterworks of art. Beyond the bedroom suite and living quarters for his household staff, there were several offices for his private secretaries, as well as a frescoed loggia, a medical clinic, and the spacious library remodeled by Benedict for his twenty thousand books. "There's room for three hundred people here!" Francis declared. "I don't need all this space." He announced—that moment—that the papal apartment would not be his home. He would use the palace for receptions but would continue to live in the Santa Marta and do most of his work there.

For years to come, official guests to Rome were thrilled to learn they would stay in the Santa Marta since it all but guaranteed an encounter with the pope. He often bought an expresso from the machine near the reception desk. Guests who were reluctant to join him in the elevator got the same response. "Come on in," he would say, motioning them in. "I won't bite." He conducted meetings in his one-room suite, which was simply furnished. Guests were invited to sit on a blue velveteen sofa. Because of his chronic back pain, Francis usually seated himself in a high-backed chair. The adjoining bedroom had a wooden parquet floor. At one end of the bed was a dark wooden headboard that bore a carved image of Christ's face.

His most controversial public comments in those first days—controversial within the Vatican, at least—involved a book Francis wanted to praise. The setting for the remarks was St. Peter's Square on the first Sunday of his papacy, when he offered a homily to the crowd from a palace window.

"Brothers and sisters, good day!" he began in his cheery Italian.

"Good day!" the delighted crowd roared back.

His address centered on the Gospels' call for tolerance. He used the words "mercy" or "merciful" twenty times in remarks that lasted only a few minutes. "God has that heart of mercy for all of us," he said. "The Lord never tires of forgiving." Then he announced a reading assignment for the crowd. "I have been reading a book by a cardinal—Cardinal Kasper, a clever theologian, a good theologian—on mercy. And that book did me a lot of good." He continued: "Cardinal Kasper says that the feeling of mercy changes everything. It is the best thing we can feel. It changes the world."

Francis laughed as he insisted that "I am not promoting my cardinals' books!" But he had done precisely that. Kasper was watching the address on television and "froze in place" when he heard the pope mention his name. Within days, he found himself regularly described as the "pope's theologian." Publishers around the world rushed to publish *Mercy* in local languages, given its papal endorsement. Within months, almost one hundred thousand copies were sold, an extraordinary number for a work of theology.

Days later, Kasper met with the pope, who seemed delighted that he had made his friend a best-selling author. Francis told him that after the address, he was approached by an elderly Italian cardinal who cautioned him that promoting Kasper's book was a mistake and might be seen as a slap at Pope Benedict. Worse, he warned, the book encouraged blasphemy by promoting tolerance for divorced Catholics, homosexuals, prostitutes, and other sinners.

"Holy Father, you cannot do this!" the old cardinal said, glowering. "There are heresies in this book!"

Francis chuckled as he assured Kasper he had ignored the warning, just as he planned to ignore much of the advice he received from the Curia. "This enters one ear and goes out the other."

38

"Who Am I to Judge?"

FRANCIS'S INSTALLATION CEREMONY was shortened, on his orders. The Mass, normally more than two hours long, was cut to less than ninety minutes. The crowd of nearly two hundred thousand included thirty-two heads of state. The United States was represented by Vice President Joseph Biden and House Democratic leader Nancy Pelosi, the country's two most prominent Catholic politicians. Benedict did not attend—an effort, he said, to prove he was living up to his commitment to remain "hidden from the world." Argentina was represented by President Cristina Kirchner, the pope's old nemesis. After releasing only a tepid statement of congratulations immediately after his election, Kirchner decided days later to present herself in Rome as the pope's greatest ally. An amused Francis played along, granting her the honor of being the first foreign leader he received as pope. He arranged for another special guest from his homeland: Sergio Sánchez, a forty-nine-year-old Buenos Aires *cartonero*, or garbage scavenger. Sánchez and the pope had been friends for years; they met when the then-cardinal was on one of his regular walking tours of the city slums. Sánchez was given a prime seat in St. Peter's Square and embraced by the pope before the ceremony. "I am surrounded by kings and princes," Sánchez marveled.

Francis was presented during the ceremony with his fisherman's ring. He decided against the traditional gold band and instead chose one in plated silver once worn by a priest who had been a private secretary to Paul VI. After the ceremony, he was patched through to loudspeakers in the Plaza de Mayo in Buenos Aires, where thousands of jubilant Argentines had gathered to watch his installation on giant video screens. He told the crowd not to "forget this bishop who is far away."

Argentine newspapers reported that the pope phoned home constantly in his first days as bishop of Rome, eager to talk to old friends. He called his dentist in Buenos Aires to cancel an appointment, as well as his newspaper delivery man to stop his subscriptions. He was eager to heal his relationship with the Society of Jesus. A day after his election, he called its Rome head-quarters to speak with the Jesuits' Spanish-born superior general, Father Adolfo Nicolás. At first, Nicolás's secretary refused to believe the pope was on the line—"If you're the pope, I'm Napoleon," she told him—but min-utes later, mortified, she put him through. Francis and Nicolás met at the Santa Marta days later. The Jesuit leader said afterward he was struck by the pope's eagerness to shake up the Vatican. Francis, he said, knew Curia bish-ops were offended by his informal style. "They criticize me, first, because I don't speak like a pope and, second, because I don't act like a king," he told Nicolás. There was a muted response to Francis's election among other Jesuits. Many were unhappy one of their own was pope, since it seemed the ultimate violation of a Jesuit's vow to reject high office. Father Nicholas King, a Jesuit lecturer at Oxford University, wrote that many in the Society

Francis meets with his longtime foe Argentine president Cristina Kirchner at his inauguration in the Vatican, March 2013. Standing directly to the pope's right is Secretary of State Tarcisio Bertone.

reacted to Francis's election with "a certain reserve, a sense that it is not the sort of thing that Jesuits should do."

Francis told deputies that as a newcomer in Rome, he would be slow in making personnel changes. Even so, he quietly settled a few scores. He ordered that his friend Victor Fernández, the Argentine theologian, be made a bishop; and the French archbishop who had blocked Fernández's university appointment in Buenos Aires was pushed out of his Curia job. The pope named his successor in the Argentine capital: Archbishop Mario Aurelio Poli, who led a rural diocese. The selection bypassed conservatives who had long maneuvered to replace then-Cardinal Bergoglio in Buenos Aires. Poli was a priest in the pope's mold. He had a graduate degree in social work and traveled everywhere by bicycle.

Four days after his installation, Francis boarded a helicopter in Vatican City for the short flight to Castel Gandolfo. He had arranged to meet with Benedict and insisted he be the one to travel out of respect for his predecessor, who would soon also be his neighbor in Rome.

The Vatican barred television cameras at the meeting but released photos that showed Francis and Benedict embracing at the helipad. Both wore white robes, although Benedict had pulled on a quilted white cassock to guard against the early spring chill. The Vatican let it be known that in the palace chapel, Benedict directed Francis to the one-man kneeler traditionally reserved for the bishop of Rome, but that Francis insisted they share a longer kneeler in the pews.

Francis said afterward that he and Benedict had a long conversation about the Vatileaks scandal and the secret report by the three cardinals. Benedict, he said, offered a summary of what was in the three-hundred-page document and knew the results of the investigation down to small, ugly details. "He had it all in his head," Francis remembered. Given what he heard from Benedict that day, Francis said he now knew the Vatileaks scandal had exposed terrible corruption and incompetence in the Curia: "There is a big problem."

The relationship between the two popes became a topic of endless speculation, the subject of books and even a big-budget Hollywood film. In public, they created the appearance of goodwill and a genuine if not particularly close friendship, but their aides admitted the relationship was always awkward and often turned tense. Over time, Benedict had trouble hiding his anger over what he saw as Francis's disrespect. That would be matched with the new pope's annoyance over what he saw as his predecessor's meddling on issues of doctrine.

The problems began within weeks of Francis's election. Benedict was infuriated, his aides said, when his successor did not tamp down an insulting public debate over whether he had been wrong to call himself "pope emeritus" and to wear the white papal wardrobe. Many church scholars agreed it was presumptuous of Benedict to give himself the title—and to continue to be addressed in conversation as "Holy Father"—since it suggested a continued tie to a post he had abdicated. A law professor at the Pontifical Lateran University in Rome wrote that "there is only one pope, and so therefore a 'pope emeritus' cannot exist." Experts on church ceremony said Benedict should have returned to wearing a cardinal's scarlet robes, or even the black robes of a bishop. Benedict's indignation was evident in a letter to a German cardinal—leaked to German newspapers—in which he bristled at the criticism and suggested that "pope emeritus" was the only logical title.*

Benedict was nearly as annoyed at what he saw as an effort to patronize him because of his age. Francis repeatedly referred to his predecessor as a "wise grandfather" even though Benedict was barely nine years older than the new pope. He was also upset by what he saw as Francis's attempt to disparage the traditional privileges of the papacy, as if Benedict had done something wrong by accepting them. He suggested Francis's efforts to prove his humility—refusing to move into the papal apartment, for example—were overdone. A pope could live in the Apostolic Palace and still be "among the people," Benedict said.

Benedict would never live completely "hidden from the world," as he had once vowed. He continued to grant interviews to admiring journalists, including another set of interviews that were turned into a book, and issue public statements that often proved controversial. In early interviews, he insisted he was "delighted" by the public excitement that Francis's papacy generated. "He is someone who is very close to the people, who stands with them," he said. With a touch of regret and envy, he added that he wished

* Among the churchmen who rejected the concept of a "pope emeritus" was John Paul II, who refused to consider abdication even as his health collapsed, since he believed only God could decide his fate. As he recovered after a 1994 hip operation, he told his surgeon that "you must heal me, and I must heal, because there is no place in the church for a pope emeritus" (Slawomir Oder, *Why He Is a Saint*, 122).

he had been less isolated as pope: "Perhaps I was not truly among the people enough." Yet Benedict's praise of his successor often came off as half-hearted and condescending. In another early interview, he revealed he had been surprised by Francis's election because he had never been particularly impressed by then-Cardinal Bergoglio, even though the Argentine had been his strongest challenger for the papacy in 2005. In their meetings in the Vatican over the years, he knew Bergoglio to be "very decisive" but not especially charismatic or otherwise memorable. It was only after Francis's election that Benedict could see the "aspect of warmth" in his personality and his "wholly personal connection to the people."

THERE HAD BEEN nothing like the global public embrace that Francis received at the start of his papacy. Even his most charismatic modern predecessors, John XXIII and John Paul II, had known only a taste of that excitement in their early months as pope. Throughout 2013, it seemed, there was no more compelling figure on the world stage than Pope Francis—a man sitting on the most exalted throne on earth who presented himself as the most humble of servants. His almost hourly gestures of humility charmed millions, Catholics and non-Catholics alike. First, there had been the simplified wardrobe and the decision to live outside the palace. Then came the announcement that he had abandoned the papal fleet of armored black Mercedes limousines, replacing them with a single blue Ford Focus sedan. He was often photographed holding the battered black briefcase he brought from Buenos Aires. Asked by a reporter what he kept in it, he laughed. "It's not the key for the atom bomb!" Inside, he said, was a razor, a pocket calendar, and, usually, a book.

Holy Week came in the first month of his papacy. By tradition, Holy Thursday Mass was conducted in one of Rome's grand basilicas. Instead, Francis held it in the city's Casal del Marmo prison for juveniles. There he carried out that day's most symbolically important ceremony—when, in the past, the pope washed the feet of twelve priests in memory of the twelve apostles—by washing the feet of a dozen young inmates, including two Muslims and two women. "I do it with all my heart, because it's my duty," he told the prisoners. In a separate Mass that day, he delivered a homily he had written in Buenos Aires and originally planned to deliver there. It called on priests to be out among the poor and oppressed and "to smell of the sheep," a phrase he used constantly as pope.

Like John Paul II, he terrified his security detail during his weekly rides in the popemobile around St. Peter's Square. He regularly jumped from the vehicle to embrace worshippers and kiss babies. Photos of those encounters were regularly splashed across newspaper front pages. Few of those pictures were more touching—or startling—than those taken one day in November when Francis stopped the popemobile to throw his arms around Vinicio Riva, a fifty-three-year-old Italian who suffered from a genetic disorder that deformed his facial bones and left his skin covered with thick, bleeding sores. "My heart was bursting," Riva said later, recalling how the pope had not flinched before kissing his face.

Francis's first extended trip out of Rome came in July, when he flew to the Italian island of Lampedusa, where thousands of African migrants, most of them Muslims, arrived each month after crossing the Mediterranean in rickety boats. He offered Mass in memory of the many desperate people drowned on the trip. "We have become too used to the suffering of others," he declared. Those remarks were denounced by right-wing Italian politicians who said he was willing to see Europe overrun by refugees. The leader of Italy's populist Northern League sneered: "It's easy to open Italy's doors while living in the Vatican."

The pope's first foreign pilgrimage was to Brazil later that month and generated an excitement not seen since the early days of John Paul II. The fact that Francis was the first Latin American pope added to the exhilaration. The highlight came when he celebrated Mass before three million people crowded on the famed white sands of Copacabana beach in Rio de Janeiro.

On the plane home, the pope held a marathon eighty-minute in-flight news conference in which he said something that many veterans of the Vatican press corps described as the single most shocking comment they had ever heard from a pope. It came when Francis was asked about Vatileaks, and specifically about reports that the investigation had identified a "gay lobby" inside the Curia.

"I haven't found anyone with an identity card in the Vatican with the word 'gay' on it," he said, chuckling. "But if someone is gay and is searching for the Lord and has goodwill, then who am I to judge?"

Who am I to judge?

No five words would be so talked about in the modern history of the church, since they seemed to undo centuries of pronouncements in which the Vatican had condemned homosexuality as an "intrinsic moral evil," in the words of Benedict XVI. That Francis used the word "gay" was itself star-tling, since he had adopted the vocabulary that gays themselves preferred.

He made other astonishing comments on the plane. He revealed plans to review the church's teachings on divorce and remarriage and suggested he would consider allowing divorced Catholics to receive Communion, the debate that Benedict had angrily insisted was closed forever. Francis was asked repeatedly about his relationship with his predecessor. "There are those who tell me: 'How can this be?'" he told the reporters. "'Two popes in the Vatican? Isn't he plotting against you?'" The answer was no, he insisted. "Pope Benedict is a man of great prudence. He doesn't interfere."

Francis never said it explicitly, but within weeks of his election it was clear he intended to undo much of Benedict's legacy. Almost overnight, years of tension between the Vatican and leaders of the world's other major religions—tension blamed mostly on Benedict—began to evaporate. The battle that Benedict waged for decades to crush liberation theology was abandoned. Days after Francis's election, he ordered the Curia to obtain sainthood for Archbishop Romero as a martyr to that cause. In April, Leo-nardo Boff, the Brazilian theologian silenced largely because of his support for liberation theology, wrote that Francis's election promised a new begin-ning for the church—"a new spiritual world." The new pope made contact with other theologians long branded as dissidents, including Hans Küng, the most famous of them all. In late 2013, Küng was astonished to receive a handwritten letter bearing the return address, in Latin, Domus Sanctae Marthae—the Santa Marta Guesthouse. It was from Francis, who thanked Küng for sending him a copy of his latest book and suggested they meet. Küng said he nearly wept, grateful that a bishop of Rome would treat him with simple courtesy after so many years as an outcast. In December, in an interview with a German magazine, he declared that Francis was the pope who might win the battle for the soul of the church begun by John XXIII at Vatican II. "Francis has introduced a paradigm shift."

While Cardinals Bertone and Müller and other Benedict loyalists remained in place in the Curia, Francis undercut their influence from the start. In April, he announced the creation of what amounted to a papal cabinet, made up of eight cardinals who would travel to Rome every two months to guide him. The members of the Council of Cardinal Advis-ers, or C-8, came from every continent. Italians in the Curia were rattled there was only one of their countrymen in the group: Cardinal Giuseppe

Bertello, who led the Vatican City municipal government. The others were from Australia, Chile, the Congo, Germany, Honduras, India, and the United States, and some were known to be harsh critics of the Curia. The American, Cardinal Sean O'Malley of Boston, was best known for his work to reform his archdiocese in the wake of the clerical-abuse scandals there.

Francis took another step toward power sharing when he announced in October he would call a synod of two hundred bishops to debate issues involving marriage and family, with no restrictions on the agenda. The synod was scheduled for the following year, with a larger gathering in 2015 to wrap up the discussions. If the pope lived up to his promise, it meant perennially taboo subjects like birth control were open for debate again.

World leaders were eager to associate themselves with Francis and to quote his words. "The pope is somebody who lives out the teachings of Christ," said President Barack Obama. The American civil rights leader Jesse Jackson compared him to Martin Luther King Jr. The British entertainer Elton John declared on stage that Francis was "my hero" because of his acceptance of gays: "Make this man a saint now, OK?" *Time* magazine, *The Times* of London, and the American gay-interest magazine *The Advocate* all declared Francis "Person of the Year" for 2013. He was the most talked-about public figure on Facebook. At the same time, Francis became a target of right-wing politicians and commentators in the US and elsewhere. The radio talk-show host Rush Limbaugh repeatedly questioned whether he was a Communist.

In August, he invited the editor of *La Civiltà Cattolica*, a Jesuit-run journal widely seen as the church's most important and prestigious publication, to his room at the Santa Marta for six hours of interviews. When published, they were seen as the most astonishing interviews ever granted by a sitting pope. Francis suggested to the magazine that while there might be no change in church doctrine, there would be a revolution in the way the Vatican presented itself to the world.

The church, he said, had become "obsessed" with hot-button issues of sexual morality—gay marriage, abortion, and birth control, in particular—and that it must end. "It is not necessary to talk about these issues all the time," he said. "We have to find a new balance." While offering his usual careful praise for Benedict, Francis rejected his predecessor's repeated suggestion as pope that the church should be ready to shrink—to force dissidents to worship elsewhere—if that kept it pure. Francis thought that ridiculous. "The church is the mother to all, not a small chapel that can hold only a small group of selected people," he explained. "I see the church as a field hospital after battle."

Prominent Catholics rushed to praise or condemn the interviews. Cardinal Timothy Dolan in New York described the pope's remarks as a "breath of fresh air." A few archconservative Curia bishops were outraged by the interviews and said so publicly. They were led by Cardinal Raymond Burke, the highest-ranking American churchman in Rome. In years to come, Burke, former archbishop of St. Louis, became the spokesman for an organized, sometimes brazenly public campaign inside the Vatican to oppose Francis. Burke sought out reporters to say he was baffled by what Francis had said to *La Civiltà Cattolica*, especially the pope's suggestion that the church was "talking too much" about abortion, which Burke called "the massacre of the unborn." On that subject, he insisted, "we can never talk enough."

Within weeks, Francis granted another interview, this time to the newspaper *La Repubblica*, in which he made a stinging attack on the Curia, suggesting it was bloated and corrupt. He said some earlier popes—he did not name them—were "narcissists" who fell prey to the flattery of power-hungry "courtiers" in the Curia. The Vatican bureaucracy, he said, had often been populated with luxury-loving "bishop-tycoons" who cared little about the poor and oppressed. "The Curia looks too inward," he said defiantly. "I will do everything I can to change it."

In November, he published a thirty-thousand-word document, *Evangelii Gaudium* (The Joy of the Gospel), a so-called apostolic exhortation, that was an even more detailed statement of his commitment to embracing mercy over punishing sin. The Vatican, he wrote, erred by speaking "more about law than about grace, more about the church than about Christ, more about the pope than about God's word." It contained passages of John XXIII's opening speech at Vatican II, including his famous plea for the "medicine of mercy" and his condemnation of the "prophets of doom." It also cited passages from the writings of Francis's countryman Bishop Fernández, who had become a frequent visitor to the Vatican that year. His influence with Francis worried Curia conservatives from the start, especially after Fernández granted interviews in which he suggested the new pope should allow priests to marry ("it is clear that mandatory celibacy is not essential") and consider the appointment of nuns to the senior ranks of the Curia—and maybe even to the College of Cardinals.

By year's end, the new pope began moving out the "prophets of doom." There was jubilation throughout the Vatican with the announcement that Bertone would step down as secretary of state, replaced by Archbishop Pietro Parolin of Italy, a mild-mannered career diplomat. In December, the pope removed Burke as a member of the Congregation for Bishops, a position that had given the American cardinal an important role in choosing bishops around the world.

Bertone took his departure badly, blaming it on the "crows and vipers" who had portrayed him as the buffoonish villain of Vatileaks. His reputation was more badly dented in retirement with the disclosure that a local children's hospital had diverted $500,000 to pay for renovation of his church-owned penthouse apartment near St. Peter's. While the cardinal was not criminally charged, the hospital's chief administrator was convicted of the Italian crime of "abuse of office" for diverting the money. Bertone, insisting he had always intended to pay for the renovation, donated $200,000 back to the hospital. In 2015, the cardinal came under scrutiny again when Francis ordered an investigation of how the Vatican Bank lost $20 million in an investment in an Italian television company run by a close friend of Bertone's. The inquiry determined that the investment had been a bad idea from the start and was approved only after the cardinal overruled the bank's directors.

Bertone's post-retirement scandals were useful to Francis since they bolstered the pope's portrayal of the Curia and much of the rest of the worldwide church hierarchy as corrupt and inept. In October 2013, he suspended and later demoted an archconservative German bishop dubbed by European tabloids as "the bishop of bling" after the disclosure that he spent $43 million to renovate his official residence in the city of Limburg. It included the installation of a $300,000, six-foot-deep fish tank, a $20,000 free-standing marble bathtub (with two headrests, since it was designed for two people), and $1.6 million in original artwork. The fifty-three-year-old bishop, Franz-Peter Tebartz–van Elst, had been installed by Benedict in 2007 and was a favorite of the German pope. He shared Benedict's most traditional views on doctrine, especially about sexuality, and made headlines when he dismissed a local priest who had offered a blessing at a same-sex wedding. The Curia found a new, low-level post for Tebartz–van Elst in Rome, where he aligned himself with Cardinal Burke and other critics of Francis's papacy. The lines of battle were forming.

39

Into the Lion's Den

FRANCIS WAS THRILLED to be pope. The "bishop who never smiles" had disappeared, apparently forever. In almost every news photo and television report that reached Argentina from Rome in 2013, Francis was shown beaming, an ear-to-ear grin that even some of his oldest friends could not recognize. From the day of his election, "a great sense of inner peace and freedom has come over me," he said several months after his election. "If you do what the Lord wants, you're happy."

One of Argentina's best-known television journalists, Nelson Castro, was shocked when he spoke with Francis during the pope's trip to Brazil. "He's another person!" Castro said. He had interviewed then-Cardinal Bergoglio years earlier and remembered his gloominess. Now, this same man was bursting with energy and joy. "I don't know if it's the Holy Spirit or what—but he's transformed." Castro suggested an explanation: the always-ambitious Bergoglio had achieved recognition beyond his wildest dreams, and he loved it. "He is a man who has always liked power," Castro said. "I think that deep inside he hoped for this kind of end to his life."

Francis continued his nightly routine of phoning old friends back home, dialing the calls himself and opening most conversations by blurting out, "It's Bergoglio!" His friends kidded him about the nonstop smiling. They also teased him about his public displays of austerity—his refusal to live in the papal palace, for example—and urged him to reconsider. They worried about his safety and thought it dangerous for him to drive around in that little, unprotected Ford sedan. Every Sunday, he continued his decade-old tradition of calling Clelia Podestá, the eighty-seven-year-old widow of

Jerónimo Podestá, the Argentine bishop who resigned in scandal in the 1960s after falling in love with her. On the basis of her unlikely friendship with the man who was now the bishop of Rome, Clelia said she was convinced that "Francis is going to turn the church upside down."

Critics back home began to refer to him as "Papa Perón," since Francis had adopted some of the same vague, crowd-pleasing populist rhetoric that his childhood hero Juan Perón had been known for. The pope had taken on some of Perón's verbal flourishes as well, referring to himself in the third person and staring out into a crowd wide-eyed while raising his voice to demand their attention. Critics also saw a Peronist-style political calculation in his constant displays of humility.

Outside Argentina, many admiring Catholics made a different comparison—to John XXIII. In June 2013, the cover of the British magazine *The Tablet* featured photos of Francis and John side by side beneath the headline: "Two of a Kind." Francis found a dramatic way to prove that he saw "the good pope" as his role model: he made him a saint. Four months after his election, Francis approved canonization for two of his predecessors: John XXIII and John Paul II. The joint announcement pleased almost everyone—progressives who saw John as their hero after Vatican II and traditionalists who cheered the Polish pope's campaign to roll back many of the council's reforms. By canonizing them together, Francis managed to honor both "the man who took the lid off and the man who tried to put it back on," said Eamon Duffy, a Cambridge University church historian.

John Paul II was made a saint nine years after his death, a tiny fraction of the time canonization normally took. That was thanks to Benedict, who fast-tracked the process. At the time of Francis's election, the Congregation for the Causes of Saints was in the final stages of evaluating John Paul's candidacy and ready to endorse it. Groups representing the victims of priestly sex abuse had been outraged for years by the idea, given John Paul's well-documented failure to deal with the abuse crisis, but the congregation was untroubled by the criticism.

Sainthood for John XXIII was trickier. His canonization had never been a priority for John Paul or Benedict. At the time of Francis's election, the congregation for sainthood claimed it could attribute only one medical miracle to John—the apparently miraculous recovery of an Italian nun from a stomach tumor in the 1960s—and not the needed two. Francis decided to bend the rules. For "the good pope," one miracle was fine.

CARDINAL KASPER ENJOYED his new celebrity as "the pope's theologian."
Since Francis was not a theologian and avoided detailed conversations about
doctrine, he decided Kasper would do it for him, and the German cardinal
was eager for the role. After the pope turned *Mercy* into an international
bestseller, Kasper rushed out another book: *Pope Francis's Revolution of Tenderness and Love*. It hailed the pope for having "breathed new life into the
church" and offered predictions of the revolution to come, beginning with
the Vatican's new relationship to other faiths. After so many years of ugly
battles with Benedict, other religious leaders were excited to work with
Francis. Jewish leaders were gratified when the new pope issued a decree in
2015 that ended the Vatican's policy of encouraging the conversion of Jews.

Even so, Kasper feared Francis risked creating disappointment: "A new
pope can renew the church but cannot invent a new church," he wrote. He
believed the pope was basically conservative on doctrine and might disappoint women especially. Francis had been adamant, in Rome as in Buenos
Aires, that women could never be priests. "That door is closed," the pope
said several months after his election when asked about the possibility of
ordaining women.

What *was* revolutionary, Kasper wrote, was that doctrine did not control
the pope. Francis believed the church needed to be flexible in enforcing its
teachings and ready to ignore them when they interfered with someone's
need for mercy. Kasper cited an early example—that of Diego Lejárraga, a
balding, soft-spoken Spanish civil servant who was born with a girl's body but
underwent a sex-change operation in 2007, at the age of forty. He wrote to
Francis in 2014, hoping the same pope who had famously asked "Who am I
to judge?" might help him remain a Catholic. "I felt he would listen to me."
The letter detailed Lejárraga's transition—of how, after surgery, he began a
new life as a man and fell in love with a woman, who was now his fiancée. He
told Francis that, in the turmoil of his life, what never changed was his devotion to Jesus. Yet after he began living as a man, his devout Catholic neighbors shunned him as a deviant sinner. His parish priest, noting the Vatican
condemned sex-change surgery, mocked him as the "devil's daughter."*

---

* In 2002, the Congregation for the Doctrine of the Faith, led by then-Cardinal Ratzinger, denounced sex-change operations and declared that they did not alter a person's
gender in the church's eyes. The decree ordered bishops to reject requests from parishioners who sought to change their sex on their baptismal records.

One afternoon that December, his cell phone rang. The caller's phone number was blocked, but the caller instantly identified himself:

"I am Pope Francis."

Lejárraga instantly recognized the gruff Argentine accent. The pope told him he had been moved by his letter—"it touched my soul"—and invited him and his fiancée to the Vatican. They met a month later in Rome. Lejárraga asked the pope whether there was "a place in the house of God for me." Francis responded by embracing him. "You are a son of God and the church loves you and accepts you as you are," he said.

AT FRANCIS'S INSISTENCE, Kasper was center stage in the preparations for the 2014 synod on the family, an event many Catholics were already comparing to Vatican II, since it was the first time since the council that the world's bishops were promised they could speak with absolute freedom.

Francis gave a strong hint of what was to come when he called the entire College of Cardinals to Rome in February, six months before the synod, for a special meeting known as a consistory and asked Kasper to speak. The consistory was itself evidence of Francis's revolution. It included an installation ceremony for the first nineteen cardinals appointed by the new pope, including several from small, impoverished nations in Africa, Asia, and Latin America. His choices signaled an end to the domination of the College of Cardinals by Europeans and North Americans. While there were nine new European cardinals, including Secretary of State Parolin and Archbishop Müller, three were over the age of eighty and could not participate in a conclave. There were no new cardinals from the United States.

Francis wanted Kasper's speech to revive the campaign he had pursued as a bishop in Germany—to allow divorced Catholics to take Communion. Kasper warned the pope that if he gave that speech, they would both be "walking into the lion's den" since it would enrage conservatives who felt the decision to bar divorced Catholics from the sacraments had been settled, most recently by Benedict. Francis laughed and replied that he welcomed the fight: "That's good! That's what we should have."

Kasper's speech, calling for the church to grant divorced Catholics a "spiritual life raft," got him the furious reaction he predicted. Cardinals close to Benedict described the proposal as an insult to the former pope, who had battled Kasper on the issue so publicly in the 1990s. Burke depicted Kasper as a self-promoting troublemaker, maybe even a heretic, who might be lying when he claimed to speak for Francis. "The pope is not mute," he said. "He can speak for himself." A conservative columnist at *The New York Times*, Ross Douthat, a devout convert, dedicated thousands of words to warn of a "Kasper-esque shift" in the Vatican that, if embraced by the pope, could lead to "civil war" in the church.

At the Congregation for the Doctrine of the Faith, Müller joined in condemning Kasper's plan. The idea of granting Communion to the divorced was a "false appeal to mercy" that undermined centuries of teachings, Müller said. He, Burke, and three other conservative cardinals hastily published a book ahead of the synod, *Remaining in the Truth of Christ*, to denounce Kasper's proposal.

The October synod signaled the launch in earnest of a well-organized internal opposition to Francis, one that would win the backing of powerful right-wing political figures outside the church, especially in the United States. The ringleaders were Burke and Müller. Burke, whose contempt for Francis was never hidden, was the more colorful of that pair—literally. The Wisconsin-born cleric was dedicated to the splendor of traditional church fashion, and his wardrobe made him a walking rejection of Francis's call for a humble church. He wore layers of silk robes, bejeweled headwear, and fur-lined scarlet gloves. In 2013, a blogger in Rome matched Burke's clothes against price lists at Vatican tailoring shops and determined that on an average day, his outer garments alone cost more than twenty-five thousand dollars.

Beneath the finery, Burke had always been a rhetorical pit bull in defending conservative doctrine, which explained why he rose so far under John Paul and Benedict. As archbishop in St. Louis from 2004 to 2006, he frequently made national headlines. In the 2004 presidential campaign, he called for the church to deny Communion to the Democratic nominee, Senator John Kerry, a Catholic, because of Kerry's support for abortion rights. In the 2008 election, he said the Democratic Party under Barack Obama was "transforming itself definitely into a party of death" because of its stand on abortion and stem-cell research. He regularly denounced homosexuality and urged Catholics to disinvite gay relatives from gatherings at which children were present.

Müller, who delighted in holding his prestigious assignment in the Curia, was never so eager to be seen as the pope's opponent, if only because he appeared to harbor hopes of being pope himself; he would not want to needlessly alienate Francis's many allies in the College of Cardinals. Still, under Müller, the congregation repeatedly put roadblocks in the way of the pope's agenda. In defending conservative doctrine, Müller became known for oddly inappropriate, even bizarre public statements. In the final weeks of Benedict's papacy, Müller created an uproar when he said the Vatican was the victim of disinformation campaigns in the United States that he compared to "pogroms against the Jews," a reference to the murderous anti-Semitic riots across Russia and eastern Europe that foreshadowed the Holocaust. The German Justice Ministry denounced his remark as "outrageously insensitive." He also made headlines for his ill-advised rush to defend archconservative friends caught up in scandal, notably the German bishop Franz-Peter Tebartz–van Elst. Müller insisted publicly that the "bishop of bling" had done nothing wrong, as if a senior cleric spending tens of millions of dollars in church funds on himself should go without scrutiny.

Francis established an early pattern in dealing with detractors inside the Vatican. He did not act against them hastily, which meant that senior Curia appointees were allowed to serve out their terms—five years, in Müller's case. He found other ways of neutralizing them. In Müller's case, he undermined the cardinal with repeated public statements in which he diminished the importance of the once-feared Congregation for the Doctrine of the Faith. Under Francis, Müller would never have the fame or authority of his predecessors. The congregation's investigations of controversial theologians dried up almost entirely under Francis. The pope also shut down what was then the congregation's most controversial investigation—of dissent by American nuns. The investigation, the one begun in 2009 under Benedict, had been criticized from the start by prominent American Catholics. The nuns' defenders included Vice President Biden, who once told Benedict in a meeting in Rome that "you are being entirely too hard on American nuns—lighten up." Under Francis, the investigation concluded with a report that praised the nuns for "a vision of religious life that is centered on the Person of Jesus Christ and is rooted in the Tradition of the Church."

FRANCIS HAD A KEEN MEMORY. His deputies in the Curia said he could remember the details of minor events, and the names of remote acquaintances, from decades earlier. A few years into his papacy, however, his memory failed him constantly when forced to confront the issue that would, more than any other, stain his legacy as pope, just as it had blackened those of John Paul II and Benedict: clerical sex abuse.

The blind spot that Francis demonstrated in Argentina was evident in Rome, too. Over time, he made several wildly inaccurate statements in trying to defend the Vatican's dismal record on the subject. In 2014, a year after his election, he brushed aside mountains of evidence to the contrary to claim that the Vatican's record in protecting children from pedophile priests had been impressive for years. "The Catholic Church is perhaps the only major public institution to have acted with transparency" in confronting child sexual abuse, he insisted. "No one has done more." (The US victims' group BishopAccountability.org, said Francis's comments were "simply delusional.")

His blind spot was evident, too, in the creation of the C-8, his papal cabinet. Most of those eight cardinals had miserable records in combatting priestly child abuse, and two were notorious: George Pell of Australia, dogged for much of his career by allegations that he himself was a child molester, and Francisco Javier Errázuriz of Chile, who had a well-established history of shielding pedophile priests. Francis was determined to have both in his cabinet, however. He and Errázuriz had been friends for years, and the brusque, no-nonsense Pell was known as an efficient manager. In 2014, Francis brought the Australian to Rome full-time and gave him an additional post, as head of a newly created Secretariat for the Economy.

Just a few months after his election, Francis was forced to deal personally with an especially grotesque child-molestation case, that of sixty-five-year-old Archbishop Józef Wesołowski of Poland, the Vatican's ambassador to the Dominican Republic. His crimes were first exposed by a Dominican television journalist, who reported that the archbishop was molesting shoeshine boys he met on the waterfront of Santo Domingo, the capital. One victim suffered from epilepsy and said that, beginning at the age of thirteen, he performed sex acts on the archbishop in exchange for his medicine. Cardinal Nicolás López Rodriguez, the country's leading churchman, flew to Rome in August 2013 for an emergency meeting with Francis and convinced the pope to recall Wesołowski to the Vatican immediately, before local police could arrest him. Francis agreed that since Wesołowski could assert diplomatic immunity, he should be prosecuted in the Vatican. The case was especially sensitive since Wesołowski billed himself as a protégé of his countryman John Paul II. The decision to recall him infuriated the

government of the Dominican Republic and resulted in damning headlines for the Vatican, especially after a seemingly carefree Wesołowski was
regularly seen strolling near St. Peter's Square as he awaited trial. He faced
charges both of child molestation and of possession of child pornography;
more than one hundred thousand images of child sexual abuse were found
on his computer. He died in 2015, reportedly of a heart attack, before he
could be tried.

In the first months of his papacy, Francis was quietly alerted to sex-abuse
allegations against another, far more senior churchman, his friend Cardinal McCarrick, and took no action. No other abuse case would so damage
Francis's reputation, especially after Vatican investigators pieced together a
timeline showing that the pope chose for years to ignore a flood of evidence
that McCarrick was a sexual predator, all the while greeting him in Rome
as an honored statesman. When confronted with that evidence years later,
Francis gave answers that were vague and incomplete, claiming he could
not remember exactly what he knew, and when, about McCarrick.

The pope *did* remember that, weeks after his election in March 2013,
he had a "brief meeting" with a former Vatican diplomat in Washington
who warned him about the allegations against McCarrick. The aide, Archbishop Giovanni Becciu, a senior Curia bureaucrat, recalled telling Francis
that the allegations were so serious that the cardinal had been ordered years
earlier to live quietly in retirement, a command he ignored.

Francis eventually acknowledged that—to his regret, he said—he did
nothing with Becciu's information, assuming it was only "gossip." Weeks
after that, he invited McCarrick to the Santa Marta guesthouse for the first
of what became regular meetings in Rome between the two. The pope
always welcomed news about McCarrick's fundraising at the Papal Foundation, the US-based charity that distributed millions of dollars a year to
worthy projects of Francis's choosing. The charity, established in 1988 by
McCarrick and Cardinal John Krol of Philadelphia, had a long record of
valuable philanthropy. It underwrote construction of churches, schools,
and medical clinics in poor countries. It also functioned as an emergency
fund that Francis, like his predecessors, could draw on.

Francis was almost entirely silent on the issue of priestly sex abuse in
the early months of his papacy, and his silence went mostly unnoticed at a
time when there was so much excitement over his election. That changed
in December 2013, when he hastily created the Pontifical Commission for
the Protection of Minors to study clerical child abuse. The initiative was

seen at the time as an obvious public-relations ploy—an effort to get ahead of a flurry of terrible headlines that month, when United Nations human-rights investigators complained they were being stonewalled by the Vatican for evidence needed for a UN study of clerical child molestation. Stung by the UN's criticism, the pope's commission was organized so quickly that on the day it was announced, the Vatican could answer few questions about the panel's mission or membership, apart from revealing its leader, Cardinal O'Malley of Boston. Advocates for child victims saw the commission as too little, too late. The US-based group SNAP, the Survivors Network of those Abused by Priests, dismissed the new panel as "toothless."

40

"Catholics Love Me"

O N APRIL 27, 2014, two massive gold-framed photographs, each twenty feet tall, were hung from the front balconies of St. Peter's Basilica. On the left, set between the rows of gray-marble columns that dominate its façade, was the handsome face of John Paul II. On the right was an uncharacteristically solemn portrait of John XXIII. Both photos had been altered to show a glowing white light just behind the men's heads, suggesting a halo. The images looked down on the thousands of spectators who had jammed into St. Peter's Square that morning to watch as the two popes were declared saints.

The huge crowd played favorites. Older Europeans, especially the Italians, cheered for their beloved John XXIII, but the cheers for John Paul II were much louder, almost deafening. That was no surprise given the estimated two hundred thousand Poles present. The Vatican later reported that seventeen hundred buses, fifty-eight charter flights, and five special trains had brought them to Rome.

Francis was even-handed in celebrating the lives of his two predecessors. He described John as a pope who demonstrated "exquisite openness" by calling the Second Vatican Council, while he praised John Paul for having brought the global family of Catholics together with his travels. A highlight came when he blessed crystal display cases containing physical relics from the bodies of the two popes—a vial of John Paul's blood taken during a transfusion shortly before his death, and a small piece of skin removed from John's corpse after it was exhumed for his beatification.

One figure in the crowd looked out of place: a disheveled, barely shaven American named Stephen K. Bannon. The sixty-year-old Bannon, a founder of the right-wing US website Breitbart News, considered his eccentric appearance a calling card—proof of how little he cared what others thought of him. He was in Rome to cover the ceremony for Breitbart and also to make contact with Curia bishops who shared his view that the church under Francis was moving in a dangerous direction. Bannon, a devout Catholic, was especially eager to introduce himself to Cardinal Burke, and they bonded during a meeting arranged on short notice by one of the cardinal's confidants in Rome. It was the beginning of an alliance between the two men that would grow into a movement in which far-right American, European, and Latin American populists joined with Francis's enemies in the Curia to undermine his papacy. Their cause was supercharged a year later when real-estate developer and television reality-show star Donald Trump announced his candidacy for the White House. Bannon would run Trump's campaign.

THE VATICAN'S NEXT BIG EVENT that year was the synod on the family, and opposition to Francis's agenda continued to mount. His critics at the October meeting were determined, above all else, to reject Cardinal Kasper's plan to allow divorced Catholics to receive Communion. The pope opened the synod with a speech to the 190 bishops in which, while not explicitly endorsing the plan, he called for the church to stop placing "intolerable burdens on the shoulders" of those who needed its mercy. He repeated the promise he made at the time he announced the synod—that there were no restrictions on what the bishops could debate: "Speak freely of everything you believe."

While the synod was closed to the public, bishops came out of the meetings to describe a rollicking, sometimes bare-knuckled debate in the spirit of the Second Vatican Council. Cardinal Luis Tagle of the Philippines said churchmen too young to have participated in Vatican II now had a sense of how thrilling the council had been. Halfway through, the synod's organizers released a stunning twelve-page summary of the early debate. It revealed that the bishops had agreed the church should provide a "welcoming home" to all people once treated as sinners. That included gays, unmarried couples who lived together, and those who had divorced and remarried. The church, it said, should recognize that gay people have "gifts and qualities to offer to the Christian community" and that same-sex unions had value when they provided a couple with "mutual aid to the point of sacrifice."

Conservative bishops were appalled and insisted the document, written by theologians selected by Francis, misrepresented the debates. According to several news reports, Müller described the document as "unworthy, shameful and completely wrong." The controversy threatened to bring the synod to a standstill, so the report was hastily rewritten to placate Müller and others. The original draft used the phrase "welcoming homosexual persons." In the revision, "welcoming" was replaced with "providing for." A reference to "partners" in same-sex relationships was changed to "these people."

The two-week synod ended inconclusively. Among the issues left unresolved was Kasper's proposal on Communion for the divorced. In his closing address, Francis criticized both conservative bishops (for "hostile rigidity") and liberals (for promoting a "false sense of mercy" that would "bandage a wound before treating it") before congratulating both sides for an uncensored debate that would continue the next year with another, larger gathering.

Cardinal Burke had seen enough, and he granted interviews that fall that represented a dramatic escalation in his rebellion against the pope. In a magazine interview, Burke said the synod proved that the Vatican under Francis had become "a ship without a rudder." The world's Catholics were feeling "seasick because they feel the church's ship has lost its way."

The Vatican announced two weeks later that Burke had been removed from his last important Curia assignment—as a judge on the Vatican's equivalent of the Supreme Court, known as the Apostolic Signatura—and given a largely ceremonial post at the Knights of Malta, the Catholic charity group. The pope insisted the move was not meant as a demotion, but the cardinal portrayed himself as a martyr. The fiercely conservative US-based newspaper the *National Catholic Register* wrote that Burke's friends believed the cardinal ("a gentle holy man who always wants to be loyal to the pope") had been treated shamefully by Francis.* A widely read ultra-

---

* The *National Catholic Register*, owned by the conservative US-based Eternal Word Television Network, is sometimes confused for the progressive *National Catholic Reporter*. The cable-television network, known as EWTN and often compared to Fox News, and its newspaper would champion Francis's opponents. EWTN bought the *Register* in 2011 from Father Maciel's scandal-plagued Legion of Christ, which had owned the paper since 1995.

traditionalist Catholic website described Burke's ouster from the court as "the greatest humiliation of a curial cardinal in living memory."

Still, Burke's allies had reason to cheer another personnel decision by the pope that year: Francis, eager for racial and geographical diversity in the Curia, named the conservative Cardinal Robert Sarah of the African nation of Guinea to head the Congregation for Divine Worship, which oversaw liturgy and religious practices. There was much to admire in the sixty-nine-year-old Sarah, a Gregorian-educated theologian who had stood up against his country's brutal dictatorship. Francis came to regret the appointment, however, since Sarah formed an alliance with Burke and openly rejected much of the pope's agenda for a more merciful church. In Rome, Sarah declared that homosexuality was of "demonic origin" and compared the gay-rights movement to "Nazi-Fascism." He described Kasper's proposal to allow divorced Catholics to take Communion as "heresy" that reflected a "dangerous, schizophrenic pathology."

FRANCIS HAD MOMENTOUS EVENTS to look forward to as he entered the third year of his papacy in 2015: a long-anticipated tour of the United States; the release of an encyclical in which he would align himself with climate scientists in calling for urgent action against global warming; and a second, climactic synod on the family. The year would be better remembered, however, for some of the most disastrous decisions of his papacy, most tied to his unwillingness to grapple with the sex-abuse crisis.

In January, the pope made what he acknowledged was the single most catastrophic personnel choice of his papacy—the naming of a bishop, Juan Barros, in the southern Chilean province of Osorno. The appointment sparked protests across Chile, since Barros had been the right-hand man to Fernando Karadima, the country's most notorious pedophile priest, for decades. Karadima's victims insisted Barros had regularly witnessed the abuse, standing only a few feet away as Karadima molested boys. "He saw it all," said Juan Carlos Cruz, a fifty-one-year-old communications executive who had been abused by Karadima as a teenager.

Barros's installation ceremony dissolved into pandemonium. Thousands of protesters gathered outside the Osorno cathedral, while several made their way inside and scuffled with the bishop's supporters. Many protesters told journalists they felt betrayed by the Vatican—and by Francis, in particular.

Two months later, a tourist in St. Peter's Square filmed an encounter between Francis and a Chilean churchman who had gone there to attend one of the pope's weekly public audiences. The two men began talking about Barros. In a chilly, contemptuous tone, the pope dismissed his critics in Chile, apparently oblivious to the fact he was being filmed. "The Osorno community is suffering because it's dumb," he said, jabbing at the church-man with his finger like a schoolmaster. "Don't be led by the nose by the leftists who orchestrated all this." He said the furor over Barros was led by *zurdos*—Communists. "I'm the first one to judge and punish someone who faces accusations of this type. But in this case? There's not a shred of evidence."

The video was broadcast by Chilean television and led to a new round of protests against the pope. Major international news organizations, includ-ing *The New York Times* and *The Washington Post*, posted the video online. "We are now seeing the real face of Pope Francis, and we demand an expla-nation," said Juan Carlos Claret, one of the Osorno protesters. The video delighted Barros, who released a statement to his parishioners: "I have great gratitude for the pope's support."

A similar scandal was brewing that year in the pope's homeland, although the details would be kept secret—on Francis's orders—since the Argentine bishop at the heart of the scandal had once been so close to him. The bishop, Gustavo Zanchetta of the rural Argentine diocese of Oran, had been an aide to then-Cardinal Bergoglio and described himself as the pope's "spiritual son." He was named a bishop in July 2013, just four months after Francis's election. In October 2015, the pope ordered Zanchetta to Rome to explain himself after lewd naked selfies of the fifty-one-year-old bishop, as well as a collection of gay pornographic images, were found on his cell phone by a church secretary. He insisted to Francis that the naked photos were fakes, an explanation the pope readily accepted even though others who saw the photos had no doubt they were real. A relieved Zanchetta went home, although his troubles had only begun. Months later, five priests in his diocese signed a joint letter accusing Zanchetta of sexual harassment of seminarians, who were regularly asked to take off their clothes and give him a massage. The pope would not act on those allegations for more than a year.

At first, Francis's five-day pilgrimage to the US in September 2015 seemed likely to be remembered as an unqualified triumph. He was wel-comed with adoring crowds first in Washington, where he met President

Obama and spoke to a joint session of Congress, then in New York and Philadelphia. Throughout the trip, he sidestepped controversial issues and stressed his call for a more tolerant church. He was careful to say nothing about that summer's landmark decision by the US Supreme Court to legalize same-sex marriage, a ruling many conservative American bishops condemned.

But there were odd stumbles during the trip that left many American Catholics questioning whether Francis was the open-minded reformer he claimed to be. In Washington, he had brief encounters with the two churchmen who, more than any others, would bring scandal to his papacy. The first, McCarrick, turned up at St. Matthew's Cathedral for midday prayers led by the pope. They greeted each other as old friends. The pope's more fateful encounter was with Viganò, the nuncio, who had organized a series of private papal audiences in Washington with Americans he thought the pope should meet. One of those meetings—between Francis and a Kentucky woman named Kim Davis, a county clerk who made national headlines weeks earlier when she defied the Supreme Court's ruling and refused to issue marriage licenses for same-sex couples—created a firestorm when it was revealed in news reports after the pope returned to Rome. In confirming the encounter, Davis claimed the pope told her to "stay strong" in her battle against gay marriage. Gay-rights activists, who once thought they had an ally in Francis, were stunned. The pope's meeting with Davis "throws a wet blanket on all the goodwill that the pontiff garnered during his US visit," said Francis DeBernardo of New Ways Ministry, an advocacy group for gay Catholics.

The Davis meeting led to a furious round of finger-pointing between the Vatican and Viganò. Francis's deputies insisted the pope had been blindsided by Viganò and had not understood the significance of meeting Davis—and did not support her views. In trying to blunt the ugly news coverage, the Vatican disclosed that in Washington the pope also met privately with a former student from Buenos Aires who now lived in the US—a sixty-seven-year-old gay man who brought along his male partner. The couple posted a video online showing the pope hugging both men.

Viganò also found himself under siege by American news organizations, which began to report on his oddly close alliance with far-right evangelical leaders opposed to gay marriage; they had introduced him to Davis. He defended himself by insisting his ties to antigay activists were consistent with the views he had always expressed about the evils of homosexuality.

Within weeks, he was summoned to Rome and found himself face-to-face with an outraged Francis, who told him his career was over.

FRANCIS RETURNED TO ROME from the US only days before the opening of his second synod on the family. The 270 bishops at the gathering reported that the debates were as fierce and freewheeling as the year before. But also like the year before, the second synod ended inconclusively. There was no endorsement of the most progressive measures before the bishops, including Kasper's proposal to grant Communion to divorced couples. The synod's final report urged that gay people be treated with "dignity," but it rejected same-sex marriage, describing it as "not even remotely analogous" to marriage between a man and a woman. Reform-minded churchmen described the synod as a failure since it had not endorsed Francis's call for greater tolerance in the church, at least not in any concrete way.

The pope was not out of options, however. By tradition, he planned to write his own report on the two synod meetings, and it would be the final word on their outcome. Kasper and other progressives were optimistic about what he would say, and Francis's closing address to the 2015 meeting gave them reason for hope. "Today is a time of mercy!" the pope declared, seeming to scold the synod bishops for cowardice. He cited a story from the Gospel of Mark about a blind beggar, Bartimaeus, who encounters Jesus and his disciples and asks for help. The disciples offer a few words of comfort to Bartimaeus, while Jesus does much more. He stops and heals the man. "None of the disciples stopped as Jesus did," the pope told the audience of bishops, who were the callous disciples in this analogy. "If Bartimaeus was blind, the disciples were deaf."

He reminded the entire church of that battle cry a few weeks later, when he declared the start of a yearlong worldwide celebration—the Jubilee of Mercy—dedicated to his belief that "mercy is the very foundation of the church's life." He announced it would begin on December 8, which was the fiftieth anniversary of the closing ceremony of Vatican II, when "the walls which for too long had made the church a kind of fortress were torn down." During the jubilee, priests around the world were given authority to grant forgiveness for abortions, a sin previously considered so grave it could be forgiven only by a bishop.

In the first months of 2016, there was frenzied speculation about what the pope would say in his report on the two synods. It was, for many Catholics, the most anticipated papal decree since *Humanae Vitae*, since it seemed likely to affect the way millions of divorced Catholics conducted their daily lives. The pope had already made their lives easier in September 2015, when he streamlined the process for divorced couples to obtain annulments, allowing them to remarry without risking sin. Before then, annulments had been so costly and time-consuming that they were largely unknown outside the US and Western Europe. Under the new rules, annulments could be approved in as little as a month.

In April, he released a 265-page document entitled *Amoris Laetitia* (The Joy of Love) that was his long-awaited report on the synods. It was written in Francis's trademark meandering style, with lots of grandfatherly wisdom and favorite bits of scripture. On first reading, it seemed to say nothing new. It was a broad proclamation of the need for sinners to be shown mercy. The church's teachings about sexual morality could not be used as "stones to throw at people's lives." Deep in the document, however, progressives found what they were looking for: a tantalizing footnote—number 351— that appeared to invite priests to find a way to enable divorced Catholics to receive Communion. Priests "could offer the help of the sacraments to those who are living in an objective situation of sin." It was a category that by most definitions included divorced men and women. Kasper certainly read it that way. The pope's document "doesn't change anything in terms of church doctrine or canon law," the cardinal said, "but it changes everything."

Cardinal Müller rushed out his own statement on behalf of the Congregation for the Doctrine of the Faith, contradicting Kasper. Insisting *he* spoke for the pope, Müller said the footnote's reference to people living in "an objective situation of sin" was not meant to include divorced Catholics. That, he suggested, was a category of sin altogether different and more serious. But Müller was *not* speaking for the pope, it became clear. Within weeks, the Catholic hierarchy in several nations set to work on guidelines for granting Communion to divorced couples. In September, Argentina's bishops submitted their proposal to the pope, citing footnote 351. He wrote back in a public letter that congratulated them because they had "completely understood" his document: "There is no other interpretation." There would soon be tearful scenes across the pope's homeland as divorced Catholics were invited to step from the pews, kneel at the altar, and accept Communion bread and wine.

The weeks that followed were compared to those after *Humanae Vitae* in

1968. Francis, like Paul VI, was denounced with rhetoric that was insulting and extreme. In an extraordinary act of disobedience, Burke and three other cardinals issued a written public challenge, known formally as a *dubia* (Latin for "doubts"), that accused the pope of creating "grave disorientation and great confusion." The four cardinals demanded that he reverse himself—and once again bar divorced Catholics from receiving the sacraments. Burke gave interviews to warn that unless Francis changed course, the church might split in two: "It could develop into a formal schism."

The furor came at a time when enemies outside the church—far-right, xenophobic populist politicians who kept winning elections around the world—were organizing against Francis. None would prove more menacing than Donald Trump, who made Francis a target on the campaign trail as he sought the presidency in 2016.

Anti-Catholic bigotry had been common in American politics since the country's founding, but there had never been anything like the 2016 campaign, when a leading presidential candidate and the bishop of Rome openly traded insults. Their battle began in February, when the pope was on a pilgrimage to Mexico and organized a Mass on the banks of the Rio Grande, along the US border. He intended to show solidarity with migrants attempting to cross illegally into the United States. Trump, whose call to build a border wall was a centerpiece of his campaign, denounced Francis on television: "I think the pope is a very political person. I don't think he understands the danger of the open border that we have with Mexico." The Mexican government was "using the pope as a pawn." (The audaciousness of Trump's attack on the pope was seen as shocking, although he had said uglier things about Benedict. "He should just give up and die," Trump said of Benedict in a radio interview in 2013. "He looks so bad.")

Francis went ahead with the border Mass, drawing almost two hundred thousand worshippers, and said nothing about Trump. On the flight home, however, he was sharply critical of the Republican candidate: "A person who thinks only about building walls, wherever they may be, and not building bridges, is not Christian."

The next day, Trump counterattacked. It was "disgraceful" for the pope to question his religious faith, said Trump, who was raised a Presbyterian. He insisted Francis did not speak for most Americans of the faith: "The Catholics love me." Several conservative evangelical leaders who were Trump backers said it was the pope, not their candidate, who crossed a line by meddling in American politics. "Jesus never intended to give instructions to political leaders on how to run a country," said Jerry Falwell Jr., the president of Liberty University, an evangelical school in Virginia.*

Trump had broad support from the nation's seventy million Catholics. In opinion polls, they sided with him, not Francis, on issues like the border wall. A handful of conservative bishops signaled they too supported Trump. Bishop Thomas Tobin of Providence, Rhode Island, wrote in a Facebook post that "only with strong Christian values can we 'Make America Great Again!'" He warned of "a toxic, anti-Catholic prejudice" in the campaign of Hillary Clinton, the Democratic candidate. Polls after Trump's victory in November showed that he received 52 percent of the Catholic vote.

Steve Bannon had been Trump's campaign manager in the final weeks of the race and, after victory, began work at the White House as the new president's "chief strategist." Bannon's rise delighted his friend Cardinal Burke, who gave interviews to welcome Trump's election. He said the new president would put the US on the "right path," especially if he lived up to his commitment to outlaw most abortions.

Trump's election alarmed Francis in a way his aides had never seen before. The pope, who felt his training as a chemist gave him insights into technology, was appalled by the disclosure that Russian Internet companies had flooded the Facebook accounts of American Catholic voters with blatantly false "news" reports that he had endorsed Trump. After the election, he asked the Vatican's scientific agency to study whether other US technology companies had allowed data collected from Catholic voters to be manipulated on Trump's behalf.†

Two days after Trump's inauguration, Francis told an interviewer for a Spanish newspaper that American Catholics should recall how Hitler came to power in Germany in the 1930s: "Hitler didn't steal the power. His people voted for him. And then he destroyed his people."

And now, working at Trump's side, was Bannon, a bombastic, self-declared "Catholic populist nationalist" whose Breitbart website had long condemned the pope as a dangerous leftist. A month after the inauguration,

* As president, Trump distanced himself from Falwell after Falwell became engulfed in a scandal centered on his wife's affair over several years with a former Miami resort pool attendant. Falwell resigned from the university in August 2020.
† He was alarmed four years later by reports that Trump's 2020 reelection campaign worked with a group called CatholicVote to collect cell-phone data from Catholics as they walked in and out of church, allowing them to be targeted for Facebook ads supporting Trump.

The New York Times published a front-page article detailing the years-long alliance between Bannon and Francis's enemies inside the Curia, including Burke.

In May, the pope met Trump at the Vatican, easily the most awkward encounter of his papacy with a foreign leader. Trump requested the meeting as part of his maiden foreign trip as president. Francis smiled warily when he was introduced to Trump but then, as official photos were taken, his face froze in a contemptuous scowl. It remained grimly set, even as an Italian tabloid photographer called out, "Sorri!" (Smile!) The pope managed what appeared to be a genuine smile when he shook hands with First Lady Melania Trump. Francis's private meeting with the president lasted exactly thirty minutes, barely long enough to get past formalities, and ended with an exchange of gifts. The pope's present to Trump was a copy of his environmental encyclical from the year before, in which Francis had warned of the catastrophe of global warming, a threat Trump dismissed. In an exchange overheard by reporters, the pope took a dig at Trump's obvious weight problem when he asked Melania what she fed her husband. "Potizza?" he asked with a chuckle, referring to the fatty nut-roll pastry of her native Slovenia. She laughed, appearing to enjoy the pope's insult of her spouse. "Yes, potizza."

Trump's election had solidified something in Francis's mind that he had felt for several years: the United States was often a destructive force in the

A scowling Pope Francis meets with President Trump at the Vatican, May 2017.

world. In his writings as an archbishop, he regularly condemned the greed and militarism of the United States and other developed nations. Now he saw the threat in a new and terrifying way—with men like Trump and Bannon, supported by an astonishing number of American Catholics, leading the Western world to reject democracy.

The pope became increasingly worried about the large number of arch-conservatives in the American church hierarchy, bishops appointed by John Paul II and Benedict and close to Cardinal Burke. None was more supportive of Trump, and openly opposed to Francis, than Archbishop Charles Chaput of Philadelphia. A month after the inauguration, Chaput suggested that the new president was being unfairly attacked by American "elites."

Francis mostly held his tongue in public about Trump, no matter how much he seethed over the new president. He did, however, want to make his feelings known about the danger he perceived in Washington. He asked two trusted friends—Father Antonio Spadaro, editor of *La Civiltà Cattolica*, and an Argentine Protestant theologian, Marcelo Figueroa—to publish an essay in *Civiltà Cattolica* to sound an alarm. Both Figueroa and the pope knew from their experience of the Dirty War what happened when Catholics sat silent in the face of tyranny.

The article was a stinging attack on the Trump administration and what the authors saw as an alliance of "hate" between American politicians and radically conservative Christians—Catholics and Protestants alike. Bannon was accused of "apocalyptic geopolitics." The authors said that Catholics and evangelical Christians had joined with Republican lawmakers in a "xenophobic and Islamophobic vision that wants walls and purifying deportations." Against this, they wrote, stood Pope Francis, who opposed this "narrative of fear."

The attack infuriated conservative American Catholics. Archbishop Chaput said the article was "an exercise in dumbing down" the legitimate views of Americans who were "merely fighting for what their churches have always held to be true."

The essay might have created a bigger uproar in Rome that summer had it not been overshadowed by momentous news about the fate of two powerful Curia cardinals. In June, Pell, the Vatican's finance chief and an original member of the papal cabinet, was charged with child molestation in his native Australia. The seventy-six-year-old cardinal, the highest-ranking Curia official ever to face criminal charges of sexual abuse, was accused of molesting two thirteen-year-old choirboys in Melbourne's cathedral in

1996, when he was the city's archbishop. Pell, who insisted he was innocent, was granted a leave of absence to go home for trial.

The other cardinal in the headlines was Müller, who was notified by Francis in July that he was being replaced as prelate of the Congregation for the Doctrine of the Faith when his five-year term ended that fall. Müller said he was dumbfounded by the news. Whatever his differences with Francis, he had expected to be reappointed for at least another five years. It was the job held by Pope Benedict, his mentor, for almost a quarter century. Müller said he was especially angry over the way Francis delivered the news—by phone, barely a minute into their conversation, and with little explanation.

That afternoon, Müller made the short journey up the hill behind St. Peter's to tell Benedict what had happened, and it was not the only dismal news the two men confronted that day. They also discussed the imminent release of a report by the Catholic diocese of Regensburg about the sexual abuse of boys in the famed choir once led by the pope's brother. The report, made public days later, concluded that 547 choirboys in the Regensburger Domspatzen were sexually or otherwise physically abused between 1945 and 1992. It condemned the "culture of silence" among Regensburg clergymen, including Georg Ratzinger, then ninety-three. It also criticized Müller, Regensburg's bishop from 2002 to 2012, for having stalled investigations of the abuse. The Vatican insisted there was no connection between the report and Müller's departure from the congregation, even if the report's findings bolstered the pope's decision to force him out.

Another cardinal learned that summer that his career would likely soon end in disgrace: McCarrick. In June, the New York City archdiocese received a phone call from a New Jersey man who wanted to report that he had been molested by a priest in 1971, shortly after his sixteenth birthday, when he was an altar boy about to participate in Christmas Mass at St. Patrick's Cathedral in Manhattan. The accuser said he knew other teenagers who had been abused by the same priest. He was known to many of them as "Uncle Ted."

41

The Network

A GROUP OF CURIA BISHOPS asked themselves the same terrible question in early 2017: Did Benedict XVI know—did he *care*—that he had put his successor's life at risk? In March, Francis announced what would be his most dangerous foreign pilgrimage—a visit to Egypt the next month. Egypt's military government had just imposed a state of emergency after a series of deadly bombings, most targeting the country's besieged Coptic Christian minority, by the terrorist network ISIS. In December 2016, a suicide bomber killed nearly two hundred people in a Coptic church in Cairo. Despite the risk, Francis insisted he would go. In announcing the trip, the Vatican revealed it had reestablished ties to the revered one-thousand-year-old Al-Azhar Mosque in Cairo, a relationship that collapsed in 2011 over what Egyptians saw as Pope Benedict's repeated insults about Islam.

Just days before Francis left for Egypt, the pope's aides were stunned to learn that Benedict, despite his promise to live "hidden from the world," had released a public statement calling on Christians to rise up against "radical" Muslims who were "creating a dangerous situation for our age." It was time for Christians to "stand up to the confrontation," he declared. His statement was read out at a conference in Poland, organized by a group of conservative theologians to honor Benedict's legacy as pope.

In Rome, commanders of the Gendarmerie, the Vatican's internal police force, were panicked by what Benedict had done. They worried that, on the eve of Francis's departure, words from his predecessor denouncing Muslims as "dangerous" and "radical" would be seized on by terrorists as proof the church under Francis remained hostile to Islam. Had Benedict forgotten what happened in 2006, when his incendiary remarks about Islam set off deadly riots throughout the Muslim world? The Gendarmerie asked foreign spy agencies, including the CIA and the National Security Agency in the US, to see if references to Benedict's statement in Poland appeared in online communications among terrorist networks. The alarm over Francis's safety only grew after he decided to announce that, in a sign of his confidence in Egypt's military, he would not wear a bulletproof vest during the trip or ride in armored cars.

The pope completed the two-day trip without incident. He was praised by his Egyptian hosts for reviving a spirit of goodwill between the Vatican and the Arab world. In Rome, aides to Francis were less angry with the ninety-year-old Benedict, who was physically frail and often appeared confused around visitors, than they were with a group of archconservative bishops close to the former pope. Those churchmen, constantly in and out of the former pope's home in the Mater Ecclesiae monastery, should have known to stop him from releasing the inflammatory message in Poland, Francis's deputies thought. By then, those Benedict loyalists were known inside the Vatican as the "Regensburg network," since so many were Germans who, like the former pope, had been associated over the years with the Bavarian city, including Cardinal Müller, its former bishop. The group's non-German members included Cardinals Burke and Sarah.

As Benedict's critics feared at the time of his abdication, the Mater Ecclesiae was increasingly seen as a rival power center to the Vatican. It was a place where opponents of Francis could gather and plot strategy, with or without Benedict's knowledge. Over time, the Regensburg network formed alliances elsewhere, including with Steve Bannon, who left the White House in August 2017. (Trump said he fired Bannon, while Bannon insisted he resigned.) Bannon found a new project in Rome. He announced he would establish a "gladiator school" in an eight-hundred-year-old monastery near Vatican City to provide theological and media training to populist Catholics who opposed Francis and other "globalists." The project was partly underwritten by a wealthy far-right German noblewoman and socialite, Princess Gloria von Thurn und Taxis (popularly known as "Princess TNT"). The party-loving princess proudly told friends that she introduced Bannon to Cardinal Müller and that they were all close to Burke, who was an official sponsor of the "gladiator school." She would also befriend Archbishop Viganò after he was dismissed as papal ambassador in Washington. Viganò, in turn, established a friendship with Bannon, as well as with Trump's disgraced former national security adviser, Michael Flynn, another devout Catholic. Viganò would also become close to Catholic leaders of the fringe American conspiracy movement known as QAnon.

WHEN DISASTER CAME to Francis's papacy, he admitted he had himself to blame. His abject failure to deal with the scandal of priestly sex abuse had allowed his enemies—churchmen like Burke as well as outsiders like Bannon—to weaponize it against him. The crisis came to a head in 2018, when evidence emerged to show that, throughout his papacy, he ignored evidence of child abuse that was covered up—and sometimes committed—by churchmen he considered friends. The uproar would not end before the careers of more than twenty cardinals and bishops were left in tatters.

The first signs of catastrophe came early in 2017, when news organizations led by the Associated Press revealed that the pope had overruled deputies and reduced the punishment given to pedophile priests. One of those decisions had already come back to haunt him. In 2014, it was revealed, he secretly granted clemency to a politically well-connected Italian priest, Father Mauro Inzoli, who was supposed to be defrocked after the Congregation for the Doctrine of the Faith determined he molested young boys. The pope quietly allowed Inzoli to remain a priest, so long as he vowed to stay away from children. In 2016, however, Inzoli was convicted in an Italian civil court of molesting several children who had not been identified in the original church investigation. In confirming the news, the Vatican sheepishly insisted the pope had simply wanted to be consistent by showing mercy to pedophile priests, just as he showed it to all other sinners. Victims' groups were incensed. By then, Francis's child-abuse commission was coming apart, with members complaining publicly that their recommendations were ignored by the pope. That March, its highest-profile member, Marie Collins, an Irish victims'-rights advocate, declared that the Vatican "thrives on silence and cover-up," and resigned.

The pope told reporters at a news conference weeks later that Collins was a "great woman" who had been right to complain. He admitted the Congregation for the Doctrine of the Faith faced a massive backlog of clerical child-abuse cases awaiting resolution, about two thousand at the time, some dating back a decade. Under Francis, the congregation had only about twenty investigators assigned to those cases, not many more than the skeleton staff under Benedict.

Then came yet another wave of abuse scandals. In June, the US State Department asked the Vatican to strip an Italian-born church diplomat of his immunity so he could be charged with distribution of child pornography. The fifty-year-old diplomat, Monsignor Carlo Capella, who had worked for the papal nuncio in Washington, was instead recalled and placed on trial in the Vatican. He was sentenced to five years in prison. In August, the Vatican announced that the pope's old friend Bishop Zanchetta of Argentina had resigned for unspecified "health reasons," when in fact it was well known among the bishop's deputies that Francis had ordered him to step down because of credible allegations that Zanchetta was molesting seminarians.*

In December, the disgraced churchman Bernard Law, the former cardinal of Boston, died in Rome at the age of eighty-six. For many Americans, Law remained the central villain of the American child-abuse crisis. Two years earlier, Hollywood had cemented that reputation with the film *Spotlight*, which explored the Boston scandal in detail and won the Academy Award for Best Picture. The cardinal's death would bring a new round of criticism of Francis, who honored Law by leading his funeral Mass in St. Peter's. In his eulogy, the pope made no mention of Law's dark legacy in the abuse crisis.

At the time, Francis was aware of the looming threat of yet another devastating scandal in the American church, this one centered on his friend Cardinal McCarrick. In September, the New York City archdiocese quietly notified the Vatican that the allegation that the cardinal had molested a teenage choirboy in St. Patrick's Cathedral in 1971 appeared to be credible. The archdiocese sought approval from Francis and Secretary of State Parolin to proceed with a full, formal investigation. Despite the request's urgency, it took Francis and Parolin weeks to reply. That strange delay was never explained, although Vatican investigators later became convinced it

---

* To the astonishment of Zanchetta's victims, his career in the church was still not over, since he continued to enjoy the pope's support. Francis moved him to Rome and appointed him to a Curia post involving Vatican finances, while insisting Zanchetta undergo psychiatric treatment. The bishop was suspended from his Curia job in 2019, when Argentine prosecutors charged him with sexually abusing two seminarians. He returned to Argentina and, in 2022, was convicted of sexual abuse and sentenced to four years in prison.

was related to another crisis facing the pope: the imminent shutdown of a corruption-plagued church-owned cancer hospital in Rome.*

The timeline of events suggests that officials in the Vatican—including, it appeared, the pope himself—held up the investigation of McCarrick because they needed the cardinal's help at that moment to secure a $25 million grant for the hospital from the Papal Foundation, the US charity that McCarrick had founded. The timeline showed that McCarrick, hoping for leniency from Francis, was eager to approve the grant.

On October 18, the pope finally replied to the New York archdiocese. Through Parolin, he ordered a full investigation of McCarrick, which would take another six months to complete. In the meantime, with McCarrick's encouragement and to the pope's relief, the Papal Foundation approved the $25 million bailout for the cancer hospital. The foundation acknowledged in a public statement there had been "division" and "disharmony" among board members about the decision.

* Like most Vatican scandals involving money, the saga of the hundred-year-old cancer hospital—the Istituto Dermopatico dell'Immacolata, which was a few minutes' drive from St. Peter's—was outrageously complicated. By 2017, however, it came down to this: the hospital was a billion dollars in debt and threatened with immediate closure, which would throw a thousand employees out of work and complicate health care for the Curia since many Vatican bureaucrats received treatment there. In the early stages of the McCarrick investigation in New York, the pope submitted an emergency request to the Papal Foundation for $25 million to keep the hospital open. The request shocked the charity's wealthy backers, since it would be far and away the single largest grant made by the foundation in its twenty-seven-year history. Individual grants were usually capped at about two hundred thousand dollars. The audit committee chairman protested, writing in an internal memo that "this is a disaster," especially since the hospital had a "dubious past" that included money-laundering scandals. He subsequently resigned from the board of directors. McCarrick, the charity's founder, was desperate to help the pope, even if his involvement in approving the grant created an obvious conflict of interest for two other members of the Papal Foundation's board: Cardinal Timothy Dolan of New York, who was overseeing the child-abuse investigation in Manhattan, and Cardinal Wuerl of Washington, nominally McCarrick's supervisor. Later, Dolan and Wuerl would deny any connection between the grant, which they also voted to approve, and any thought of leniency for McCarrick.

42

The Year of Living Desperately

T HE FRAYING, blood-stained cincture had been brought to Rome at Pope Francis's request. A type of ornamental priestly belt made of strands of rope, it had been loosely tied around the waist of Archbishop Óscar Romero on the day of his assassination in 1980. Like other items of Romero's clothing that day, the cincture had been gathered up and treasured as a relic of his godliness.

It would be worn again on October 14, 2018, by the pope, when he oversaw the ceremony in St. Peter's to proclaim Romero a saint. By wearing the cincture, Francis said, he hoped to feel closer to the flesh-and-blood sacrifice that Romero had made. During months of planning, the pope said he wanted the canonization ceremony to be one of the great events of the year, since he saw the murdered archbishop as the embodiment of "the poor church" that Francis championed.

In reading the files from the Congregation for the Causes of Saints, Francis was startled by how Romero's sainthood had been stalled for decades by bishops in Rome and El Salvador. "He was defamed, slandered, his memory despoiled—even by his own brothers in the priesthood," Francis told a group of Salvadoran pilgrims. "How many times those who have given their lives continue being struck with the hardest stone there is—the tongue!"

For that reason alone, the pope felt a special kinship with Romero that year. He would later describe 2018 as *el año desesperado*—the desperate year, when his papacy came under siege and he too felt defamed. By year's end, there would be open calls for his resignation from other churchmen. The central allegations made against him were not so different from those during Argentina's Dirty War—that he ignored the evil in front of him.

The year began with the most disastrous foreign trip of his papacy—to Chile. Before setting off, he had been assured by his old friend Cardinal Errázuriz that he would be welcomed there joyfully, and that the scandal over Bishop Barros had blown over. Francis arrived to chaos, however. In the week before his arrival in Santiago, three churches in the Chilean capital were firebombed in protest over his visit. Leaflets left outside the churches declared in broken English: "We attack with the fire of combat, exploding your disgusting morals. Pope Francis, the next bombs will be attached to your robes!" Riot police had to break up anti-Francis protests elsewhere in the city that focused on the child-abuse crisis.

On his first full day in Santiago, the pope paid a visit to the presidential palace and offered apologies to Chileans for the crimes of pedophile priests: "I cannot help but express the pain and shame that I feel over the irreparable harm caused to children." If that earned him any goodwill, however, it vanished hours later when he led an open-air prayer service, attended by an estimated four hundred thousand Chileans, and celebrated Mass alongside the much-hated Barros. The image of the two men embracing, broadcast live on Chilean television, resulted in a new wave of protests, which became angrier later in the trip, after the pope offered a new, impassioned defense of the embattled bishop. "The day someone brings me proof against Bishop Barros, then I will act," he told reporters. "But there is not one single piece of evidence. It is all slander. Is that clear?"

The pope's claim was patently false, and he should have known it. Days later, the Associated Press and *The New York Times* reported that, in 2015, Francis had been presented personally—by Cardinal O'Malley, president of his child-abuse commission—with an eight-page letter listing the detailed, credible allegations against Barros. The list, prepared by one of Karadima's victims, had first been obtained by several lay members of the papal commission, who then gave it to O'Malley, who said he chose to hand-deliver it to the pope as a demonstration of how serious the allegations were.

While Francis was still in Chile, O'Malley issued a stunning public rebuke of the pope. He said Francis's defense of Barros, and the suggestion the bishop's accusers were lying, was "a source of great pain for survivors of sexual abuse." O'Malley flew to Santiago and confronted the pope, who realized his mistake. Meeting with reporters on the flight back to Rome,

Francis apologized for remarks in Chile that were "a slap in the face to victims."

Days later, he dispatched the Vatican's most experienced investigator in sex-abuse cases, Archbishop Scicluna, to Chile. Scicluna returned to Rome to report that child molestation by Chilean priests was rampant and that the national church hierarchy had covered it up for decades. It was clear Errázuriz had lied to Francis for years about the situation. Scicluna produced a twenty-three-hundred-page report detailing the abuse, including the complicity of Barros in Karadima's crimes.

In April, a chagrined Francis issued a letter to Chile's bishops in which he effectively accused the entire hierarchy of lying. He summoned the country's thirty-four cardinals and bishops to Rome the following month. Ahead of the meeting, the pope demanded letters of resignation from all of them, so he could dismiss the worst offenders immediately. He began by ousting three bishops, including Barros, then sacked four more later that year. Two were defrocked. In December, he unceremoniously removed Errázuriz—and Cardinal Pell, then awaiting trial in Australia—from the C-8.

The move by a pope to oust so many bishops from a single country was unprecedented in modern times. Francis made a more personal show of remorse by inviting three of Karadima's victims to Rome to live with him for several days at the Santa Marta, so he could hear their stories personally. The trio said they were moved by the pope's apologies during hours of wrenching conversations. "I have never met someone so contrite," said Juan Carlos Cruz, one of the three. "The pope said, 'I was part of the problem. I caused this.'" When the three Chileans returned home, they released a statement thanking Francis. "For almost ten years we have been treated as enemies because we fought against sexual abuse and cover-up in the church," they wrote. "These days, we met the friendly face of the church."

The pope's decisive action in Chile did not quiet the criticism of his failure to grapple with the crisis elsewhere. In May, the Vatican received the final, damning report from the New York archdiocese about Cardinal McCarrick, confirming that he had molested a teenage boy. Cardinal Dolan told the pope that McCarrick should be ordered immediately into a life of "prayer and penance." Archbishop Becciu, the same Curia aide who first warned Francis in 2013 that McCarrick might be a sexual predator, briefed the pope on the findings of the New York investigation. Days later,

Francis ordered McCarrick to withdraw from public life permanently and face a church trial that could end in his excommunication.

The pope's decision was revealed in June by the New York archdiocese. The same day, the hierarchy in New Jersey acknowledged it had known for years about McCarrick's abuse of seminarians there. Initially, there was no public acknowledgment by the Vatican that Francis had also known—for years—about the allegations. The scandal grew darker that summer, as more victims came forward to report that they, too, had been molested by McCarrick as boys. Although the cardinal continued to insist on his innocence, he resigned from the College of Cardinals in July and agreed to live the rest of his life in seclusion.

Other child-abuse scandals erupted across the US that summer. In August, a Pennsylvania grand jury released a searing report that charged the state's Catholic bishops had covered up for more than three hundred child-molesting priests. The report detailed several especially sordid cases, including that of a priest who raped a seven-year-old girl while she was in the hospital recovering from having her tonsils out. In another case, a priest impregnated a thirteen-year-old girl, then arranged her abortion. A key target of the report was Cardinal Wuerl, McCarrick's successor in Washington. The grand jury cited several instances in which Wuerl, as bishop of Pittsburgh in the 1990s, moved pedophile priests from parish to parish rather than deal with their crimes.

By year's end, several American bishops had resigned or hurriedly retired. Wuerl stepped down. In September, Bishop Michael Bransfield of West Virginia, former president of the Papal Foundation, was ousted after a church investigation determined that he had been molesting seminarians and young priests for years.

In the midst of so much other turmoil, Archbishop Viganò stepped forward to exact his revenge on the pope. Living in retirement in Italy, he knew much of the truth about the McCarrick scandal was still being hidden—by Francis. Friends agreed that Viganò burned with hatred for the pope and found allies in that cause in the Regensburg network. That summer, he drafted a timeline of what he remembered about McCarrick's misconduct, a document he called his "testimony." He had evidence to back up his most damaging allegations. He had copies of the 2006 and 2008 memos he had sent to Cardinal Bertone, and through Bertone to Pope Benedict, about McCarrick's "wicked acts."

By August, he had finished his seven-thousand-word account and turned it over to two conservative Catholic websites in the US, which agreed to publish it in full. While his document included wild exaggerations and outright falsehoods, Viganò's central allegation—that the pope had known for years about the abuse allegations against McCarrick—was true. Viganò claimed he had warned Francis face-to-face in June 2013, three months after his election, that McCarrick had molested generations of seminarians and that the Vatican had a "thick dossier" documenting the abuse dating back decades, and yet the pope had done nothing.

Viganò named twenty other cardinals and bishops who, he said, participated in the cover-up, including Bertone, Sodano, and Wuerl. The one senior Vatican official spared Viganò's rage was Benedict.* Much of the rest of the document was a homophobic rant. "Homosexual networks present in the church must be eradicated," he wrote, suggesting he was ready to "out" several cardinals and bishops who were "active homosexuals."

Despite Viganò's over-the-top language, major news organizations portrayed the allegations as devastating for Francis. *The New York Times* said the McCarrick revelations "threaten not only Francis's agenda but his entire papacy." Viganò's document was posted online just hours before the pope was scheduled to fly home after a difficult two-day pilgrimage to Ireland, where the child-abuse crisis had demoralized the local church. On the plane, the shaken pope sidestepped questions about Viganò. "I will not say a single word about this," he said in an in-flight news conference.

To a degree unheard of in the modern history of the church, senior churchmen decided to side with a bishop against the pope. More than twenty American cardinals and bishops put out statements vouching for Viganò, with the clear suggestion that it was the pope who was lying. Opinion polls showed that Francis's popularity in the United States began to plummet. In Rome, Cardinal Burke offered his support to Viganò, and then Steve Bannon entered the debate. He announced he would organize an independent tribunal to investigate the charges against Francis, which Bannon described as "an existential threat to the heart of the institution of the Catholic Church."

---

* Viganò's document suggested that he was unaware at the time of how often Benedict had been warned, explicitly, over several years, about the sexual-abuse allegations made against McCarrick.

AFTER THE INITIAL SHOCK of Viganò's allegations, Francis seemed to
know his papacy would survive the uproar, no matter how much uglier the
McCarrick scandal got. The pope's aides saw a cold-blooded calculation
in his strategy to get through the crisis. From what Francis knew of the
excitable Viganò, the archbishop's credibility would be challenged almost
immediately. There were easily refuted allegations in Viganò's document,
including his claim that Benedict had secretly disciplined McCarrick and
banished him from Rome. In fact, official photos showed the pope and the
cardinal greeting each other at the Vatican in the final year of Benedict's
papacy, including at an April 2012 reception at which McCarrick presented
the pope with a cake to congratulate him on his eighty-third birthday.

In October, Francis ordered a "thorough study" of church archives for
other evidence of McCarrick's crimes. An American lawyer close to the
Vatican was hired to run the investigation. He was directed to interview
all of the still-living churchmen implicated in the scandal, including both
Benedict and Francis. He was given no deadline, which suggested Francis
could keep his silence indefinitely about McCarrick, arguing that he should
say nothing until the lawyer had finished his investigation. As it turned out,
the inquiry dragged on for more than two years.

The announcement of the investigation came exactly a week before
Francis oversaw the ceremony to proclaim Archbishop Romero a saint,
and the timing was not coincidental. It was more than a little cynical, in
fact. By then, Francis knew enough about the Vatican press corps to realize that news of the investigation would distract reporters for days. He
intended to use that week of relative calm to try to push thoughts about
McCarrick's miserable, wasted life out of his mind—- and to reflect instead
on the saintliness of Romero and another churchman to be canonized at
the same ceremony: Pope Paul VI. He intended to present these two new
saints as champions of the tolerant, merciful church that Vatican II—and
Francis—had promised.

The day of the ceremony was Rome at its autumn best, with crisp sun
and a cloudless sky. Almost seventy thousand people had gathered in
St. Peter's Square, including an estimated eight thousand from El Salvador.
Six thousand miles away in their homeland, the ceremony was being shown
live on video screens outside the cathedral in San Salvador, where Romero
was interred.

As Francis joined the procession into the square, he looked relieved to be free of his other burdens for one glorious day. He wore Romero's cincture, as planned, and in honor of Paul VI he walked with the late pope's silver crozier—a type of ornamental hooked staff—and used Paul's favorite chalice for the Mass. In his homily, he first honored Paul, saluting him as the "wise helmsman" of Vatican II. After the council, the church "turned outwards to the world—looking to those far away and taking care of the poor." Romero, Francis said, was the embodiment of what a priest should be, willing to sacrifice his own life to serve God and the poor. During the ceremony, small flecks of Romero's dried blood fell onto the pope's white robes. Francis later told his deputies that he took it as a sign from God of all that he, too, needed to be ready to sacrifice.

43

A Papacy "Begins Anew"

IN THE DAYS just before Christmas in 2022, doctors attending to Benedict XVI made hourly visits to the former pope's bedside, and they knew his death was near. After decades of chronic health problems, his ninety-five-year-old body was shutting down. In public audiences in December, Pope Francis called for prayers for his dying predecessor, a request he repeated to his eighteen million followers on Twitter: "Let us #PrayTogether."

By then, Francis, who turned eighty-six on December 17 and was about to mark his tenth anniversary as pope, regularly pondered his own mortality and asked whether he, like Benedict, should abdicate instead of dying in office. In a newspaper interview in December, he revealed for the first time that he had already signed a preemptive resignation letter, which his staff would act on if he became too ill to carry out his duties. By 2022, he had also quietly settled on the logistics of his funeral and burial. He had decided not to be laid to rest alongside more than one hundred of his predecessors in the grottoes beneath St. Peter's. Instead, he wanted to be entombed in the fifth-century Basilica of Santa Maria Maggiore in central Rome. As pope, he had treated the beloved basilica almost as his parish church and often visited to pray before its Byzantine icon of the Virgin Mary.

Increasingly, Francis could not hide his own health problems, including painful sciatica that often forced him to use a wheelchair at public events; he complained of constant stomach discomfort as a result of surgery in 2021 to remove an inflamed portion of his large intestine. Still, he regularly told reporters his overall health was fine. He laughed off a well-organized whispering campaign at the end of 2022—led, many Vatican journalists knew, by a prominent, well-connected cardinal in Rome who demanded anonymity when he eagerly shared the rumor with reporters—that Francis was near death from a fatal, undisclosed illness.

On December 31, only hours before the new year arrived, Benedict died at his home at the Mater Ecclesiae Monastery. His corpse was immediately draped in red robes, the traditional color for papal funeral vestments, and readied for transfer to St. Peter's Basilica, where it would lay in state for three days before the funeral. That afternoon, the Vatican released a copy of his will, which he entitled "My Spiritual Testament," in which he thanked family and friends and asked forgiveness "from the bottom of my heart from all those whom I have wronged in some way." Most of the rest of the seven-hundred-word will had a similarly gracious tone, although a paragraph near the bottom seemed jarringly out of place—spiteful, even. It was a deathbed attempt to settle professional scores. The passage denounced, by name, a trio of progressive twentieth-century German religious scholars, including the late Rudolf Bultmann, a renowned Lutheran theologian who theorized that Jesus's biography in the New Testament was mostly legend, not fact. Benedict's will claimed that the "seemingly unshakeable" theories of Bultmann and other "existentialist" and "Marxist" theologians had "collapsed" over time.* The will made no reference, at least by name, to the theologian who would always be considered his greatest professional rival, Hans Küng, who had died the year before at the age of ninety-three. In the days after Küng's death, Cardinal Walter Kasper revealed that, weeks earlier, at Francis's request, he had telephoned Küng, then in the final stages of Parkinson's disease, to relay a message of the pope's support as he faced the hereafter. "Hans had been overjoyed" by the pope's comforting words, Kasper told reporters. The cardinal said that, despite his own bitter professional clashes with Küng, the Swiss theologian would be remembered with admiration for "helping many people to find their faith."

Whatever the truth about the relationship between the two popes, Benedict's death was seen across Rome as a turning point for Francis, since

---

* In his writings over decades, Benedict regularly—and his critics thought, obsessively—denounced Bultmann (1884–1976), who was otherwise widely respected among German theologians, including those who disagreed with him. He was also remembered with admiration in Germany for the bravery he showed in the 1930s, when he publicly protested Nazi laws that targeted Jews for economic and political discrimination.

the months that followed were among the most momentous of his papacy. While Benedict was alive, even after he became so frail and confused that he vanished entirely from public view, archconservative churchmen had continued to rally round him as the living symbol of the traditional church that they wished to revive after Vatican II. With Benedict gone, however, Francis seemed unbound—emboldened to make sweeping changes in church teachings and in the structure of the Curia that he had resisted while his predecessor was still alive. Alberto Melloni, an Italian church historian, said he detected the change almost instantly after Benedict's death: "The pontificate of Francis starts anew."

The first evidence of it came at Benedict's funeral in St. Peter's on January 5, which was attended by an estimated fifty thousand mourners, a tiny fraction of the audience at the funerals of his modern predecessors. Francis presided over the Mass and delivered a homily that was so brief and impersonal that many of Benedict's admirers were convinced it was meant as a thinly veiled insult to the dead pope. The eulogy lasted barely seven minutes and referred to Benedict by name only once. Francis offered no direct praise for his predecessor apart from describing him as a "faithful friend" to Christ. The conservative American writer Rod Dreher described Francis's homily as an "act of disrespect explicable only as an exercise in banked contempt." The former pope's allies were also offended when Francis, reportedly citing his bad knees, declined to walk down to the grottoes beneath the basilica to witness Benedict's interment.

In retirement, Benedict said nothing publicly that amounted to direct criticism of Francis, even as he continued to suggest he was troubled by his successor's outreach to divorced and gay Catholics. After his death, however, Benedict loyalists tied to the Regensburg network stepped forward to claim that, in private, he condemned much of his successor's agenda and often felt personally betrayed by Francis. A week after the funeral, Benedict's private secretary, Archbishop Georg Gänswein, gave interviews in which he revealed that Francis "broke Pope Benedict's heart" and that, behind the scenes, the two popes had always had serious doctrinal differences. Gänswein said Benedict had been alarmed especially by a 2021 papal decree in which Francis sharply limited the use of the Latin Mass, effectively reversing Benedict's decision fourteen years earlier to revive the ancient language. "It hit him hard," Gänswein said. Benedict's friend and biographer Peter Seewald, who often visited him in retirement, backed up Gänswein's account. He said the late pope had been "bitterly disappointed" with Francis, who had "set out to erase much of what was precious and dear" to his predecessor.

Francis angrily dismissed the claims from Gänswein and Seewald and insisted he had no sharp disagreements with Benedict. The late pope was not "embittered" in retirement, Francis told reporters in late January. Benedict's friends who claimed otherwise "don't have ethics," he went on. "It's bunk."

The pope had another ugly reminder of the opposition he faced inside the Vatican when, two weeks after Benedict's death, Cardinal Pell of Australia died in Rome of a heart attack. The eighty-one-year-old Pell had returned permanently to the Vatican in 2020, when he was freed from an Australian jail after his child-molestation conviction was overturned on appeal. (In 2018, a jury in Melbourne found him guilty of abusing two thirteen-year-old boys in the city's cathedral in the mid-1990s. Australia's highest court overturned the verdict two years later after determining that the jury had failed to consider all the evidence.) After returning to Rome, the cardinal claimed publicly that he was loyal to Francis and grateful for the pope's support during his legal ordeal. As soon as Pell died, however, journalists revealed that, behind the scenes, the Australian had actually become a vicious critic of the pope; the cardinal was revealed to be the author of a widely read, anonymous essay circulated months earlier that described Francis's leadership as a "catastrophe." Journalists acknowledged that Pell had also been their key off-the-record source for the rumor that Francis was dying—a rumor that Pell seemed to hope was true.

That spring, Francis moved decisively to dismantle the Regensburg network and other organized opposition to his papacy. It began with the demotion or ouster of several churchmen close to Benedict. In May, Francis met face-to-face with Gänswein and ordered him to vacate his apartment in Rome and return home to Germany to live as a private citizen, without any sort of church appointment, at least initially. The sixty-six-year-old Gänswein, once seemingly assured of promotion to cardinal, told colleagues he was humiliated by his exile.

Another Benedict loyalist, Cardinal Burke, still Francis's most vocal critic inside the Curia, was removed from the Vatican payroll entirely and stripped of other privileges, including his spacious church-subsidized apartment in Rome. Seewald described the moves against Gänswein, Burke, and others as a "purge" in which Benedict's friends were "guillotined." By then, another prominent member of the Regensburg network, Archbishop

Viganò, who had become increasingly erratic in his public statements after his forced retirement in 2016, aligning himself with fringe populist movements and antivaccine conspiracy theories, faced a church trial on charges of schism over his rejection of the pope's legitimacy.[*]

On Francis's orders, the building that had become the brick-and-mortar symbol of the opposition—the Mater Ecclesiae—was converted back into a full-time monastery. He invited an order of Benedictine nuns from his native Argentina to move in. He pledged that, even if he abdicated and remained in Rome, he would never live in the monastery. He said he would look for a much smaller, more modest home in retirement.

In July, he announced the most important, and most shocking, personnel decision of his papacy: a new leader for the agency known until 2022 as the Congregation for the Doctrine of the Faith. (In a Curia reorganization that year meant to end rivalries, Francis renamed all congregations as "dicasteries," so it became the Dicastery for the Doctrine of the Faith). His choice was his protégé Archbishop Víctor Fernández of the Argentine city of La Plata, the Gregorian-educated theologian who had become the pope's principal ghostwriter. In calling him to Rome, Francis announced that Fernández would also be named a cardinal that fall, which led to instant speculation that the pope saw his countryman as a possible successor.

Fernández, sixty, succeeded Cardinal Luis Francisco Ladaria Ferrer, a Spanish Jesuit whose retirement was portrayed as routine since he was about to turn eighty. In fact, Francis had long seemed eager to replace the Spaniard, whose public pronouncements put him at odds with the pope's message of tolerance. Francis had been taken aback when Ladaria Ferrer issued a 2021 decree in which the congregation said priests were forbidden from offering blessings at same-sex marriages, since those ceremonies defy "the Creator's plan." The document was condemned by gay-rights activists who questioned again whether the pope—who famously asked "Who am I to judge?"—was a hypocrite.

In a public letter to Fernández after the appointment, Francis called for a radical change in the mission of the Dicastery for the Doctrine of the Faith, still so closely associated with twentieth-century heresy-hunters

---

[*] In July 2024, the Vatican announced that Viganò, who refused to attend the trial, had been found guilty of schism and excommunicated, which barred him from accepting the sacraments, including Communion, or officiating at a Mass.

like Joseph Ratzinger and Alfredo Ottaviani. In the letter, Francis condemned the "immoral methods" used by the agency throughout its history. He called on Fernández to promote "a new way of thinking about a God who loves, who forgives, who saves, who liberates."

Fernández's appointment was "an ecclesial earthquake," in the words of the English magazine *The Tablet*. He was known among parishioners in Argentina as boldly, even radically progressive. In Argentina, he had not hidden his contempt for the Curia agency he would now lead. He readily acknowledged that, during Benedict's papacy, he had been the target of a secret, nearly two-year-long investigation by the Congregation for the Doctrine of the Faith. He described the investigation—begun in 2009 after then-Cardinal Bergoglio nominated him to lead the Pontifical Catholic University of Argentina—as a "painful experience" in which he was required to answer detailed, often pointless questions about his writings from decades earlier, including a thirty-year-old essay in which he had promoted tolerance for gay people. "I spent months on this nonsense," he said.

His appointment to Rome was the subject of a furious public debate almost from the moment it was announced—so furious that many Curia bishops assumed Francis would have to withdraw Fernández's name. There was controversy first after news reports from Argentina suggested that Fernández, as archbishop of La Plata, had tried in 2019 to cover up child-abuse allegations against a local priest, Eduardo Lorenzo, who had been accused of molesting at least five children. Despite an aggressive police investigation, Fernández kept the priest in place for months and alleged his accusers were lying in a "crude battle" to destroy an innocent man. In December 2019, hours after the police issued a warrant for his arrest, Lorenzo committed suicide. In a brief statement that offered no words of comfort to the alleged victims, Fernández said the priest killed himself "after long months of enormous tension and suffering." The American victims' rights group BishopAccountability.org said that, on the basis of the Lorenzo case alone, it was outrageous for Francis to appoint Fernández to lead the Vatican agency responsible for investigating all clerical sex-abuse cases around the world. "Fernández should have been investigated, not promoted," the group said.

Days later, there was an even more ferocious dispute after it was discovered that Fernández's official Vatican biography was suspiciously incomplete. A supposedly comprehensive list of his published works failed to include his sexually charged 1995 book *Heal Me with Your Mouth*, in which he celebrated the joys of passionate open-mouth kissing and sensual touch.* Conservative Catholic news organizations reprinted long excerpts from the book, including the erotic poems signed by "Tucho," Fernández's nickname, as well as its detailed checklist for proper kissing techniques: "The penetrating kiss is when you suck and slurp with the lips."

The Italian-based conservative Catholic website Daily Compass described the book as "porno-theology." Phil Lawler, director of the American website Catholic Culture, thought the book, written at a time when Fernández was a thirty-three-year-old priest bound by chastity vows, raised legitimate concerns about his personal conduct: "When a celibate shows an inordinate interest in how young people express physical affection, there is cause for concern."

In a flurry of posts on his Facebook account that had a panicky tone, Fernández, still weeks away from his transfer to Rome, seemed to believe his appointment was in jeopardy. He acknowledged, in vague terms, that he had mishandled the case of Father Lorenzo: "Today I would certainly act differently." As for *Heal Me with Your Mouth*, he insisted that the contents of "this little book of mine" did not reflect any personal sexual experience—he was repeating what he had been told by parishioners, he said—and was intended to remind young couples that there were pleasurable alternatives to sexual intercourse. He thought attacks on the book were part of a long-running campaign by Francis's opponents to undermine the pope: "By attacking me, they want to attack Francis."

From all appearances, Francis was unconcerned about the controversies and eager to have Fernández by his side, wearing the scarlet robes of a cardinal, as soon as possible. By late summer, Fernández was in Rome permanently, working in the same suite of offices in the Palace of the Holy Office from which predecessors like Ratzinger and Ottaviani had once exercised such outsized power over the lives of millions of Catholics.

* Months later, it was revealed that Fernández had left a second book off the list. Entitled *La Pasión Mística: Espiritualidad y Sensualidad* (Mystical Passion: Spirituality and Sensuality), it was published in Mexico in 1998, when Fernández was thirty-eight. It was seen by some of his critics as even more troubling than *Heal Me with Your Mouth* since *La Pasión Mística* included a detailed anatomical description of human genitalia and of the physiology of orgasms, which Fernández compared to the mystical rapture of Catholic saints. Advocates for victims of clerical sex abuse said they were alarmed about a passage in which Fernández appeared to describe his conversations with a sixteen-year-old Argentine girl who reported a vision of a "passionate encounter" with Jesus in which she kissed him on the mouth and caressed his flesh.

From the moment Fernández settled in, he was constantly in and out of meetings with the pope at the Santa Marta guest house. They were regularly seen hunched over in private conversation, chattering away quietly in their native, rapid-fire Spanish. The fact that they conversed in the language's Argentine dialect, which is strikingly different from Spanish spoken elsewhere, with its own vocabulary and pronunciation for common words, meant that even some Spanish-speaking Curia bishops could not easily understand them. That fed the suspicion among Francis's archconservative opponents in Rome that he and Fernández—"the Gauchos," as they became known—were up to no good. On September 30, in a ceremony in St. Peter's, Fernández was ordained a cardinal, wearing his red robes for the first time, alongside twenty other new members of the College of Cardinals, representing sixteen countries.

By then, Fernández had been hard at work for weeks on two early assignments from the pope. The first was no secret: Fernández was helping Francis with logistics for another worldwide bishops' synod, scheduled to open in October. The pope's ultimate plans for the new two-year synod were a mystery, reflected in its almost comically meaningless name, the "Synod on Synodality," but many progressive churchmen hoped he would use it as a vehicle to make the sort of reforms he had resisted before Benedict's death. After the synod meetings in 2014 and 2015, Francis had invited divorced Catholics to return to the altar for Holy Communion; this time, reformers hoped, Francis would go much further to cement his legacy.

No matter what happened at the Synod on Synodality, the meetings were guaranteed to be history-making since Francis had decided to allow nuns and other Catholic women—fifty-four of them—to participate for the first time as full, voting members of a synod, alongside about three hundred cardinals and bishops. It appeared to be the first time in the recorded history of the church that women had been given a formal vote on its future.

Fernández's second, early assignment *was* a secret, and he was thrilled by it. He had been asked that summer to draft a formal decree, to be issued by the Dicastery for the Doctrine of the Faith late that year, that would be easily the most groundbreaking—and incendiary—of Francis's papacy.

FRANCIS NEVER SAID IT explicitly but, after a decade on the throne of St. Peter, he must have known he had been a disappointment to millions of Catholics who had once been so excited about his election. John XXIII, the predecessor he cited as his role model, had been responsible—not always intentionally—for historic, even revolutionary change. John's great project, Vatican II, had ended the church's isolation from the modern world. Under "the good pope," ancient church teachings, notably the Vatican's once formal endorsement of the ugliest sort of anti-Semitism, were overturned.

But as Francis entered his second decade as bishop of Rome, he could claim no such accomplishments, at least none that were guaranteed to outlast his papacy. Like Pope John, he had dramatically changed the tone of Vatican debates, with an emphasis always on promoting mercy over punishing sin. But little had changed in terms of formal church teachings. Francis's promise to reconsider the doctrine of priestly celibacy had gone nowhere; South American churchmen were heartbroken when he rejected a proposal approved by two-thirds of the bishops at a 2019 synod to allow the ordination of married men in the vast Amazon River basin, where the priest shortage had always been dire.

Under Francis, the church's ban on birth control remained in place, even if it was more widely mocked and ignored than ever. Despite his vow to promote women to the Curia, there was still only token representation of women at the highest reaches of the Vatican. He had shown mercy to divorced Catholics by allowing them to remarry more easily through annulments and to receive Communion, but a future pope could erase those initiatives as easily as Francis had put them into place.

His greatest failure, like that of John Paul II and Benedict XVI, was his refusal to grapple with the clerical sexual abuse crisis. After the 2018 Chilean abuse scandals, he regularly claimed that the horrors exposed in Chile had jolted him into realizing how much more he needed to do. "That was my conversion," he said later. "That's when the bomb went off, when I saw the corruption of many bishops in this." But those words were never met with decisive action, especially when abuse allegations were made against churchmen he knew. The fact that his protégé Fernández had badly mishandled the most serious child-molestation case he confronted as an archbishop in Argentina did not block his appointment by Francis in 2023 to lead the Curia agency responsible for policing all abuse cases. That same year, many journalists in the Vatican press corps wrote constantly about a brewing scandal over Francis's refusal to end the career of a notorious sexual predator—Father Marko Rupnik, a Jesuit theologian and world-famous mosaic artist accused of abusing more than twenty women in Rome and his native Slovenia. Even after the Jesuits determined in 2019 that the allegations were credible, Rupnik was invited the following year to be the principal lecturer at Francis's Lenten retreat for the Curia, among the highest honors a pope can bestow on any Catholic scholar. In January 2022, a few months before he was permanently expelled from the Jesuits, Rupnik, who remained a priest, was invited to Rome for what appeared to be a friendly private chat with the pope; the meeting was documented in an official Vatican publicity photo. At the time, there was no public evidence to suggest that the pope intended to defrock—or even demote—his old friend Bishop Zanchetta in Argentina, even though Zanchetta had been sentenced to prison the year before, following his conviction on charges of molesting seminarians. Online court-record databases maintained by major victims' rights groups showed that hundreds of priests and other church workers around the world continued to be arrested and convicted of child molestation and other sex crimes each year.

STILL, AT THE START of his second decade as pope, Francis seemed confident and cheerful—giddy, even—in public discussions about the state of the church. While he would never again experience the sort of joyous frenzy that greeted his election in 2013, he could comfort himself with the knowledge that he remained wildly popular among most of the world's Catholics. He attracted huge, enthusiastic crowds in 2023 during pilgrimages to France, Portugal, Hungary, and the Congo. He was also greeted warmly that year in Mongolia, home to fewer than two thousand Catholics, which he visited in hopes of encouraging one of the world's newest Catholic communities. He remained alarmed about what he saw as the disobedience of some "reactionary" and "backward" Catholic clerics in the United States—he dismissed Bishop Joseph Strickland of Tyler, Texas, in November 2023 after Strickland denounced Francis as dangerously progressive, especially on sexual issues—but the pope was otherwise widely admired in the country. Opinion polls consistently showed that more than three quarters of American Catholics viewed him favorably. The scandals tied to the disgraced former Cardinal McCarrick, seen a few years earlier as a grave threat to Francis's survival as pope, were mostly forgotten, even among McCarrick's former parishioners in Washington.[*]

[*] In 2019, on Francis's orders, McCarrick, then eighty-eight and living in seclusion in a Catholic friary in Kansas, was defrocked and finally appeared ready to disappear forever from public view.

Over time, Francis's public image also benefited by comparison to what had become the increasingly tarnished legacy of most of his modern predecessors, especially Benedict XVI and the now-sainted John Paul II. In January 2022, eleven months before Benedict's death, a Munich law firm issued its long-awaited, church-sponsored report on clerical child abuse in the local archdiocese and accused Benedict of "wrongdoing" when, as the city's archbishop, he failed to act against at least four pedophile priests, including the notorious child molester Peter Hullermann. The authors of the 1,900-page report alleged that Benedict, who offered written testimony to the investigation that was later shown to be demonstrably untrue, lied when he claimed he could not remember the cases. The head of the German Bishops' Conference, Bishop Georg Bätzing of Limburg, accepted the report's damning conclusions and called on Benedict to plead for forgiveness from abuse victims: "He must set aside the recommendations of his advisors and say clearly and simply: I bear guilt, I have made mistakes." As requested, Benedict did issue a public apology—"I can only express to all the victims of sexual abuse my profound shame"—even as he complained about his many critics who cited the report "to label me a liar."

There had been a similar, damning reappraisal of John Paul II in his homeland. In 2023, many Poles were stunned by a deeply researched book and television documentary that detailed how then-Cardinal Wojtyła had shielded child-molesting Polish priests from local law enforcement in the 1970s, including two who eventually served jail time. Polish church leaders denounced the book and documentary, noting they relied in part on files from Communist-era spy agencies, but some national politicians said they were horrified by what they saw as credible evidence of John Paul's wrongdoing and called for his name to be stripped from Polish buildings and streets.

The legacy of Pius XII, the revered pope of Francis's youth, continued to be battered by the work of historians given access to the Vatican's World War II archives. The six-decade-long campaign to have Pius declared a saint appeared to have collapsed once and for all after the 2022 publication of a bestselling book by Pulitzer Prize–winning American scholar David Kertzer, who uncovered long-secret documents in the archives that bolstered the now widely held view among respected church historians—that Pius had incontrovertible evidence of the genocide in the early days of the war and still said nothing in protest, even though his voice would have saved lives. "As a moral leader, Pius XII must be judged a failure," Kertzer concluded.

IN THE MONTHS after Benedict's death, Francis suddenly abandoned talk of abdicating. So long as his health permitted and he remained mentally fit, he intended to die as pope, and he began to speak excitedly of legacy-shaping projects that he wanted to see to completion. He hoped to remain pope long enough to bestow sainthood on two great churchmen he had known personally, both hailed as champions of liberation theology: Bishop Angelelli of Argentina, assassinated at the height of the Dirty War in 1976, and Pedro Arrupe, the Jesuit leader who had been so instrumental in Francis's early career. Both Angelelli and Arrupe had been considered serious candidates for canonization for years; Francis personally approved Angelelli's beatification in 2019, declaring him a "martyr to the cause of justice."

Francis also spoke eagerly of his hope for more travel, including home to Argentina for the first time since his election. That he had avoided returning home for more than a decade had always confounded some of his Curia deputies and embarrassed the Argentine church hierarchy, since he made papal pilgrimages to every other major Latin American nation. When pressed by reporters why he never went home, he claimed he was wary of returning to Argentina because it would be seen as interference in the country's always tumultuous national politics. That explanation became harder to justify, however, after so many of the Argentine politicians he had once tangled with were out of the public eye, especially his old nemesis Cristina Kirchner, the former president, who was sentenced to prison in 2022 following her conviction on corruption charges. In 2023, her party's presidential candidate was trounced by a maverick economist and self-proclaimed "anarcho-capitalist," Javier Milei, who pledged to undo Peronist patronage networks loyal to Kirchner. Almost as soon as he took office, the wild-eyed, shaggy-haired Milei, who denounced Francis on the campaign trail as an "imbecile" and a "representative of the Evil One on earth" because of what he saw as the pope's Marxist economic views, reversed himself and began to court Francis to return home in a show of national unity. Weeks after his inauguration, Milei flew to Rome, where he was photographed embracing the pope before they met privately for more than an hour. Afterwards, Francis suggested he would soon accept Milei's invitation home.

AFTER BENEDICT'S DEATH, the late pope's archconservative admirers in Rome, including what remained of the Regensburg network, had good reason to fear what Francis would do with the rest of his papacy. The agenda for the Synod on Synodality, expected to conclude at the end of 2024, included debates on all the most contentious issues that had faced the Vatican during Francis's lifetime, from birth control to priestly celibacy to the role of women and gay people in the church.

Archconservatives had fresh evidence to justify their fears when, in December 2023, just days before the first anniversary of Benedict's death, Fernández released a document—issued under his name but "based on the pastoral vision of Pope Francis"—that granted priests the right to offer blessings to same-sex couples seeking to marry. The document, which directly contradicted the guidance issued two years earlier by Fernández's predecessor, landed like a thunderbolt and became easily the most controversial teaching document of Francis's papacy. Entitled "On the Pastoral Meaning of Blessings," it declared that, while the church still recognized a true marriage as one between a man and a woman, priests could meet with same-sex couples before or after a wedding to assure them of God's blessing. Fernández wrote that the church needed to promote a message of "transcendence, mercy, and closeness to God" to all couples who found love. DignityUSA, the Catholic gay rights group, whose members had been barred by then-Cardinal Ratzinger even from gathering in a Catholic church in the 1980s, welcomed Fernández's document as a sign of "meteoric" progress. Predictably, there was a furious reaction from conservative church leaders, especially those who had been close to Benedict, who had never backed away from his description of homosexuality as an "intrinsic moral evil." Cardinal Müller, Fernández's embittered predecessor, now living in semi-retirement in Rome, said that priests who followed Fernández's instructions would be committing a "blasphemous act." There was something like a continent-wide revolt against Francis and Fernández when most of Africa's bishops issued a joint statement to announce they would not offer blessings to gay couples, since same-sex unions were "contrary to the will of God." In response, Fernández said that while the Vatican would grant African bishops time to adjust to the instructions, they could not bar local priests who wished to bestow the blessings from doing so.

Fernández was widely criticized for having bungled the document's release, since he shared it with few churchmen in Rome or anywhere else ahead of publication—a violation of the spirit of consultation that he had promised when he arrived at the Vatican. Many Curia theologians who were otherwise supportive of Fernández felt blindsided. Even so, if the pope was upset with his protégé, he offered no evidence of it in public. In interviews, Francis defended Fernández's document and said its critics where "hypocrites" who failed to understand that the Gospels' merciful message applied to all, including gay people. "I bless two people who love each other," he said. "And I also ask them to pray for me."

Despite the initial, fierce opposition to the gay-blessing document, the controversy quieted within a few weeks—so quickly, in fact, that Francis's allies were convinced it was proof of just how successful he had been in diluting the power of the Regensburg network after Benedict's death. Earlier in Francis's papacy, his friends agreed, the debate would have convulsed the Vatican for months, if not years.

And the pope signaled he was likely to dilute his enemies' influence further, and quickly, especially in the body that would choose his successor: the College of Cardinals. With the appointment of Fernández and seven-

Pope Francis prays before the remains of Saint John XXIII during a ceremony in St. Peter's Basilica to mark the sixtieth anniversary of the opening of Vatican II, October 11, 2022.

teen other voting-age cardinals in 2023, and then another twenty in 2024, Francis had named 80 percent of the cardinals who would participate in the next conclave—a supermajority if they stood together. As had been true throughout his papacy, the men he promoted to the college that year were far more geographically and racially diverse than those they replaced. By 2024, almost exactly half of the world's voting-age cardinals came from outside Europe and North America.

Despite those numbers, there had always been wishful thinking among the pope's enemies that bubbling outrage over the scandals of his papacy would lead the college to elect a successor who would reverse course on the most progressive parts of his agenda. As Francis entered his final years as bishop of Rome, however, his calm and self-confidence suggested he knew better. He seemed convinced that the next bishop of Rome would share his vision of a more tolerant, open-minded church—one that dispensed the "medicine of mercy" that his hero the now-sainted John XXIII had promised at Vatican II.

It became the subject of a baffling little joke that Francis began to make repeatedly when pressed on the subject after 2014, the year he raised both John XXIII and John Paul II to sainthood. Not surprisingly, he always refused to speculate about the identity of the likely candidates in the horse race to succeed him, But whenever he was asked by other churchmen or journalists in the Vatican press corps to predict what might happen at the next conclave, he often confounded them by referring to his successor by his papal name—as if the next bishop of Rome, whomever he was, whatever his nationality or other background, had only one divinely inspired choice when it came time to ascend the throne of St. Peter and select a name. Francis would casually utter the next pope's name, without context, as if there were simply no doubt about what it would be.

It would not be John Paul III, he made clear. Nor Paul VII. Nor Benedict XVII or Pius XIII. And certainly not Francis II.

It would be John XXIV, in honor of "the good pope" who had launched the battle for the church's soul that Francis and his allies still intended to win.

Acknowledgments

In a long career in investigative journalism, I have often reported on secretive and powerful organizations—from spy agencies like the CIA and the Mossad, to banking syndicates in Switzerland and the Cayman Islands, to American organized-crime families—but I have never encountered anything like the Roman Catholic Church.

It is often described as the world's last true absolute monarchy, and it can threaten its internal enemies, at least the truly devout ones, with the ultimate sanction: the damnation of their eternal souls. That helps explain why, in the church's two-thousand-year history, there have been so few senior churchmen or church-women willing to step forward to expose corruption and other wrongdoing. I was startled when a Latin American bishop close to Pope Francis told me he was certain that, if he spoke out against the Vatican in a critical way, even mildly, even anonymously, he risked banishment to hell.

I am especially grateful then to the many prominent Catholic clerics, including several influential cardinals and bishops in Rome and elsewhere, who took the risk of speaking to me for *Jesus Wept*, most on the understanding that I would not reveal their names. Those off-the-record sources proved invaluable to me in the hunt for *on-the-record* evidence to back up the most contentious material in this book. They directed me to long-forgotten church records, interview transcripts, private journals, unpublished manuscripts, video and audio recordings of once-confidential meetings, court records, and obscure foreign news reports that allowed me to verify the accuracy of information that the Vatican has long been determined to hide, especially about the priestly child-abuse crisis.

As a result of that digging, there are more than 1,200 endnotes at the back of this book, as well as a bibliography of more than 400 church-related books that now crowd the shelves of my home library. One more thing about anonymous sources:

during more than two decades at *The New York Times*, I came to appreciate the paper's policy of barring the use of pejorative quotations from unnamed people, and I followed that policy here. I am pleased that there are almost no anonymous quotations, pejorative or otherwise, in this book.

I am grateful, too, to the many theologians, Bible scholars, historians, prosecutors, criminal defense lawyers, judges, legal researchers, social scientists, psychiatrists and psychologists, victims-rights advocates, and fellow journalists who *are* identified by name in this book, either because they spoke to me on the record or because I made use of their writings, as documented in the notes.

One churchman was an especially important early guide for me in trying to understand the modern church: the late Father John W. O'Malley, a Jesuit theologian at Georgetown University who wrote authoritative histories of Vatican II and the First Vatican Council. I tested his patience during hours of conversations in his sunny Georgetown office before his death in 2022.

Sadly, four other renowned Catholic scholars instrumental in my research also died before I could thank them here: Father Michael Fahey, a Jesuit theology professor at Boston College; Father Thomas Stransky, a great American champion of interfaith dialogue; the Canadian theologian Gregory Baum; and John T. Noonan Jr., a former federal judge and Notre Dame law professor who was a member of the papal birth-control commission established by John XXIII. As young priests in Rome in the early 1960s, Stransky and Baum helped draft some of the key documents of Vatican II that ended the church's isolation from other faiths. I was also sad to learn of the 2024 death of Sister Theresa Kane, the former president of the Leadership Conference of Women Religious, who also offered me her wisdom.

My conversations with the famed psychotherapist Richard Sipe, who died in 2018, and former Oklahoma governor Frank Keating, an old reporting contact of mine from his years at the Justice Department, helped me understand the origins of the child-abuse crisis. Jim Nicholson, the U.S. ambassador to the Vatican from 2001 to 2005, was generous in helping me chronicle the final years of John Paul II's papacy.

In several trips to Argentina, two savvy former aides to then-Cardinal Bergoglio were essential in my research in Pope Francis's homeland: Father Guillermo Marcó and Federico Wals. I had extraordinary research help in Buenos Aires from two talented young Argentines: Felicitas Ruiz Guiñazú, who organized and helped translate important interviews, and Santiago del Carril, then of the *Buenos Aires Herald*. Santiago's journalism career has done the memory of his late grandfather—the great human-rights champion Emilio Mignone—proud.

In Chile, three victims of the notorious pedophile priest Fernando Karadima—Juan Carlos Cruz, James Hamilton, and José Andrés Murillo—agreed to long interviews in which they offered the wrenching details of how Karadima shattered their youth and how the Chilean church hierarchy and the Vatican nearly covered it all up.

The staff of the Salt + Light Catholic media organization in Toronto spent hours with me in their offices and provided me with valuable research material. In New York, Patrick Hayes, Ph.D., archivist of the Redemptorists clerical order, helped me locate treasures in the personal papers of Father Francis X. Murphy, the former *New Yorker* correspondent who wrote under the pseudonym Xavier Rynne in his newsmaking, gossipy chronicles of Vatican II. Father Charles Curran, the renowned theologian, welcomed me to his office at Southern Methodist University in Dallas. Dr. Joel Brence, a Colorado psychiatrist who once studied under then-Professor Joseph Ratzinger at the University of Tübingen, provided insight about that part of the career of the future Benedict XVI.

I have enormous respect for several historians and journalists who came before me in trying to piece together the church's modern history. That would include the indispensable and indefatigable John L. Allen Jr., the de facto American dean of the Vatican press corps, whose work for the *National Catholic Reporter* and the website *Crux*, as well as his eleven books, changed the way I thought about the church. The investigative reporter Jason Berry, also best known for his work at the *National Catholic Reporter*, will be remembered as one of the great American journalists of the last century because of his groundbreaking reporting over decades on the clerical sex-abuse crisis.

No one can claim to understand the papacy's modern history without reading the works of the authors Austen Ivereigh, Paul Vallely, David Kertzer, Elisabetta Piqué, Peter Seewald, Father James Martin, Father Richard McBrien, Peter and Margaret Hebblethwaite, Robert Blair Kaiser, John Cornwell, Garry Wills, Vittorio Messori, and Massimo Faggioli. While I might fundamentally disagree with the views of the author George Weigel, his deeply researched biographies of John Paul II were important additions to my library.

The gracefully written—and unusually revealing—memoirs of Father Gerald O'Collins, the former theology dean of the Gregorian, were a godsend in my research, as were the phone interviews he granted me from his home in Australia. The writings of Bart D. Ehrman of the University of North Carolina and the theologian Bill Huebsch helped me make sense of the densest passages of the Bible and of the documents of Vatican II. I deeply admire the eye-opening work about the Gnostic Gospels written by Elaine Pagels, the Princeton University religious historian.

I made constant use of the archives of the *National Catholic Reporter*, the UK-based journal *The Tablet*, the Associated Press, *The New York Times*, *The Washington Post*, *Time* magazine, *America* magazine, and the *Buenos Aires Herald*, the English-language newspaper that bravely stood up to the junta during Argentina's Dirty War. The journalists Nicole Winfield of the AP; Laurie Goodstein and Jason Horowitz of *The New York Times*; Kristen Lombardi, formerly of *The Boston Phoenix*; Sandro Magister of *L'Espresso*; Robert Mickens of *La Croix International*; Michael Sean Winters and Christopher White of the *National Catholic Reporter*; Philip Pullella of Reuters and Gerald O'Connell and Colleen Dulle of *America* magazine deserve special praise for their reporting and commentary on the church.

The reporting of the Argentine journalists Horacio Verbitsky, Hugo Alconada Mon of the newspaper *La Nación*, and Uki Goñi was key to my understanding of the Dirty War and of the modern Argentine church hierarchy. I regularly consulted the databases maintained by two victims-rights groups—SNAP, the Survivors Network of Those Abused by Priests, and BishopAccountability.org—and by the crusading American victims-rights lawyer Jeff Anderson.

I am grateful to Paul Murphy, son of the late Boston journalist Paul I. Murphy, for sharing the backstory of his father's tantalizing 1983 book *La Popessa*, the biography of Sister Pascalina that has never attracted the attention it deserved. The book's editor, Reid Boates, was also generous with his time.

Two publishing industry legends were essential partners of mine in this book: My brilliant, brave and ever-patient literary agent Kathy Robbins, who kept up my spirits at times when this project threatened to overwhelm me, and Richard Cohen, the renowned editor and author (and world-class fencing champion), who devised the essential structure of this book, tried valiantly to streamline it, and came up with its spectacular title. I am indebted to Kathy's colleagues at the Robbins Office, including Janet Oshiro, Alexandra Sugarman, and Grace Garrahan. David Halpern, who offered me smart counsel at the Robbins Office, struck out on his own in 2023, and I was sorry to see him go.

At Alfred A. Knopf, I am grateful to the editors and executives who guided this project, including the wise and unflappable Todd Portnowitz (aka Nico's proud dad), Jonathan Segal, and the late Sonny Mehta. Their colleagues at Knopf proved smart and resourceful, a list that includes Isabel Frey Ribeiro, Cassandra Pappas, Kevin Bourke, Patrick Dillon, Ben Shields, Sarah Perrin, Kelly Shi, and Anna Noone. Kathy and Richard led me to the talented and imaginative British photo researcher Cecilia Mackay, who tracked down the wonderful images found throughout these pages.

In writing much of this book in Washington at the height of the Covid pandemic, I was allowed to camp out for months by the staff of two of the city's great hotels, the Conrad and the Fairmont, who permitted me to work in their pretty lounges and gardens at a time when there was almost nowhere else to go. I am eternally thankful to my mother, Philippa Shenon, and my four brothers and sisters (Michael, Carol, Linda, and Chris) and my seven nieces and nephews for their support during my long, mysterious absences from home in the Bay Area. My brilliant friends Jerónimo J. Cassarino, Neil A. Lewis, Elisabetta Melandri, Daniela Giganti, Susan Howells, and Carol J. (who asked me not to use her full name since "I will always fear the wrath of my church") cheered me on during the long years of writing and editing this book.

Notes

INTRODUCTION

5 Inside Vatican City: There is no full, authoritative staff list of the Roman Curia, which means that it is possible only to estimate the size of the Vatican's bureaucracy and its makeup by nationality, gender, and race.

I. THE SILENT POPE

16 Cardinal Domenico: Tardini, *Pio XII*, 72. Also see "French Cardinal Condemned Nazis," *The New York Times*, February 26, 1964, 41.

16 Cardinal Eugène Tisserant: Phayer, *The Catholic Church*, 175.

17 "It wasn't that": Murphy, *La Popessa*, 2. Despite its unflattering and sometimes shocking portrait of Pius XII, *La Popessa* was praised by reviewers after its publication in January 1983 by Warner Books, a leading American publishing house then associated with the Warner Brothers film studio. Andrew Greeley, a Catholic priest who was also a bestselling novelist and frequent contributor to *The New York Times*, hailed *La Popessa* as a "powerful and moving love story, no less interesting because the two lovers were chaste celibates, one a pope." In a 2023 interview, the book's editor, Reid Boates, said he was unaware of any challenge to its accuracy from the Vatican, Pascalina, or anyone else. He said Warner Books had great confidence in the integrity of the author, the late Paul I. Murphy, who reported that he spent more than thirty hours in conversation with Pascalina, and that the book had been carefully fact-checked. Professor David Kertzer of Brown University, a Pulitzer Prize–winning historian who has chronicled the papacy of Pius XII, said in a 2023 interview that he was familiar with *La Popessa* and that he, too, had never heard of any dispute over its accuracy. The only detailed public challenge to the book came in 2017 in *The Godmother: Madre Pascalina, a Feminine Tour de Force*, a self-published book by Father Charles Murr, an American who said that he had been close to Pascalina. He suggested she had only one brief encounter with Murphy and had never bothered to read *La Popessa*, which meant that "she was unaware just how awful it was." Muir alleged that *La Popessa* was full of "lies, half-truths and vile innuendo." In a strange coincidence that gave birth to conspiracy theories among Murphy's friends, he and Pascalina died within two weeks of each other in late 1983, less than a year after *La Popessa*'s publication.

18 "He was the kind": Ibid., 270.
18 "I want people": Hebblethwaite, *Paul VI*, 739.
18 "I pitied": Murphy, *La Popessa*, 248.
19 "Go quell": Ibid., 52.
19 She later remembered: Ibid., 200.
19 When in 1943: Szulc, *Pope John Paul II*, 106. Also see Guenter Lewy, "Pius XII, the Jews and the German Catholic Church," *Commentary*, February 1964, https://www.commentary.org.
20 "If you cannot": Murphy, *La Popessa*, 202.
20 In 1946: Ventresca, *Soldier of Christ*, 242.
20 In 1949: Frank J. Coppa, "Morality and Diplomacy," *Journal of Church and State*, Summer 2008, 543. Also see Ventresca, *Soldier of Christ*, 243.

2. "A CHURCH OF NO, NOT YES"

21 He taught: Küng, *My Struggle*, 17.
22 As a teenager: Ibid., 34.
22 In 1954: *Sacra Virginitas, Encyclical of Pope Pius XII on Consecrated Virginity*, March 25, 1954, https://www.vatican.va.
24 That had been: Ratzinger, *Milestones*, 25.
24 They made sure: Ratzinger, *Salt*, 43.
24 There was "nothing mystical": Ibid., 54.
24 He said the idea: Ibid., 49.
26 He thought he met: Benedict XVI, *Last*, 135.
26 In his review: Küng, *My Struggle*, 138.
26 Küng remembered: Ibid., 229.
26 Pressed to explain: Küng, *What I Believe*, 90.
27 "With his perfect": Küng, *My Struggle*, 51.
27 He was an untraveled: Murphy-O'Connor, *An English Spring*, 30.
27 Curia bishops: Ibid., 10.
27 Instead of celebrating: Ibid., 16.
27 The Holy Office: *On the Ecumenical Movement. An Instruction of the Holy Office*, December 20, 1949. Some theologians thought Küng overreacted to the document, since it did allow continued dialogue with non-Catholic Christians, although with strict limits.
28 Whatever it called: Küng, *My Struggle*, 99.
28 The Vatican under: Ratzinger, *Theological Highlights*, 6.
28 In writings early: Ibid., 35.
29 He thought: Ibid., 27.
29 "Kindness is": Allen, *Benedict XVI*, 310.
29 True Christians: Cahill, *Pope John XXIII*, 94.
30 "For the first": Küng, *My Struggle*, 99.
30 Then in the middle: Jerry L. Walls, "The Problems of Bad Popes," *Perichoresis: The Theological Journal of Emanuel University* 18.5 (2020), 97.
31 "It was a crash": Kasper, *Cardinal Walter Kasper: Spiritual Writings*, 204.
31 "I learned in": Kasper, *A Celebration*, 127.
32 and wondered why: Kasper, *Cardinal Walter Kasper: Spiritual Writings*, 123.
32 "This alleged doctor": Murphy, *La Popessa*, 264.
33 He called a news: "Old Method Used to Embalm Pope," *The New York Times*, October 15, 1958, 3.
35 In a pivotal scene: Rolf Hochhuth, *The Deputy*, 155.

3. A POPE FOR ALL THE WORLD

40 "I blessed Rome": Hebblethwaite, *John XXIII, Pope of the Century*, 146.

40 "He was this": Curran interviews.

40 After years of: Küng, *My Struggle*, 171.

41 "About half": Hebblethwaite, *John XXIII, Pope of the Century*, 198.

41 "Anybody can be": Fesquet, *Wit*, 112.

41 The thought of: John XXIII, *Journal*, 204.

41 Even so: Ibid., 220.

41 he was dispatched: Ibid., 232.

42 His chef: Cahill, *Pope John XXIII*, 147. Also see Alden, *A Man Called*, 70.

42 His Parisian: Cahill, *Pope John XXIII*, 147.

42 In an address: Hebblethwaite, *John XXIII, Pope of the Century*, 118.

42 "I am excited": John XXIII, *Journal*, 283.

43 He said later: Hebblethwaite, *John XXIII, Pope of the Century*, 141.

43 the new pope: Küng, *My Struggle*, 176.

43 He ordered: Cahill, *Pope John XXIII*, 171.

43 The model: John XXIII, *Journal*, 309.

44 "Under Pius": Hebblethwaite, *John XXIII, Pope of the Century*, 156.

44 When he caught: Joseph McAuley, "When a Pope Met a First Lady," *America* magazine, September 18, 2015, https://americamagazine.org. Also see "Pope John XXIII's New Pentecost," *Time*, January 4, 1963, https://time.com.

44 "Open up": Cushing, *Call*, 56.

45 He revealed that: Cahill, *Pope John XXIII*, 174.

45 When asked later: Hebblethwaite, *John XXIII, Pope of the Century*, 192.

45 "The secret": John XXIII, *Journal*, 299.

46 Instead, he wrote: Ibid., 201.

46 The idea occurred: William Grimes, "Obituary: Loris Francesco Capovilla, Pope John's Aide and Spiritual Son, Dies at 100," *The New York Times*, May 26, 2016, 19.

47 Cardinal Giacomo: Cahill, *Pope John XXIII*, 177.

47 In Germany: Ratzinger, *Milestones*, 120.

47 He understood: Ibid., 132.

48 "I could hardly feel": Ibid., 112.

48 "We could not": Colberg, *The Theology of Walter Kasper*, 278.

48 Despite happy: Küng, *My Struggle*, 256.

49 After a lecture: Ibid., 231.

49 For Küng: "A Second Reformation, for Both Catholics & Protestants," *Time*, June 8, 1962, https://time.com.

50 Küng wrote in: Küng, *My Struggle*, 266.

50 A few weeks later: Ibid.

50 "My friends tell": Ibid., 256.

4. TO SUMMON A COUNCIL

53 The Vatican's only: Clifford, *Oxford Handbook of Vatican II*, 510. Also see Cushing, *Call*, 142.

53 In a 1944 sermon: Hebblethwaite, *John XXIII: Pope of the Century*, 95. Also see Faggioli, *John XXIII*, 78.

53 "We are all sons" Oesterreicher, *The Bridge*, 17. Also see Lapide, *Three Popes*, 322.

53 The Vatican stood: Cornwell, *Hitler's Pope*, 70. Also see Richard Cohen, "A Pope Who Was No Saint," *The Washington Post*, September 20, 1999, https://www .washingtonpost.com.

53 ambiguous passage: Matthew 27:25, "Then answered all the people, and said, His blood be on us, and on our children."

54   At a time: Charles King, "Refugees on the Bosphorus," *Slate*, September 24, 2014, https://slate.com. Also see Joseph D'Hippolito, "Pope John XXIII and the Jews," August 20, 2004, as posted on the website of the International Raoul Wallenberg Foundation, https://www.raoulwallenberg.net.

54   The next year: Hebblethwaite, *John XXIII: Pope of the Century*, 94.

54   In June 1960: John L. Allen Jr., "60 Years Ago, a Pope Met a Jewish Icon," *Crux News*, June 14, 2020, https://cruxnow.com.

55   One of his brightest: Stransky interviews. Also see Thomas F. Stransky, "The Catholic-Jewish Dialogue: Twenty Years After 'Nostra Aetate,'" *America* magazine, February 8, 1986, https://www.americamagazine.org.

55   On the day: *Address of His Holiness Pope Benedict XVI to Parish Priests and the Clergy of Rome*, February 14, 2013, https://www.vatican.va.

56   The language: Ratzinger, *Theological Highlights*, 42.

56   Unless the drafts: Ibid., 20.

56   As he once told: Hebblethwaite, *Paul VI*, 285.

58   the pope telling him: Suenens, *Memories*, 109.

58   Suenens said: Ibid., 80.

61   "Celibacy is a sacrifice": "The Case Against Celibacy," *Time*, August 28, 1964, https://time.com. Also see Wagoner, *The Seminary*, 111.

61   In his diary: John XXIII, *Journal*, 251.

61   In 1962: Kaiser, *Whistle*, 65.

61   The document: *Crimen sollicitationis* (Crime of Solicitation): *Instruction of the Supreme Sacred Congregation of the Holy Office on the Manner of Proceeding in Cases Involving the Crime of Solicitation*, March 16, 1962, https://www.vatican.va.

63   He was ordained: Maciel, *Christ*, 46.

63   After reviewing: Berry, *Render*, 176.

63   In the two weeks: Ibid., 158.

5. PLANNING THE GREAT DEBATES

65   He had an early: Kaiser, *Pope, Council*, 48.

65   She pointed: Hebblethwaite, *John XXIII: Pope of the Century*, 248.

66   Instead, he vented: Cahill, *Pope John XXIII*, 207.

66   "People believe": O'Malley, *What Happened*, 113.

66   There was: Benedict XVI, *Last*, 126.

67   "I notice in my body": John XXIII, *Journal*, 319.

67   Perhaps, he wrote: Ibid., 214.

69   "I feel fed up": Congar, *My Journal*, 410.

69   He realized again: Ibid., 143.

69   He saw Ottaviani: Ibid., 419.

69   In his diary: Ibid., xliii.

69   And then there: Ibid., 77.

69   An American magazine: Kaiser, *Vatican II Journal*, September 26, 2012, web.archive .org/.

70   Bishop Joseph: Kaiser, *Clerical*, 108.

6. THE MEDICINE OF MERCY

71   "Who do men say that I am?": Mark 8:27.

71   In one case: Congar, *My Journal*, 720.

71   Another, a Mexican: Ibid.

72   Even late in life: Benedict XVI, *Last*, 126.

73   "That man has": *Draft of a Dogmatic Constitution on Chastity, Marriage, the Family and*

Virginity. The original document is not readily available in Vatican archives. A copy translated into English appears on the website of the Catholic University theologian Joseph A. Komonchak (https://jakomonchak.wordpress.com).

73 He was nagged: Ratzinger, *Theological Highlights*, 19.

73 Ratzinger, witnessing: Seeward, *Benedict XVI: A Life, Volume I*, 404.

74 One of the Protestant: Moorman, *Vatican*, 15.

74 "Bea came to be": Ibid., 19.

75 Moorman was put: Ibid., 34.

76 He turned his head: Küng, *My Struggle*, 273.

76 "Dear children": Cahill, *Pope John XXIII*, 203.

77 Küng could hear: Küng, *My Struggle*, 277.

77 To Ratzinger: Ratzinger, *Theological Highlights*, 24.

77 "If we don't": Rynne, *Vatican Council II*, vii.

78 They addressed: Ratzinger, *Theological Highlights*, 36.

79 "These beautiful rites": Kaiser, *Pope, Council*, 132.

79 "Latin is dead!": Ibid., 134.

79 The most powerful Catholic: Hebblethwaite, *John XXIII: Pope of the Century*, 232. Also see Rynne, *Vatican Council II*, 65.

79 "Are the bishops": Rynne, *Vatican Council II*, 69.

80 "The forces": Ratzinger, *Theological Highlights*, 39.

80 "I pray": Hebblethwaite, *John XXIII: Pope of the Century*, 213.

81 At the council: Moorman, *Vatican*, 21.

81 "I am overcome": Congar, *My Journal*, 141.

81 He was especially: Ibid., 316.

81 He had long admired: Ibid., 366.

81 Still, to Congar: Ibid., 847.

82 Congar agreed: Ibid., 367.

82 "I speak 'Câmara'": Suenens, *Charismatic*, 3.

82 "When I give": Camara, *Dom Helder Camara*, 11.

83 Since a baby's: Ibid., 129.

83 He believed: Ibid., 75.

83 European settlers: Ibid., 73.

7. DEATH BE NOT PROUD

85 When they met: Hebblethwaite, *John XXIII: Pope of the Century*, 251.

85 At about the same: "The Gospel According to St Matthew: No. 10 Best Arthouse Film of All Time," *The Guardian*, October 20, 2010, https://www.theguardian.com.

85 "At the moment": "The Text of the Will Left by Pope John XXIII," *The New York Times*, June 7, 1963, 2.

86 Shortly after President: Cahill, *Pope John XXIII*, 205.

86 He said later: Ibid., 205.

86 The encyclical called: *Pacem in Terris* (Peace on Earth): *Encyclical of Pope John XXIII on Establishing Universal Peace in Truth, Justice, Charity, and Liberty*, April 11, 1963, https://www.vatican.va.

86 "As a Catholic": "President Kennedy's Address at Boston College Centennial Celebration, 20 April 1963," John F. Kennedy Presidential Library, https://www.jfklibrary.org.

87 Bishop Moorman: Moorman, *Vatican*, 50.

88 The decision: Rynne, *Vatican Council II*, 142.

88 He said Ottaviani's: Schner, *The Church*, 83. Also see Gregory Baum, "The End of the Beginning," *Commonweal*, October 7, 2022, https://www.commonwealmagazine.org.

88 The paper's dense: Kaiser, *Inside*, 158.
88 "No one knows": Baum interviews. Also see Gregory Baum, "The End of the Beginning: On Liturgy, Secrecy, and the Second Vatican Council," *Commonweal*, October 7, 2022, https://www.commonwealmagazine.org.
89 *L'Osservatore Romano*: "People," *Time*, December 14, 1962, https://time.com. Also see "Pope's Health Better, Communiqué Reports," *The Montreal Star*, December 3, 1962, 29.
90 looked up to the window: Küng, *My Struggle*, 323.
90 "A new freedom": George Duggan, "Council's Impact on Church Hailed," *The New York Times*, December 6, 1962, 24. Also see Küng, *My Struggle*, 301.
90 He gave standing-room: Ibid., 304.
90 The bishop of: Ibid., 310.
90 The Washington newspaper: Mary McGrory, "Chat with Kennedy Caps Father Küng's Tour," *The Boston Globe*, May 1, 1963, 27.
91 "I drive": Küng, *My Struggle*, 314.
91 Ushered into the: Ibid., 316.
91 He was summoned: Ibid., 322.
91 "My time on earth": Hebblethwaite, *John XXIII: Pope of the Century*, 256.
91 John asked him: Cahill, *Pope John XXIII*, 212.
92 Despite the pain: Clancy, *Apostle*, 155. Also see Novak, *The Open Church*, 27.
92 Once, when he was: Hebblethwaite, *John XXIII: Pope of the Century*, 257.
93 In Israel: Lapide, *The Last Three Popes*, 344.
93 The Vatican reported: Clancy, *Apostle*, 217.
94 Ratzinger later insisted: Benedict XVI, *Last*, 127. Also see Ratzinger, *Theological Highlights*, 57.
94 Normally, church law: Küng, *My Struggle*, 324.
94 Cardinal Cushing: Cushing, *Call*, 76.
95 Cardinal Giuseppe Siri: Hebblethwaite, *The Year*, 142. Also see Margaret Hebblethwaite, "The Solitude of the Succession," *The Tablet*, June 10, 2023, https://www.thetablet.co.uk; and Hoffman, *Anatomy*, 129.

8. THE HAMLET POPE

99 His inaugural lecture: Seewald, *Benedict XVI: A Life, Volume I*, 425.
99 He published: Allen, *Pope Benedict XVI*, 91. Also see Joseph Ratzinger, "Free Expression and Obedience in the Church," in Hugo Rahner and Karl Rahner, eds., *The Church: Readings in Theology*, 212.
99 He would prepare: Ratzinger, *The Ratzinger Reader*, 210.
101 At the moment: König, *Open*, 15.
101 Montini was nearly: Ibid.
102 He referred to: Hebblethwaite, *Paul VI: The First Modern Pope*, 50.
102 But Montini hesitantly: König, *Open*, 15.
102 In fact, he: Chiron, *Paul VI*, 8. Also see Hatch, *Pope Paul VI*, 6.
103 He first set: Küng, *My Struggle*, 195.
103 A Church of England: Hebblethwaite, *Paul VI: The First Modern Pope*, 262.
103 Montini did not: Ibid., 304.
104 He insisted: Zuccotti, *Under*, 59. Also see Hebblethwaite, *Paul VI: The First Modern Pope*, 196.
104 In a speech in: Weldon Wallace, "Pope Plan to Reform Rome Curia," *The Baltimore Sun*, September 22, 1963, 1. Also see Arnaldo Cortesi, "Pope Offers More Powers to Bishops," *The New York Times*, September 22, 1963, 1.
104 Ratzinger saw: Guerriero, *Benedict XVI*, 159.
104 Once the council: Küng, *My Struggle*, 357.

105 Then, suddenly: Ibid., 139. Also see Fesquet, *The Drama*, 139.
105 Parente gave: Küng, *My Struggle*, 352.
105 His days: Ibid., 399.
105 "Küng charges": Congar, *My Journal*, 369.
106 He introduced: *Solenne Inizio della Seconda Sessione del Concilio Ecumenico Vaticano II: Allocuzione del Santo Padre Paolo VI* (Solemn Beginning of the Second Session of the Second Vatican Ecumenical Council: Address of the Holy Father Paul VI), September 29, 1963, https: https://www.vatican.va.
106 "It was the first": Moorman, *Vatican*, 68.
107 Döpfner's contempt: "Roman Catholics: The Unfinished Reformation," *Time*, February 7, 1964, https://time.com.
109 He wrote a single: Küng, *My Struggle*, 364.
109 Patriarch Maximos: Fesquet, *The Drama*, 150.
110 "Do not take": Ratzinger, *Theological Highlights*, 86. Also see Congar, *My Journal*, 373.
110 "With trepidation": O'Malley, *What Happened*, 180.
111 He vowed: Rynne, *Vatican Council II*, 221. See also O'Malley, *What Happened*, 192.
112 "The Curia has no": Rynne, *Vatican Council II*, 232. Also see Allen, *Pope Benedict XVI: A Biography of Joseph Ratzinger*, 65, and O'Malley, *What Happened*, 192
112 Ottaviani was incensed: Allen, *Pope Benedict XVI*, 65. Also see Congar, *My Journal*, 417, and O'Malley, *What Happened*, 193.

9. THE NEW POPE STRUGGLES

115 The cardinal often: Hamilton, *Cardinal Suenens*, 100. Also see Rynne, *Vatican Council II*, 198.
116 Egypt's government: Howard, *The Faiths*, 192.
117 "How can we?": Congar, *My Journal*, 484.
118 The patriarch told: Hebblethwaite, *Paul VI: The First Modern Pope*, 372.
118 His remarks were: Robert C. Doty, "The Deputy is Here," *The New York Times*, February 23, 1964, 1. Also see Chiron, *Paul VI*, 354.
119 As he told: Hebblethwaite, *Paul VI: The First Modern Pope*, 340.
119 "I don't want": Ibid.
120 "The Holy Father": Küng, *My Struggle*, 400.
120 *The Economist*: Rynne, *Vatican Council II*, 288.
120 *The New York Times*: "Vatican II: Final Session,"reprinted in *The Kansas City Star*, September 16, 1965, 34. Although the original *New York Times* article was republished by the *Star* and other newspapers, it appears to have been inadvertently deleted from the online archives of *The New York Times*.
121 "He spoke to me": Suenens, *Memories*, 189.
122 There was a "thawing": Ibid., 316.
122 "A new spirit": Küng, *My Struggle*, 406.
122 He thought the: Ratzinger, *Theological Highlights*, 138.
122 In a meeting: Küng, *My Struggle*, 138.
123 In the meantime: "Pope Paul's Remarks on Birth Control," *The New York Times*, June 24, 1964, 3.
123 While the women: "Woman in the News; U.S. Nun at Council Mother Mary Luke," *The New York Times*, October 3, 1964, 11.
123 He warned against: "Council Opens Today," *The Boston Globe*, September 13, 1964, 9.
125 Modern Jews needed: F. E. Cartus, "Vatican II & the Jews," *Commentary*, January 1965, 305. Also see Rynne, *Vatican Council II*, 305.
125 He decided to: Küng, *My Struggle*, 421.

126 The ban: Hamilton, *Cardinal Suenens*, 118. Also "Text of Patriarch Maximos IV Saigh on Marriage, Family," as published online by the Catholic News Service, https://vaticaniiat50.wordpress.com.

127 "I beg": Rynne, *Vatican Council II*, 367. Also see Hebblethwaite, *Paul VI: The First Modern Pope*, 459.

128 "Let's not stand": "The Vatican Council: The Pope Runs the Church," *Time*, November 27, 1964, https://time.com.

128 He announced that: O'Malley, *What Happened*, 245.

10. A POPE "IN AGONY"

129 Many German bishops: Ratzinger, *Theological Highlights*, 201.

129 The debates: Ibid., 158.

129 The reporting: Rynne, *Vatican Council II*, 430.

129 He accused: Ibid.

130 This "hoarding": Rynne, *Vatican Council II*, 428. Also see "Pope Donates Crown to Aid World's Poor," Associated Press, *Los Angeles Times*, November 14, 1964, 14.

130 *L'Osservatore Romano*: "Papacy: Paul Is First Pope to Visit Asia," *Los Angeles Times*, December 6, 1964, 108.

131 He used a blur: Paul VI, *The Pope Speaks*, 20.

131 He told parishioners: Robert C. Doty, "Pope Opens an Era by Celebrating Mass in Italian," *The New York Times*, March 8, 1965, 1.

131 At a news conference: Robert C. Doty, "New Jesuit Leader Sets Forth Goals," *The New York Times*, June 15, 1965, 10.

132 In April: "Comment on Jews by Pope Clarified," *The New York Times*, April, 8, 1965, 2.

132 "Catholics do not": Harriet Pilpel, "The Right of Abortion," *The Atlantic*, June 1969, https://www.theatlantic.com.

132 In an interview: Fesquet, *The Drama*, 658.

133 Because she was: McClory, *Turning Point*, 7.

133 The husband wrote: Ibid., 72.

134 Patty tried to: Ibid., 67.

134 The four Gospels: Noonan interviews. Also see McClory, *Turning Point*, 112.

134 He told them: Kaiser, *The Encyclical*, 135.

135 Küng was not: Küng, *My Struggle*, 416.

135 Within days: Ibid., 417.

135 "He loves the": Congar, *My Journal*, 733.

135 Paul had a surprise: *Inizio della Quarta Sessione del Concilio Ecumenico, Vaticano II. Allocuzione di Sua Santità Paolo VI* (Start of the Fourth Session of the Second Vatican Ecumenical Council. Address of His Holiness Paul VI), September 14, 1965, https://www.vatican.va.

136 If the synod: Ratzinger, *Theological Highlights*, 206.

136 Ultimately, he suspected: Küng, *My Struggle*, 418.

136 "This right": *Declaration on Religious Freedom. Dignitatis Humanae. On the Right of the Person and of Communities to Social and Civil Freedom in Matters Religious*, December 7, 1965, https://www.vatican.va.

137 "No more war": *Address of the Holy Father Paul VI to the United Nations*, October 4, 1965, https://www.vatican.va.

137 Columnist Walter Lippmann: Walter Lippmann, "The Pope at the U.N.," *Lincoln Star Journal* (Lincoln, Nebraska), October 9, 1965, 4.

138 The pope tried: Wills, *Papal Sin*, 122.

138 Ratzinger said later: Ratzinger, *Theological Highlights*, 253.

138 Küng was: Küng, *My Struggle*, 418.

139 At exactly 12:00: Ibid., 426.
140 It would be: Ibid., 429.
140 Since his four years: Congar, *My Journal*, 737.
141 "Basically, I love": Ibid., 739.
141 By the end: Ibid., 714.
141 In 1965: Ibid., 739.
141 He was especially: *Pastoral Constitution on the Church in the Modern World. Gaudium et Spes*, December 7, 1965, https://www.vatican.va.
142 He said he believed: F. E. Cartus, "Vatican II & the Jews," *Commentary*, January 1965, https://www.commentary.org.
142 The American Jewish Committee: "The Vatican Council: A Vote Against Prejudice," *Time*, October 2, 1965, https://time.com.
142 It came in a speech: John Cogley, "Middle-of-Road Pope; Paul VI Setting Church's Course Between Two Doctrinal Extremes," *The New York Times*, November 20, 1965, 25.
143 "Women priests": Fesquet, *Drama*, 707.
144 "The pope got": Congar, *My Journal*, 874.
144 He was shown: Ibid., 868.

11. YOU MUST TRUST ME

145 He warned: Hebblethwaite, *Pope Paul VI: The First Modern Pope*, 446.
146 "They recognized": Küng, *My Struggle*, 429.
146 "Evidently, the Holy Father": Ibid.
147 He and his: Ratzinger, *Milestones*, 136.
147 He was defensive: Küng, *Disputed*, 12.
148 The messages: Ibid., 41.
148 "It's in the nature": Godfrey Anderson, "Once-Rigid Dutch, Vatican Near Schism on Doctrine," Associated Press, *The Minneapolis Tribune*, July 13, 1969, 32.
148 The idea: The Dutch catechism was published in English as *A New Catechism: Catholic Faith for Adults*, 1967. Also see "Roman Catholics: Catechism in Dutch," *Time*, December 1, 1967, https://time.com.
149 In New York: John Cogley, "Priestly Celibacy: Five Years Have Sharply Changed Attitudes of Catholic Clergymen," *The New York Times*, December 16, 1966, 16.
150 In a 1962 letter: Pamela Schaeffer, "Karl Rahner's Secret 22-Year Romance," *National Catholic Reporter*, December 19, 1997, https://natcath.org.
151 The relationship: Roy Larson, "In the 1980s, a Chicago Newspaper Investigated Cardinal Cody," *Nieman Reports*, Spring 2003, https://niemanreports.org.
151 Clarence Tripp, a respected: Mark McCain, "Book on Spellman Sparks Feud," *The Boston Globe*, August 12, 1984, 2. Also see Rich Hampson, "Cardinal Spellman: 'The American Pope,'" Associated Press, September 28, 1984, https://apnews.com; and Ron Dreher, "Cardinal Mary," *The American Conservative*, February 9, 2019, https://www.theamericanconservative.com. Some of the most detailed reporting on the book controversy was done by writer Michelangelo Signorile for his article "Cardinal Spellman's Dark Legacy" in the *New York Press*, April 23, 2002, which is found online at his website: https://www.signorile.com.
151 "Spellman put his": Lucian K. Truscott IV, "I Was Groped by a Man Called 'Mary,'" *Slate*, February 9, 2019, https://www.salon.com.
151 There was no little: Andy Newman, "Accusation of an Affair Leads Priest to Resign," *The New York Times*, August 12, 2005, B1.
152 Years after: James Carroll, "The Cardinal of Repression," *The Atlantic*, July 1992, https://www.theatlantic.com.
152 He said that: Weakland, *A Pilgrim*, 44.

152 "No one": Ibid.
152 Their departure: Ibid., 199.
153 When he left: Ibid., 198.
153 In June, he: *Sacerdotalis Caelibatus* (Of Priestly Celibacy),*Encyclical of Pope Paul VI on the Celibacy of the Priest,* June 24, 1967, https://www.vatican.va.
154 Patty Crowley: Kaiser, *The Encyclical,* 206.
154 The Vatican had: Ibid., 214.
155 Lifting the birth-control ban: Hebblethwaite, *Paul VI: The First Modern Pope,* 472.
155 He said Paul VI's: "Theologian Leaving R.C. Church," *The Guardian,* December 21, 1966, 1. Also see Kaiser, *The Encyclical,* 230.

12. "A THORN IN MY FLESH"

157 In November 1965: Gregg, *Challenging,* 182. Also see "Strong Papal Warning," *The Miami Herald,* November 25, 1965, 101.
158 The statement was: Jon Sobrino, "The Urgent Need to Return to Being the Church of the Poor," *National Catholic Reporter,* March 24, 2010, https://www.ncronline.org.
158 "The images": Suenens, *Memories,* 182.
159 As a young man: Guzmán, *Camilo Torres,* 14.
159 "The duty": Ibid., 144.
159 "I have taken": Ibid., 292.
160 Father Michael: Burns, *Francis,* 124.
160 Rembert Weakland: Weakland, *A Pilgrim,* 152.
160 He would always: Bishop, *Pedro Arrupe,* 187.
161 At the order's 1966: Robert C. Doty, "Pontiff Rebukes Group in Jesuits for 'Sinister' Acts," *The New York Times,* November 17, 1966, 1.
161 "I do not want": McRedmond, *To the Greater,* 307.
162 In 1967, he: *Populorum Progressio. Encyclical of Pope Paul VI on the Development of Peoples,* March 26, 1967, https:www.vatican.va. Other authoritative translations are written in clearer English.
162 For a pope normally: Peter Steinfels, "An Unsparing View of Economic Ills," *The New York Times,* February 20, 1988, 5. Also see Woodward, *Getting Religion,* 202.
163 The pope complained: Hebblethwaite, *Paul VI: The First Modern Pope,* 487.
163 He insisted: Robert C. Doty, "Pope Tells Synod Church Is Periled," *The New York Times,* September 30, 1967, 1.
163 Weeks later: "Roman Catholics: A Cardinal for a Leper Colony," *Time,* November 17, 1967, https://time.com.
164 The meeting was: Hebblethwaite, *Paul VI: The First Modern Pope,* 506.
164 Küng responded: Küng, *Disputed,* 67.
165 They differed: Ratzinger, *Milestones,* 135.
165 Küng could be: Küng, *Disputed,* 79.
165 He felt students: Ibid., 123.
166 "My whole Swiss": Ibid., 117.
166 They were "like": Ibid., 118.
166 Küng came: Ibid., 119.
166 Ratzinger later compared: Ratzinger, *Milestones,* 137.
166 Others at the university: Ibid., 138.
167 "Your intentions": Küng, *Disputed,* 119.
167 Still, he came: Ibid.
167 He phoned: Ibid., 122.
167 He replied: Ibid., 128.
167 He was disappointed: Ratzinger, *Milestones,* 141.
168 Densely written: Ratzinger, *Introduction,* 41.

168 "Has our theology": Ibid., 27.
168 "Perhaps I should": Küng, *Disputed*, 230.
168 The result was: Ratzinger, *Introduction*, 11.
169 He remembered: Rachel Donadio, "Pope Benedict Says Blame the '60s for Priests' Abuse," *The Atlantic*, April 12, 2019, https://www.theatlantic.com.
169 He regularly claimed: "Full Text of Benedict XVI Essay: 'The Church and the Scandal of Sexual Abuse,'" Catholic News Service, April 10, 2019, https://www.catholic newsagency.com.

13. "STANDING BEFORE THE WORLD ALONE"

170 he declared: "The Papacy: The Bones of the Fisherman," *Time*, July 5, 1968, https://time.com.
171 In March: Hebblethwaite, *Paul VI: The First Modern Pope*, 510.
171 "He was simultaneously": Ibid., 505.
171 Then a copy: "Roman Catholics: A Stern No to Birth Control," *Time*, August 2, 1968, https://time.com.
171 The seventy-five-hundred-word: *Encyclical Letter. Humanae Vitae* (Of Human Life), *of the Supreme Pontiff Paul VI to His Venerable Brothers the Patriarchs, Archbishops, Bishops and Other Local Ordinaries in Peace and Communion with the Apostolic See, to the Clergy and Faithful of the Whole Catholic World, and to All Men of Good Will, on the Regulation of Birth*, July 25, 1968, https://www.vatican.va.
172 The church's new: John Leo, "Dissent Is Voiced," *The New York Times*, July 30, 1968, 1.
172 Thomas Roberts: Ibid.
172 The US bishops': "Major Points of Pastoral Letter," *The Boston Globe*, November 16, 1968, 7.
172 In London: Rynne, "Letter from Vatican City," *The New Yorker*, October 25, 1968, https://www.newyorker.com.
173 John Marshall: Ibid.
173 "It burst": Küng, *Disputed*, 104.
173 He was careful: Ibid., 106.
173 The pope: Ibid.
173 "This, our encyclical": Robert C. Doty, "Paul Tells of Dilemma," *The New York Times*, August 1, 1968, 1.
175 At an open-air: "Pope's Address to Peasants and Excerpts from His Second Speech," *The New York Times*, August 24, 1968, 2.
176 While the holiday: Robert C. Doty, "Pope Voices Pessimism in Christmas Message," *The New York Times*, December 20, 1968, 1.
176 At the end: Edward B. Fiske, "Paul: Uneasy Heir to a Revolution," *The New York Times*, December 8, 1968, E7.
177 The pope: Hebblethwaite, *Paul VI: The First Modern Pope*, 532.
177 Paul VI, he declared: Henri Schoup, "Cardinal Denies Disrespect to the Vatican," *The Guardian*, June 24, 1969, https://www.theguardian.com.
177 In an interview: "The Cardinal as Critic," *Time*, August 1, 1969, https://time.com.
178 The newly named: John L. Hess, "Cardinal Rebukes Critics of Rome," *The New York Times*, July 6, 1969, 8.
178 His friends: "French Church Attacks Reports Cardinal Died in Woman's Room," *The New York Times*, June 25, 1974, 2.
178 The mysteries: "Bishop Who Died in a Hotel in Paris Cleared by Church," *The New York Times*, February 20, 1975, 7.
178 Papal powers: "Pope Rejects Challenge to His Absolute Role," *The Boston Globe*, October 6, 1969, 20.

178   The pope's defense: Robert C. Doty, "French Cardinal Defends Supremacy of the Pope," *The New York Times*, October 17, 1969, 5.

180   It trailed: John L. Hess, "Dutch Council Asks End of Priestly Celibacy Rule," *The New York Times*, January 8, 1970, 1.

180   There was good: C. C. Pecknold, "The call for married priests is nothing new," *Catholic Herald*, October 29, 2019, https://catholicherald.co.uk.

181   Suddenly, however: Tom Harpur, "Theologian Rocks Catholic Church," *Toronto Star*, September 11, 1971, 85.

181   An Italian-language: Alan McElwain, "Is Infallibility Fallible?" *The Sydney Morning Herald*, February 25, 1971, 7.

181   Walther von Loewenich: Küng, *Disputed*, 170.

181   He said that: Ibid., 158.

182   Ratzinger, in his: Ibid., 164.

182   The pope's decision: "Rome: Reaction to Pope's Reforms," *The Tablet*, December 5, 1970, 1192. Also see Hebblethwaite, *The Next Pope*, 67.

182   Simonis refused: "Vatican's Choice of Bishop Widens Conflict with Dutch," *The New York Times*, January 5, 1971, 2.

183   The choice of: "The Gijsen Affair," *Time*, July 24, 1972, https://time.com.

183   In 2014: "Second Deceased Dutch Bishop Outed as Sexual Abuser," *The Tablet*, May 1, 2014, https://www.thetablet.co.uk.

14. THE CHURCH'S FRONT LINE

184   "I felt I was": Arrupe, *Itineraire*, 131.

184   "Arrupe did not": Jim McDermott, "Three Jesuits Who Knew Pedro Arrupe Reflect on His Legacy," *America* magazine, November 12, 2007, https://www.americamagazine.org.

186   In 1970, the Vatican: Alfred Friendly Jr., "Vatican Assailed for Secular Role," *The New York Times*, March 9, 1970, 8.

186   In 1973, a Jesuit: "Jesuit Hails China for Birth Control," *The New York Times*, November 18, 1973, 47.

186   Similarly, many: Paul Hofmann, "Jesuit University Ousts Professor," *The New York Times*, February 25, 1973, 5.

187   The encounter occurred: Câmara, *Understanding*, 96. Also see Pique, *Pope Francis*, 58.

187   Growing up: Ivereigh, *The Great Reformer*, 25.

187   His family: Câmara, *Understanding*, 28.

187   "I felt like": Ivereigh, *The Great Reformer*, 35.

188   Years later: Valley, *Pope Francis: The Struggle*, 59.

188   Too many priests: Pique, *Pope Francis*, 109.

189   The family sat: Ibid., 17.

189   She did not: Pope Francis, *A Future of Faith*, 267.

190   That choice: Vallely, *Pope Francis: The Struggle*, 58.

190   Bergoglio was required: Câmara, *Understanding*, 57.

190   He once revealed: Clancy, *Apostle*, 218.

190   In 1960, he wrote: Pique, *Pope Francis*, 46.

191   The school's textbooks: Vallely, *Pope Francis: The Struggle*, 68.

191   He listed his failings: Ivereigh, *The Great Reformer*, 100.

194   Perez warned friends: Burns, *Francis*, 130.

194   "He had a cool head": Ivereigh, *The Great Reformer*, 109.

194   "At that time," Ibid., 118.

195   He was offended: Vallely, *Pope Francis: The Struggle*, 38.

195   "I was only": Antonio Spandaro, "A Big Heart Open to God: An Interview with Pope Francis," *America* magazine, September 30, 2013, https://www.americamagazine.org.

196 Bárbaro denied his group: Barbaro interviews.
196 The motto of: Iacopo Scaramuzzi, "Bergoglio: 'One ear to the Gospel and One to the people' is the advice that Angelelli gave me," *La Stampa* (Turin, Italy), October 29, 2018, https://www.lastampa.it.
197 Bergoglio was impressed: Pope Francis, *Only Love*, 57.
197 He said he felt: Vallely, *Pope Francis: Untying the Knot*, 53.
198 Father Guillermo: Vallely, *Pope Francis: The Struggle*, 90; Marco interviews.

15. "WALKING IN MUD"

199 In a public audience: Hebblethwaite, *Paul VI: The First Modern Pope*, 595.
200 He said he wanted: "Stumble Saved the Pope," *The Guardian*, January 14, 1971, https://www.theguardian.com.
200 A year later: Paul Hofmann, "Pietà Damaged in Hammer Attack," *The New York Times*, May 22, 1972, 1.
200 His personal confessor: Hebblethwaite, *Paul VI, The First Modern Pope*, 600.
201 A friend of Wojtyła's: Acosta, *Karol Wojtyła's Personalist Philosophy*, 106. Also see Sandro Magister, "Twenty Years as a Bishop," *L'Espresso*, May 14, 2004, https://lespresso.it.
202 "We are walking": "Pope Paul Asserts 'Sensual Pleasure' May Lead to Drugs," *The New York Times*, September 14, 1972, 9.
202 In a much-ridiculed: "Pope Exhorts Hairdressers," *The New York Times*, April 20, 1971, 9.
202 He compared departing: Paul Hofmann, "Pope Paul Compares Defecting Priests to Judas," *The New York Times*, April 9, 1971, 3.
203 In Los Angeles: "Religion: Priests and Nuns: Going Their Way," *Time*, February 23, 1970, https://time.com.
203 Two years later: Paul Hofmann, "A Nun from India Is Extolled by Pope at Peace Prize Rite," *The New York Times*, January 7, 1971, 14.
204 "This is a giant step": Kennedy interviews. Also see George W. Cornell, "Reactions Mixed to Vatican Stand on Sexual Ethics," Associated Press, *St. Petersburg Times*, January 24, 1976, 52.
204 The actor: Martel, *In the Closet*, 185. Also see Peter Kwasniewski, "Why We Need Not (and Should Not) Call Paul VI 'Saint,'" *One Peter Five*, October 12, 2018, https://onepeterfive.com. In his bestselling 2019 book on homosexuality among senior Catholic churchmen, Martel, a French journalist, reported that he believed evidence of Paul VI's alleged homosexuality was inconclusive, especially since police reports in Milan that supposedly documented the pope's relationship with Paolo Carlini were never made public, if they existed at all.
205 The allegations: "Pope Paul Denounces 'Horrible Insinuations,'" *The New York Times*, April 5, 1976, 12.
206 In 1972, the national: Eugene C. Kennedy, *The Catholic Priest in the United States*, (Washington: United States Catholic Conference of Bishops Publications Office), 1972.
207 The book erred: *Sacred Congregation for the Doctrine of the Faith. Declaration (regarding two works of Professor Hans Küng)*, February 15, 1971, www.vatican.va.
207 On the day: Paul Hofmann, "Vatican Says Küng, Rebel Theologian, Rejects Church Dogma," *The New York Times*, February 21, 1975, 2.
207 In fact: Küng, *Disputed*, 226.
208 It was the: "Obituary: Professor Hans Küng, Catholic Theologian Banned from Teaching Theology by the Vatican," *The Telegraph*, April 7, 2021, https://www.telegraph.co.uk.
208 A reviewer: Andrew M. Greeley, "Hans Küng: Embattled Teacher and Priest," *The New York Times Book Review*, December 19, 1976, 2.

208 He wrote that: Allen, *Pope Benedict*, 128.
208 His death: Küng, *Disputed*, 346.
209 Ratzinger remembered: Ratzinger, *Milestones*, 152.
209 "Auer had": Ibid.
210 Several years after: Allen, *Pope Benedict*, 120.
210 "I didn't dodge": Ratzinger, *Salt*, 83.

16. THE DIRTY WAR

211 He insisted: "Vatican said Pinochet killings were 'propaganda', U.S. Cable Shows," *The Telegraph*, April 8, 2013, https://www.telegraph.co.uk.
213 "This is a national": Pope Francis, *On Heaven*, 195.
214 "I hate to use": Uki Goñi, "Admiral Emilio Massera Obituary," *The Guardian*, November 10, 2010, https://www.theguardian.com.
214 "As many people": Adam Bernstein, "Jorge Rafael Videla, Argentine Junta Leader, Dies at 87," *The Washington Post*, May 17, 2013, https://www.washingtonpost.com.
214 "At one time": Nicholas Caistor, "General Jorge Rafael Videla: Dictator Who Brought Terror to Argentina," *The Independent*, May 17, 2013, https://www.independent.co.uk.
215 A crudely lettered: Juan de Onis, "Argentine Extremists Kill 46 in 2 Mass Murders," *The New York Times*, August 21, 1976, 47.
216 It was revealed: Feitlowitz, *A Lexicon*, 255.
217 "There were bishops": Pope Francis, *On Heaven*, 194.
217 He, by comparison, learned: Ibid., 196.
217 "I was taking": Pope Francis, *Life*, 84.
218 "She was a widow": Rubin and Ambrogetti, *Pope Francis: Conversations*, 202.
218 "For six months": Pope Francis, *A Future*, 273.
218 Bergoglio adamantly denied: Pope Francis, *Life*, 84.
219 "They put on": Uki Goñi, "Pope Francis and the Missing Marxist," *The Guardian*, December 11, 2013, https://www.theguardian.com.
220 "Perhaps I didn't": Pope Francis, *Life*, 89.
221 The response from: "Salvador Rightist Group Threatens to Kill Jesuits Unless They Leave Nation," *The New York Times*, July 18, 1977, L5.
221 He told Magee: John Magee, "La Vita Quotidiana de Paolo VI," in *Paul VI et la modernité dans l'Église* (Rome: Collection de l'école française de Rome, 1983), 135. Also see Hebblethwaite, *Paul VI: The First Modern Pope*, 815.
221 He often told Magee: Hebblethwaite, *Paul VI: The First Modern Pope*, 820.
222 "I write to you": Ibid., 823.
223 Magee recalled: Ibid., 832.
223 Küng issued: Küng, *Disputed*, 388.
223 The funeral services: "In Search of a Pope," *Time*, August 21, 1978, https://time.com.
226 The two got along: Ratzinger, *Salt*, 85.
226 He did not expect: Seewald, *Benedict XVI: A Life, Volume Two*, 119.
226 "My room": Suenens, *Memories*, 322.

17. THE SMILING POPE

229 He was the first: "Religion: Compassionate Shepherd," *Time*, September 4, 1978, https://time.com.
229 He seemed wary: Sigmund, *Liberation*, 101.
230 When the world's first: "Religion: A Swift, Stunning Choice," *Time*, September 4, 1978, https://time.com.

230 "I am truly": Küng, *Disputed*, 392.

230 The younger nun: Gerard O'Connell, "Pope John Paul I, 'The Smiling Pope,' Is on the Path to Sainthood," *America* magazine, November 4, 2017, https://www.america magazine.org.

231 He believed Magee: John Cornwell, "How the Death of a Pope Was Constructed," *The Sydney Morning Herald*, May 15, 1989, https://www.smh.com.au.

18. THE SUPERSTAR POPE

235 "He could never be": Weigel, *Witness*, 253.

236 "We wanted": Szulc, *Pope John Paul II*, 276.

236 In Germany: Küng, *Disputed*, 399.

238 He insisted he was: Louis B. Fleming, "John Paul II Vows to Pursue Church's Reform Program," *Los Angeles Times*, October 18, 1978, 1.

238 On October 23: Szulc, *Pope John Paul II*, 291. Also see Kelly-Gangi, ed., *Pope John Paul II*, 9.

238 In November: *Address of His Holiness John Paul II to Members of the International Union of Superior Generals*, November 16, 1978, https://www.vatican.va.

238 Days after his election: Marjorie Hyer, "Pope Tightens Rules Against Priests' Marrying," *The Washington Post*, October 29, 1980, https://www.washingtonpost.com. Also see Nicholas P. Cafardi, "Loose Canons," *Commonweal*, January 25, 2011, https://commonwealmagazine.org.

238 Of thirty-two thousand submitted: Weigel, *Witness*, 328.

239 Küng's eyes widened: Küng, *Disputed*, 400.

239 News reports: Szulc, *Pope John Paul II*, 358.

240 In 1941, the Jesuits': Vázquez de Prada, *The Founder*, 387.

240 By the 1970s: "Vatican Clarifies Order on Opus Dei," *The New York Times*, September 5, 1982, 4. Also see Coleman McCarthy, "The Right Hand of the Church," *The Washington Post*, November 7, 1992, https://www.washingtonpost.com.

240 In 1974: Martin Lee, "Their Will Be Done," *Mother Jones*, July/August 1983, https://www.motherjones.com. Also see Allen, *Opus Dei*, 237.

240 In a confidential: Kwitney, *Man*, 305.

241 The priest said he was: Kenneth Woodward, "A Questionable Saint," *Newsweek*, January 12, 1992, https://www.newsweek.com. Also see Felzmann, *A Journey*, 33.

241 Fearing it would be: Michele Dolz, "John Paul II and Opus Dei," *Studi Cattolici*, April 2011; republished in English on the Opus Dei website, https://opusdei.org.

242 They knew he: Oder, *Why He Is a Saint*, 173.

243 Maciel convinced: Gerald Renner, "Accusers' Victory Not Complete," *Hartford Courant*, May 21, 2006, 1. Also see Yallop, *Beyond Belief*, 60.

243 The evidence: Berry and Renner, *Vows of Silence*, 1. Berry and Renner did groundbreaking investigative reporting on Maciel over several years.

19. GOSSIP AND SIN

245 A week after his election: "A Foreign Pope," *Time*, October 30, 1978, https://time.com.

245 As archbishop in Krakow: "Pope John Paul Letters Reveal 'Intense' Friendship with Woman," BBC News, February 15, 2016, https://www.bbc.com/news. The respected American journalist Robert Blair Kaiser, a former Vatican correspondent for *Time* magazine and the author of several books about the church, wrote in his diary in 2001 about the existence of an ongoing, long-term romantic relationship between the pope and a Polish woman from Krakow who "came to live in the Vatican ten years ago." Kaiser, who died in April 2015, did not name the woman or

identify her further, except to say that she "really loves him." Kaiser's self-published diary (*My Rome Diary: 1999–2005*) appeared in e-book form on his personal blog, which was taken down after his death. The author of this book printed out a copy of *My Rome Diary* in August 2015, when it was still available online. The e-book has no page numbers. The references to the woman from Krakow appear in Kaiser's diary entries from 2001.

246 In 1976, two years: Justin Wm. Moyer, "John Paul II 'Secret Letters' Reveal Connection to Married Woman," *The Washington Post*, February 16, 2016, https://www.washingtonpost.com.

246 It allowed him: Peter Stanford, "John Paul II's Scapular: A Roman Catholic version of a rabbit's foot," *The Independent*, February 17, 2016, https://www.independent.co.uk.

247 A friend of hers: "'Intimate Relationship' Tests John Paul's Faith," *The Times*, February 14, 2016, https://www.thetimes.co.uk.

247 In the mid-1970s: Küng, *Disputed*, 385.

247 "Marianne is a stroke": Ibid., 387.

247 In 1974, he published: The book, *Jesus the Christ*, which was published in an English translation in 1976, is considered by many theologians to be the most important of Kasper's many books.

248 "There is no question": John Cooney, "Thomas Merton: The Hermit Who Never Was," *The Irish Times*, November 9, 2015, https://www.irishtimes.com.

249 "I learned a great deal": Sipe interviews.

20. ON THE ROAD

250 Churchmen who worked: Martel, *In the Closet*, 278. Also see Andrew Sullivan, "The Corruption of the Vatican's Gay Elite Has Been Exposed," *New York*, February 22, 2019, https://nymag.com.

251 "Liberation theology is": Alan Riding, "Over a Million in Mexico City Excitedly Greet the Pope," *The New York Times*, January 27, 1979, 1.

251 He rejected the idea: George Vecsey, "Pope Warns Bishops Against Political Role by Clergy," *The New York Times*, January 29, 1979, D8.

251 Suddenly there was: "Pope Assails Political Activism," *The Star (Minneapolis)*, January 29, 1979, 2. Also see "Pope Speaks Over Hissing," United Press International, *Omaha World-Herald*, January 29, 1979, 3.

251 One Mexican writer: Murphy, *The Papacy*, 190. Also see Kwitny, *Man*, 314.

252 The conference released: "Religion: Weighing Words," *Time*, February 26, 1979, https://time.com.

252 In March, he released: *John Paul II Supreme Pontiff Encyclical Letter, Redemptor Hominis* (Redeemer of Man), March 4, 1979, https://www.vatican.va.

253 His first target: "Pope Condemns a Book; First Such Act Since '67," *The New York Times*, April 4, 1979, 8.

253 That fall: Henry Tanner, "Liberal Theologian Queried at Vatican," *The New York Times*, December 14, 1979, 5.

253 In December: Henry Tanner, "Vatican Condemns Book by U.S. Priests," *The New York Times*, December 9, 1979, 21. Also see Marjorie Hyer, "Catholic Study on Sexuality Stirs Debate," *The Washington Post*, June 9, 1977, https://www.washingtonpost.com.

254 "You couldn't tell": Inocencio Alas, "The Reluctant Conversion of Oscar Romero," *Sojourners*, March-April 2000, https://sojo.net/magazine.

254 "The conflict is": Gene Palumbo, "Archbishop Oscar Romero: Setting the Record Straight," *National Catholic Reporter*, October 10, 2018, https://www.ncronline.org.

254 Bishop Pedro Arnoldo: Alan Riding, "Latin Church in Siege," *The New York Times Magazine*, May 6, 1979, 32.

255 At the end: Romero, *A Shepherd's Diary*, 214.

256 "What rumors?": Weakland, *A Pilgrim*, 239.

256 "He never": Rembert G. Weakland, "Insider Accounts from a Lonely Man," *National Catholic Reporter*, May 27, 2009, https://www.ncronline.org.

257 In a speech: Kenneth A. Briggs, "Pope Calls on Poles to Set Christian Example," *The New York Times*, June 9, 1979, 2.

257 The planning: *Funeral Mass for Cardinal Alfredo Ottaviani, Homily of His Holiness John Paul II*, August 6, 1979, https://www.vatican.va.

258 The evangelical preacher: "The Pope in America," *Time*, October 15, 1979, https://time.com.

258 In advance: "Catholics in U.S. Strongly Approve of John Paul's Leadership, Poll Says," *The Arizona Republic*, October 1, 1979.

259 the all-male priesthood: "The Pope in America," *Time*, October 15, 1979, https://time.com.

259 She read out: Marjorie Hyer, "A Challenge from Nuns," *The Washington Post*, October 7, 1979, https://www.washingtonpost.com. Also see "Religion: Aftershock from a Papal Visit," *Time*, October 22, 1979, https://time.com.

21. PUNISHING A THEOLOGIAN

260 From what the cardinal: Seewald, *Benedict XVI: A Life, Volume II*, 190.

261 "The child": Pursell, *Benedict*, 115. Also see Mark Landler, "A Future Pope Recalled," *The New York Times*, April 22, 2005, 12.

261 He was eager: Seewald, *Benedict XVI: An Intimate Portrait*, 79.

261 But Metz: Allen, *Pope Benedict XVI*, 125.

261 In discussing: Stephen R. Haynes, "Christian Holocaust Theology: A Critical Reassessment," *Journal of the American Academy of Religion* 62, no. 2 (Summer 1994), 553–85.

261 "You had no reason": Allen, *Cardinal Ratzinger*, 125.

262 Küng suggested: Hans Küng, "Pope John Paul II: His First Year," *The New York Times*, October 19, 1979, 35.

262 Several German bishops: Küng, *Disputed*, 437.

262 "A cardinal": Ibid., 438.

263 "Dear Herr Küng": Ibid., 440.

263 Three days later: Ibid., 452.

264 While Küng suffered: Walter J. Burghardt, "Rome and Rebellion," *The New York Times*, April 8, 1980, 15.

264 "I am deeply": "Texts of Vatican Declaration and Priest's Statement," *The New York Times*, December 19, 1979, 8.

264 He interrupted: Paul Hofmann, "Five German Prelates Meet with Pope on the Kung Case," *The New York Times*, December 30, 1979, 3.

265 "Küng had a big mouth": Benedict XVI, *Last*, 150.

265 "In previous years": Ibid., 159.

265 "This is a betrayal": Küng, *Disputed*, 490.

265 The Jesuits, he said: Robert Blair Kaiser, "Jesuits' Chief, at Pope's Request, Orders a Curb on 'Shortcomings,'" *The New York Times*, December 7, 1979, 1.

266 "We need you": Benedict XVI, *Last*, 166.

267 Archdiocese records: Nicholas Kulish and Katrin Bennhold, "Memo to Pope Described Transfer of Pedophile Priest," *The New York Times*, March 25, 2010, 1.

267 Fahr wrote: Ibid.

268 In April, the Congregation: *Inaestimabile Donum* (A Priceless Gift), *Instruction Concerning Worship of the Eucharistic Mystery*, prepared by the Sacred Congregation for the Sacraments and Divine Worship, April 17, 1980. The decree is not available on the Vatican's official website but has been republished on the Catholic affairs website New Advent, https://www.newadvent.org.

270 She admitted: David Van Biema, "Mother Teresa's Crisis of Faith," *Time*, August 23, 2007, https://time.com.

270 In a diary entry: Romero, *A Shepherd's Diary*, 466.

270 "I prefer it": Wright, *Óscar Romero*, 126.

270 In a sermon: Sobrino, *Romero*, 28.

270 He wrote in: Kwitny, *Man*, 353.

271 "He was acting": Ibid. Also see Colman McCarthy, "It's Their Way or No Way," *The Baltimore Sun*, January 18, 1998, 71.

271 In a telegram: Kwitny, *Man*, 354.

272 He repeatedly hailed: "Pope to Visit Six African Nations," *Los Angeles Times*, March 27, 1980, 6.

272 He rejected pleas: Gregory Jaynes, "Huge Crowds Greet Pope in Zaire," *The New York Times*, May 3, 1980, 1.

272 "Sometimes there": Kwitny, *Man*, 358.

273 In one speech: Richard N. Ostling, "Religion: Building Bridges in Brazil," *Time*, July 21, 1980, https://time.com.

273 "We are not": Ibid.

273 After the last: "Pope Breaks Silence, Prays for Poland," *New York Daily News*, August 21, 1980, 2.

22. CARDINAL RATZINGER RISES

275 There was a moment: "U.S. Bishops' Stand on Birth Control Hit," Associated Press, *Los Angeles Times*, October 1, 1980, 4.

275 In his weekly audience: "Religion: Tempest in a Cappuccino Cup?" *Time*, October 27, 1980, https://time.com.

276 The next week: "Pope Praises Couples for Self-Control," Associated Press, *The Baltimore Sun*, October 13, 1980, 2.

276 Germany's Catholic: Kenneth A. Briggs, "Pope's Tour: Mixed Signals," *The New York Times*, November 21, 1980, 7.

276 Ratzinger would claim: Allen, *Pope Benedict XVI*, 123. Also see "Youth Leader Lectures Pope," Associated Press, *The Miami Herald*, November 20, 1980, 69.

277 On December 7: Weigel, *Witness*, 405.

278 "We had kind of a": Kengor, *The Judge*, 173.

279 In August, over: "Religion: Half Alive," *Time*, January 25, 1982, https://time.com.

279 "I wanted first": Henry Tanner, "Pope out of Hospital, Back at Vatican," *The New York Times*, August 15, 1981, 3.

280 In Germany: George W. Cornell, "Jesuits to Elect New Leaders," Associated Press, *The Atlanta Constitution*, September 10, 1983, 25.

280 Many of Ratzinger's: Seewald, *Benedict XVI, A Life, Volume II*, 153.

281 If he went out: Guerriero, *Benedict*, 292.

282 "Then the pope": Ibid., 297. See also Ratzinger, *Salt*, 9.

282 "He was very slight": Ratzinger, *My Brother*, 63.

283 And so they again: Ibid., 133.

283 He recalled how: Ibid., 134.

23. BANISHING A JESUIT

284 Bergoglio's legacy: Burns, *Francis*, 179.

285 "I joined": Pique, *Pope Francis*, 83.

285 He was given: Ibid., 85. Also see Ivereigh, *The Great Reformer*, 179.

285 Father Rafael Velasco: Velasco interviews.

286 Bergoglio praised: Pepinster, *The Keys*, 75. Also see Ivereigh, *The Great Reformer*, 83.

288 *Iglesia y Dictadura:* The book was published in English in 1988 with the title *Witness*

to the Truth: The Complicity of Church and Dictatorship in Argentina (Maryknoll, NY: Orbis Books, 1988).

288 Father Andrés Swinnen: Vallely, *Pope Francis: The Struggle*, 101.

289 What Bergoglio later: James Carroll, "Who Am I to Judge?," *The New Yorker*, December 15, 2013, https://www.newyorker.com.

24. THE DISTRACTED POPE

290 Now freed: Küng, *Disputed*, 847.

290 It was not: Ibid., 510.

290 "You're doing well": Ibid., 515.

291 The meeting proved: Ibid., 516.

291 They discussed: Ibid.

291 The Italians: Ratzinger, *The Ratzinger Report*, 67.

291 "Postponing things": Ibid., 69.

292 Because Gutiérrez's writings: Allen, *Pope Benedict XVI*, 153.

293 "I declare": Boff, *Liberation Theology*, 95. Also see "Theologian in Brazil Says He Is Silenced," *The New York Times*, May 9, 1985, 21.

293 Among them: Marlise Simons, "Vatican Reported to Have Sought Rebukes for 2 Other Latin Clerics," *The New York Times*, September 11, 1984, 14.

293 One of them: Michael Novak, "The Case Against Liberation Theology," *The New York Times Magazine*, October 21, 1984, 51.

294 The article: Allen, *Pope Benedict XVI: A Biography of Joseph Ratzinger*, 154. Also see Aidan Nichols, "The Rise and Fall of Liberation Theology, *New Blackfriars* 72, no. 853 (October 1991).

295 *Time* magazine: "Religion: Purifying Heat," *Time*, May 7, 1984, https://time.com.

295 That fall: *Instruction on Certain Aspects of the Theology of Liberation*, prepared by the Congregation for the Doctrine of the Faith, August 6, 1984, https://www.vatican.va.

295 The report was: Thomas Sheehan, "The Vatican Errs on Liberation Theology," *The New York Times*, September 16, 1984, 23.

297 The cardinal jokingly: John Hooper, "Is the pope a reactionary or a prophet?" *The Guardian*, March 23, 2010, https://www.theguardian.com.

297 "He would leave": Peter Hebblethwaite, "The Emperor of Rome," *The Guardian*, May 22, 1982, https://www.theguardian.com.

298 Messori, who hadn't: Ratzinger, *The Ratzinger Report*, 15.

298 Ratzinger told Messori: Ibid., 34.

298 After Vatican II: Ibid., 29.

298 He dismissed: Ibid., 162.

298 He offered: Ibid., 95.

298 They had: Ibid., 103.

298 He had contempt: Ibid., 100.

299 He condemned: Ibid.

299 He was outraged: Ibid., 87.

299 "There are zingers": Ralph McInerny, "The Ratzinger Report," *Crisis* magazine, December 1, 1985, https://crisismagazine.com.

299 Fergus Kerr: E. J. Dionne Jr., "A Voice of Conservatism with the Pope's Ear," *The New York Times*, August 4, 1985, section 4, page 3.

299 George Lindbeck: George A. Lindbeck, "But if One Despairs," *Commonweal*, November 15, 1985, https://www.commonwealmagazine.org.

299 Monika Hellwig: Monika K. Hellwig, "I Respect but Deplore," *Commonweal*, November 15, 1985, https://www.commonwealmagazine.org.

299 When asked: O'Collins, *On the Left Bank*, 202.

299   While holding: "Ratzinger's Sad Book," *The Tablet*, July 13, 1985, 723.
300   After attending several: O'Collins, *Midlife Journey*, 346.
300   The pope: O'Collins, *On the Left Bank*, 146.
300   Like many churchmen: O'Collins, *From Rome*, 8; O'Collins interviews.
300   Father Richard: Peter J. Boyer, "A Hard Faith," *The New Yorker*, May 16, 2005, https://www.newyorker.com.
301   Catholic bishops: E. J. Dionne Jr., "Catholics at Odds over Call for Synod," *The New York Times*, October 2, 1985, 12.
302   In advance: E. J. Dionne Jr., "The Pope's Guardian of Orthodoxy," *The New York Times Magazine*, November 24, 1985, 40.
302   The cardinal: Pamela Schaeffer, "Maverick Catholic Scholar Speaks Out Again," *St. Louis Post-Dispatch*, October 31, 1985, 19.
302   The conservative Swiss: Ibid.

25. "SO MUCH FILTH"

303   When it erupted: Benedict XVI, *Light*, 58.
303   He claimed the: Ibid., 38.
304   In that case: "Catholic Church Documents: The Handling of Stephen Kiesle," *The Mercury News*, October 24, 2018, https://www.mercurynews.com.
304   He would later: Jesse McKinley and Katie Zezima, "Oakland Priest's Accuser Describes Sexual Abuse," *The New York Times*, April 11, 2010, 13.
305   The letter, which raised: Laurie Goodstein and Michael Luo, "Pope Put Off Punishing Abusive Priest," *The New York Times*, April 9, 2010, 1.
306   One victim: Evan Moore, "Church Abuse Case Haunts Lawyer," *Daily World* (Opelousas, Louisiana), October 5, 2013, 1.
306   Doyle discovered: Kaiser, *Whistle*, 33.
307   That telex: Ibid., 34.
307   By July 1985: Ibid., 38–39.
308   Doyle was struck: Thomas P. Doyle, "Records Show That John Paul II Could Have Intervened in Abuse Crisis—But Didn't," *National Catholic Reporter*, April 25, 2014, https://www.ncronline.org.
309   A respected American: Allen, *Pope Benedict XVI*, 171.
309   Ratzinger's critics: "Ruling Said Difficult for Alcoholic Priests," Associated Press, *Daily Hampshire Gazette* (Northampton, Massachusetts), June 29, 1984, 18.
311   In a 1981 book: Cox, *The Silencing*, 52. Also see Berry, *Render*, 157.
311   The book did not: Allen, *Pope Benedict XVI*, 156.
311   It was a story: Cox, *The Silencing*, 27.
311   "I am in Rome": Ibid., 25.
312   "Aha, is this": Ibid., 97.
312   He said the movement's: Ibid., 54.
313   Boff said he was saddened: "Theologian Turns Other Cheek," *The Sydney Morning Herald*, March 22, 1985, 7.
313   At a meeting: Richard N. Ostling, "Religion: A Lesson on Liberation," *Time*, April 14, 1986, https://time.com.
313   A delighted Boff: Allen, *Cardinal Ratzinger*, 162.
313   The Vatican's power: Tony Judt, "Holy Warrior," *The New York Review of Books*, October 31, 1996, https://www.nybooks.com.
314   Ratzinger believed: Ratzinger, *The Ratzinger Report*, 83.
314   In the 1984 US: "O'Connor Critical of Ferraro Views," Associated Press, *The New York Times*, September 9, 1984, 1.
314   He had openly: Curran interviews. Also see Curran, *Loyal Dissent*, 237.
315   Ratzinger directed: Curran and McCormick, eds., *Dissent in the Church*, 359.

315 Häring had known: Bernard Häring, "The Curran Case," *CrossCurrents* 36, no. 3 (Fall 1986), 332–43.
315 He brought: Curran, *Loyal Dissent*, 124.
315 Curran had gone: Ibid., 121.
316 Ratzinger replied angrily: Curran interviews. Also see Curran, *Loyal Dissent*, 124.
316 One journalist asked: Ibid., 127.

26. RATZINGER'S CRUSADE

319 "A proposal for": Allen, *Pope Benedict XVI*, 205.
319 Hunthausen replied with: McCoy, *A Still*, 176.
320 A handful of American bishops: Joseph Berger, "Bishops and Vatican: U.S. Prelates Tread a Fine Line," *The New York Times*, September 18, 1986, B15.
320 Father John McNeill: Briggs, *Holy Siege*, 73.
321 "What is technologically": Michael D. Schaffer, "Test-tube Births Are Condemned," *The Philadelphia Inquirer*, March 11, 1987, 1.
321 "I admired his": "Benedict XVI: I Knew During His Life That John Paul II Was a Saint," Catholic News Agency, April 23, 2014, https://www.catholicnewsagency.com.
323 In the interview, Ratzinger: Ari L. Goldman, "Cardinal's Views Assailed by Jews," *The New York Times*, November 18, 1987, 25.
323 The American Jewish Committee: Ibid. Also see Marjorie Hyer, "Interfaith Summit Postponed," *The Washington Post*, November 21, 1987, https://www.washingtonpost.com.
323 The cardinal, stung: John Dart, "Cardinal Tries to Mollify Jewish Leaders," *Los Angeles Times*, January 30, 1988, 42.
324 The experience taught: Bellm and Krieg, *Cardinal Walter Kasper*, 113.
325 This was a "shotgun": Clyde Haberman, "Pope Picks Conservative Cardinal for Cologne," *The New York Times*, December 21, 1988, 6.
325 The protests began: "Remembering the Cologne Declaration," *National Catholic Reporter*, January 15, 1999, https://www.ncronline.org.
326 In one interview: Allen, *Pope Benedict XVI*, 69.
326 The "oath of fidelity": Michael Hirsley, "'Loyalty Oath' Troubles Schools," *Chicago Tribune*, April 21, 1989, 8.
326 The seventy-five-hundred-word: *Instruction. Donum Veritatis. On the Ecclesial Vocation of the Theologian*, May 24, 1990, https://www.vatican.va.
326 It was time: William D. Montalbano, "Vatican Warns Theologians Not to Dissent," *Los Angeles Times*, June 27, 1990, 1.

27. POLISHING AN IMAGE

330 "Never even heard": O'Collins, *Midlife*, 328; O'Collins interviews.
331 Under Ratzinger, it had abandoned: O'Collins, *Catholicism*, 125.
331 Under Ratzinger, O'Collins said: O'Collins, *On the Left Bank*, 208.
331 O'Collins believed: Ibid., 152; O'Collins interviews.
332 He said he cited: Benedict XVI, *Last*, 174.
332 "The *Panzer-Kardinal*": "Interview with Peter Seewald, *Faith Magazine*, January/February 2016, https://faithmag.com.
332 In 1996, he gave: Ratzinger, *Salt*, 86.
332 He expressed pride: Ibid., 44.
332 "It was the kind": Ratzinger, *Milestones*, 27.
333 When a Nazi pogrom: Allen, *Pope Benedict XVI*, 15.
333 The writer Luise: Ibid., 16.

333   "The horrors": Ibid., 15.
333   Despite the: Ratzinger, *Milestones*, 42.
333   "A theme which seldom": O'Collins interviews. Also see O'Collins, *On the Left Bank*, 196.
333   The cardinal: Seewald, *Benedict XVI: A Life, Volume I*, 156.
334   He repeatedly claimed: "Vatican Mistaken on Condom Controversy," *The Miami Herald*, October 27, 2003, 29.
335   Days later, the pope: Dennis Coday, "A Cardinal Is Accused: The Groër Case," *National Catholic Reporter*, April 4, 2014, https://www.ncronline.org.
335   He believed the church: John L. Allen Jr., "The Vatican in Full-Court Ecumenical Press," *National Catholic Reporter*, January 25, 2008, https://www.ncronline.org.
336   In 1993, Kasper and two: Thomas D. Williams, "When Ratzinger Said No: A History of the Kasper Proposal," *Crisis* magazine, October 23, 2015, https://crisis magazine.com.
337   Lehmann produced: Maike Hickson, "Cardinal Lehmann's Memoirs: On His Humanae Vitae Dissent and the Conduct of Some Popes," *OnePeterFive*, March 14, 2018, onepeterfive.com.
337   The following year: *Congregation for the Doctrine of the Faith. Letter to the Bishops of the Catholic Church Concerning the Reception of Holy Communion by the Divorced and Remarried Members of the Faithful*, September 14, 1994, https://www.vatican.va.
337   The 1998 decree: His Holiness Pope John Paul II, Apostolic Letter Issued "Motu Proprio," *Apostolos Suos. On the Theological and Juridical Nature of Episcopal Conferences*, May 21, 1998, https://www.vatican.va. Also see Larry Stamer, "Pope Issues Edict Limiting Power of Bishops," *Los Angeles Times*, July 24, 1998, 31.
338   Another member: Seewald, *Benedict XVI: A Life, Volume II*, 265. Also see Ivereigh, *The Great Reformer*, 257, and Edward Pentin, "Still Controversial: Cardinal Danneels and the Conclave of 2005," *National Catholic Register*, November 5, 2015, https://www.ncregister.com.
338   He came to describe: Seewald, *Benedict XVI: A Life, Volume Two*, 264.
339   As for the world's: David O'Reilly, "Reading the Pope in the Right Context," *The Philadelphia Inquirer*, April 24, 2005, 1.
340   In another book-length: Ratzinger, *Salt*, 244.
340   The penalty: Diego Ribadeneira, "After Pilgrimage, Law Sees 'New Cuba,'" *The Boston Globe*, January 31, 1998, 14.
341   In a review: Gerald O'Collins, "Review: Paths to God," *The Tablet*, January 24, 1998, 110.
341   He knew nothing: O'Connell, *Do Not Stifle*, 199.
342   "The joy": Ibid., 150.
342   "One would have": O'Collins, *On the Left Bank*, 220.
342   Dupuis used: Ibid., 219.
342   "The misgivings": Ibid., 227.
343   König's initial: Franz König, "In Defense of Fr. Dupuis," *The Tablet*, January 16, 1999, 76.
343   His letter: Joseph Ratzinger, "Cardinal Ratzinger Replies," *The Tablet*, March 13, 1999, 385.
344   "He can hardly": O'Collins interviews.
344   Was Ratzinger suggesting: O'Collins, *On the Left Bank*, 234. Also see O'Connell, *Do Not Stifle*, 71.
345   Most of the thirty-six-page: Congregation for the Doctrine of the Faith, *Declaration. Dominus Iesus. On the Unicity and Salvific Universality of Jesus Christ and the Church*, August 6, 2000, https://www.vatican.va.
345   The Lutheran World: Mannion, ed., *Church and Religious 'Other,'* 134.

345 The World Council: Richard Boudreaux, "Vatican Declares Catholicism Sole Path to Salvation," *Los Angeles Times*, September 6, 2000, 1.

345 In Milan: Ibid.

345 Hans Küng described it: Edmund Doogue and Stephen Brown, "*Dominus Iesus* a 'Public Relations Disaster' for Ecumenism Say Critics," *Christianity Today*, September 1, 2000, https://www.christianitytoday.com.

345 He eventually issued: John Norton, "Pope Reassures Reformed Leaders," Catholic News Service, *Lake Shore Visitor* (Erie, Pennsylvania), September 22, 2000, 2.

345 Ultimately, the congregation's: O'Connell, *Do Not Stifle*, 197.

28. BERGOGLIO IN EXILE

347 He was assigned: Câmara, *Understanding*, 147.

347 Father Victor Zorzín: Vallery, *Pope Francis: The Struggle*, 205.

348 Ricardo Spinassi: Câmara, *Understanding*, 169.

349 Velasco thought: Vallely, *Pope Francis: The Struggle*, 104; Velasco interview.

350 "But I'm very comfortable": Ivereigh, *The Great Reformer*, 223.

350 "He didn't even": Vallely, *Pope Francis: The Struggle*, 201; Marco interviews.

350 Quarracino was criticized: Paul Vallely, "Pope Francis puts people first and dogma second. Is this really the new face of Catholicism?," *The Independent*, August 1, 2013, https://www.independent.co.uk.

351 He received a visit: Bergoglio, *On Heaven*, 76. Also see Pique, *Pope Francis*, 100.

352 Father Fernando Giannetti: Ivereigh, *The Great Reformer*, 224.

353 Bergoglio walked to the Casa Rosada: Aguilar, *Pope Francis*, 100. Also see Ivereigh, *The Greater Reformer*, 241.

354 Bergoglio's homily: Burns, *Francis*, 214.

354 "Everyone was in tears": McCarten, *The Pope*, 60.

354 "The least serious sins": Pope Francis, *A Future of Faith*, 173.

354 "That does not mean": Ibid., 54.

355 "Some priests": Ibid., 174.

355 "What you see": Rubin and Ambrogetti, *Pope Francis*, 154.

355 "In my diocese": Pope Francis, *On Heaven*, 50.

355 "Even one Catholic priest": Pope Francis, *A Future of Faith*, 155.

359 Late that year: Christopher White, "How Sept. 11 Inadvertently Paved the Way for the Future Election of Pope Francis," *National Catholic Reporter*, September 9, 2021, https://www.ncronline.org.

359 In a series: Vallely, *Pope Francis: The Struggle*, 174.

29. THE CRISIS IN BOSTON

360 The problem was: Wilson interviews. Also see Laurie Goodstein and David M. Halbfinger, "Church Office Failed to Act on Abuse," *The New York Times*, July 1, 2010, 1. See passim Robertson, *The Case of the Pope*, which contains the detailed analysis of the legal consequences of the Vatican's mishandling of priestly child-abuse cases.

361 He would claim: Benedict XVI, *Last*, 199.

362 Many Austrians were appalled: Dennis Coday, "A Cardinal Is Accused: The Groër Case," *National Catholic Reporter*, April 4, 2014, https://www.ncronline.org.

362 In January 2001: Berry and Renner, *Vows of Silence*, 274.

362 In his remarks: *Address of John Paul II to the Legionaries of Christ and the Members of the Regnum Christi Movement*, January 4, 2001, https://www.vatican.va.

362 In the United States: Gerald Renner and Jason Berry, "Head of Worldwide Catholic

Order Accused of History of Abuse," *Hartford Courant*, February 23, 1997, 1. Also see Daniel J. Wakin and James C. McKinley Jr., "Abuse Case Offers a View of Vatican's Politics," *The New York Times*, May 2, 2010, 1.

362   She organized: Alma Munoz, "Marcial Maciel, Pedrasta, Determina el Vaticano," *La Jornada* (Mexico), May 19, 2006, https://www.jornada.com.mx.

363   "By all means": Kevin Clarke, "Cardinal Bernard Law, the face of the church's failure on child sexual abuse, dies at 86," *America* magazine, December 19, 2017, https//www.americamagazine.org.

364   In 1996, the cardinal: Walter V. Robinson and Matt Carroll, "Documents Show Church Long Supported Geoghan," *The Boston Globe*, January 24, 2002, 1.

364   In a letter to the world's priests: "Sex-abuse scandals cast 'dark shadow'—Pope," *The Irish Times*, March 21, 2002, https://www.irishtimes.com.

365   *The New York Times*: Daniel J. Wakin, "Scandals in the Church: McCarrick Is Public Voice of U.S. Group," *The New York Times*, April 25, 2002, 28.

365   Archbishop Julián Herranz: Garry Wills, "Forgive Not," *The New Republic*, May 18, 2010, https://newrepublic.com. Also see Laurie Goodstein, "A Vatican Lawyer Says Bishops Should Not Reveal Abuse," *The New York Times*, May 18, 2002, 1.

365   Ratzinger's former deputy: Barry James, "Priests and pedophilia: A scandal not only in America," *The International Herald Tribune*, April 19, 2002, https://www.nytimes.com.

365   He charged that he: Laurie Goodstein, "Pope Has Gained the Insight to Address Abuse, Aides Say," *The New York Times*, April 23, 2005, 1. Also see "Cardinal Ratzinger Sees a Media Campaign Against Church," ZENIT news agency, December 3, 2002, https://zenit.org.

366   Richard Sipe, the psychotherapist: Sipe interviews.

367   He had one task: *Report on the Holy See's Institutional Knowledge and Decision-Making Related to Former Cardinal Theodore Edgar McCarrick*, November. 20, 2020, 131, https://www.vatican.va.

367   A promotion for McCarrick: Ibid., 141.

367   One, Edward Hughes: Ibid., 152.

367   On July 4: Ibid., 166.

368   Through a friend: Ibid., 169.

369   Other news reports in 2001: "Documents Allege Abuse of Nuns by Priests," *The New York Times*, March 21, 2001, 10.

369   In resigning: Keating interviews. Also see Alan Cooperman, " 'No Apology' as Keating Leaves Panel," *The Washington Post*, June 17, 2003, https://www.washingtonpost.com.

369   A year after that: Alan Cooperman, "Bishops Accused of Backsliding in Sex Abuse Scandal," *The Washington Post*, May 11, 2004, https://www.washingtonpost.com.

369   The study, by the John Jay: *The Nature and Scope of Sexual Abuse of Minors by Catholic Priests and Deacons in the United States: 1950–2002*, John Jay College of Criminal Justice, February 2004. Available on the website of the United States Conference of Catholic Bishops, https://www.usccb.org.

370   Under Ratzinger's leadership: Kilian McDonnell, "The Ratzinger/Kasper Debate: The Universal Church and Local Churches," *Theological Studies*, May 2002, 227.

370   He portrayed Ratzinger: Walter Kasper, "On the Church," *America* magazine, April 23, 2001, https://www.americamagazine.org.

370   He described his shock: Joseph Ratzinger, "The Local Church and the Universal Church," *America* magazine, November 19, 2001, https://www.americamagazine.org.

30. THE SAINT FACTORY

374 Sainthood for the pair: John Rivera, "Divided Opinion on Beatification of 2 Popes," *The Baltimore Sun*, September 3, 2000, 1.

374 As part of the campaign: Jason Berry, "Money paved way for Maciel's influence in the Vatican," *National Catholic Reporter*, April 6, 2010, https://www.ncronline.org.

374 Father Richard Neuhaus: Richard Neuhaus, "Feathers of Scandal," *First Things*, March 2002. The article is no longer available on the *First Things* website but has been republished on the website of the victims rights group BishopAccountability .org, https://www.bishop-accountability.org. Also see Michael Shnayerson, "The Follieri Charade," *Vanity Fair*, September 3, 2008, https://www.vanityfair.com, and Jason Berry, "How Father Maciel Built His Empire," *National Catholic Reporter*, April 12, 2010, https://www.ncronline.org.

375 According to the Justice Department: Jason Barry, "The last bull: Cardinal Sodano goes out," *National Catholic Reporter*, December 27, 2019, https://www.ncronline .org.

376 "Only the angels and saints": Edward Pentin, "Cardinal Sodano Discusses Vatican Leaks," *National Catholic Register*, June 6, 2012, https://www.ncregister.com.

376 Schönborn said that: Christa Pongratz-Lippitt, "Schonborn spells out shocking reality of clerical sex abuse," *The Tablet*, November 27, 2019, https://www.thetablet .co.uk.

376 After returning to Rome: Shawn Boburg, Robert O'Harrow Jr., and Chico Harlan, "Ousted Cardinal McCarrick Gave More Than $600,000 to Fellow Clerics, Including Two Popes," *The Washington Post*, December 26, 2019, https://www.washington post.com.

377 McCarrick knew: *Report on the Holy See's Institutional Knowledge and Decision-Making Related to Former Cardinal Theodore Edgar McCarrick*, November 20, 2020, 203, https://www.vatican.va.

377 McCarrick donated: Shawn Boburg and Robert O'Harrow Jr., "Cardinal McCarrick Secretly Gave Nearly $1 Million to Group Led by Cleric Accused of Sexual Misconduct," *The Washington Post*, February 17, 2020, https://www.washingtonpost.com.

378 He said he: *Report on the Holy See's Institutional Knowledge and Decision-Making Related to Former Cardinal Theodore Edgar McCarrick*, November 20, 2020, 393, https://www .vatican.va.

31. THE CARDINALS' "MAFIA"

379 Kasper lived at: "Can a Shy Theologian Transform into a Pope for the People?," *Der Spiegel*, April 25, 2005, https://www.spiegel.de/international.

379 He felt blindsided: Bellm and Krieg, *Cardinal Walter Kasper*, 126.

380 Cardinal Murphy-O'Connor: Murphy-O'Connor, *An English Spring*, 175.

380 In a bow to the children's: Paul Elie, "The Year of Two Popes," *The Atlantic*, January/February 2006, https://www.theatlantic.com.

381 He made one trip: Ibid.

381 Ratzinger offered a surprising: Benedict XVI, *Light*, 20.

381 Former Soviet leader: David Van Biema, "Defender of the Faith," *Time*, April 3, 2005, https://time.com.

381 In Germany, Hans Küng: Hans Küng, "The Pope's Contradictions," *Der Spiegel*, March 26, 2005, https://www.spiegel.de/international.

381 "Americans clearly loved": David Van Biema, "Defender of the Faith," *Time*, April 3, 2005, https://time.com.

382 "Of course, my name": Benedict XVI, *Last*, 183.

382 The Brazilian newspaper: Ivereigh, *The Great Reformer*, 280.

383 Eager to overcome: *Funeral Mass of the Roman Pontiff John Paul II, Homily of His Eminence Card. Joseph Ratzinger,* April 8, 2005, https://www.vatican.va.

383 The two cardinals denied it: Jeff Diamant, "Whither Thou Goest," Newhouse News Services, *Honolulu Star-Bulletin,* April 10, 2005. Also see "Opposition Mounting to Ratzinger as Pope," *Deutsche Welle,* April 14, 2005, https://www.dw.com, and Greeley, *The Making of the Pope,* 160.

384 "Shy, reserved": Rubin and Ambrogetti, *Pope Francis: Conversations,* xix.

384 "My reaction was": Ibid., 165.

385 He spent much of that year: Molano, *In the Land of Silver,* 86. Also see "Swiss Probe Asked of Kirchner's Accounts," *The Miami Herald,* November 6, 2004, 12.

385 At the annual Mass: John Lyons, Ken Parks, and Matthew Cowley, "'Father Jorge' Rose from Modest Roots," *The Wall Street Journal,* March 14, 2013, https://www.wsj.com. Also see Vallely, *Pope Francis: The Struggle,* 170.

385 Asked the next day: Marco interviews. Also see Vallely, *Pope Francis: The Struggle,* 170.

385 "He depicted himself": Horacio Verbitsky, "How I made the chilling discovery that exposed 'Pope of Dictatorship,'" *The Daily Mail,* March 16, 2013, https://www.dailymail.co.uk. Also see "Pope Francis's Junta Past: Argentine Journalist on New Pontiff's Ties to Abduction of Jesuit Priests," *Democracy Now,* March 14, 2013, https://www.democracynow.org.

386 By 2004, Verbitsky had: Horacio Verbitsky, *El Silencio. De Paulo VI a Bergoglio. Las relaciones secretas de la Iglesia con la ESMA* (Buenos Aires: Editorial Sudamericana, 2005).

386 The cardinal now had: Burns, *Francis,* 172.

387 The Italian newspaper: Jorge Covarrubias, "Complaint on '76 Kidnappings," Associated Press, *The Boston Globe,* April 17, 2005, 13.

387 Marco, the cardinal's spokesman: Ibid.

32. THE UNWELCOME CHALLENGER

391 The 2005 conclave: Clyde Haberman, "Cleansed of Centuries of Grime, Sistine Ceiling Shines Anew," *The New York Times,* March 29, 1990, C17.

392 At least one participant: Nicole Winfield, "Shedding Some Light on Secret Conclave," Associated Press, *Chicago Tribune,* September 24, 2005, 3.

392 "We each wrote": Murphy-O'Connor, *An English Spring,* 170.

393 The account of what: "Martini: Benedict XVI's Resignation and the 2005 Conclave," *La Stampa* (Turin, Italy), July 18, 2015, https://www.lastampa.it. Also see Robert Mickens, "Letter from Rome," *Commonweal,* August 26, 2015, https://www.commonwealmagazine.org.

394 After a third: Murphy O'Connor, *An English Spring,* 171.

395 He acknowledged that: Benedict XVI, *Last,* 184.

395 He said he felt: Benedict XVI, *Light,* 19.

396 Before the conclave: John Hooper, "Pope vows to defend Catholic church's 'pro-life' doctrine," *The Guardian,* May 8, 2005, https://www.theguardian.com.

396 The large American victims-rights: Gerald Renner, "Familiar Face on Abuse Issues," *Hartford Courant,* April 20, 2005, 10.

396 Still, Küng held: Richard Boudreaux, "An Agenda, Certainly, but Which?" *Los Angeles Times,* April 20, 2005, 1.

396 A few weeks earlier: *Report on the Holy See's Institutional Knowledge and Decision-Making Related to Former Cardinal Theodore Edgar McCarrick,* November 20, 2020, 227, https://www.vatican.va.

397 The day after: Gayle White, "U.S. Cardinals Voice High Praise of Pope," *The Atlanta Constitution,* April 21, 2005, 7.

397 He backed up: Shawn Boburg, Robert O'Harrow Jr., and Chico Harlan, "Ousted Cardinal McCarrick Gave More Than $600,000 to Fellow Clerics, Including Two Popes," *The Washington Post*, December 26, 2019, http://www.washingtonpost.com.

397 Still, he insisted: *Report on the Holy See's Institutional Knowledge and Decision-Making Related to Former Cardinal Theodore Edgar McCarrick*, November 20, 2020, 233, https://www.vatican.va.

398 In a statement released: Ian Fisher, "Old Foes, Pope and Dissident, Meet to Find Shared Ground," *The New York Times*, September 27, 2005, 3.

398 He declared that every: Benedict XVI, *Last*, 185.

398 His red papal shoes: Ashley Fetters Maloy, "The Hidden Meanings of Pope Benedict XVI's Ruby-Red Shoes," *The Washington Post*, December 31, 2022, http://www.washingtonpost.com.

398 He wore costly: Peter Popham, "Discreet endorsement: Pope Inc. A dedicated follower of fashion," *The Independent*, April 27, 2006, https://www.independent.co.uk.

399 He opened negotiations: Daniel J. Wakin, "Pope Benedict XVI Signs with Geffen," *The New York Times*, August 5, 2009, https://www.nytimes.com.

399 Under new regulations: Daniel Williams and Alan Cooperman, "Vatican Document Sets New Rules on Gays in Seminaries," *The Washington Post*, November 22, 2005, http://www.washingtonpost.com.

399 "But it's better": James C. McKinley Jr., "Pope-to-Be Reopened Mexican Sex Abuse Inquiry," *The New York Times*, April 23, 2005, https://www.nytimes.com.

400 It was prompted instead: Jason Berry, "Legion of Christ's Deception," *National Catholic Reporter*, February 18, 2013, https://www.ncronline.org.

400 In May 2005, barely a month: Ian Fisher, "Vatican Says Mexican Priest Will Not Face Abuse Trial," *The New York Times*, May 22, 2005, https://www.nytimes.com.

401 The young man: *Report on the Holy See's Institutional Knowledge and Decision-Making Related to Former Cardinal Theodore Edgar McCarrick*, November 20, 2020, 257, https://www.vatican.va.

401 "If there had been any": Ibid., 235.

402 In a glowing: Michelle Boorstein, "McCarrick's Approachability, Civility Translated into Popularity," *The Washington Post*, May 16, 2006, http://www.washingtonpost.com.

402 He had been widely mocked: Paddy Agnew, "Cardinal to Rebut *The Da Vinci Code*," *The Irish Times*, March 16, 2005, https://www.irishtimes.com.

33. A SPEECH IN REGENSBURG

403 The emperor sneered: *Lecture of the Holy Father. Faith, Reason and the University. Memories and Reflections*, University of Regensburg, Germany, September 12, 2006, https://www.vatican.va.

404 The deputy leader: Anthony Shadid, "Remarks by Pope Prompt Muslim Outrage, Protests," *The Washington Post*, September 15, 2006, http://www.washingtonpost.com.

404 The violence went on: Ali Daraghmeh, "Five Churches Attacked in West Bank," Associated Press, *The Arizona Republic*, September 17, 2006, 4.

404 An Italian nun working: Tracy Wilkinson, "Pope Issues a Rare 'Sorry,'" *Los Angeles Times*, September 18, 2006, 1.

404 Osama bin Laden: Ian Fisher, "Vatican Rejects bin Laden Tape, but Officials Voice Concern," *The New York Times*, March 20, 2008, https://www.nytimes.com.

404 Benedict frantically tried: "Pope Sorry About Muslim Reaction, Urges Dialogue," *The New York Times*, September 27, 2006, https://www.nytimes.com.

404 The Regensburg disaster: Alexander Smoltczyk, "How the Pope Angered the Muslim World," *Der Spiegel*, November 24, 2006, https://www.spiegel.de/international.

405   Even with the revision: John L. Allen Jr., "The Auschwitz Visit," *National Catholic Reporter*, June 11, 2006, https://www.ncronline.org.

405   Just a year after: Ian Fisher and Laurie Goodstein, "Vatican Punishes a Leader After Abuse Charges," *The New York Times*, May 19, 2006, https://www.nytimes.com.

406   In November, he received: *Report on the Holy See's Institutional Knowledge and Decision-Making Related to Former Cardinal Theodore Edgar McCarrick*, November 20, 2020, 261, https://www.vatican.va.

406   The subject line: Ibid., 262.

407   Even so, he told Bertone: Ibid., 268.

407   On the flight from Rome: John Holusha and Ian Fisher, "Pope Begins U.S. Visit; Says He Is Ashamed of Sex Scandal," *The New York Times*, April 16, 2008, https://www.nytimes.com.

408   Sipe wrote: Richard Sipe, "Statement for Pope Benedict XVI about the Pattern of the Sexual Abuse Crisis in the United States," April 21, 2008, as posted on the website of the victims-rights group BishopAccountabiliy.org, https://www.bishop-accountability.org.

408   The letter also recommended: *Report on the Holy See's Institutional Knowledge and Decision-Making Related to Former Cardinal Theodore Edgar McCarrick*, November 20, 2020, 283, https://www.vatican.va.

34. THE POPE STUMBLES

410   George Weigel: Rachel Donadio and Nicholas Kulish, "Amid Scandals, Questions of Where the Pope's Focus Lies," *The New York Times*, February 16, 2009, https://www.nytimes.com.

410   Father Keith Pecklers: Michael Paulson, "Vatican Grants a Revival for Old-Style Latin Mass," *The Boston Globe*, July 8, 2007, 29.

411   The prayer, dropped when: Tracy Wilkinson and Rebecca Traunson, "Pope Elevates Latin Mass, Leaving Some Polarized," *Los Angeles Times*, July 8, 2007, 3.

411   The International Council for Christians and Jews: Jonathan Petre, "Pope's Plan to Revive Latin Mass 'Could Damage Links with Jews,'" *The Daily Telegraph*, April 28, 2007, 14.

411   The Anti-Defamation League: Jason Burke, "Pope's move on Latin mass 'a blow to Jews,'" *The Observer*, July 8, 2007, https://www.theguardian.com.

411   Instead of referring: Ian Fisher, "Pope's Rewrite of Latin Prayer Draws Criticism From 2 Sides," *The New York Times*, February 6, 2008, https://www.nytimes.com.

411   He told the audience: Ian Fisher, "Pope Tries to Quell Anger over Speech He Gave in Brazil," *The New York Times*, May 23, 2007, https://www.nytimes.com.

412   "It was all lies": Philip Willan, "Pope readmits Holocaust-denying priest to the church," *The Independent*, January 25, 2009, https://www.independent.co.uk.

412   In Germany, Cardinal Lehmann: Rachel Donadio, "Vatican Move on Bishop Exposes Fissures of Church," *The New York Times*, February 5, 2009, https://www.nytimes.com.

412   Rabbi Marvin Hier: Victor L. Simpson, "Pope Tells Bishop to Recant," Associated Press, *The Baltimore Sun*, February 5, 2009, 10.

413   A wounded Benedict: Rachel Donadio, "Vatican Move on Bishop Exposes Fissures of Church," *The New York Times*, February 4, 2009, https://www.nytimes.com.

413   "there was a huge propaganda": Seewald, *Benedict XVI: A Life, Vol. II*, 395.

414   In 2007, a classified cable: "US embassy cables: Vatican's 'moral megaphone' is faulty," *The Guardian*, December 10, 2010, https://www.theguardian.com.

414   "Listen to me carefully": Joachim Frank, "Kardinal Joachim Meisner: Wie soll das gehen? Ein Papst im Ruhestand!" *Frankfurter Rundschau* (Frankfurt, Germany), February 11, 2013, https://www.fr.de. Also see John L. Allen Jr., "A critical tone

among cardinals begins to emerge," *National Catholic Reporter*, February 15, 2013, https://www.ncronline.org.

414 "He certainly was no diplomat": Benedict XVI, *Last*, 226.

414 The memorial's chairman: "The Failed Papacy of Benedict XVI," *Der Spiegel*, June 4, 2010, https://www.spiegel.de/international.

414 George Weigel, the American writer: Peter Steinfels, "From the Vatican, a Tough Read," *The New York Times*, July 17, 2009, https://www.nytimes.com.

414 A religion writer for *The New York Times*: Ibid.

415 He declared that the order: Benedict XVI, *Light*, 52.

416 Many boys described: Geir Moulson, "Report: Hundreds of Boys Abused at German Choir," Associated Press, *The Spokesman-Review* (Spokane, Washington), July 19, 2017, 7.

416 The *Times* tracked down: Nicholas Kulish and Katrin Bennhold, "Doctor Asserts Church Ignored Abuse Warnings," *The New York Times*, March 18, 2010, 1.

417 And that trial: Laurie Goodstein, "Vatican Declined to Defrock U.S. Priest Who Abused Boys," *The New York Times*, March 24, 2010, 1.

417 The longest-serving Catholic bishop: John A. Dick, "Belgian bishop insists he is not a pedophile," *National Catholic Reporter*, April 22, 2011, https://www.ncronline.org.

417 They charged that: Laurie Goodstein, "Abuse Victims Ask Court to Prosecute the Vatican," *The New York Times*, September 13, 2011, 15.

418 As the pope listened: Lewis Smith, "Preacher likens treatment of Pope to the Holocaust," *The Independent*, April 3, 2010, https://www.independent.co.uk.

418 Germany's Central Council: Victor L. Simpson, "Pope's Preacher Sets Off Storm," Associated Press, *The Detroit Free Press*, April 3, 2010, 14.

418 Two days later: John Hooper, "Pope receives Easter Day backing of cardinal amid sex abuse storm," *The Guardian*, April 4, 2010, https://www.theguardian.com.

418 "When we speak up": Guy Dinmore, "Child abuse overshadows Pope's Easter," *Financial Times*, April 4, 2010, https://www.ft.com.

418 "If a pope": Benedict XVI, *Light*, 44.

418 The Vatican said: Delina Castelanos, "Vatican Says Nuns' Group Must Reform," *Los Angeles Times*, April 20, 2012, 7.

419 In 2011, however, she was forced: "Change of Leadership or Change of Direction?" *America* magazine, March 14, 2011, https://www.americamagazine.org.

419 He blamed Benedict: Hans Küng, "Church in worst credibility crisis since Reformation," *The Irish Times*, April 16 2010, https://www.irishtimes.com.

419 In response, the Vatican: George Weigel, "An Open Letter to Hans Küng," *First Things*, April 2, 2010, https://www.firstthings.com.

35. THE VATICAN VS. BUENOS AIRES

420 Father Marco: Patricia Montemurri, "Pontiff Holds First News Conference," Knight Ridder Newspapers, *The Tampa Tribune*, April 24, 2005, 15; Marco interviews.

421 "If we have to sell": Pique, *Pope Francis*, 115.

421 His office issued: Vallely, *Pope Francis: The Struggle*, 36.

421 His visit in November: Ingrid D. Rowland, "The Fall of the Vice-Pope," *The New York Review of Books*, June 16, 2014, https://www.nybooks.com.

422 "He's been totally": Nick Miroff, "Pope Francis Was Often Quiet on Argentine Sex Abuse Cases as Archbishop," *The Washington Post*, March 18, 2013, https://www.washingtonpost.com; Moreau interviews.

422 After his conviction: Vallely, *Pope Francis: The Struggle*, 483.

423 He believed the Kirchners: Philip Pullela, "Pope says Argentina government wanted 'my head' when he was in Buenos Aires," Reuters, May 9, 2023, https://www.reuters.com.

423 Bergoglio made a final: John Corvino, "A Papal Surprise: Humility," *The New York Times*, July 30, 2013, https://www.nytimes.com.

424 During his occasional: Pique, *Pope Francis*, 133.

424 The region's church: Ernesto Cavassa, "On the Trail of Aparecida: Jorge Bergoglio and the Latin American Ecclesial Tradition," *America* magazine, October 30, 2013, https://www.americamagazine.org.

424 Fernández, then forty-four: Fernández, *The Francis Project*, 107.

425 The book, which even: Colleen Dulle, "Same-sex blessing, the 'kissing book' and abuse," *America* magazine, July 6, 2023, https://www.americamagazine.org.

425 He was offered: Magena Valentie, "Bergoglio's Neighborhood; The Home That No Longer Waits for Father Jorge," *La Gaceta* (Tucumán, Argentina), March 16, 2013, https://www.lagaceta.com.ar.

426 The package ended: Edward Pentin, "Cardinal Müller Confirms Vatican Doctrinal Office Had File Warning About Archbishop Fernández," *National Catholic Register*, July 6, 2023, https://www.ncregister.com.

426 When it became clear: Sandro Magister, "Amoris Laetitia Has a Ghostwriter," *L'Espresso*, May 25, 2016, http://www.chiesa.espressonline.com.

36. WHAT THE BUTLER SAW

427 "We are dealing with": Mark Hallam, "Catholic Cover-ups," Deutsche Welle, December 3, 2010, https://www.dw.com.

427 She could identify: "Cardinal's Plea: Forgive the Church," Associated Press, *Tampa Bay Times*, December 4, 2010, https://www.tampabay.com.

428 "We *all* knew": Jack Crowe, "Bishop: 'We All Knew' of McCarrick's Abuse," *National Review*, August 30, 2018, https://www.nationalreview.com.

428 A confidential memo: *Report on the Holy See's Institutional Knowledge and Decision-Making Related to Former Cardinal Theodore Edgar McCarrick*, November 20, 2020, 352, https://www.vatican.va.

429 At a charity dinner: Ibid., 370.

429 The following month: Leo Cendrowicz, "Tolerant Dutch Shocked by Accusations the Church Forced Castrations," *Time*, March 23, 2012, https://time.com.

429 In a widely mocked: John L. Allen Jr., "Pope sees the Devil behind timing of sex abuse crisis," *National Catholic Reporter*, June 11, 2010, https://www.ncronline.org.

431 Viganò told: Jason Horowitz, "Archbishop at Center of Mystery of Papal Meeting with Kim Davis," *The New York Times*, October 2, 2015, 3.

431 He was stung: Tony Paterson, "German satirical magazine in trouble over Papal 'leaks,'" *The Independent*, July 22, 2012, https://www.independent.co.uk.

432 According to Fausti: Gian Guido Vecchi, "Quando Martini disse a Ratzinger: La Curia non cambia, devi lasciare" (When Martini said to Ratzinger: "The Curia doesn't change, you have to leave"), *Corriere della Sera* (Milan, Italy), July 16, 2015, https://www.corriere.it.

432 "No one had tried": Benedict XVI, *Last*, 24.

433 He did not despair: Ibid., 15.

433 The church "is 200 years": John Hooper, "Italy mourns cardinal who said Catholic church was 200 years out of date," *The Guardian*, September 3, 2012, https://www.theguardian.com.

433 "That will be the worst": Markus Grill, "'I Don't Cling to This Life,'" *Der Spiegel*, December 12, 2013, https://www.spiegel.de/international.

433 "I can do it like Socrates": Jimmy Burns, "Frank Exchanges," *The Tablet*, February 1, 2014, 6.

433 He was sad only: Markus Grill, "'I Don't Cling to This Life,'" *Der Spiegel*, December 12, 2013, https://www.spiegel.de/international.

434   He compared Benedict: Hans Küng, "A Putinization of the Catholic Church," *Der Spiegel*, September 21, 2011, https://www.spiegel.de/international.

434   It was a promise: Kasper, *Mercy*, 15.

436   He refused to discuss publicly: Benedict XVI, *Last*, 230.

436   He originally considered: Ibid., 17.

436   "I felt my stomach": Leo Cushley, "A monsignor sobbed, then silence fell: an eye-witness account of Pope Benedict XVI's resignation," *Catholic Herald*, February 11, 2015, www.catholicherald.co.uk.

437   German chancellor Merkel: Kevin Cote, "'A Sense of Duty': Germany Reacts to Pope Benedict XVI's Resignation," *Time*, February 11, 2013, https://time.com.

437   The left-leaning: "It Is Good That Benedict Is Gone," *Der Spiegel*, December 2, 2013, https://www.spiegel.de/international.

437   Days later, Hans Küng: Hans Küng, "A Vatican Spring?," *The New York Times*, February 27, 2013, 29.

437   He said he was departing: Alessandro Speciale, "Pope Benedict Defends Choice to Resign in Last Public Address," *The Washington Post*, February 27, 2013, http://www.washingtonpost.com.

438   There was an obvious: Murphy-O'Connor, *An English Spring*, 224.

439   In 2010: Steven Erlanger, "Belgian Church Leader Urged Victim to Be Silent," *The New York Times*, August 29, 2010, https://www.nytimes.com.

37. "CARNIVAL TIME IS OVER"

443   Father Fernández: Fernández, *The Francis Project*, 108.

443   They thought it might explain: Within weeks of Bergoglio's election as pope in 2013, *El Jesuita* was translated into English and published with the title *Pope Francis: Conversations with Jorge Bergoglio, His Life in His Own Words* (New York: G. P. Putnam's Sons, 2013).

443   While he always denounced: Rubin and Ambrogetti. *Pope Francis: Conversations*, 109.

444   He recalled reading: Ibid., 87.

444   "Benedict had surely": Pope Francis, *Life*, 174.

444   The lobbying began: Murphy-O'Connor, *An English Spring*, 224.

445   "There was stillness": Ibid., 227.

445   Ouellet of Canada, a rival: Christopher Lamb, "No longer prisoners of the past," *The Tablet*, October 26, 2017, https://www.thetablet.co.uk.

446   "Ah, mercy": Thomas Ryan, "Kasper's book: Mercy has been 'criminally neglected,'" *National Catholic Reporter*, October 8, 2014, https://www.ncronline.org.

446   The rumors of: Pique, *Pope Francis*, 26.

446   An Indian cardinal: Ibid., 28.

446   Bergoglio later acknowledged: Antonio Spadaro, "A Big Heart Open to God: An Interview with Pope Francis," *America* magazine, September 30, 2013, https://www.americamagazine.org.

446   The cardinal seated: Michael Collins, *Francis*, 102.

447   "Those words came": Joshua J. McElwee, "Pope Francis: 'I would love a church that is poor,'" *National Catholic Reporter*, March 16, 2013, https://www.ncronline.org.

447   "No, thank you": John A. Allen Jr., "Yet another mystery emerges about what the Pope actually said," Crux News, November 19, 2023, https://cruxnow.com.

448   Benedict picked up: O'Connell, *The Election*, 358.

449   A *New York Times*: Elisabetta Povoledo and Rachel Donadio, "Francis Vows to Serve 'Poorest, Weakest' and Urges Leaders to Offer Hope," *The New York Times*, March 19, 2013, 12.

449   "There's room for": Vallely, *Pope Francis: The Struggle*, 265.

451   "Holy Father, you cannot": David Gibson, "Cardinal Kasper, the 'pope's theolo-

gian,' downplays Vatican blast at U.S. nuns," *National Catholic Reporter*, May 6, 2014, https://www.ncronline.org.

38. "WHO AM I TO JUDGE?"

452 He decided against: Joshua J. McElwee, "Pope Francis uses recycled ring from era of Paul VI," *National Catholic Reporter*, March 18, 2013, https://www.ncronline.org.

453 "They criticize me": Ivereigh, *Wounded*, 70.

453 Father Nicholas King, a Jesuit lecturer: Nicholas King, "Habemus Papam Franciscum," Thinking Faith, the Online Journal of Jesuits in Britain, March 15, 2013, https://www.thinkingfaith.org.

454 "He had it all": *Apostolic Journey to Rio de Janeiro on the Occasion of the XXVIII World Youth Day, Press Conference of Pope Francis During the Return Flight*, July 28, 2013, https://www.vatican.va.

455 A law professor: David Gibson, "Is Benedict XVI the REAL Pope? Four Factors Fueling Vatican Conspiracy Theories," *The Washington Post*, November 26, 2014, http://www.washingtonpost.com.

455 A pope could live: Benedict XVI, *Last*, 31.

455 With a touch of regret: Ibid.

456 "It's not the key": Draper, *Pope Francis*, 34.

456 "I do it": Vallely, *Pope Francis: Untying*, 187.

457 "My heart was": Carol Glatz, "Pope's embrace was heavenly, says man with disfiguring disease," *National Catholic Reporter*, November 19, 2013, https://www.ncronline .org.

457 "We have become": Vallely, *Pope Francis: Untying*, 186.

457 "I haven't found anyone": *Apostolic Journey to Rio de Janeiro on the Occasion of the XXVIII World Youth Day, Press Conference of Pope Francis During the Return Flight*, July 28, 2013, https://www.vatican.va.

458 In April, Leonardo: Hesselmans and Teubner, *An Analysis*, 66.

458 In December, in an interview: Markus Grill, "'I Don't Cling to This Life,'" *Der Spiegel*, December 12, 2013, https://www.spiegel.de/international.

459 "The pope is somebody": David Jackson, "Obama 'Hugely Impressed' with Pope Francis," *USA Today*, October 2, 2013, https://www.usatoday.com.

459 The British entertainer: "Pope Francis should be canonised for reaching out to gay people," Associated Press, *The Guardian*, October 29, 2014, https://www.theguardian .com.

459 The church, he said: Antonio Spadaro, "A Big Heart Open to God: An Interview with Pope Francis," *America* magazine, September 30, 2013, https://www.america magazine.org.

460 Cardinal Timothy Dolan: Lisa W. Foderaro, "Dolan Calls Pope's Tone on Sexual Morality a 'Breath of Fresh Air,'" *The New York Times*, September 22, 2013, 17.

460 On that subject: David Gibson: "Pope Francis's Vatican reforms may prompt curial pushback," *National Catholic Reporter*, December 17, 2013, https://www.ncronline .org.

460 He said some earlier: Laurie Goodstein, "Pope Assails Bureaucracy of Church as Insular," *The New York Times*, October 1, 2013, 6.

461 Bertone took his: Tom Kingston, "I Was Surrounded by Vipers," *The Daily Telegraph* (London), September 3, 2013. Also see Vallely, *Pope Francis: The Struggle*, 271.

461 In October 2013: Terrence McCoy, "How the 'Bishop of Bling' Spent $43 Million Renovating This House," *The Washington Post*, March 28, 2014, http://www .washingtonpost.com.

39. INTO THE LION'S DEN

462 From the day: Ivereigh, *The Great Reformer*, 365.

462 "He's another person": Pique, *Pope Francis*, 275.

463 In June 2013: John Borelli, "Two of a Kind," *The Tablet*, June 15, 2013, https://www.thetablet.co.uk.

463 By canonizing them: Jim Yardley, "Sainthood for 2 Predecessors Allows Pope to Straddle Divide," *The New York Times*, April 26, 2014, 1.

464 Even so, Kasper: Gerald O'Connell, "After a conclave that demanded reform, a year of 'fresh air,'" *National Catholic Reporter*, March 8, 2014, https://www.ncronline.org.

464 "That door is closed": Diane Winston, "Pope Francis's Woman Problem," *Los Angeles Times*, August 6, 2013, 40.

464 "I felt he": Ana B. Hernández, "El Bendito Encuentro Entre Francisco y Diego" (The Blessed Meeting Between Francis and Diego), *Hoy* (Badajoz, Spain), January 25, 2015, https://www.hoy.es. Also see Thomas C. Fox, "Report: Pope Francis meets with, hugs transgender man," *National Catholic Reporter*, January 30, 2015, https://www.ncronline.org.

466 "The pope is not": Liz Dodd and James Roberts, "Burke lashes out at Kasper over divorce and remarriage," *The Tablet*, October 1, 2014, https://www.thetablet.co.uk.

466 A conservative columnist: Ross Douthat, "A Catholic Dilemma," *The New York Times*, May 9, 2014, https://www.nytimes.com. Also see Ross Douthat, "The Pope's Marriage Endgame," *The New York Times*, September 12, 2015, SR11.

466 He, Burke, and three other: Robert Dodaro, ed., *Remaining in the Truth of Christ: Marriage and Communion in the Catholic Church* (San Francisco: Ignatius Press, 2014).

467 In the final weeks: "Muller Compares Mood Toward Catholic Church to Anti-Jewish Pogroms," *La Stampa* (Italy), February 2, 2013, https://www.lastampa.it. Also see "Top Vatican Cleric Criticized for 'Pogrom' Remark," *Der Spiegel*, April 2, 2013, https://www.spiegel.de/international.

467 The nuns' defenders: Jason Horowitz, "Biden, a Catholic School 'Kid,' Praises Nuns Under Fire from the Vatican," *The New York Times*, September 17, 2014, 22.

468 "The Catholic Church": E. J. Dionne Jr., "Pope Francis's First Year Underlines His Commitment to the Needy," *The Washington Post*, March 12, 2014, http://www.washingtonpost.com.

468 Just a few months: Laurie Goodstein, "For Nuncio Accused of Abuse, Dominicans Want Justice at Home, Not Abroad," *The New York Times*, August 23, 2014, 1.

469 The pope *did* remember: *Report on the Holy See's Institutional Knowledge and Decision-Making Related to Former Cardinal Theodore Edgar McCarrick*, November 20, 2020, 415, https://www.vatican.va.

40. "CATHOLICS LOVE ME"

471 He described: *Holy Mass and Rite of Canonization of Blessed John XXIII and John Paul II*, *Homily of Pope Francis*, April 27, 2014, https://www.vatican.va.

472 One figure in the: Jason Horowitz, "Steve Bannon Carries Battles to Another Influential Hub: The Vatican," *The New York Times*, February 7, 2017, 1.

472 He repeated the: Elisabetta Povoledo, "Pope Francis Calls for Candor at Meeting on Family Issues," *The New York Times*, October 6, 2014, 4.

473 According to several news reports: Müller later denied making the remark after it was widely attributed to him by Italian journalists. Members of the Vatican press corps were convinced that, whatever his precise words, the quotation accurately reflected his views.

473 A reference to: Elizabeth Dias, "Vatican Changes Draft Report Translation About Welcoming Gays," *Time*, October 16, 2014, https://time.com.

473 In his closing: John A. Allen Jr., "Divided bishops water down welcome to gays and the divorced," Crux News, October 18, 2014, https://cruxnow.com.

473 In a magazine interview: Josephine McKenna, "Burke: Church under Francis is a 'ship without a rudder,'" *National Catholic Reporter*, October 31, 2014, https://www .ncronline.org.

473 The fiercely conservative: Vallely, *Pope Francis: The Struggle*, 276.

474 In Rome, Sarah: Jeffrey Gettleman and Laurie Goodstein, "A More Conservative Catholic Church Awaits Pope Francis in Africa," *The New York Times*, November 25, 2015, 12.

474 "He saw it": Cruz interviews.

475 "The Osorno community": Adam Taylor, "Pope Francis Says Chilean Protests over Alleged Child Abuse Cover-Up Are 'Dumb,'" *The Washington Post*, October 8, 2015, https://www.washingtonpost.com.

475 "We are now seeing": Pascale Bonnefoy, "Calling Protesters in Chile 'Dumb,' Pope Francis Sets Off Uproar," *The New York Times*, October 7, 2015, 12.

476 In confirming the: David Gibson, "Pope Francis Met Kentucky Clerk Kim Davis: 'Stay Strong!'" *The Washington Post*, September 30, 2015, https://www.washington post.com.

476 The pope's meeting: Patrik Jonsson, "Pope Francis Met Kim Davis: Why It Matters in Fight over Religious Freedom," *The Christian Science Monitor*, September 30, 2015, https://www.csmonitor.com.

477 The synod's final report: *XIV Ordinary General Assembly. The Vocation and Mission of the Family in the Church and in the Contemporary World. The Final Report of the Synod of Bishops to the Holy Father*, October 24, 2015, https://www.vatican.va.

477 "Today is a time": *Holy Mass for the Closing of the XIV Ordinary General Assembly of the Synod of Bishops. Homily of His Holiness Pope Francis*, October 25, 2015, https://www .vatican.va.

477 He reminded the entire: *Misericordiae Vultus, Bull of Indiction of the Extraordinary Jubilee of Mercy*, April 14, 2015, https://www.vatican.va.

478 In April, he released: *Post-Synodal Apostolic Exhortation Amoris Laetitia of the Holy Father Francis to Bishops, Priests and Deacons, Consecrated Persons, Christian Married Couples and All the Lay Faithful on Love in the Family*, March 19, 2016, https://www .vatican.va.

478 The pope's document: Christopher Lamb, "Cardinal Walter Kasper: Amoris Laetitia 'changes everything,'" *The Tablet*, April 14, 2016, https://www.thetablet.co.uk.

478 Insisting he spoke: Cindy Wooden, "Four Cardinals are asking Pope Francis to clarify his teaching on Communion for divorced," *America* magazine, November 14, 2016, https://www.americamagazine.org.

478 In September, Argentina's bishops: Christopher Lamb, "Pope praises Argentinian bishops' correct interpretation of Amoris Laetitia," *The Tablet*, September 13, 2016, https://www.thetablet.co.uk.

479 In an extraordinary act: Edward Pentin, "Four Cardinals Formally Ask Pope for Clarity," *National Catholic Register*, November 14, 2016, https://www.ncregister .com.

479 Burke gave interviews: Robert Mickens, "Another embittered cardinal threatens the pope," *La Croix International*, December 1, 2017, https://international.la-croix.com.

479 "I think the pope": Rebecca Kaplan, "Donald Trump Calls Pope Francis 'A Very Political Person,'" CBS News, February 11, 2016, https://www.cbsnews.com.

479 "He should just": David A. Fahrenthold, "New Clips Show Trump Talking about Sex, Rating Women's Bodies, Reminiscing about Infidelity on Howard Stern's Show," *The Washington Post*, October 14, 2016, https://www.washingtonpost.com.

479 On the flight: Harriet Sherwood, "Pope Francis appears to criticize Trump's Mexico border wall plan," *The Guardian*, February 8, 2016, https://www.theguardian.com.

479   It was "disgraceful": Patrick Healy, "Donald Trump Fires Back at Sharp Rebuke by Pope Francis," *The New York Times*, February 18, 2016, 1.

480   "Jesus never intended": Francis X. Rocca and Felicia Schwartz, "Pope Francis and Donald Trump Spar Over Immigration," *The Wall Street Journal*, February 18, 2016, https://www.wsj.com.

480   Bishop Thomas Tobin: Katherine Gregg, "R.I. Priest: Vote for Clinton Would Put 'Immortal Soul' in Peril," *The Providence Journal*, October 27, 2016, https://www.providencejournal.com.

480   He said the new president: Josephine McKenna, "Cardinal Burke: Trump will defend human life from conception," *National Catholic Reporter*, November 10, 2016, https://www.ncronline.org.

480   Trump's election alarmed: Craig Silverman, "This Analysis Shows How Viral Fake Election News Stories Outperformed Real News on Facebook," BuzzFeed News, November 16, 2016, https://www.buzzfeednews.com.

480   Two days after: "Pope Francis warns against rise in populism," BBC News, January 22, 2017, https://www.bbc.com/news.

481   The pope managed: Mark Moore and Ruth Brown, "Pope to Melania: What Are You Feeding Trump?" *The New York Post*, May 24, 2017, https://nypost.com.

482   A month after: Michael J. O'Loughlin, "Philly archbishop says the press is being too hard on President Trump," *America* magazine, February 13, 2017, https://www.americamagazine.org.

482   The article was: Antonio Spadaro and Marcelo Figueroa, "Evangelical Fundamentalism and Catholic Integralism in the USA: A surprising ecumenism," *La Civiltà Cattolica*, July 13, 2017, https://www.laciviltacattolica.com.

482   Archbishop Chaput said: "Archbishop Chaput: *Civiltà Cattolica* article was an 'exercise in dumbing down,'" *Catholic Herald*, July 19, 2017, https://catholicherald.co.uk.

483   It condemned the: Melissa Eddy, "'Culture of Silence' Abetted Abuse of at Least 547
483   Choir Boys, Inquiry Finds," *The New York Times*, July 18, 2017, 10.

41. THE NETWORK

484   Just days before: Filip Mazurczak, "Benedict XVI Warns of 'Dangerous Situation' with Radical Atheism and Radical Islam," *National Catholic Register*, May 1, 2017, https://www.ncregister.com.

485   He announced he: Ben Munster, "The Last Stand at Steve Bannon's 'Gladiator School,'" *The New Yorker*, May 24, 2021, https://www.newyorker.com.

486   The first signs: Nicole Winfield, "Pope Quietly Trims Sanctions for Sex Abusers Seeking Mercy," Associated Press, February 25, 2017, https://apnews.com.

486   That March, its highest: "Sex Abuse Survivor Marie Collins Quits Pope Francis's Commission to Protect Minors," CBS News, March 2, 2017, https://www.cbsnews.com.

486   The pope told: Nicole Winfield, "Pope Acknowledges 2,000-Case Backlog in Sex Abuse Cases," Associated Press, May 13, 2017, https://apnews.com.

488   The foundation acknowledged: Francis X. Rocca, "U.S. Donors Balk at $25 Million Vatican Request," *The Wall Street Journal*, February 23, 2018, https://www.wsj.com.

42. THE YEAR OF LIVING DESPERATELY

489   "He was defamed": "Romero 'Defamed,'" *America* magazine, November 4, 2015, https://www.americamagazine.org. Also see Philip Pullella, "Pope Denounces Clergy Who Criticized Romero," Reuters, October 30, 2015, https://www.reuters.com.

490   Leafets left outside: Pascale Bonnefoy, "Pope Faces Turmoil in Chile Over Indigenous Group and Sex Abuse," *The New York Times*, January 12, 2018, 6.

490   "The day someone": "Pope Francis 'slander' comment angers Chile abuse victims," BBC News, January 19, 2018, https://www.bbc.com.

490   Days later: Nicole Winfield and Eva Vergara, "AP Exclusive: 2015 Letter Belies Pope's Claim of Ignorance," Associated Press, February 5, 2018, https://apnews .com; and Elizabeth Povoledo, "Letter Suggests Pope Knew About Abuse Complaints, Despite Denials," *The New York Times*, February 5, 2018, 5.

490   He said Francis's: Joshua McElwee, "Cardinal O'Malley: Pope caused 'great pain' for abuse survivors in Chile," *National Catholic Reporter*, January 20, 2018, https://www.ncronline.org.

490   Meeting with reporters: Rick Noack, "Pope Admits 'Grave Error,' Apologizes for Not Believing Chilean Sex Abuse Victims," *The Washington Post*, April 12, 2018, https://www.washingtonpost.com.

491   "I have never": Interviews with Juan Carlos Cruz, James Hamilton, and José Andrés Murillo. Also see Elisabetta Povoledo, "Abuse Victims Meet with Pope Francis: 'We Need Concrete Actions,'" *The New York Times*, May 2, 2018, 9.

493   Viganò claimed: Chico Harlan, Stefano Pitrelli, and Michelle Boorstein, "Former Vatican Ambassador Says Popes Francis, Benedict Knew of Sexual Misconduct Allegations Against McCarrick for Years," *The Washington Post*, August 26, 2018, https://www.washingtonpost.com.

493   "I will not": Daniel Burke, "The 'Coup' Against Pope Francis," CNN, August 27, 2018, https://www.cnn.com.

493   He announced he: Megan Keller, "Bannon wants to see sexual abuse tribunal instead of pope's resignation," *The Hill*, September 9, 2018, https://thehill.com.

495   In his homily: *Holy Mass and Canonization of the Blessed. Paolo VI, Óscar Romero, Francesco Spinelli, Vincenzo Romano, Maria Caterina Kasper, Nazaria Ignazia di Santa Teresa di Gesù, Nunzio Sulprizio, Homily of His Holiness Pope Francis*, October 14, 2018, https://www.vatican.va.

43. A PAPACY "BEGINS ANEW"

496   In a newspaper: Cindy Wooden, "Pope Reveals He Prepared Resignation Letter in Case of Impairment," *National Catholic Reporter*, December 19, 1992, https://www .ncronline.org.

497   That afternoon, the Vatican: Benedict XVI, *My Spiritual Testament*, December 22, 2022, https://www.vatican.va.

498   Alberto Melloni: Chico Harlan and Stefano Pitrelli, "Historic But Spare Funeral for Pope Benedict XVI," *The Washington Post*, January 5, 2023, https://www.washington post.com.

498   Francis presided over: *Homily of His Holiness Pope Francis*, January 5, 2023, https://www.vatican.va.

498   The conservative American: Rod Dreher, "Lessons from Pope Benedict's Funeral," *The American Conservative*, January 5, 2023, https://www.theamericanconservative .com.

498   A week after: Simon Caldwell, "Curbs on Traditional Latin Mass 'Broke Pope Benedict's heart,'" *The Catholic Herald*, January 4, 2023, https://catholicherald.co.uk.

498   Benedict's authorized biographer: AC Wimmer, "'Benedict Trusted Francis. But He Was Bitterly Disappointed,' Biographer Says," EWTN Vatican, December 29, 2023, https://www.ewtnvatican.com.

501   Fernández's appointment: Christopher Lamb, "Francis Orders Regime Change at Doctrine Office," *The Tablet*, July 2, 2023, https://www.thetablet.co.uk.

501   He described the investigation: "The Congregation for the Doctrine of the Faith

'Even Investigated Me,'" *Katholisches* (Catholic) magazine, July 5, 2023, https://katholisches.info.

501 The American victims': Peter Pinedo, "Bishop Accountability Group Voices Concerns About Archbishop Fernández Appointment," Catholic News Agency, July 3, 2023, https://www.catholicnewsagency.com.

502 The Italian-based: Luisella Scrosati, "Orgasm Like Paradise, Fernández's Porn-Theology," *The Daily Compass*, January 1, 2024, https://newdailycompass.com.

502 Phil Lawler: Phil Lawler, "With This Appointment, the Pope Repudiates His Predecessor," Catholic Culture, July 18, 2023, https://www.catholicculture.org.

504 "That was my conversion": Nicole Winfield, "Pope Opens Up on Sex Abuse Cases, Says Church Must Do More," Associated Press, January 23, 2023, https://apnews.com.

506 The head of: "Top German Bishop Again Calls for an Apology from Retired Pope Benedict," *National Catholic Reporter*, January 31, 2022, https://www.ncronline.org.

506 As requested, Benedict: *Letter of Pope Emeritus Benedict XVI Regarding the Report on Abuse in the Archdiocese of Munich-Freising*, February 6, 2022, https://press.vatican.va.

506 In 2023, many Poles: Shaun Walker and Katarzyna Piasecka, "'What Did the Pope Know?' Poles Divided Over John Paul II Abuse Cover-Up Claims," *The Guardian*, May 16, 2023, https://www.theguardian.com.

507 "As a moral leader": Jason Berry, "Historian's New Book Highlights Pius XII's Moral Failures," *National Catholic Reporter*, July 2, 2022, https://www.ncronline.org.

508 Entitled "On the Pastoral Meaning": *Fiducia Supplicans: On the Pastoral Meaning of Blessings*, December 18, 2023, https://www.vatican.va.

509 In interviews: Cindy Wooden, "Pope Francis: I Don't Bless a 'Homosexual Marriage.' I Bless Two People Who Love Each Other," *America* magazine, February 7, 2024, https://www.americamagazine.org.

Bibliography

Abbott, Walter M. *Twelve Council Fathers*. New York: Macmillan, 1963.

Acosta, Miguel, and Adrian Reimers. *Karol Wojtyła's Personalist Philosophy*. Washington: Catholic University of America Press, 2019.

Aguilar, Mario. *Pope Francis: His Life and Thought*. Cambridge: The Lutterworth Press, 2014.

Alberigo, Giuseppe. *A Brief History of Vatican II*. Maryknoll, NY: Orbis Books, 2006.

Allen, John L. Jr. *All the Pope's Men: The Inside Story of How the Vatican Really Thinks*. New York: Doubleday, 2004.

———. *Cardinal Ratzinger: The Vatican's Enforcer of the Faith*. London: Continuum, 2001.

———. *Opus Dei*. New York: Image Books, 2007.

———. *Pope Benedict XVI: A Biography of Joseph Ratzinger*. New York: Continuum, 2000.

———. *The Rise of Benedict XVI*. New York: Doubleday, 2005.

Ambrogetti, Francesca, and Sergio Rubin. *Pope Francis: His Life in His Own Words*. New York: New American Library, 2014.

Anonymous. *Against Ratzinger*. New York: Seven Stories Press, 2008.

Armstrong, Karen. *The Bible: A Biography*. New York: Grove Press, 2007.

Arrupe, Pedro. *Itinéraire d'un Jésuite* (Itinerary of a Jesuit). Paris: Le Centurion, 1982.

———. *Pedro Arrupe: Essential Writings*. Maryknoll, NY: Orbis Books, 2004.

———. *Recollections and Reflections of Pedro Arrupe, S.J.* Wilmington, DE: Michael Glazier, 1986.

Aslan, Reza. *Zealot: The Life and Times of Jesus of Nazareth*. New York: Random House, 2013.

Augias, Corrado. *The Secrets of Rome: Love and Death in the Eternal City*. Milan: Rizzoli, 2007.

Baigent, Michael, Richard Leigh, and Henry Lincoln. *Holy Blood, Holy Grail: The Secret History of Christ*. New York: Bantam Dell, 2004.

Bea, Augustin (Cardinal). *The Church and the Jewish People: A Commentary on the Second Vatican Council's Declaration on the Relation of the Church to Non-Christian Religions*. New York: Harper & Row, 1966.

———. *The Way to Unity After the Council*. London: Geoffrey Chapman, 1967.

Bellitto, Christopher M. *Popes and the Papacy*. Mahwah, NJ: Paulist Press, 2008.

Bello, Omar. *El Verdadero Francisco* (The Real Francis). Buenos Aires: Ediciones Noticias, 2013.

Benedict XVI, Pope, with Peter Seewald. *Last Testament in His Own Words*. London: Bloomsbury, 2016.

———. *Light of the World: The Pope, the Church and the Signs of the Times*. San Francisco: Ignatius Press, 2010.

Bergoglio, Jorge Mario. *Education for Choosing Life: Proposals for Difficult Times*. San Francisco: Ignatius Press, 2014.

———. *The Way of Humility: Corruption and Sin*. San Francisco: Ignatius Press, 2013.

Bergoglio, Jorge Mario, and Abraham Skorka. *On Heaven and Earth*. New York: Image, 2013.

Bermúdez, Alejandro, ed. *Pope Francis: Our Brother, Our Friend*. San Francisco: Ignatius Press, 2013.

Bernstein, Carl, and Marco Politi. *His Holiness: John Paul II and the History of Our Time*. New York: Penguin Books, 1996.

Berrigan, Daniel. *To Dwell in Peace: An Autobiography*. New York: Harper & Row, 1987.

Berry, Jason, and Gerald Renner. *Vows of Silence: The Abuse of Power in the Papacy of John Paul II*. New York: Free Press, 2004.

Berry, Jason. *Lead Us Not into Temptation: Catholic Priests and the Sexual Abuse of Children*. New York: Doubleday, 1992.

Berryman, Phillip. *Liberation Theology: The Essential Facts About the Revolutionary Movement in Latin America and Beyond*. New York: Pantheon Books, 1987.

Bishop, George. *Pedro Arrupe SJ*. Leominster, UK: Gracewing, 2007.

Boeve, Lieven, and Gerard Mannion. *The Ratzinger Reader*. London: T & T Clark, 2010.

Boff, Clodovis. *Feet-on-the-Ground Theology: A Brazilian Journey*. Maryknoll, NY: Orbis Books, 1987.

Boff, Leonardo. *Francis of Rome, Francis of Assisi*. Maryknoll, NY: Orbis Books, 2014.

———. *Liberation Theology: From Dialogue to Confrontation*. New York: Harper & Row, 1986.

———. *Saint Francis: A Model for Human Liberation*. New York: Crossword, 1982.

Borghesi, Massimo. *The Mind of Pope Francis*. Collegeville, MN: Liturgical Press Academic, 2017.

Briggs, Kenneth A. *Holy Siege: The Year That Shook Catholic America*. San Francisco: HarperSanFrancisco, 1992.

Brockman, James R. *Romero: A Life*. Maryknoll, NY: Orbis Books, 2005.

Brown, Robert McAfee. *The Ecumenical Revolution*. Garden City, NY: Doubleday, 1969.

Brown-Fleming, Suzanne. *The Holocaust and Catholic Conscience*. Notre Dame, IN: University of Notre Dame Press, 2006.

Burke, Raymond Leo. *Hope for the World: To Unite All Things in Christ*. San Francisco: Ignatius Press, 2015.

Burns, Charles. *The Election of a Pope*. Rome: Catholic Truth Society, 2005.

Burns, Jimmy. *Francis, Pope of Good Promise*. New York: St. Martin's Press, 2015.

Cahill, Thomas. *Pope John XXIII*. New York: Viking, 2002.

Câmara, Hélder. *The Desert Is Fertile*. Maryknoll, NY: Orbis Books, 1974.

———. *Hoping Against All Hope*. Maryknoll, NY: Orbis Books, 1984.

———. *Revolution Through Peace*. New York: Harper Colophon, 1972.

———. *A Thousand Reasons for Living*. Philadelphia: Fortress Press, 1981.

Cámara, Javier, and Sebastian Pfaffen. *Understanding Pope Francis*. Scotts Valley, CA: CreateSpace Independent Publishing, 2015.

Capovilla, Loris. *The Heart and Mind of John XXIII*. New York: Hawthorn Books, 1964.

Carpenter, Edward. *Archbishop Fisher: His Life and Times*. Norwich, Norfolk, UK: Canterbury Press, 1991.

Carroll, James. *An American Requiem: God, My Father and the War that Came Between Us*. Boston: Mariner Books, 1996.

———. *Constantine's Sword: The Church and the Jews*. Boston: Mariner Books, 2002.

Catoir, John T. *Encounters with Holiness.* New York: St. Paul's, 2007.

Cavallari, Alberto. *The Changing Vatican.* Garden City, NY: Doubleday, 1967.

Cessario, Romanus. *Boston's Cardinal: Bernard Law, the Man and His Witness.* Lanham, MD: Lexington Books, 2002.

Chaput, Charles J. *Living the Catholic Faith, Rediscovering the Basics.* Ann Arbor, MI: Servant Publications, 2001.

Charamsa, Krzysztof. *La Prima Pietra* (The First Stone). Milan: Rizzoli, 2016.

Chesterton, G. K. *Saint Francis of Assisi.* Nashville, TN: Sam Torode Book Arts, 1924.

Chiron, Yves. *Paul VI: The Divided Pope.* New York: Angelico Press, 2022.

Clancy, John G. *Apostle for Our Time: Pope Paul VI.* New York: P. J. Kenedy & Sons, 1963.

Clarke, Kevin. *Oscar Romero: Love Must Win Out.* Collegeville, MN: Liturgical Press, 2014.

Clifford, Catherine E., and Massimo Faggioli, eds. *The Oxford Handbook of Vatican II.* Oxford: Oxford University Press, 2023.

Colberg, Kristin M., and Robert A. Krieg, eds. *The Theology of Walter Kasper.* Collegeville, MN: Liturgical Press, 2014.

Collins, Michael. *Francis, Bishop of Rome: A Short Biography.* Collegeville, MN: Liturgical Press, 2013.

———. *Pope Benedict XVI: Successor to Peter.* New York: Paulist Press, 2005.

———. *The Vatican: Secrets and Treasures of the Holy City.* New York: DK Publishing, 2014.

Collins, Paul. *Absolute Power.* New York: PublicAffairs, 2018.

———. *From Inquisition to Freedom.* New York: Simon & Schuster, 2001.

———. *God's New Man: The Election of Benedict XVI and the Legacy of John Paul II.* London: Continuum, 2005.

———. *Papal Power.* London: Fount, 1997.

Colonna, Marcantonio. *The Dictator Pope: The Inside Story of the Francis Papacy.* Washington: Regnery Publishing, 2017.

Conde, Angeles, and David J. P. Murray. *The Legion of Christ: A History.* North Haven, CT: Circle Press, 2004.

Congar, Yves. *My Journal of the Council.* Collegeville, MN: Liturgical Press, 2012.

Cooney, John. *The American Pope: The Life and Times of Francis Cardinal Spellman.* New York: Times Books, 1984.

Cornwell, John. *Breaking Faith: Can the Catholic Church Save Itself?* New York: Penguin Compass, 2002.

———. *Hitler's Pope: The Secret History of Pius XII.* New York: Viking, 1999.

———. *A Thief in the Night: The Mysterious Death of Pope John Paul I.* New York: Simon & Schuster, 1989.

Cox, Harvey. *The Silencing of Leonardo Boff.* Oak Park, IL: Meyer-Stone Books, 1988.

Curran, Charles E. *Christian Morality Today.* Notre Dame, IN: Fides Publishers, 1966.

———. *Loyal Dissent: Memoirs of a Catholic Theologian.* Washington: Georgetown University Press, 2006.

———. *The Moral Theology of Pope John Paul II.* Washington: Georgetown University Press, 2005.

Curran, Charles E., and Richard A. McCormick, eds. *Dissent in the Church.* Mahwah, NJ: Paulist Press, 2011.

Cushing, Richard (Cardinal). *Call Me John: A Life of Pope John XXIII.* Boston: Daughters of St. Paul, 1963.

———. *Richard Cardinal Cushing: In Prose and Photos.* Boston: Daughters of St. Paul, 1965.

Cutie, Albert. *Dilemma: A Priest's Struggle with Faith and Love.* New York: Celebra, 2012.

Cutler, John Henry. *Cardinal Cushing of Boston.* New York: Hawthorn Books, 1970.

Dal Maso, Leonardo B. *Rome of the Popes: St. Peter's and the Vatican.* Rome: Bonechi, 1980.

Dassin, Joan, ed. *Torture in Brazil: A Shocking Report on the Persuasive Use of Torture by Brazilian Military Governments, 1964–1979, Secretly Prepared by the Archdiocese of São Paulo.* New York: Vintage Books, 1986.

del Carmen Tapia, María. *Inside Opus Dei: A True, Unfinished Story*. New York: Continuum, 2006.

Del Carril, Mario, *La vida de Emilio Mignone: Justicia, catolicismo y derechos humanos* (The Life of Emilio Mignone: Justice, Catholicism and Human Rights). Avellaneda, Argentina: Grupo Editorial Planeta, 2011.

Dodaro, Robert, ed. *Remaining in the Truth of Christ: Marriage and Communion in the Catholic Church*. San Francisco: Ignatius Press, 2014.

Döpfner, Julius. *The Questioning Church*. Westminster, MD: The Newman Press, 1964.

Dorril, Stephen. *MI6: Inside the Covert World of Her Majesty's Secret Intelligence Service*. New York: Touchstone Books, 2000.

Doyle, Thomas P., A. W. Richard Sipe, and Patrick J. Wall. *Sex, Priests and Secret Codes*. Los Angeles: Volt Press, 2006.

Draper, Robert. *Pope Francis and the New Vatican*. Washington: National Geographic, 2015.

Dussel, Enrique. *A History of the Church in Latin America, Colonialism to Liberation*. Grand Rapids, MI: Eerdmans, 1981.

Dziwisz, Stanisław, Czeslaw Drazek, et al. *Let Me Go to the Father's House*. Boston: Pauline Books, 2006.

Dziwisz, Stanisław. *A Life with Karol*. New York: Doubleday, 2008.

Eco, Umberto, and Cardinal Carlo Maria Martini. *Belief or Nonbelief? A Confrontation*. New York: Helios Press, 2012.

Ehrman, Bart D. *Did Jesus Exist? The Historical Argument for Jesus of Nazareth*. New York: HarperOne, 2012.

———. *How Jesus Became God*. New York: HarperOne, 2014.

———. *Jesus Interrupted: Revealing the Hidden Contradictions in the Bible*. New York: HarperOne, 2009.

———. *Misquoting Jesus: The Story Behind Who Changed the Bible and Why*. New York: HarperOne, 2005.

Elliott, Lawrence. *I Will Be Called John: A Biography of Pope John XXIII*. New York: Reader's Digest Press, 1973.

Escriva, Josemaria. *The Way*. New York: Image Books, 1982.

Faggioli, Massimo. *John XXIII: The Medicine of Mercy*. Collegeville, MN: Liturgical Press, 2014.

———. *Pope Francis: Tradition in Transition*. New York: Paulist Press, 2013.

Falasca, Stefania. *The September Pope: The Final Days of John Paul I*. Huntington, IN: Our Sunday Visitor, 2021.

Farina, Raffaele (Cardinal), ed. *The Vatican Secret Archives*. Flanders, Belgium: VDH Books, 2009.

Feitlowitz, Marguerite. *A Lexicon of Terror: Argentina and the Legacies of Torture*. New York: Oxford University Press, 2011.

Fenton, John H. *Salt of the Earth: An Informal Portrait of Richard Cardinal Cushing*. New York: Coward-McCann, 1965.

Fernández, Victor Manuel, and Paolo Rodari. *The Francis Project: Where He Wants to Take the Church*. Mahwah, NJ: Paulist Press, 2016.

Fesquet, Henri, ed. *Wit and Wisdom of Good Pope John*. New York: Signet Books, 1965.

Fox, Matthew. *The Pope's War*. New York: Sterling Ethos, 2011.

Francis, Pope. *The Joy of Love*. Erlanger, KY: Dynamic Catholic Institute, 2015.

———. *Only Love Can Save Us*. Huntington, IN: Our Sunday Visitor Publishing, 2013.

———. *Open Mind, Faithful Heart*. New York: Herder & Herder, 2013.

Francis, Pope, and Austen Ivereigh. *Let Us Dream: The Path to a Better Future*. New York: Simon & Schuster, 2020.

Francis, Pope, with Fabio Marchese Ragona. *Life: My Story Through History: Pope Francis's Inspiring Biography Through History*. New York: HarperOne, 2024.

Francis, Pope, with Antonio Spadaro. *Open to God, Open to the World*. London: Bloomsbury Continuum, 2018.

Francis, Pope, and Andrea Tornielli. *The Name of God Is Mercy*. New York: Random House, 2016.

Francis, Pope, with Dominique Wolton. *A Future of Faith*. New York: St. Martin's Essentials, 2018.

Frossard, André. *Be Not Afraid: Pope John Paul II Speaks Out*. New York: St. Martin's Press, 1984.

Gaeta, Saverio, and Slawomir Oder. *Karol Il Santo* (Karol the Saint). Milan: Paoline, 2014.

Gannon, Robert I. *The Cardinal Spellman Story*. Garden City, NY: Doubleday & Company, 1962.

Goethals, Jozef. *Ponderings of an Old Theologian: Vatican: A Life-Shaping Event*. London: Austin Macauley, 2023.

Gormley, Beatrice. *Pope Francis: The People's Pope*. New York: Aladdin, 2017.

Graham-Yooll, Andrew. *A State of Fear: Memories of Argentina's Nightmare*. London: Eland Publishing, 1986.

Gramick, Jeannine, and Pat Furey. *The Vatican and Homosexuality*. New York: Crossroad, 1988.

Granfield, Patrick. *The Papacy in Transition*. Garden City, NY: Doubleday & Company, 1980.

Greeley, Andrew M. *The Making of the Pope 2005*. New York: Little, Brown and Company, 2005.

Gregg, Samuel. *Challenging the Modern World*. Lanham, MD: Lexington Books, 1999

Griffin, Michael, and Jennie Weiss Block. *In the Company of the Poor: Conversations with Dr. Paul Farmer and Fr. Gustavo Gutiérrez*. Maryknoll, NY: Orbis Books, 2013.

Guerriero, Elio. *Benedict XVI: His Life and Thought*. San Francisco: Ignatius Press, 2016.

Guest, Ian. *Behind the Disappeared: Argentina's Dirty War Against Human Rights*. Philadelphia: University of Pennsylvania Press, 1990.

Guimaraes, Atila Sinke. *Vatican II, Homosexuality and Pedophilia*. Los Angeles: Tradition in Action, 2004.

Guitton, Jean. *The Pope Speaks: Dialogues of Paul VI with Jean Guitton*. New York: Meredith Press, 1968.

Guzmán, German. *Camilo Torres*. London: Sheed and Ward, 1969.

Hagerty, James. *Cardinal John Carmel Heenan: Priest of the People, Prince of the Church*. Leominster, Herefordshire, UK: Gracewing, 2012.

Hales, E. E. Y. *Pope John and His Revolution*. Garden City, NY: Doubleday & Company, 1965.

Hall, Mary. *The Spirituality of Dom Helder Câmara: The Impossible Dream*. Maryknoll, NY: Orbis Books, 1980.

Hammer, Richard. *The Vatican Connection*. New York: Charter Books, 1983.

Häring, Bernard. *Free and Faithful: My Life in the Catholic Church*. Liguori, MI: Liguori/Triumph, 1998.

Häring, Hermann, and Karl-Josef Kuschel. *Hans Küng: His Work and His Way*. Garden City, NY: Image Books, 1980.

Harris, Sam. *The End of Faith: Religion, Terrorism and the Future of Reason*. New York: W. W. Norton, 2004.

Hasler, August Bernhard. *How the Pope Became Infallible: Pius IX and the Politics of Persuasion*. Garden City, NY: Doubleday & Company, 1981.

Hatch, Alden. *A Man Named John: The Life of Pope John XXIII*. New York: Hawthorn Books, 1963.

———. *Pope Paul VI*. New York: Random House, 1966.

Hatch, Alden, and Seamus Walshe. *Crown of Glory: The Life of Pope Pius XII.* New York: Hawthorn Books, 1957.

Hebblethwaite, Peter. *In the Vatican.* Oxford: Oxford University Press, 1986.

———. *John XXIII: Pope of the Century.* London: Continuum, 1994.

———. *The New Inquisition: Schillebeeckx and Küng.* Glasgow: Collins Fount Paperbacks, 1980.

———. *The Next Pope.* San Francisco: HarperSanFrancisco, 1995.

———. *Paul VI: The First Modern Pope.* London: HarperCollins, 1993.

———. *Pope John XXIII: The Definitive Biography of Angelo Roncalli.* Garden City, NY: Doubleday & Company, 1985.

———. *The Runaway Church: Post-Conciliar Growth or Decline.* New York: Seabury Press, 1975.

———. *Synod Extraordinary.* Garden City, NY: Doubleday & Company, 1986.

———. *The Year of Three Popes.* London: Fount, 1978.

Heenan, John C. (Cardinal). *Council and Clergy.* London: Geoffrey Chapman, 1966.

———. *A Crown of Thorns: An Autobiography, 1951-1963.* London: Hodder and Stoughton, 1974.

Heim, Maximilian Heinrich. *Joseph Ratzinger: Life in the Church and Living Theology.* San Francisco: Ignatius Press, 2007.

Hesselmans, Marthe, and Jonathan Teubner. *An Analysis of Gustavo Gutiérrez's 'A Theology of Liberation.'* London: Macat Library, 2017.

Hill, Roland. *Lord Acton.* New Haven: Yale University Press, 2000.

Hochhuth, Rolf. *The Deputy.* Baltimore: Johns Hopkins University Press, 1964.

Hofmann, Paul. *Anatomy of the Vatican: An Irreverent View of the Holy See.* London: Robert Hale, 1985.

———. *O Vatican! A Slightly Wicked View of the Holy See.* New York: Congdon & Weed, 1984.

———. *The Vatican's Women: Female Influence at the Holy See.* New York: St. Martin's Griffin, 2002.

Howard, Thomas Albert. *The Faiths of Others: A History of Interreligious Dialogue.* New Haven: Yale University Press, 2021.

Huebsch, Bill. *Vatican II in Plain English: The Council.* Notre Dame, IN: Ave Maria Press, 1996.

———. *Vatican II in Plain English: The Decrees and Declarations.* Notre Dame, IN: Ave Maria Press, 1997.

Huebsch, Bill, and Paul Thurmes. *Vatican II in Plain English. The Constitutions.* Notre Dame, IN: Ave Maria Press, 1997.

Ivereigh, Austen. *The Great Reformer: Francis and the Making of a Radical Pope.* New York: Henry Holt and Company, 2014.

———. *Wounded Shepherd: Pope Francis and His Struggle to Convert the Catholic Church.* New York: Picador, 2019.

Jalics, Franz. *The Contemplative Way: Quietly Savoring God's Presence.* New York: Paulist Press, 2011.

Jens, Walter, Karl-Josef Kuschel, and Hans Küng. *Dialogue with Hans Küng.* London: SCM Press, 1997.

John Paul II, Pope. *Crossing the Threshold of Hope.* New York: Alfred A. Knopf, 1995.

———. *Gift and Mystery: On the Fiftieth Anniversary of My Priestly Ordination.* New York: Image, 1999.

———. *In God's Hands. Spiritual Diaries, 1962-2003.* New York: HarperOne, 2017.

———. *Rise, Let Us Be On Our Way.* New York: Warner Books, 2004.

John XXIII, Pope. *Journal of a Soul: The Autobiography of Pope John XXIII.* New York: Image Books, 1980.

———. *Mission to France: Memoirs of a Nuncio, 1944–1953.* New York: McGraw-Hill Book Company, 1966.

———. *Pope John XXIII: Essential Writings.* Maryknoll, NY: Orbis Books, 2008.

———. *Pope John XXIII: Letters to His Family.* New York: McGraw-Hill Book Company, 1970.

Johnson, Paul. *A History of Christianity.* New York: Touchstone Books, 1976.

Kaiser, Robert Blair. *A Church in Search of Itself: Benedict XVI and the Battle for the Future.* New York: Vintage Books, 2006.

———. *Clerical Error: A True Story.* New York: Continuum, 2002.

———. *Inside the Jesuits: How Pope Francis Is Changing the Church and the World.* Lanham, MD: Rowman & Littlefield, 2014.

———. *Pope, Council and World.* New York: Macmillan, 1963.

———. *Whistle: Tom Doyle's Steadfast Witness for Victims of Clerical Sexual Abuse.* Thiensville, WI: Caritas Communications, 2015.

Kasper, Walter. *Cardinal Walter Kasper: Spiritual Writings.* Maryknoll, NY: Orbis Books, 2016.

———. *A Celebration of Priestly Ministry.* New York: Herder & Herder, 2007.

———. *The God of Jesus Christ.* New York: Crossroad, 1992.

———. *An Introduction to Christian Faith.* Ramsey, NJ: Paulist Press, 1980.

———. *Jesus the Christ.* Mahwah, NJ: Burns & Oates, 1977.

———. *Mercy: The Essence of the Gospel and the Key to Christian Life.* New York: Paulist Press, 2013.

———. *Pope Francis's Revolution of Tenderness and Love.* New York: Paulist Press, 2015.

———. *That They May All Be One: The Call to Unity Today.* London: Burns & Oates, 2004.

———. *Wo Das Herz Des Glaubens Schlagt* (Where the Heart of Faith Beats). Freiberg: Herder, 2008.

Katz, Robert. *Days of Wrath: The Ordeal of Aldo Moro.* New York: Doubleday & Company, 1980.

Kelly, Geffrey B., ed. *Karl Rahner: Theologian of the Graced Search for Meaning.* Minneapolis, MN: Fortress Press, 1992.

Kelly, George A. *Battle for the American Church.* San Francisco: Ignatius Press, 1995.

Kengor, Paul, and Patricia Clark Doerner. *The Judge: William P. Clark, Ronald Reagan's Top Hand.* San Francisco: Ignatius Press, 2007.

Kennedy, Eugene C. *The Catholic Priest in the United States.* Washington: United States Catholic Conference of Bishops Publications Office, 1972.

Kertzer, David I. *The Pope Against the Jews: The Vatican's Role in the Rise of Modern Anti-Semitism.* New York: Knopf, 2001.

———. *The Pope and Mussolini: The Secret History of Pius XI and the Rise of Fascism in Europe* New York: Random House, 2014.

———. *The Pope at War: The Secret History of Pius XII, Mussolini and Hitler.* New York: Random House, 2022.

Kilby, Karen. *Karl Rahner: A Brief Introduction.* New York: Herder & Herder, 1997.

Kolodiejchuk, Brian. *Mother Teresa: Come Be My Light.* New York: Doubleday, 2007.

König, Franz. *Open to God, Open to the World.* London: Burns & Oates, 2005.

Krieg, Robert A. *Catholic Theologians in Nazi Germany.* New York: Continuum Books, 2004.

Küng, Hans. *Can We Save the Catholic Church?* London: William Collins, 2013.

———. *The Catholic Church: A Short History.* New York: Modern Library, 2013.

———. *The Council in Action: Theological Reflections on the Second Vatican Council.* New York: Sheed and Ward, 1963.

———. *The Council, Reform and Reunion.* Garden City, NY: Image Books, 1965.

———. *Credo: The Apostles' Creed Explained for Today.* New York: Doubleday, 1993.

———. *Disputed Truth: Memoirs.* London: Continuum, 2008.

———. *Great Christian Thinkers*. New York: Continuum, 1994.

———. *Infallible? An Inquiry*. Garden City, NY: Doubleday & Company, 1983.

———. *Justification: The Doctrine of Karl Barth and a Catholic Reflection*. Philadelphia: Westminster Press, 1981.

———. *My Struggle for Freedom: Memoirs*. Grand Rapids, MI: William B. Eerdmans Publishing, 2003.

———. *On Being a Christian*. New York: Doubleday & Company, 1976.

———. *That the World May Believe*. London: Sheed and Ward, 1963.

———. *What I Believe*. London: Continuum, 2010.

Küng, Hans, Yves Congar, and Daniel O'Hanlon. *Council Speeches of Vatican II*. Glen Rock, NJ: Original Deus Books, 1964.

Küng, Hans, and Leonard Swidler. *The Church in Anguish*. New York: Harper & Row, 1987.

Kwitny, Jonathan. *Man of the Century: The Life and Times of Pope John Paul II*. New York: Henry Holt and Company, 1997.

Lamb, Christopher. *The Outsider: Pope Francis and His Battle to Reform the Church*. Maryknoll, NY: Orbis Books, 2020.

Lapide, Pinchas E. *The Last Three Popes and the Jews*. London: Souvenir Press, 1967.

LaPierre, Albert, Edward Wetterer et al., eds. *The Church: Readings in Theology*. New York: P.J. Kennedy & Sons, 1964.

Lehmann, Karl. *Mit Langem Atem* (With a Long Breath). Freiburg: Herder, 2018.

Lehnert, Sister M. Pascalina. *His Humble Servant: Sister M. Pascalina Lehnert's Memoirs*. South Bend, IN: St. Augustine's Press, 2014.

Lennon, J. Paul. *Father Marcial Maciel: Pedophile, Psychopath and Legion of Christ Founder*. Self-published, 2014.

Lentz, Harris M. III. *Popes and Cardinals of the 20th Century: A Biographical Dictionary*. Jefferson, NC: McFarland & Company, 2002.

Lewis, Brenda Ralph. *A Dark History: The Popes*. New York: Metro Books, 2009.

Lewis, Paul H. *Guerrillas and Generals: The "Dirty War" in Argentina*. Westport, CT: Praeger Publishers, 2002.

Lindbeck, George A. *Dialogue on the Way: Protestants Report from Rome on the Vatican Council*. Minneapolis: Augsburg Publishing House, 1965.

Livingston, James C., and Francis Schussler Fiorenza. *Modern Christian Thought: Volume II, The Twentieth Century*. Upper Saddle River, NJ: Prentice Hall, 2000.

Lopez Vigil, Maria. *Oscar Romero: Memories in Mosaic*. Washington: Epica, 2000.

Luciani, Albino (Pope John Paul I). *Illustrissimi: Letters from Pope John Paul I*. Boston: Little, Brown and Company, 1978.

Lytton, Timothy D. *Holding Bishops Accountable*. Cambridge, MA: Harvard University Press, 2008.

Maciel, Marcial. *Christ Is My Life*. Manchester, NH: Sophia Institute Press, 2003.

Madges, William, and Michael J. Daley, eds. *Vatican II: Fifty Personal Stories*. Maryknoll, NY: Orbis Books, 2012.

Malinski, M. *Pope John Paul II: The Life of My Friend Karol Wojtyła*. London: Burns & Oates, 1979.

Mannion, Gerard, ed. *Church and Religious 'Other.'* London: T&T Clark, 2008.

Marchak, Patricia. *God's Assassins: State Terrorism in Argentina in the 1970s*. Montreal: McGill-Queen's University Press, 1999.

Marr, David. *The Prince: Faith, Abuse and George Pell*. Collingwood, Australia: Black Inc., 2014.

Martin, James. *Building a Bridge: How the Catholic Church and the LGBT Community Can Enter Into a Relationship of Respect, Compassion and Sensitivity*. New York: Harper Collins, 2017.

———. *James Martin: Essential Writings*. Maryknoll, NY: Orbis Books, 2017.

———. *My Life with the Saints*. Chicago: Loyola Press, 2006.

Martin, Malachi. *The Jesuits: The Society of Jesus and the Betrayal of the Roman Catholic Church*. New York: Simon & Schuster, 1987.
———. *Three Popes and the Cardinal*. New York: Farrar, Straus and Giroux, 1972.
Martini, Cardinal Carlo M., and Georg Sporschill. *Night Conversations with Cardinal Martini*. New York: Paulist Press, 2012.
Martini, Carlo Maria. *The Joy of the Gospel: Meditations for Young People*. Collegeville, MN: Liturgical Press, 1994.
Marty, Martin. *Martin Luther*. New York: Viking, 2004.
Matthews, Rupert. *Popes: Every Question Answered*. New York: Metro Books, 2013.
McBrien, Richard P. *Catholicism*. New York: HarperSanFrancisco, 1994.
———. *The Church: 101 Questions and Answers*. New York: Paulist Press, 1996.
———. *The Church: The Evolution of Catholicism*. New York: HarperOne, 2008.
———. *Lives of the Saints*. New York: HarperSanFrancisco, 2001.
———. *Report on the Church: Catholicism After Vatican II*. San Francisco: HarperSanFrancisco, 1992.
McCarten, Anthony. *The Pope: Francis, Benedict, and the Decision That Shook the World*. New York: Flatiron Books, 2019.
McConahay, Mary Jo. *Playing God: American Catholic Bishops and the Far Right*. Brooklyn, NY: Melville House, 2023.
McCoy, John A. *A Still and Quiet Conscience: The Archbishop Who Challenged a Pope, a President and a Church*. Maryknoll, NY: Orbis Books, 2013.
McDannell, Colleen. *The Spirit of Vatican II: A History of Catholic Reform in America*. New York: Basic Books, 2011.
McDonagh, Francis, ed. *Dom Helder Câmara: Essential Writings*. Maryknoll, NY: Orbis Books, 2009.
McManners, John, ed. *The Oxford Illustrated History of Christianity*. Oxford: Oxford University Press, 1992.
McNeill, John J. *The Church and the Homosexual*. Boston: Beacon Press, 1993.
McRedmond, Louis. *To the Greater Glory: A History of the Irish Jesuits*. Dublin: Gill and Macmillan, 1991.
Mignone, Emilio F. *Witness to the Truth: The Complicity of Church and Dictatorship in Argentina*. Maryknoll, NY: Orbis Books, 1988.
The Millenari (Pseudonym). *Shroud of Secrecy: The Story of Corruption within the Vatican*. Toronto: Key Porter Books, 2000.
Modras, Ronald. *Ignatian Humanism: A Dynamic Spirituality for the 21st Century*. Chicago: Loyola Press, 2004.
Molano, Walter Thomas. *In the Land of Silver: 200 Years of Argentine Economic and Political Development*. Scotts Valley, CA: CreateSpace Independent Publishing, 2013.
Moorman, John. *Vatican Observed: An Anglican Impression of Vatican II*. London: Darton, Longman & Todd, 1967.
Müller, Gerhard, and Carlos Granados. *The Cardinal Müller Report: An Exclusive Interview on the State of the Church*. San Francisco: Ignatius Press, 2017.
Murphy, Francis X. *The Papacy Today: The Last 80 Years of the Catholic Church*. New York: Macmillan Publishing, 1981.
———. *Patristic Heritage: In the Renaissance and the Modern World*. Tappan, NY: Shepherd Press, 1989.
Murphy, Gerald T. *Maximos IV at Vatican II: The Quest for Autonomy*. West Roxbury, MA: 2011.
Murphy, Paul I., and R. Rene Arlington. *La Popessa: The Controversial Biography of Sister Pascalina, the Most Powerful Woman in Vatican History*. New York: Warner Books, 1983.
Murphy-O'Connor, Cormac. *At the Heart of the World*. London: Darnton, Longman and Todd, 2004.
———. *An English Spring: Memoirs*. London: Bloomsbury Continuum, 2015.

Murr, Charles Theodore. *The Godmother: Madre Pascalina, a Feminine Tour de Force*. Scotts Valley, CA: CreateSpace Independent Publishing, 2017.

Neuhaus, Richard John. *Appointment in Rome: The Church in America Awakening*. New York: Herder and Herder, 1999.

Nicholson, Jim. *The United States and the Holy See*. Rome: Trenta Giorni Societa, 2004.

Noonan, John T. Jr. *A Church That Can and Cannot Change*. Notre Dame, IN: University of Notre Dame Press, 2005.

Noonan, Peggy. *John Paul the Great: Remembering a Spiritual Father*. New York: Penguin Books, 2005.

Nowell, Robert. *A Passion for Truth: Hans Küng, A Biography*. London: Collins, 1981.

Nuzzi, Gianluigi. *Merchants in the Temple: Inside Pope Francis's Secret Battle Against Corruption in the Vatican*. New York: Henry Holt and Company, 2015.

O'Collins, Gerald. *Do Not Stifle the Spirit: Conversations with Jacques Dupuis*. Maryknoll, NY: Orbis Books, 2017.

———. *The Election of Pope Francis*. Maryknoll, NY: Orbis Books, 2019.

———. *From Rome to Royal Park*. Ballarat, Australia: Connor Court Publishing, 2015.

———. *Living Vatican II: The 21st Council for the 21st Century*. New York: Paulist Press, 2006.

———. *A Midlife Journey*. Leominster, UK: Gracewing, 2012.

———. *On the Left Bank of the Tiber*. Leominster, UK: Gracewing, 2013.

———. *Portraits: Popes, Families and Friends*. Redland Bay, Australia: Connor Court Publishing, 2019.

———. *Second Journey: Spiritual Awareness and the Mid-Life Crisis*. Leominster, UK: Gracewing, 1995.

O'Collins, Gerald, and Edward Farrugia. *A Concise Dictionary of Theology*. New York: Paulist Press, 1991.

O'Collins, Gerald, and Michael A. Hayes. *The Legacy of John Paul II*. London: Burns & Oates, 2008.

O'Connor, Garry. *Subdued Fires: An Intimate Portrait of Pope Benedict XVI*. Strout, UK: History Press, 2013.

———. *Universal Father: A Life of Pope John Paul II*. New York: Bloomsbury USA, 2005.

Oder, Slawomir, and Saverio Gaeta. *Why He Is a Saint*. New York: Rizzoli, 2010.

O'Malley, John W. *The First Jesuits*. Cambridge, MA: Harvard University Press, 1993.

———. *A History of the Popes: From Peter to the Present*. Lanham, MD: Sheed & Ward, 2010.

———. *The Jesuits: A History from Ignatius to the Present*. London: Rowman & Littlefield, 2014.

O'Meara, Thomas F. *A Theologian's Journey*. New York: Paulist Press, 2002.

O'Toole, James M. *Militant and Triumphant: William Henry O'Connell and the Catholic Church in Boston, 1859–1944*. Notre Dame, IN: University of Notre Dame Press, 1992.

Pallenberg, Corrado. *Inside the Vatican*. New York: Hawthorn Books, 1960.

Parrinder, Geoffrey. *Jesus in the Quran*. London: Oneworld Publications, 2013.

Paul VI et la modernité dans l'Église, Actes du Colloque (Paul VI and Modernity in the Church, Conference Proceedings). Rome: Collection de l'école française de Rome, 1983.

Pawley, Bernard C., ed. *The Second Vatican Council: Studies by Eight Anglican Observers*. London: Oxford University Press, 1967.

Pepinster, Catherine. *The Keys and the Kingdom: The British and the Papacy from John Paul II to Francis*. London: Bloomsbury, 2017.

Pepper, Curtis Bill. *An Artist and the Pope*. New York: Giniger Books, 1968.

Pham, John-Peter. *Heirs of the Fisherman: Behind the Scenes of Papal Death and Succession*. New York: Oxford University Press, 2004.

Phayer, Michael. *Pius XII, the Holocaust and the Cold War*. Bloomington, IN: Indiana University Press, 2008.

Pique, Elisabetta. *Pope Francis: Life and Revolution.* Chicago: Loyola Press, 2013.

Pitre, Brant. *The Case for Jesus: The Biblical and Historical Evidence for Christ.* New York: Image Books, 2016.

Politi, Marco. *Pope Francis Among the Wolves.* New York: Columbia University Press, 2015.

Powell, Mark E. *Papal Infallibility: A Protestant Evaluation of an Ecumenical Issue.* Grand Rapids, MI: William B. Eerdmans Publishing, 2009.

Purdy, W. A. *The Church on the Move: The Characters and Politics of Pius XII and John XXIII.* New York: The John Day Company, 1966.

Purdy, William. *The Search for Unity: Relations between the Anglican and Roman Catholic Churches from the 1950s to the 1970s.* London: Geoffrey Chapman, 1996.

Pursell, Brennan. *Benedict of Bavaria: An Intimate Portrait of the Pope.* London: Circle Press, 2008.

Quinn, John R. *The Reform of the Papacy.* New York: Herder and Herder, 1977.

Rahner, Hugo, ed. *The Church: Readings in Theology.* Baltimore: P.J. Kenedy, 1963.

Rahner, Karl, and Joseph Ratzinger. *The Episcopate and the Primacy.* New York: Herder & Herder, 1963.

Ratzinger, Georg. *My Brother, the Pope.* San Francisco: Ignatius Press, 2012.

Ratzinger, Joseph. *Church, Ecumenism and Politics.* San Francisco: Ignatius Press, 2008.

———. *Introduction to Christianity.* San Francisco: Ignatius Press, 2004.

———. *Milestones: Memoirs, 1927-1977.* San Francisco: Ignatius Press, 1998.

———. *The Nature and Mission of Theology.* San Francisco: Ignatius Press, 1995.

———. *Principles of Catholic Theology.* San Francisco: Ignatius Press, 1987.

———. *The Spirit of the Liturgy.* San Francisco: Ignatius Press, 2000.

———. *Theological Highlights of Vatican II.* New York: Paulist Press, 2009.

———. *Truth and Tolerance: Christian Belief and World Religions.* San Francisco: Ignatius Press, 2004.

———. *Values in a Time of Upheaval.* San Francisco: Ignatius Press, 2006.

———. *What It Means to Be a Christian.* San Francisco: Ignatius Press, 2005.

Ratzinger, Joseph, with Vittorio Messori. *The Ratzinger Report.* San Francisco: Ignatius Press, 1985.

Ratzinger, Joseph, and Marcello Pera. *Without Roots: The West, Relativism, Christianity, Islam.* New York: Basic Books, 2006.

Ratzinger, Joseph, and Peter Seewald. *Salt of the Earth: The Church at the End of the Millennium.* San Francisco, Ignatius Press, 1997.

Reese, Thomas J. *Archbishop: Inside the Power Structure of the American Catholic Church.* New York: Harper & Row, 1989.

———. *Inside the Vatican: The Politics and Organization of the Catholic Church.* Cambridge, MA: Harvard University Press, 1996.

Richards, Clare. *Roman Catholic Christianity.* Oxford: Heinemann, 1995.

Riemer, George. *The New Jesuits.* Boston: Little, Brown and Company, 1971.

Rigert, Joe. *An Irish Tragedy: How Sex Abuse by Irish Priests Helped Cripple the Catholic Church.* Baltimore: Crossland Press, 2008.

Robertson, Geoffrey. *The Case of the Pope: Vatican Accountability for Human Rights Abuse.* London: Penguin Books, 2010.

———. *Confronting Power and Sex in the Catholic Church.* Collegeville, MN: Liturgical Press, 2008.

———. *For Christ's Sake: End Sexual Abuse in the Catholic Church.* Mulgrave, Australia: Garratt Publishing, 2013.

Rock, John. *The Time Has Come: A Catholic Doctor's Proposals to End the Battle Over Birth Control.* New York: Alfred A. Knopf, 1963.

Romero, Oscar. *A Shepherd's Diary.* Cincinnati: St. Anthony Messenger Press, 1993.

———. *The Violence of Love.* Maryknoll, NY: Orbis Books, 2010.

Rooney, Francis. *The Global Vatican: An Inside Look at the Catholic Church, World Politics and the Extraordinary Relationship between the United States and the Holy See.* Lanham, MD: Rowman & Littlefield, 2013.

Roper, Lyndal. *Martin Luther: Renegade and Prophet.* New York: Random House, 2016.

Rosales, Luis, and Daniel Olivera. *Francis: A Pope for Our Time.* Boca Raton, FL: Humanix Books, 2013.

Rubin, Sergio, and Francesca Ambrogetti. *Pope Francis: Conversations with Jorge Bergoglio.* New York: G. P. Putnam's Sons, 2010.

Rynne, Xavier. *Letters from Vatican City: Vatican II (First Session).* New York: Farrar, Straus & Company, 1963.

Schmidt, Stjepan, ed. *Augustin Cardinal Bea: Spiritual Profile.* London: Geoffrey Chapman, 1971.

Schner, George P. *The Church Renewed: The Documents of Vatican II Reconsidered.* Lanham, MD: Rowan & Littlefield, 1986.

Seewald, Peter. *Benedict XVI: A Life. Volume I: Youth in Nazi Germany to the Second Vatican Council, 1927–1965.* London: Bloomsbury Continuum, 2020.

———. *Benedict XVI: A Life. Volume II: Professor and Prefect to Pope and Pope Emeritus, 1966– The Present.* London: Bloomsbury Continuum, 2021.

———. *Benedict: An Intimate Portrait.* San Francisco: Ignatius Press, 2007.

———. *Pope Benedict XVI: Servant of the Truth.* San Francisco: Ignatius Press, 2005.

Segundo, Juan Luis. *Theology and the Church: A Response to Cardinal Ratzinger and a Warning to the Whole Church.* San Francisco: Harper & Row, 1987.

Shannon, James Patrick. *Reluctant Dissenter: An Autobiography.* New York: Crossroad Publishing, 1998.

Shelley, Bruce. *Church History in Plain Language.* Nashville: Thomas Nelson Publishers, 1995.

Shriver, Mark. *Pilgrimage: My Search for the Real Pope Francis.* New York: Random House, 2016.

Sigmund, Paul E. *Liberation Theology at the Crossroads: Democracy or Revolution?* London: Oxford University Press, 1990.

Simmons, William Paul. *Joyful Human Rights.* Philadelphia: University of Pennsylvania Press, 2019.

Sipe, A. W. Richard. *A Secret World: Sexuality and the Search for Celibacy.* New York: Brunner / Mazel Publishers, 1990.

Sobrino, Jon. *Romero: Martyr for Liberation.* London: Catholic Institute for International Relations, 1982.

Spadaro, Antonio, ed. *Encountering Truth: Meeting God in the Everyday.* New York: Image, 2015.

Suenens, Leon-Joseph, and Dom Helder Câmara. *Charismatic Renewal and Social Action: A Dialogue.* London: Darton Longman and Todd, 1980.

Szulc, Tad. *Pope John Paul II: The Biography.* New York: Scribner, 1995.

Tal, Uriel. *Christians and Jews in Germany.* Ithaca, NY: Cornell University Press, 1975.

Thavis, John. *The Vatican Diaries.* New York: Viking, 2013.

Thornton, John F., and Susan B. Varenne, eds. *The Essential Pope Benedict XVI.* San Francisco: HarperSanFrancisco, 2007.

Tittmann, Harold H. *Inside the Vatican of Pius XII: The Memoir of an American Diplomat During World War II.* New York: Image Books, 2004.

Trigilio, John Jr., and Kenneth Brighenti. *The Catholicism Answer Book.* Naperville, IL: Sourcebooks, 2007.

Vallely, Paul. *Pope Francis: The Struggle for the Soul of Catholicism.* New York: Bloomsbury USA, 2015.

———. *Pope Francis: Untying the Knots.* London: Bloomsbury, 2013.

Vardey, Lucinda M. *John XXIII: A Saint for the Modern World.* New York: Paulist Press, 2014.

Vázquez de Prada, Andrés. *The Founder of Opus Dei. The Life of Josemaría Escrivá. Volume II: God and Daring.* Strongsville, OH: Scepter Publishers, 1997.

Ventresca, Robert A. *Soldier of Christ: The Life of Pope Pius XII.* Cambridge, MA: Belknap Press, 2013.

Verbitsky, Horacio. *Confessions of an Argentine Dirty Warrior.* New York: The New Press, 2005.

———. *The Flight: Confessions of an Argentine Dirty Warrior.* New York: The New Press, 1996.

Vereb, Jerome-Michael. *Because He Was a German: Cardinal Bea and the Origins of Roman Catholic Engagement in the Ecumenical Movement.* Grand Rapids, MI: William B. Eerdmans Publishing, 2006.

Vermes, Geza. *Jesus the Jew: A Historian's Reading of the Gospels.* Philadelphia: Fortress Press, 1981.

Von Kempis, Stefan, and Philip F. Lawler. *A Call to Serve: Pope Francis and the Catholic Future.* New York: Crossroad Publishing, 2013.

Wagoner, Walter D. *The Seminary: Protestant and Catholic.* London: Sheed and Ward, 1966.

Walsh, Michael J. *The Popes: 50 Extraordinary Occupants of the Throne of St. Peter.* London: Quercus, 2007.

Weakland, Rembert. *A Pilgrim in a Pilgrim Church: Memoirs of a Catholic Archbishop.* Grand Rapids, MI: William B. Eerdmans Publishing, 2009.

Weigel, George. *The End and the Beginning.* New York: Image Books, 2010.

———. *Letters to a Young Catholic.* New York: Basic Books, 2004.

———. *The Truth of Catholicism.* New York: Perennial, 2001.

———. *Witness to Hope: The Biography of Pope John Paul II.* New York: Harper Perennial, 2005.

West, Morris. *The Shoes of the Fisherman.* New Milford, CT: Toby Press, 2003.

Widmer, Andreas. *The Pope and the CEO: John Paul II's Leadership Lessons.* Steubenville, OH: Emmaus Road, 2011.

Wilhelm, Anthony. *Christ Among Us: A Modern Presentation of the Catholic Faith.* New York: Paulist Press, 1975.

Willebrands, J. G. M. *You Will Be Called Repairer of the Breach: The Diary of J. G. M. Willebrands.* Leuven, Belgium: Peeters Publishers, 2009.

Willey, David. *God's Politician: Pope John Paul II, the Catholic Church and the New World Order.* New York: St. Martin's Press, 1992.

Williams, Thomas D. *Knowing Right from Wrong: A Christian Guide to Conscience.* New York: Faith Words, 2008.

Wills, Garry. *The Future of the Catholic Church with Pope Francis.* New York: Viking, 2015.

———. *Papal Sin: Structures of Deceit.* New York: Doubleday, 2000.

———. *Saint Augustine.* New York: Viking, 1999.

———. *What the Gospels Meant.* New York: Penguin Books, 2009.

———. *Why I Am a Catholic.* Boston: Mariner Books, 2003.

———. *Why Priests? A Failed Tradition.* New York: Viking, 2013.

Wiltgen, Ralph M. *The Inside Story of Vatican II.* Charlotte, NC: TAN Books, 1978.

Witham, Larry. *Curran vs. Catholic University: A Study of Authority and Freedom in Conflict.* Riverdale, MD: Edington-Rand, 1991.

Wojtyła, Karol. *Love & Responsibility.* San Francisco: Ignatius Press, 1993.

———. *Sources of Renewal: The Implementation of the Second Vatican Council.* London: Collins, 1980.

Woodward, Kenneth L. *Getting Religion: Faith, Culture and Politics from the Age of Eisenhower to the Era of Obama.* New York: Convergent Books, 2016.

———. *Making Saints: How the Catholic Church Determines Who Becomes a Saint, Who Doesn't, and Why.* New York: Simon & Schuster, 1990.

Wright, Jonathan. *God's Soldiers: A History of the Jesuits.* New York: Image Books, 2004.

Wright, Scott. *Oscar Romero and the Communion of the Saints.* Maryknoll, NY: Orbis Books, 2009.

Wynn, Wilton. *Keepers of the Keys: John XXIII, Paul VI and John Paul II.* New York: Random House, 1988.

Yallop, David. *Beyond Belief: The Catholic Church and the Child Abuse Scandal.* London: Constable & Robinson, 2010.

———. *In God's Name: An Investigation into the Murder of Pope John Paul I.* New York: Basic Books, 2007.

———. *The Power and the Glory: Inside the Dark Heart of John Paul II's Vatican.* New York: Carroll & Graf, 2007.

Zuccotti, Susan. *Under His Very Windows: The Vatican and the Holocaust in Italy.* New Haven: Yale Nota Bene, 2002.

Index

Page numbers in *italics* refer to illustrations.

ILLUSTRATION CREDITS

ILLUSTRATIONS IN THE TEXT

Wikimedia Creative Commons,
Attribution-Share Alike 2.0 Generic
Licence

481: Photo: Evan Vucci / AP / Alamy

509: Photo: Paolo Galosi / Romano
Siciliani / KNA

COLOR INSERT

page 1

Photo: Farabola / Bridgeman Images

page 2

[top row] Pius XII. Photo: © KNA-
Bild / KNA; John XXIII with First
Lady Jacqueline Kennedy. Photo:
Bettmann / Getty Images

[bottom row] Paul VI with
Archbishop Óscar Romero. Photo:
History & Art Collection / Alamy;
John Paul I with Cardinal Karol
Wojtyla. Photo: Vatican Media /
Romano Siciliani / KNA

page 3

[top row] Father Joseph Ratzinger
with his sister, Maria. Photo:
Levan Ramishvili / Flickr Creative
Commons; Pope Benedict XVI with
Father Georg Ratzinger. Photo:
Abaca Press / Alamy

[bottom row] John Paul II and
Cardinal Joseph Ratzinger. Photo: ©
KNA-Bild / KNA; John Paul II and
Mother Teresa. Photo: RealyEasyStar
/ Fotografia Felici / Alamy

page 4

[top row] Cardinal Hans Hermann
Groër. Photo: APA Picture Desk /
Alamy; Father Gilbert Gauthe.
Photo: AP / Alamy; Father Stephen
Kiesle. Photo: Police handout

[middle row] Father Marcial Maciel.
Photo: CNS

[bottom row] Father Theodore
McCarrick with victim. Photo:
Family handout; Cardinal McCarrick
with President Bush and Chief
Justice Roberts. Photo: dpa picture
alliance / Alamy

page 5

[top row] The assassination attempt
on John Paul II. Photo: Farabola /
Bridgeman Images; The funeral of
Archbishop Óscar Romero. Photo:
Étienne Montes / Gamma-Rapho /
Getty Images

[bottom row] Friar Leonardo Boff.
Photo: Bernard Bisson / Sygma /
Getty Images; Father Orlando Yorio.
Photo: Mónica Hasenberg / Archivio
Hasenberg Quaretti, Buenos Aires;
Father Franz Jalics. Photo: dpa
picture-alliance / Alamy

page 6

[top row] Cardinal Jorge Bergoglio
with Cardinal Tarcisio Bertone.
Photo: Agencia Rio Negro; Cardinal
Raymond Burke. Photo: Archive PL
/ Alamy

[bottom] Benedict XVI with Cardinal
Walter Kasper and Secretary of State
Tarcisio Bertone. Photo: Abaca Press
/ Alamy

page 7

[top row] Pope Francis with Pope
Emeritus Benedict XVI. Photo:
Abaca Press / Alamy; Still from the
2019 film *The Two Popes*. Photo:
Peter Mountain, courtesy Netflix

[bottom row] Francis washes the feet
of refugees. Photo: Abaca Press /
Alamy; Francis with President Joseph
Biden. Photo: Sipa US / Alamy

page 8

Photo: Maykova Galina /
Shutterstock

A NOTE ABOUT THE AUTHOR

PHILIP SHENON, is an award-winning investigative reporter and bestselling author who spent more than twenty years at *The New York Times*. As a Washington correspondent for the paper, he covered the Pentagon, the Justice Department, the State Department, and Congress. As a foreign correspondent, he reported from more than sixty countries and several war zones. He is the author of two *New York Times*–bestselling books: *A Cruel and Shocking Act: The Secret History of the Kennedy Assassination* and *The Commission: The Uncensored History of the 9/11 Investigation*. A native of San Francisco, he now lives in Washington, DC.

A NOTE ON THE TYPE

This book was set in Janson, a typeface long thought to have been made by the Dutchman Anton Janson, who was a practicing typefounder in Leipzig during the years 1668–1687. However, it has been conclusively demonstrated that these types are actually the work of Nicholas Kis (1650–1702), a Hungarian, who most probably learned his trade from the master Dutch typefounder Dirk Voskens. The type is an excellent example of the influential and sturdy Dutch types that prevailed in England up to the time William Caslon (1692–1766) developed his own incomparable designs from them.

Printed and bound by Berryville Graphics,
Berryville, Virginia

Composed by North Market Street Graphics,
Lancaster, Pennsylvania

Designed by Cassandra J. Pappas